# NEITHER BLACK
# NOR WHITE
# YET BOTH

# NEITHER BLACK NOR WHITE YET BOTH

*Thematic Explorations
of Interracial Literature*

WERNER SOLLORS

New York   Oxford

OXFORD UNIVERSITY PRESS

1997

Oxford University Press

Oxford   New York
Athens   Auckland   Bangkok   Bogotá   Bombay
Buenos Aires   Calcutta   Cape Town   Dar es Salaam   Delhi
Florence   Hong Kong   Istanbul   Karachi
Kuala Lumpur   Madras   Madrid   Melbourne
Mexico City   Nairobi   Paris   Singapore
Taipei   Tokyo   Toronto

and associated companies in
Berlin   Ibadan

Library of Congress Cataloging-in-Publication Data
Sollors, Werner.
Neither black nor white yet both: thematic explorations
of interracial literature / Werner Sollors.
p   cm.
Includes bibliographical references and index.
ISBN 0-19-505282-X
1. Race in literature.  2. Miscegenation in literature.
3. Mulattoes in literature.  4. Passing (Identity) in literature.
5. Literature, Comparative—History and criticism.  I. Title.
PN56.R16S66   1996   809'.93355—dc20   96-7162

As this page cannot legibly accommodate all the copyright notices,
pages xi–xii constitute an extension of the copyright page.

1 3 5 7 9 8 6 4 2

Printed in the United States of America
on acid-free paper

*Per Alide*

# Acknowledgments

The idea for this book presented itself over a decade ago when I was preparing a new course, "Black and White in American Drama," that became part of the larger enterprise of focusing on the reading of African American texts comparatively, historically, embedded in cross-cultural and transgeneric approaches, and with an interest in intertextuality and in interracial themes. The pursuit of the project took me to many texts that I had never read, and many more that I had never heard of. The completion of this study has been made possible by the support of many individuals and institutions and has profited from the suggestions I received from colleagues and generations of students as well as from the inspiration of such pioneering texts in the field as those by Sterling Brown, Penelope Bullock, Caroline Bond Day, Eva Dykes, James Hugo Johnston, Sidney Kaplan, J. A. Rogers, George Schuyler, Frank Snowden, Wylie Sypher, and Louis Wirth as well as other more recent work in several different disciplines. Selected secondary literature on the field is listed at the end of the book. Some of the authors are very well known—for example, Hannah Arendt, Anthony Barker, Urs Bitterli, David Dabydeen, Jean Devisse, Ann duCille, Gerald Early, George Fredrickson, Sander Gilman, Nathan Huggins, Winthrop Jordan, Richard and Sally Price, Marc Shell, Doris Sommer, Joseph Washington, and Joel Williamson—and I also found especially helpful the scholarship presented in such pioneering essays as those by Daniel Aaron, Tilden Edelstein, William McKee Evans, Claude Julien, Milton Mayer, Simone Vauthier, Judith Wilson, and Jules Zanger, as well as some outstanding unpublished dissertations, such as those by Wen-Ching Ho, Jonathan David Little, Ratna Roy, Earlene Stetson, Simone Vauthier, and Richard Yarborough. The recent interventions by such scholars as George Hutchinson, Dana Nelson, and Naomi Zack have confirmed me in my approach. As always, I find most helpful the combination of American Studies, with its interdisciplinary openness toward many fields that may shed light on an issue, and Comparative Literature, with its readiness to pursue problems of literary representation across national and linguistic boundaries and through long historical trajectories.

To the following libraries, museums, and archives I owe special thanks: Biblioteca nazionale Marciana, Venezia (Marino Zorzi); Öster-reichische Nationalbibliothek, Vienna (Christa Bader); Burgerbibliothek Bern; Schweizerische Landesbibliothek (Christoph Vogel-Gsell); Stadt-und Universitätsbibliothek Bern; Bibliothèque nationale, Paris; Universitätsbibliothek Heidelberg (Dr. Winfried Werner); Bayerische Staatsbibliothek, München; Staatsbibliothek, Berlin; Deutsche Bibliothek, Frankfurt (Frau Stoll); Stadt-und Universitätsbibliothek Frankfurt; Kongelige Bibliotek, Copenhagen; Hans Christian Andersen Hus, Odense (Niels Oxenvad); Orange County, Florida, Library System (R. B. Murray and Carol Testut); and the Image of the Black project of the Menil Foundation (Karen Dalton). Most important, this study could not have been written without the facilities of Harvard University's Widener Library; Houghton Library; Hilles Library (Steve Love); the Harvard University Theatre Collection (Jeannette T. Newlin); Audio-visual Services (Cynthia Cox); and the outstanding work of the Inter-library Loan Division (Daryl Boone, Michelle Duroche, and Maria McEachern). Judith Jackson was my first research assistant on this pro-ject and laid the groundwork for my growing interracial library which has become the basis for the present book; among the other students who worked for me on *Neither Black Nor White Yet Both* are Maxine Senn-Yuen,Valarie Moses, Jonathan Veitch, Adam Lifshey, Lauren Gwin, Tanya Ponton, Minh-Trang Dang, and Breda O'Keeffe.

I have had many opportunities to discuss ideas that went into this work or to correspond about bibliographic leads with friends, colleagues, writers, and students, among them most notably Daniel Aaron, Doris Abramson, William Andrews, Anthony Appiah, Mia Bay, Sacvan Bercovitch, Warner Berthoff, Urs Bitterli, David Blight, Emily Budick, Carla Cappetti, Hazel Carby, Anna Maria Carpi, Jules Chametzky, Martin Christadler, Kathleen Diffley, Ann duCille, Gerald Early, Geneviève and Michel Fabre, Jeffrey Ferguson, Thomas Ferraro, Barbara Fields, Henry Finder, Shelley Fisher Fishkin, Winfried Fluck, Herbert Gans, Henry Louis Gates, Jr., Nathan Glazer, Philip Gleason, Susan Gillman, Robert Gooding-Williams, Farah Griffin, Margaret Gullette, Fritz Gysin, Stuart Hall, Olaf Hansen, Beatrice Hanssen, Phillip Brian Harper, Heather Hathaway, Patricia Hills, Léon-François Hoffmann, Heinz Ickstadt, Josef Jařab, Charles Johnson, Adrienne Kennedy, Randall Kennedy, Martin Kilson, Angelika Krüger-Kahloula, Jutta Klebe, Vera Kutzinski, Andrea Lee, Günter Lenz, Kathryne Lindberg, John Maynard, Deborah McDowell, Nellie McKay, Jeffrey Melnick, Sheldon Meyer, James Miller, Sidney Mintz, Sandra Naddeff, Charles Nichols, Robert O'Meally, Berndt Ostendorf, Anthony Pagden, Nell Irvin Painter, Orlando Patterson, David Perkins, Sergio

Perosa, Pierre-Yves Petillon, Joel Porte, Alessandro Portelli, Dorothy Porter, Arnold Rampersad, Ishmael Reed, David Riesman, Shlomith Rimmon-Kenan, Ugo Rubeo, Marc Shell, Doris Sommer, Robert Stepto, Jurij Striedter, Eric Sundquist, Thomas Underwood, Enrica Villari, Lynn Weiss, Cornel West, Doris Wilkinson, Theodore Widmer, John Wright, Jean Fagan Yellin, Rafia Zafar, Shamoon Zamir, Rosella Mamoli Zorzi, and many others. I am deeply indebted to my editor Sheldon Meyer for the longstanding and patient support that he has extended to me over the years, and am grateful to Stephanie Sakson for her help in suggesting cuts and in copyediting the manuscript.

Some sections of the book were also read or heard by others, and I wish to acknowledge special comments and suggestions as follows:
*Introduction:* Dorrit Cohn and Menachem Brinker for discussions of thematics; Remo Ceserani and Frank Trommler for comments on theming Chesnutt; Gary Kulik and Jerry Watts for suggestions on Zora Neale Hurston's Cold War nonfiction writings; my son David Sollors for some suggestions; the students in two seminars at Harvard and one in Berlin, and the contributors to the volume *The Return of Thematic Criticism* for ideas on thematics; Fritz Gysin, Elisabeth Bronfen, and other members of the Swiss Association for University Teachers of English for comments on *The Rabbit's Wedding*. A more detailed account of the issues of "theming" appears in "La critica tematica oggi," *L'Asino d'oro* 5.9 (1994): 156–81; and in "Thematics Today," in *Thematics Reconsidered: Essays in Honor of Horst S. Daemmrich*, ed. Frank Trommler (Amsterdam: Rodopi, 1995), 13–32; an expanded discussion of Zora Neale Hurston's conservative anticommunist essays was published under the title "Of Mules and Mares in a Land of Difference; or, Quadrupeds All?," in *American Quarterly* 42.2 (June 1990): 167–90.
*Origins:* Peter Hartwig Graepel and Paul Rathgeber for information on the interracial paradise painting.
*Natus Æthiopus:* Beatrice Hanssen, Barbara Rosenkrantz, Doris Sommer, and Jan Ziolkowski. The discussion following a presentation of this chapter at the Columbus Circle of Columbia University was particularly helpful, and I wish to thank Carla Cappetti, Andrew Delbanco, Robert O'Meally, and Priscilla Wald, as well as Anna Brickhouse, Michael Eliot, Tina Gianquitto, Aviva Taubenfeld, and other graduate students.
*Curse of Ham:* Daniel Aaron, Bob Allison, Patricia Baudoin, Hedda Ben-Bassat, Larry Benson, Miriam Bodian, Juan Bruce-Novoa, Randall Burkett, Ursula Brumm, Isabel Caldeira, Jules Chametzky, Paolo Costa, Gregory Dowling, Geneviève Fabre, Franco Fiorentino, Winfried Fluck, Steven Gillies, Sherice Guillory, David Hollinger, William Hutchison, Heinz Ickstadt, John T. Irwin, Barbara Johnson, J. Lorand Matory, Barry Mazur, Wilson Moses, Anthony Pagden, David Perkins,

Adriano Prosperi, Enrico Pugliese, Albert Raboteau, Allen Reddick, Barbara Rosenkrantz, Irene Santos, Marc Shell, Jürgen Trabant, M. Lynn Weiss, Hana Wirth-Nesher, Larzer Ziff, and Rosella Mamoli Zorzi for suggestions. The comments of the conference participants at the Fondazione Malatesta, at Coimbra University, and of the faculty and students at the Harvard University Center for Literary Studies, at the University of Michigan, at the John F. Kennedy-Institut of the Freie Universität Berlin, at Tel Aviv University, and at the Université de Paris Charles V are much appreciated, as are the questions of a student group at the Massachusetts Institute of Technology. An Italian version of this chapter appeared in *Il razzismo e le sue storie*, ed. Girolamo Imbruglia (Napoli: Edizioni Scientifiche Italiane, 1992), 183–205. A Portuguese translation by Ângela Maria Moreira was published in *Actas do XIV encontro da A.P.E.A.* (Coimbra: Associação Portuguesa de Estudos Anglo-Americanos, 1995), 17–49.

*Calculus of Color:* Manuel Alvar, Barry Mazur, and Sidney Mintz.

*Fingernails as a Racial Sign:* I am grateful for questions and suggestions I received from colleagues and students at the Tudor Room, Johns Hopkins University, at the W. E. B. Du Bois Institute, Harvard University, and from the MERGE group at the University of Umeå (Sweden), as well as from Aleksandra Ålund, Brother Blue, Robert Bone, Jeanne Clegg, Heather Hathaway, John T. Irwin, Steven James, Russell Larkin, Andrea Lee, Grace Dane Mazur, Francesco Orlando, Thomas Pavel, Carl-Ulrik Schierup, Jamie Wacks, and Larzer Ziff. An earlier, slightly different version of this chapter appears in Claude Bremond, Joshua Landy, and Thomas Pavel, *Thematics: New Approaches* (Albany: State Univ. of New York Press, 1995).

*Retellings:* American Studies Association Convention panelists Deborah Pickman Clifford, Carolyn Karcher, Jean Fagan Yellin, Rafia Zafar, as well as Jules Chametzky; Barbara del Mercato, Shaul Bassi, and the group for postcolonial studies at the University of Venice; Raoul Granqvist, University of Umeå; Jochen Achilles, Carmen Birkle, Elizabeth Fox-Genovese, Ulla Haselstein, Udo Hebel, Klaus Lubbers, and other participants in the International Symposium on (Trans)Formations of Cultural Identity in the English-Speaking World at the Johannes-Gutenberg-Universität Mainz; Ernest May and the participants in a colloquium at the Charles Warren Center, Harvard University.

*Passing:* Harvard freshman seminar participants 1992 and 1994; the late Nathan Austern, the late Nathan Irvin Huggins, Barbara Antoniazzi, Cynthia Blair, Marina Cacioppo, Adrienne Kennedy, Glenn Loury, Robert O'Meally, Nell Irvin Painter, Kathleen Pfeiffer, Barbara Rosenkrantz, Jack Salzman, Jamie Wacks, Gayle Wald, and Mary Waters. A short excerpt drawn from this chapter appeared in the *Encyclopedia of African-American Culture and History*, ed. Jack Salzman,

David Lionel Smith, and Cornel West (New York: Macmillan, 1995).

*Incest and Miscegenation:* Viola Sachs and the workshop on the Occult in American Culture, 1987; and David Barron, Mary Dearborn, David Kurnick, Marc Shell, Simone Vauthier, and Doris Y. Wilkinson.

*Illustrations:* Cynthia Bond, Karen Dalton, Patricia Hills, and Judith Wilson.

For final proofreading and help with the preparation of the index I am indebted to Maria Chung, Valerie Jaffee, and Katherine Wagner McCoy.

Cambridge, Frankfurt, Venezia                                     W. S.
Winter 1995/96

## Permissions

The author and publisher wish to thank the following for permission to reproduce copyrighted material:

Antikensammlung München for the reproduction of "Komasten und Hetären: Rauschtanz und sexuelles Vergnügen" (Amphore v. 560 v.C., gezeigt in der Ausstellung Sonderausstellung: *Kunst der Schale, Kultur des Trinkens,* Juni 1991, Nummer 37).

The Bancroft Library of the University of California for permission to reproduce "Un Anglais de Barbade vend sa Maîtresse" (1798), Inkle and Yarico (1808), and Trudge and Wowski: "Come, Let Us Dance and Sing."

Bayrische Staatsbibliothek München for permission to reproduce "Philippa Cataniensis," Jean Fouquet's illumination of the marriage of Philippa of Catania to Raymond de Campagne, from Boccaccio, *Des cas nobles hommes et femmes,* fol. 347, Cod. gall. 6 (1458).

Margaret Benton, Theatre Museum, London, for the reproduction of the photograph by J. W. Debenham of Paul Robeson and Flora Robson in the 1933 London production of *All God's Chillun Got Wings.*

The Bibliothèque nationale de France, Service de reproduction, for permission to reproduce "On l'entraîne, elle se lamente," illustrations from Boulenger de Rivery's *Inkle et Yarico* in *Fables et contes* (Paris, 1754) and from François Gérard, *Ourika* (1824; Alfred Johannot's steel engraving), Cabinet des Estampes, inventory number DCC 55.

Burgerbibliothek Bern for the reproduction of "Feirefiz and Parzival embrace," Bern Codex of *Parzival,* Cod. AA 91, fol. 158$^V$ (746, 12) (1467).

Dutton's Children's Books and Orchard Books for the reproduction of a panel from Jane Ray, *The Story of the Creation* (© 1992).

Editions Rodopi, for an extract from Werner Sollors, "Thematics

Today" in *Thematics Reconsidered: Essays in Honor of Horst S. Daemmrich*, ed. Frank Trommler (© 1995).

Genesis 9, from *Bible moralisée, Codex Vindobonensis 2554* (13th c.), "Negativ aus dem Bildarchiv der Öesterreichischen Nationalbibliothek Wien," with permission of Gerhard Gut.

Richard Landwehrmeyer, Staatsbibliothek Berlin, Preußischer Kulturbesitz Berlin, for the reproduction of a detail from the "Beginning of a genealogy of Christ," rotulus from St. Patricks-Kathedrale Soest (ca. 1230).

Erich Lessing and Fritz Molden Verlag for the illustration of the Chartres stained glass window representing the three estates, as it appeared in Erich Lessing, *Die Arche Noah in Bildern* (© 1968).

The Museum of Fine Arts, Boston, for the reproduction of *Standing Pair Statue*, Egyptian, Old Kingdom, Dynasty 5, Painted Limestone, H: 7m, Harvard University/MFA Expedition, MFA 06.1876.

National Urban League, New York City, for the reproduction of the *Opportunity* October 1925 cover illustration entitled "The Vanishing Mulatto."

The Newberry Library for the reproduction of the "T-O map" from Isidore of Seville's *Etymologiae* (Augsburg, 1472).

Österreichische Nationalbibliothek and Akademische Druck- und Verlagsanstalt, Graz, 52 for an illumination from *Codex Vindobonensis*, 7=fol. *3v (Genesis 9).

Peabody Museum, Harvard University, for the reproduction of the genealogy "C21 DU BOIS" (PLATE 50) from Caroline Bond Day, *A Study of Some Negro-White Families in the United States* (© 1932).

Estill Curtis Pennington, Curator of Southern Painting, and Morris Museum of Art for the reproduction of Thomas Satterwhite Noble's painting *The Price of Blood* (1868).

Herr Rathgeber and Museum der Stadt Calw for the reproduction of "Gemälde aus der Alten Apotheke Nr. 9 (Tierreich)."

Simon and Schuster, for extracts from Werner Sollors, "Passing," in *Encyclopedia of African-American Culture*, eds. Jack Salzman, David Lionel Smith, and Cornel West (© 1996).

The State University of New York Press, for Werner Sollors, "The Bluish Tinge in the Halfmoons" in *Thematics: New Approaches*, eds. Claude Bremond, Joshua Landy, and Thomas Pavel (© 1995).

Richard M. Ticktin and the estate of Garth Williams for permission to reproduce the front cover and double page from *The Rabbits' Wedding* (© Garth Williams 1958 and 1986).

Every effort has been made to trace all copyright holders, but if any have been inadvertently overlooked the publisher will be pleased to make the necessary arrangement at the first opportunity.

# Contents

# Illustrations

## Endings

# NEITHER BLACK
# NOR WHITE
# YET BOTH

You go long! No more nigger dan you be, Miss Rosa. . . . You seem to tink yourself white folks. You an't nerry one, black *nor* white, I'd like to be one or turrer.

—Dinah to Rosa in Harriet Beecher Stowe's *Uncle Tom's Cabin* (1852)[1]

I can't be white and coloured at the same time; the two don't mingle, and I must consequently be one or the other.

—Clarence Garie [Jr.] in Frank Webb, *The Garies and Their Friends* (1857)[2]

The result of such an anomalous position was, that the boy was neither a white person nor a negro. The white race, to which he bore the nearest kinship, repudiated him utterly; while the blacks could not rightfully claim him as belonging to them. He had no people.

—Tully's background in *Sisters of Orleans* (1871)[3]

[Children of a white man and a black woman] are neither white nor black, neither French nor African, neither curly-haired nor straight. Unfortunately, they are something nonetheless.

—Albert Londres, *Terre d'ébène: La traite des Noirs* (1929)[4]

Mongrel. 4 *transf.* Of persons, things, classes: Of mixed origin, nature, or character; not referable to any definite species or type: that is "neither one thing nor the other." Chiefly in contemptuous use.

—*Oxford English Dictionary*

I am white and I am black, and know that there is no difference. Each one casts a shadow, and all shadows are dark.

—Walter White, "Why I Remain a Negro" (1947)[5]

So, I thought, you are neither black nor white.
You are neither male nor female.
And you are that most ambiguous of citizens, the writer.

—Samuel R. Delany, *The Motion of Light in Water* (1988)[6]

What is to become of that large class of which I am a part, that class which is neither white nor black and yet both?

—A Professor in a Western Negro College (1908)

# Introduction
## Black—White—Both—
## Neither—In–Between

Neither black nor white yet both may be nothing more than a cliché. It does appear with some frequency in interracial literature, and is one recurrence among many that give that literature a special quality. The tracing of similar such recurring features is the subject of this book. By "interracial literature" I mean, on the following pages, works in all genres that represent love and family relations involving black-white couples, biracial individuals, their descendants, and their larger kin—to all of whom the phrasing may be applied, be it as couples, as individuals, or as larger family units. I find the term "interracial" preferable to some others.[1] Although it may be understood as inadvertently strengthening a biological concept of "race" that it promises to transcend—and I do not wish to employ it in the sense that would emphasize the "racial" more than the "inter-" (or the "bi-")—this may, in any case, be a lesser semantic burden to bear than the heavy historical load that weighs down much of the problematic vocabulary applied to interracial relations and that will be subjected to some etymological and semantic scrutiny: it includes not only such words as "Mulatto," "miscegenation," "mixed race," and "hybrid," but also, for that matter, "black" and "white." One has only to remember Joel Williamson's remarkable statement, "There are, essentially, no such things as 'black' people or 'white' people."[2] Despite their histories and inaccuracies, such terms may be unavoidable and even useful and helpful at times, as they have also been adopted and reappropriated for a variety of reasons, including their specificity, their ability to redefine a negative term from the past into one positively and defiantly adopted in the present, or simply the absence of better terms.[3]

An interracial focus, however, might serve specific ends. Since there are no "races" nor widely agreed upon definitions of "race," understanding the cultural operations which make them seem natural or self-evident categories may be desirable.[4] Instead of only looking at interracial relations as those interactions that are often prohibited between people from "different races," we might also regard intermarriage bans—and the denial of legitimacy to biracial individuals—as important building blocks in the construction of "race."[5] The hackneyed notion of "pure blood" always rests on the possibility and the reality of "mixed blood"—though violent "cleansing" may be deemed necessary to constitute "purity." The time may have come to stop avoiding the interracial theme in literature, to investigate it, and to unpack its semantic fields.

Black-white interracial love and family relations have been—especially in the modern period, from the French and Haitian Revolutions to the aftermath of World War II—a subject likely to elicit censure and high emotions, or at least a certain nervousness. The attacks on the fact that black male customers had the right to go to white prostitutes led to the South African system of racial segregation that became known as "apartheid." In the United States, the mere presence of a white woman and a black man in the same space could justify mob violence or terror.[6] Such familiar questions as "Would you like your daughter to marry one?" have functioned as central, and not always ineffective, attacks on racial equality and integration. And in various opinion polls taken in the U.S. South from 1962 to 1982, the majority of respondents has never been opposed to laws prohibiting interracial marriage.[7]

What is subjected to socially approved attempted or legalized bans in real life is often also censored, suppressed, denied, or rejected in symbolic representations. In 1930, the state of Mississippi, for example, enacted a criminal statute that made punishable the "publishing, printing, or circulating any literature in favor of or urging interracial marriage or social equality."[8] (Simply representing interracial marriage, or criticizing its criminalization, was often perceived to be the same as "favoring" or "urging" it.)[9] Vladimir Nabokov succinctly expressed the belief that the theme of "a Negro-white intermarriage which is a complete and glorious success resulting in lots of children and grandchildren" is "utterly taboo" in literature (as are, he asserts, pedophilia, and the happy and contented atheist who gets to be 102 years old and dies in his sleep).[10] In the face of its opposition, does interracial literature exist at all?

The answers of the past would seem to lean toward the negative, and the working hypothesis of many readers (and that includes my own expectations before embarking on this project) has been that inherently controversial texts about interracial alliances must have been very rare indeed. For example, a Mark Twain critic started an essay on *Pudd'nhead Wilson* (1894) with the assertion that in its treatment of miscegenation, the novel "considers a theme which was totally avoided in nineteenth century American literature."[11] The editor of another nineteenth-century American text, of an autobiographical nature, claimed that the work had remained obscure for over a century because of its "unabashed representation of an interracial marriage, a liaison from which the novel's protagonist was an offspring." This was so because interracial marriage "was not a popular subject for representation in either antislavery or proslavery novels."[12] The author of an often-cited essay on the literature of American abolitionism deemed it "hardly surprising that, at least so far as I am aware, no antislavery fiction admits to the possibility of a white woman loving or wedding a black man."[13] And in a valuable survey of sixty American novels on the theme of racial "amalgamation" (including two very early, six proslavery, and at least ten antislavery novels before 1860), another author expressed the belief that such fictions were "unique to American literature" and "foreign to European culture."[14]

To be sure, stories of black-white sexual and family relations have run against various taboos. Texts from Masuccio Salernitano's *Novellino* (1475) to Richard Hildreth's *The Slave* (1836) were, for example, put on the Catholic Church's *Index Expurgatorius* of forbidden books, though it was probably the representation of sexual frankness, adultery, or incest, and not the interracial nature of the relationships, that was decisive in such bans. When Eugene O'Neill's play *All God's Chillun Got Wings* was first produced in New York City in 1924, the censors intervened, prohibiting the staging of the first scene (involving the interracial friendship of children), and the playwright received personal threats from the Ku Klux Klan—that he answered courageously and succinctly. The 1930s movie production code forbade the theme of miscegenation. And Alexandra Ripley, the author of *Scarlett*, a 1991 sequel to Margaret Mitchell's *Gone With the Wind* (1936), had "almost" complete aesthetic freedom in her work; the only restriction that the Mitchell estate put on her efforts was the injunction: "don't include miscegenation or graphic sex." Many such interferences could be registered in the production of interracial literature.[15]

There is, for example, the case of Maria Edgeworth, who, at the request of her own father, struck out of the revised 1810 edition of her novel *Belinda* (first published in 1801) an interracial marriage subplot in which the black servant Juba weds Lucy, an English farmer's daughter. Edgeworth wrote in a letter to Anna Barbauld on 18 January 1810:

> In the second volume, "*Jackson*" is substituted for the husband of Lucy instead of "*Juba*," many people having been scandalized at the idea of a black man marrying a white woman; my father says that gentlemen have horrors upon this subject, and draw conclusions very unfavorable to a female writer who appeared to recommend such unions; as I do not understand the subject, I trust his better judgment, and end with—for Juba read Jackson.[16]

Harriet Martineau, in her *Retrospect of Western Travel* (1838), mentioned the fate of *Belinda*'s scandalous subplot in the United States:

> Miss Edgeworth was denounced as a woman of no intelligence. . . . The incident is so subordinate that I had entirely forgotten it; but a clergyman's lady threw the volume to the opposite corner of the floor when she came to the page. . . . Miss Edgeworth is worshipped throughout the United

States; but it is in spite of this terrible passage, this clause of a sentence in *Belinda*, which nobody in America can tolerate, while no one elsewhere ever, I should think, dreamed of finding fault with it.[17]

Short of removing interracial marriage plots or subplots completely from literary texts so as not to appear to "recommend" such alliances, authors could decide to resolve their plots in such a way that what looked like an interracial romance at the beginning would turn out to be an intraracial one at the end. Ratna Roy has called one version of this formula "Mulatto-Proved-White" and analyzed it in Joseph Holt Ingraham's *The Quadroone; or, St. Michael's Day* (1841) and in James S. Peacocke's *The Creole Orphans* (1856).[18] Roy's formula may only be the unusual variation of the cultural norm in the modern United States according to which a "Mulatto" is really (and does not have to be proved) "black."

This norm has come to be shared by black and white alike. Naomi Zack has subjected this cultural logic to scrutiny and taken a statement by Zora Neale Hurston as a point of departure—who claimed, "I am a mixed-blood, it is true," only to proceed a little later with the following self-description: "I maintain that I have been a Negro three times—a Negro baby, a Negro girl, and a Negro woman."[19] Zack questions how Hurston, "if she sees herself as mixed race, . . . can *logically* identify herself as a Negro. . . . Hurston illustrates all too well how morally good American identities of mixed race collapse into black racial identities. Such black identities may be admirable, but they are not logically or in fact identities of mixed race."[20] Whether the interracial character is proved white or black, in either case the "mixed-race" space is cleared in favor of a monoracial occupancy. And it is not a foregone conclusion that, for example, African American or biracial writers would be more relaxed in approaching interracial themes than their white colleagues.

Even classics of the past and the most respectable modern writers who have represented the interracial theme were subjected to public criticism. Shakespeare's *Othello* was, of course, a permanent provocation. For example, Abigail Adams confessed in 1786 that she was upset by "the sooty appearance of the Moor" and added: "I could not separate the African from the man, nor prevent that disgust and horror which filled my mind every time I saw him touch the gentle Desdemona"; and in 1835 her son John Quincy Adams wrote that the great "moral lesson of *Othello* is that black and white blood cannot be intermingled without a gross outrage upon the law of Nature; and that, in such violations, Nature will vindicate her laws."[21]

In his book *Race Orthodoxy in the South* (1914) Thomas Pearce Bailey, a professor of psychology and the dean of the department of education at the University of Mississippi, expressed his belief that one reaches the "the real *crux* of the question" when one asks: "may not all the equalities be ultimately based on potential social equality, and that in turn on inter-marriage?" Bailey was therefore discouraged to discover that "even the high-souled Tennyson, in 'Locksley Hall,' draws a picture of the reck-less, disappointed youth who has an impulse to wed a dusky maiden and rear a dusky brood."[22] Simply by representing this theme, Tennyson seems to have made the task of Bailey's educational program more diffi-cult.

> It is just because primary race feeling is *not* deeply based in human instinct, whereas the mating instinct is so based, that a secondary racial feeling, race-pride, comes in from a more developed reflective consciousness to minimize the natural instinct for amalgamation.

Bailey is honest enough not to claim a "race instinct"[23] but, on the con-trary, a mating instinct that knows no racial boundaries. And Tennyson's poem does, indeed—in its uncut version—contain the lines spoken by the lover who, spurned by his cousin Amy, dreams of an escape from the West of technology and book-learning to an Oriental island paradise:

> There the passions cramped no longer shall have scope and breathing space;
> I will take some savage woman, she shall rear my dusky race.
>
> Iron jointed, supple-sinew'd, they shall dive, and they shall run,
> Catch the wild goat by the hair, and hurl their lances in the sun;
>
> Whistle back the parrot's call, and leap the rainbows of the brooks,
> Not with blinded eyesight poring over miserable books.[24]

Bailey disapproved of these lines in Tennyson's poem, and they remind-ed the educator of the need to curb certain instincts—implicitly, by restricting access to racially discouraging works of literature.[25]

In view of the palpable and formidable social opposition, is there enough "interracial" literature to make it the subject of a study? Some investigations of "miscegenation" have, at times inadvertently, turned into restatements of the power of the taboo against it (in order to suggest that it could not have existed and hence did not exist).[26] This is as if read-ers took at face value Mrs. Hayes-Rore's reaction to Helga Crane's story in Nella Larsen's novel *Quicksand* (1928):

> The woman felt that the story, dealing as it did with race intermingling and possibly adultery, was beyond definite discussion. For among black people, as among white people, it is tacitly understood that these things are not mentioned—and therefore they do not exist.[27]

Yet this statement appears in a novel that *does* mention "these things," and many other writers have chosen to include the representation of social obstacles to their interracial family stories. It seems evident that—

despite legal prohibition, religious denunciation, moral indignation, or social opposition from political conservatives, liberals, or radicals—more literary works about "forbidden" couples and their descendants have been written, published, read, and debated than is usually assumed, and some attempts have also been undertaken to survey, catalog, and describe the vast materials that are in existence.[28] Far from appearing exclusively in the literature of the United States, interracial themes have been present in writing from antiquity and the middle ages to the Renaissance and the present, with a pronounced increase since the late eighteenth century. Texts can be found, not only in English, German, French, Spanish, and Portuguese, but also in Greek, Latin, Italian, Danish, Russian, Arabic, and Middle High German. The topic was neither "minor" nor was it the special province of bad, unknown, or unimportant writers; and a library adhering to Bailey's idea of "Race Orthodoxy" would have to keep an impressive list of authors and works under lock and seal in order to prevent readers from being tempted by their own instincts: Heliodorus, Wolfram von Eschenbach, Masuccio Salernitano, Giraldi Cinthio, Shakespeare, *Thousand and One Nights*, Heinrich von Kleist, Victor Hugo, Aleksandr Sergeevič Puškin, Honoré de Balzac, Gustave de Beaumont, Victor Séjour, Hans Christian Andersen, Eugène Sue, Walt Whitman, Alexandre Dumas, Lydia Maria Child, Mayne Reid, William Wells Brown, Frank Webb, Charles Baudelaire, William Dean Howells, Theodor Storm, Rebecca Harding Davis, John William De Forest, Louisa May Alcott, Wilkie Collins, Guy de Maupassant, Cirilo Villaverde, George Washington Cable, Bernardo Guimarães, Pierre Loti, Aluísio Azevedo, Albion W. Tourgée, Lafcadio Hearn, Joel Chandler Harris, Frances E. W. Harper, Mark Twain, Kate Chopin, Charles Waddell Chesnutt, Pauline Hopkins, W. E. B. Du Bois, Thomas Dixon, Ellen Glasgow, Eugene O'Neill, Claire Goll, Paul Green, Langston Hughes, William Faulkner, Lillian Smith, Sinclair Lewis, and many, many other famous, recently rediscovered, or still little-known writers and works. There is a considerable body of works in all genres in which interracial couples, biracial individuals, or their descendants are crucial, central, or otherwise noteworthy. Any doubtful reader may easily ascertain the varieties of interracial literature by glancing at the preliminary chronology appended to this book: it shows that the theme is very much present in literature, though this may not be the most widely recognized (let alone universally applauded or critically studied) presence. As a comparative glance at the chronology of intermarriage bans (that is also appended) will show, the stories of black-white families did not stop appearing in places on the globe where such unions were banned; they were even produced in states that prohibited the distribution of literature "advocating" racial intermingling or social equality. They have been a prominent feature of American literature, and a pervasive element in writing by African Americans, so that the present book is also an attempt

***Figure 1a*** U.S. stamp commemorating the
French Revolution (1989)

at offering some new international and historical contexts for black and
white literature of the United States.

The same holds true for visual representations of interracial alliances
and families, and I have chosen to illustrate this book, which is primarily
concerned with *texts*, with interracial images, some of which are little
known. There may also be a similar tendency at work in not circulating
such images widely. To take just one obvious example, the discussions
about the 1989 United States postage stamp commemorating the French
Revolution revealed that the Postmaster General preferred to represent
the two children embracing each other as part of the allegory of
"Fraternity" in an identical silvery color rather than follow the original
image, an allegorical representation of 1792, and show one black and one
white child—as Charles Cordier did in his *Aimez-vous les uns les autres ou
Fraternité* (1867), and as the French post office managed to do on a simi-
lar-sized stamp (Figs. 1a, 1b).[29]

***Figure 1b*** French
*fraternité* stamp (1989)

The evidence suggests that "racial mixing" has its tradition, an inter-racial tradition that deserves to be explored and analyzed.[30] By making the interracial theme a constant, the persistence and scope of the litera-ture can begin to be sketched; at the same time, many other variables are left open, inviting comparisons across literary genres and periods. While the most recent impulse in writing literary criticism has been to continue working within national frames that are at times corrected by an alterna-tive focus on gender or race, more international comparisons could vali-date or make questionable some hypotheses of national, ethnic, or gen-der-based idiosyncrasies in writing. Ironically, interracial plot lines have been marginalized not only in national literatures but also in their sup-posed correctives, the literary studies dedicated to explore ethnicity and gender; and interracial stories, after all, involve male, female, black, white, and biracial characters.[31] These are works of literature that chal-lenge by definition the boundaries within which literature is being stud-ied; yet neither have they played a central role in comparative literary studies. The critical literature of the past often focuses on representa-tions *within* national and ethnic boundaries, a fact which has freed me to write a study in which the shared elements as well as the differences in works from many lands, and cross-cultural historical changes, can be introduced to (and, hopefully, enrich) the study of literature of the United States.

Once denounced for threatening the principle of ethnic purity from the white conservative side, such works are now at times criticized by lib-erals and radicals for not being consistently nonwhite enough; and, once attacked for subverting the white man's burden or undermining the "race instinct," they are now rejected for supposedly serving the "hegemonies" of Eurocentrism or patriarchy.[32] Furthermore, interracial texts are at times discussed as if they were related only to "nature" and not also to other texts and to variously imaginable literary series; and, finally, when they are discussed, they are more often "themed"—Gerald Prince's term for identifying themes—for a black-white *contrast* of "either/or" than for an interracial realm of "neither, nor, both, and in-between."[33] Is there such a thing as "amalgophobia" or "mixophobia"? As Diana Williams observed, it is still hard for Americans to recognize "racial mixing, both between and within persons."[34]

## Theming "Race"

A good example for the theming history that has resulted in the disap-pearance of "mixed race" is Charles W. Chesnutt's "The Wife of His Youth" (1898).[35] The story focuses on Mr. Ryder, a light-skinned mid-dle-aged man of partly African ancestry who plays a leading role in the "Blue Vein" Society, an upwardly mobile social club of "individuals who were, generally speaking, more white than black" in a city recognizable as Cleveland, Ohio. At the beginning, the narrative is close to Ryder's consciousness, describes his light features and career as an employee of a railroad company, and develops his social views as a representative of people of mixed blood:

> "I have no race prejudice," he would say, "but we people of mixed blood are ground between the upper and the nether millstone. Our fate lies between absorption by the white race and extinction in the black. The one doesn't want us yet, but may take us in time. The other would welcome us, but it would be for us a backward step."[36]

Ryder is reading Tennyson in order to find some appropriate verses that he can use at a ball he is preparing to give in honor of a young light-skinned widow, Mrs. Molly Dixon, because he intends to propose marriage to her. Suddenly an old woman appears at his door who turns out, as the reader soon learns and Mr. Ryder has undoubtedly recognized sooner, to be 'Liza Jane, to whom Ryder (this is an assumed name, and he used to be called Sam Taylor) was married in slavery days in Missouri, a fact he and the narrator seem to have forgotten until 'Liza Jane appears. She is everything the Blue Veins have tried to repress about their past: she speaks in dialect, is very dark, has old-fashioned clothes, and so forth. For twenty-five years she has been looking for her husband, whom she would recognize anywhere, she says; she had helped him get away when the people he worked for planned to sell him (even though he was a free-man); and she was whipped and sold down the river as a punishment for warning him. She shows him an old daguerreotype of Sam that he studies. Then he says noncommittally—and without lying outright—that he knows no one "who goes by that name," but promises to help her find her husband and writes her address on the fly-leaf of his Tennyson edition. When she leaves, he looks at the mirror for a long time. The final scene takes place later that night, at the ball at which Ryder had intended to ask for Molly Dixon's hand. He had planned to speak in praise of women's fidelity and devotion before making the announcement, but now he tells his own story—as a hypothetical case, but told in the "soft dialect, which came readily to his lips" (whereas in reading poetry "his pronunciation was sometimes faulty"). "Suppose that this husband," he tells the assembled Blue Veins,

> was young, and she much older than he; that he was light, and she was black; that their marriage was a slave marriage, and legally binding only if they chose to make it so after the war. . . . Suppose, too, that, as the years went by, this man's memory of the past grew more and more indistinct, until at last it was rarely, except in his dreams, that any image of this bygone period rose before his mind. (21)

He asks what that man should have done when Mrs. Dixon, at whom Ryder looks "with a mingled expression of renunciation and inquiry," answers: "He should have acknowledged her" (23). Ryder now brings 'Liza Jane into the ballroom from an adjacent chamber. The story ends with his declaration, "This is the woman, and I am the man, whose story I have told you. Permit me to introduce to you the wife of my youth."

Typical for the reception that Chesnutt's story found among his contemporaries was the reading of "The Wife of His Youth" in the context of the generalization "Mulatto" that Mr. Ryder and the "Blue Veins" were seen to embody. Thus William Dean Howells praised Chesnutt for the novelty of the story's material,

> for the writer dealt not only with people who were not black enough to contrast grotesquely with white people,—who in fact were of that near approach to the ordinary American in race and color which leaves, at the last degree, every one but the connoisseur in doubt whether they are Anglo-Saxon or Anglo-African.

Howells was fascinated by Chesnutt's portrayal of "that middle world" and commended him for acquainting "us" (presumably white readers)

> with those regions where the paler shades dwell as hopelessly, with relation to ourselves, as the blackest negro. He has not shown the dwellers there as very different from ourselves.[37]

By contrast with Howells's theming of the middle world, Nancy Huston Banks thought in 1900 that "The Wife of His Youth" constituted a critique of Ryder, "vain, conceited, puffed up over his small measure of success, thinking over-much of his white blood." She deplored Chesnutt's "careless approach to the all but unapproachable ground of sentimental relations between the black race and the white race"—that is, interracial marriage—in another story and concluded with regret that Chesnutt "has not held to the themes well within his scope."[38] Banks thus used Chesnutt's choice of the "all but unapproachable" interracial theme as a touchstone of a negative evaluation. As late as 1965, Hugh Gloster themed the "Mulatto" explicitly, but positively, in Chesnutt's story and described "The Wife of His Youth" as "a masterful study of the Blue Vein Society" presenting

> a cultured mulatto who respectfully but not enthusiastically acknowledges an ignorant black woman whom he married before the Civil War and who helped him to escape to freedom.[39]

After the book was reissued in the 1960s, however, it received new readings as a "black" text; and the new racial theming generally substituted a black-white contrast for Ryder's, Chesnutt's, and Howells's intermediate "mixed-blood" terms so that Mr. Ryder was now typically described as "black." Cleanth Brooks, R. W. B. Lewis, and Robert Penn Warren, for example, underwrote the statement that the story's concern was "with the problems of the black man free in a white world."[40] Robert

Bone, in a more sustained theming, focused on "race" in the sense of the political and psychological conflict between assimilationism and nationalism, so that a social science paradigm—developed by Abram Kardiner and Lionel Ovesey's book *The Mark of Oppression* (1951)—became the context for theming. Bone was particularly clear in identifying the theme:

> The danger of internalizing the white ideal is Chesnutt's major theme. Up to a point, he warns, the black man can play at being white, but in the end reality will overtake him. The story thus amounts to an attack on the assimilationist perspective and an exposure of its source in fantasy and wish-fulfillment.[41]

Ryder thus became a black everyman, and his acceptance of his black "reality" through his decision not to "play at being white" was found to be the primary theme. Bone also wrote that "Mr. Ryder's dilemma is essentially that of the 'voluntary Negro' who is light enough to pass and therefore free to choose his race."[42] If Mr. Ryder's situation was seen in analogy to stories renouncing the option of racial "passing," then that choice could be placed into the larger context of an admirable intraracial cross-class union that would appear to be celebrated at the end of the story. This is, of course, a plausible reading; yet what concerns us here is the fact that Chesnutt's "Mulatto" is thus folded into a black identity.

Many readers have followed Bone's pioneering work. William Andrews also saw Ryder's choice as the theme of the story. Looking at it politically rather than through the lens of social psychology, he believed the choice to be moral and commendable since it results in bridging class divisions within the black community.[43] This provided the story with the political theme of W. E. B. Du Bois's concept of the "talented tenth," applied to Chesnutt's Blue Veins—seen in relation to "the rest of the race" (implying also that Mulattoes are *eo ipso* part of the "black race"). The theme of the dilemma of the middle world had been replaced by the need for black unity. Sylvia Lyons Render also isolated the theme of a happy resolution of intraracial relations, adding that Mr. Ryder's action provided "a pattern of behavior which no doubt Chesnutt hoped more advantaged blacks would follow."[44] And Eric Sundquist, too, strongly emphasized community solidarity and the healing of an intra-black class rift as themes and set Ryder into a direct relationship with Chesnutt, who thus appeared as the biographical contextualization that validates the hero's moral choice in favor of "the community."[45]

Strikingly, the context of British Victorian literature that is so strongly present in the text of the story that shows Ryder reading and quoting Tennyson has typically been invoked only to build up a *contrast* with Chesnutt's themes. For example, Sundquist writes that 'Liza Jane stands "in stark contrast to" Ryder's "fantasy of a social world represented by Tennyson's poem, 'A Dream of Fair Women.'"[46] The textual presence of Tennyson is thus subordinated to the theme of racial contrast. Yet "The Wife of His Youth" could also be linked with Tennyson, whose presence in the text may be the result of Chesnutt's pervasive employment of intertextual irony.

To be sure, Chesnutt does juxtapose Tennyson's language and 'Liza Jane's; and he contrasts "divinely fair" and "rather ruddy."[47] But he also develops—in Tennyson's terms—a contrast between art and life; and he continues Tennyson's (and Chaucer's) themes of looking at the past and singing about good women. Chesnutt does not quote Tennyson randomly or one-dimensionally, and "The Dream of Fair Women" is not merely a white contrast for the colored world of Mr. Ryder.[48] Though he excerpts the Helen section from the poem that seems to highlight all the contrasts in complexion with such phrasings as "chiselled marble" and "most divinely fair," one of Tennyson's "fair women"—the adjective has a *moral* meaning and does not denote complexion—was Cleopatra, the queen "with swarthy cheeks and bold black eyes." Chesnutt's narrator states that Ryder's "volume was open at 'A Dream of Fair Women'"— and it was exactly on that page that Cleopatra's image was reproduced, above the poem's title, in the most famous illustrated edition of Tennyson's poems (Fig. 2). This Cleopatra, rendered by the pre-Raphaelite artist John Everett Millais, looked rather dark, reflecting Tennyson's description of her as "swarthy." In fact, her appearance so

***Figure 2***   John Everett Millais, *Cleopatra* (1866)

reminded Tennyson of *racial* difference that he complained about Millais's choice of making Cleopatra a "Mulatto."[49] Chesnutt may well have been aware of Millais's illustration when he chose "The Dream of Fair Women" for incorporation in his tale. The presence of Cleopatra in "The Wife of His Youth" may also extend to Shakespeare's *Antony and Cleopatra*, the play in which the queen of Egypt offers a messenger to kiss her "bluest veins" if he brings her the tiding that Antony is alive.[50] And even the poem "Margaret" (1832) that begins with the address to her as "rare" and "pale," cited by Chesnutt, continues with a contrast between Adeline and the "darker" Margaret.[51] When Chesnutt lets Mr. Ryder write down 'Liza Jane's address "on the fly-leaf of the volume of Tennyson" (17), he might ironically be questioning common racial distinctions between black and white. It is precisely this questioning that marks an interracial location, and it is a location that has often been sacrificed to black-white dualism.

"The Wife of His Youth" has been read, more often than not, as a story that has a happy ending, giving the Blue Veins and Mr. Ryder the opportunity to reconcile past and present, upward aspirations and slave memories, mobility and dialect, and so forth, as the forward-looking upstart with only a last name and the backward-looking allegory of memory with only a first name publicly reaffirm their alliance. While this seems true for the moment of the acknowledgment scene itself, the story chooses not to represent what happens *after* the dramatic disclosure, and it seems doubtful whether a permanent healing of class and color rifts within the black community can justly be inferred from the story's conclusion. Though several thematic interpretations seem to take for granted that an ultimate class-healing is what will follow the ending, it is also possible to imagine other conclusions. Readers who have themed Ryder's psychological dilemma rather than his function in promoting racial unity have looked at the ending as a problem: Richard Watson Gilder, for example, wrote Chesnutt in a letter that it seemed to him as though the "poor fellow were entitled to a compromise of some sort. I don't know just what it would be, but the precise outcome hardly seems humanly right."[52] And A. Robert Lee wrote that "Ryder's nominal gesture towards the oneness of black Americans, having denied his blackness for an adult lifetime, doesn't carry much conviction."[53] What might also be assumed to follow the ending is Mr. Ryder's demotion as "dean" of the Blue Veins, or even his expulsion from the exclusive association, as a result of his revelation, or of his humiliation of Molly Dixon, on the Saturday morning after the wonderfully moving last toast in the ballroom on Friday night.

If the case of Chesnutt's "Wife of His Youth" is representative, one may infer that available contexts for theming have been limited. Of course, race is neither an illegitimate nor a forced theme to be identified in a collection subtitled "and Other Stories of the Color Line."[54] Yet it is

Chesnutt's special way of treating this theme that might deserve more attention because it distinguishes his aesthetic method—which often aims at questioning any easy distinction between "black" and "white"—from that employed in countless other thematizations of race. Chesnutt *did* represent a middle world and took no metaphysical assurance from such terms as "black" or "white."[55] In its growing focus on race—understood as black-white contrast—the development in theming "The Wife of His Youth" (whether psychological, political, or biographical) may parallel the disappearance of interracial categories on American census forms after 1920, or contemporary scholarly discussions of "miscegenation" that are tellingly (and without any apparent awareness of the irony of such a move) placed under the heading "Black Life."[56]

## Thematic Explorations

The approach I chose for this study is "thematic,"[57] and I have already been using such terms as "theme" or "theming," and implied that the literature studied here is "about" something. This assumption is shared with critical practice in much, if not most, of the flourishing literary scholarship dedicated to ethnic, racial, and gender issues. Many works in these fields are, in fact, thematic studies, even if this may not be widely acknowledged. For example, no one, to my knowledge, has analyzed "The Wife of His Youth" solely as a *formal* vehicle or a specific kind of narrative structure; in other words, all published interpretations of the tale are at least partly and, in most cases, predominantly, if not exclusively, thematic.[58]

Of course, "there is no 'in-and-of-itself' in the theme,"[59] and even a single uncomplicated sentence can be *absolutely* or *relatively* "about" something, as Menachem Brinker illustrated:

> The sentence "the book is on the table" is absolutely about the book, the table, and the fact that the book is on the table. Yet relative to the information received this morning, according to which "if Peter buys the book he will leave it on the table," the first sentence . . . is also about Peter and about the fact that he bought the book and left it on the table. By implication it may also be about the fact that Peter keeps his promises, that the book has arrived in Israel, and so on and so forth.[60]

If this is true for a simple statement of fact, how much more complicated must it be to say what the theme of a literary work may be? A variety of mixed-up, often unconscious interests may guide the process of theming—for example, aesthetic, logical, statistical, political, moral, genealogical, psychoanalytical, structuralist, nationalistic, or autobiographical motives.[61] It is the contexts and, especially, the debates about legitimate and unpredictable contexts that help to determine the themes of a given work, and the contexts surrounding interracial themes may be particularly strong.

"Black" and "white" could serve as such forceful agents that they have had the power to eclipse, or racialize, what they referred to; and the metaphoric significance of color could be more important than the ostensibly represented subject. Just as the "Mulatto" could be themed *away* in the case of Chesnutt, so an interracial theme could also be inserted *into* texts that were hardly "absolutely about" this topic. For example, a postcard, probably from the early part of the century, portrayed two cats, a black one in a man's bathing suit, and a white one in a dress, dancing in the shallow ocean waters on the edge of a beach, and other cats are visible in and near beach tents in the background. The card was titillatingly entitled "Mixed Bathing" (Fig. 3). The cats' colors and costumes—or, put differently, the way in which they were coded by race and gender—are the only aspects that could conceivably make the subject risqué, while the postcard's heading may also represent an attempt to turn potential tension into humor.[62] In this instance, we do not know why the manufacturer chose the title he did over such other possibilities as "Cats by the Seaside," "The New Beach Apparel," "Family Vacation," or "Summer." In each case, however, it would be the title, a *text*, that would give the central theme to the image: the image would seem to be "about" different things, dependent on the heading it received. In any event, the postcard was not, as far as I know, enmeshed in a theming controversy such as the one that emerged in the Alabama Public Library system and that will be discussed shortly.

In the last years of legalized racial segregation in the United States animal fables applied to the human situation seem to have flourished, as

**Figure 3** *Mixed Bathing*, postcard

is evidenced, for example, by Zora Neale Hurston's little-studied conservative essays of the period in which she denounced the fight for legal desegregration, with her rejection of the supposedly integrationist fable of mules running after a white mare, as a communist plot for interracial marriage.[63] When she used it in the *Orlando Sentinel*, the story was illustrated with a little cartoon depicting a luring white mare with a question mark over her head and a sign reading "desegregation," while across the fence a black mule is thinking, "I just want my own pasture improved" (Fig. 4).[64]

**Figure 4**    *Orlando Sentinel*, cartoon (1955)

Characteristic of the mood of the time was the small crisis generated by a children's book published in 1958. It was written and illustrated by Garth Williams (who may be best known for his visual work in E. B. White's novel *Charlotte's Web*) and entitled *The Rabbits' Wedding*. It is the story of two little rabbits who live in a forest and happily play with each other, hopping, skipping, and jumping around. Their happiness is only interrupted by one of the rabbits' recurring moods of pensiveness, brought on by his wish that he could always be with the other one. The other rabbit says that if he really wishes that, she will be his forever; then they pick flowers together and put them in each other's ears. They get married in a wedding circle of all the other rabbits, and the animals of the forest come to watch the wedding dance. The married rabbits live happily ever after. The book was pitched for an audience of three- to seven-year-olds, and the well-balanced *New York Times* reviewer felt that children would hug the book tightly "if only for the bold pictures of frisky, fluffy bunnies romping in the forest. The tale of this bashful suitor and his lady fair, however, is too low-keyed for many readings."[65]

**Figure 5** Garth Williams, *The Rabbits' Wedding*, cover illustration (1958)

*The Rabbits' Wedding* seems thematically unrelated to the topic of the present study. Yet the brief reference to "lady fair" contains the important clue: as in the case of Hurston's mules and mares and that of the cat postcard, it was the *color* of the rabbits that suggested the human context: one rabbit (the male one, too) was black, the other one white (and, yes, a female one—it *was* 1958) (Fig. 5). In the world of the 1950s U.S. South, divided by the issue of racial integration, this was sufficient evidence to invite readings of this book as a contribution to the interracial theme. The presence of the categories black/male and white/female helped to override the species difference between the book's subjects and its readers, and *The Rabbits' Wedding* could thus be themed as *really* about an interracial marriage, an event that, at the time of the book's publication, was still illegal in more than half of the United States. The book also appeared three years after the Virginia supreme court, in *Naim v. Naim*, had sustained the miscegenation statute and ruled that the state's legislative purpose was "to preserve the racial integrity of its citizens" and to prevent "the corruption of blood," "the obliteration of racial pride," and the creation of "a mongrel breed of citizens."[66]

Once it was themed "interracially," pictures and text of a children's book could appear different from what they seemed, not harmless and joyful but positively dangerous; the representation of the hopping characters could now be deemed taboo, and the images of their physical closeness suggestive of the corruption of (more than rabbit) blood and

**Figure 6**  Garth Williams, *The Rabbits' Wedding*, illustration (1958)

hence inappropriate for children (Fig. 6). An Alabama (White) Citizens' Council used its organ, the weekly *Montgomery Home News*, for a sharp, front-page critique of the book for promoting integration, spelling out its fears and its method of theming in the headline: "What's Good Enough for Rabbits Should Do for Mere Humans."[67] The book was thus thought not just to represent a certain course of action but (again) to "recommend" it to human readers. The columnist Henry Balch followed suit and condemned *The Rabbits' Wedding* in the *Orlando Sentinel*—the same paper that had carried Hurston's white-mare attack on integration four years earlier—as "propaganda" for mixing races and as the "most amazing evidence of brainwashing":

> As soon as you pick up the book and open its pages you realize these rabbits are integrated.
>
> One of the techniques of brainwashing is conditioning minds to accept what the brainwashers want accepted.
>
> Where better to start than with youngsters in the formative years in the South?[68]

Balch's phrasing suggested the danger that the very term "integrated" must have contained. The fear of brainwashing (a term that had become popular during the Korean War) made the children's book look as if it were part of a plot of weakening the defensive potential of the next generation, a danger that was all the more momentous since Balch saw the book in the children's section of one of the Florida public libraries where the dangerous work had been checked out so many times since its arrival that a waitlist had to be opened for those interested in reading the book. The segregationist Alabama State Senator E. O. Eddins of Marengo

County continued Balch's attack on the book with a focus on public libraries and declared aggressively that "this book and many others should be taken off the shelves and burned," specifying that he meant books "of the same nature" (presumably integrationist) and those that "are communistic."[69]

*The Rabbits' Wedding* was thus publicly themed as a dangerous text promoting racial integration, and the fact that it did not represent humans at all could make it seem all the more subversive for spreading its illegal message surreptitiously—and to minors, too, who would have access to it through taxpayer-financed public libraries. As we have already seen, it is very difficult to say with any degree of certainty that a given text is not, at least *relatively*, about a particular theme, and the southern context simply suggested that this was one way in which the book would be read by many others, now that it had been looked at as an interracial marriage tale by anti-integrationists. This situation put public pressure on the Alabama library system, and Emily Wheelock Reed, the director of the State Public Library Service (which provided books for local libraries), was personally questioned by the Demopolis Senator Eddins, to whom she also had to make budget requests in the legislature. Pointing out that the book had not been banned, she came up with the Solomonic decision of neither leaving *The Rabbits' Wedding* in the agency's normal open shelves nor taking it completely out of circulation, but putting it on a special, closed shelf "for works on integration or those considered scatological."[70] The effect was that local librarians were permitted to take *The Rabbits' Wedding* to their branches only upon special request. (Libraries that had their own copies of the book were not affected and could keep them on the shelves.) In the line of fire for the possible accusation of making available dangerous literature, Reed had chosen the diplomatic course of not prohibiting "circulating the book to anyone, but then again . . . not peddling it." She acknowledged that she had been under indirect pressure and that her action was taken "in view of the troubled times in which we live." She accompanied her directive with a tart statement: "We were surprised that such a motive (integration) could be read into what appears to be a simple animal story using black and white illustrations to differentiate characters."[71] Yet, her disclaimer notwithstanding, Reed's action had the effect of sanctioning the interracial theming of *The Rabbits' Wedding*. Thus Alabama legislators who privately opposed the restriction, or even ridiculed it, were afraid to express their opinion in public and "declined to be quoted by name." If they criticized in the press Reed's measure or Eddins's theming of the book, "their position might be misconstrued as pro-integration."[72] The thematic interpretation of the Citizens' Council had surely prevailed if public opposition to the restricted access to a children's book about rabbits could become associated with the offense of promoting racial integration.

All of this brought national attention to the case and generated a broad, often overtly humorous coverage of the relatively minor near-suppression. The *New York Times* reported the scandal under the title "Children's Book Stirs Alabama: White Rabbit Weds Black Rabbit," and *Time* opened its article with excerpts from the book and the statement: "It seems incredible that any sober adult could scent in this fuzzy cotton-tale for children the overtones of Karl Marx or even of Martin Luther King." *Time* also ironically captioned the reproduction of an excerpt of the cover illustration of the book, with an allusion to Balch, "Anyone can see they're integrated."[73] A reader of the *Orlando Sentinel* suggested sarcastically that Balch should also worry about such children's classics as *Black Beauty*, in which "many fair skinned horses . . . want to nuzzle up to that black horse," or *Heidi*, in which—this reader believed—there "is a brown goat that gets a yen for a white goat," and that Balch should therefore form a "committee of one to ferret out all this diabolical trash and to see that from now on the only literature allowed in our public library is about 100pct. white animals who wouldn't spit on the best part of a darker one."[74] The book's author Garth Williams also commented on what *Time* called "the nonsense of it all":

> *The Rabbits' Wedding* has no political significance. I was completely unaware that animals with white fur, such as white polar bears and white dogs and white rabbits, were considered blood relations of white human beings. I was only aware that a white horse next to a black horse looks very picturesque—and my rabbits were inspired by early Chinese paintings of black and white horses in misty landscapes.
>
> It was written for children from two to five who will understand it perfectly. It was not written for adults, who will not understand it because it is only about a soft furry love and has no hidden message of hate.[75]

This episode in the cultural history of racial segregation reads like a version of "The Emperor's New Clothes," in which our "normal," commonsense perception of reality is restored through the voice of an honest child that is still free of adult scheming. We may, however, be merely laughing off the problem of theming which is not settled even in this easy-seeming case.

For, upon closer scrutiny, we must admit that there is no safe intellectual ground on which we could offer a *principled* objection to a reading of *The Rabbits' Wedding* as an allegory for a human story. Obviously, animal stories have been read for a very long time, from Aesop's fables to Uncle Remus's Brer Rabbit, as allegories for human tales. Garth Williams's rabbits are, furthermore, quite anthropomorphic; they decorate themselves with dandelions, get married, and the little black rabbit is repeatedly saddened by the thought (the reasons for which are not explained in the text but make sense in the context of *Brown v. Board of Education*) that he might not always be with the white rabbit. (Interestingly, a similar worry does not seem to cloud the white rabbit's *joie de vivre*, though she is ready to marry the black one if that will only dispel his sadness.)

In attempting to refute the "human" reading, Reed had to speak about "a simple animal story" (as if that excluded the possibility of human allegory), and Garth Williams and Reed offered the explanation that black and white were used merely to differentiate characters, following a Chinese tradition. *Time*'s glibly cosmopolitan ridiculing, and the author's attempt to make absurd, the human theming of the book drew on the impact of invoking animal varieties (horse, dog, and rabbit) and features ("fuzzy" or "fur") in order to build up contrasts between human and animal, adult and child, and hate and love—all of which actually ended up as an oblique criticism of segregation in the same breath as any political motive and significance were denied. Better to have the "soft furry love" of this "cottontale" (an effective pun, as it alludes to Beatrix Potter's famous *Peter Rabbit* and unites storytelling and animal features) than the hard segregationist logic of columnists and politicians that makes "whites" out of polar bears, dogs, and rabbits. It may thus have been the "fit" between ideology and representation that permitted liberals to laugh at the segregationists' paranoia. It probably would have constituted a breach of faith, but it certainly would have made the segregationists seem less ridiculous, if their opponents had spelled out and conceded the potential for human dimensions of the book. Yet in this controversy there also does not seem to have been a single ardent segregationist who would have supported the circulation of literature representing intermarriage (whether as an animal allegory or in human form) on the principle of Free Speech. And there was no criticism of the notion that the representation of certain themes *eo ipso* constituted a "promoting" or "recommending" of what was represented. All of these may be the effects of a politicized discussion; there is little need to replicate it now. Instead, we might draw the conclusion from the incident that it is hard to predict in which contexts themes will be discovered in texts that are not overtly (though they may be at least "relatively" if perhaps not "absolutely") "about" these themes.[76] In the case of *The Rabbits' Wedding*, a book which has stayed in print from its first publication to the writing of these pages, one could identify such themes as love and marriage, the animal kingdom, or sadness and happiness, but it would be hard to categorically *exclude* the interracial theme on the grounds that this is simply an animal tale, and that "animals with white fur" cannot be "blood relations of white humans."

This is not to say that theming is a random process. The method of using an absurdly chosen theme in order to mark the limits of theming is also a good one—though it was more convincing on ideological than on intellectual grounds in this case. Nilli Diengott once took the effective example of Ezra Pound's "In a Station of the Metro" as a poem that may *not* be said to be about the maxim that we should drink milk regularly.

More modestly, Erwin Panofsky observed that the ceiling of the Sistine Chapel can be understood better if we recognize that Michel-angelo represents the fall and not a "déjeuner sur l'herbe."[77] Yet the social pressure exerted by the milk industry on Pound interpretation, or by Manet scholars on the iconography of Renaissance art, is undoubtedly less forceful than the political context that has surrounded the interracial theme and, as we have already seen, denied its legitimacy and its very existence. One could, of course, also imagine a situation in which Pound *could* symbolize milk-drinking: for example, in a hypothetical society that banned both Pound's poetry and lactic nutrition, a resistance movement might be provoked to use "In a Station of the Metro" as a toast-in-code before surreptitiously defiant social milk-drinking. Politically motivated milk-drinking rituals did take place in the French Revolution, when right on the ruins of the Bastille a statue much like that of the "fraternity" stamp provided nourishment from her breast, thus creating among the diverse drinkers a sense of citizenship as siblinghood, of *fraternité*.[78] Yet even in this situation it might be hard to argue that the poem was actually "about" the maxim that we should drink milk regularly, though a person reciting it might be charged with "urging" his audience to drink milk. Absurdly random public theming is by no means uncommon. Still, the process of theming is negotiated by debate, and, in order to be justifiable, the result has to appear plausible *in the text*, and not just in the power generated by public contexts, be they advanced by governments, ideologues, or critics. Random theming may lead to tyranny.

## Uniting Texts

The search for the theme of a text, Brinker has suggested, "is always a quest for something that is not unique to" one specific work since the theme is what may unite "different texts."[79] For example, in theming Nella Larsen's novel *Passing* (1929), we would probably not settle for an enumeration of details such as Gertrude Martin's overtrimmed georgette crepe dress, Clare Kendry's handwriting and purple ink, Brian Redfield's restlessness, or the ridiculous Japanese print on the wall, nor would we be likely to choose a formulation like the following: Larsen's novel thematizes "a series of successive causally related events bringing about crucial changes in the lives of several human beings." The first option would stick too closely to the details of only this novel, the second would seem so abstract as to apply to too many works.

This recognition suggests that a "theme" must be the right "size." As an abstraction that is drawn from a work, it should be neither too global nor too tiny. In fact, however, theming may focus on rather large and widely disseminated concepts as well as on some very small details, as long as they link the specific work with others, or refer *out* of the text. It is for this reason, I believe, that the distinction between "thematics"—the thematic study of a single work—and "thematology"—the investigation of a theme in many texts—that Raymond Trousson proposed has not been widely adopted, since even the theming of a single text implies the existence of other texts in the context of which theming proceeds.[80]

Larsen's text signals a "larger" theme, "passing," in its title and may thus be themed as a representation of the relationship between Clare Kendry, a woman who has crossed the color line, and Irene Westover Redfield, a woman who does it only sporadically. This theming would lend special significance to the explicit passages about passing in the text. For example, the narrator says about Irene:

> She wished to find out about this hazardous business of "passing," this breaking away from all that was familiar and friendly to take one's chance in another environment, not entirely strange, perhaps, but certainly not entirely friendly. What, for example, one did about background, how one accounted for oneself. And how one felt when one came into contact with other Negroes. But she couldn't. She was unable to think of a single question that in its context or its phrasing was not too frankly curious, if not actually impertinent. (157)

This passage announces a social theme, and the narrator both explains passing ("this breaking away . . .") and keeps it mysterious, though Irene gets to ask some of her questions anyway, and her questions typically refer *out* of the novel, to the "world" mediated by a variety of other texts.

What is true for the overarching theme that Larsen announces in her title is also true for some quite minute details in the text that call attention to themselves. For example, Larsen ticks off a whole repertoire of recurrent thematic aspects in interracial literature such as fingernails as a racial sign (178), the curse of Ham (188), or the biracial mother's fear of giving birth to a darker-skinned descendant (197). No "larger" than the ones that stayed too "close to the novel" to count as thematic elements, these recurrences—they could be regarded as *motifs*—are "thematic," not only because they "cluster" around and intensify the central theme of "passing" in the novel but also because, like "passing," they inevitably refer us *out* of the novel and toward relationships with other texts and discourses. Such thematic recurrences and their clustering may help to create the illusion of reality in the novel, and, as we shall see, they appear in texts with some frequency. In fact, the fear of a much darker-skinned descendant (that emerged at times in the *Natus Æthiopus* motif), the "Curse of Ham," "Fingernails as a Racial Sign," and "Passing" are all among the noteworthy recurrences of interracial literature that will be examined at some detail in this study.

It is because of the outward-looking character of thematic recurrences that what may seem intriguing or cryptic in an individual work may be clarified by considering other literary and nonliterary texts; what may appear radically innovative in one text may actually be widely shared by many earlier literary texts and other documents; what is praised as the accomplishment (or what the New Critics might call the "thematic unity") of a single text may be more fairly viewed as the nuanced refiguring of themes that are familiar from many other texts; what is regarded as the defining motif of a certain ethnic group may really be a shared feature of many other ethnic and national literatures; what is looked at as a startling and noteworthy "subversion" of a traditional element may actually be in itself a traditional commonplace, and so forth. Furthermore, what may not at all appear to be a problem in a single text may turn out to be recognizable as an "alteration," as an "omission" of crucial elements of an earlier text—so that one suddenly perceives, and can make plausible, an *absence* in a given text. One only has to recall the example of the 1989 stamp on the French Revolution to recognize that, looked at in isolation, the two silvery children do not call attention to themselves: they become identifiable as "versions" of an interracial family theme only in an intertextual line-up that suggests a "thematics of absence" in this case. (If stamps are examined only within national boundaries, or within the genre of the vertical or the horizontal stamp format, or without consideration for "models" and "precursor images" or for non-postage-stamp images with related themes, such comparative theming is inhibited.)

The examples of the representation of biracial individuals who pass, or of interracial siblinghood, suggest the relevance of the field of thematic criticism known as "imagology," typically devoted to studies of the "image," "mirage," or "stereotype" of one social group in the literature written by another.[81] Though the name "imagology" may not be widely familiar, imagological work may actually be the dominant form of thematic criticism practiced in the areas of ethnic and gender studies. It is not an unproblematic field and has, in its little-known past, produced contrastive, at times Manichean, approaches that are, perhaps, too easily and at times inadvertently generated by such topics as, for example, the image of the Jew on the German stage.[82] A study explicitly dedicated to interracial themes would seem to offer a needed corrective, as it might help to provoke further explorations of an area that seems particularly suited to make questionable the one-dimensional character of some imagological work and generate a sense of dialectic.[83] In interracial literature, no single image is totally in or totally out, auto-image or heteroimage: black-white couples, biracial individuals, and their descendants are (or at least may be seen as) both, and a real dialectic is all the more possible with a topic that makes many writers and readers simultaneously both insiders and outsiders.[84] In any event, the body of works is defined here by a shared *thematic* orientation rather than by the national and ethnic origins or sex of authors.

Interracial literature announces itself with recurrences—Francesco Orlando calls them "constants"—such as the word plays on black, white, neither, and in-between.[85] By focusing attention on a small number of such "constants," as well as "variants" and "versions," this study puts many texts and images into a relation with each other—and potentially, it is hoped, with many other possible works that could not be investigated here.

This process of searching for similarities is not always unproblematic. For example, the investigator of visual images of interracial couples will be happy to find such Egyptian Fifth Dynasty limestone images (of approximately 2400 B.C.) as *Tenti and His Wife* or *Standing Pair Statue* (Fig. 7). Yet in Egyptian representations of couples the man is often shown in a reddish brown (the male color), and the woman in an ocher yellowish tint (the woman's color); hence interracial appearance is the *rule* rather than the exception in Egyptian art and is due to a code of gender differentiation, not of racial representation. To some extent, this is also true for the coloring of Greek vases, which used black and red figures for aesthetic differentiation, though this difference, once established, could also serve to represent race. For example, the intoxicated dances and sexual encounters of satyrs and hetaerae on amphoras of about 560 B.C. show how the formal principle has been put to the use of a sense of racial difference (Fig. 8). For this reason it is often necessary to discuss recurring themes in their different contexts.

This book presents some of these thematic "recurrences" (as I have already started to call them) comparatively and thus begins to sketch some of the clusters that have constituted the recognizability of interra-

***Figure 7***   Standing Pair Statue (ca. 2400 B.C.)

*Figure 8*    Comasti and Hetaerae (ca. 560 B.C.)

cial literature. Whether because of their apparently referential character and their deceptive familiarity, or because of the fact that—in the absence of thematic comparisons—they may appear to be self-evident or to pose no problem, some such recurring features have remained unstudied. The present study aims at subjecting some commonplaces to scrutiny and thus making them visible.[86] If the larger units may be referred to as "themes" and the smaller ones as "motifs," there is also a third type of recurrence, the rhetorical commonplaces—such as "one drop" or "neither black nor white"—that may be called "topoi" (topos in the singular).

In a phrasing that is of interest both for the method and for the subject of the present study, Brinker argued that themes inhabit the "intertextual space created by the partial overlapping of artistic fictional texts and other cultural texts" and are therefore "rightly suspected of extraliterary origins or at least of impure (literary) blood." He adds: "Yet literature is always inescapably contaminated with their existence."[87] In this sense it is the goal of this study to pursue both the theme of "mixed blood" and the theme as the "impure (literary) blood" of artistic and other cultural texts by putting literary works and many other texts into a relationship with each other. A thematic approach may be ideal for the kind of interdisciplinary work that interracial literature would seem to require.

The contexts for the literature of "neither black nor white yet both" are often, as has already become clear, political, and in many cases they originate in a social *world*. They may come from myth, history, society, individual psychology, religion, sciences, and laws as well as from elements of the physical environment. It is in this sense that one might expect the thematological analysis of "neither black nor white yet both" to work best, since debated historical problems and issues such as slavery, racism, and family relations typically come into play in the texts. Hence such diverse disciplines as history, history of science, philology, sociology, anthropology, law, theology, gender and family studies, and always, of course, thematology and the iconological tradition in art history may prove helpful in analyzing them as part of the history of interracial representation. The most varied nonpoetic contexts, ranging from biblical commentaries to Enlightenment encyclopedias, from biological theories to debates on statistics, from travel accounts to sociology handbooks, and from etymologies to legal commentaries, may thus have a thematic bearing on the texts.

Yet in a second sense interracial writings are also part of an aesthetic *tradition*, and much of the literature investigated here is deeply anchored in its own literary ancestry from the Bible and the classics to medieval romances, renaissance novellas, *Othello, Thousand and One Nights*, and early modern literature. For this reason some retellings of similar story lines are investigated, as they may illuminate the development of a tradition of interracial literature as well as the historical and cultural constraints surrounding some representations of the themes. Here the discussion of contexts benefits from selected work in classical and medieval philology, and from the study of modern and comparative literature.

This book takes a first step toward acknowledging the largely unrecognized scope of interracial literature and toward suggesting some of its systemic qualities (the recurrences in various texts) as well as some of its historical unfoldings and transformations (represented in a few selected moments of revision, change, and rupture). This format permits a focus on some aesthetically outstanding, historically significant, innovative, influential, culturally resonant, or otherwise interesting texts and authors as well as on clusters of motifs and themes that were found to recur in several—and, at times, in many, many—works.

What follows is neither a comprehensive thematic history nor a systematic study of interracial literature, but—literally—a series of *explorations* of interracial themes in literature. The book starts with a chapter investigating some notions of "Origins" of racial difference, both in historical-mythical accounts and in the context of family stories. Chapter Two, "*Natus Æthiopus/Natus Albus*" focuses on the representation of the unusual cases of the births of children whose color differs from that of their parents. Chapter Three, "The Curse of Ham," presents the history of a theme that takes its point of departure from a biblical passage that was racialized and transformed from its origins in order to account for the emergence of "blackness" within a family that has often been taken for "the human family." Chapter Four, "The Calculus of Color," explores some racial terminologies and taxonomies and traces such terms as "Mulatto." Chapter Five, "Fingernails as a Racial Sign," examines a very small motif in interracial literature both structurally and historically. Chapter Six takes the *Code noir* as an instance of the theme of law in literature and highlights the first African American short story by Victor Séjour and the little-known play "The Mulatto" by Hans Christian Andersen against some other uses of the *Code noir* in retellings of similar plot elements. Chapter Seven, "Mercenaries and Abolitionists," pursues retellings of a changing tale in different, at times antithetical versions, focusing centrally on Lydia Maria Child. Chapter Eight is an excursus that investigates and questions the uses and abuses of the term "Tragic Mulatto" in literary criticism. Chapter Nine regards the theme of "Passing" in literature, history, and sociological writing. Chapter Ten explores the puzzling thematic cluster of "Incest and Miscegenation" in interracial literature, culminating in William Faulkner's novel *Absalom, Absalom!* The book concludes with an investigation of alternative endings that have been proposed for certain interracial themes, at times by the same authors, at times in a rewriting process undertaken by others, revealing a recurring ambivalence about how and where interracial works can be given closure. The text of the study is followed by two appendices that list interracial literature and prohibitions of interracial marriage and cohabitation chronologically, by a selective list of the most important secondary literature, and by the index.

Interspersed throughout the text, and at times simply listed without commentary, are many quotations from the literature that make the argument more vivid, or so I hope. In some cases, the excerpts seem to enter a dialogue just by being placed near each other. Similarly, the book is accompanied by many visual images, only a few of which are discussed at detail. The book pursues many different lines of argument but adheres to the overall method of making one variable, the "interracial theme," the constant that is complemented by an investigation of further recurrences within this overarching thematic field. It is hoped that the various forays into the vast area of interracial literature may stimulate further work.

# Origins; or, Paradise Dawning

And wherefore wouldst thou repulse my love, Maria? I am a king, and my brow rises above all that are human. Thou art white, and I am black: but day must be wedded to night to give birth to the aurora and the sunset, which are more beautiful than either.

> —The rebel Bug-Jargal to Marie, the betrothed of the narrator of Victor Hugo's novel *Bug-Jargal* (1826)[1]

Black, white, green, yellow—nothing will prevent intermarriage. Position, wealth, family, friends—all sink into insignificance before the God-implanted instinct that made Adam, awakening from a deep sleep and finding the woman beside him, accept Eve as bone of his bone; he cared not nor questioned whence she came. So it is with the sons of Adam ever since, through the law of heredity which makes us all one common family.

> —Dr. William Thornton in Pauline E. Hopkins, "Talma Gordon" (1900)[2]

The skeletal remains of early man show unmistakable evidence of racial intermixture.

> —E. B. Reuter, "Amalgamation" (1937)[3]

[The Mulatto] designates the moment of origins, when black and white met on a footing of *sexual equality*. . . .

> —Simone Vauthier, "Textualité et stéréotypes" (1980)[4]

A dam and Eve were a black-white couple. This is at least the way in which they appear to have been portrayed on an eighteenth-century door panel of the *Alte* (formerly Gärtnersche) *Apotheke*, a pharmacy in Calw near Stuttgart, Germany. The panel—part of a series on the realms of nature from which medicines are taken—depicts the animal kingdom (*regnum animale*) as a paradise scene in which a landscape that opens to a bay is cheerfully populated with various land and air animals, including a stag and a lion (in the foreground center), birds, monkeys, a sheep, a goat, and a dog. Under a leafy tree on the lower right of the painting, a seated white and presumably male nude is seen from behind looking up at another nude figure, a black woman who is leaning against the tree. Both are pointing with one hand each at the Edenic landscape (Fig. 9). In 1954, the *Scientific American* offered the following theming of the picture:

> Adam and Eve in the Garden of Eden were painted by an unknown artist.... Contemplating the races, this pious artist or his patron deduced that the original parents of mankind must have been of different hues. Thus he placed in Paradise two progenitors of the most colorful dissimilarity to explain the persisting diversity.[5]

The anonymous German drugstore artist's vision was paralleled by that of a contemporary American prose writer. In Hugh Henry Brackenridge's satirical novel *Modern Chivalry* (1792–1815), the narrator, Captain John Farrago, reflects upon the origin of human diversity, rejects several other explanations, and concludes:

> I am of opinion that Adam was a tall, straight limbed, red haired man, with fair complexion, blue eyes, and an aquiline nose; and that Eve was a negro woman. For what necessity to make them both of the same colour, feature, and form, when there is beauty in variety. Do not you see in a tulip, one leaf blue, and another white, and sometimes the same leaf white and red?
>
> As God made Adam in his own likeness, so it is to be supposed, that Adam begat some in his; and these were red haired, fair complexioned,

***Figure 9*** Door panel, Alte Apotheke, Calw,
known as *The Animal Kingdom* (ca. 1770–1780)

blue eyed, proportionably featured boys and girls; while, on the other
hand, some took after the mother, and became negro men and women.
From a mixture of complexion, the offspring, at other times, might be a
shade darker, in one case, than the father; and a shade lighter, in another
case, than the mother; and hence, a diversified progeny, with a variety of
features; from the bottle-nose to the mire-snipe; which is that of the people in the west of Ireland; and from the auburn of the Corsican hair, to the
golden locks of the Caledonian beauty; and from the black eye, to the hazel
and the grey.[6]

Brackenridge's quixotic novel, written for *the people*, for "Tom, Dick, and
Harry, in the woods," here makes fun of the deliberations of the
American Philosophical Society.[7]

Nearly a century later, Charles Chesnutt led his story "The Fall of
Adam" (1886), step by step, to a similar conclusion. In the tale, Brother
Elijah Gadson visits the preacher Gabriel Gainey and asks him for biblical answers to some questions, among them "what caused de diffe'nce
'twix' white folks an' black folks."[8] Brother Gabriel gives his answer on
the next Sabbath:

de Lawd nevuh made nobody black. 'Fac' de Lawd nevuh made nobody but Adam an' Eve—de yuthuhs wus all bawn. O' co'se if Adam uh anybody else gwine' do anything to make deyse'ves black, de Lawd wan' gwin have nothin' tuh do wid it; he made 'em once, an' he nevuh do his wuk twice. So dis 'splains de diffe'nce. When Adam jump' ovuh de sun, de fiah wus so hot, its scawched 'im black as a crips, an' curled up his ha'r so he nevuh couldn't git it straight agin. An', 'cawdin' to de laws ob nachah

Jes' so de tree fall, jes' so it lie.

Jes' so de sinner lib, jes' so he die.

An' so Adam nevuh turn' white no mo', but stayed black all de rest of 'is life. All Adam an' Eve's chillun bawn fo' de Fall wus white, an' dey wus de fo'fathers ob de white race o' people—all Adam an' Eve's chillun bawn aftuh de Fall wus black, an' dey wus de fo'fathers ob de black race of people. (181–82)

After inquiring whether Adam lived with Eve after the fall, too, and learning that there was nobody else to live with, Bre'r Isham comments: "Well, it kindah 'peahs to me, elder, dat unduh all de sarcumstances ob de case dem chillun bawn aftuh de Fall oughtah be'n mullatahs" (182).

All three representations establish a myth of origins that harmonizes a biblical theme with modern scientific interest in rules of descent that was to culminate in Gregor Johann Mendel's work in the ratio of possible combinations. The son and grandson of the original owners of the Calw pharmacy were botanists whose pioneering work on fruits and seeds was cited by Mendel and Darwin;[9] Brackenridge's satire is directed at the Philosophical Society's learned discussions of issues of descent and race; and Chesnutt's Br'er Isham has subversive interracial knowledge. All three interracial paradise scenes also contain elements of white-black hierarchy: in the painting only the white man is seated; in Brackenridge the suspiciously Irish-looking Adam is presumed to resemble God more than does the black Eve (who is also described at much less detail); and in Chesnutt, Adam's turning black is ironically associated with the fall, and the original human color is imagined to be a prelapsarian white. Yet such tales of origins also strike the modern reader for the ways in which they are oblivious of, or attempt to subvert, thinking in fixed racial categories by imagining a primal sexual contact between black and white (white man and black woman for the anonymous artist and Brackenridge, and black man and white woman for Chesnutt). If modern race-thinking rests on the denial, prohibition, and tabooization of interracial sexual contacts, then the representation of a racially mixed pair as the primal parents of us all may be hard to reconcile with the modern belief in essential racial difference. Winthrop Jordan concludes that "the intermixture implied in Brackenridge's burlesque of Genesis was precisely what Americans could not accept."[10] How could human origins be connected with stories of what came to be considered a "forbidden couple"?

**Figure 10**    Jane Ray, *The Story of Creation*, illustration (1992)

As biologically based racial thinking has been on the decline for some time and is no longer overtly supported by very many intellectuals, one may perhaps expect more visualizations of interracial paradise scenes in the years to come. Jane Ray's beautiful children's book *The Story of the Creation: Words from Genesis* (1992) may be a case in point, as it shows a dark, frizzy-haired Adam and a lighter-skinned, golden-haired Eve in Paradise, surrounded not only by sun, moon, stars, animals, and plants but, in one image, also by collage-style scraps of old maps, writing in many languages, and flaglike ornamentation, suggesting a theme of cosmopolitanism.[11] A reviewer simply noted, without further comment, that the book "ends with a honey-colored Eve and a dusky Adam tenderly companionable in a pre-serpent Eden" (Fig. 10).[12] The debacle about *The Rabbits' Wedding* seems to be a matter of the distant past.

## Cleobulus's Riddle, Aurora, and Competing Myths of Origins

There may be something about representations of interracial couples and their descendants that provokes audiences to read them as myths of origins, *foundational* stories rather than stories about just *any* couple.[13] Thus a glance at images like the Spanish ethnographic paintings or the genealogical photographs appended to volumes by Charles B. Davenport or Caroline Bond Day may generate a sense of a collective family romance. Such images constitute an invitation to view them as pictures of ancestors rather than just of contemporaries or of any family.[14]

This is also true for works of literature. In some cases they anchor the foreground of the action in an interracial coupling of the past. In Lydia Maria Child's *Romance of the Republic* (1867), for example, there is the story of the "original" mixed couple, "Papito" Royal (who dies in the second chapter) and "Mamita" Gonsalez (who passed away before the novel opens), the founding parents of the two generations of descendants who form the cast of the novel and who are neatly assembled in a family tableau at the end. Of course, an exotic tropical paradise setting often suggested itself for an interracial romance—such as Surinam in Captain John Gabriel Stedman's *Narrative of a Five Years Expedition Against the Revolted Negroes of Surinam* (1796), accompanied by appropriate lines from *Paradise Lost* and illustrated in an American abolitionist collection of 1834.

It may not always be an Edenic beginning, as the revelation in C. W. Mary (Andrews) Denison's *Old Hepsy* (1858) of the original love story between Old Colonel Hollister's daughter and his slave (and illegitimate son) Fred Keene, an affair crowned by the birth of a child, shows, for this is a novel that culminates in the ruin of the house. Or it may be only a more hopeful beginning, as with the love story of Clarence and Emily Garie in Frank Webb's novel *The Garies and Their Friends* (1857), who go from Georgia to Philadelphia in order to live as a legitimate couple— only to fall victim to a satanic schemer who manipulates the city institutions and rouses a mob against the former plantation owner and his invisibly nonwhite spouse.

The original couple may also be the ancestors of the narrator, as in Madame Reybaud's novella "Les Épaves" (1838), in which the Creole woman Zoe who tells the story claims to be directly descended from the spirited French noblewoman Cécile de Ratèl and her heroic mixed-race husband Donatien. At other times, the author's own myth of origins (putative or fictional though it may be) seems transposed into an interracial union; thus Langston Hughes incorporated elements of his struggle against his own father into the drama of a rebellious son in an interracial family in *Mulatto* (1935), and Eugene O'Neill used aspects of his parents' parental strife (and their names) in creating the racially mixed couple that leads a tortured marriage in *All God's Chillun Got Wings* (1924). One might speak, in such cases, of an "interracialization" in the representation of œdipal and marital conflicts. Whether Adam and Eve are imagined happily in paradise or as the ones whose fall has been bequeathed to all after generations, they do matter as "origins" for characters within texts. They are the capital-A ancestors from whom descent lines are dated and generations are counted.[15] Certain representations of interracial families may evoke a sense of a beginning, from which originate plots that may unfold by developing the consequences of these beginnings for the descendants—be these consequences blessings, curses, or just changing times and the course of history.

In the sixth century B.C. on the Greek island of Rhodes, not far from Asia Minor and what had once been Troy, there lived the thinker Cleobulus, who was celebrated as one of the Seven Sages of Greece. He is known as the author of three thousand riddles, but only a few of them have survived, among them the following famous one:

There is one father and twelve children. Each of these has twice thirty children of different aspect; some of them we see to be white and the others black, and though immortal, they all perish.[16]

The obvious answer to the riddle is that the *year* is the father of twelve *months*, each of whom have thirty *days* and thirty *nights*. Because of the cyclical nature of time, each night, day, month, and year passes only to begin anew. The riddle thus transforms calendar time into a three-generation family story of a father, twelve children, and 720 grandchildren. For the person who has solved the poetic riddle, time can no longer be indivisible and immeasurable flux, but has become organized, memorizable, and predictable. We remember that the biblical creation story is also accompanied by the division of day and night and by a sense of the time of the days of the week.

Cleobulus's family imagery is not unusual, nor is his casting nights and days in terms of black and white. Cleobulus presents an origin of black and white as well as an answer to the riddle of time.[17] In the repeated deaths of those immortal grandchildren he confers a particular meaning to the twilight zone between night and day: to dusk and dawn, the periods that are neither day nor night, yet also both day and night. The mythic figures embodying such transitional moments can contain all the ingredients of a story of origins—time, human difference, and a family saga—in concentrated fashion.

This seems true of the goddess of Dawn, who is between black and white as much as between night and day. The Greek Eos was derived from the Indian goddess Ushàs. Ushàs/Eos, the daughter of the Titans Hyperion and Theia and the sister of both Helios (the god of the sun) and Selene (the goddess of the moon), who are also incestuously married to each other, ultimately became the Roman Aurora. Aurora marries Tithonos, with whom she goes to Æthiopia. She rises every morning from his bed to bring light to the world,[18] and she is often described as winged. Her child (in Ovid's version, from a black Æthiopian[19]) is Memnon, a chief or ancestor[20] of the Æthiopians, who helps Troy against the Greeks, kills Antilochos and, in Homer's version,[21] is killed by Achilles. Aurora's tears for Memnon are the morning dew.[22] He is often explicitly represented as black.[23] The first volume of *The Anglo-African Magazine* (1859) has the Virgilian motto of a black Memnon on the front page—"et nigri Memnonis arma." And in Pauline Hopkins's novel *Of One Blood; or, The Hidden Self* (1902–3), a Professor explains that Memnon symbolizes the link between Egypt and Ethiopia and the land of the upper Nile, for "Memnon personifies the ethnic identity of the two races."[24] A Theban statue of Memnon sounded in the morning, which was interpreted as the son's greeting to his mother, Dawn.

Zeus grants Aurora's request to give Tithonos immortality, but, since they forget to request eternal youth, Tithonos shrivels and is finally transformed into a cicada (which may be interpreted as a representation of the greyness of day after the red of sunrise).[25] The myth of rose-fingered Dawn thus contains one beginning of the theme of a being between black and white.[26] Aurora's three-generation family story also helps to explain human variety against the background of the contrasts between night and day and moon and sun.

Though few modern writers probably believe in a goddess of Dawn, she is often invoked in literature; and several biracial characters bear her name. Versions of "Aurora" (who also is known for abducting beautiful young men) are thus common in interracial literature. Aurore is the name of the titular heroine in Mayne Reid's novel *The Quadroon*. Characters in George Washington Cable's novel *The Grandissimes* (1879–80) and in Frank Yerby's novel *The Foxes of Harrow* (1946) are also named Aurora or Aurore, whereas Muriel Spark chose the name "Dawn" in "The Black Madonna" (1958). Both interracial marriages and biracial characters are symbolically located between night (black) and day (white).

Since the ancestral quality that designates origins inheres not only in interracial couples, but also in some individual characters who are neither black nor white, it was possible to imagine that mankind was of one intermediate color at the dawn of time and that other more extreme hues were developed only later. Some theorized explicitly that the first color was neither black nor white but in-between. In 1744, for example, John Mitchell thought that

> Noah and his sons were of a complexion suitable to the climate in which they resided, as well as all the rest of mankind; which is the colour of the southern Tartars of Asia, or northern Chinese, at this day perhaps, which is a dark swarthy, a medium between black and white: from which primitive colour the Europeans degenerated as much on one hand, as the Africans did on the other.[27]

Mitchell also addresses possible opposition to his argument in a manner that accentuates his view of human origins in the "medium between black and white" from which both black and white "degenerated":

> The grand obstacle to the belief of this relation between white and black people is, that, on comparing them together, their colours seem to be so opposite and contrary, that it seems impossible that one should ever have been descended from the other. But, besides the falsity of this supposed direct contrariety of their colours, they being only different, though extreme degrees of the same colour . . . ; besides this, that is not a right state of the question; we do not affirm that either blacks or whites were originally descended from one another, but that both were descended from an intermediary tawny colour; whose posterity became more and more tawny, i.e. black, in the southern regions, and less so, or white, in the northern climes.

John Winthrop IV, a professor of mathematics at Harvard, similarly wrote in 1759:

> [I]t has long seemed most probable to me, that the original complexion of mankind, considering the climate they lived in, was swarthy or tawny; as, I suppose, that of the greater part of the Asiatics and Americans is at this day; and that our color and that of the Africans are equal deviations from this primitive color toward the opposite extremes of whiteness and blackness.[28]

The intermediate category "neither black nor white" could thus also designate the origin of the "opposite extremes" of the black and white "deviations" from it.[29]

Black-white founding myths—whether visualized in an original black-white couple or in a beginning that is between black and white—let later interracialism appear as the repetition and continuation of long-established, even original practice; polygenetic theories may look at "black" and "white" as "contrary" and thus cast racial mingling as a novel—and perhaps threatening—departure from differently conceived origins, or as the repetition of a feared transgression in the past. The polygenetic myth imagines races as prior and original and views interracial categories as secondary and later phenomena.

Of course, many other explanations of racial difference in human origins have been given. One option was to assume that human difference was a result of the process of creation. For example, according to a Cherokee myth of origins, God created men by baking human figures that he made out of dough in an oven. Impatiently, he took out the first one too soon: "It was sadly underdone—pale, an unlovely color. But for better or worse, there it was, and from it are descended the white people." The second one, taken out just at the right time, was well built and richly browned, "the ancestor of the Indians"; it corresponded so much to the creator's ideal that he forgot the third one in the oven "until he smelled it burning. He threw open the door, only to find this last one charred and black. It was regrettable, but there was nothing to be done; and this was the first Negro."[30]

Another option was to assume that color difference came later. It could be the result of a slow or rapid transformation brought about by climate, genetic mutation, or a time-lapse effect implanted in the first human beings. Unlike the myth of origins with a black-white couple, many alternative stories of human beginnings start with only one parent who would have had to contain all human difference that would come to visible fruition only in later generations. Chesnutt's story—which so ironically corrected the one-ancestor model—drew on an important tale of this kind in order to explain black skin color: the classical myth of Phaëthon.

A son of the god of the sun Helios[31]—which makes Phaëthon also Aurora's nephew—Phaëthon is ridiculed for the story of his ancestry and asks his mother Clymene (who is married to the Egyptian king Merops) about his parentage. She invites him to talk to his father Helios himself. Phaëthon finds him, Helios grants him a wish as a sign of his paternity, and Phaëthon requests to drive the sun chariot through the sky for a day. He starts well but panics and crashes, scalding the earth and drying up rivers:

> And that was when, or so men think, the people
> Of Africa turned black, since the blood was driven
> By that fierce heat to the surface of their bodies.[32]

Zeus kills him with a thunderbolt to save the earth. Ovid's version of the myth of Phaëthon may be considered the prototype of the "climate theory" of accounting for variations in human skin color, though it imagines a catastrophe rather than the steady climate differences caused by the varying power of the sun. In a version by Hyginus, however, the Phaëthon story bears certain resemblances to the biblical story of Noah and Ham. Here Phaëthon takes the chariot *without* his father's permission, and Zeus has to quench the fire by starting Deucalion's Flood, which drowns all mankind.[33]

Thomas Browne referred to the story of Phaëthon's "deviation of the sun" only briefly and expressed more general reservations about the climate theory in his *Pseudodoxia* (1646):

> For *Negroes* transplanted, although into cold and phlegmatick habitations, continue their hue both in themselves, and also their generations; except they mix with different complexions; whereby notwithstanding there only succeeds a remission of their tinctures; there remaining unto many descents a strong shadow of their Originals; and if they preserve their copulations entire, they still maintain their complexions. As is very remarkable in the dominions of the Grand Signior, and most observable in the *Moors* in *Brasilia*, which transplanted about an hundred years past, continue the tinctures of their fathers unto this day. And so likewise fair or white people translated in hotter Countries receive not impressions amounting to this complexion.[34]

Large-scale migration made the climate theory much less attractive.[35] Which other options were there?

In the Islamic tradition, the Koran mentions only the creation of heaven and earth and the diversity of languages and colors as Allah's signs (Sura 30:22). As Gernot Rotter has shown, later traditions expand this short statement in two ways in order to explain color diversification in Adam's descendants.[36] According to a passage cited by Ibn Sa'd (d. 845), the prophet is to have said: "Adam was made of three [kinds of] dust, black, white and dark."[37] A more frequently given elaboration is "In truth, God created Adam out of a handful [of clay], which he took from the whole earth. Therefore Adam's children turned out according to the earth. The reds, whites, and blacks emerged, and among them the soft and the rough ones, the mean and the good ones."[38] This resembles the Cherokee myth in positing three original human types, but differs from it in making all three types present in one single human ancestor. An African genesis from Dogon suggests that the blacks were created in full sunlight, whereas the whites were made by the light of the moon whence they took their larva-like appearance.[39]

It was not always father Adam who functioned as the single origin to account for later diversity. There was also, for example, the assumption of one original mother with different sets of eggs. The idea goes back to Epicure via Lucretius, and Le Cat gave a free translation of the decisive passage. Modernized, this was the theory of Pierre Louis Moreau de Maupertuis, the president of the Berlin academy of sciences at the time of Friedrich II, according to which two sets of eggs of one mother had a different coloration, one set white and the other one black. For a long time only the white eggs were fertilized, and only several generations later did the other races of mankind emerge, one at a time.[40] All the white people were believed to emerge from the white eggs and all the Negro people from the black eggs.[41]

### Who Is the Parent?

Interracial family stories may orient readers toward beginnings; they also may address specific questions and puzzles concerning human origins, such as, "Who is the more important parent, a mother or a father?" Interracial stories could thus help to clarify the relative importance of a father and a mother in giving shape to their progeny. What has often fascinated readers in stories about mixed couples and their descendants is not only that contrasts (or at least the cultural perceptions of them) make good beginnings, but also that such stories may illuminate the (often-obscured) fact that mothers as well as fathers matter for the makeup of their progeny.[42] A black-white family beginning with descendants is—unlike the monadic monoracial alternatives—a perfectly dialectical illumination of the fact that descendants take features of both parents, a fact that some ideas of "pure" identity have to obscure in the name of unilateral parentage, of one "unadulterated" sex or of one race, and, hence, with the general quest for only *one* origin embodied in such questions as: Who is *the* parent? Is it the male or the female parent who matters more, or even exclusively? This issue has been debated in texts at least since *The Eumenides*, the last play of Aeschylus's trilogy *Oresteia* (458 B.C.).

The question has also not infrequently been addressed in interracial literature. A character like the "piebald" Feirefiz in Wolfram's *Parzival* (ca. 1200) visualizes not only his biracial origin in his white father

***Figure 11***   Feirefîz and Parzival embrace, Bern
codex (1467)

Gahmuret and his black mother Belacâne, but also illustrates generally
that any child is the offspring of a father and a mother, both of whose
traits combine in their descendant (Fig. 11).

> And a thousand times she kissed him where white as his sire's skin.
> And she named the babe of her sorrows [Feirefîz Anschevîn].
> And he was a woodland-waster, many spears did he shatter fair,
> And shields did he pierce—as a magpie the hue of his face and hair.
> (57: 15–28)[43]

It is exactly this dimension in stories of interracial couples and their
descendants that has also been stressed as a way of understanding human
origins. Just as migration reduced the plausibility of the Phaëthon theory, so did it generate a new sense of how color change does take place
over generations: through interracial relations.

It is in this fashion that the Dominican friar Jean-Baptiste Labat in his
*Nouveau voyage aux Isles de l'Amérique* (1722) uses a (not altogether sympathetic) description of West Indian Mulattoes in order to argue that
they combine the traits of both of their parents. Labat defines Mulattoes
as "children descended from a black mother and a white father or from a
black father and a white mother, the latter case being rare." He points
out that their color has "something of the white and something of the
black" (121). A little later he argues openly, playing the observer in what
he seems to think of as a scientific experiment:

> Some of our doctors may assert that the two sexes do not contribute equal-
> ly to the generation of a child, & that women are like hens who have eggs
> in their bodies by nature, & that the man, like the rooster, does nothing

but loosen them and perfect the seed. If this were the case, then a Negro woman would always give birth to black children, no matter what the color of the man might be. Our experience, however, contradicts such an assumption, since we see that she generates blacks with a black man and Mulattoes with a white man.[44]

Labat's observation of the generation of Mulattoes and their descendants serves his interest to demonstrate the equal force of the male and the female parent.[45] Yet this understanding was also often denied, as maternal descent of slave status became the rule in the New World, and as racial myths were invented, established, and put into law, according to which parentage, grandparentage, and, finally, any form of ancestry were determined, and could be overruled, by race. If Orestes was, according to the Furies, first of all Clytaemnestra's boy, and, according to Apollo, descended most significantly from Agamemnon, so slaves were identified—by legal fiat—exclusively by their maternal origins, and, in the United States, biracial persons were equally unilaterally defined by only the black side of their ancestry. African slaves in the New World were deprived of the name of the father, and under the rules of race they belonged to the category "black," no matter how many white ancestors they might also have had. Thus, while Labat still found evidence in interracial family stories that both parents matter for the makeup of children, the system of racialism gave rise to the paradox that race—or "black blood"—could acquire the power to overrule either parent's role. Following the Roman principle of *partus sequitur ventrem*, the status of the mother determined that of the child in modern slaveholding societies as well.[46] In the United States, however, the racial principle of descent—since it often excluded a biracial category and other intermediate identities—was that a "white" parent (male or female) might generate a "black" or a "white" child, but that a "black" parent (male or female) could usually generate only "black"—and under only very few circumstances "white"—descendants.

The consequence was the maxim which was actually formulated in the French colonies (that *did* establish intermediate racial categories): *partus colorem sequitur*.[47] Whiteness was thus symbolically identified as the color of all possible origins (and freedom), blackness (into which interracial identity was often folded) as the source of only black origins (and slavery). This set up a contradictory system of accounting for familial identity and for racial identity, so that some of the closest blood relatives and even a majority of ancestors might be omitted in determining race—and conversely, so that race could be used to establish a semblance of kinship—complete with such terms as "brother" and "sister." This contradiction at the core of family relations, making some relatives count more than others (and "race" more than any of them), subjected interracial families to culturally constructed conflicts, as kin relations could be obscured in the name of race, a category that ironically tended to usurp the terms of blood and kinship. F. James Davis has described how this state of affairs creates a strain in interracial families of today: "It is as if the child has only African ancestors, as if the white parent's family and white ancestry do not exist."[48] The "dominant" color that was given the cultural position of symbolizing universal origin also may be less than "recessive" and not matter at all as origin. There is a dissonance between race and family, reflected in semantic confusions. This is an all the more significant cultural feature since it was established in cultural contexts that otherwise emphasize family relations and exaggerate the certainty with which kinship can be established.[49]

## Slavery, Patriarchy, and the Denial of Paternity

In many cases, the conflict between family and race resulted in the denial of "white" paternity of "black" children in cultures otherwise dominated by patrilineage. Mixed-race descendants were often classified as belonging to a different "race" from that of the father, and therefore not to his "family." This is what Simone Vauthier calls the silence of the father, and what Lillian Smith terms a ghost story: the denial of white paternity. Such denials have been read in the general context of patriarchy.[50] To be sure, slavery has been famously imagined by slaveholders and critics as a modern enactment of a core patriarchal institution. William Byrd II, for example, described his slaveholding status in a well-known passage of 1726:

> I have a large Family of my own, and my Doors are open to Every Body, yet I have no Bills to pay, and a half-a-Crown will rest undisturbed in my Pocket for many Moons together. Like one of the Patriarchs, I have my Flocks and my Herds, my Bond-men and Bond-women, and every Soart of trade amongst my own Servants, so that I live in a kind of Independence on every one but Providence.[51]

For Byrd, leading the good life of a biblical Patriarch, complete with bond-men and bond-women, was blissful and made him free of market pressures. In March 1861, Mary Helen Chesnut in her Civil War diary took a darker view of the matter, yet she, too, drew the same biblical comparison in order to portray slavery as patriarchal:

> God forgive us, but ours is a monstrous system, a wrong and an iniquity! Like the patriarchs of old, our men live all in one house with their wives and their concubines; and the mulattoes one sees in every family partly resemble the white children. Any lady is ready to tell you who is the father of all the mulatto children in everybody's household but her own. Those, she seems to think, drop from the clouds. My disgust sometimes is boiling over. Thank God for my country women, but alas for the men! They are

probably no worse than men everywhere, but the lower their mistresses, the more degraded they must be.[52]

Thomas Satterwhite Noble's painting *The Price of Blood* (1868) made an even sharper, visual critique of the patriarchal presumptuousness of a slaveholder. The painting shows a well-dressed patriarchal-looking father who sells his barefooted Mulatto son in front of a painting showing Abraham's sacrifice of Isaac (Fig. 12). Modern patriarchs sacrifice their own sons—and not for any divine command but merely for a little money.[53] Whereas Byrd idealized patriarchal slaveholding for its independence from money, Noble imagined the patriarch as so money-dependent or profit-hungry as to be ready to put up for sale his own son.

Slaveholding was experienced and represented as patriarchal, for better or worse. In addition, the legal control of interracial relations was, under the rules of slavery in the English continental colonies, biased in favor of white men: thus, whereas white women were generally punished for bearing children by black or Mulatto men, white men were typically not penalized for impregnating black or Mulatto women, "unless they married them."[54] But was slavery simply an aspect of patriarchy?

Max Weber may have been the first to spell out that whereas unbroken patriarchal power left the father completely at liberty to decide whether he wanted to confer freedom upon any children of slave women, this patriarchal leeway was curtailed as status groups closed themselves off endogamously and the rule that only endogamously generated children were accepted as equal members of the community prevailed over patriarchal privilege.[55] Regarding the modern slavery society of the United States in this light, William McKee Evans found the slaveholding

*Figure 12*   Thomas Satterwhite Noble, *The Price of Blood* (1868)

patriarch still in a position from which he might grant preference over members of his own legitimate family to a person "who possesses neither legal rights nor social status," and "this option serves to bring legitimate members of his family under tighter control."[56] Yet the members of the legitimate family, who typically outnumber the patriarch, may resent, and react to, this situation, even violently, and thus restrain the father.[57] Evans therefore summarizes that "slaveholding societies are characterized by a tension between two elite-class, ideological tendencies: paternalism, associated with the patriarch, which functions toward the elimination of slaves as a distinct status group within the hierarchy of the patriarchal family; and legitimacy, associated with the free, dependent members of the household, which incubates traditions, myths, and sexual taboos serving to protect old distinctions of status and privilege." The cultural construction that the mother's slave status could outweigh the father's freedom, or that any parent's "black" origins could make meaningless the other parent's "whiteness," may thus actually represent a social *curtailment* of the father's unlimited patriarchal power of deciding either who can be a legitimate heir or who among the illegitimate family members may receive a standing equal to the legitimate family.[58] Not just the mores, or the pressures of legitimate white family members, but the laws of various countries often intervened. One could thus extend Weber's argument that the curtailment of unfettered patriarchy was brought about by the rise of slavery and racial identification which restrained the father from deciding unilaterally who should be free, who an heir.

Thus considered, slavery was not only an extension of, but also at odds with, patriarchy and could constitute a curbing of the father's limitless powers—including even the simple power of naming some of his own descendants or permitting them to address him as their father. Property, inheritance, acknowledgment, access to education, and conferral of rights were all connected with this conflict between patriarchy and matrilineal racial slavery. On the cultural level, the belief in "blackness" and in "whiteness" and in their differing powers in determining descent may constitute the most severe interference with a dialectical understanding of reality in which at least *two* origins matter, and for which the family provided an existential model.[59]

Abolitionist melodrama (and its critical descendants in the twentieth century) could transform the patriarchically imagined father into the all-powerful villain whose evil nature alone would explain everything, but eighteenth- and nineteenth-century slaveholders may also have been forced into denying or sacrificing their own descendants by a social system that had reduced their patriarchal power.

Though much less frequent, the denial of maternity is also an occurrence that commands attention in texts and deserves some cultural contextualization. Paternity is well understood as an uncertainty principle in literature; but maternity may also be far from indisputable in texts.[60] Whereas paternity may become questionable not only by a father's failure to recognize his offspring (or by the social pressure exerted by the legitimate family or community that restrained him from doing so), but also by adultery or promiscuity stories; maternity is in doubt not only in the cases of orphans or foundlings but also, for example, as a result of baby-switching (a common theme in interracial literature) or of the action of a mother who (perhaps—there may be uncertainty even about *that* in the stories) denies or covers up her maternity in order to let her son or daughter have a white identity or spouse. In any event, the proof of motherhood may lie in such peripheral and easily forged signs as a monogram (Charles Chesnutt, "Her Virginia Mammy"), a found document (George Washington Cable, "'Tite Poulette"), tattooed initials (Lydia Maria Child, *Romance of the Republic*), a lotus-lily on the breast (Pauline Hopkins, *Of One Blood*), or a dual set of old fingerprints (Mark Twain, *Pudd'nhead Wilson*) that are needed, for example, to determine that the nurse mother should be called not "mammy" but "mother." Ultimately, maternity may also depend on untrustworthy assertions and hence remain undecidable (Margaret Deland, "A Black Drop").

Race may disturb kinship recognition; yet it may also be invoked as a factor in the attempt to establish the presence or absence of kin relations. This is easily apparent in stories of children who do not resemble (one or both of) their (putative) parents as much as we expect them to. Johann Friedrich Blumenbach (1752–1840), in examining this expectation, noted:

> Remarkable too is the constancy with which offspring born from parents of different colours present a middle tint made up as it were from that of either parent. For although we read everywhere of single specimens of hybrid infants born from the union of different *varieties* of this sort, who have been of the colour of one parent alone, still, generally speaking, the course of this mixture is so consistently hereditary, that we may suspect the accuracy of James Bruce about the Ethiopians of some countries in the kingdom of Tiger, who keep their black colour unadulterated, although some of the parents were of one colour and some of another; or about the Arabians, who beget white children with the female Ethiopians like the father alone.[61]

It is the "remarkable constancy" with which children come out somewhere between their parents that provides partial reassurance about the uncertainty of parentage and makes suspect the exceptional stories of the kind Blumenbach mentions here. More than that, if we believed that children in general did *not* resemble both their parents, the exceptional stories would not be the cause of wonder or the starting point for complicated explanations.[62] Such cases of surprising births have been discussed since antiquity.

# CHAPTER TWO

# *Natus Æthiopus / Natus Albus*

I am as uplifted and reassured by it as a mother who has given birth to a white baby when she was awfully afraid it was going to be a mulatto.

—Mark Twain to William Dean Howells,
about Howells's review of *Roughing It* (1872)[1]

I'm afraid. I nearly died of terror the whole nine months before Margery was born for fear that she might be dark. Thank goodness, she turned out all right. But I'll never risk it again. Never! The strain is simply too—too hellish.

—Clare Kendry in Nella Larsen, *Passing* (1929)[2]

About the only group in which an Othello in black makeup performed with a white cast in the 1920s was New York City's Yiddish Art Theatre Company, known for exploring the anguish of distorted family relationships. But here the director added a silent character: a young daughter of Emilia and Iago. Her complexion was dusky and her features resembled Othello's. Iago now had compelling conjugal reasons for seeking Othello's destruction.

—Tilden G. Edelstein, "Othello in America" (1982)[3]

Listen, I don't have a black baby.

—Bill Clinton (1992)[4]

A light woman gives birth to a dark child. A dark mother gives birth to a light child. In both cases the husband is the same color as the mother. What are the questions asked, the actions undertaken? In antiquity, as Frank Snowden has shown, Aristotle (384–322 B.C.), Ovid (43 B.C.–17 A.D.), Pliny the Elder (c. 23–79), Martial (c. 40–104), Plutarch (c. 46–120), Juvenal (c. 55–c. 140), the second-century rhetor Calpurnius Flaccus, and Heliodorus's third-century *Æthiopica* contributed to a discussion that was circumscribed by a small range of options, including the reaction of wonder, the suspicion or accusation of adultery, and attempts at an explanation, made at times by the mother or her lawyers, ranging from an exonerating genealogy (of mother *or* father) to the magic of "maternal impression."[5]

The question goes back to Aristotle, who argued that "children are like their more remote ancestors from whom nothing has come, for the resemblances recur at an interval of many generations, as in the case of the woman in Elis who had intercourse with the Æthiop; her daughter was not an Æthiop but the son of that daughter was."[6] Aristotle used the story of the woman of Elis in order to offer the explanation of what came to be called *atavism*, literally, "great-grandfather-ism," a descendant's surprising "resemblance to grand-parents or more remote ancestors rather than to parents."[7] Physical traits may skip one, two, or even many generations.

Interestingly, Ovid used a story of Aurora's giving birth to Memnon in a similar way and implied that this may have been a case of adultery since the poet addresses Aurora and wishes that he could also hear from her husband Tithonus. Here is Horace Gregory's English version of the respective lines:

> Invidious Aurora!
>        Why race through heavens
> at your ungodly hour?
> The warning was your son,
> unhappy Memnon,
> born black, the color of his mother's heart!

> If Tithonos, your husband, had a voice,
> O what a story
> the old man could tell
> complaining of young Cephalus and the like.[8]

Plutarch related another story about a Greek woman, but also with the explicitly formulated detail that her black baby caused her to be accused of adultery:

> [A]s the warts and birth-stains and freckles of fathers, not appearing in their own children, crop out again in the children of their sons and daughters; as a certain Greek woman, giving birth to a black child, when accused of adultery, discovered that she was descended in the fourth generation from an Æthiopian; . . . so not infrequently earlier generations conceal and merge ancestral habits and dispositions, while afterward and through later generations the inherited nature comes to flower, and reproduces the family tendency to vice or virtue.[9]

The association with adultery became common enough to prompt Martial to speak of black children (of the white mother Marulla) in an epigram on adultery.[10] Juvenal suggested in a sarcastic address to a husband that he should rejoice that abortions reduced the number of adultery-generated dark babies (described as *Æthiops* and *decolor*).[11]

Calpurnius Flaccus pursued the question of the mother charged with adultery at considerable length. It is his *declamatio Natus Æthiopus* ("born black" or "the black child") that gave the name to the motif, and in this two-part piece the arguments for and against adultery were juxtaposed. The married woman who is accused of adultery because she has given birth to a black child is charged with indiscriminate love that might have fed on itself. The possible defense of atavism is acknowledged: "Children are not always born similar to their parents." Yet it is rejected with the questions:

> What good does this line of argument do you, except to demonstrate more clearly that you have done wrong? Do we marvel at nature's law, that the looks of the parent are passed on to the child, that these aspects (*species*) are preserved as though they were recorded in writing?

Looking at ethnic diversity in different countries the accusation concludes that whereas "groups of men are different, no one is different from his own group." It thus seems more plausible to ask, "Did she love a black man?" This leads to the following plea:

> Sometimes, men of the jury, bad things have their own charm, and [repulsive] things hold a certain delight. Are you shocked that someone loves unwisely, when falling in love itself is quite unlike a wise person? Concede, for a moment, that the woman has healthy eyes: no adulterer is handsome. When womanly virtue is about to perish, the method by which it will perish is the least of worries. When shame has once faltered, the soul, inclined

toward wrong, finds no ruin disgraceful. It is characteristic of unholy lust to be unaware of where it falls. In the end, he pleased her lust, because with him she could not excite her husband's suspicion.

The defense takes the very fact that the woman was willing to give birth as a sign of her chastity. Having apparently raised the possibility of atavism early, the defense rests its case against the charge of adultery on wonder:

Fortune has great power, even in the womb. You see skin that is scorched by a flaw in the blood, and you think it is the complexion. Perhaps this was an injury to the infant. A discoloration has dyed the skin dark, but the child's long life will thin out the color. The sun often darkens snow-white limbs, and the body loses its paleness. And shade makes limbs grow white, though they are naturally dark. Time is capable of just as much as you think nature is.[12]

If nature can tan skins or make darker limbs grow white, the child's darkness may have many causes other than adultery. What the court had to decide then was whether, given that by the law of nature parents transmit their own appearance to children and that love is neither reasonable nor sane, the mother must have made love to an Æthiopian; or whether the child's color may be due to other causes, since the blood may have changed the child in the uterus just as weather can alter the color of our skins, which might change again when the child grows up.

The addition of the suspicion of adultery to Aristotle's tale changed the focus on parentage and ancestry from a curious interest in atavism to a possible defense strategy for a married woman. For Calpurnius Flaccus, the defense rested principally on wonder (though atavism and a rudimentary version of maternal impression are also mentioned), and for Plutarch, on genealogy: if the investigation of the woman's lineage showed that she was in the "fourth generation" descended from (hence the great-granddaughter of) an Æthiopian, then such a genealogy could exonerate the mother who was suspected of adultery because her child was *Natus Æthiopus*.

Pliny's account of the boxer Nicæus, whose mother was no different from the others (white) but whose grandfather, whom Nicæus resembled, was Æthiopian, includes adultery in the past, but he uses the story in a discussion of strange resemblances so that no cloud of suspicion hangs over the mother:

Some women have children like themselves, some like their husband, while others again bear children who resemble neither the one nor the other. In some cases the female children resemble the father, and the males the mother. The case of Nicæus, the celebrated wrestler of Byzantium, is a well-known and undoubted instance. His mother was the produce of an act of adultery, committed with a male of Æthiopia; and although she herself

differed in no way from the ordinary complexion of other females, he was
born with all the swarthy complexion of his Æthiopian grandfather. [13]

The explanation that a child may "regenerate the Æthiopian grandfather" (*avum regeneravit Æthiopem*) was the familiar one of atavism. The
rivaling interpretation of maternal impression was also given by Pliny in
this instance: "A great many likenesses that appear accidental were influenced by sense impressions of sights and sounds received at the time of
conception."[14] Thomas Browne merely paraphrased Pliny when he
defined "maternal impression" as "the power of the imagination which
produceth effects in the conception correspondent unto the phancy of
the Agents in generation; and sometimes assimilates the Idea of the
Generator into a reality in the thing ingendred."[15]

Maternal impression is described nowhere more fully than in
Heliodorus's *Æthiopica* which presents the symmetrically opposite case
of a child born white (*Natus Albus*) to an Æthiopian mother married to a
black husband. The African magus Calasiris finds the testimony given in
writing by Persina, queen of the Æthiopians, to her daughter Chariclea:

> But thou wert born white, which colour is strange among the Ethiopians. I
> knew the reason, that it was because, while my husband had to do with me,
> I was looking at the picture of Andromeda brought down by Perseus naked
> from the rock, and so by mishap engendered presently a thing like to her.
> But counting it certain that thy colour would procure me to be accused of
> adultery, and that none would believe me when I told them the cause, I
> determined to rid myself of shameful death and to commit thee to the
> unstableness of fortune, which was a thing far to be preferred to present
> death or to be called a bastard. Telling my husband therefore that thou
> wert straightway dead, I have privily laid thee forth with the greatest riches
> that I had, as a reward for him who shall find thee and take thee up. And
> besides those other things I have wrapped thee in this band, wherein is
> contained the story of both our fortunes, which I have written with tears
> and blood that I have shed for thee, since I have thee and fell into much
> sorrow for thee at one and the same time.[16]

Here the suspicion of adultery would seem to outweigh any possible
social credibility of a maternal impression tale in which the poet, however, may believe; otherwise Persina would not act the way she does, pretending that her child was dead and abandoning it.

In the modern period, many of the elements of the classical discussion
of the topic remained available. Dr. James Parsons in 1765 reported to
the Royal Society of London a number of cases of "deviation of the
colour in the child, from the contrary hue of both parents," one of which
he described in terms of wonder as "very singular, and something preternatural." In this case of *Natus Albus*, the descendant is called—despite
appearances—"White Negro."[17] The most elaborate instance of *Natus*

*Albus* reported by Parsons appears in a story that he heard from a family who had lived in Virginia:

> [I]n a small plantation near to that of this family, which belonged to a widow, 2 of her slaves, both black, were married; and the woman brought forth a white girl, which this lady saw very often; and as the circumstances of this case were very particular, he makes mention of them here, both for the entertainment of the Society, and to show that this is exactly similar to the case of this boy [i.e., the "White Negro"]. When the poor woman was told the child was like the children of white people, she was in great dread of her husband, declaring, at the same time, that she never had any thing to do with a white man in her life; and therefore begged they would keep the place dark that he might not see it. When he came to ask her how she did, he wanted to see the child, and wondered why the room was shut up, as it was not usual; the woman's fears increased when he had it brought into the light; but while he looked at it he seemed highly pleased, returned the child, and behaved with extraordinary tenderness. She imagined he dissembled his resentment till she should be able to go about, and that then he would leave her; but in a few days he said to her, "You are afraid of me, and therefore keep the room dark, because my child is white; but I love it better for that: for my own father was a white man, though my grandfather and grandmother were as black as you and myself; and although we came from a place where no white people ever were seen, yet there was always a white child in every family that was related to us."[18]

This account of *Natus Albus* strongly resembles the classical cases; wonder is accepted; an exonerating genealogy—somewhat untypically, the husband's—clears the mother of the feared suspicion of adultery; and the quality of "whiteness" is a matter of appearance, not of descent. Olaudah Equiano also described, in his *Interesting Narrative* (1789), an interracial family scene that he viewed and presented as an exemplary wonder:

> Soon after my arrival in London, I saw a remarkable circumstance relative to African complexion, which I thought so extraordinary, that I beg leave just to mention it: A white negro woman, that I had formerly seen in London and other parts, had married a white man, by whom she had three boys, and they were every one mulattoes, and yet they had fine light hair.[19]

As late as 1843, a case with the classical elements of wonder, suspicion of adultery, and atavism was recorded:

> Two white parents in New Jersey, were very much astonished to find in their child unequivocal marks of the African race and blood. . . . His wife protested her innocence in terms so strong and solemn, that he was finally led to believe in her integrity. Still, no explanation of the phenomenon appeared. At length he sailed for France, and visited a town on its frontiers where her family had resided for generations, and found, to his joy, that his wife's *great grandfather* was an African.[20]

In New Jersey of the 1840s a mother's African genealogy could still exonerate her from the suspicion of adultery.[21]

Maternal impression also still made its appearance, although it was, of course, rejected by Enlightenment thinking.[22] For example, in *Le Moyen de parvenir* François Beroalde de Verville (1558–1612) put the following tale into the mouth of the devil: The wife of the Parisian bureaucrat Livet, a man who never left his writing desk, engineered an affair with a young Moor under the pretext that she had a stomach ache that needed curing and that his skin would be warmer than that of a Frenchman. When the wife gives birth to a black baby, the scheming midwife tells Livet that he has a beautiful child and asks him whether he has ever made love to his wife near his writing desk. When he exclaims, "more than thirty times," she explains that because of some spilt ink he must have generated a child that is as black as a Moor.[23] As this last example suggests, however, the secret of adultery could more and more generally be assumed by writers to be the true story behind "maternal impression" tales—the opposite of what was the case in Heliodorus. A Virginia judge in 1840, for example, presumed adultery in a *Natus Æthiopus* case and admitted as evidence the professional opinion "that, according to the course of nature, a mulatto child cannot be the offspring of two white persons."[24] Reflecting the opinion of modern liberal scientists, the porter Dixon argues in J. A. Rogers's novel *From "Superman" to Man* (1917):

> This canard of the apparently unmixed white couple with the coal-black baby is like ghosts. Most everyone believes in them, but no entirely sane person has ever seen one. . . . If no white woman ever went with Negroes, I could accept that story of a white couple with a Negro child as due to atavism. But you'll find any number of white women, married and otherwise, having mulatto children as the result of intercourse with Negroes. Why, then, go to the moon for an explanation of the white couple with a black baby when a logical reason lies right under our nose.[25]

## Puškin's Use of the Motif

No modern text shows better the interconnectedness of adultery and the theme of *Natus Æthiopus/Natus Albus* than does Aleksandr Sergeevič Puškin's unfinished historical novel, *Arap Petra Velikogo*, or "The Blackamoor of Peter the Great" (1827–28).[26]

Puškin (1799–1837) is certainly an appreciated hero of interracial literature. For example, the narrator of Frances Harper's novel *Iola Leroy; or, Shadows Uplifted* (1892) calls him the "Byron of Russian literature" and a "prominent figure in fashionable society" and mentions that one "of his paternal ancestors was a negro who had been ennobled by Peter the Great."[27] Mr. Solomon Sadler, one of the Blue Veins in Chesnutt's *The Wife of His Youth* (1899) "who was supposed to know everything worth knowing concerning the colored race . . . could give the pedigree of Alexander Pushkin" and "the titles of scores of Dumas's novels."[28] And many others, from Victoria Earle Matthews in "The Value of Race Literature" (1895) to Richard Wright in *White Man, Listen!*, have invoked Puškin and his illustrious maternal great-grandfather, Abram Hannibal.[29]

*Arap Petra Velikogo* was Puškin's first experiment at writing prose fiction, and he was trying out an omniscient narrator, care for psychological details, and an impersonal narrative voice of ironic detachment from all characters.[30] The subject was, as the title suggests, an imaginative version of the story of Puškin's ancestor, who is here called Ibrahim.[31] The story opens as Peter the Great's godson Ibrahim, who has received his military training in Paris and become a war hero, returns to Paris in about 1720 and delays going back to Russia. He is twenty-seven years old (as was the author when he wrote this), becomes part of fashionable society, is known as "le Nègre du czar," and falls in love with Léonore, the Countess D., who is "married to a man to whom she had not had time to grow attached." The countess was reputed to have had lovers but had kept her good name "simply because she could never be accused of any ridiculous or scandalous episodes" (12).

Unlike others, she has not looked at the young black man as if he were a wonder.[32] Instead, Countess D. treats him "politely but without fanfare, which flattered him." Ibrahim is at this point embittered, and his pride is offended, for he is regarded as "a kind of rare animal" (13), whereas he only wishes to attract nobody's attention. Countess D., who has grown tired of the "endless jests and subtle insinuations of French wit," is drawn to Ibrahim's "simple and demure" conversation; he often comes to her house, and she becomes used to his appearance, even "finding something attractive in that curly head, standing out with its blackness among the powdered wigs in her drawing room" (13).

Slowly, their mutual affection grows, fueled by their difference, and the narrator takes delight in analyzing the process:

> The idea of love had not crossed his mind, but to see the Countess daily was becoming a necessity to him. He sought her out everywhere, and meeting her seemed to him an unexpected favor from heaven each time. The Countess recognized his feelings before he himself did. Whatever you say, love without aspirations and demands touches the feminine heart more surely than all the wiles of seduction. When she was with Ibrahim, the Countess followed every movement he made and listened carefully to every word he said; in his absence she grew thoughtful and sank into her habitual distractedness. Merville was the first to notice this mutual inclination, and he congratulated Ibrahim. Nothing inflames love so much as the encouraging remark of an outsider. Love is blind, and distrustful of itself, eagerly grasps any support. Merville's words awakened Ibrahim. Until then the idea that he might possess the woman he loved had not even

occurred to him; now hope suddenly lit up his soul; he fell madly in love. The Countess, frightened by the violence of his passion, tried to counter with friendly exhortations and prudent admonitions, but all in vain; she herself was weakening. Incautiously granted favors followed one another in quick succession. And at last, carried away by the force of the passion she had herself inspired, overpowered by its moment, she gave herself to the ecstatic Ibrahim. . . . (13–14)

I have quoted this section fully because it conveys the extent to which Puškin is able to investigate ironically, even clinically, the growth from infatuation to consummation in a few lines that leave far behind the sociological specter of black-white love that so seems to have haunted the imaginary of the modern West.

Puškin has sketched the outline of the story that he now continues with a new look at the social world in which the Countess and Ibrahim also had to live. Their liaison becomes common knowledge: "Some ladies were surprised by her choice, but many found it perfectly natural." Double entendres and allusions make the Countess worry that Ibrahim's passionate defenses of her might further implicate her social reputation, and she begs him not to defend her.

At this point Puškin introduces her pregnancy that will lead to his version of a *Natus Æthiopus* story. Recognizing her situation, the "consequence of her imprudent love," the Countess thinks that "her ruin was inevitable, and waited for it in despair." The conflict is set up in such a way that the world of the lovers, justified in its own way but not socially legitimated, is threatened by the social world of common talk that will suspect adultery the moment the child is born.

> Ladies of sensibility moaned with horror; men took bets on whether the Countess would give birth to a white or black baby. Epigrams proliferated at the expense of her husband—the only person in Paris who knew nothing and suspected nothing. (14)

This is a nicely satirical application of the classical *Natus Æthiopus* scenario. Interracial adultery seems to suggest a certainty of parentage that can have disastrous effects for the mother unless the defense is good. Meanwhile Russian—like Latin—epigram writers may make fun of the hardly individualized figure of the cuckolded husband who serves only as a social type.[33] By constructing his conflict in such a way, Puškin has also created suspense and made the reader await eagerly the "fateful moment" of the delivery scene. The buildup of nervous tension reaches its high point as Countess D. feels the first pains. The narrator states: "Measures were taken quickly. A pretext was found for sending the Count away. The physician arrived." How is the Countess going to get out of the scandal that must be imminent?

Puškin takes his authorial liberty in going back in time in order to signal the way out of the dilemma at hand: by switching babies. "A couple of days before, a destitute woman had been persuaded to give up her new-born son; now a trusted agent was sent to fetch him" (14). After Ibrahim, from whose point of view the reader experiences the delivery scene, has agonized in "horror" for a long time during the Countess's labor, the feeble cry of a child can be heard, and he rushes into her room:

> A black baby lay on the bed at her feet. Ibrahim went up to it. His heart throbbed violently. He blessed his son with a shaking hand. The Countess gave a faint smile. (15)

After this brief and touching family scene the camouflage is enacted for the husband. The baby is taken away, through a secret staircase, and—unlike in the case of Heliodorus's Chariclea—the reader never hears of the child again, except when Ibrahim invokes it as a memory; and in its stead the other child is placed in the cradle. The reader, who may have been expecting this child to become of ancestral importance for the poet, feels surprised at this moment.

Ibrahim's reaction is odd after the emotional blessing that he gives his son: he "left somewhat reassured." Ultimately, social rules matter more than private feelings. When the husband returns, Ibrahim is satisfied, and the public "which had anticipated an uproarious scandal, was frustrated in its expectations and had to content itself with mere vilifications" (15). While it seems that everything has returned to normal, Ibrahim is now plagued by a new sense of a presentiment of jealousy, and in order to prevent it from becoming a reality, he decides to go back to Petersburg, writing the Countess a long letter explaining his motives.

> Your tranquility is dearest of all to me, and you could not enjoy it while the gaze of society was fixed on us. Remember everything you have suffered through, all the humiliations, all the torments of fear; remember the terrifying birth of our son. Just think: should I subject you to the same worries and dangers even longer? Why struggle to unite the fate of such a tender and graceful creature with the unlucky lot of a Negro, a pitiful being, scarcely granted the title of man? (17)

Playing the race card again in asking her to think sometimes "of the poor Negro," he bids his farewell and promises that he will devote himself from now on to hard work in gloomy Russia.

Favored by his godfather Peter the Great who is awaiting Ibrahim at the border, he *does* work hard and becomes attached to his Tsar. Paris seems almost forgotten—though Ibrahim sometimes shudders at the thought that Countess D. might have made a new liaison: "Jealousy began to seethe in his African blood, and burning tears were ready to course down his black face" (21). When his friend Korsakov arrives from France and reports the news that the "lanky Marquis of R." has actually replaced Ibrahim in Léonore's heart he is numb with depression, and Korsakov asks him, "But what are you staring at me for with those Negro eyeballs of yours? . . . Don't you know that lasting grief is not in the nature of human beings, especially of a woman?" (22). In all these instances, the description of racialized physical details is associated with jealousy. Life at the court continues, with Korsakov playing the part of the foppish young man with French airs.

The second half of the novel fragment concerns the marriage plot for Ibrahim that is devised by the Tsar, who makes a surprise visit to the aristocrat and descendant of an ancient lineage of boyars, Gavrila Afanasevich Rževskii, asking him to give his daughter Natasha in marriage to Ibrahim. Puškin uses the scene for more social satire: after the Tsar has left, Gavrila's family is trying to guess what the Tsar's proposal might be; and when Gavrila reveals it, adding that it is the duty of vassals to obey, the noise of Natasha's fainting can be heard outside the room. She has overheard and deeply resents the plan since she is secretly in love with a Valerian about whom she fantasizes in her feverish weakened state.

Ibrahim, just as surprised by the Tsar's plan, discusses the marriage plans with Korsakov who—true to the convention of the literary topos—advises him *not* to marry, reminding him not so subtly of the possibility of adultery—that is now specifically linked to Ibrahim's Africanness:

> "Don't you remember our Parisian friend, Count D.? One cannot rely on woman's fidelity; lucky the man who can contemplate the matter with indifference. But you? Should you, with your passionate, brooding, and suspicious nature, with your flat nose and thick lips, and with that kinky wool on your head, throw yourself into all the dangers of matrimony?"
>
> "I thank you for all the friendly advice," Ibrahim interrupted him coldly, "but you know the saying: it's not your duty to rock other people's babies."
>
> "Take care, Ibrahim," answered Korsakov, laughing, "take care not to let it happen that you should illustrate this proverb in a literal sense." (37)

Foppish and ridiculous though Korsakov may be, his function here seems to be to foreshadow what Puškin had planned to represent in the unfinished part of the novel, for Natasha is also given the advice by a midget to take a broader view of the marriage plans:

> Even if you have to marry the blackamoor, you will have your freedom. Today it's not as it used to be: husbands don't lock up their wives. The blackamoor, they say, is rich; your house will be like a cup brimming over; you'll live in clover. . . . (39)

Apparently, it was Puškin's intention to bring the novel to the symmetrically opposite development of letting Natasha give birth to a white baby—and, as her punishment, having her banned to a monastery[34]—so that Ibrahim would indeed be literally rocking other people's babies in a narrative that juxtaposed a *Natus Æthiopus* opening with a *Natus Albus* sequel. Ibrahim would have doubled as lover of a married woman and as cuckolded husband, as the one who felt relieved having given away the son that he blessed only to become legal father to a child that was not his.

Puškin does not seem to have sought a filiopietistic myth of ancestry, and in the writer's hands, the racial difference of his capital-A ancestor mattered most especially in providing him with verisimilitude for a double adultery plot. The fact that Puškin's *Arap Petra Velikogo* has remained a fragment is a great loss to interracial literature. The narrator's ironic relationship to the psychology and sociology of human motivation is free of the heaviness and paranoia that have often attached themselves to the theme before and after his time. His narrative style of reporting in a neutral and objective way, avoiding emotionality, rhetorical questions, amazed exclamations, and the like, gave Puškin's prose force and clarity.[35]

## The Origin of "Species"

All the continuities of the *Natus Æthiopus/Natus Albus* motif from Aristotle to Puškin notwithstanding, there were differences between the "classical" and the "modern" view that sharpened in the eighteenth and nineteenth centuries, affected the meaning of the details of the theme, and ultimately redefined the role of *genealogy* in the tales of *Natus Æthiopus/Natus Albus*. These changes are most easily apparent if we return to the classical cases and compare them with a few modern ones.

In his discussion of Pliny's text about the boxer Nicæus, Lloyd A. Thompson observed: "What was quite obviously *not* the yardstick by which the perception of membership of the category *Aethiops* operated was 'negro blood.'"[36] Thompson noted that the boxer's mother

> though white, was (after the birth of her son) believed to be the daughter of a black man, just as the suspected adulteress of Plutarch's account retained her identity as a *Greek* (and white) woman after it came to be understood that she was the great-granddaughter of a black African.

According to Pliny, she was "no different from the others." Her African genealogy cleared her of the suspicion of adultery, but it did *not* define her as "black." This is precisely what separates the modern view from the Roman examples, as Thompson also made clear:

> [I]n Roman society, the quality of Aethiopian-ness which distinguished the *Aethiops* from white men was merely a matter of outward physical appearance—*species*, as Christian writers would later express it.[37]

"Species" had not yet become an abstraction removable from, and in potentially contradictory relation to, a "mask-like" "appearance." In fact, a philosophical system of abstracting was necessary to take mankind from *species* as *aspect* to "species" as an "essential division of kind." Again, it was an animal story that mattered in this transformation. Citing Boethius, Meletius, Athanasius, and Augustine, Thompson argued:

> Christian leaders were reflecting a long-standing Roman attitude when, in their discussions on the "essential" and the "accidental" qualities of man, they supported their doctrine by (*inter alia*) the argument that, although a black horse and an *Aethiops* both share the same "accidental" quality of blackness, the removal of this blackness leaves the horse still a horse, but entirely eliminates the quality of the *Aethiops* from the *Aethiops*, who thereby becomes "a white man like other men" (*erit eius species candida, sicut etiam aliorum hominum*).[38] These Christian arguments . . . are clearly characteristic of a culture in which the defining quality of the *Aethiops* was simply physical appearance (*species*), irrespective of ancestry and parentage.[39]

Thompson's analysis highlights what from the "modern" view appears as a paradox:

> The Pliny text indicates that the black boxer's mother is white, even though she is separated from their common black ascendants by a narrower generation-distance than her own son who is black, and the distance separating the latter from his white relations is merely one of somatic appearance, not a social distance. Nor does the presence of a black relation in any way socially distance his white family members from their white peers outside the family circle.[40]

In Greece or Rome, a man could "regenerate" his black African maternal grandfather without affecting the "race" of his Greek mother.

This was no longer quite the case in the "remarkable circumstance" mentioned by Equiano, who intriguingly described the mother as a "white negro woman." "White" obviously designated her appearance (*species* in the classical sense) and "Negro" defined her "species" (close to the genealogical abstraction "race" in the modern sense) that made itself known in her descendants. In other words, Equiano's example implied that the mother's "race" was no longer just a matter of appearance, but also of genealogy. The oxymoron "white negro" was used here in order to give expression to this tension.[41] In antiquity the wonder was that a white woman should give birth to a black child; in the modern period—the time of the African slave trade—it seemed wondrous that a woman proven to be "Negro" by her ascendant and descendant should look so deceptively white.[42]

It is this historical difference in racial identity embedded in the word "species" that makes difficult—if not impossible—a continued and unchanged recurrence of the theme of *Natus Æthiopus/Natus Albus* in the modern world. Calpurnius Flaccus used the term "species," meaning aspect, in his *declamatio* on the topic, and Augustine stated that there are not "several species of men as there are species of herbs."[43] In 1770, however, Virginia statutes were enacted in order to deter white women from a "confusion of species," which meant from sexual relations with other human beings, namely, black men.[44] Similarly, the instructions for French colonial governors from 1760 to 1780 recommended that one "could not keep too much distance between the two species" of blacks and whites.[45]

That "species" began to connote "essential qualities of a class of persons or things as distinguished from genus on the one hand and the individual on the other"[46] is due to an adaptation from the language of logic.[47] The stabilization of "species" as an essential subdivision of the human *genus* was completed only in the course of the eighteenth and nineteenth centuries. Like Augustine, both Buffon and Blumenbach regarded humans as one *species* that was subdivided by "varieties," and invoked as proof that in physical appearance there was as much difference among Africans as between "negroes and other varieties of the human species."[48] For Kant in 1785 the proof for the existence of a single human species lay in the fact that people of all races could procreate with each other, producing fertile offspring.[49] By contrast, and apparently much more influentially, in 1774 Edward Long may have been the first to suppose, against all evidence, that Mulattoes were "defective and barren" when they "intermarried with those of their own complexion," which was to become a much-needed core assumption in the belief that racial differences were not distinctions of "varieties" but really "species" differences. In fact, Long was fully aware of this implication of his argument, believed that "the White and the Negroe had not one common origin," and stated explicitly "that the White and the Negroe are two distinct species."[50] In 1799 Charles White drew on Long and argued systematically that human varieties were really differences in "species." It was another animal tale that served to make his point, since he could not believe that all dogs had descended from one origin:

> I should rather suppose that the different kinds of dogs, which, from time immemorial, have preserved their distinctive qualities, are in reality separate species of animals; and that all others are only varieties, or mongrels, produced by the intermixture of species, and which, like the mule, in one, two, or more generations in the mongrel line, lose their prolific quality, and consequently become extinct.[51]

The role of interracial family structures was thus crucial in setting up a theoretical definition of "race" *as* "species": if the descendants of black-white sexual unions were not able to generate, then the difference between black and white was one not merely of "variety" but of *kind*, or "species" in the modern sense.[52] And the dog story also suggested the usefulness for racial thinking of the "polygenist" assumption of many origins. Race differences could now be described as species differences by writers like James Kirke Paulding, who determined in a proslavery book of 1836 that the differences between whites and blacks were "equivalent to those which separate various species of animals."[53]

In the first half of the nineteenth century Julien-Joseph Virey and Josiah Clark Nott pulled these various strands together and devised the intellectual backbone of biological racism. Virey argued in his *Histoire naturelle du genre humain* (1824) that there were two human *species*, "whites" and "blacks" (including Africans, Indians, and Asians), and in 1841 he exalted "Caucasians" and argued that their enslaving of others was "natural."[54] Whereas Virey went for the biological approach of skull-measuring and anatomical contrasting, it is not without interest for an understanding of the emergence of "race" out of the denial of the "interracial" and "biracial" realms that one of Nott's first attempts at making the move toward race as species appeared in the *American Journal of Medical Sciences* in 1843 under the title "The Mulatto a Hybrid—probable extermination of the two races if the Whites and Blacks are allowed to intermarry." Defining the "Mulatto" as a "hybrid," Nott explicitly claimed that this meant "the offspring of two distinct species—as the mule from the horse and the ass." And he invoked evidence from Edward Long to a faulty reading of American census data in order to make his case for the "unnatural" character of interracial sexual relations and the "degeneracy" of their offspring. As of yet, he did not care whether to adopt a monogenetic or a polygenetic line:

> The Caucasian, Ethiopian, Mongol, Malay, and American may have been distinct creations, or may be mere varieties of the same species, produced by external causes acting through many thousand years; but this I do believe, *that at the present day the Anglo-Saxon and Negro races are, according to the common acceptation of the terms, distinct species, and that the offspring of the two is a Hybrid.*[55]

Nott's focus was on the distinction to be made in the present, and it did not matter whether his assumption of racial difference might imply that separate species can *emerge*. After the encounter with other racialists, however, Nott may have become the first American scientist to suggest the separate creation of races (understood as if they were species in the modern sense) when he set out to claim "that there is a Genus, Man, comprising two or more species—that physical causes cannot change a White man into a Negro, and that to say this change has been affected by a direct act of providence, is an assumption which *cannot be proven, and is contrary to the great chain of Nature's laws.*"[56] To say "species" meant that the difference was not only more than one in appearance but also more than one in degree[57]—and that implied that the "degrees" and "varieties" between black and white had to be declared nonexistent or unnatural.

In making this argument, Nott virtually had to stand on its head the classical distinction between "essential" and "accidental" qualities: whereas skin color had been the prototypical accidental trait in antiquity, it now became the sign of an essential difference.[58] Nott viewed races as "radically distinct" and demanded in 1854 that "the superior races must be kept free from all adulterations, otherwise the world will retrograde, instead of advancing, in civilization."[59] Worried that the popular meaning of the term "species" "might apply as readily to mere varieties," Nott invokes Samuel George Morton's definition: "SPECIES: *a primordial organic form.*"[60] The purity of species was endangered by "adulteration" that could, however, be detected. Nott specifically claimed that black ancestry could generally be recognized: "I have rarely if ever met an individual tainted with black blood," he wrote, "in whom I could not detect it without difficulty."[61]

In Charles Darwin's *On the Origin of Species* (1859), a whole chapter is devoted to "Hybridism" that clarifies the normal distinction between sterility of "hybrids"—the offspring of different "species"—and the fertility of "mongrels"—generated by different "varieties," while also questioning this differentiation and noting that sterility and fertility are not universal and various in degree. Still, Darwin kept in place the rule of thumb that it was only the test of fertility that could distinguish between hybrids and mongrels.[62] A 1990 encyclopedia defines species as "group of physically and genetically similar individuals that interbreed under natural conditions."[63] The idea of "genetic" (a word first used in the biological sense in France in 1846[64] and adopted by Darwin) similitude was the new element; and, as we shall see in Chapter Four, the pressing question whether blacks and whites "interbreed under natural conditions" was precisely what became the center of a racialist argument that wished to view "race" as synonymous with "species" and had to look for "natural" signs in order to detect the "essential" (but often invisible) difference. The term "species" has traveled a long way, indeed.

An annotation of 1912 to Aristotle's tale of the woman of Elis is characteristic of the changing modern meaning of genealogy:

> It is possible that this story *may* be true. . . . In the absence of details we cannot even say exactly what is meant here; the daughter, for instance, might have been an albino and her son a quadroon, which would be enough to start the story, and then there would be nothing remarkable about it. But such tales are recklessly invented in America to this day.
>
> Granting it to be true in its obvious and strongest meaning, it would *not* be a case of Mendelism. For if black were the dominant character, how could the daughter be white? And if white were dominant how could her son be black?[65]

"Black" and "white" had become genealogically imagined "essences," independent of "aspect." Now the woman of Elis could not possibly have been "white"—no matter what she looked like—if, married to a Greek, she could give birth to a "black" child, and if giving birth to the "black" child was accounted for by her ancestry, then that would only confirm her identification as "black," regardless of her "white" appearance. In arguing a scenario that would, by casting her as an albino, leave "nothing remarkable" about the episode, this commentator presented the two sides of the modern approach of making "wonder" scientifically explainable and of viewing racial essence as if it were a stable scientific category.

### From Wonder to Horror:
### Some Modern Versions of *Natus Æthiopus*

In stories of atavism that appeared in a concentrated fashion in the late nineteenth and the early twentieth centuries, these racial essences were also imagined in a hierarchical arrangement (compatible with the enslavement and subjugation of Africans) so that the symmetry of *Natus Æthiopus/Natus Albus* no longer prevailed. Only the birth of a child that was *darker* than its parents would now be perceived as a problematic, bad, and even disastrous event.[66] It is obvious why this should have been a convenient fiction for shrill white racialists. In Robert Lee Durham's novel *The Call of the South* (1908), for example, set a few years into the future from the date of its publication, Helen Phillips, a daughter of the liberal-seeming President of the United States, falls in love and marries the Harvard-educated war hero Hayward Graham, whose great-grandfather was the African Guinea Gumbo. Helen gives birth to a baby boy, and her father reacts very strongly to the "flesh-and-blood terror" that he sees in little Hayne Phillips's face, "many, many shades darker than the face of Hayward Graham."

> With a hope that was faltering indeed had he prayed for the miracle that might deliver Helen entirely from the consequences of her thoughtless folly, but with all his faith had he besought a merciful Heaven that the child which would come to her should not fall below a fair average of its parental graces. Even that were a torture, that were horrible enough: that Helen's blood should be *evenly* mixed and tainted with the baser sort. But this recession below the father's type!—this resurgence of the negro blood, with its "vile unknown ancestral impulses!"—there came to him an almost overpowering desire, such as had come of late with increasing frequency but never with such physical weakness as now: the desire to lie down at full length to rest.[67]

The motif of *Natus Æthiopus* has become an element of horror in the tormented white grandfather's perspective whose soul cries against fate, "why, oh, why should atavism have thought to play its tricks and assert its prerogative here!" As he sees the "tight-shut baby fist that was almost black" coming out of the white coverlet, he almost flees, but in response to his daughter's request, he sits down beside the boy:

Pulling the covering a little away, he took the tiny hand in his, and grand-father and grandson looked for the first time each into the face of the other.

It was a negro baby: the colour that was of Ethiopia, the unmistakable nose, the hair that curls so tightly, the lips that were African, the large whites of the eyes. Verily a negro baby: and yet in an undefinable way a likeness to Helen, a caricature of Helen, a horrible travesty of Helen's features in combination with—with whose? Helen's and whose? . . . Mr. Phillips could not answer his own question—he had never seen Guinea Gumbo.

It is telling that this description connects the child's essence to that of the distant capital-A ancestor Guinea Gumbo, while finding the mother's features only caricatured in the baby. The closer and much more dominant white ancestry becomes mask-like compared with the overpowering genealogical memory of blackness. Shortly after this scene, Mr. Phillips dies of a heart attack.

As represented by Durham, Phillips's fate serves to prove right the extremist segregationist hate speech by Senator Evans Rutledge that is quoted at length near the center of the novel:

When the blood of your daughter or your son is mixed with that of one of this race, however *risen*, redolent of newly applied polish or bewrapped with a fresh culture, how shall sickly sentimentalities solace your shame if in the blood of your mulatto grandchild the vigorous red jungle corpuscles of some savage ancestor shall overmatch your more gentle endowment, and under your name and in a face and form perhaps where a world may see your very image in darker hue there shall be disported primitive appetites, propensities, passions fit only to endow an Ashanti warrior or grace the orgies of an African bacchanalia?[68]

A grandparent's fear of not recognizing himself in his descendant is exploited for the worst racist sentiments. Although Rutledge had sharply criticized Phillips for inviting two black leaders to lunch at the White House,[69] it turns out that Phillips secretly agreed more with Rutledge than he publicly admitted. When Helen finds out, after her father's death, that he had written the comment "UNTHINKABLE!"[70] next to this passage in his copy of the *Congressional Record* (giving Durham the occasion to quote Rutledge a second time), the recognition that she may be responsible for her father's death drives her to give up the child and to go insane in self-torment. While her sister Elise is getting ready to marry Rutledge, Helen utters blood-curdling screams at her husband in her hospital room:

*Go away!* The poison of your blood is in my veins and will not come out! It is polluted, forever polluted! A knife—*a knife!* Give me a knife, doctor, that I may let it out. . . . Kill me—*save me!* My blood is *unclean*, and he did it!

My baby was black, *black!*—and its negro blood is in my veins! A knife, doctor! A knife!! Oo-o-a-ugh!! I'll tear it out, then.[71]

When the doctor explains to Hayward Graham that Helen is actually *sane* in those moments, and insane only when her mind is happily wandering, her shaken husband reenlists in the army.

In the hands of a racialist radical, the *Natus Æthiopus* motif changed into the white horror of horrors. Underneath the Gothic machinery, however, one still recognizes the issues of the past in their transformation: atavism explains a child's color, but in a cultural context in which it could be asserted that black and white must never be related in a family structure. *Wonder* is replaced by *horror* (further enhanced by the character of Guinea Gumbo, who fits the worst expectations); adultery seems to have completely disappeared; "essential" racial difference cuts even fully legalized family relations; and the birth of a dark child can now affect two generations of white ascendants, since not only the child's mother, but also the mother's father seem fatally marked by the birth. One of Rutledge's political competitors also implicates Helen's sister Elise—but there even Rutledge draws the line and gallantly defends Elise, thus opening the way to their ultimate marriage. White daughters who love segregationist senators look forward to a happy married life; those who intermarry Harvard-educated men[72] with invisible black ancestry go under and take their fathers with them.

The adoption of such a position by racist novelists may explain why extended discussions of atavism have been important to liberal social scientists.[73] Yet the thematic field constituted by *Natus Æthiopus* also provides a context for more liberal literary texts that have been claimed for progressive readings. As an example, I wish to focus on Kate Chopin's well-known short story "Désirée's Baby" (1893) as a decidedly modern version of *Natus Æthiopus*. The story was actually entitled "The Father of Désirée's Baby" when it was first published in *Vogue*, and it appeared there under the general title "Character Studies."[74]

Désirée, an orphan who was found near a Louisiana plantation and raised by the Valmondés, marries the planter Armand Aubigny, of one of the oldest and proudest families, who has fallen in love with her "as if struck by a pistol shot" (70). Some time after the birth of their son, Madame Valmondé comes to look at the baby; and when she sees it she exclaims "in startled tones," "This is not the baby!" (70)—inspecting it near the lightest window. Yet Désirée is without guile or suspicion and answers Madame Valmondé's charged question, "What does Armand say?," with a glowing account of the family's happiness. Suddenly, however, when the child is about three months old, everything changes menacingly. After some unaccountable visits by neighbors and a general air of mystery, the bubble begins to burst:

When [Armand] spoke to her, it was with averted eyes, from which the old love-light seemed to have gone out. He absented himself from home; and when there, avoided her presence and that of her child, without excuse. And the very spirit of Satan seemed suddenly to take hold of him in his dealings with the slaves. Désirée was miserable enough to die. (71)

One afternoon, one of La Blanche's Quadroon boys is fanning the baby when Désirée finally notices something herself:

She looked from her child to the boy who stood beside him, and back again; over and over. "Ah!" It was a cry that she could not help; which she was not conscious of having uttered. The blood turned like ice in her veins, and a clammy moisture gathered upon her face. (71)

When she asks Armand for help—and this may be the closest the story comes to admitting "wonder"—he accuses *her* of not being white. Désirée courageously denies it:

"It is a lie—it is not true, I am white! Look at my hair, it is brown; and my eyes are gray, Armand, you know they are gray. And my skin is fair," seizing his wrist. "Look at my hand—whiter than yours, Armand," she laughed hysterically.
    "As white as La Blanche's," he returned cruelly; and went away leaving her alone with their child. (71)

She writes to Madame Valmondé, who invites Désirée to "come home" with the child. In a conversation with Armand he harshly tells her to go; she walks away with the baby, and "disappeared among the reeds and willows that grew thick along the banks of the deep, sluggish bayou; and she did not come back again."
    The socially ostracized mother who disappears in the water with her child formed a well-known motif of romantic literature.[75] Yet Chopin's story does not end on this note. What follows (after a line of asterisks) is a brief appendix of sorts, a second ending that sets the record straight. A few weeks after the main action, Armand has made a bonfire, and the Negroes are throwing in all reminders of Désirée and the baby—marriage trousseau, clothes, cradle, and all—a kind of ethnic cleansing. The last thing to go in is a package of Désirée's letters to Armand, and in the back of the drawer from which he takes them the remnant of one emerges.

But it was not Désirée's. It was part of an old letter from his mother to his father. He read it. She was thanking God for the blessing of her husband's love;
    "But, above all," she wrote, "night and day, I thank the good God for having so arranged our lives that our dear Armand will never know that his mother, who adores him, belongs to the race that is cursed with the brand of slavery." (74)

This is the surprising way in which the story ends. No wonder that it was originally entitled "The Father of Désirée's Baby." Jon Erickson has analyzed the function of the double ending:

> The circumstances that lead to the suicide of the heroine—the first ending—argue that fairytale solutions to real social problems are unviable. But the second ending, reflecting on the first, asks if they are really as unviable as it seems.[76]

Armand seems a perfect target for an antipatriarchal reading. He is horrible and blames his innocent, orphaned wife for the child's blackness—thus also illuminating the fact that Désirée is always externally defined by the roles of daughter, wife, mother, and discarded woman. Armand is moody, can be satanically mean to the slaves on the plantation, and may well be having sexual relationships with other women. Characteristic is his iron-clad adherence to a brutal racial code that makes interracial relations incompatible with family relations. Armand's cruel application of racial logic hardly makes him a sympathetic character. He is so bad, in fact, that some readers even surmised (without any textual evidence) that Armand must have known about his own racial background earlier and kept this knowledge from Désirée; others hypothesized that La Blanche may have been an earlier wife who had been discarded when proven black—making him a sort of racially motivated Bluebeard. At first glance, the conclusion therefore may seem to be bringing about the satisfying punishment of a hypocrite, following the logic of a fairy tale.

Is the ending truly convincing, however, or is it a deus ex machina? Carlos Baker unambiguously thought it was the latter. He argued that it is "a trick which mars" Chopin's "frequently anthologized (and not very typical) study in race relations." He finds that the story "satisfies the reader's sense of justice while disappointing him with a contrived conclusion."[77] Armand blames Désirée undeservedly and gets his just deserts, but the mechanism of bringing it about is not plausible and seems almost an afterthought. Furthermore, it is the time-worn device of the found, fragmentary document that authenticates Armand's racial background.

It is noteworthy that the paternity of "The Father of Désirée's Baby" is never in doubt, though it might be: *Natus Æthiopus* did, after all, yield the suspicion of adultery—which is here (as it was in Durham) suppressed so totally as not to occur to the narrator or any character; it is a possibility that was scarcely mentioned by readers.[78] "Black blood" understood as genealogical essence is such a liability (not only in sufferable social terms, but also in unbearable psychological ones) in the world of the story that it seems UNTHINKABLE that any white woman might voluntarily associate with a black man.[79] Adultery is simply not in the picture. Yet is there a residue of the old thematic cluster somewhere? For one, Armand's certainty in assuming that Désirée must be blamed would have made more sense in an adultery story than in a tale of mysterious racial origins—that makes the ancestry of husband, wife, or both worth exploring. Furthermore, could it be that the emotions that are conventionally attached to a husband's reaction to his wife's adultery—whether expressed by horrified surprise, jealous rage, or cynical coldness, there is always his sense of having been ridiculed and "dishonored" that may generate the need to purge the experience by a hostile, and at times violent, purification ritual—are now *displaced* onto the discovery of the wife's supposed "impure blood," the "violation" of *racial* purity, or her deception about it? The violent recoiling from the racial "stain," the blot, the impurity, the *adulteration* of the beloved, that is typically overdrawn in the literature, may borrow some of its structure and intensity from the reaction to an *adultery* plot.[80] The word "adulteration" was, as we saw, employed by Blumenbach and Nott, but it was Long who still used it in a way that signaled an appeal to marital legitimacy as well as to white racial purity: he thought it better for Britain and Jamaica

> if the white men in that colony would abate of their infatuated attachments to black women, and, instead of being "grac'd with a *yellow offspring not their own*" [Pitt's Virg. Aen. vi. 293], perform the duty incumbent on every good cittizen, by raising in honourable wedlock a race of unadulterated beings.[81]

"Adulteration," which marked a contrast with purity (and especially, racial purity), still announced its etymological origin by also standing in opposition to fidelity in wedlock.

His reaction permits Armand not only to recoil from the once romantically desired spouse, tellingly named "Désirée"—not looking at her and answering her only reluctantly and coldly—as if she had deceived him, had betrayed him, by her supposed invisible essence, with another *race*, so to speak, but it also makes him take a brutal distance from his own child as if it were no longer his at all: He "avoided [Désirée's] presence and that of her child"—not "their" child.[82] (This is also a reaction one might expect more in the case of a husband who suspects his wife of adultery so that the child would be that by another father.) The narrator explains Armand's emotions when he sends Désirée away:

> He thought Almighty God had dealt cruelly and unjustly with him; and felt, somehow, that he was paying Him back in kind when he stabbed thus into his wife's soul. Moreover he no longer loved her, because of the unconscious injury she had brought upon his home and his name.
>
> She turned away like one stunned by a blow, and walked slowly towards the door, hoping he would call her back.
>
> "Good-by, Armand," she moaned.
>
> He did not answer her. That was his last blow at fate. After it was dealt he felt like a remorseless murderer. (74)[83]

Armand acts with the cold-hearted and murderous impulses of the irascible deceived husband, and the bonfire of all remnants that could remind him of his family is the ritual by which he attempts to exorcise their memory from his mind. Strangely, his murderous coldness and the fire he makes bring back in a perverted form the initial metaphors of his falling in love "as if struck by a pistol shot" and with a passion that "swept along . . . like a prairie fire." The clustering of racial "adulteration" and marital "adultery" emotionalizes the representation so that the suppression and change of other plausible elements of the *Natus Æthiopus* motif could go unnoticed.

Most dramatically, what is taken for granted in the story is the unquestioned power of the new rule that genealogy can no longer exonerate—but that it implicates. In antiquity the suspicion of adultery could be allayed by an appropriate African genealogy of the mother, and atavism could help in building up the case. In Chopin, the absence of an ascertainable white genealogy is enough to condemn Désirée in Armand's eyes for her adulterated blood. When Désirée recognizes their legal "white" son and heir's similarity to La Blanche's "Quadroon boy" (who might well have been fathered by Armand as well[84]), she asks him—in his sullenness—what that means. The question could raise the expectation that its answer might lead toward a story of Armand's marital infidelity or of switched babies.[85] Yet such plot possibilities, too, are not realized in the story, as Armand's response makes clear: "'It means,' he answered lightly, 'that the child is not white; it means that you are not white'" (71). This may be the epiphanic moment of the short story; but it is, of course, also a very modern syllogism that would not have seemed plausible to Pliny, either as a set of individual propositions or as a logical sequence. It takes a sense of inward racial essentialism to overrule *appearance* for child and mother. (It is also a sequence that would hardly have come to Count D.'s mind had he returned earlier for his wife's *accouchement*.)

The poetic justice that the ending seems to promise only intensifies the universal rule of an implicating genealogy: the found document is taken to establish firmly that although he has discarded Désirée for reasons of her putative "race," it is really Armand who is genealogically "black."[86] Interestingly, what makes the baby "black" is never clearly represented—only that in some way the boy resembles that of La Blanche.[87] The birth of the child sets up the need to ask for an explanation. The *Natus Æthiopus* motif could hardly be expected to connect any longer with "maternal impression": it was too hard to imagine that "essences" could get transmitted in such a haphazard way, and heredity was far too important for environmental explanations. What the birth of the child makes necessary is to resolve the problem of ascertaining who is black and who is white: for in a society in which racial identity is all-important but not necessarily visible, not a function of "species" in the classical sense, it is certain that each person must be either black or white—though it may not be clear which.[88] Armand's logic is also the logic of the story: if a "white" child looks like a "Quadroon boy" (whose mother may look white and have a name that means "the white one," yet who is "black"), a parent must also not be "white." Chopin's story plays hide-and-seek with its reader about her characters' race. First the reader is led to assume that Désirée, the orphan and foundling, must be the one whose genealogical uncertainty would invite the expectation that she is not "white." ("Orphan"—as well as "double"—function as racial magnets in race fiction that values genealogy over appearance.[89]) Then the authority of the document identifies Armand as "black"—and by implication restores Désirée's "whiteness" and innocence. In this *Natus Æthiopus* story, black genealogy exonerates only the parent who does *not* have it. (The assumption that both parents may be "black" is not invited by the text.[90]) On one level this makes Armand a tragic character. As Erickson argued, "Armand finds out that in order to expunge the guilt, he would have to expunge himself."[91] The ending brings the certain identification of Armand's race, but—since it is based on circumstantial evidence surprisingly found—also the knowledge to the reader that any "white" person could find such a letter hidden in a drawer. Yet the story hardly constitutes an attack on racial certainties in calling attention to the vagaries of genealogical information.

A strange side-effect of the melodramatic closure is that what wins out is not only a genealogy that damns Armand but also a racial undertone. Emily Toth argued that in "the end Armand, not Désirée, is the tragic octoroon" since he plays the male type who is "militant, rebellious, melancholy, at the mercy of fierce passions."[92] Yet the reader is also assured at the end that it is the evil, satanic character who is at fault; conveniently, he is also the one who definitely has the "black blood"; by contrast, the one wrongly accused of blackness is perhaps really whitewhite-white and innocent and good. This raises the question of whether all the "liberal" sentiments are undone when Armand turns out to be "black" (and perhaps *therefore* so bad all along—as a racist reading might insist). Perhaps Chopin goes for the melodramatic experience of wholeness in seeing someone totally innocent and powerless going under. Yet it seems doubtful whether this necessarily evokes the reader's protest against the status quo; in fact, not only the sharp Manichean polarity of good and bad, but also the specific cultural content with which it is filled supports a racial axis of white = good and desirable vs. black = Satanic and vicious, though it may be devilishly deceptive, not immediately recognizable, and even capable of making "white" appear "black" for a good while. It is also worth remembering that Désirée has internalized the black-white hierarchy and, like all other characters in the story, seems to assume that it is not desirable, in fact, horrifying, and a sort of curse, to be black. African genealogy now dooms.

### *Natus Æthiopus* and a Happy Intermarriage

This point of view was hardly one that many nonwhite writers could be expected to share, and the examples of Pauline E. Hopkins and George Schuyler will serve to illustrate the ways in which they rearranged the existing materials. Hopkins's short story "Talma Gordon" (1900)[93] at first merely seems to contain all the familiar elements of the *Natus Æthiopus* motif. At the center of it is the story of *wonder* and of some white persons' *horror* in reaction to the birth of Jonathan Gordon's third child—the much wished-for boy. This reaction is signaled by a doctor's comment, "Captain Gordon, there is something strange about this birth. I want you to see this child" (286). Gordon reacts with surprise:

> Quelling my exultation I followed him to the nursery, and there, lying in the cradle, I saw a child dark as a mulatto, with the characteristic features of the Negro! I was stunned. Gradually it dawned upon me that there was something radically wrong. I turned to the doctor for an explanation.
> "There is but one explanation, Captain Gordon; there is Negro blood in this child." (286)

This diagnosis sends Gordon seeking for causes of this birth. As in the case of "The Father of Désirée's Baby," the mother of the child turns out to be an orphan, and unlike in Chopin's version, it is *her* background that ultimately provides the explanation (again, hardly an exonerating genealogy in the eyes of some *but not all* white characters) though the accusation of adultery is also voiced by Jonathan Gordon against his first wife Isabel Franklin of Boston:

> "There is no Negro blood in my veins," I said proudly. Then I paused—*the mother!*—I glanced at the doctor. He was watching me intently. The same thought was in his mind. I must have lived a thousand years in that cursed five seconds that I stood there confronting the physician and trying to think. "Come," I said to him, "let us end this suspense." Without thinking of consequences, I hurried and accused her of infidelity to her marriage vows. I raved like a madman. (286)

After the mother falls into convulsions and is in danger of dying her "parents" are sent for, and they reveal the truth.

> They were childless. One year while on a Southern tour, they befriended an octoroon girl who had been abandoned by her white lover. Her child was a beautiful girl baby. They, being Northern born, thought little of caste distinction because the child showed no trace of Negro blood. They

determined to adopt it. They went abroad, secretly sending back word to their friends at a proper time, of the birth of a little daughter. No one doubted the truth of the statement. (286–87)

Again as in Chopin, the mother and "the unfortunate babe" die—though the crisis is brought about by the traditional elements of the adultery charge followed by the story of an exonerating genealogy.

Hopkins's tale is embedded in a complex narrative structure, and the revelation at the core of it affects other family members and seemingly unrelated characters as well. In fact, it is in a four-fold frame narrative that the doctor's comment to Gordon appears, and the *Natus Æthiopus* story has a bearing on the other layers of the tale. The outer frame, told by a third-person narrator, opens and closes the tale with a description of a meeting of the Canterbury Club at Dr. William Thornton's house on Boston's Beacon Street. Thornton leads the discussion of the subject "Expansion; Its Effect Upon the Future Development of the Anglo-Saxons Throughout the World" into the direction of interracial marriage when he asks the assembled gentlemen to consider "both sides" of the issue—not just the economic and political benefits but also the following question: "Did you ever think that in spite of our prejudices against amalgamation, some of our descendants, indeed many of them, will inevitably intermarry among those far-off tribes of dark-skinned peoples, if they become a part of this great Union?" (272). Asked to elaborate this point, he gladly obliges, and the story moves into the next frame, constituted by Doctor Thornton's first-person singular narrative. Taking his point of departure from the universality of the mating instinct,[94] Thornton now tells the story of the Mayflower descendant Jonathan Gordon, his second wife, and his second little son who were murdered under mysterious circumstances on a stormy night in Gordonville, Massachusetts. Jonathan and Isabel also had two older daughters, Jeannette and (the title heroine) Talma, who were treated badly by their stepmother and who now become the sole heirs to the Gordon fortune; the suspicion for the murder falls on Talma, who is, however, acquitted for lack of evidence. The daughters go to Europe, and Jeannette dies in Rome. Talma returns to New England, refuses to accept her suitor Edward Turner's marriage proposal, and gives Dr. Thornton, as an explanation, a letter she had received from Jeannette; this five-page document constitutes the third frame. Yet this narrative, in which Jeannette describes overhearing a conversation between her father and the second Mrs. Gordon, only prepares the reader for the next layer of narration, Jonathan Gordon's tale of *Natus Æthiopus*, which forms the core of the tale. The story of the birth of the first Gordon son is thus the direct speech of the father to Jeannette, cited in Jeannette's letter to Talma that is quoted in Dr. Thornton's narration at the Canterbury

Club meeting. The effect of the revelation is that it brings the moment of truth for the whole family: Talma understands now that the ancestry of her mother Isabel Franklin affects *her* and makes her comprehend her stepmother's cruelties as racially motivated. Edward Turner recoils from her in *horror*, for, as in Durham, "black blood" is worse than the suspicion of being a murderess: "I could stand the stigma of murder, but to add to that the pollution of Negro blood! No man is brave enough to face that!" (288). The triple murder is cleared up as the revenge of Simon Cameron for some of Captain Gordon's misdeeds as a pirate.[95] Now the tale moves back into the outer frame; and the punch line of the ending that closes all frames brings a surprising twist to the familiar elements. Unlike Chopin, and unlike Durham, Hopkins ends with a happy interracial couple, as Dr. William Thornton takes the Club members to the drawing room in order to introduce them to his wife "—*née* Talma Gordon" (290). With this surprise ending Hopkins ran against the kind of story lines that Chopin had told: by moving the intermarriage tale that was Armand's parents' secret that had to be consummated in the past and in France to the open revelation in Boston society in the present, she had put what would be UNTHINKABLE to Durham right at the high point of the story's cheery ending. Hopkins may thus be said to have redirected the emotional energies of the modern racialist contexts of the *Natus Æthiopus* motif toward normalizing an interracial marriage plot.

## Satire's Counterattack

George Schuyler's novel *Black No More: Being an Account of the Strange and Wonderful Workings of Science in the Land of the Free, A.D. 1933–1940* (1931) did more than any other literary text to dismantle and ridicule the race-obsessed modern uses of the motif.[96] It reads almost as if it were a conscious rewriting of both Durham's and Chopin's versions. Like *The Call of the South*, Schuyler's satirical novel is set in the near future, presents a "what if. . ." scenario, and casts a political leader's daughter named Helen as the wife of a character with a black past. And as in "The Father of Désirée's Baby," the question of the mother's and the father's racial past arises when Helen gives birth to a child. When the doctor sees the father, Matthew Fisher, né Max Disher, in the hospital waiting room, he holds his "finger to his lips," motions Matthew to another room, and says:

> I'm very sorry to have to tell you this, Mr. Fisher, that something terrible has happened. Your son is very, very dark. Either you or Mrs. Fisher must possess some Negro blood. It might be called reversion to type if any such thing had ever been proved. Now I want to know what you want done. If you say so I can get rid of this child and it will save everybody concerned a lot of trouble and disgrace. Nobody except the nurse knows anything about this and she'll keep her mouth shut for a consideration. Of course,

it's all in the day's work for me, you know. I've had plenty of cases like this in Atlanta. (188)

Matthew is in a quandary. Since he has earlier undergone a treatment that turned him white, the doctor's offer to have the child removed for a mere bribe of the nurse would not provide an answer.[97] Matthew worries about the future: "Must he go on forever in this way? Helen was young and fecund. Surely one couldn't go on murdering one's children, especially when one loved and wanted children." He is tempted by an inner angel to tell the truth about himself when the newspaper arrives with the headline "Democratic Leaders Proved of Negro Descent," and Helen's father is among those leaders. This deus ex machina is as contrived as Chopin's letter; and it makes the devil in Matthew come out and declare to the doctor that "there is something to that reversion to type business," though his motto remains, "you never can tell." When Helen finds herself proven black by headline, she faints and then denounces "fate and father." The narrator's sarcastic intervention pokes fun at the worries that have animated much serious discussion and fictional representation.

> With that logicality that frequently causes people to accept as truth circumstantial evidence that is not necessarily conclusive, she was assuming that the suspiciously brown color of her new-born son was due to some hidden Negro drop in her veins. (191)[98]

Helen pleads with her husband to forgive her and not to leave her, and Matthew is moved to say (what Armand never could have said to Désirée) that she has not "disgraced" but "honored" him with a beautiful son, and finally coming out with his confession: "You're not responsible for the color of our baby, my dear. I'm the guilty one." When he has told her his story, Helen is relieved:

> There was no feeling of revulsion at the thought that her husband was a Negro. There once would have been but that was seemingly centuries ago when she had been unaware of her remoter Negro ancestry. She felt proud of her Matthew. She loved him more than ever. They had money and a beautiful, brown baby. What more did they need? To hell with the world! To hell with society! Compared to what she possessed, thought Helen, all talk of race and color was damned foolishness. (192–93)

Schuyler's fictional scheme is to take genealogical definitions of race to the point at which no "white" person in America could be sure of "racial purity" any more. This recognition could help explode racism, and for good. The troubling concerns of *The Call of the South* and "The Father of Désirée's Baby" seem directly addressed and comically overcome in *Black No More*, a book that signals through romantic irony—"This sounds like a novel," a character chuckles—that it is an ironic examination of the fictions of race.[99] Schuyler's satire has many targets, among them the suggestion that the abuse of the Bible has been as disastrous for race relations as the abuse of science. Whereas blackness had appeared like a "stain" to Durham's Helen and like a "curse" in Armand's mother's letter, it is nothing of the sort in *Black No More*, which ends with a newspaper photograph of the sun-tanned Fisher family at Cannes, all "quite as dusky as little Matthew Crookman Fisher who played in a sandpile at their feet."

This association of color with a curse[100] sounds like a religious idea. The Bible is relatively reticent in the matter of suggesting origins of human color variety. There is, of course, no biblical basis for the intermarried version of Adam and Eve, yet as has often been observed, the Bible does have its resonant intermarriage stories: Moses had an Ethiopian wife; the Bride, sometimes identified with the Queen of Sheba, opens the Song of Solomon with the poetic lines "I am black *and*"—though translations after the Septuagint substituted the culturally charged conjunction *but*—"comely";[101] Joseph was married to an Egyptian woman;[102] Jeremiah thought that the Ethiopian's skin was as changeable—or unchangeable—as "leopard's spots"; and St. Paul's universalism envisioned a world that was "neither bond nor free." Yet we are not told how people became "white" and "black." It is perhaps for this reason that Bible readers have provided additional myths of origins not given in the text of the book.

Far more widespread than any alternative belief was the perhaps self-flattering assumption in Western culture that mankind's initial color must have been white—and the problem thus became how to explain, not the diversity of human pigmentation as such, but most especially the appearance of *blackness*. This bias in favor of a supposedly original whiteness that was imagined to have been disrupted by the emergence of blackness—a notion that found its reinforcement in the denial that whiteness could be descended from any black origins—can be noticed in many versions of tales of origins. Among attempts to anchor the rise of blackness within the frame of shared family origins, the bias makes itself manifest in that it sometimes explains the racial differentiation within a family in sharply hierarchical ways, for example, as the result of a crime or a curse which can have the long-range effect of effacing stories of one origin by myths of several separate origins. The most widely disseminated set of apocryphal stories that fulfilled this function connected the origins of color difference with the biblical figures of Cain, Ham, or Canaan: Schuyler, for example, spoke of "the much maligned Sons of Ham" (132). Whatever else that tale implies (and I shall in the following chapter investigate the sinister as well as absurd sides of it), it still rests on a single origin of mankind in a family story and relates the present to the past as the fulfillment of a curse. In any event, the story of Ham, often used to justify slavery, had no firmer authority in scripture than the vision of the black Adam or Eve, though it has been invoked far more frequently, in contexts ranging from discussions of slavery to comments on black-Jewish relations. And yet, as we shall see, elements of a feared story of black-white couplings recur in some of the worst versions of that story which may also be considered to constitute the transformation from *Natus Æthiopus* to *Damnatus Æthiopus*.[103]

# CHAPTER THREE

# The Curse of Ham;
# or, From "Generation" to "Race"

We have it in our power to begin the world over again. A situation, similar to the present, hath not happened since the days of Noah until now. The birth-day of a new world is at hand, and a race of men perhaps as numerous as all Europe contains, are to receive their portion of freedom from the events of a few months.

—Thomas Paine, *Common Sense* (1776)[1]

In-this-re-publi-can-land-all-men-are-born-free-and-equal. . . .
Except-the-tribe-of-Hamo.

—Herman Melville, *Mardi and a Voyage Thither* (1849)[2]

*A son of Ham, I had to scram!*

—Melvin Tolson, *Harlem Gallery* (1965)[3]

[In classical striptease narrative] all the excitement is concentrated in the *hope* of seeing the genitals (the schoolboy's dream) or of knowing the end of the story (the novelistic satisfaction). . . . [I]t is an Oedipal pleasure (to denude, to know, to learn the beginning and the end), if it is true that all narrative (all unveiling of the truth) is a staging of the Father (absent, hidden, or suspended)—which would explain the consubstantiality of narrative forms, family structures, and interdictions on nudity, all brought together in our culture in the myth of Noah's nakedness covered by his sons.

—Roland Barthes, *The Pleasure of the Text* (1973)[4]

Bawdy songs fill the valley of Ararat in a one-act play, first published in New York in 1927. It presents the origin of black skin color within a family drama. Ham is a character reminiscent of Bacchus and Pan; he likes to sing about feeling like a young goat in the spring; he drinks, dances, and arrives late at his father Noah's tent. Relieved that the flood is over, Noah enjoys the dance of Ham and Eve (Ham's wife) and drinks heavily with them from a goatskin of wine: "Pour again, Eve, and Ham sing on and dance and drink—drown out the waters of the flood if you can. . . . Drink wine, forget water—it means death, *death!*" (54). Shortly thereafter Ham is heard "laughing raucously" inside Noah's tent; he comes out and reports: "Our father has stripped himself, showing all his wrinkles. Ha! Ha! He's as no young goat in the spring. . . . The old Ram, Ha! Ha! Ha! He has had no spring for years" (55).

This prompts the scheming and hypocritical shrew Mrs. Shem into action. She needles her husband to "regain his birthright" and tells him to cover Noah's nakedness: "Oh (she beats her breast) that I should live to see a father so mocked and shamed by his son to whom he has given all his vineyards!" (55). Mrs. Japheth sends her husband along with Shem; they cover their father and wake him up, while Mrs. Shem and Japheth weep ostentatiously. Mrs. Shem tells Noah that he has been shamed, but not by whom; and Shem asks Noah: "Shall the one who has done this thing hold part of thy goods after thee?" The scheme seems to work, and, instigated by Shem, Noah excludes the guilty one from his share of the inheritance. Yet, still somewhat drunk, Noah goes on: "He shall be accursed. His skin shall be black! Black as the nights, when the waters brooded over the Earth!" Mrs. Noah attempts in vain to intervene. All are trying to undo the curse by making Noah "unsay it all" (56). Shem accuses his covetous wife of causing all the trouble, which prompts Noah to comment that "Shem's wife is but a woman" (56). Mrs. Shem is remorseful: "We coveted his vineyard, but the curse is too awful for him" (56). Yet despite all their prayers, Jehovah does not send another rainbow sign, and the curse cannot be unspoken. Shem and Mrs. Shem have manipulated and controlled the patriarch, and the play is a perfect example of the emerging distinction between a legitimate and an illegitimate family. When the singing Ham reappears "they see that he is black. They shrink back terrified. He is laughing happily. Eve approaches him timidly. . . . She touches his hand, then his face: 'Look at thy hands, thy feet. Thou art cursed black by thy Father'" (57). Shem does not want to be touched by Ham; and even his mother averts her face. When Eve brings their boy in her arms, he has also turned black, and the other children jeer and pelt him. Finally Noah sternly expels the pleading Ham: "Thou art black. Arise and go out from among us that we may see thy face no more, lest by lingering the curse of thy blackness come upon my seed forever." The play—entitled *The First One*—ends as Eve and a somewhat cynical Ham leave in order to go to "the end of the Earth" "where the sun shines forever" while Mrs. Noah prays and sobs. The curse on Ham that is thematized in this play belongs to the group of motifs and themes that originate in a text: the play has at its obvious point of departure Genesis 9, a very complex biblical passage that makes, however, despite the play's assumption, no mention of skin color, but provides slavery as punishment for Ham's transgression.[5]

## Scripture and Exegeses

And Noah began to be an husbandman, and he planted a vineyard:
    And he drank of the wine, and was drunken; and he was uncovered without his tent.
    And Ham, the father of Canaan, saw the nakedness of his father, and told his two brethren without.
    And Shem and Japheth took a garment, and laid it upon both their shoulders, and went backward, and covered the nakedness of their father; and their faces were backward, and they saw not their father's nakedness.
    And Noah awoke from his wine, and knew what his younger son had done unto him.
    And he said, Cursed be Canaan; a servant of servants shall he be unto his brethren.
    And he said, Blessed be the LORD God of Shem; and Canaan shall be his servant.
    God shall enlarge Japheth, and he shall dwell in the tents of Shem; and Canaan shall be his servant.

—Genesis 9:20–27

In the Pentateuch,[6] Canaan is cursed by Noah to become a "slave of slaves." Theologians have been baffled by this passage. Noah's malediction promises a punishment that not only seems out of proportion with

Ham's transgression (seeing his father's nakedness) but that also is meted out not to Noah's son Ham, the man who did not avert his eyes from the scene of his father's nakedness, but to one (and only one) of Ham's rather innocent sons. When Calvin addressed the question "why among the many sons of Ham, God chooses one to be smitten," he answered with a warning against too much human curiosity concerning the "great deep" of God's judgments, yet he also tried to rationalize this puzzle in concluding: "While God held the whole seed of Ham obnoxious to the curse, he mentions the Canaanites by name, as those whom he would curse above all others." The contrasting prophecies that Canaan was to be a servant to his brethren and that Shem and Japheth were to be served are also difficult to reconcile, since Canaan was their *nephew* rather than their brother. The strange and unexplained confusion between Canaan and Ham was a particularly odd element in the context of a new beginning after the deluge. In addition, why is Ham called "father of Canaan" at a time when Canaan was not yet born? Ambrose (340–97) may have been the first to raise this question. Yet another textual difficulty stems from the contradictory position that Ham holds: he is listed between Shem and Japheth (in Genesis 6:10 or 7:13)—suggesting that he was between his brothers in age—yet he is here described as Noah's youngest son. Von Rad points out that Noah's sons were married in the ark; and now they are young and live in their father's tent. Furthermore the utterance against Canaan was made not by God but by a human being who had just woken up from the first biblically recorded instance of drunkenness; and Noah curses him only shortly after God had explicitly blessed Noah and his sons (Genesis 9:1). Should the phrase "servant of servants" be read figuratively as referring to the lowest of servants, or could it mean, more literally, that Canaan was to be a slave of Shem and Japheth, who (or at least one of them, Shem, if one reads Genesis 9:27 that way) might themselves be enslaved?[7]

Is it something in particularly problematic texts that invites the obvious intrusion of nontextual matter into the process of theming and interpreting? Or is it the cultural-historical context that helps to generate specific readings? From the earliest exegetical attempts to those of the modern age, Genesis 9 seems to have encouraged Jewish, Christian, Muslim, and secular readers to explain away or harmonize the incongruities in this passage. Interpreters were variously tempted to ignore Noah's drunkenness or the fact that the malediction was not divine but pronounced by a man, to reinstate Ham as the recipient of the curse, or to argue that "Ham" was a later substitution for what originally must have been "Canaan," to magnify the nature of Ham's transgression, and to offer some more elaborate explanation of the punishment of (some) later generations. The oddities and difficulties of this passage were frequently placed into contexts that would seem to provide plausibility for

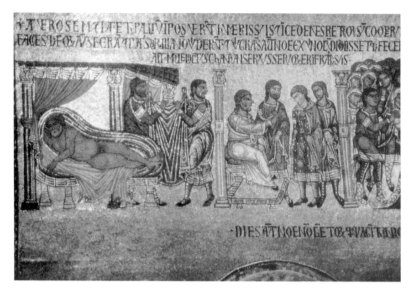

**Figure 13**   San Marco, Venice, mosaics (ca. 1240–1250)

nonscriptural and historical reasons. In this case, the contexts could certainly be more important than the text that was the origin of the theme
that is the subject of this chapter.

For example, Islamic sources typically make no reference to the
prominent fact of Noah's inebriation.[8] By contrast, many Christian
artists welcomed the theme of intoxication, and seemed to be especially
attracted to the opportunity of portraying Noah in the nude, for example
in the thirteenth-century atrium mosaics of San Marco or in Michelangelo's panel in the Sistine Chapel (Figs. 13 and 14).[9] Nachmanides (ca.
1195–1270), who explains the whole passage as a warning against drunkenness, cites various explanations of the phrase "unto his brethren" as
"his father's brothers" (as in Genesis 14:14).[10] The bishop of Bristol
Thomas Newton (1746) suggests an emended text in which Noah says
"Cursed be [Ham the father of] Canaan."[11] Josephus Flavius (37–90), in
the *Antiquities of the Jews*, writes differently that Noah "did not curse
[Ham], by reason of his nearness in blood, but cursed his posterity: and
when the rest of them escaped that curse, God inflicted it on the children
of Canaan."[12] U. Cassuto (1949), who carefully and systematically
describes some of the difficulties in interpreting this passage, concludes
that Noah's utterance was directed not against Ham, or Canaan, but
against "the Canaanite *people*":

> This is not a case, therefore, of a son being punished for his father's sin: the
> perspective is much wider. . . . The Canaanites were to suffer the curse and
> the bondage not because of the sins of Ham, but because they themselves

*Figure 14*   Michelangelo, Sistine Chapel, ninth ceiling panel (1508–1512)

acted like Ham, because of their own transgressions, which resembled those attributed to Ham in this allegory.[13]

It is in their reflections upon the specific consequences of the curse and the nature of the crime that might have called for them that readers of Genesis have gone beyond the text in the most dramatic and culturally resonant ways. According to Samuel Bochart's *Phaleg, Canaan, et Hierozoicon* (1692), a book that harmonizes biblical and classical stories, Cham was related to (and perhaps even etymologically connected with) alchemy and with the Egyptian God Am as "Jupiter Hammon," and Canaan was a figure parallel to Mercury: both had to travel a lot, and Mercury's wings were an allusion to Canaan's sails.[14] Augustine (354–430) took as his point of departure the "wicked" Ham's position as Noah's middle son who "remained between, neither belonging to the first family of Israel nor to the fulness of the gentiles" and hence signifies the "heretics hot with the spirit . . . of impatience";[15] Gregory of Tours (ca. 540–94) linked the descendants of Ham with the invention of devilish magic, with idolatry, and with Zoroastrianism;[16] Venerable Bede (ca. 672–735) associated them with the inhabitants of Sodom; Rabanus Maurus (776–856) saw Ham as the progenitor of infidels; and both Bede and Rabanus identified Ham typologically with the Jews. Their fanciful exegeses made Noah's drunkenness the *type* to which Christ's passion was the *antitype*; Shem's and Japheth's covering of Noah's nakedness prefigured the worshipful gesture of the believers, and Ham's action the irreverent attitude that the Jews took toward Christ's passion.[17] The orthodox views of Bede and Rabanus are beautifully visualized in the illuminated thirteenth-century

**Figure 15** *Bible moraliseé,*
*Codex Vindobonensis* 2554
(13th c.)

Vienna *Bible moralisée* in which scenes from the Old Testament are
directly juxtaposed with elements they are believed to foreshadow or
"mean." Noah's planting of the vineyard thus "means" Christ who
"plants the Jews and drinks the chalice during his passion," whereas
Noah's sons prefigure "the Jews who uncovered Christ's shame and the
Christians who covered him" (Fig. 15) .[18] These may be early instances
of a structural analogy between anti-Semitism and that other prejudice
that no one seems to have called anti-Hamitism and for which legitimacy
was also sought in the same passage of Genesis 9.

The story of Noah's family had important consequences. Many histories drew their own lineage from Japheth, and the famous "T-O" map of
Isidore of Seville (560–632) from the 1472 Augsburg edition of the
*Etymologiae* divides the whole known world into three geographic areas
defined by Noah's sons: Asia is associated with Shem, Africa with Ham,
and Europe with Japheth (Fig. 16).[19] Many other histories and geogra-
phies of populations and languages followed this pattern, though there
are also some imaginative exceptions.[20] An Irish legend, for example,
gives the Celts a lineage that goes back to Japheth, whereas Ham is the
ancestor of a race of giants that, led by Albion the son of Neptune, drove
the Celts out of what then became England.[21] A medieval interpretation
of the meaning of Noah's three sons—visualized in the glass windows of
1235–40 in the Cathedral at Chartres—turned them into symbols of the
three estates on which the feudal order rested: those who prayed (the

europa & affrica      De. Asia

Oriens

MARE

·ASIA·

Son

Mare magnum sine

EVROPA    AFRICA

Iafech    Cham

Occidens

giones·quaru breuiter nomina et situ
a paradiso ¶Paradisus est locus in c

**Figure 16**    T-O map (1472)

priesthood), those who fought (knighthood), and those who worked (serfs and working classes) (Fig. 17).[22] And the fourteenth-century sculpture of Noah and his sons that forms the southeast corner relief of the Palazzo Ducale in Venice suggests a separation of one son (Japheth?) who gets a position equivalent to that of Noah, whereas the other two

**Figure 17**    Chartres cathedral, glass window (1235–1240)

***Figure 18***   Ducal Palace, Venice,
southeast corner relief (14th c.)

sons (one definitely Ham, looking at his father, one probably Shem) take
a subordinate position (Fig. 18). The scene of the curse of Ham functioned literally as a cornerstone for the Venetian republic; and since the
other two corner reliefs represent the Fall and the Judgment of Solomon,
John Ruskin, who also made drawings of the Noah scene, probably from
daguerreotypes, asked in his diary: "I wonder why two of the chief corner
stones of the Doge's Palace should be representations of human weakness?"[23]

Probably the most widespread uses that have been made of Genesis 9
concern themselves not only with slavery (which is, after all, present in
the text), class structure, or human weakness, but also, and from a textual
point of view quite surprisingly, with debates about the origin of black
skin color.[24] It is the story of the accursed Ham or Canaan that has
often—as in the play *The First One*—served as a myth of origin of black
people. It has also been invoked as a specific justification of the enslavement of Africans, of modern racial segregation, and the prohibition of
interracial marriages. This makes interpretations of Genesis 9 versions of
a particularly problematic interracial story, as they tried to account for
the emergence of color variation within a single family. How did blackness enter into the readings?[25]

Jewish, Christian, and Muslim exegeses have been scrutinized for an
answer to that question. As has been widely asserted by modern scholars,
an assertion comprehensively criticized by David Goldenberg, Talmudic

and Midrashic sources from as early as the second to the sixth centuries assumed that Ham's curse affected his skin.[26] *The Babylonian Talmud*, for example, contained the rabbinical view that "Ham was smitten in his skin." The meaning is far from clear, however, and only a much later note to this passage adds: "I.e., from him descended Cush (the negro) who is black-skinned."[27] The readings collected in the *Midrash Rabbah*, among them the sixth-century *Bereshit Rabbah*, suggest a variety of contexts for Noah's curse; according to a statement by the Rabbis Huna and Joseph that was not related to the ark story but that the editor of *Genesis Rabbah* joined with other interpretations, Ham came out of the ark blackskinned.[28] The late mystical *Zohar* writes that

> Ham represents the refuse and dross of the gold, the stirring and rousing of the unclean spirit of the ancient serpent. It is for that reason that he is designated the "father of Canaan," namely, of Canaan who brought curses into the world, of Canaan who was cursed, of Canaan who darkened the faces of mankind. For this reason, too, Ham is given a special mention in the words, "Ham, the father of Canaan," that is, the notorious world-darkener. . . .[29]

While this passage has often been cited as a source for the curse on Ham, David Goldenberg has stressed that the Aramaic original describes Canaan, not Ham, and that the term "world darkener" refers not to skin color but to the introduction of death (brought about by the snake).

Other exegeses followed. In the Christian tradition, Ambrose reintroduced the theme of Ham's curse.[30] Saint Ephrem of Nisibis (d. 373) has been credited with the following paraphrase of Noah's words: "Accursed be Canaan, and may God make his face black."[31] This may be the very first association of blackness with the curse, but the passage is of dubious authority (as it is recorded only in later Arabic translations) and somewhat ambiguous (in its conjunction "and" that does not necessarily imply a causal relation). Dark skin color was often traced to Ham, Canaan, or Cush—for example, by Isidore of Seville or by Rodericus Ximenius de Rada (circa 1170–1246), the archbishop of Toledo—though this appeared only rarely as the result of Ham's curse.[32] A parchment roll with a genealogy of Christ (1230) originally in the Cathedral of St. Patroklus in Soest briefly mentions the curse upon Ham's children and portrays Chus's (or Cush's), but *not* Canaan's, children as blacks and without making a connection between the two stories (Fig. 19). This is also the case with the atrium mosaics at San Marco which show a darker-looking descendant (Cush?) in the Tower of Babel scene, followed by God's ordering the division the peoples into the three great families, and opposite to the wall on which the curse of Ham is represented—but the stories are not linked in any recognizable way (Fig. 20).

Jean Devisse argued that the development of genealogies that are divided between a truly chosen descent line and unimportant lateral lines may be regarded as a step toward polygenetic theory.[33] Genealogies are

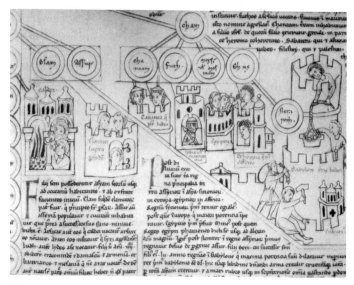

**Figure 19** Genealogy of Christ (1230)

**Figure 20** San Marco, Venice, mosaics
(ca. 1240–1250)

crucial; they are also ambiguous instruments as they can instruct different users about the common family origins of all mankind (e.g., in Noah) as well as about the sources of current differences (e.g., in Noah's descendants); readers can contemplate human unity in the image of the ark or heterogeneity with the story of the Tower of Babel (appropriately associated with Nimrod, one of Ham's descendants).

Muslim genealogies also ranged from interrelated tables of peoples to those stressing protoracial divisions; and there is controversy surrounding the role of Islamic writing in the association of blackness with the curse of Ham.[34] In its version of the story of the deluge and the ark, the Koran contains only a veiled reference to an unnamed son of Noah whose demise was preordained:

> Noah cried to his son who had gone aside, "O my boy! ride with us and be not with the misbelievers." Said he, "I will betake me to a mountain that shall save me from the water." Said he, "There is none to save to-day from the command of God, except for him on whom He may have mercy." And the wave came between them, and he was amongst the drowned.[35]

The text lets God voice a threat rather than Noah pronounce a curse; the son dies during the flood, and there is no reference to blackness or slavery. The Koran's version was difficult to apply to Ham, since Noah's postdiluvian malediction could hardly have been directed at a son who had already drowned (Mas'ūdi (d. 956) in *Les prairies d'or* calls that son Yâm.)[36] Muhammad lashed out against pride in family lineage, and his tolerance was expressed in his view that linguistic and racial differences could be understood only as the result of divine miracles.[37] Yet Islamic genealogies describing the peoples that followed the flood showed a variety of contradictory uses. Some accepted the story of the curse without associating it with blackness; others derived blackness from the line of Ham, yet never mentioned a curse.[38] Ğawzī, for example, wrote that Ham's children turned black, but stressed that Ham also had many other nonblack descendants, and explicitly rejected any connection between curse and skin color.[39] Ibn Qutayba (828–89, writing in 879–80 and drawing on Wahb ibn Munabbih) thought that Ham was white, God changed his color and the color of his descendants because of his father's curse, and he moved away; his children followed him: those were the Sūdān.[40] The Persian historian al-Ṭabarī (ca. 838–923) also presented a very mixed and somewhat phenotypally defined genealogy; furthermore, in his *History of al-Ṭabarī (Ta'rīkh a rusul wa'l-mulūk)*, he invokes sources that ascribe evil only to the descendants of *Japheth*:

> Noah begat three, each one of whom begat three: Shem, Ham, and Japheth. Shem begat the Arabs, Persians, and Byzantines, in all of whom there is good. Japheth begat the Turks, Slavs, Gog, and Magog, in none of whom there is good. Ham begat the Copts, Sudanese, and Berbers....
> Ham begat all those who are black and curly-haired, while Japheth

begat all those who are full-faced with small eyes, and Shem begat everyone who is handsome of face with beautiful hair. Noah prayed that the hair
of Ham's descendants would not grow beyond their ears, and that wherever his descendants met the children of Shem, the latter would enslave
them. . . . The people of the Torah claim that Shem was born to Noah
when the latter was five hundred years old.[41]

This is an example of a genealogy that is moving into the direction of
identifying peoples by "racial" features; it shows, however, that the postdiluvian story can also be read into the direction of anti-Japhethism, as
Japheth's descendants are here the only ones in whom there is no good.
By contrast, and in what may be an exception in early Islamic exegesis,
the eleventh-century *Abrégé des merveilles* states: "The traditionalists say
that Noah cursed Ham, praying to God that Ham's descendants might
become horrible and black and that they be subjected as slaves to those of
Shem. He had a son, after Kanā'ān, Kush, who was black. . . . Kanā'ān
had a son Sūdān, who was black."[42] Here the features of curse, skin color,
and slavery are all assembled, though once again, the conjunction "and"
leaves some ambiguity. Yet there were voices that sharply contradicted
the uses of a curse as an explanation for human difference. The climatic
explanation of color, already contained in the etymology of *Æthiops* =
"burnt face" (and visualized in the story of Phaëthon) was explicitly
invoked in the *Muḳaddima* by Ibn Ḳhaldūn against the curse-of-Ham
theory:

> Certain genealogists, ignorant of the nature of things, imagined that the
> Sūdān, who are the descendants of Ḥām b. Nūh (Ham, son of Noah), are
> set apart (from other men) by their black color as a result of the curse
> (which Noah) laid upon their father Ḥām. According to them, Ḥām's
> black color as well as his slave condition were decreed by that curse of
> God. Noah's malediction of his son Ḥām is reported in the Tawrat
> (Torah). In that book this is not at all a question of black color. The curse
> has no other aim than to make Ḥām a slave of his brothers' descendants,
> and that is all.
>
> To connect the black color of the Sūdān with (the curse laid upon)
> Ḥām is to fail to understand the nature of heat and cold, and of their influ-
> ence on climate and on the condition of animal life.[43]

Islamic sources in support of the curse of Ham were thus balanced by
close textual reading and by the countervailing climate theory that was to
remain one of the most frequently used alternative explanations of
human diversity. Aḥmad Bābā of Timbuktu argued most comprehensively against the curse's application to blacks and rejected it on the
ground that it was incompatible with the Islamic rule that only infidels
could be enslaved (whereas the curse of Ham might justify the enslavement of black Africans who were Muslims); he invokes Ǧawzī, mentions

the tradition that Adam was made out of three kinds of earth, and cites Ibn Khaldūn's theory of natural influences on color change.[44]

The curse on Ham does appear in an explicitly racial manner in the tale of "The Man of Al-Yaman and His Six Slave-Girls" in *Thousand and One Nights*. The man from Yemen lets the six slave girls who embody such contrasts as "fat" and "lean" perform some kind of aggressive game of exegesis: they are asked to sing and praise themselves and attack their opposite numbers, always drawing on the Koran. In the course of this very balanced bantering the white handmaid denounces the black one by citing the Koran (Sura 27:12 and Sura 3:103), by offering a poetic praise of whiteness denouncing blackness, and drawing on a version of Noah's curse:

> And indeed it is told in certain histories, related on the authority of devout men, that Noah (on whom be peace!) was sleeping one day, with his sons Cham and Shem seated at his head, when a wind sprang up and, lifting his clothes, uncovered his nakedness; whereat Cham looked and laughed and did not cover him: but Shem arose and covered him.
>
> Presently, their sire awoke and learning, what had been done by his sons, blessed Shem and cursed Cham. So Shem's face was whitened and from him sprang the prophets and the orthodox Caliphs and Kings; whilst Cham's face was blackened and he fled forth to the land of Abyssinia, and of his lineage came the blacks. All people are of one mind in affirming the lack of understanding of the blacks, even as saith the adage, "How shall one find a black with a mind?"[45]

The text seems to adhere to the belief that there was an original color that must have been neither black nor white, since Shem is whitened just as Ham is blackened. Japheth has disappeared, though he played such an important moral part earlier in al-Ṭabarī; Noah's drunkenness is not mentioned; and Ham's action has been magnified from the account in Genesis. What is also noteworthy is not only the sharply polemical way in which the motif is used—the older slave stereotypes of lasciviousness, laziness, and so on have now become racial stereotypes in the story—but also the balancing of its import in the story as a whole: thus the Yemenite comments that the white girl has "given us sufficient and even excess," and the white slave's black counterpart immediately retaliates with an equally sharp attack on *whiteness* by citing the Koran which mentions night before day (in Sura 92:1–2) and by associating whiteness with aging (gray hair) and death, leprosy (as in Numbers 12:9–10), and icy hell. In any event, *Thousand and One Nights* is, of course, hardly a representative text of the Islamic tradition.[46]

Omitting al-Ṭabarī's reference to the evil nature of the descendants of Japheth, one interpreter of the "sons-of-Ham" motif, William McKee Evans, uses al-Ṭabarī's account to argue that the odyssey toward Western uses of the curse as a justification of African slavery went through the all-important transmission of Islamic theology. By contrast, Thomas Gossett writes that these legends were "the most famous example of racism among the Jews." J. R. Willis and Winthrop Jordan also locate the origin in Jewish writers, and their highly problematic statements have been reiterated with vituperative and ethnicizing undertones by some Afrocentric politicians and professors. Finally, Bernard Lewis stresses that it was the *Christian* Ephrem who preceded any Jewish interpreters and believes only Islam developed the full features of a curse with slavery and blackness.[47] Is the curse of Ham the responsibility of Muslims, Jews, or Christians? Such questions and the attempts made at answering them may have a strange, inadvertently exculpatory effect when it comes to discussing modern uses of Ham as a justification of African slavery: Do we really wish to believe that modern racism simply seems to have *inherited* an ideological system from isolated and pre-racist fragments that were articulated by early saints and Church fathers, anticipated by the Talmud, or further developed in Islamic texts? In interpretations of morally charged genealogical origins the genealogy of themings may also carry unrecognized moral implications.

## Early Modern Instances

No matter how impressive a Judeo-Islamic lineage can be developed for the curse on Ham, and how many early Christian readings of Genesis may have contained materials that could be used later on, the view that the Africans' skin color was a result of Noah's curse on Canaan appears to have been developed most fully in the modern world, starting near the end of the Middle Ages, and it has been most pervasive in Europe and North America for the past four hundred years.[48] Even though several modern interpreters have shown that they were conscious of Jewish, early Christian, and Muslim readings of the text,[49] the notion of the curse of Ham seems to have flourished not because it had occasionally been in evidence in older exegetical literature but only as it became enmeshed in debates about the African slave trade, black slavery, and that new word, "race," that was to become at times a subcategory of, and at other times a synonym for, "species" (in its new abstract sense). The *Oxford English Dictionary* gives the first English equivalent for Italian *razza*, Spanish and Castilian *raza*, and Portuguese *raça* in the sixteenth century; for example, Foxe, 1570: "Thus was the outward race & stocke of Abraham after flesh refused." This instance supports the theory that the obscure roots of "race" may lie in the word "generation."[50] In any event, "race" and "generation" remained synonyms for some time in such languages as English and French. Sir Thomas Browne wrote in 1646 that "complexion was first acquired, it is evidently maintained by generation," and Le Cat made a similar argument in 1765 that even at the poles of the earth Moors "keep their black skins without any change from generation to generation" (*de race en race*).[51] The development from "generation" to "race" slowly resolved the ambiguity in genealogies against family connectedness and in favor of human divisions. Verena Stolcke has stressed that the word "race" suggested different dimensions: it meant "the succession of generations (*de raza en raza*) as well as all the members of a given generation"; it often took a close connection of "quality" and "nobility of blood," yet it was also "confused in the middle of the fifteenth century with the old Castilian *raza* which meant 'a patch of threadbare or defective cloth,' or, simply, 'defect, guilt,'" obtaining a meaning exactly opposite to "nobility," namely, "taint" and "contamination," which is why the word appeared in Castilian, with a negative meaning, in connection with the doctrine of purity of blood (*limpieza de sangre*), "understood as the quality of having no admixture of the races of Moors, Jews, heretics, or *penitenciados* (those condemned by the Inquisition)."[52]

A frequently cited early modern author who used the curse on Ham in order to explain black descent and African slavery was the Portuguese chronicler Gomes Eanes de Azurara (or Zurara), not a traveler but a scholar who put travelers' accounts into a learned global perspective. In his *Chronicle of the Discovery and Conquest of Guinea* (*Crónica dos Feitos da Guiné*, 1441–48) he informs Prince Henry the Navigator:

> these blacks were Moors like the others, though their slaves, in accordance with ancient custom, which I believe to have been because of the curse which, after the Deluge, Noah laid upon his son Cain [*sic*], cursing him in this way:—that his race should be subject to all the other races of the world. And from this race these blacks are descended. . . .[53]

Azurara, perhaps influenced by attempts to link the line of Ham with descendants of Cain, literally merges Canaan and Cain.[54] Azurara also shows his learning by invoking Josephus Flavius and Rodericus Ximenius de Rada; and he uses the Portuguese word for "generation" in the sense the English translator renders as "race."[55]

Azurara provided a comprehensive rationale for African slavery; yet, as William McKee Evans stresses, it is still tempered by his view that non-Muslim Africans, though black, had souls and were "Gentiles." They shared human "essentials" and differed only in "accidentals." Furthermore, as Raoul Allier points out, it was a rationale not widely applied before the sixteenth century: for example, it appears *not* to have been adopted (though this was later attributed to him) by Bartolomé de Las Casas, the man whose humanitarian pleas on behalf of the Indians of the New World to the Spanish kings Ferdinand II and Charles V led to the systematic and large-scale African slave trade to the New World in 1517. Las Casas (who also knew Azurara's work) was familiar with the modern uses of the curse of Ham. In a polemic against Sepúlveda, he particularly mentioned the story of how God "avenged the injury the

Semites suffered from the Hamites by wiping out the offspring of Ham in keeping with the oath taken by Noah's sons." Las Casas believed, however, that the interpretation of biblical passages should not be taken out of their specific context and "particular circumstance" of referring to the biblical Canaanites: if applied to the modern world, such a reading

> opens the way for tyrants and plunderers to cruel invasion, oppression, spoliation, and harsh enslavement of harmless nations that have neither heard of the faith nor known whether belief in Christ is in accord with reality or whether the Christian religion can be discovered, and all this under the pretext of religion.

Las Casas is outstanding in shifting the focus from textual exegesis to the naming of political motives that it may serve. Invoking Saint Thomas, he also points out that while the Bible forbade Jews intermarriage with Canaanites (Deuteronomy 7:2–3), it permitted them to marry women of "the other idolatrous nations." As his first illustration, he mentions the case of Joseph (Genesis 41:45), who "chose as his wife the daughter of Potiphar, a priest of the Egyptian idols."[56]

What was characteristic of many proslavery exegeses that followed was (as in Azurara) the identification of curse, slavery, and skin color. For example, the entry on "Nigritien oder das Land der Schwartzen" in Johann Heinrich Zedler's *Universallexikon* (1732–54) relates that many scholars have found the origin of blackness in Noah's cursing of his son Ham; Augustin Calmet, the author of the *Dictionary of the Bible*, wrote in 1801 "that *Noah* having cursed *Ham* and *Canaan*, the effect was, that not only their posterity became subject to their brethren, and was born, as we may say, in slavery, but likewise that the colour of their skin suddenly became black. . . ."[57] Azurara, Thomas Newton, and some other proslavery speculators upon the crime of Ham have already been cited among the supporters of the story who often engaged in biblical readings, at times with elaborate citations of their precursors, that aimed at sanctioning modern practices in biblical prototypes. In 1578, George Best combined the biblical with an emerging biological view when he wrote: "Thus you see, that the cause of the Ethiopians blacknesse is the curse and naturall infection of blood, and not the distemperature of the Climate."[58]

Other writers endorsed the story of Ham's curse, often in relation to the Atlantic slave trade and American slavery. Among them were Richard Jobson (1623), Jean-Louis Hannemann (1677), Thomas Herbert (1677), an anonymous *Relation universelle de l'Afrique ancienne et moderne* (1688), and William Byrd (1736).[59] The example of Hugh Jones (1724) may suffice to illustrate the self-serving nature of such applications:

> To the *white* Posterity of *Japheth*, viz. to the *Europeans* in particular are *Noah*'s Words (*Gen.* ix. 27.) very applicable. . . ; which [seem] fulfilled in

our Possession of Lands in the *East* and *West-Indies,* the Tents of the Sons of *Shem,* where *Canaan* or the *Negroe* is our Servant and Slave; and as it is said of him in the 25th Verse, a *Servant of Servants is* Canaan *unto his Brethren.*

For the *Negroes* seem evidently to be Descendants from some of the Sons of *Canaan.*[60]

It is somewhat ironic that in justifying the subjugation of "Ham," the full pride of the chosen lineage has been transferred from the children of Shem to the descendants of Japheth, the Northern Europeans in whom the Persian al-Ṭabarī at least had seen little good.

Many inconsistencies, contradictions, and ironies notwithstanding, the curse of Ham was useful to proslavery writers. In 1818, for example, Senator William Smith from South Carolina invoked the curse of Ham in order to support a proposal for a fugitive slave bill.[61] The notion of a hereditary curse helped to suggest that while blacks were still part of one human race descended from Adam and Noah, they were also cursed with a difference that put them forever below the realm of the "chosen people," a metaphor that was slowly transferred from religious believers (Jews, Christians, or Muslims) to the religiously neutral term "whites" that gave speakers empowerment for more than their lifetime and sanctioned enslavement and tyranny; furthermore, "whiteness," unlike religious beliefs, but like the notion of aristocratic blue blood, could not be spread by missionary efforts. (In fifteenth- and sixteenth-century Spain, however, Christian religion was, as Verena Stolcke puts it, "converted into a natural—and hence, hereditary—attribute," as the Inquisition examined genealogies for possible "stains."[62])

In Dion Boucicault's play *The Octoroon* (1859), Zoe describes herself as marked by "the ineffaceable curse of Cain," continuing the familiar confusion between Canaan and Cain; its social manifestation is Zoe's ineligibility to marry her white suitor and first cousin George Peyton. Similarly, M. E. Braddon writes about Cora in her novel *The Octoroon* (serialized in the 1860s): "One drop of the blood of a slave ran in her veins, poisoned her inmost life, and stamped her with the curse of Cain."[63] Once slavery was cast as the punishment for Ham's act and as the fulfillment of Noah's curse; now it seemed to have become a genealogical origin that may make whites shudder and with which they must not be linked in marriage. The curse of Ham served both as a myth of origin and as a racist description: blacks had become black because of some misdeed and malediction in the past; their blackness was result and proof as well as permanent punishment. This tautological procedure was hard to combat. James Baldwin described the feeling of being enclosed by the story of Ham's curse in *The Fire Next Time* (1963):

> I realized that the Bible had been written by white men. I knew that, according to many Christians, I was a descendant of Ham, who had been

cursed, and that I was therefore predestined to be a slave. This had nothing to do with anything I was, or contained, or could become; my fate had been sealed forever, from the beginning of time.[64]

If one were to amend Baldwin one could say that it was less the Bible than a certain tradition of misreading it that was responsible for the "sealing" of his fate to which he gave such eloquent expression. Enslavement (or, in its aftermath, hereditary lower-caste status) was a very serious punishment, indeed, to be derived from certain themings of a sacred text; but for what, according to the logic of these stories, was it imagined to be a punishment?

### What Could Ham Have Done?

This question has remained central to many exegetical attempts. The punishment is symmetrical: the son looks at his patriarchal origin—and the son's descendant is doomed. Yet such structural symmetry alone hardly constitutes a satisfactory explanation. A son's gaze at his father's nakedness, though it seemed an insufficient transgression to some readers, may have constituted a particularly offensive violation of *a special taboo*. The Ugaritic epic of Danel and Aqhat has been cited in this connection because it suggests that the "disgrace of a drunken father was considered by the Canaanites to be a crime of the utmost gravity."[65] Yet it seems to have been hard for exegetes to settle upon a literal interpretation of Ham's sin in the context of cultural relativism. No matter what Noah's curse meant, the feeling among readers was that there *had* to be more to Ham's transgression than was told in Genesis. This tendency came to a head in the debate on African slavery when abolitionists sometimes felt that they had to play down Ham's putative transgression, whereas proponents were inclined to elaborate and magnify it. In opposing the curse of Ham, the American antislavery writer Stephen Vail came to believe that Ham had "just opened his eyes and then turned away as any pure-minded man would."[66] The proslavery authors appear to have been less modest in their reinterpretations of the text.

The connection between filial disobedience and the matter of sexuality that is suggested by Noah's nakedness (and that may have prompted Roland Barthes's view of this scene as the origin of striptease) also inspired readers to go far beyond literal readings of the text. The versions in Josephus's *Antiquities of the Jews*, in *Thousand and One Nights* or in the play *The First One*, modestly added Ham's laughing at his father's nakedness, and the proslavery writer Josiah Priest saw Ham "yelling and exploding with laughter at his sleeping father;"[67] according to the *Azhār* of Jalálu 'l-Din al-Suyutī (1445–1505), Ham had looked *shamelessly* at his father while he was washing.[68] Many other renditions were far less restrained, and Ham has been found guilty of a considerable variety of remarkable crimes that were to account for Noah's malediction of Canaan.[69]

### Intercourse in the Ark

One way of correlating filial disobedience and sexual transgression was to assume that Ham had violated a command of chastity for the duration of the time that was spent in the ark. This was the view cited in the *Babylonian Talmud*:

> three copulated in the ark, and they were all punished—the dog, the raven, and Ham. The dog was doomed to be tied, the raven expectorates [his seed into his mate's mouth], and Ham was smitten in his skin.[70]

This motif also appears in Islamic sources: for example, Dimšqī's *Nuḥba* (or al-Dimashqī's *Nukhbat*—he lived from 1256 to 1327), and the *Kitāb at-tiğān fī mulūk* report traditions according to which Ham's crime was that of approaching a woman in the ark despite Noah's prohibition, whereupon Nūḥ "cursed him and prayed to God to modify his seed."[71]

According to the previously mentioned problematic extrapolation from Rabbis Huna and Joseph, Noah was kept from fathering more children after the deluge (because of Ham's fornication in the ark?), which is why he said to Ham: "You have prevented me from doing something in the dark [sc. cohabitation], therefore your seed will be ugly and dark-skinned."[72] Some added the speculation that since Ham kept Noah from having a fourth son, Noah pronounced the malediction upon Ham's fourth son.[73] Ham's reputed copulation in the ark was at times supposed to have been undertaken for the ulterior motive of stealing the birthright for his son. George Best (cited briefly a bit earlier), a companion of Martin Frobisher's on his voyage to Cathay, whose account of 1578 was later included in *Hakluyt's Voyages*, gave one of the most elaborate, fanciful, and racially charged versions, according to which Noah

> straitely commaunded his sonnes and their wives, that they should with reverence and feare beholde the justice and mighty power of God, and that during the time of the floud while they remained in the Arke, they should use continencie, and abstaine from carnal copulation with their wives: and many other precepts hee gave unto them, and admonitions touching the justice of God, in revenging sinne, and his mercie in delivering them, who nothing deserved it. Which good instructions and exhortations notwithstanding his wicked sonne Cham disobeyed, and being perswaded that the first childe borne after the flood (by right and Lawe of nature) should inherite and possesse all the dominions of the earth, hee contrary to his fathers commandement while they were yet in the Arke, used company with his wife, and craftily went about thereby to dis-inherite the off-spring of his other two brethren: for the which wicked and detestable fact, as an

example for contempt of Almightie God, and disobedience of parents, God would a sonne should bee borne whose name was Chus, who not onely it selfe, but all his posteritie after him should bee so blacke and lothsome, that it might remaine a spectacle of disobedience to all the worlde. And of this blacke and cursed Chus [a rare reference to Cush as accursed] came all these blacke Moores which are in Africa. . . .[74]

The association of Ham's putative transgression with some sexual activity took even more elaborate forms than this.

### Castration of Noah/Indulgence of Ham's Lust Upon His Father

The *Soncino Chumash*, a popular rather than a scholarly work, suggests the following readings of Genesis 9:22: "Some say that [Ham] castrated [Noah]; others that he indulged a perverted lust upon him."[75] It is this reading to which the writers James Baldwin and Ralph Ellison were to allude in the 1950s and 1960s.[76] Rabbinic opinion has also included the view that it was Canaan who had committed this act, and that Canaan may actually have been Noah's fourth and youngest son.[77] Graves and Patai merged differing versions into their castration tale according to which Canaan "mischievously looped a stout cord about his grandfather's genitals, drew it tight, and unmanned him," or Ham himself unmanned Noah, or a sick lion dealt Noah's "genitals a blow."[78] Arthur Frederick Ide offered an extensive and imaginatively detailed homosexual reading that expands the theme of sodomy sounded in the *Soncino Chumash*.[79] Other readers went for even more lurid possibilities.

### Incest

The entry "Cham" in Zedler's *Universallexikon* (1733) reports some fabled versions of Ham's sin, and adds to the castrating of his father, committing incest with his mother.[80] The American proslavery writer Josiah Priest (1845) also imagined, at much greater detail, that Ham's real "lascivious" crime was incest with his mother, a reading that is based on an application of Leviticus 18:8 (in which "father's wife" seems differentiated from "mother" of the previous verse, thus extending the incest taboo to a father's wife who may not be the addressee's mother).

> The word [Ham], doubtless, has more meanings than we are *now* acquainted with, *two* of which, however, besides the first, we find are *heat* or *violence* of temper, exceedingly prone to acts of ferocity and cruelty, involving murder, war, butcheries, and even *cannibalism*, including beastly lusts and lasciviousness in its *worst* feature, going beyond the force of these passions, as possessed in common by the other races of men. Second, the word signifies deceit, dishonesty, treachery, low mindedness, and malice. . . .
>
> As it respects the crime of Ham, the youngest son of Noah, . . . it is

believed by some, and not without reason, that it did not consist alone in the seeing his father's nakedness as a *man*, but rather in the abuse and actual *violation* of his own mother.

This opinion is strengthened by a passage found in Levit. xviii.8, as follows: "The nakedness of thy father's wife shalt thou not uncover: it is thy *father's* nakedness." On account of this passage, it has been believed that the crime of Ham did not consist alone of seeing his father in an improper manner, but rather of his own mother, the wife of Noah, and violating her.

If this was so, how much more horrible, therefore, appears the character of Ham, and how much more deserving the *curse*, which was laid upon him and his race [again, "generation" and "race"], of whom it was foreseen that *they* would be like *this*, their lewd ancestor.

All Egypt, the Sodomites, the Canaanite nations, with all the negro heathen countries, practised these outrages upon good order, (as stated by Moses, see Levit. xviii.3, and chap. xx.23) without shame or remorse, as if, indeed, they considered themselves as being no better than the cattle on the fields.

For these things, as foreseen, they were adjudged judicially, together with Ham, as an inferior race of men, and could never be elevated on account of their natures.[81]

Whereas incest remains Ham's central transgression for Priest, he also gives him a whole catalogue of other sins, from violence and lasciviousness to cannibalism and treachery, in order to express his feelings towards the "inferior race" of Ham. Priest's book also contains "The family of Noah, including Ham," the only visual example I have encountered in which Ham is represented as black (Fig. 21).[82]

Frederick W. Bassett has taken up the issue of incest. He notes that Noah in verse 24 refers to Ham's offense as a *deed*, and—again by invok-

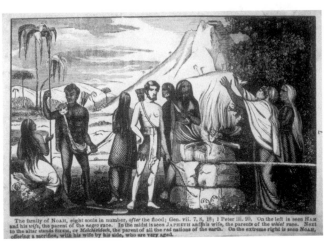

*Figure 21*   Josiah Priest, *The Family of Noah, including Ham* (1845)

ing Leviticus—suggests that the Hebrew for "to see the nakedness of someone" means "to have sexual intercourse with someone," and that the redactor or a later editor may have missed the idiom and "added the reference to the brothers' covering their father's nakedness with a garment." Since "seeing one's father's nakedness" could also mean having sexual intercourse with one's father's wife, Bassett, assuming that "father's wife" means "mother," speculates that the seriousness and nature of this possible offense would explain why Noah cursed only one of Ham's several sons, if it is further assumed that "Canaan was the fruit of such a case of incest."[83] Perhaps it is not necessary to add that this reading, though it starts from a shaky exegetical move similar to Priest's, could help to undermine any racial readings of the consequences of the curse.

### Intermarriage with a Descendant of Cain

Another American proslavery writer accused Ham of having been the first to enter an interracial marriage with a woman descended from Cain—thus once again merging the curses on Cain and Canaan, though in a new way. In 1852 John Fletcher, a northern-born Louisianian who had become an ardent advocate of slavery, cited Jewish, Christian, and Muslim sources and supposed first of all that Cain's mark was blackness:

> Now, for a moment, let us suppose that Ham did marry and take into the ark a daughter of the race of Cain. If the general intermixture of the Sethites with the Cainites had so deteriorated the Sethites, and reduced them to the moral degradation of the Cainites, that God did not deem them worthy of longer encumbering the earth before the flood, would it be an extraordinary manifestation of his displeasure at the supposed marriage of Ham with one of the cursed race of Cain, to subject the issue of such marriage to a degraded and perpetual bondage?
>
> But again, in case this supposed marriage of Ham with the race of Cain be true, then Ham would be the progenitor of all the race of Cain who should exist after the flood; and such fact would be among the most prominent features of his history. . . .
>
> In case Ham had married a female of the race of Cain, he had also identified himself with that race, and might well be called by his father, especially at a moment of displeasure, by a term emphatically showing, yea announcing prophetically, his degradation through all future time,—the degradation to which that connection had reduced him. (445)

Fletcher is explicit about the need to go beyond the text as he rejects the idea that Ham's conduct toward his father could have been the reason for the curse.

> The ill-manners could have no so great effect. And let us inquire, where are we to find an adequate cause for the immediate degradation of an

unborn race, unless we find it in intermarriage? His intermarriage, then, could have been with no other than the race of Cain? (446)

Fletcher's hypothetical interpretation illustrates the strength of the intermarriage taboo in the mind of a mid-nineteenth-century American slavery advocate. (His thinking also suggests how central this taboo was to any definition of "race.") His proof lies in modern times, and another circle closes:

> Suppose, even at this day, a descendant of Japheth should choose to amalgamate with the Negro, could not his father readily foretell the future destiny of the offspring,—their standing among the rest of his family?[84]

Genealogy could sanction a modern practice (racial slavery) and a modern sentiment (aversion to interracial marriage). A contemporary feeling ("Would you like your descendant to marry one?") was enlarged as the genealogy gave this sentiment an illusory depth and antiquity—in short, legitimacy. Fletcher's extreme exegesis was not a solitary undertaking, and not all interpreters of his mindset used the subjunctive. In 1860, for example, the president of Dartmouth and slavery supporter Nathan Lord also believed in Ham's "forbidden intermarriage with the previously wicked and accursed race of Cain."[85] Perhaps with even more public (if not scholarly) authority Jefferson Davis argued in a speech to the United States Senate of April 1860:

> [W]hen the low and vulgar son of Noah, who laughed at his father's exposure, sunk by debasing himself and his lineage by a connection with an inferior race of men, he doomed his descendants to perpetual slavery. Noah spoke the decree, or prophecy, as gentlemen may choose to consider it, one or the other.[86]

Davis tellingly substituted an "inferior race" for the generation of Canaan.

### Bestiality

Canaan was not only compared with the raven on the ark; in the *Sachsenspiegel* (ca. 1200)[87] he was also presumed to have been the offspring of Ham's copulation with the raven—making his blackness both a proof of and punishment for his father's bestiality.

Anchoring the defense of slavery in scripture, Thornton Stringfellow had suggested a "beastly wickedness" that made Ham's character "a true type of the character of his descendants."[88] This may still have been somewhat metaphoric. By the late nineteenth century, however, the concept of "race" had moved from biblical "generation" toward biological "species," in the modern sense, and other "races" could therefore be viewed in extra-species terms. Charles Carroll's *The Negro a Beast* (1900), for example, did, indeed, mean its title *literally*. Applying this idea to a racially paranoid reading of the Bible, Carroll maintained that at the time of the Flood, Noah and his wife were the only pure whites left on the earth; but there was a pair of Negroes among the *beasts* on the Ark, and amalgamation resumed after the Flood. Christ was then sent to "redeem man from atheism, amalgamation, and idolatry" and to "rebuild the barriers which God erected in the Creation between man and the ape."[89] Miscegenation had literally become identified with extra-species relationship.

Bestiality was thus added to incest and miscegenation on Ham's putative record (though he resorted to it in some instances *after* being cursed already).[90] By staring at a complicated passage in Genesis while experiencing human difference in racial terms, readers may have projected some of their most feared transgressions onto Noah's sons, both as a cause or an explanation and as the result of difference.

### Is There a Redemption?

It was characteristic of the folklore of curses (for example, in the Flying Dutchman tale), that various versions would begin to offer resolutions of a curse in some form of a redemption. The curse of Ham is no exception. In the Islamic tradition several authors explain the exemption of some descendants of Ham from the curse by adding stories of the lifting of the curse. In the Byzantine tradition, Pentecost was the antitype to the Tower of Babel, hence also a form of redemption from the consequences of the curse on Ham.[91] Yet the fact that white Christians believed that blacks stood in need of a more specific redemption is suggested by the request that a group of missionary bishops made at the first Vatican Council of 1870, "asking the pope to release the Negro race from the curse which, it seems, comes from Ham."[92]

Another, even stranger example of a proposal for lifting the curse on blacks was made by Modesto Brocos (1852–1936) in his painting *Redenção de Cã* ("The Redemption of Ham"), which won the first gold medal at the Brazilian Fine Arts Exposition in 1895 and is now in the Museo de Belas Artes in Rio de Janeiro (Fig. 22). Here the resolution represented is a white sexual partner, as the succeeding generations— arranged on a diagonal line from upper left to the center of the painting—look lighter and lighter.[93] What the American John Fletcher viewed as the cause of Ham's curse, the Brazilian Modesto Brocos thus saw as the way of lifting it. Despite the endorsement of interracial relationships, this is hardly a view free of preconceptions, as it presumes the identification of whites as a racially chosen people. Even the (rare) redemptions of the curse may thus show what Patrick Girard has called "pigmentocracy."[94] Yet these examples of "redemption" still deserve to

**Figure 22**   Modesto Brocos, *Redenção de Cã* (1895)

be contrasted with the view of the Georgia-born writer Maurice Thompson, who composed a work entitled "The Voodoo Prophecy" (ca. 1889):

> You seed of Abel, proud of your descent,
> And arrogant, because your cheeks are fair,
> Within my loins an inky curse is pent
> To flood
> Your blood
> And stain your skin and crisp your golden hair.[95]

Thompson formulated what one might regard as a secularized version of the curse on Cain/Ham: it has become the "inky curse," ineffaceable and threatening as pollution of the blood stream via "miscegenation" and *Natus Æthiopus*. "Race" may partly function in analogy to the distinction between unbelievers and believers; yet, as has already been noted, it does not permit conversion.

### "Cain, Harry, Dick or Tom": Great Refutations

The manifold reflections upon the curse of Ham lent this legend verisimilitude and even a reality that, despite the weak textual basis and the incongruities in the various exegeses, seemed to evoke a sense of "truth" when alluded to. Numerous writers participated in the debate about the curse of Ham, which may have spread through refutations as well as endorsements.[96] If it was an easier story to assert than to prove (as Thomas Browne observed), it was also a difficult tale to "refute," and some partial refutations helped to support other parts of the story.[97]

Some writers opposed Ham's curse on the ground of mere technicalities: thus Samuel Sewall—who also argued, without success, against a Massachusetts "Act for the Better Preventing of a Spurious and Mixt Issue"—thought (like Las Casas before him) that the prophecy had been "accomplished in the Extirpation of the *Canaanites*" (1700) and hence could have no bearing on Africans; Charles W. Gordon (1887) and John W. Tyndall (1927) singled out the problem that Noah's words were human and not divine; Elihu Coleman (1733) invoked the injunction that "the son should not bear the iniquity of the father, and the father should not bear the iniquity of the son" against the curse of Ham, but conceded in his refutation that "negroes might not have the understanding that some other nations have"; and Ralph Sandiford (1729) emphasized that the curse of Canaan was not so extensive as to serve as a "suitable original for the Negro Trade." Several readers stressed that neither Ham nor Cush are cursed by Noah but only Canaan, so that there actually is no biblically sanctioned "curse of Ham" and that the presumably light-skinned Canaan was actually cursed to be servant of the Ethiopian Cush.[98] Others appealed to reason in a very general fashion: thus de Pauw (1770) and John Woolman (1774) saw in the legend a "pious extravagance" and a "Supposition too gross to be admitted into the Mind of any Person, who sincerely desires to be governed by solid Principles."[99]

An early principled question was raised in Dimšqī's *Nuhba*: after reviewing the explanations of the malediction because of Ham's intercourse on the ark or seeing his father's nakedness, Dimšqī comments: "But in truth, the fact is that the nature of their country demands that their characteristics should be as they are, contrary to those connected with whiteness, for most of them inhabit the south and west of the earth."[100] This environmental approach was followed by many scholars who offered a climatic explanation for color difference. Thus John Mitchell argued in 1744 that "different colours of people have been demonstrated to be only the necessary effects, and natural consequences of their respective climes, and ways of life." From this premise he concluded

that the black colour of the negroes of Africa, instead of being a curse denounced on them, on account of their fore-father Ham, as some have idely imagined, is rather a blessing, rendering their lives, in that intemperate region, more tolerable, and less painful: whereas, on the other hand, the white people, who consider themselves as the primitive race of men, from a certain superiority of worth, either supposed or assumed, seem to have the least pretensions to it of any, either from history or philosophy; for they seem to have degenerated more from the primitive and original complexion of mankind, in Noah and his sons, than even the Indians or negroes; and that to the worst extreme, the most delicate, tender, and sickly.[101]

Some strikingly comprehensive or witty refutations were offered by Thomas Browne and in Hugh Henry Brackenridge's novel *Modern Chivalry*. Browne mentions the whole gamut of familiar objections, from the confusion between Ham and Canaan, the calculation that of eleven sons of Canaan, "five only were condemned and six escaped the malediction" (383), and the vast number of nonblack descendants of Ham (including Italians), to the imperfect descent lines that make it difficult to say who is Ethiopian. Browne also adds an important argument for cultural relativism, however, when he writes:

> Whereas men affirm this colour was a Curse, I cannot make out the propriety of that name, it neither seeming so to them, nor reasonably unto us; for they take so much content therein, that they esteem deformity by other colours, describing the Devil, and terrible objects, white.

Browne draws on the familiar example of animals in order to show that color—in the classical tradition—is an accidental aspect, not essential to any definition of beauty: "Thus horses are handsome under any colour, and the symmetry of parts obscures the consideration of complexions."[102]

Captain John Farrago, the narrator of Hugh Henry Brackenridge's previously cited novel *Modern Chivalry* (1792–1805), argues amusingly:

> Some supposed, that it was the curse pronounced upon Canaan, the son of Noah, for looking at his father's nakedness. They got rid by this means of the difficulty of the flood; but by Moses' own account, the Canaanites were the descendents of Canaan; and we do not hear of them being Negroes; which, had it been the case, we cannot doubt would have been laid hold of by the Israelites as a circumstance to justify their extirpating, or making slaves of them. . . . [103]

What role could authors of African ancestry play in this debate? Gernot Rotter has argued that blacks, in the context of the Islamic Ham legends and slavery—where their color alone could be seen as "proof" of the curse—found it difficult to criticize the curse except in two ways: by a denial of descent from Ham or a more general denial of the transferability of traits by descent.[104] Yet a number of African American writers did respond rather memorably within as well as outside such constraints as their writings helped to transcend the loop, the circle, the rhetorical prison that the interpretation of the curse of Ham had helped to "seal" them in.[105]

David Walker, in his famous *Appeal in Four Articles* (1829), used the story of Joseph's marriage to the Egyptian Asenath (Genesis 41:45)—

that Las Casas had previously invoked—in order to isolate American slavery with its intermarriage prohibition from Old Testament proto-types; "show me a page," he writes, "which maintains, that the Egyptians heaped the *insupportable insult* upon the children of Israel, by telling them that they were not of the *human family*." Walker therefore also goes to Noah, the root of the story of family connectedness of mankind, and argues:

> Shem, Ham, and Japheth, together with their father Noah and wives, I believe were not natural enemies to each other. When the ark rested after the flood upon Mount Arrarat in Asia, they were all the people which could be found alive in all the earth—in fact if scriptures be true (which I believe are) there were no other living men in all the earth, notwithstand-ing some ignorant creatures hesitate not to tell us, that we, (the blacks) are the seed of Cain, the murderer of his brother Abel. But where those igno-rant and avaricious wretches could have got their information, I am unable to declare. Did they receive it from the Bible? I have searched the Bible as well as they, and have never seen a verse which testifies whether we are the seed of Cain or of Abel.— Yet those men tell us that we are of the seed of Cain and that God put a dark stain upon us, that we might be known as their slaves!!! Now I ask those avaricious and ignorant wretches, who act more like the seed of Cain, by murdering, the whites or the blacks? How many vessel loads of human beings have the blacks thrown into the seas? How many thousand souls have the blacks murdered in cold blood to make them work in wretchedness and ignorance, to support their families?— However, let us be the seed of Cain, Harry, Dick or Tom!!! God will show the whites what we are yet.[106]

Walker's powerful indictment of Christian hypocrisy and juxtaposi-tion of American self-made rhetoric against the biblical justification of slavery combine effectively to deflate the opponents' position. Walker also suggests that the rhetoric of ancestry-free Harry, Dick, or Tom may actually *rest on* Cain and Ham, who seem forever ancestrally bound. In a country that has modeled its beginnings on Noah's rainbow covenant after the flood, the "tribe of Hamo" seems excluded from partaking in this promise of a new start.

Frederick Douglass wrote in his *Narrative* (1845):

> [T]he slaveholder, in cases not a few, sustains to his slaves the double rela-tion of master and father. . . . It was doubtless in consequence of a knowl-edge of this fact, that one great statesman of the south predicted the down-fall of slavery by the inevitable laws of population. Whether this prophecy is ever fulfilled or not, it is nevertheless plain that a very different-looking class of people are springing up at the south, and are now held in slavery, from those originally brought to this country from Africa; and if their increase will do no other good, it will do away the force of the argument, that God cursed Ham, and therefore American slavery is right. If the lineal descendants of Ham are alone to be scripturally enslaved, it is certain that

slavery at the south must soon become unscriptural; for thousands are ush-
ered into the world, annually, who, like myself, owe their existence to
white fathers, and those fathers most frequently their own masters.[107]

Like Walker, Douglass insisted upon the family connection, that old
side of the meaning of "generation" that had been sacrificed to "race";
and he used *himself* as proof against the curse of Ham (when the tautological presupposition would have been that his blackness had somehow
"proved" it); and if white segregationists invoked the curse of Ham in
order to inhibit racial amalgamation, Douglass uses the fact of racial mixing in order to suggest the absurdity of applying the curse of Ham to
Afro-American slaves.

Alexander Crummell developed a very scholarly and perhaps the most
systematic refutation of the curse of Ham in his essay "The Negro Race
Not Under a Curse: An Examination of Genesis ix.25" (published in
revised form in 1862). Reviewing some of the theological literature, past
misreadings and elucidations, Crummell concludes:

1. That the curse of Noah was pronounced upon Canaan, not upon Ham.
2. That it *fell* upon Canaan, and was designed to fall upon him only.
3. That neither Ham, nor any of his three sons, was involved in this curse.
4. That the Negro race have not descended from Canaan; were never
   involved in the curse pronounced upon him; and their peculiar suffer-
   ings, during the last three centuries, are not the results or evidences of
   *any* specific curse upon them.
5. That the fact of slavery in the Negro race is not peculiar to them as a
   people; but a *general* evil existing in the whole human family; in which,
   in God's providence, the Negro family have latterly been called to suffer greatly, and doubtless for some high and important ends.
6. That the geographical designations of Scripture are to be taken in good
   faith; and that when the *"Land of Canaan"* is mentioned in the Bible, it
   was not intended to include the Gold Coast, the Gaboon, Goree, or
   Congo.

Crummell also arrives at the collateral conclusions that Genesis ix.25
*"does not imply mental degradation and intellectual ineptitude,"* that the
*"'principle of chattelism' is not the correlative of the curse of Canaan,"* and that
his examination *"nullifies the foolish notion that the curse of Canaan carried
with it the sable dye which marks the Negro races of the world.* The descendants of Canaan in Palestine, Phoenicia, Carthage, and in their various
colonies, were not *black*. They were not Negroes, either in lineage or
color."[108]

A similarly impressive and cogent refutation, entitled "Noah's Malediction," was published by Edward Wilmot Blyden in the same year,
1862. He notes that the argument is a posteriori, he invokes Acts 17, and
then focuses on attempts to gloss over the disparity between Ham's
action and Canaan's punishment by inserting "Ham the father of" into

the line with the curse on Canaan. Invoking many biblical instances he asks: "But would there have been any thing more unjust in this, than in other instances in which God has visited the iniquity of the fathers upon their impenitent children?" He therefore resolves the issue in the following manner:

> Every one knows the severe bondage which the Israelites endured in Egypt under the Egyptians. The Egyptians were the descendants of Ham; the Jews the descendants of Shem; the Jews were in servitude to the Egyptians, therefore Shem was the servant of Ham—a palpable reversion of the male-diction, if it be true that it included all the posterity of Ham.

Blyden also recalls having been exposed to a racialized curse-on-Canaan sermon when he was eighteen, which gave him "an intuitive revulsion of mind never to be forgotten."[109]

For a final example, one of many possible others, in Charles W. Chesnutt's story "The Fall of Adam" (1886)—mentioned in Chapter One—Brother 'Lijah Gadson wonders about the possible origin of the difference "'twix' white folks an' black folks." Gadson explains:

> I be'n 'flectin' dat subjic' over a long time, and axin' 'bout it; but nobody doan' seem to know nuffin' surtin' 'bout it. Some says it's de cuss o'Caanyun but I never could'n' understan' 'bout dis here cuss o' Caanyun. I can['t] see how de Lawd could turn anybody black jes' by cussin' 'im; 'case 'fo I j'ined de church—dat was 'fo de wah— I use' ter cuss de overseah on ole marse's plantation awful bad—when he was'n' da—an' all de darkies on the plantation use'ter cus 'im, an' it didn' make de leas' changes in 'is com-plexion.[110]

This thoroughly ironic rereading of the relationship of curse and complexion, extended by the already cited answer that Bre'r Gab'l and Bre'r Isham give on the next Sabbath, suggesting that Adam and Eve must have been a black-white couple, their descendants Mulattoes, affirms Chesnutt's belief in the power of folk voices to come up with the same arsenal of refutations as scholars as well as his openness to interra-cial stories.

The fact that the black literary tradition is far from homogeneous, however, even when it comes to refutations of the curse of Ham, is illus-trated by the play *The First One* that I described at the beginning. It was written by Zora Neale Hurston, and it can probably be read in many different ways. Robert Hemenway has viewed it as "a comedy about [Ham's] curse and exile" and added: "In effect, the play pokes fun at all those who take seriously the biblical sanction for racial separation."[111] Yet Hurston's drama, however comical its effect, by making Ham's black pigmentation the result of Noah's curse, also may have provided a belat-ed literary support to the central racial transformation of the biblical story. Another writer from the African American tradition, Pauline

Hopkins, drew on the story (though not the cursing) of Ham in order to account for the human diversity of divinely planned distinct races and to establish an Egyptian myth of origins for black Americans.[112]

### "No Relationship": The End of Ham's Usefulness

Unfortunately, some of the best rebuttals came at a time when secularizing tendencies were weakening theology.[113] Race thinking began to rely less and less upon biblical justification. Theodore Weld wrote in *The Bible Against Slavery* (fourth edition, 1838) that the "prophecy of Noah is the *vade mecum* of slaveholders, and they never venture abroad without it."[114] The story of Noah, Ham, and Canaan provided a terrain that both proslavery writers and abolitionists could contest—as Ron Bartour has shown—by drawing on Hebrew grammar and biblical studies, though both camps tended to distort the key passage from Genesis.[115] Blyden relates a New York Thanksgiving Day sermon of 1850 in which the Reverend J. B. Pinney invoked the "decree" of the curse on Canaan in order to defend the Fugitive Slave Law and characterize all efforts at elevating the African as futile.[116] Undoubtedly, the curse of Ham has been invoked in support of such causes as racial segregation, and well into the twentieth century.[117] With the ascent of nineteenth-century racism, however, the subjugation of blacks could be anchored in biology rather than in theology (as has already become apparent). At that point in history the curse of Ham could be attacked even by *supporters* of slavery and in the name of racial inequality. In *Two Lectures on the Natural History of the Caucasian and Negro Races* (1844) Josiah C. Nott shifted the proslavery argument from biblical to racial-biological sources and hence could simply dispense with the Canaan-Ham stories:

> Negroes existed in Africa before this date of the flood [2348 B.C.], and . . . there is reason to believe they did not descend from Noah's family. . . . (213)
>
> Shem and Ham were twin brothers—the word Shem, means white, and Ham, means dark, or swarthy, but not black. It is probably therefore, that there was the same difference between them, that we often see between brothers here. Many have supposed Ham to be the progenitor of the negro race. There was no curse upon him, and there is nothing in the Bible which induces such a belief; but this point is settled by the fact which I shall prove, that the Egyptians were not Negroes.
>
> The curse of heaven fell upon Canaan, but we have no reason to believe that the curse was a physical one. Canaan took possession of Palestine, and not any part of Africa; and his descendants were Caucasians.[118]

In Nott's eyes mankind no longer had one, but many origins, human history had to transcend the biblical time frame, and blacks were understandable as a different species whose origins may well have been outside scriptural history and biblical time altogether. Nott stressed that "no relationship can be traced between them and Noah's family" (236) and focused on studying *difference*[119] that disconnected members of the human family until races reached the proximity of other species: "The difference to an Anatomist, between the Bushman or Negro and the Caucasian, is greater than the difference in the skeletons of the Wolf, Dog and Hyena, which are allowed to be distinct species" (224). Hybrids (like the mule) were the proof of this difference; and it became Nott's concern to prevent the further human "adulteration of blood" that generated hybrid offspring (like the Mulatto) and to return to mankind's original diversity.[120] The new focus on difference inspired even Bible readers to discover new ways to disconnect blacks and whites from a shared family story. In 1860, Samuel A. Cartwright (who had previously dissented from Nott and advocated a single human origin, putting the emphasis on the curse on Canaan in order to advocate racial hierarchy) offered a new polygenetic account of mankind, according to which Negroes (as well as Indians) were created before Adam and Eve; the snake (Hebrew, "Nachrash") in the garden was not a serpent but a "negro gardener" since the word supposedly also means "to be or to become black." Cain intermarried with these pre-Adamite Negroes: "That they were black . . . is inferred from the mark they put on Cain. The hybrids were so exceedingly wicked that the Lord determined to destroy them in the flood." Blacks must have been on the ark, however, since Cartwright thought that Ham was not the father of Canaan, but "the headmaster or overseer of the Nachrash race of which Canaan was a member."[121] The shriller Charles Carroll also could not possibly accept any family relationship between blacks and whites, and felt compelled to develop a grandiose refutation of the notion that Noah could have changed Canaan into a Negro: Carroll doubted that Noah had such power or authority and believed that a merciful God would not have permitted the punishment of an "unoffending individual" as a result of Noah's "drunken desire." Carroll also thought it quite absurd to imagine Canaan's physical transformation into a black and pointed out (fourteen years after Chesnutt's "Fall of Adam") that since no female was similarly cursed, Canaan's descendants "would not have been negroes, but halfcastes—mulattoes." Furthermore, Noah's curse was never fulfilled:

> It is a matter of scriptural record that while the Israelites, who were a branch of the family of Shem, were in bondage to the Egyptians, who were a branch of the family of Ham, the descendants of Canaan, whom Noah cursed, were the masters of one of the finest countries in the world; a country which God described as "a godly land"; "a land flowing with milk and honey."[122]

So much for the "absurd church theory of the Hamitic origin of the Negro" (81).

The concept of "race" that had perhaps developed out of the biblical "generations" and genealogical tables had fiercely emancipated itself from its own genealogical beginnings. Blacks were now being excluded even from a second-rate nonblessed membership in the human family story going back to Noah. The family curse of Ham had turned into the notion of permanent racial difference that extended back to the very beginning of mankind. And as the importance of theology began to wane, genealogical interests shifted from the attempt to locate the origins of human diversity in scripture to the search for scientific definitions of racial identity.

# The Calculus of Color

Mixed bloods, they are suspended between two races,—mulattoes, quadroons, musters, mustafinas, cabres, griffies, zambis, quatravis, tresalvis, coyotes, saltatras, albarassados, cambusos—neither white nor black, but Negroes.

—[Charles S. Johnson,] "The Vanishing Mulatto" (1925)[1]

Strictly in terms of genetic contribution, the child of one white parent and one black parent had the same claim to being classified as white as he did to being classified as black. He was neither, either, or both. One could decide to call such half/half mixtures mulattoes, but that merely raised the question of classification again in the next generation. Was the child of a mulatto and a white to be deemed mulatto or white? Or should another name, like quadroon, be devised for such a person?

—A. Leon Higginbotham, Jr., and Barbara K. Kopytoff, "Racial Purity and Interracial Sex in the Law of Colonial and Antebellum Virginia" (1989)[2]

There are only two qualities in the United States racial pattern: white and black. A person is one or the other: there is no intermediate position. . . . [I]n Brazil the children of a white and black couple are neither black nor white.

—Carl Degler, *Neither Black Nor White* (1971)[3]

In Latin America whoever is not black is white: in teutonic America whoever is not white is black.

—James Bryce, *The American Commonwealth* (1893)[4]

lassification schemes of racial names were an eighteenth- and early nineteenth-century obsession. The Enlightenment promise of using empirical methods in order to overcome the tyranny of clergy and hereditary aristocracy raised the hope that science would put an end to the superstitions of theology. Yet as has become apparent in the substitution of the curse of Ham by scientific racialism, the efforts of bringing the light of reason to "race" were deeply compromised at times. On the one hand, in the English-speaking world it was partly due to the dual forces of revolutionary Enlightenment thinking and romantic evangelical movements that the African slave trade and slavery were ultimately abolished; and the whole framework of antiracist scholarship rests on, and is unthinkable without, the Enlightenment legacy. On the other hand, there is undoubtedly a double-edged quality to much eighteenth-, nineteenth- and twentieth-century thinking about the races of people, their various crosses, and the future of mankind, however scientifically such thinking may have been presented. The following text of 1815 is representative of the problem:

As the issue has one-half of the blood of each parent, and the blood of each of these may be made up of a variety of fractional mixtures, the estimate of their compound in some cases may be intricate; it becomes a mathematical problem of the same class with those on the mixtures of different liquors or different metals; as in these, therefore, the algebraical notation is the most convenient and intelligible. Let us express the pure blood of the white in the capital letters of the printed alphabet, the pure blood of the negro in the small letters of the printed alphabet, and any given mixture of either, by way of abridgment in MS. letters.

Let the first crossing be of $a$, a pure negro, with A, pure white. The unit of blood of the issue being composed of the half of that of each parent, will be $\frac{a}{2} + \frac{A}{2}$. Call it, for abbreviation, $h$ (half blood).

Let the second crossing be that of $h$ and B, the blood of the issue will be $\frac{h}{2} + \frac{B}{2}$, or substituting for $\frac{h}{2}$ its equivalent, it will be $\frac{a}{4} + \frac{A}{4} + \frac{B}{2}$, call it $q$ (quarteroon) being $\frac{1}{4}$ negro blood.

Let the third crossing be of $q$ and C, their offspring will be $\frac{q}{2} + \frac{C}{2} = \frac{a}{2} + \frac{A}{8} + \frac{B}{4} + \frac{C}{2}$, call this $e$ (eighth), who having less than $\frac{1}{4}$ of $a$, or of pure negro blood, to wit $\frac{1}{8}$ only, is no longer a mulatto, so that a third cross clears the blood.

From these elements let us examine their compounds. For example, let $b$ and $q$ cohabit, their issue will be $\frac{b}{2} + \frac{q}{2} = \frac{a}{4} + \frac{A}{4} + \frac{a}{8} + \frac{A}{8} + \frac{B}{4} = \frac{3a}{8} + \frac{3A}{8} + \frac{B}{4}$, wherein we find $\frac{3}{8}$ of $a$, or negro blood.

Let $b$ and $e$ cohabit, their issue will be $\frac{b}{2} + \frac{e}{2} = \frac{a}{4} + \frac{A}{4} + \frac{a}{16} + \frac{A}{16} + \frac{B}{8} + \frac{c}{4} = \frac{5a}{16} + \frac{5A}{16} + \frac{B}{8} + \frac{c}{4}$, wherein $\frac{5}{16}$ $a$ makes still a mulatto.

Let $q$ and $e$ cohabit, the half of the blood of each will be $\frac{q}{2} + \frac{e}{2} = \frac{a}{8} + \frac{A}{8} + \frac{B}{4} + \frac{a}{16} + \frac{A}{16} + \frac{B}{8} + \frac{C}{4} = \frac{3a}{16} + \frac{3A}{16} + \frac{3B}{8} + \frac{C}{4}$ wherein $\frac{5}{16}$ of $a$ is no longer a mulatto, and thus may every compound be noted and summed, the sum of the fractions composing the blood of the issue being always equal to unit. It is understood in natural history that a fourth cross of one race of animals with another gives an issue equivalent for all sensible purposes to the original blood. Thus a Merino ram being crossed, first with a country ewe, second with his daughter, third with his granddaughter, and fourth with his great-granddaughter, the last issue is deemed pure Merino, having in fact but $\frac{1}{16}$ of the country blood. Our canon considers two crosses with the pure white, and a third with any degree of mixture, however small, as clearing the issue of the negro blood. But observe, that this does not re-establish freedom, which depends on the condition of the mother, the principle of the civil law, *partus sequitur ventrem*, being adopted here. But if $e$ be emancipated, he becomes a free *white* man, and a citizen of the United States to all intents and purposes.

The premise of such a text would seem to be that "race" was foremost a mathematical problem, and that "algebraical notations" could resolve some of the political issues of mankind. Hence a social assumption could be presented as if it were a mathematical law: "a third cross clears the blood." Yet there are odd things about this text. The animal story (perhaps alluding to the beast with two backs in *Othello*) that is employed in order to present "natural" evidence that a "fourth cross" is equivalent to "the original blood"—in order, really, to argue *against* the "one-drop rule"—turns, allegorically considered, into a tale of repeated incest committed by the Merino ram, first with his own daughter, then his granddaughter, and finally his great-granddaughter. The real individual disappears behind images of "blood" and "generation" that are no less metaphoric for being expressed in precise fractions. The mathematics obscures more than it clarifies: it is a way of saying, in so many formulae, fractions, and equations, that there is a dividing line, a cutoff point for "whiteness" that does not, however, always "coincide" with freedom—an issue decided by historical matrilineage and law, not by the "natural" realm of fractions.[5]

The fractions, especially the more intricate ones that serve to draw out the nuances of the only boundary that matters, are likely to intimidate the nonexpert. The text embodies the dialectic of Enlightenment, though in its attempt at systematizing interracial locations it expresses not so much the curiosity of the scientist or his or her service in the description of knowledge as the perhaps unconscious desire to make the findings compatible with the existence of an ultimate racial boundary that would support the notion of racial difference. The mathematical approach moves into the realm of "science" what amounts to little more than the telling of an animal story that serves as a complex legitimation of racial hierarchy (though "slavery" was theoretically differentiated from "race" in the text). It is thus a case of scientism in the service of establishing "race." Tellingly, the "purity" of the "original" lower-case and upper-case races is simply taken for granted as constituting a genetic 100 percent of itself. In other words, the formulae direct the reader's attention to the later mingling while simply assuming as an unstated given that $a$ and $A$ are not so much specific human beings as merely "pure black" and "pure white" specimens.[6] The pseudoscience of amalgamation may thus help to establish the original existence of pure races in analogy to pure metals and liquids. As a result of the magic of the fractions of "amalgamation," "race" becomes as primal as a chemical element.

It is precisely this aspect of such models that has been attacked by modern writers like Jean Toomer, who in an unpublished essay entitled "The Americans" denounced this use of a scientistic analogy and argued:

> This new race is neither white nor black nor red nor brown. These are the old terms for old races, and they must be discarded. This is a new race; and though to some extent, to be sure, white and black and red and brown strains have entered into its formation, we should not view it as part white, part black, and so on. . . . Water, though composed of two parts of hydrogen and one part of oxygen, is not hydrogen and oxygen; it is *water*, a new substance with a new form.[7]

And while this statement may simply be using another form of scientism in praise of "chemical fusion" rather than of "pure elements," Toomer also added perceptively that "there are no differences between the blood of a Caucasian and the blood of a Negro as there are between hydrogen and oxygen."

The example of 1815 may sound absurd indeed. Yet are these the idiosyncratic shortcomings of one specific text—that tells a repeated animal incest story in order to give "race" a valence of "species" in the modern sense, impresses the reader with scientistic formulae, and quietly establishes original, pure, and hierarchically arranged races as an unquestioned and unquestionable hypothesis—or are these features shared by all, or many, attempts at classifying races and interracial relations? Would our exemplary text be qualitatively different if it did *not* use the term "Quarteroon"—or, conversely, if it drew on more terms such as "Octoroon" instead of saying "eighth"? And how do the different mathematical classifications translate into literary texts?

## *Mestizaje* and Racial Dualism

Some recent appoaches have offered the names and terms associated with the classifications of interracial mingling evoked by the Spanish term *mestizaje* as quasi-utopian concepts that would run against and subvert the sharpness and terror of dualistic racial societies and their systems of domination.[8] It is true that proliferating terms can offer a powerful challenge to the binarism of "either black or white" and that some systems were established with the best scientific intentions. For example, as we have seen, Jean-Baptiste Labat's interest in observing the generation of Mulattoes and their descendants was to demonstrate the equal force of the male and the female parent. In fact, Labat continued his argument with an imagined generational sequence:

> If one marries Mulattoes, male or female, with whites, the children emerging will be much whiter, their hair much less curly. In the third generation one will only recognize them by the white of the eyes which always tends to look a bit hazy. . . . Should one ally them with blacks, they would return in the same number of generations to their previous blackness.[9]

Labat thus sketched a three-generation process and a minimal classification system. And the sets of eighteenth-century paintings of mixed families in the Ethnological Museum of Madrid and the Ethnographic Museum of Trocadero that Manuel Alvar describes and partly reproduces in his *Lexico del mestizaje en Hispanoamerica* (1987) similarly serve the interest of classification and of rules that has its counterpart in an apparently precise semantic system of terms for each combination: for example, from an anonymous series, *De Mulato y Mestiza nace Cuarterón* ("From a Mulatto Man and a Mestiza (half-Indian) Woman Is Born a Quadroon")[10] or, from another series by Ignacio de Castro, *De Español y Mulata nace Morisco* ("From a Spaniard and a Mulatta a "Morisco" Is Born") (Figs. 23 and 24).[11] Such paintings may not only convey a sense of collective origins to multiracial societies but also help to normalize interracial generations by giving them names and connecting them to the daily lives of different castes of people. We can readily imagine the effect of such images on children and adolescents in racially segregated societies if we remember Durham's capitalized term "UNTHINKABLE" to describe interracial alliances or recall the demands to suppress even a representation of a black and a white *rabbits'* wedding. Judith Wilson concluded that even while these portraitures of the "elaborate taxonomies" of *las castas* "document social distinctions and at times the racial stereotypes that reinforced them" and do *not* offer any evidence

**Figure 23** *De Mulato y Mestiza nace Cuarterón*
(18th c.)

**Figure 24** Ignacio de Castro, *De Español y Mulata nace Morisco* (18th c.)

that their painters meant to "criticize the prevailing system," it is still important to observe that "corresponding works by North Americans are few" since the subject of "miscegenation" was too controversial in the United States.[12] Marc Shell also accentuated the positive in Latin American racial terminologies when he argued that these terms can have "certain practical benefits" as they suggest "the reality of racial miscegenation (which the United States did not)" and as they also "allow for the conceptual distinction of race from class."[13] These advantages may, however, be offset by problems in the legacy of *mestizaje*.

For example, Julien-Joseph Virey's influential system, in his *Histoire naturelle du genre humain* (1801), goes beyond dualism, shares some features with our initial example, and is relatively uncomplicated in its definition of intermediate, fractionally defined "products or castes" that are between white (*blanc*) and black (*noir*).

| Parents | Produits ou castes | Degrés de mélanges | |
|---------|--------------------|--------------------|---|
| Blanc et noir | Mulâtre | $\frac{1}{2}$ blanc | $\frac{1}{2}$ noir |
| Blanc et mulâtre | Terceron saltatras | $\frac{3}{4}$ blanc | $\frac{1}{4}$ noir |
| Noir et mulâtre | Griffe ou zambo | $\frac{3}{4}$ noir | $\frac{1}{4}$ blanc |
| Blanc et terceron | Quarteron | $\frac{7}{8}$ blanc | $\frac{1}{8}$ noir |
| Noir et terceron | Quarteron saltatras | $\frac{7}{8}$ noir | $\frac{1}{8}$ blanc |
| Blanc et quarteron | Quinteron | $\frac{15}{16}$ blanc | $\frac{1}{16}$ noir |
| Noir et quarteron | Quinteron saltatras | $\frac{15}{16}$ noir | $\frac{1}{16}$ blanc[14] |

Virey's scheme uses a relatively small number of racial terms (but more than just two or three), and the numerical progression might suggest, at first glance, a more natural harmony between "race" and the tortured mathematics than in the first example. This impression is, however, undercut by the use of such blatantly racist terms as "saltatras"—or "jumpback"—which reveal the underlying sense of a sharp white-black hierarchy.[15] In 1774 Edward Long used the English equivalent "RETRO-GRADE" in his discussion of the "different castes" that the "intermixture of Whites, Blacks, and Indians" has generated in Jamaica; Hensley Woodbridge reports a gloss of the Venezuelan term "salta atrás" according to which the "offspring is so-called, because instead of advancing somewhat (i.e. in whiteness), it goes backward to a great or lesser degree."[16] This highlights the first general problem with such classification systems: they may imagine a progression *from* black *to* white (in this aspect also resembling the phrase, "clearing the blood"), while the opposite movement that the scheme also represents is believed to be "regressive," leading to "throwbacks."

This is precisely what Michèle Duchet notices and criticizes in the schemes of de Pauw and Buffon. Focusing on the tension between their perfect respect for arithmetical proportions (to the point of "delirium of rationality") and their authoritative enunciation of racial typologies and divisions, Duchet reminds the student of racial mathematics that the underlying social question was *not* the experimental division of genetic matter in people whose position could best be described in certain fractions, but the decision whether real individuals would be free or enslaved—and, if free, what their social status would be. This is what already struck Alexander von Humboldt when he reported the calculus of color in New Spain and found that in the constitution of a new pseudoaristocracy on the basis of color it became important for vanity and public recognition that the percentage of European blood that was ascribed to each social caste would have to be determined most precisely.[17]

De Pauw's four-generation system, for example, is beautifully visualized (again, with some different terms) in John Stedman's *Narrative of a Five Years Expedition Against the Revolted Negroes of Surinam* (1796) as a perfectly symmetrical arrangement of a progression from white to black and from black to white, entitled "Gradation of Shades Between Europe & Africa"[18] (Fig. 25). From the "Mulatto" position at the center the model offers two diametrically opposed directions of "gradation": three generations of alliances either with whites or with blacks lead to the category "White" on the left and to the term "Black" on the right side. Stedman's image thus visualizes "Black" and "White" as separated by four generations and, apparently, united in the central and perhaps original position of the Mulatto. Yet despite the implicit claims of a unity of the human species in such a chart and the occasional assertion by some intellectuals that crossing races may ennoble and perfect humanity, the presumed superiority of the white race strongly suggested that, even though the symmetry of the reversible mathematical formulae could work in either direction, what was really at stake was the whitening of blacks, and hardly the reverse.[19] An underlying question was: How many generations would it take to move from black to white?

In this question a second problem with classification schemes becomes apparent. In their differing quests for cutoff points and dividing lines, they may indeed take mathematics to the point of delirium in determining at what stage the goal of whiteness could be reached: three, four, five, six, seven, or more generations? Though Virey's system lacked animal references or an excessive use of overly complicated formulae, the sense is even more pronounced there than in the opening example that this form of counting could go on ad infinitum since there is no point at

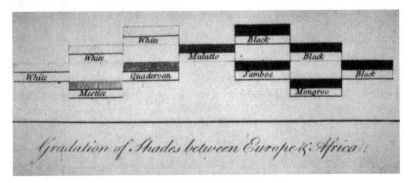

**Figure 25** John Stedman, "Gradation of Shades between Europe and Africa" (1796)

which black ancestry does *not* seem to matter—as would be the case independent of the issues of slavery and matrilineage.

This issue becomes clear in the next example, the novel *Bug-Jargal* (second edition, 1826), in which Victor Hugo gives the following explanation of the term "Griffe":

> An accurate definition of terms will perhaps be necessary to the understanding of this word. M. Moreau de Saint Méry, developing the system of Franklin, has classed in generic species the different tints which the mixture of the colored population presents. He supposes man to form, by the union of whites with whites and blacks with blacks, a totality capable of division into one hundred and twenty-eight parts. Proceeding on this principle, he affirms that an individual is near or distant from either color, as he approaches or recedes from the sixty-fourth term, which constitutes the proportional mean. According to this system, every man who is not eight parts white is accounted black. From black to white nine principal stocks are distinguished, with intermediate varieties according to the greater or less number of parts which they retain of one or the other color. These nine species are the sacatra, the griffe, the marabout, the mulatto, the quadroon, the mongrel, the mamelouc, the quateronne and the sang-mêlé. The sang-mêlé, continuing its amalgamation with the white blood, is finally lost in it. We are assured, however, that there is always perceptible on a particular part of the body the ineffaceable trace of its origin. The griffe is the result of five combinations, and may possess from twenty-four to thirty-two parts white blood, and from eighty-six to one hundred and four black. (26–27n)[20]

Hugo explicitly states here that he adheres to Médéric-Louis-Élie Moreau de Saint-Méry's well-summarized, comprehensive scientific system of classification, revised from Franklin's, as Hugo claims.[21] Moreau de Saint-Méry's startling system, fully developed in his *Description topographique, physique, civile, politique et historique de la Partie Française de l'Isle Saint-Domingue* (1797), looks at times like a parody of Enlightenment algebra. Moreau takes nearly twenty pages of charts, calculations, and classifications in order to distinguish thirteen basic nuances of color, each of which can be arrived at through several different types of interracial mixing, yet all this machinery, including the 128 parts that are presumed to constitute each individual's seven-generation ancestry, only helps to draw (once again) an ultimate cutoff point of convenience rather than any absolute, let alone "scientific," demarcation. The only problem is that the cutoff point for white may begin to approach the mystical, as Moreau finds the *Sang-mêlé* with $\frac{1}{64}$ black blood "steadily approaching the White"—though he added in the manuscript "without ever merging with him absolutely."[22] And in what may be the most extreme instance in which racial ancestry has been registered, short of the mathematical infinity implied in the phrasing "any ascertainable trace" or its more popular synonym "one drop," is in Moreau de Saint-Méry's assertion that in

Santo Domingo there are mixed-bloods who have only $\frac{1}{512}$ of African blood.[23]

That this sort of record-keeping approached infinity was noticed by George Washington Cable. Commenting on the persistence of the white American's view of the black as "alien," Cable wrote in "The Freedman's Case in Equity" (1889):

> The occasional mingling of his blood with that of the white man worked no change in the sentiment; one, two, four, eight multiplied upon or divided into zero still gave zero for the result. Generations of American nativity made no difference; his children and children's children were born in sight of our door, yet the old notion held fast.[24]

The calculus of color seems to place its fractions between zero and infinity, and by inserting "zero," Cable works within the mathematical context yet drives home the critical point that racial mingling is not at all a matter of fractions but of attitudes. Simone Vauthier noted that such attempts to define precisely what "admixture of black blood makes a person a Negro" can "have but a *legal* value,"

> for it cannot help displacing the problem, with percentages varying from 1/4th to 1/8th, 1/16th, "one drop of Negro blood," until one comes full circle to the *imaginary* underlying point; when "*any ascertainable* trace of Negro blood" is enough to define the non-white, one is still left with the boggling uncertainty of the ascertainable trace.[25]

The fact that the smallest fractions and invisible parts can have status-defining power highlights the next problem with *mestizaje* schemes. The symmetry of an outline like Stedman's is not suggestive of equality, as the "nonwhite blood" seems to carry more genetic weight than "white blood." Why should 75 percent of white blood not weigh more than 25 percent black blood, Léon-François Hoffmann wonders, and gives the answer that unsymmetrical ancestry-counting reveals the absurdity of racist philosophy. Which exchange rate, Hoffmann asks sarcastically, should be established between the "purifying European blood cells" and the "corrupting Senegalese plasma"?[26] The implausibility of racial quantifications becomes clear in statements like that made by Zoe to her beloved George Peyton in Dion Boucicault's play *The Octoroon* (1859), a text from the United States that gives much weight to a racial location between black and white:

> Of the blood that feeds my heart, one drop in eight is black—bright red as the rest may be, that one drop poisons all the flood; those seven bright drops give me love like yours—hope like yours—ambition like yours—life hung with passions like dew-drops on the morning-flowers; but the one black drop gives me despair, for I'm an unclean thing—forbidden by the laws—I'm an Octoroon![27]

The very insistence on the mathematics of fractions taken to the melo-dramatic point of an articulation that aims at evoking audience empathy suggests that what is at work is primarily cultural (an internalization of power relations and prejudice) and not "scientific" (a matter of genealog-ical percentages and precise mathematical fractions). As Hoffmann sum-marized the French exercises in "haematological science," they repre-sented a West Indian terminology that was incorporated into French in order to measure the degree of impurity in the blood of each Mulatto—and this was not an abstract scientific issue but one quite practically felt in political and social life since the Haitian revolution.[28] In his emphasis on asymmetry, Hoffmann's critique of an intricate terminological scheme resembles that made by Naomi Zack of racial dualism, for Zack sees in it an asymmetrical schema that "logically precludes the possibility of mixed race because cases of mixed race, in which individuals have both black and white forebears, are automatically designated as cases of black race."[29] (It is from the point of view of such critiques, however, that *mestizaje* models sometimes seem to contain more verisimilitude.)

Theoretically speaking, it is, of course, not necessary to assume that any attempt at classifying racial mixing, at devising a terminology for the language of *mestizaje*, would have to be compromised by the simultane-ous establishment of a presumed initial purity, of a racial hierarchy embodied in a movement from black to white, and of a principle of exclu-sion expressed in near-mystical mathematical formulae that would give unequal weight to the black and white parts. In practical terms, however, many efforts at creating such systems of racial mixing and their impres-sive varieties of names for mixed-race persons emerged in the context of colonialism and bear the mark of an interest that could also—and at times seemed specifically designed to—support racially based domina-tion. In empirical history, both sets of assumptions—*mestizaje* and racial dualism—were seriously implicated in the construction of race as a legit-imation of slavery and caste hierarchy. This is also what some compar-isons of dualistic and *mestizaje* systems have concluded.

It should of course be noted that the Latin American classification sys-tems have varied greatly from country to country, in the course of their historical development, and that there is a difference between termino-logical schemes and actual usage: many terms may have been applied only very rarely in any strict sense. Marvin Harris, for example, tested the precision of the Brazilian terms and in 1970 reported what he called "Referential Ambiguity in the Calculus of Brazilian Racial Identity."[30] According to Harris, most terms were used imprecisely, and Brazilians called "almost any combination of racial features by the terms *moreno* or *mulato* with a high but unpatterned frequency." Harris accounts for his findings by noting that the function of such terms may serve not "the maintenance of orderly distinctions" but the "maximization of noise and ambiguity in the calculus under discussion" (12). He argues that "there is a correspondence between class and race in Brazil . . .; the more negroid the phenotype, the lower the class." Hence the "noise" of all the various terms that may help prevent "the development of racial ideology may very well be a reflex of the conditions which control the development of class confrontations," with the result that whereas the lower class is fragmented by race in the United States, it has tended to be united in the Brazilian system. Harris draws an interesting distinction between racial dualism and the nomenclature of *mestizaje*:

> "Black power" in the United States lacks the revolutionary potential of the preponderant mass; "black power" in Brazil contains this potential. The ambiguity built into the Brazilian calculus of racial identity is thus, speculatively at least, as intelligible as the relative precision with which blacks and whites identify each other in the United States.[31]

For Harris the calculus of color differentiation is as "intelligible" as a strictly biracial arrangement since it also obscures class and power relations, only in a different way, which is presumably why it would seem progressive from a North American point of view.[32] Verena Stolcke describes eighteenth-century society in the Spanish colonies as "a complex and multicolored human mosaic of inequalities—the result of the interaction between the criteria of class and race to the benefit of some (Creole and Spanish-born whites) and the detriment of everyone else," and Magnus Mörner finds that socioracial terminology "always reflected disdain."[33]

Dualistic as well as *mestizaje* arrangements could be used for the construction of racial hierarchies, though the latter tended to give more room to class simply by differentiating racial categories to the point at which class factors could permit racial reclassifications: "money bleaches" is the appropriate Brazilian proverb that does not equally apply to dualistic societies.[34] Dualistic models—though they were probably somewhat less rigidly applied than is often believed—did not allow for such fluidity and tended to make invisible the fact of interracial mingling. The appeals to symmetry made by both systems were often illusory.

What speaks for Duchet's (and Humboldt's) argument that classification schemes are primarily *social* instruments—and not the scientific or biological findings that they appear to be—is the fact that such genealogies are hardly part of a continued scientific interest from antiquity to the modern age, but are probably creations of the fifteeenth and sixteenth centuries, the period of the discovery of America and the beginning of the African slave trade. Thus many of the earliest examples for the thinking in racial fractions and the invention of new terms to go along with them, as they are explored in Manuel Alvar's comprehensive study, fall into the period after the second half of the sixteenth century: after a few isolated instances of this term or that, it appears to have been the Peruvian historian Garcilaso de la Vega (1539–1616), called "el Inca," who developed the first attempts at a more comprehensive terminology in 1605, gave a precise definition of "Creole," and is credited with having coined such terms as "Quarterón, or Quatratuo."[35] While the true mathematical systems proliferated in the second half of the eighteenth and the first half of the nineteenth century, many different terms were invented to name the various interracial locations. The Spanish terms were rich in suggesting all kinds of European-African-Indian mixes, and in the ethnographic paintings we have already encountered such words as "Mestizo"—a term used by Garcilaso that originated in vulgar Latin *mixticius*, "mixed," and from which *mestizaje* is, of course, derived, as are the English terms "Mustee" and "Mestee."[36]

When it comes to black-white crosses, there were essentially two ways of naming, both based on forms of generational counting. According to the first method, descendants who are two, three, four, five, or more generations away from a founding, interracial moment that is taken as the point of origin receive names like *Tercerón*, *Quarterón*, or *Quinterón*—the way Long or Virey proceeded. The second and more popular method (adopted by de Pauw, Buffon and many other intellectuals, and the way our first text was organized, without, however, using names exhaustively) was to find terms that are the equivalents of half, quarter, eighth, and smaller fractions.[37] It appears that only this second method has elicited significant semantic echoes in the United States, where some detailed distinctions were drawn in the law-books, especially in sections prohibiting intermarriage, but where the most dramatic and only truly significant opposition has remained (or become) that between "white" and "non-white."[38] Thus contemporary census forms discourage biracial or multiracial identification.[39]

Characteristic of this tendency toward racial dualism is the following dialogue from a purported letter by Augusta to her sister in Anna Dickinson's novel *What Answer?* (1868):

> "'You will not deny that you are a negro, at least a mulatto.'
>
> "'Pardon me, madam,' she replied; 'my father is a mulatto, my mother was an Englishwoman. Thus, to give you accurate information upon the subject, I am a quadroon.'
>
> "'Quadroon be it!' I answered, angrily again, I fear. 'Quadroon, mulatto, or negro, it is all one. . . .'" (153)

And almost a century later, Frank Yerby in *The Foxes of Harrow* (1946) lets the dialogue between Stephen and his son Etienne follow similar lines:

> "But I must say ye've become quite democratic, 'Tienne—crossing swords with mulattoes."
>
> "Mulattoes!"
>
> "Aye—but then he's probably a quadroon or an octoroon—I don't

know how to draw those nice distinctions in blood lines like a native Louisianian." (268)

Here a difference is made between the United States model and the Louisiana way. Invoking rationalistic mathematical fractions does not really work, as Mark Twain suggested in *Pudd'nhead Wilson*. Characterizing the fair-complexioned and soft-haired Roxy, he writes:

> To all intents and purposes Roxy was as white as anybody, but the one sixteenth of her which was black outvoted the other fifteen parts and made her a negro.[40]

It may seem paradoxical to Mark Twain's narrator that Roxy should be classified as "Negro," but he does not choose a more subtle terminology to resolve the problem at hand. Unlike Hugo, who could draw on such terms as "Griffe" or *Sang-mêlé*, authors of the United States did not very often use racial names for characters whose precise racial composition was nonetheless described. For example, in the novel *Crescent Carnival* (1942), by Frances Parkinson Keyes, Anna expresses the need for a term for someone with one-sixteenth black blood in order to "define" Laure, who, though a cousin, was born "on the wrong side of the blanket": "An octoroon—no not an octoroon, for Laure was only one-sixteenth colored. What did you call a girl who was only one-sixteenth colored?" (401). The novel provides no answer to that question.

## Quadroon, Octoroon, Mulatto, and Hybrid

Although in the United States terms such as "Quadroon" and "Octoroon" were sometimes used (and other terms very infrequently), the distinctions were often blurred, were perhaps even more imprecise than those terms Harris observed in Brazil. The English word "Quadroon" was derived from the Spanish *Cuarterón*, a term which goes back to Garcilaso in his *Historia de la Florida* (1605)—who, however, called the person with one-fourth of Indian ancestry "Quarterón," which became the standard French word.[41] The term could refer to one-quarter admixture of either white or black (or Indian) blood, and hence to a person with one grandparent of a different race. The title of Lydia Maria Child's short story "The Quadroons" (1842) suggests that in the United States the term was metaphoric rather than indicative of a precise genealogical location, since both a mother and her daughter by a white man are referred to by that name. The explanatory move that the narrator makes in Joseph Holt Ingraham's novel *The Quadroone; or, St. Michael's Day* (1841) at first seems similar to Victor Hugo's invoking of Moreau de Saint-Méry, though Ingraham apparently feels that he owes a particular definition of the term in his title. Yet the author clearly does *not* draw on scientific works while draping his narrative voice in merely the invocation of their authority—with slightly comical results that might be obvious even to a casual reader who has ever pondered any aspect of family genealogy:

> A Quadroon, strictly, is one whose blood is four part European and one part African. This amalgamation is expressed in the French words *Quatre et une*, or *Quatr'une*, from which comes the Anglo corruption of QUADROON. Those, however, who retain even a tenth part of the African blood, and, to all appearance, are as fair as Europeans, and undistinguished from them save by the remarkable and undefinable expression of the eyes, which always betrays their remote Ethiopian descent, come also under the general designation of "Quadroon" (ix).

Unlike Hugo, Ingraham does not indicate a scientific source, and judging by the nature of the information he offers it is doubtful whether he has consulted one. In any event, his etymology was probably improvised; and his mathematics for the calculus of color is startlingly uninformed by the most basic recognition that it is hard to convert ancestry-counting (which—barring incest—has to run 2, 4, 8, 16, 32, 64, 128, 256—and, at least for Moreau de Saint-Méry, 512—based on the number of parents, grandparents, and their more distant antecedents) into a (decimal?) system that would include such units as "tenth" and "fifth." For Ingraham, the function of the term "Quadroon" obviously was not that it established a precise genealogical position but that it provided a name for characters who, "to all appearance, are as fair as Europeans," even though they retain what he somehow calculated to be "a tenth part of the African blood." The term "Quadroon" thus marks a character with some "black" ancestry who could be taken for "white"—a situation which has plot consequences in courtship situations.[42] It is probably for this reason that Ingraham also attempted to launch an English gender differentiation in the term:

> As Quadroons are of both sexes, and the English word is not distinctive, the author, in order to avoid confusion, has restored the feminine termination, *e*, of the French phrase, which is *quatr'une* feminine, but *quatr'un* masculine, distinguishing them throughout the volumes as Quadroon and Quadroone, according to sex. (ix)

Ingraham's purpose in making this distinction becomes clearer in such chapter titles as "Scene in a Quadroone's Boudoir." Though contemporary critics have occasionally reawakened a gender distinction between "Mulatto" and "Mulatta," Ingraham's differentiation of "Quadroon" and "Quadroone" appears to have remained without many successors.[43]

The word "Octoroon," according to the *Oxford English Dictionary* a "non-etymological formation" from Latin *octo* and on the analogy of "Quadroon," may actually derive from the Spanish *Ochavón* (first documented in 1740 in Joseph Gumilla's *El Orinoco Ilustrado*) and the French *Octavon*, which—together with "Quarteron"—was used by Cornelius de Pauw (1774) and accepted by Buffon (1777).[44] "Octoroon" originally referred to one-eighth admixture of either white or black blood, and hence to a person with one great-grandparent of another race. In the United States the word was probably made most popular by Dion Boucicault's play *The Octoroon* (1859). The term often became connected with what has been called the stereotype of the "Tragic Mulatto"; thus in *Kingsblood Royal* (1947), Sinclair Lewis makes fun of the Octoroon clichés, when he lets Sophie say to Neil:

> Mister, don't you realize what I am? I'm that beautiful convent-trained New Orleans octoroon, the passionate slave-girl with the lambent eyes and long raven tresses, standing on the block with hot blushes, and practically nothing else on, before the leering planters (or theatrical agents) with their beaver hats and beaver watch-chains. But one young man there, young Nevil Valhoun Kingsblood of Kingsblood Corners, Kentucky, pities her, and soon, along the gal'ry of a mysterious old mansion nigh Lexington, there is to be seen a veiled figure gliding—lookit her glide, lookit her, the *nebig*! (150)

One perhaps exceptional case in which the distinction between the categories "Quadroon" and "Octoroon" was plot-constitutive was Charles Chesnutt's novel *The House Behind the Cedars* (1900). Advised by Judge Straight, John Walden, who wants to be a lawyer, learns that although he is "black" in North Carolina where the color line is drawn "at four generations removed from the negro," he could still be "white" in South Carolina where the law stipulates that it is justifiable to consider a person "white in whom the admixture of African blood did not exceed one eighth." The judge adds: "They're more liberal there, perhaps because they have many more blacks than whites, and would like to lessen the disproportion."[45] The young man follows the advice and becomes a lawyer in the state with the more liberal cutoff point.

The apparently neutral logic of mathematical fractions implied in the terms "Octoroon" and "Quadroon" is at odds with the etymology of others. A closer look at the various names given to the "racial crosses" of *mestizaje* reveals that *saltatras* is not an exception, and that the animal imagery of our first example is pervasive. This is most obvious in the case of the most frequently used word for the person who is at the half-way point between races. Such terms as *Mestizo* or *Métif* (English "Mustee") could perhaps mark this point semantically, but the word that was far more popular in many languages—and the only one that was widely used in the British colonies—was "Mulatto."

The word "Mulatto," of sixteenth-century Spanish origin, documented in English since 1595, and designating a child of a black and a white parent, was long considered etymologically derived from "mule"; yet it may also come from the Arabic word *muwallad* (meaning "Mestizo" or mixed).[46] The zoological analogy with mules may thus not have been the word's original, or exclusive, etymological source, but the term "Mulatto" certainly did become intertwined with the animal that was a cross between two *species*; and numerous texts have explicated, or alluded to, the etymology. Thus Samuel Johnson's *Dictionary* (1755) defined the word as "one begot between a white and a black, as a mule between different species of animals."[47] And the parallel was echoed in the foundational statements of racism such as Edward Long's proclamation that Mulattoes seem to be "of the mule-kind" (1774) and Josiah Clark Nott's already cited declaration that Mulattoes were "the offspring of two distinct species—as the mule from the horse and the ass" (1843).[48] As late as 1916, J. E. Wodsalek argued in the *Biological Bulletin* that "the Negro is fully as far removed from the white man as is the ass from the horse."[49]

Given this context, it is not surprising that as early as in Victor Hugo's *Bug-Jargal* (1826) there is evidence that the word "Mulatto" was looked upon as a term of contempt that some "men of color" (*hommes de couleur*) would not apply to themselves. "If you were really a mulatto . . . you would not make use of the term," the revolutionary Rigaud tells a character; and Hugo annotates: "It must be remembered that the men of color indignantly rejected this nomenclature, which was invented by the whites in derision, they said."[50] Hensley Woodbridge also reports that in Cuba, Brazil, Argentina, and the West Indies the term "has an unpleasant connotation for some people."[51] Hortense Spillers would seem to second this point, when she stated: "Neither the enslaved man/woman, nor the fugitive-in-freedom would call *himself/herself* 'mulatto/a.'"[52] In the 1980s and 1990s, however, the term seems to have been adopted again by writers and intellectuals. For example, Trey Ellis reported in "The New Black Aesthetic" (1989) that the kinds of contradictory responses he received made him adopt a symbolic identification as "Mulatto": "It wasn't unusual for me to be called 'oreo' and 'nigger' on the same day. . . . I realized I was a cultural mulatto."[53] And Jimmy Pierre stated in *Black, White, Other* (1994), seemingly drawing on the putative Arabic etymology of the term:

I have an ex-girlfriend, she was telling me, "You're not mulatto, you're black."

I said, "No, I'm not." I said, "I'm a mulatto," which means a mixture of colors in Spanish. . . .

It's not like you just have to make a stand, you know, like it used to be with Black Power? *Black Power! Black Power!*

*Mulatto Power! Mulatto Power!* There's not a lot of that going on, but I do want actively to be involved with things that have to do with being interracial. I think it's great.[54]

The call for "Mulatto Power!"—voiced by Pierre in explicit analogy to

"Black Power"—may mark a turning point in racial symbolism of the United States, which may be moving in the direction of the Latin American models at this moment. If the term "Mulatto" may thus be undergoing a reevaluation, this is even more the case with the recent uses of the word "hybridity."

The popular version of the etymology of Mulatto is widely familiar and often mentioned in the secondary literature; but those scholars and writers who have adopted the more neutral-seeming term "hybridity" in order to articulate their opposition to the binarism of black-white race thinking (at times accompanied by an explicit valorization of *mestizaje*) might be surprised to find in the *Oxford English Dictionary* that the origin of "hybrid," derived from Latin "*hybrida*, more correctly hibrida (ibrida)," is the "offspring of a tame sow and a wild boar; hence, of human parents of different races, half-breed." It was Isidore of Seville who illustrated the progeny of different parent animals ("bigenera") with such examples as the mule (Latin *mulus*, of mare and male donkey), the hinny (Latin *burdo*, of stallion and female donkey), and the hybrid (Latin *hybrida* of sow and boar).[55] The sow-and-boar origin of the word thus makes the word "hybrid" no more human than its popular etymology makes "Mulatto." Josiah Nott's consequential essay of 1843 was, after all, entitled "The Mulatto a Hybrid—probable extermination of the two races if the Whites and Blacks are allowed to intermarry." Nott's reason for this startling headline and the basis for his segregationist argument was the "Mulatto sterility hypothesis" as a quasi-logical extension of the popular etymology of "Mulatto."

## Mulatto Sterility vs. Hybrid Vigor

The Mulatto sterility hypothesis that has much to do with the rejection of the term by some writers is only half as old as the word "Mulatto." Apparently, it goes back to a text that has commanded our attention before. I mean Edward Long's anonymously published *The History of Jamaica* (1774) which, as we saw, made the double claim that "the White and the Negroe are two distinct species" and that Mulattoes seem to be "of the mule-kind." Long's "proof" lay in his belief that Mulattoes are supposedly "not so capable of producing from one another as from a commerce with a distinct White or Black." On the one hand Long thought that Mulattoes were suited to form the "centre of connexion between the two extremes." On the other, although he referred to Mulattoes as a "species," he perceived them not as a fixed grouping but as a short-lived intermediary category. The story that Long tells deserves to be cited at length:

> The Mulattoes are, in general, well-shaped, and the women well-featured.
> . . . Some few of them have intermarried here with those of their own com-

plexion; but such matches have generally been defective and barren.... [I]t seems extraordinary, that two Mulattos, having intercourse together, should be unable to continue their species, the woman either proving barren, or their offspring, if they have any, not attaining to maturity; when the same man and woman, having commerce with a White or Black, would generate a numerous issue. Some examples may possibly have occurred, where, upon the intermarriage of two Mulattos, the woman has borne children, which children have grown to maturity: but I never heard of such an instance; and may we not suspect the lady, in those cases, to have privately intrigued with another man, a White perhaps?

Long's story reveals the extent to which ideological desire overwhelms possible empirical counterevidence; he was an observer who knew West Indian life—and yet he could make a claim that ran against any experience, though it did confirm the putative etymology of the word "Mulatto." He offered the familiar adultery supposition in order to account for the generative ability of mixed-race people, and his remarkable qualification of the Mulattoes' supposed "infertility"—that their children would grow to "maturity"—was one "that no reputable scientist applied to other hybrids."[56] Long is furthermore quite aware of how his view of things tends to support the possibility "that the White and the Negroe had not one common origin," a rethinking he explicitly associates with the Copernican challenge that polygenism presented to ecclesiastical doctrine.[57]

What is noteworthy for the questions posed earlier in the present chapter is the fact that Long articulated his consequential hypothesis in a book that also gave room to a modified *mestizaje* scheme: hence one centerpiece of modern racism emerged *not* in the context of pure racial binarism, but in a (West Indian rather than a fuller Latin American) system of interracial generation—which, however, led its author to the conclusion that from Mulatto and Mulatto, *nobody* was born (or, at least, no one who would survive for two generations).[58] It has already been stressed that this belief found widespread support. In 1799 Charles White accepted Long's hypothesis in a passage previously cited.[59] Josiah Clark Nott was inspired by Long's theory to misinterpret the census of 1840 so as to find Mulattoes disappearing and thus helped to promulgate the Mulatto sterility hypothesis (he stressed the version that they supposedly had a low life expectancy).[60] Nott's argument is very strange: he realizes that he is off the mark once he mentions New Orleans, and so he simply posits a biracial system constituted only of Anglo-Saxons and Negroes (excluding the French, who were obviously "white" yet whose Creole offspring of all colors showed no signs of sterility). Nott's dream was that of a classless white master race. Although his democratic (or perhaps more precisely, upwardly mobile) animus was directed against hereditary hierarchy, he thought of whites as a new aristocracy: "*nature's noblemen*...often spring from the families of the backwoodsmen, or the sturdy mechanic." Blacks, however, were a different "species," forever determined by heredity.[61] And Mulattoes who had to serve as the proof of the difference were argued out of existence. Suggesting at least a "weakening" of the offspring of amalgamation thus became crucial to racial theory. This counterfactual ideology probably spread more easily as it exploited, and seemed to legitimate, hostility to interracial alliances.

In 1860, W.W. Wright argued, in an essay anonymously published in *De Bow's Review* and entitled "Amalgamation," that the so-called "prejudice of color" should be more properly termed *"aversion to hybridity . . . on the part of the whites, that will preserve the black and white races from destroying one another by amalgamation, and prevent all of those evils which we have shown to be everywhere entailed upon the mulatto breed."* The scientific justification of Wright's strenuous opposition to what he perceived to be the amalgamationist's wish to turn the United States into "a model republic" came from Nott.[62]

In 1863, the year of the Emancipation Proclamation, the Swiss-American Harvard Professor Louis Agassiz, one of the inventors of scientistic racism, developed his racial views in a series of letters addressed to the former abolitionist Dr. Samuel Gridley Howe, who had become a member of the American Freedman's Inquiry Commission and requested scientific advice.[63] While Agassiz expressed his conviction that the black race would endure in America, perhaps in black states in the South, he doubted whether racial mixtures would be able to survive.

On the one hand, Agassiz warned Howe against any policies that might transform the United States from a "manly population descended from cognate nations" into "the effeminate progeny of mixed races, half indian, half negro, sprinkled with white blood." He alluded to the fearful example of Mexico where the Spaniards could no longer be rescued "from their degradation" and concluded with an expression of horror at the prospect of a similar development north of the border: "In whatever proportion the amalgamation may take place, I shudder from the consequences" (10 August 1863). The biologist considered amalgamation simply "unnatural."[64] "History speaks equally loudly in favor of the mixture of closely related nations, as it condemns the amalgamation of remote races," he argued.

On the other hand, however, Agassiz was also convinced that in the United States the problem would resolve itself by the "natural" weakness of the hybrid offspring, which he repeatedly described in terms of "effeminacy" as opposed to the "manliness" of pure races. His analogy between race and sex summons an image of "unnatural" half-bloods that resembles some popular negative representations of homosexuals, and his language also evokes the sense of incest-toned sterility that is at times associated with aristocrats in bourgeois literature.[65] Agassiz believed that the existence of half-breeds was "likely to be only transient" and recommended that "all legislation with reference to them . . . be regulated with this view & so ordained as to accelerate their disappearance from the Northern States" (10 August 1863). Viewing "pure" races in analogy to *species* and regarding mixed breeds as hybrid aberrations, he thus wrote on 9 August 1863:

> Among the characteristics of halfbreeds one of the most important is their sterility or at least their reduced fecundity. This shows the connections to be contrary to the normal state of the races, as it is contrary to the preservation of the species in the animal kingdom.

Agassiz gave expression to his belief in the Mulattoes' "sickly physique and their impaired fecundity" and viewed Mulattoes only as the "unnatural" progeny of different *species*.

Dr. Samuel Gridley Howe, the addressee of Agassiz's letters, was also among the Commissioners on the Freedman who addressed queries to Congress "as to the capacity and condition of the mulatto, his offspring, and their tendency to bodily and mental decay."[66] Howe concluded, along Agassiz's lines, that "Mulattoism" had impaired "the purity of the national blood taken as a whole," and that given the Mulattoes' susceptibility to disease and relative infertility, "without the continuance of mulatto breeding, in the South. . . mulattoes would soon diminish . . . [and] Mulattoism would fade out from the blood of the Northern States."[67] Samuel Sullivan Cox's congressional speech of 17 February 1864 is typical of the parliamentary mood concerning this issue:

> The physiologist will tell the Gentleman [the authors of the pamphlet *Miscegenation*] that the mulatto does not live; he does not recreate his kind; he is a monster. Such hybrid races by a law of Providence scarcely survive beyond one generation.[68]

In 1869 Benjamin Apthorp Gould of the United States Sanitary Commission confirmed the "well known phenomenon" of the Mulatto's "inferior vitality," and in 1875 Jedediah Hyde Baxter of the Provost Marshall-General's Bureau corroborated this view.[69] In the nineteenth and the first half of the twentieth century the belief that Mulattoes were "feeble" or unable to procreate among themselves, or that their children would be impaired in fertility, had so much political, scientistic, and general intellectual support that it may be called the "dominant opinion" of the period. It permeated intellectual life from local history writing to pronouncements by nationally celebrated scientists. Thus Benjamin Hobart's *History of the Town of Abington* (1866) relates the story of a racially mixed family whose first mixed progenitor, Josiah Thompson, "(it was believed) never became a great-grandfather" (257). Such prominent scientists as the Harvard geologist and paleontologist Nathaniel Southgate Shaler (one of W. E. B. Du Bois's professors) in 1904 invoked general presumption, experience in so far as it has been subjected to any kind of scientific analysis, a large number of physicians, and the observations of his own father in Cuba and the slave-holding South, who stated "that he had never seen mulattos, that is, a cross between pure white and pure black, who had attained the age of sixty years, and that they were often sterile."[70] And the widely read statistician Frederick L. Hoffman cited literature from Nott to Gould in order to arrive at the conclusion, presented to the public under the imprimatur of the American Economic Association, that "the mixed race is physically the inferior of the white and pure black, and as a result of this inferior degree of vital power we meet with a lesser degree of resistance to disease and death among the mixed population."[71]

The obvious argument against Long, Nott, and their descendants was that mixed offspring was "as fruitful as its parents."[72] And indeed, intellectuals from Kant to Buffon made interracial procreation the pivotal element in their approaches to the concept of race. Yet, perhaps animated by the thesis it opposed, a countervailing exaggeration emerged, according to which mixed races were *superior* to their parent stocks. It is the theory that became known as "Hybrid vigor" (the very term a response to the gendered view of Mulatto "effeminacy") and that was, for example, tentatively articulated by Lionel W. Lyde (1911):

> While race blending is not everywhere desirable, yet the crossing of distinct races, especially when it occurs with social sanction, often produces a superior type; certainly such crossing as has occurred tends to prove absurd the conclusion that the dilution of the blood of the so-called higher races by that of the so-called lower races will either set the species on the highway to extinction, or cause a relapse into barbarism.[73]

The theory of "Hybrid vigor" emerged at just about the same time as Long's hypothesis. A famous early example was, once again, Moreau de Saint-Méry's *Description*, the book that set up the 128–part classification system that Hugo invoked in *Bug-Jargal*. Moreau wrote:

> Of all the combinations of white and black, the mulatto unites the most physical advantages. It is he who derives the strongest constitution from these crossings of race, and who is best suited to the climate of St. Domingo. To the strength and soberness of the negro he adds the grace and form of the whites, and of all the human beings of St. Domingo he is the longest lived. [74]

When the *Anglo-African Magazine* responded to Moreau, it was appreciative and tried to stress the visible existence and vitality of racially mixed persons in the New World. A piece from the *Anglo-African Magazine* explicitly cites Moreau de Saint-Méry. J. Dennis Harris draws on heterogeneous sources in order to make his case against the notion prevailing in the United States "that the mulatto has no vitality of race; that after three or four generations he dies out":

This race, if on the white side it derives its blood from either the English or French stock, possesses within itself a combination of all the mental and physical qualities necessary to form a civilized and progressive population for the tropics, *and it is the only race yet found of which this can be said.*[75]

*The Anglo-African* also goes on to argue that it does not want to be considered "Defender of the Mulattoes," but that there should be talk of one *colored nationality* rather than a stress on the divisions between Negroes and Mulattoes.

Other abolitionists praised the Mulatto as a superior human type with less restraint in this respect: Theodore Parker thought in the 1850s that African, Indian, and Anglo-Saxon racial mixing would "furnish a new composite tribe, far better I trust than the old."[76] C. G. Parsons maintained in 1855 that the Mulattoes "are the best specimens of manhood found in the South," offering a reason (as did Moreau) that only reinstated the power of their different racial origins: "The African mothers have given them a good physical system, and the Anglo-Saxon fathers a good mental constitution."[77] Moncure Daniel Conway thought that the "mixture of the blacks and whites is good" because "the person so produced is, under ordinarily favorable circumstances, healthy, handsome, and intelligent." Conway believed that "such a combination would evolve a more complete character than the unmitigated Anglo-Saxon."[78]

A lively debate was generated by the question of whether racial mixing brings down civilization (the familiar racialist position) or stimulates and invigorates cultural activity (Charles Darwin, Thorstein Veblen, the early Havelock Ellis, Robert Park, Everett Stonequist).[79] When Frederick Douglass inserted himself vigorously into such a debate in 1860, he took a sane middle course of supposing equality between "pure" and "mixed" races. Selecting a reader's inquiry to the *Herald of Progress* for his intervention, he claimed that whatever a white "whole" man could do, a Mulatto "half" man could match. Examining height, weight, physical stamina, and so forth, Douglass concluded that there was "not much difference between the '*half*' and the '*whole.*'"[80]

This debate did, of course, have consequences for artistic creation. In simply representing Mulatto characters, writers were inevitably taking sides, and literature functioned as an active participant in an ideological debate. The very choice made by an author whether to create mixed characters *with* families and descendants or to represent them as single, ill, with a low life expectancy, and without children, resonated with cultural expectations and political interests in the real world. One author who openly shows his awareness of such implications is Richard Hildreth, whose narrator states in the expanded versions of his novel, *The White Slave* and *Archy Moore* of 1852 and 1856 (and clearly and explicitly directed against Nott's position), about Archy's son:

I need only add, that Montgomery follows with profit, at Liverpool, the mercantile pursuits to which he had been educated, and that a family of five beautiful and promising children, of which he and Eliza are the happy parents, does not afford much countenance to the nonsensical physiological theory that the mixed race is hybrid and sterile, under which certain American statesmen are endeavoring to find shelter against the growing inevitable danger by which their favorite system of slavery is threatened.[81]

This might be considered a proto-Brechtian incorporation of the explicit terms of the political debate into the literary work itself. Literature is not always this blunt in suggesting the cultural contexts in which plots, characters, and metaphors are devised; yet the relationship undeniably exists.[82] In his novel *Georges* (1843), Alexandre Dumas describes the protagonist Georges Munier in terms that echo the debate, first seemingly making a concession by suggesting his "lack of physical strength," and then mentioning his "vigour."[83] The character Vance states in Epes Sargent's novel *Peculiar* (1864): "The French Quadroons are handsome and healthy, and are believed to be more vigorous than either of the parent races from which they are descended."[84] And Mark Twain's choice to note in Roxy's description "the rosy glow of vigorous health in her cheeks" may constitute a somewhat more subtle participation in this discussion.[85] The function of literature as ideological debating ground was made explicitly thematic in Claude McKay's story "Near-White," when Mrs. Miller says to her daughter Angie:

> You know what they say about us light-colored, what they *write* about us. That we're degenerate, that we're criminal—and their biggest bare-faced lie, that we can't propagate our own stock. They hate us more than they do the blacks. For they're never sure about us, they can't place us.[86]

Perhaps the eeriest emanation is in Fannie Hurst's *Imitation of Life*, in which the mixed-race character Peola actually has herself sterilized—a startling plot development of a novel that was published in the same year that Madison Grant, the president of the New York Zoological Society, stressed the importance of racial segregation and of making knowledge of "methods of Birth Control . . . universally available to the Blacks."[87] The life expectancy of Mulatto characters, their health, strength, and ability to generate a line of descendants, thus inevitably became contributions to a debate.

### Milton Bradley Spin-Top and Forceps

Charles B. Davenport's amazing book *Heredity of Skin Color in Negro-White Crosses* (1913)[88] looks like it was invented in a novel by Ishmael Reed or Charles Johnson. It is a positivistic exercise with charts, interracial family photographs, and genealogical tables, undertaken and completed by one of the leading eugenicists, who was identified in this study as director of the Department of Experimental Evolution at Cold Spring Harbor, and who placed the documentation of his researches in the Eugenics Record Office.[89]

Davenport's project was to determine the heredity of skin color by studying interracial families. Since he found U.S. genealogical records of "colored" people too unreliable or too difficult to obtain he undertook a comparative study of Louisiana, Jamaica, and Bermuda. He was assisted by a Miss Florence H. Danielson, "who had already spent an entire year in field work upon pauper families in rural districts and had been markedly successful in her work" (2). The method was dependent upon an objective scale with which the color of persons of identifiable racial genealogies could be measured and compared. Davenport explains:

> The color determinations were made in the following manner: Miss Danielson visited the homes of the colored people and obtained all of the genealogical data that could be furnished. Then the sleeve was rolled up above the elbow and a part of the skin that is usually covered from the sunlight was thus exposed. The arm was placed on the table by a good light and a Bradley color-top was spun close to the arm and the disks adjusted until they matched, when spun, the color of the skin. Various combinations of black (N), red (R), yellow (Y), and white (W) gave a close approximation to the skin color.[90]

Davenport emphasizes the "courtesy with which our fieldworker was everywhere received." Then he clarifies the measuring device; and, yes, it is the familiar children's toy that has been reshaped for his scientific experiment:

> The *color-top*, made by the Milton Bradley Company, Springfield, Massachusetts, is a little device for expressing color quantitatively. Disks of standard black, red, yellow, and white are arranged so that varying proportions of each are exposed as sectors of the whole circle. When the top is spun the colors blend. By varying the proportions of the sectors (with a small dissecting forceps) the color of the blend is altered. (2–3)

The forceps applied to the children's toy spun next to the unexposed skin of the informants provided Miss Danielson with a four-way color code for all individuals examined. This information was then combined with the genealogical data, and family stories of the following type resulted:

PEDIGREE 7. F. FAMILY
Black x White Mating
I *Gen.*—T.F., son of an Englishman and a white Bermudian; blue eyes; brunet; married a very black woman, who knows of no white blood in her ancestry; typically kinky hair; skin 77, 15, 3, 5. They have six children, of whom five are living (II 1–6).
II. *Gen.*—

1. ♂ C.F., 9 years. Hair very dark, coarse, curly but not woolly; skin 43, 35, 7, 15.
2. ♂ E.F., 7 years. Hair dark brown, very curly, almost woolly; skin 39, 35, 10, 16.
3. ♀ ———, † 3 months. Skin was like the baby's, No. 6.
4. ♂ J.F., 4 years. Hair dark brown, very wavy, not woolly; skin 43, 26, 10, 21.
5. ♂ A.F., 2 years. Hair dark brown, golden on its curly ends, otherwise straight and soft; skin 42, 28, 11, 16.
6. ♂ H.F., 3 months. Hair black and straight; skin 30, 28, 18, 24. (51)

It is immediately apparent that the "white" person is not subjected to a spintop measurement here and that in the second generation the numbers for the black circle on the spintop are about half of those of the mother. Of course, Davenport rejoiced in the exactness of his procedure: "Of the delicacy of the method there can be no question; in a good light the proportions N 55, R 40, W 5 can be readily distinguished from N 53, R 42, W 5" (3). Yet he did have to concede that in "poor light" the difference between "N 54, R 34, Y 6, W 6, and N 48, R 40, Y 6, W 6 is not striking." Of course, he also had to worry about such problems as the changing intensity of skin color in an individual's lifespan, eye fatigue of the researcher, variations in the color-top's speed, and the possibility of illegitimacy (for his genealogical conclusions). Among the many scientific texts on race that seem like inadvertent self-parodies, Davenport's stands out.[91]

Yet despite all of his scientistic machinery that would seem to reduce people to racial formulae resembling British or Canadian postal codes, Davenport is honest enough to report some findings which must have run counter to the assumptions of his reference group.[92] He finds that the male and the female matter equally in matters of human heredity that are his concern: "The determiners of skin color carried in the egg and those carried in the sperm are alike" (25). He sees no evidence for atavism, or "reversion," and attempts a general rational explanation (as folklore) of some *Natus Æthiopus* cases that Miss Danielson collected (29–30): "The tradition that a person with negro blood who passes for white may have, by a white consort, a child with a black skin color probably depends on the observation that two 'light-colored persons' may have a medium-colored child" (47). And perhaps most heretically for the context of American racism, Davenport objects to the "ancient tradition" (that he traces back to Edward Long) that "mulattoes are unprolific" (46). As the black/white genealogy cited indicates, he included large interracial families, and he offered the following explicit conclusion:

Our own records afford no support to the view of the inferior fecundity of the black x white crosses. Even $F_1$ crosses are fully fecund. . . . There is no support in our data for the notion of lack of fecundity of negro x white crosses, not of their deficient viability. . . . It is not generally true that hybrids between whites and blacks are relatively infertile; some such hybrids show an exceptionally high fecundity. (46–47)

The articulation of these findings places the eugenicist Charles Davenport's study much closer than one would think to the efforts undertaken by liberal social scientists such as Caroline Bond Day or E. Franklin Frazier, who arrived at similar conclusions in subsequent decades.

Day, for example, shows respect for the subjects investigated, and she identifies them by name. Yet the effect of the racial genealogy-construction is not that dissimilar from that of Davenport's study, as Bond's following calculus of color of Du Bois's family suggests (Fig. 26).

C21 DU BOIS (PLATE 50)

W.E.B. Du Bois, 5/8N 3/8W, apparently a third generation cross, has a light brown skin color with frizzly black hair, Grade A9. His nose is narrow-bridged, long, convex with moderate alae and a narrow tip. His lips are medium thickness, the lower being slightly heavier than the upper. He married Nina Gomer, 7/16N 9/16W, also a probable third generation cross on the paternal side. Her mother was a French woman.

She has skin color #12, straight, rather coarse hair of exceedingly great length and abundance. It has a high natural gloss. Her features are medium, the nose being slightly thick at the tip.

They had two children, the eldest, a son, being the dominant, with a yellow skin color, light brown, curly hair, and gray-brown eyes. The daughter is the recessive, being light brown in color with frizzly hair and a nose unlike either father or mother. Her lips are medium.

The family is notable for the appearance in the daughter of distinctly more negroid features than occur in either parent.

*Figure 26*  Du Bois genealogy assembled by Caroline Bond Day (1932)

Biographies of known or unknown persons were equally subjected to a racial-genealogical reading in which a few semiotic details became the features on which the scientists' exclusive interest was riveted. In her general classifications, e.g. "*Quadroons (2/8N 6/8W)*," Day sounds much like the long tradition of color calculus, though she finds no physical traits of black ancestry after the *second* generation. Thus she writes: "*Octoroons (1/8N 7/8W)*: In the few examples of octoroons which I have studied I have been able so far to see no traces whatever of Negro admixture."[93]

It is ironic that Davenport's spin-top method should have been part of what helped to turn the tide against the racial theory that rested on vilifying interracial and biracial locations. In 1911 Dr. Jean Baptiste de Lacerda put the issue surrounding the definition of "race" in relation to the sterility hypothesis very clearly:

> The one test by which we can distinguish races from species is the fertility or infertility of the offspring which results from crossing the two species in question. If their progeny continue to reproduce in successive generations, the parents constitute a race. If, on the contrary, they prove sterile, the parents which were crossed must be considered species.
>
> Admitting the principle, which seems to me sounder physiologically and more natural than any of the others, I have no difficulty in granting that the white man and the black man are merely two races, and not two distinct species.[94]

Though the Mulatto sterility hypothesis was restated in much serious scientific literature, and though some modern writers discussed it seriously, the hypothesis was finally put to rest.[95] The pioneering work of Franz Boas called attention to a higher fertility rate among mixed than among pure Indian women. Robert E. Park began to remind scholars not only that all so-called races go back to mixings and that ancient Greece had been the result of the positive effect of a melting pot, but also theorized that "marginal men" were more likely to achieve great accomplishments in the arts and in modern life in general, since they were the vanguard of modernism. In 1933 E. Franklin Frazier refuted the infertility theory with massive data that were accepted in the scholarly world. Even Davenport spoke in 1930 of "hybrid vigor" (in the case of the Chinese Hawaiians). And summarizing the discussion, Louis Wirth and Herbert Goldhamer concluded in 1944: "Certainly it can at least be said that there is no satisfactory evidence that the mulatto shows a lowered reproductive capacity."[96] Finally, Melville Herskovits—who argued somewhat sarcastically that as "far as has been ascertained, there are no crosses between human groups which carry lethal determinants for the offspring"[97]—furthermore showed that "the chances of estimating a person's ancestry accurately from skin color alone" were slight. Herskovits summarized the resolution to the longstanding debate:

Whether crossed types are better or worse than pure bloods is another moot question. The concepts of "harmonic" and "disharmonic" crosses have been applied to those individuals where the crossing has resulted happily or unhappily; the difficulty in the use of words bearing evaluative connotations such as these lies in the definitions behind them.[98]

In his work Herskovits used—as Wirth and Goldhamer summarized— "more refined measuring techniques than those employed by Day." They included, in fact, an improved Davenportian color wheel.[99] The double legacy of the Enlightenment interest in the calculus of color has led to the scientistic excesses of eugenicism and fascism as well as to the scientific knowledge that helped to dismantle segregation and apartheid.

### It Was Thomas Jefferson

Some of the examples of racial science are as amazing as if they were found poetry. Writers from Hugo on have drawn on racial classification schemes, and while no writer to my knowledge has ever made such strange experiments as Davenport's spin top the subject of fiction, at least one contemporary author has incorporated the text with which this chapter opened into an interracial novel. The writer is Barbara Chase-Riboud, the novel is *Sally Hemings* (1979);[100] and after quoting the full text as cited above, the narrator continues with a description of the patriarch who wrote it:

> His long legs under the full-length gray frockcoat shifted position, itching for the feel of his horse Eagle between them. He was seventy-two years old. His presidency was six years behind him and those six years had been spent here at home, in retirement, surrounded by those he loved most in the world: his women, his children, his slaves, his neighbors, his kin. (20)

In the morning light, the letter writer looks at the view from his house, and the chapter ends with the lines:

> He stared for a moment more at the west lawn, noting several figures gamboling on it—children, he supposed. He smiled. Whoever they were, black or white, they belonged to Monticello. And to him.
>     He turned his eyes away and picked up his pen. Absently, he massaged his wrist before signing: *Thomas Jefferson.* (20–21)

The Enlightenment mathematician was, indeed, Thomas Jefferson, and the text is from his letter to Francis Gray of 4 March 1815.[101] The African American expatriate Chase-Riboud drew on the never completely confirmed and never completely refuted tale of Jefferson's slave lover and mixed descendants that had first been circulated by Callender, put into verse by Thomas Moore—cited by Henry Adams—and fictionalized in the first Afro-American novel, William Wells Brown's *Clotel; or, The*

*President's Daughter* (1853), a text Chase-Riboud specifically acknowledges.

If Nott stylized whites as "nature's noblemen," it followed that non-whites should be considered "naturally" different—and, of course, less noble. Once interracial locations were taken to fall under the definition of "non-whites" the need emerged for more and more complicated physical recognition and detection schemes for an increasingly invisible difference that was yet felt to be natural and essential. The belief in one of them—a rather strange and perhaps unsuspected one that has been so pervasive in literary texts as to be invisible to thematic approaches—is the subject of the next chapter.

# The Bluish Tinge
# in the Halfmoon; or,
# Fingernails as a Racial Sign

A black child that is being born is neither black nor white, but of a reddish color. It is only after about two or three days that the skin begins to darken; but from birth the root of his nails and his scrotum are black. A European is no whiter at birth, but reddish like the Negro.

—Le Cat, *Traité de la couleur de la peau humaine* (1765)[1]

Mixed blood women can be distinguished from white women only by certain imperceptible signs.

—Eugène Sue, *Les Mystères de Paris* (1843)

The largest matters on earth are brought about by things that we disregard, small causes that we overlook and that finally cumulate.

—Georg Christoph Lichtenberg, *Sudelbücher* (1765–1770)

I n a great variety of French, American, German, and English literary texts that were published from the mid-nineteenth to the mid-twentieth century and that have as one of their themes interracial couples or their descendants, a small but startling detail recurs with some frequency.[2]

Sir Walter Murph comments, in Eugène Sue's immensely popular novel *Les Mystères de Paris* (1843ff), on the American Mulatto woman Cecily's charm:

> It would require a Creole's pitiless eye to detect the *sang mêlé* ["mixed blood"] in the imperceptible dark shade that lightly colors the crowns of that Mulatto woman's rosy fingernails; our fairest Northern beauties do not own a more transparent complexion, nor a whiter skin.[3]

The Irish-American Dion Boucicault's play *The Octoroon* (1859) is set on the Louisiana plantation Terrebonne. The fair-skinned title heroine Zoe describes herself as ineligible for matrimony with her white cousin George Peyton because she feels separated from him by a gulf that she does not only ascribe to the curse of Cain and to the "one drop" of blood but that she also explains to George in the following way:

> ZOE: . . . George, do you see that hand you hold? look at these fingers; do you see the nails are of a bluish tinge?
> GEORGE: Yes, near the quick there is a faint blue mark.[4]

Boucicault's Zoe interprets these and other signs as "dark, fatal" marks that point to her slave descent and cause her to feel racial shame (and, as we saw, regard herself as cursed and unclean). She has thus accepted a racial hierarchy within her own constitution.

In Theodor Storm's North German novella "Von jenseit des Meeres" ("From Across the Sea," 1865), the architect Alfred describes how, when he was still a boy, he first met Jenni, the beautiful young girl from overseas, and he gives a particularly detailed account of the mark:

Then, when I inadvertently looked upon her slender little white fingers that held mine captive, something about them, I don't know what, seemed different from the way I had perceived it before. And suddenly, while pondering upon it, I saw what it was. The small half moons at the roots of her nails were not, as ours are, lighter than the rest of the nails, but darker and bluish. I had not yet read then that this is considered the identifying sign of America's frequently very beautiful pariahs in whose veins even a mere drop of slave blood is coursing; but it was a strange sight, and I could not take my eyes off it.

A conversation ensues in which Alfred asks Jenni about those dark moons, and once she realizes what he means after comparing her and his hands she says that in St. Croix all people had such fingernails, adding, "My mother, I believe, had much darker ones."[5] Years later when they meet again, and their serious courtship begins, Alfred once again notices "the little dark moons on her nails." He tells his cousin, the frame narrator of the novella: "I don't know why I was almost so startled by them that my eyes were enthralled. When Jenni noticed this she withdrew her hand quietly into the shadow. . . ."[6]

In Rudyard Kipling's short story "Kidnapped" (1887), set in India, young Peythroppe is prevented by his friends from marrying the "Spanish"-complexioned Miss Castries whose "little opal-tinted onyx at the base of her finger-nails" reveals her racial identity "as plainly as print."[7]

Around 1884 Mark Twain composed a sketch in which a nameless character decides to pass for white: "At last, seeing even the best educated negro is at a disadvantage, besides being always insulted, clips his wiry hair, wears gloves always (to conceal his telltale nails,) & passes for a white man, in a Northern city." In Mark Twain's novel *Pudd'nhead Wilson* (1894), Roxana (who is one-sixteenth black) is upset that her son "Tom" Driscoll has refused a duel; she berates him and then mutters to herself: "Ain't nigger enough in him to show in his finger-nails, en dat takes mighty little—yit dey's enough to paint his soul."[8]

In Gertrude Atherton's novel *Senator North* (1900), the white heroine Betty Madison encourages her illegitimate Mulatto half-sister Harriet Walker to pass for white (instructing her, however, as we saw earlier, to tell the truth before getting married so as to avoid a *Natus Æthiopus* surprise). Looking at Harriet's fingernails, Betty notices something: "There was a faint bluish stain at the base of the nails; and she remembered. It was the outward and indelible print of the hidden vein within. The nails are the last stronghold of negro blood."[9]

In Thomas Dixon's novel *The Sins of the Father* (1912), the foundling Helen is told by her beloved Tom's father that she is descended from blacks. She is startled and horrified:

She stopped suddenly and lifted her hand, staring with wildly dilated eyes at the nails of her finely shaped fingers to find if the telltale marks of negro blood were there which she had seen on Cleo's. Finding none, the horror in her eyes slowly softened into a look of despairing tenderness.[10]

Dorothy Canfield writes in her novel *The Bent Twig* (1915) that the segregated black Washington Street school in the midwestern town of La Chance

> was filled with laughing, shouting children, ranging from shoe-black through coffee-color to those occasional tragic ones with white skin and blue eyes, but with the telltale kink in the fair hair and the bluish half-moon at the base of the finger-nails.[11]

The proud white mother Mrs. Elliot, in the novella "The Vengeance of the Gods" (1922) by William Pickens, expresses her belief that "blood will tell" and that one can always determine whether a person is white or black. "If the nails or the hair of the neck don't tell, the very spirit will tell."[12] Her more skeptical sister suggests, however, that a tattoo is a better identifier.

In his short story "Elly," written in 1929 and published in 1934, William Faulkner focuses on the title heroine's rebellion against the restrictions imposed upon her life by her cold grandmother. Elly is provocatively flirtatious and necks with numerous men until she finds herself drawn to Paul de Montigny, whom the inhabitants of Jefferson suspect to be a Negro. Elly is partly attracted to Paul because a relationship with him would signal her defiance of the ultimate southern taboo; yet while she obviously assumes Paul is a Negro in her dealings with him, she denies it when speaking with her grandmother—whereupon the grandmother tells Elly, without going into further details: "Look at his hair, his fingernails, if you need proof."[13]

In Fannie Hurst's best-selling novel *Imitation of Life* (1933), the black woman Delilah Johnston explains why her daughter Peola is so light:

> Her pap jes' had style mixed in, I guess, wid a teaspoonful of white blood back somewheres, an' it got him through life an' three wives widout ever turnin' them lily-pink palms of his. Style, but not a half-moon to his finger nails, and doan' you forget it.[14]

*The Foxes of Harrow* (1946), a novel by the popular African American writer Frank Yerby, includes a dialogue between Stephen and his son Etienne that takes the following turn: "All I do know is that Aupre Hippolyte has a touch of the tarbrush about him. Ye should have studied his nails."[15]

Such descriptions of fingernails appear in texts set in India, Germany, France, Britain, and—most frequently—the United States; they can be found in short stories, novellas, novels, autobiographies, plays, and nonfiction, and are particularly prevalent in popular literature. More examples could undoubtedly be found, and some others will be cited later.

What are we to make of the recurrence of this element?[16] Two broad approaches most readily offer themselves. One is a systematic-structural-synchronic method that searches for constants and variants (and their patterns), and the other a historical-genealogical-diachronic procedure that investigates changes—origins, transformations, substitutions and disappearances—in the context of cultural history.[17] Using this example, I shall in this chapter attempt to sketch both approaches.

## Patterns of a Motif

Surveying the instances of a motif one notices shared features as well as differences among the texts; this invites the construction of certain groupings of the motif. In the case of the fingernail motif, the inspection of the nails is expected in most instances to yield clues to a character's nonwhite racial ancestry, however remote it may be and how white the person in question may look. Yet the variations are considerable.

The fingernail sign may need description and explanation. This is the case in Storm's story, which presents the visual recognition as taking place *before* Alfred had read anything about the sign, and in Boucicault's dialogue, where Zoe's lengthy explanation retards dramatic action. Atherton lets the narrator intercede with an explanatory description even though the argument is made in the text that the sign is instinctually recognizable. The description of the sign varies, too, from a dark shade to a bluish tinge and from an opal-tinted onyx to a half-moon.

Upon other occasions the reader's familiarity with the motif seems to be taken for granted, hence requiring no description beyond the quickest reference to "telltale nails" (Mark Twain, Dixon, Pickens, Faulkner, Hurst, or Yerby). In some borderline cases, the mark may be assumed to be known to readers even when it is *not* explicitly mentioned in the text. For example, in Kate Chopin's *Natus Æthiopus* story "The Father of Désirée's Baby" (1893)—which, we remember, does *not* represent the baby's "blackness"—the rapid growth of the child's fingernails is explicitly commented upon as Désirée tells Madame Valmondé: "Look at his legs, mamma, and his hands and finger-nails, real finger-nails. Zandrine had to cut them this morning." Though it is not made a more explicit "sign" in the story, Kate Chopin may have counted on her readers' (and Madame Valmondé's and Zandrine's) knowledge of the fingernail as a racial clue. After all, Désirée seems to be the last to find out that her baby is "not white," whereas her foster mother, everyone in the household, and her husband have been able to read the signs earlier.[18] Similarly, in Ross Lockridge's epic novel *Raintree County* (1948), the disturbed Susanna Shawnessy spends a long time looking at her newborn child's "little hands and feet and its blue eyes," inquiring whether there was, perhaps, another child, a twin that had been thrown away.[19] Such cases constitute a thematics of *absence*—according to which we look at a given text in a certain way by drawing on details that are, however, fully present only in other works.[20]

Some texts presuppose that there really is such a mark in nature (for example, Sue, Boucicault, Storm, Atherton, Kipling, Dixon) and that it is proof of racial identity. Others (fewer in number) imply or state that there is no such sign in reality and that looking for it yields unreliable results. Thus the very light-skinned African American Walter White told the Jamaican-born novelist Claude McKay stories of his experiences in passing for white, and McKay reports in his autobiography *A Long Way from Home* (1937):

> To me the most delectable was one illustrating the finger-nail theory of telling a near-white from a pure-white. White was traveling on a train on his way to investigate a lynching in the South. The cracker said, "There are many yaller niggers who look white, but I can tell them every time."
>
> "Can you really?" Walter White asked.
>
> "Oh sure, just by looking at their finger nails." And taking White's hand, he said, "Now if you had nigger blood, it would show here on your half-moons."

McKay concludes:

> That story excited me by its paradox as much as had the name and complexion of Walter White. It seemed altogether fantastic that whites in the South should call him a "nigger" and whites in the North, a Negro. It violates my feeling of words as conveying color and meaning. . . . For me a type like Walter White is Negroid simply because he closely identifies himself with the Negro group—just as a Teuton becomes a Moslem if he embraces Islam. White is whiter than many Europeans—even biologically. I cannot see the difference in the way that most of the whites and most of the blacks seem to see it. Perhaps what is reality for them is fantasy for me.[21]

McKay views "race" in analogy to religion and the possibility of "conversion." McKay also contrasts race as "species" in the classical sense with its modern interpretation as genealogy that may make race invisible and thus create the desire for other signs by which it may be detected.

The sign may also be believed to be generally reliable, but not in specific cases. The generational novel *Crescent Carnival* (1942) by Frances Parkinson Keyes, for example, has a subplot involving the dark strain in the family. When Laure first appears, the white southerner Breck explains to his New England wife Anna: "That girl you saw is one-sixteenth colored. It won't ever show in her hair or her skin or her eyes—not even in her fingernails, and they're the greatest giveaway." For Keyes, the fingernail mark—while expected to work in principle—fails to identify fourth-generation descendants. Put another way, in such works as *Crescent Carnival* (as well as in *Pudd'nhead Wilson* or *Imitation of Life*), while the fingernail mark is viewed as evidence of "blackness," its absence is no proof of "whiteness."[22] (By contrast, in Dixon's *Sins of the Father*, the absence of the fingernail mark on Helen seems to be evidence that she is really white.)[23]

For some authors the sign is permanent, indelible, ineffaceable. According to others, it can be covered, erased, deleted, or otherwise removed; thus Mark Twain lets his character always wear gloves. In Edith Pope's *Colcorton* (1944), a Florida version of James's *Aspern Papers*, the white writer Clement Johnson has fingernails that are "the whitened colour of their moons"; Johnson instinctively suspects that the heroine Abby Clanghearne is partly black. Abby, who has been living in the Florida family homestead Colcorton yet passing for white all her life, recalls how she reacted after finding out her true ancestry:

> She remembered the frights she had had when she thought folks looked at her kind of queer. Many's the day she had nearly scrubbed her skin off fancying it was getting black; and the times she had studied her fingernails, and that once—she was young then and right foolish—she had bruised them with a stone to make white marks come that she could play like they was moons; and how she had baked her brains to a frazzle going bareheaded so as to bleach her hair.

Abby does not stop short of self-mutilation, and in order to let her nephew Jad—who was born prematurely and "without fingernails hardly"—escape from the disadvantages of a public discovery of his racial identity and a family history of passing, Abby encourages her sister-in-law Beth to go North with him and change their names.[24]

Such coverup may not always be successful since other characters may be able to see through it. For example, Atherton has Betty's friend Sally explain how she knew about Harriet's "true" racial identity: "I *felt* it. So vaguely that I scarcely put it in words until lately. And I never saw such an amount of pink on finger-nails in my life" (166). Atherton thus suggests that the use of nail-polish may be a possible cover for the racial mark of the fingernails; it is a useless effort, however, since the suspicious Sally finds out about Harriet anyway. When Robert Jones, the narrator of Chester Himes's *If He Hollers Let Him Go* (1945), looks at his light-skinned girlfriend Alice Harrison, he comments on her fingers:

> I watched the fluid motion of her long slender fingers as she absently fiddled with the steering wheel and thought wonderingly that I'd never noticed before how beautiful they were. Then I thought of what they said about being able to tell a Negro by the half-moons in their finger-nails, and reflected half laughingly on what they'd have to do if the nails were painted.[25]

In some texts the sign is readable "as plainly as print" (Kipling). In others it is ambiguous. In Sinclair Lewis's social satire *Kingsblood Royal*

(1947), for example, the bigoted royal-ancestry-hunting Minnesotan banker Neil Kingsblood discovers that Xavier Pic, his great-great-grand-father, was not, as he had hoped, a white French aristocrat, but a black man born in Martinique. Neil immediately thinks of examining his body for possible clues to this ancestry:

> [H]e wanted to stop and look at his hands. He remembered hearing that a Negro of any degree, though pale of face as Narcissus, is betrayed by the blue halfmoons of his fingernails. He wildly wanted to examine them. But he kept his arms rigorously down beside him (so that people did wonder at his angry stiffness and did stare at him) and marched into the elevator. He managed, with what he felt to be the most ingenious casualness, to prop himself with his hand against the side of the cage, and so to look at his nails.
>
> No! The halfmoons were as clear as [his daughter] Biddy's.

Lewis's Neil keeps investigating his nails nervously, "tapping his teeth with his fingernail, occasionally looking suddenly at that nail again" or dropping his hand in his lap, studying his nails and wondering: "Was it this mercury vapor light, or was there really a blue tinge in the half-moons?"[26] Neil's nails have acquired an indeterminable quality. This quality is also apparent in Robert Penn Warren's novel *Band of Angels* (1955), in which the light-skinned narrator Amantha Starr, who grew up white, is sold down the river upon her father's death. As she is going from Kentucky to Louisiana on a steamboat, she ponders her new condition and the history of her identity:

> I remembered how my father, back when he held me on his lap and played pattycake, had looked at my hands and then kissed each finger. Had he been secretly looking all the time for the tell-tale blue half-moons on my fingernails—the sure mark, they said, of black blood, even if only a spoon-ful?
>
> Now in the cabin, I looked at my fingers. They told me nothing I could be sure of.[27]

The mark on the fingernail may be noticed in a character's self-exam-ination that Sinclair Lewis, for example, represents with an allusion to Narcissus. Dixon's, Pope's, and Warren's heroines, too, inspect them-selves for the mark. The sign may also be detected by another character (Kipling) or a real or hypothetical trained observer (Sue).

It may be recognized by a narrator or character and serve to classify the person who carries it (Storm, Kipling). However, looking at the sign can also identify the observer who does not have it but whose gaze is directed at it on another character: in Sue the description of the nail is combined with a critique of the pitiless gaze of a Creole observer (ren-dered by an English translator as "a slave-driver's practiced eye"). To cite some further examples, Mary E. Braddon's *The Octoroon* (ca. 1862), a derivative though not unsuspenseful novel written in the wake of Mayne

Reid and Dion Boucicault, introduces the fingernail motif in the very first chapter when Mortimer Percy discusses the beautiful woman—who turns out to be the Octoroon Cora Leslie—with the British artist Gilbert Margrave, who later is destined to marry Cora. Percy says:

> Had you been a planter, Gilbert, you would have been able to discover, as I did, when just now I stood close to that lovely girl, the fatal signs of her birth. At the extreme corner of the eye, and at the root of the finger nails, the South American can always discover the trace of slavery, though but one drop of the blood of the despised race tainted the object upon whom he looked.[28]

Percy both identifies the woman's racial background and ascribes the ability to detect the sign to a special group of southern planters. (By "South Americans" the hurried pulp novelist Braddon apparently meant U.S. southerners).

Paul Bourget's *Cosmopolis* (1893) contains an episode on the racially mixed descendants of Napoléon Chapron in which the habit of inspecting fingernails for racial clues is considered peculiarly *American*. The twelve-year-old Florent Chapron is being educated in an English country college where he is simply known as the grandchild of a great French officer (that he truly is); his fellow students are unaware of any racial difference between them and Florent. The narrator adds, quite in Sue's manner, and in a possibly clichéd phrasing that resembles Storm's: "It would have taken a Yankee's glance to notice that very small drop of black blood, already so far removed, under the fingernails of this beautiful and slightly tanned youth."[29] For this reason, Florent is scared when an American who has come to the college seems to give him the disdainful glance to which he had often been subjected in the United States. It turns out, however, that this American student, Lincoln Maitland, was in fact raised by his English mother in an environment as little American as possible and lived outside the United States since he was five, so that he has no difficulties in becoming Florent Chapron's close friend. Once again, rather than the mark on the nails itself, the *gaze* that is directed at them serves as a sign of group membership, here in the category "Yankee."

This is also the case, though for the category of the Anglo-Indian, in George Aberigh-Mackay's *Twenty-One Days in India* (1881). In the chapter "The Eurasian; a Study in Chiaro-Oscuro" he writes that the "Anglo-Indian has a very fine eye for colour":

> He will tell you how he can detect an adulterated European by his knuckles, his nails, his eyebrows, his pronunciation of the vowels, and his conception of propriety in dress, manner, and conduct.[30]

The fingernail motif is intricately linked to race and gender. The characters thus marked are more likely to be women, but there are also some male figures who bear the sign (in the texts by Bourget, Mark Twain, Faulkner, White, and Lewis); significantly for the function of the mark as an impediment to an alliance, the characters who bear it are often young and in a situation of courtship (Sue, Boucicault, Braddon, Kipling, Atherton, or Faulkner). Yet in other instances they may also be babies (Chopin), children (Bourget), in midlife (Lewis), or in advancing years (Pope). They may be entering a crisis because of the death of a father (Warren), because they have attempted to "pass" racially (Pope), or because their aristocratic pretensions make them search for ancestors (Lewis). The sign may work as a marriage impediment (in Kipling, one version of Boucicault's play, or Faulkner) or not (in another version of Boucicault's *Octoroon*, in Braddon, or in Storm[31]). While the belief in the sign may cause antiracist amusement (Larsen and Himes) or criticism of an American "fantasy" (McKay), the mark's recognition in texts that presuppose its real existence may cause romantic fascination (in Storm's Alfred, who could not take his eyes off it) or racist revulsion (in Atherton's Betty Madison, who, upon looking at her stepsister Harriet's fingernails, "dropped the hand and covered her face with her muff").[32]

As a motif, the fingernail as a racial sign is sometimes linked with other signs that transform the body into a text and that are presumed to be racial indicators—such as hair, skin, or eyes; the sign is very strongly determined racially, and the instances where even its absence functions as a racial marker suggests that some of the texts imply a reader who shares certain ideas about race. The motif is intimately connected with the theme of passing; there are also clusters in which "fingernails" are linked to such diverse other motifs as Narcissus, twins, the gaze, and the rhetoric of reading (or "studying") print language. The contexts of the motif are very varied, indeed.

No single instance contains all elements of the motif, and some instances share only very few or no elements with some others.[33] The various examples may thus be grouped regardless of chronology: it does not matter whether an example originated earlier or later than another one. This changes when we approach the motif historically.[34]

## The History of a Motif

A historical procedure might start with the observation that virtually all the evidence presented so far comes only from the century or so that separates the work of Eugène Sue from that of Robert Penn Warren. It is in the period from the 1840s to the 1950s that the fingernail motif seems to have been conventionalized and stabilized as a peculiarly racial sign. What are the origins that could have led to this motif's emergence? What functions could it have fulfilled? How did stabilization set in? What may have led to its disappearance?[35]

One point of departure might be the exploration of literary and other texts from the time before the motif had become conventionalized. In 1839, just four years before Sue's *Mystères de Paris* began to be serialized, "Les Épaves" ("The Wrecks"), a little-known historical novella of the *Revue de Paris* of 1838, was placed into a new collection with a narrative frame that links the various stories; and it is the discussion in the frame narrative of this collection by Madame Reybaud, entitled *Valdepeiras*, that illustrates the status of the fingernail motif *before* stabilization set in. At the end of the tale the storyteller, the Creole woman Zoe, commences a conversation with the audience of the frame narrative. In response to the listeners' question she authenticates the interracial love-and-marriage story by saying that she was that couple's great-grand-child and emphatically concluding: "there is Mulatto blood in my veins." Since she is white-looking, she puts forth her little hands, and the frame narrator comments: "they were refined, delicate, and charming, but around her fingernails there was a light brownish tinge."[36] However, Reybaud uses the revelation of Zoe's fingernails not primarily as a general racial proof of the narrator's "Mulatto blood" but as the sign of Zoe's own specific individual identity and hence of the authenticity and veracity of her tale. The mark that serves as evidence of her heroic descent is, of course, a sign of honor; racial identification was not the absolute, freestanding, self-important, and all-determining matter that it was to become, say, in Atherton, but served primarily as a device calculated to support the authenticity of a tale.

Zoe's gesture of stretching forth her hands as proof of her racial background as well as of her truthfulness may go back to Victor Hugo's already cited historical novel *Bug-Jargal* (second edition, 1826), set at the time of the Haitian Revolution. It is also a text which suggests the moment before motif-stabilization had set in and which, as it turns out, takes a pivotal place in the textual interaction between scientific and literary discourses.

In Hugo's novel, an unnamed Haitian planter—often presumed to be of mixed descent by his peers but so resentful of such suspicions that he once challenges the narrator Léopold d'Auverney, who voices it—falls into the hands of black rebels. Ever an opportunist, he tries to convince Biassou, the leader of his captors, that they have seized not a white but a man of mixed blood:

> "Monsieur Commander-in-chief, this black circle which you can see about my nails proves that I am a *sang-mêlé*."
> Biassou pushed his hand away.
> "I have n't the skill in such matters that the chaplain has, who can tell who you are by looking at your hand."[37]

The gesture of stretching forth one's hand in order to demonstrate truthfulness and racial identity (that Reybaud's Zoe performs more convincingly) is here made by a parvenu for whom the narrator has few sympathies.

Hugo's is the earliest literary text I have found in which the fingernail motif is used. But did Hugo make up the fingernail sign? He does seem unsure of his readers' knowledge of the matter and—perhaps in the service of verisimilitude—adds a clarifying footnote: "Many *sang-mêlés* bear this mark at the root of the nails; it is effaced by age, but reappears in their children."[38] Hugo thus explicates the mark as something that reveals—though not with absolute certainty, since only "many" *Sang-mêlés* are said to bear it—what language may obscure. This makes nails what one might call "ascriptive clues"; they have the status of circumstantial "evidence" that can support, or be held against, a person's claim in order to classify and define that person.[39] In the context of a modern political revolution during which a semiotic "proof" of whose side characters were on could seal their fates, the offering of the fingernails as evidence goes together with the planter's politically unwise choice of the word "Mulatto" to describe himself.

From where did Hugo get this notion? Hugo's footnote suggests that this sign of mixed racial identity wanes with the subjects' age, though Hugo did not hesitate to use it in a fully grown character (rather than a newborn child). This contradiction between text and authenticating footnote directs the reader toward other footnotes in the novel. And it is in these notes that Hugo's text positions itself in such a way as to make an intertextual approach plausible even to the most exacting demands made by scholars who require *textual* evidence for an author's putative knowledge of other discourses.

In one of his notes (cited in full before), Hugo explicitly states that he adheres to Moreau de Saint-Méry's system of classification of 1797 that was examined in "The Calculus of Color" and that works with fractions of 128 that constitute a person's seven-generation ancestry. Moreau thus arrives at an unusually elaborate racial nomenclature that includes, for example, twelve possibilities of being a Mulatto, including four ways of arriving at an exactly divided heritage of 64 white to 64 black ancestral parts.[40] In Moreau de Saint-Méry's system, a *Sang-mêlé* has between $\frac{125}{128}$ and $\frac{127}{128}$ parts of white blood (and, correspondingly, only $\frac{3}{128}$ to $\frac{1}{128}$ black ascendants). In other words, a *Sang-mêlé* may be seven (or, in the instance of $\frac{1}{512}$ African blood that was already cited, even *nine*) generations removed from any black ancestry. And still, Hugo claims in *Bug-Jargal* that the "*sang-mêlé*, continuing its amalgamation with the white blood, is finally lost in it. We are assured, however, that there is always perceptible on a particular part of the body the ineffaceable trace of its origin."[41] There is a tension in Hugo's scientist strategy that contradicts some of his own fictional logic, though the contradiction might not necessarily catch the eye of the reader. Hugo's "always" stands in a contradictory relation to his statement, cited earlier, that "many *sang-mêlés*" bear the mark. This suggests that fictions of racial difference may express a yearning for permanence, especially in Creole societies, while a text that represents such yearning may at the same time recognize the absence of any such permanence. What reconciles the contradiction between the reader's wish for verisimilitude and the text's ambivalence are such phrases as "we are assured" or "it is said" that were also noticeable in several of the later texts cited and that invoke scholarly, and especially scientific, discourse as an authenticating device.[42]

Hugo's text thus contains noteworthy contradictions: the sign is present in all *Sang-mêlés*; in many *Sang-mêlés*. It appears on infants and disappears later in life; it is ineffaceable and may be found on an adult planter. As we have already seen, later writers followed those different possibilities, with some choosing newborn characters (Chopin and Lockridge) and most others writing about adults; with some writers believing in the absolute permanence of the sign, and many others representing various degrees of impermanence, or even unreality, of the sign.

The contradictoriness of the descriptive detail is reconciled by Hugo's footnotes that refer the ignorant or skeptical reader to scientific discourse; and Moreau de Saint-Méry—whom Hugo specifically invokes— also offers the by now familiar observation of the nails as a racial sign:

> At the time of birth black children have a skin in which a reddish tinge would leave their color undecided, were it not for a small blackish rim which one can observe around the areas which shame wants covered, as well as along the roots of the nails.[43]

Moreau's observations were similar to those made by many other writers of scientific and travel literature of the eighteenth century such as de Pauw, Labat, Le Cat, Gumilla, and Buffon. Ultimately they seem to go back to an anatomical report to the French Royal Academy of 1702. This report describes Alexis Littré's efforts to test the assumption advanced by Marcello Malpighi that black skin coloration was caused by an internal liquid.[44] Finding Malpighi's theory untenable and connecting blackness instead to exposure to air, Littré is said to have noticed— according to the Academy report—that children of Moors were born white, and that

> when male children of Moors are born, they have, at the tip of the penis, a small black sign which then extends on the top of the uncovered gland, and even to the whole body, and extends, if one wishes, through the action of air. . . . We note in passing that, apart from that little sign which only appears in boys, all Moorish infants have at birth nails which are black at the extremity.[45]

The anatomist's gaze is here focused on the symbolic source of blackness and on the borderline between covered and uncovered skin. In these parts male "Moors" are defined at birth, and *all* "black" children are believed to carry a sign in another borderline area. While the general association of fingernails and sexuality was frequently made in the texts here examined, such an explicit description of the male sexual organ was to remain rare in nonanatomic writing. Some eighteenth-century writers believed that it was only the boys' genitals (Le Cat focused on the scrotum rather than the penis) that carried the racial signs, others thought that boys and girls had the sign in the area that "shame wants covered," for example, Bernard Romans; but most saw the fingernails as an analogous but more easily accessible—and for some, more universal—indicator of a newborn child's racial identity.[46]

Different writers approached this detail with heterogeneous questions in mind. Littré and the anatomists were interested in the development of all babies' skins during the first days and weeks of life. Count Georges Louis Leclerc de Buffon, who was curious about the relation of heredity and climatic environment in the case of skin pigmentation, notes:

> it has been observed, that the children of Negroes, as soon as they come into the world, have black genitals, and a black spot at the roots of their nails. The action of the air, and the jaundice, may, perhaps, help to expand this colour; but it is certain that the rudiments of blackness are communicated by their parents; that in whatever part of the world a Negro is brought forth, he will be equally black as if he had been born in his own country.[47]

Buffon ends his observations with the thought that this does not imply that color will always continue the same: he speculates that, if transported to a northern province, the descendants of blacks in the eighth, tenth, or twelfth generation "would be much fairer and perhaps as white as the natives of that climate."[48]

Jean-Baptiste Labat, who, as we saw, placed himself in an Aristotelian tradition, was interested in children of mixed couples as proof that both father and mother have a decisive influence on progeny; it is in such a context that he looked at the fingernail sign as a way of telling black children from Mulatto children at birth. In a chapter on Mulattoes for his *Nouveau voyage aux Isles de l'Amérique* (1722), he takes his point of departure from the observation that all children are universally born light and that black skin pigmentation emerges only eight to ten days after birth. In order to predict blackness one can look at the color of the babies' genitals (for him, of both boys and girls), which are, Labat writes, black in Negro children but white or nearly white in Mulatto children. He also recommends the simpler method of ascertaining race by observing, immediately upon delivery, the baby's nails at the point where they grow out of the flesh.

> [I]f they are black in this area, the child will also become black, according to this infallible mark; should this spot, however, be white or nearly white, one may say with certainty that the child is a Mulatto, whether descended

from a white man and a Negro woman or a white woman and a Negro man.[49]

From such sources variants of this notion proliferated in historical, philosophical, and numerous other works of the eighteenth century.[50]

Fingernails—whether their extremities or their roots—were thus established in the eighteenth-century texts not just as a general "sexual symbol" of sorts, but expressly as a substitute for, and even a more legible improvement over, genitals—whether the French Academy's "penis" or Le Cat's "scrotum." Sexual organs are, of course, symbolically associated with the realms of ancestry and descent; yet fingernails, too, seem to extend beyond the individual's lifespan, as they grow before birth and continue growing even after death.

The Royal Academy's, Gumilla's, Le Cat's, de Pauw's, and Buffon's mark (*tache*, *seña*, *marque*, or *signe*) of the fingernails served mainly to make distinctions at birth, not between Mulattoes and whites but between Negroes and all others;[51] Labat looked explicitly for a method of distinguishing newly born Mulattoes *from blacks*. Though Le Cat insisted on the universal reddish birth, some of the repeated descriptions and their variations also served the purpose of representing nonwhite skin as if it were the result of the "loss" of "original whiteness." As we have seen, the eighteenth-century authors often made attempts at offering systematic classifications of racial mixture with an appropriately scientific terminology, though most classify as white a person who is three, four, or at most five generations away from a black ancestor. Such was not the case, however, for Moreau de Saint-Méry, Hugo's central source, who, as we saw, cited a Sang-mêlé who was $\frac{1}{512}$ black. Inspired by his source, Hugo also made the fingernails the mark that distinguishes racially mixed people who are very light-skinned not from darker-skinned blacks, but from *whites*. This is a dramatic departure from the earlier scientific literature, and, as has been mentioned, despite his footnote that authenticates the sign in newborn children, he contradictorily makes fictional use of the motif in a grown-up man. Perhaps because of the background of the Haitian revolution in *Bug-Jargal*, the distinction between white and Mulatto nonwhite appears to have become more relevant than other differentiations; it was more useful in this novel (that includes no child character) if he could apply it to adults. Hugo's way of drawing the distinction, however, was to become crucial in biracial societies like the United States where the difference between only two categories—"white" and "nonwhite"—came to be established more sharply than in societies which recognized three or more gradations of difference.

With this development it became conveniently possible to imagine a definition of "whites" as "people without marks on their fingernails" and to believe in the possibility of a life-long detection of even distant nonwhite ancestry in others.[52] Such an identification may also have been desirable because it helped to define who was slave and who was free in societies that made the status of the mother alone the touchstone of her descendants' enslavement or liberty; and with the rise of Jim Crow segregation it could be stabilized in support of the construction of racial difference in borderline cases. The motif of the fingernail is thus yet another ideological element that helped to fix racial categories against "appearance"—and give away to the trained observer what Atherton would call "the indelible proof of the hidden vein within."

Hugo's choice was all the more momentous since his text may have had the position of a funnel that gathered forms of other discourses and utilized them, however contradictorily, in fiction; his work, through the dissemination of *Revue de Paris* novellas (like "Les Épaves") and feuilleton fiction (like *Les Mystères de Paris*) may thus have been one literary Ur-text of the motif under scrutiny. A vast number of nineteenth-century readers (and writers) may have noticed and remembered the sentence in a footnote by Sue that appears as motto to this chapter and that, again, contains the contradiction between the statement that *métisses* differ from whites only in certain signs and the qualification that these signs are "imperceptible."

### "No Truth"

In the course of the nineteenth century, the use of the motif generally developed from the belief in a method of distinguishing at birth who was to become darker-skinned or lighter-skinned within days or weeks, into a supposedly life-long, essential difference between people without any, and those with, black ancestry, no matter how white they may be in appearance. The sign helped to make natural (it "naturalized") socially constructed group distinctions. It was, in fact, exactly this hope of finding such a permanent natural mark "indicating Race and Temperament" that made Francis Galton develop the fingerprint technique. Instead he discovered that "English, Welsh, Jews, Negroes, and Basques, may all be spoken of as identical in the character of their finger prints; the same familiar patterns appearing in all of them with much the same degree of frequency, the differences between groups of different races being not larger than those that occasionally occur between groups of the same race," a formulation that echoes the argument Blumenbach had made for the unity of the human species.[53]

Fingernails, initially the object of a predominantly classificatory interest in a sign that was presumed to be universally readable—though it appeared differently to various observers—turned into an element that could evoke first a romantic shiver of wonder and fascination and then a racist shudder of disgust, as it also began to require a specially trained eye to be decoded. Like the much less frequently represented physical signs for which it substituted, the fingernail mark was viewed as a symbol of attraction and repulsion. Especially prominent in plot situations involving courtship, the motif also became part of the arsenal of ideological strategies that helped to legitimate and make natural the feeling of a racial hierarchy crowned by white superiority. The mark of the fingernails was occasionally used to authenticate a character or a tale; it was inverted to identify the person who *stares* at fingernails as white Creole or American; it appeared in stories of "passing" in connection with various possibilities of camouflaging the mark that might otherwise give away a "suspicious looking brunette" (Atherton) or a "tanned" young man (Bourget); and, finally, it receded into uninterpretability or into the dimension of folkloric hearsay knowledge of a by now largely forgotten white superstition. The story of the fingernail motif may thus also be a *pars pro toto* of the history of changing notions about race, about reading, and about specialization; its tellings include romantic, realistic, and modernist versions.

Once universally readable—and in the case of Moreau de Saint-Méry, precisely the means to decide the undecidable—and then telling to the specialist or identifying the viewer as Creole, American, Southern, Anglo-Indian, or simply biased, the fingernails (like other signs in the twentieth century) have become enmeshed in indeterminacy. By the mid-twentieth century they had become telltale nails that tell nothing. They no longer yield any certainties; they merely symbolize the problematic way in which a daughter reads her father's relationship to her, or the strange reflection of neon light.

Taking seriously the original substitution for sexuality that is involved in the fingernail sign also means reading some of the passages anew. The area "shame wants covered" extends to Harriet's fingernails in the case of Atherton's heroine, who is tellingly described as "Southern to her fingertips." In Pope's *Colcorton* Abby Clanghearne who once tried to efface her fingernails also has no progeny. The hand, so often the symbol of a possible matrimonial connection, in fictions thematizing the racialized fingernail also becomes an image of a taboo, suggestive of the dialectic of attraction and repulsion.[54] To introduce some final examples, Elizabeth Madox Roberts writes in *My Heart and My Flesh* (1927) about the heroine Theodosia Bell, who was to find out about her father's dark past and her unsuspected relatives in the course of the novel:

> Theodosia would watch the long brown hand with its yellow shadowed nails when Lucas passed a plate of some food at her side. While she helped herself to a serving her eyes would cling to the hand where it folded at the edge of the plate, the thumb near the food, and she would remember the baby on the quilt in Aunt Deesie's yard. An exquisite disgust of the hand would make the food taste doubly sweet in her mouth when the hand was withdrawn.[55]

In quite a different context, Gustave Flaubert describes the first encounter between Charles and Emma in *Madame Bovary* (1857) when the shy Charles sees Emma sewing and does not dare to look directly at her face:

> Charles was much surprised at the whiteness of her nails. They were shiny, delicate at the tips, more polished than the ivory of Dieppe, and almond-shaped.[56]

And in his epistolary novel *Blason d'un corps* (1961), dedicated to the relationship between the French narrator and the Creole woman Mayotte, [René] Etiemble devotes the bulk of a long letter (dated October 1944) to a retrospective exploration of his changing attitude toward his own fingernails and their significance for his sexual maturation and identity. Etiemble's text, while it does not regard nails as a racial sign, constitutes an encyclopedic investigation of the motif in the narrator's life. Having bitten his fingernails to the point that his father covered them with mustard and, upon the doctor's diagnosis of a case of onychophagy, let the boy sleep with tied hands at night, the narrator finally abandons this habit but looks quite discouraged at his own nails:

> Reddish, like a blood sausage, the flesh of my fingers obscured the half moons for which I envied Jacqueline, my oldest sister, and which I admired in Maryse, my favorite sister. For months I tried to convince myself that this white halfmoon was a "girls' thing." Experience taught me differently. Many of my high school comrades resembled my sisters at least in having half moons on their fingernails.[57]

Associating the fingernails with sexual prowess, the narrator (who was circumcised as a punishment when his father discovered him masturbating) interprets *onycho* as "eunuch"[58] and relates instances in which his fingernails interfered with sexual exploits. He wears gloves, goes to manicurists, uses fingernail drops, discovers spots (but no moons) on his nails, admires American artificial nails, and, as a twenty-year-old, takes to a woman whom he chose "exclusively for the reason that her half moons fascinated [him], as they covered a third of her fingernails." Only Mayotte's loving treatment of his "martyr's hands" ends his agony and reconciles him with his nails that he buries happily in her breasts. Why, he asks, does he finally accept the "fingernails' slow, vegetative life of sulphurous hardening" in the age of teletype and wireless picture transmission? His own answer is that it must be for love.[59]

Such examples (as well as those of Chopin and Lockridge) illustrate the possibility that one can encounter instances, in the course of such a sweeping survey of a detail, which throw light on the whole development without actually constituting an explicit part of it. Fingernails may function as gender identifiers, as symbols of attraction and repulsion, or as metaphors of erotic energy and substitutes for sexuality, and texts in which racialized contempt is lacking may make this function all the more apparent.

Even though it was, in different versions, early propagated by scientists, Jesuits, travelers, and scholars, and changed, adopted as factual, and conventionalized by many writers, and though it was useful to racialists in helping to create the illusion that racial distinctions are permanent, natural, objective, biological, and always subject to discovery, the literary motif of the telltale "dark moons" on the fingernails does not seem to be based upon any anatomical facts. It may be the elite equivalent to the kind of folk superstitions recorded by Newbell Niles Puckett in 1926:

> [Some] Negroes say that the number of white spots under your finger nails betokens the number of friends you have. In England yellow spots on the nails of fingers indicate coming death. They are sometimes called "death-mould"; the Negro calls them "death-moles" or "death-mules," and sometimes says they are blue spots instead of yellow ones, but always the sign is death.[60]

There is also a superstition that the growth of fingernails is the result of original sin.[61]

In his essay "The Future American" (1900), Charles Chesnutt characterized as a "race fallacy," a "delusion," and a "snare" the belief that the "telltale mark at the root of the nails" constitutes "an infallible test of Negro blood." In 1932, Samuel Monash, who deplored the absence of any "systematic study of pigmentation of the nails of the Negro," published an illustrated examination of the fingernails of 296 Negroes of all age groups. He noted "longitudinal stripes running the length of the nails" which are not usually present at birth, but may appear at any age, so that, contrary to Victor Hugo's assumption (derived from eighteenth-century scholarship), their frequency *increases* during the span of a life. Monash, who was, incidentally, working with Charles Davenport's color-top method, also emphasized that there "is no deeper pigmentation of the nail bed under these pigmented stripes" and that among "the lighter Negroes such pigmentation is uncommon."[62] When asked by a literary critic whether the motif of the dark moons in characters of mixed blood referred to a real phenomenon, Dr. Monash replied in a letter: "I can assure you that there is no truth in the statement that Negro blood shows in the moons of any person."[63]

Seven years after Monash had published his study, the white drummer Johnny Otis was permitted to attend a blacks-only dance with Count Basie's band at the World's Fair near San Francisco—only after a Mississippi-born policeman had "examined Otis's fingernails and concluded that he was black."[64] In a 1951 account of the Rhinelander case, the author remarked that "in those days whites thought that a Negro woman had certain ineradicable marks of race on their bodies and dark half-moons in the fingernails"—in order to explain why Alice Jones was asked by her lawyer to disrobe in front of the jury.[65] And the biracial journalist Zenobia Kujichagulia writes that when she went to a Nation of Islam mosque in San Francisco in the late 1960s, "they looked at my fingernails to see if I had dark enough rings around my nails."[66] She was deemed "black enough" to enter. Though the belief in fingernails as a racial sign was a cultural invention, forms of social practice have certainly been based on it.

The sciences—from the algebra and mathematical fractions to dermatology and human cuticle formation—have contributed to the many scholarly justifications invoked in the search for racial distinctions. Yet perhaps no other scholarly field was as implicated in making practicable the distinction of who was to be slave and who free, who black and who white, and who could or could not marry whom, as was the discipline of law. The activities of law-making bodies in the modern world have been extensive; and Appendix B on "Prohibitions" conveys a first impression of the range of legal efforts in this direction. The following chapter touches upon a few provisions of the *Code noir* that were invoked at climactic moments in literary texts.

# Code Noir and Literature

Any slave who strikes his master, his mistress, the husband of his mistress, or their children, causing bruises or effusion of blood shall be punished by death.

—*Code noir*, invoked in Victor Séjour, "Le Mulâtre" (1837)

Any slave who marries a white woman is free by law.

—*Code noir*, cited in Fanny Reybaud, "Les Épaves" (1838)

And the law is: that when a free-born woman
Of noble ancestry really chooses a slave to marry,
Then he is free; and his slave chain
Is hung in the church's nave. Forgiven
Is all earlier guilt; the husband
Of the Lady receives equal rights,
The same rank and standing that she
Occupies. He is free! Yes, free!

—*Code noir*, cited in Hans Christian Andersen, *Mulatten* (1840)

According to the *Code noir*, which you know better than I do, the sale of a masterless slave is void if the master presents himself . . . and the master am I!

—*Code noir*, cited in Eugène Scribe, *Le Code noir* (1842)

L aw is a thematic element that could and did become central to literary works. The varying descriptions of fingernails in interracial literature concerned a detail that recurred in many texts but that rarely if ever constituted a decisive, pivotal element without which the works would not have been what they are. It was a motif that was unlikely to become plot-constitutive and that remained a minor aspect of the works in which it occurred. "Law" as a theme functioned differently. George Washington Cable, for example, famously referred to Louisiana law as a marriage impediment when he let Madame Delphine say memorably: "'Tis dad *law*! Dad *law* is crezzie! Dad law is a fool!" and let Père Jerome explain that they made the law "to keep the two races separate." Without this law, prohibiting intermarriage, the plot of "Madame Delphine" could be quite different. And in the story of Bras-Coupé that forms the historical backdrop to Cable's novel *The Grandissimes*, the narrator describes its climactic moment by referring to the law:

> The master swore a Spanish oath, lifted his hand and—fell, beneath the terrific fist of his slave, with a bang that jingled the candelabras. Dolorous stroke!—for the dealer of it. Given, apparently to him—poor, tipsy savage—in self-defence, punishable, in a white offender, by a small fine or a few days' imprisonment, it assured Bras-Coupé the death of a felon; such was the old *Code Noir*.[1]

Bras-Coupé's resistance is also what leads to his death, as an article of the *Code noir* stipulates that any slave who strikes his master, "causing bruises or effusion of blood," shall be punished by death.[2] Here again, the law has a significant, plot-determining quality.

In the present chapter I shall examine the ways in which the *Code noir* was explicitly invoked or implied at such climactic moments and with such a decisive function for the resolution of the central conflicts that one text ultimately took as its title the name of the French law code governing slaves that was first devised in 1685 and repeatedly supplemented and amended from 1716 to 1762.[3] Though many other writers have drawn on the *Code noir* I shall here focus closely on four texts, two prose narratives and two plays that were published in the five-year span from 1837 to 1842: Victor Séjour, "Le Mulâtre," Fanny Reybaud, "Les Épaves," Hans Christian Andersen, *Mulatten*, and Eugène Scribe, *Le Code noir.* The issue that is of interest to a thematic investigation is whether the presence of a single element, in this case, some paragraphs of the French legal code of slavery, is connected with other recurrences; it will be addressed once a closer look has been taken at the four texts. Since English versions of these texts are not readily available, relatively detailed descriptions will be provided.

## The First African American Short Story—in *French*

The search for recovering texts written by Afro-Americans before the twentieth century has led to an impressive search-and-reprint activity that began in the late 1960s and has accelerated in the 1980s and 1990s. However, the work of the New Orleans-born and -raised writer whose full name was Jean François Louis Victor Séjour Marcou Ferrand (1817–74) has not benefited much from such activities, probably because he wrote and published in French rather than in English. Victor Séjour's father Juan Francisco Victor Séjour Marcou was a free man of color from Santo Domingo; his mother Eloise Phillippe Ferrand was a Mulatto born in New Orleans. Victor's baptismal record at the Cathedral Saint-Louis identifies him as *quarteron libre* (free Quadroon).[4] The father had a shop on Chartres Street, and Victor studied with the famous tutor Michel Séligny, attended Sainte-Barbe Academy, and in 1836 continued his education in Paris. Yet once there, he must have decided to stay, for he spent most of his lifetime as a well-known playwright and poet in France. He knew Alexandre Dumas (père), who supported him. His ode "Le Retour de Napoléon" (1841) was included in the famous Creole anthology *Les Cenelles* (1845);[5] among his many interesting dramas are "Les Noces Vénitiennes" (1855, presented in English as "The Outlaw of the Adriatic"), "The Brown Overcoat" (1858, revived in New York in 1972), and such problem plays as "Diégarias" (1844), a drama praised by Théophile Gautier, and "La Tireuse de Cartes" (1859), a performance of which was attended by Napoleon III. The text of a drama entitled "L'Esclave" (The Slave), on which Séjour was known to be working, has not been found. He also had connections with Victor Hugo, and the preparation of Séjour's dramatization of the life of John Brown was announced in 1861.[6] He may have married a New Orleans woman when he returned for a visit, and he also brought his parents back to live with him to Paris. He died of tuberculosis and was buried at Père-Lachaise.

Séjour's first literary publication, written shortly after his arrival in Paris at age nineteen and published in the *Revue des Colonies* (March 1837), the organ of a radical society of People of Color and edited by

Cyrille Charles Auguste Bissette, was the fascinating short story "Le Mulâtre." Unless an earlier text will be found in the future, this is the first published short story by an author of African ancestry born in the United States.[7]

The frame of the tale that begins with the aurora motif of the first rays of dawn is provided by a first-person singular narrator who approaches Saint-Marc, a small town in Santo Domingo, "now the Republic of Haiti," as the narrator adds so as to suggest immediately the Haitian Revolution as the significant historical background to the story. The narrator meets Antoine, an old black man who greets him as "master" and who, when reminded of an earlier promise, agrees to tell the story of his friend Georges. The old man's narrative, told from a close to omniscient point of view, and full of vivid dialogues and descriptions, forms the remainder and the bulk of the tale, which does not return to the frame narration at the end.

In the days before the end of slave sales, the estate Saint-M***, which Antoine points out to the narrator, was used as a market where husband was separated from wife, and brother from sister. There the twenty-two-year-old Alfred, one of the richest planters of the island, was bidding for a young Senegalese beauty and ended up purchasing her for a very high price. She is an orphan whose name is Laïsa, and when Alfred's driver Jacques Chambo speaks with her as he is taking her to the plantation they recognize each other as siblings and embrace each other in tears. Alfred is furious when he sees them in each other's arms and whips Jacques bloody.[8]

A tough and heartless master, Alfred takes violent possession of Laïsa, but finding her proud and cold, loses interest in her before she gives birth to his child, a boy she names Georges and whom Alfred never acknowledges. Mother and child are relegated to the meanest cabin on the plantation. When Georges grows up without ever hearing the name of his father mentioned he becomes curious about the mystery of his origin, but his mother guards the secret, promising him only that he will learn his father's name at age twenty-five. However, Laïsa dies, and leaves Georges as his heirloom only a sack containing a portrait of his father; the son has to promise to his dying mother not to open it before his coming of age on his twenty-fifth birthday.

As Georges grows older he keeps this promise despite his curiosity. By coincidence he learns one night that a group of robbers ("brigands") who have been killing planters are planning Alfred's assassination, and Georges immediately warns his master. Alfred, mistrustful like all tyrants, suspects the loyal Georges, but four assassins arrive, and in the ensuing fight Georges saves his master's life, is seriously wounded, and carried to his cabin. Antoine interrupts the flow of his narration because he forgot to mention that Georges had a wife, the young and beautiful Mulatto woman Zélie; and when Georges's life was still in danger, Alfred often came to visit him in his cabin and became enamored of Zélie, who rejected the master's advances with humble dignity. Alfred is piqued by the thought that the Sultan of the Antilles would be turned down by a slave woman, and he orders her to his chamber where he assaults her, despite all her pleas, and she, as a last resort, pushes him away—but she does it so forcefully that he loses his balance and injures his head falling down. The unfortunate Zélie immediately understands that this means that she will have to die. Alfred obviously calls upon the same paragraph of the *Code noir* that Bras-Coupé's master invoked in the novel published forty years later. Knowledge of the *Code noir* is so much taken for granted by Séjour's characters and narrator that it does not have to be explicitly named or fully cited in the text.[9]

In tears Zélie tells her incredulous husband what has happened though he, in his weakened state, cannot do anything to help. Ten days later Zélie's execution is being prepared in front of a crowd of heartless spectators. Georges pleads in vain for Alfred's pardon, reminding him of the promises he made when his life had been saved. When Alfred remains immovable, Georges accuses him of wanting Zélie hanged only because she had refused him. Georges threatens to kill Alfred, he rushes into the forest where he finds and joins the slave rebels, and Zélie is executed.

The ending of the story, set three years later, brings home the violence of the family tragedy to the master's mansion. Georges has heard that Alfred has married and that his wife has given birth to a son; he secretly approaches and manages to enter the master bedroom, having first put poison into the mistress's broth. He makes himself known to the frightened Alfred and congratulates him sarcastically on the birth of his son. Georges also asks him whether it isn't horrible to die when one is happy. When Alfred asks for mercy "in the name of your father," Georges relents for a moment and asks Alfred whether he knows who his father is. But now the wife cries for water, and Georges keeps Alfred from helping his wife, whose screams of agony soon fill the room. He shows Alfred the drops that could serve as antidote to the poison, but smashes the bottle against the wall because he wants his master to watch his wife dying. Finally Georges takes a hatchet in order to decapitate Alfred whose last pleading words are, "since you have poisoned her, you may as well kill your fa—"—at which moment the head is separated from the body; but rolling away, the father's head audibly mumbles the last syllable, "—ther" (302). Georges cannot believe his ears, opens the bag and exclaims that he is doomed. The next morning his body is found next to that of Alfred. Séjour ends the story abruptly on this high point: What could a return to the frame narrator and Antoine have added at such a moment?

Séjour's tale is a strong concentration of the horrors of slavery told from a point of view of antislavery urgency, and it was published at a time when English-language abolitionist fiction in the United States had not yet contributed anything resembling the force of this tale. Especially effective is Séjour's mythic method of locating the deep tragic themes of the son's search for the name of the father and of the father-son conflict culminating in a lurid, unknowingly committed patricide in an interracial family structure in which a modern Oedipus or Job endures the loss of his mother and his wife, and has to make the agonizing discovery that the tyrant and villain he has decapitated in revenge is his own father. As Simone Vauthier has observed in her reading of another text, "oedipal fantasies of parricide and the dream of social redress" may get "fused" in such mythic tales, resulting in images which have, "at the same time, psychoanalytic significance and revolutionary relevance."[10] Georges becomes a political rebel to the extent that he opposes his own father, a fact which heightens the revolutionary spirit of the tale as does the seemingly limitless array of injustices that Alfred is able to commit before— brought about by the master's incestuously toned desire for his own son's wife and his revenge on her through the ruthless application of the *Code noir*—the Faustian Georges finally opposes him with equal violence. The *Code noir* is also the father's law, and Alfred's application of it forces his son to become an outlaw.

Yet while the clash between father and son is central to Séjour and marks the gory climax of the tale, the stark presentation of the fates of the two women at the hand of the master is also remarkable. In Séjour's world the sexual aggression that the tyranny of slavery implies leaves few choices to the enslaved women, single or married: Laïsa's "coldness" prompts Alfred to banish her, and Zélie's resistance makes him invoke the deadly extremes of the *Code noir*.[11] And the property owner's jealousy toward "his" slave woman's brother (Laïsa's Jacques) or husband (Zélie's Georges) demonstrates the rawness and violence of the possessive urge that is unleashed by slavery. The reference to Alfred as the "Sultan of the Antilles" connects the attack of tyranny with the orientalist critique of the slave owner's desire for a harem. Séjour's "Le Mulâtre" is a brief tale for so much and for such spectacular action, and the characters are defined by their actions and by their constellation to each other more than by psychological depth, but the story is undoubtedly effective in energizing antislavery sentiment toward a revolutionary overthrow of the status quo.

### Two White Women in Love With the Same Mulatto Man

Published in February 1838, less than a year after Séjour's grim short story, the novella "Les Épaves" by Madame Charles Reybaud (1802–71) again invokes the *Code noir*, in fact, does so repeatedly and explicitly, as we shall see. The little-known author was a prolific and once popular French "regional" writer, born in Aix-en-Provence. Her maiden name was Henriette-Etiennette-Fanny Arnaud, and she published many novellas and novelettes that were seemingly marketed to railway passengers.[12] Reybaud undoubtedly takes a more moderate and optimistic position than did Séjour. This is apparent in the narrative situation, for instead of having a black storyteller who relates the story to a white frame narrator and thus offers a formal reminder of the theme of racial hierarchy, this novella—in the book version of 1839—is told by a descendant of the happy interracial union that is constituted at the end of the story. We have seen earlier how the narrator Zoe uses her fingernails as proof of the story's authenticity. Reybaud's novella was slightly expanded and newly framed as part of the novella cycle *Valdepeiras* (1839), entitled after a place near Arles in which the first novella, "Une famille de parias," is set.[13] In "Salvador," the subsequent tale of that collection, the narrator of "Les Épaves" is identified as the grandfather of Zoe, a beautiful Creole woman (104). Hence the fiction is established that in "Les Épaves" Reybaud is merely reproducing a story told by Zoe, who, in turn, is reading from her grandfather's manuscript. And what the Creole woman's tale supposedly goes to show is the firmness and devotion of women's hearts (104). This is, however, not necessarily the first conclusion that would suggest itself to an attentive reader or listener. After all, the main plot line focuses not only on the growth of pure love between the noble French heiress Cécile de Kerbran, countess of Rethel, and the multitalented Mulatto Donatien but also on the emergence of carnal attraction between Éléonore, unhappily and childlessly married to the cold, jealous, and vindictive Belgian slaveholder M. de la Rebelière, and Donatien. In other words, contrary to the critical wisdom of the 1980s and 1990s, Reybaud produced a story, set in Martinique around Christmas of 1720, in the course of which not one but two white women fall in love with the beautiful and accomplished Mulatto genius who is also the protagonist.

Éléonore de la Rebelière, the "typical" Creole, is unlike Cécile, who remains unalterably French, French here understood as synonymous with being open-minded and humanitarian. Like her Belgian husband (an upstart from plebeian origin with whom she, who comes from the best families of Martinique, has otherwise an all but harmonious relationship), she seems to have lost a sense of empathy for the victims of the plantation system; Rebelière's ward Cécile, by contrast, sympathizes very strongly with the slaves. For example, Cécile inquires about the runaway ex-slave Palème, a slave without master whom she calls a "white slave" (*esclave blanc*—two years after Richard Hildreth's *Archy Moore* popularized that term around the world): Rebelière replies that there are no "white slaves" and denounces Palème as the product of an unhealthy melting pot, "such a confusion of all races that even the devil would not recognize his own children there" (111). Little does he expect that his own ward Cécile will contribute to this melting pot by marrying a

Mulatto man—and even less that his own wife is also deeply attracted to that same man!

While Rebelière is away on a trip, Éléonore and Cécile take shelter from a storm in Donatien's residence.[14] Their host considerately sets the table only for the two women so as not to embarrass them by his presence.[15] After the meal, however, Cécile asks Donatien to sit at the table with them, and he unleashes all his charm, stunning the women with the irresistible beauty of a handsome and refined, slightly bronzed, and fashionably dressed man in his late twenties whose regular features make him resemble a figure from antiquity. Donatien explains that the beautifully executed paintings on the wall portray the brothers Énambuc-du-Parquet, and Éléonore concludes that Donatien must be the natural son of Énambuc and a slave woman of mixed blood. This, the narrator (the grandfather, Zoe, or Madame Reybaud?) adds, did not change Mme. de la Rebelière's opinion of Donatien, since she believes in the "one-drop" theory: "Had he been the first-born of a king, one drop of black blood under his skin would have sufficed to make him sink to a rank below that of the most common white" (123).[16]

Soon Cécile and Éléonore meet Donatien frequently, though he never comes *into* their house. One day the women venture alone into the wilderness and are surprised by Palème, who formerly belonged to the Rebelières. He plays the part of the wild man, shows them his scars from slavery days, and threatens to take revenge by making Mme. de la Rebelière share his hut with him; he already invites both of them to eat his fried bananas with him, crudely and disrespectfully asking Éléonore: "Do you want to eat, mistress?" (129).[17] Significantly, the young and innocent Cécile does not understand the threat that is signified by the very fact that Palème addresses them so directly and (unlike Donatien) invites them to *eat* with him. In any event, Donatien appears, and the situation immediately loses its danger. Donatien warns Palème not to touch the women.

Éléonore begins to notice symptoms of having fallen in love (132), though a feeling of indomitable pride and fierceness enters into her mind as well. Cécile, untouched by the Creole contempt for Mulattoes and unable to understand the subtle distinctions which make a Negro out of a nearly white man (133), is beginning to show signs of infatuation, too. The narrator also intimates that if Donatien's heart beat for one of the women he knew how to hide such emotions.

When M. de la Rebelière hears that a Mulatto has been the women's guide, he is startled and expresses his contempt for the mixed race which now seems to be everywhere though once there were only blacks and whites (137–38).

Rebelière's passionate jealousy is aroused one night when he finds that his wife, who is "ignorant like a Creole woman,"[18] does not know how to express herself, and can only barely hold a plume, has filled a great sheet of paper with ciphers, flaming hearts and, again and again, the name Donatien. Instead of reaching for his knife, Rebelière employs the *Code noir* as his way of obtaining his revenge: he can order the *épave*[19] (the term after which the story is entitled, meaning a "masterless slave" ) killed.

Rebelière seizes some Negroes as well as the Mulatto Donatien, who resists the arrest violently and is injured. Cécile challenges Rebelière with the question by which right he has arrested a man who "belongs to nobody." This gives Rebelière the occasion to cite the *Code noir* triumphantly: "What right? The right to ask him what he is, ask for his free papers, and if he cannot produce them, to declare him *épave* and put him up for sale. That is the law: the *Code noir* is precise" (149–50). Cécile understands: as in Séjour, the supposition is that everyone knows the provisions of the *Code noir*, and again it is shown in the hands of a tyrannical father figure who uses it as an instrument of obtaining personal revenge. Yet Reybaud's *Code noir* is no longer only the coldhearted master's law.

Rebelière humiliatingly puts Donatien up for sale in front of the church of St. Pierre on Sunday, suggesting the Church's complicity with the slave trade; and he refuses Cécile's request to buy Donatien. Looking at his wife, Rebelière swears that he will have the Mulatto killed by the overseer's whip. When Cécile tries to appeal to his religious sense toward the unhappy one who, too, was made in God's image, the colonist Rebelière tells his French ward Cécile that after some years in Martinique she will forget her French "prejudices" and come to a better understanding "of our superiority over the Negro race; those people are brutes" (151). The (implied French) reader is thus mobilized against the evil upstart's racial prejudices. When the Rebelières go off to rest, like a Gothic couple, both hiding their secrets (respectively, hatred and love for Donatien), Cécile takes the keys from under Rebelière's pillow, and goes secretly, together with the slave woman Fémi, into the sugar mill in which the injured Donatien is imprisoned. The sudden dream-like apparition of the young, rich, and beautiful noblewoman in his terrible cell makes Donatien doubt his sanity (156). Cécile advises Donatien to play along with his own sale so that she will be able to buy him, and she promises that they'll be in France together. He responds with deep emotion, puts his fate in her hands, and describes himself from now on as truly her "slave"[20] (158), but also points out to Cécile that he *is* legally free: he claims the right which gives freedom to all who have touched French soil. This is the second invocation of the law and may allude not to the *Code noir*, but to the French Court of the Admiralty's decision, on 31 March 1762, to grant freedom and 750 livres in back pay to Louis, a Mulatto slave from Santo Domingo who thus won a law suit against his Parisian master, Jean Jacques de Febre, and for the reason that he had been brought on French soil.[21] The realm of the law is thus more divided than it was in Séjour, and Donatien even thinks that a legal appeal might help, but Cécile again tells him that going through with the sale will provide the only method by which he can be saved—purchase by her.

After Cécile has left the cell, Palème appears through a secret passageway (161)[22] and offers to lead Donatien straight into freedom. Yet Donatien refuses to go and says that his friends would save him. He also does not accept Palème's knife. Palème calls him a fool for trusting the words of a white woman (163). Donatien rejects all of Palème's revolutionary revenge schemes, including one of setting fire to the Rebelière mansion and explains that he, too, might be able to kill M. de la Rebelière in fair combat, but that he could never regard the white women as enemies.

Fémi recognizes the letter "R" under a ducal crown tattooed onto Donatien's arm (as onto her own); it is the mark of the count of Rethel, on whose possession Donatien must have been born. Taking the lamp closer to Donatien, Fémi also recognizes his face: his mother was Bécouya, a Caribbean woman.[23] Rebelière's father, a poor man, had sold her to count Rethel. Now Donatien remembers, too, how, when he was very young, he was hiding in the forest with his mother, without clothes, and often hungry. One time, his mother rested under a palm tree and never got up. He stayed with her until hunters led him to the house of Énambuc.

Returning to her mistress, Fémi tells Cécile that Donatien is hers "by birth" (174), because he was born on her estate and bears her mark. Fémi also adds some reminiscences of Donatien's mother, and, as for Donatien's father, she says that there was only one white man on the plantation, the count of Rethel, Cécile's uncle (175). Worried about Rebelière's plans Cécile hurries to get advice about the *Code noir.*

The service in the church of Mouillage is in process just as the culminating scene of the auction is about to begin.[24] Donatien and four or five Negroes are awaiting their fate. Yet it is not the sale—as Cécile and Éléonore thought—but the *Code noir,* twice invoked before in the story, and now subjected to several further interpretations, that will decide Donatien's fate and force the denouement of the story.

Donatien is barefoot, dressed in slave cassack, and hiding his face in his hands. The proud Éléonore says boldly that though she knows her husband intends to buy him, Donatien is still the most beautiful man she has ever seen (178). The sale is like that of a prize horse, and when Rebelière inspects the slaves, he asks Donatien to get up and walk a bit for inspection. Donatien ignores the request, and the angry planter threatens and insults him, whereupon Donatien offers a beautiful rhetorical speech: If he is a slave it is only due to the contempt of natural laws and justice, and he attacks the supposed "master" as a self-made nobleman who hid his lowly origins and made himself "M. de la Rebelière" though his father, an indentured cooper, still was named after his profession, "Rebel le tonnelier." And he concludes: "It is more honorable to be a slave like me than to be a nobleman like you!" (180). Just as Donatien only has a first name, so Rebelière seems to have only a last name—and one that was made up.

Pélagie (who is representing Éléonore) and Rebelière start bidding, driving the price up to 12,500 livres, when Cécile has the auction stopped on the legal ground that a slave whose ownership can be ascertained may not be sold. The administrator offers documentary proof of Donatien's birthdate and of the identity of his mother, pointing out the Rethel mark on the Mulatto's arm, opens the *Code noir*, and is about to read the appropriate paragraph, when Rebelière concedes this point of law—thus revealing a rift between the tyrant and his law book. Of course, he still wants to get control of Donatien. First he offers to buy Donatien from Cécile (now for a mere 3000 livres, as the upstart seems to be thrifty even at the moment of wishing to take jealous revenge). But when Cécile continues to turn down his offers because she intends to give freedom to Donatien, Rebelière again resorts to the *Code noir*. Having told Cécile that she will never be able to set Donatien free legally, Rebelière invokes the law which requires that the governor must assent to the emancipation—and he would never do that. When Cécile replies that she intends to take Donatien to France, Rebelière, in rage, exclaims that those who walk around with the *Code noir* in their hands must also know another paragraph of the *Code noir* which makes a slave who insults a free white man liable to punishment by twenty-nine lashes. That is the law, he proclaims, and before Cécile should be able to do anything else with Donatien, he *must* receive his due punishment for having insulted Rebelière with words and gestures. What can still save Donatien?[25]

It is of course, once again, the *Code noir*. Turning toward Rebelière, Cécile briefly and firmly tells him not to touch Donatien whom she, Cécile de Kerbran, now surprisingly declares she will—*marry*. This unexpected move at the last moment of the story means that Donatien is free, and that his freedom takes effect immediately: "Read, read the article of the *Code noir*: 'any slave who marries a white woman is free by law'" (184).[26] Christ's miracle at the wedding of Cana could not have produced a greater amazement in the crowd than the words with which a free woman, a white woman, a noble woman addressed a man of color, a slave. For even if there was a similar provision in the *Code noir*, it was conceived for religious reasons in order to legitimate concubinage between master and slave woman—and not to encourage young noblewomen to invoke on the day they come of age in order to marry and free a man of color![27] Everyone is petrified. (The fact that Cécile and Donatien are probably first cousins is never mentioned.) And only now does the narrator also involve Donatien in this denouement-by-*Code noir*. Cécile formally asks him to give her his arm (184), Donatien rises without answering, and the narrator adds that there are emotions and situations in life which leave one speechless.

Éléonore, too, is stunned and silent at first; but a sentiment of justice and generosity slowly wins over her passion for Donatien that is no longer a secret to her husband. She has to renounce her love, but she is at least contented to see that her husband is raging in his unfulfilled dream of revenge. Conversely, Rebelière is comforted by seeing tears in his wife's eyes; but then he understands that her love for Donatien was strong and "devoted" (184) enough that she could consent with joy that another, happier woman might save him. This single moment avenged Éléonore for everything she has suffered, and in cold triumph she asks her husband sarcastically whatever happened to his promise to let Donatien die under the lash. Here the inside story comes to an end (as does the original *Revue de Paris* version); in the novella collection *Valdepeiras* the frame continues in which the narrator Zoe does not mention her grandfather again, but now identifies her mother as the great-granddaughter of Donatien and Cécile (and shows her nails).

As in Séjour, the *Code noir* governs the land. Yet unlike in "Le Mulâtre," in which the law—invoked only once—is firmly identified as Alfred's, as the white master's effective and unambiguous instrument that can easily bring death to his slaves, for Reybaud the law opens a realm of dispute that divides the whites so that different possibilities of invoking various paragraphs can have enormous plot consequences (though the grimmest options that were used by Séjour, by Andersen, and later by Cable, are *not* brought up here). As the legal dispute between women and men, and between the aristocratic and upstart wings within the master class grows, and the fine points of legal exegesis are developed, however, the agency of the heroically idealized mixed-race protagonist declines, and Donatien is reduced at the end—which is, to a large extent, a dispute about property and its right ownership—to be *chosen* as a husband without so much as saying a single word (184). These issues will come up again, for Reybaud's tale inspired several dramatic adaptations, two of which I would like to examine in the remainder of this chapter.

## Before "The Ugly Duckling"

In an address on "The Value of Race Literature," delivered by Victoria Earle Matthews at the First Congress of Colored Women of the United States on 30 July 1895, the forceful ex-slave woman from Georgia admonished her Boston audience not to consider race literature synonymous with self-flattery, or with "things uttered in praise of ourselves, wherein each goose thinks her gosling a swan." The reference to the transformation of a lesser fowl into a swan is probably an allusion to one of the most famous modern Danish fairy tales, Hans Christian Andersen's "The Ugly Duckling" (1843), with which Matthews's listeners were likely to be familiar (and which has occasionally been themed or retold as a comment on "race").[28] Andersen was well known as a brooding and somewhat somber man; for example, when Frederick Douglass met Andersen in England, he described "the Swedish poet" as "singular in his silence." Douglass continued: "His mind seemed to me all the while turned inwardly. He walked about the beautiful garden as one might in a dream."[29]

What is less widely known is that Hans Christian Andersen (1805–75), the world-famous author of this and other modern fairy tales, also acquired considerable experience and recognition as a playwright; it was, in fact, the hostile reaction to one of his plays that inspired him to write "The Ugly Duckling."[30] It is even less well known that among his plays is a "romantic drama" that he composed in 1839 at age thirty-four and that was first produced at the Danish Royal Theatre in Copenhagen in 1840, entitled *Mulatten* (The Mulatto).[31] It was a success, was translated into Swedish and into German, and it was revived on the stage in 1868 and 1873.

Andersen's drama was, as Frederick Marker has argued, part of the romanticization of the European stage in the first half of the nineteenth century. In France, the emergence of the new romantic drama coincided with the July Revolution and the rise of Louis Philippe; in many European countries it had strong political implications. The romanticization also went hand in hand with new theaters that had modern mechanical devices and scenic stage sets at the high point of the "panoramic" mode. At the same time, while the theater was being professionalized (with, for example, more rehearsals before a production opened), plays were increasingly and soon almost exclusively reviewed by journalists in rapidly spreading daily and weekly newspapers (rather than, as was previously the case, in more scholarly criticism by specialists). The Danish Royal Theatre on Copenhagen took part in all these developments and played such a prominent role in Danish society that the philosopher Søren Kierkegaard commented on it in 1848 with the statement that in "Denmark there is but one city and one theatre."[32]

The play *Mulatten* by the Danish writer who is now best remembered as a children's author is easily recognizable as a very close adaptation of Reybaud's "Les Épaves," the novella upon which Andersen—who first read it in the February 1838 issue of the *Revue de Paris*—admittedly based his play. At an 1843 Paris soirée at which Balzac also was present, Andersen met Madame Reybaud and amused her by telling her about his dramatic adaptation of her story and its performances.[33] Andersen structured his five acts largely along the flow of Reybaud's novella, and apart from Donatien, whom he (in a Shakespearean mood) renamed Horatio, he generally kept the characters' names, altering only the spelling.[34] Just like the novella, the play builds up toward the climactic moment of the auction scene at the end; in fact, it was the thematic novelty of the

Reybaud-inspired slave market in the play that convinced one influential man to throw "the last necessary *yes* in the urn for the acceptance of 'The Mulatto'"—making its production possible.[35] Given the extent to which Andersen followed Reybaud, it is not surprising that there were Danish reactions to his play criticizing him for failing to indicate "on the printed title-page" "that the material was merely borrowed"—especially since the subtitle of *Mulatten* promised an "original romantic drama in five acts."[36] In the wake of this debate, the *Portefeuillen* also published a Danish translation of Reybaud's novella, and Andersen decided to write a new play, *Maurerpigen* (The Moorish Maiden), that was original and all his own.[37]

When Andersen's *Mulatten* was first performed at the Royal Danish Theatre in Copenhagen on 3 February 1840, it received an overwhelmingly positive response from the audience and, on the whole, favorable notices in the Danish press, confirming Andersen's own feeling that his true literary career had started with "The Mulatto."[38] During a Danish-language performance in the Swedish city of Malmö, *Mulatten* was awarded an enthusiastic welcome by the students of Lund, where Andersen was later celebrated. A Swedish version also had a successful run at the Royal Theater in Stockholm.[39] *Mulatten* was first scheduled to be produced on 3 December, 1839, but because of the sudden death of King Frederick VI on that day, the theaters were closed for two months. The published version was dedicated with a four-line poem to the new king, Christian VIII. (Since 1838, Andersen had been the recipient of a generous annual royal stipend for writers.) Between the first and second act the concert overture "The Hebrides," composed in 1830 by Felix Mendelssohn-Bartholdy, was played in the first production.

Like the story, the play is set on the island of Martinique. Skipping Reybaud's first section, Andersen starts *in medias res*, as Eleonore and Cecilie seek refuge from a storm in Horatio's abode. The parallels are very strong, making quite unnecessary a new plot summary, yet there are also changes that Andersen made in adapting his source, from the altered sense of time to some variations in the characters, and from the employment of a highly stylized poetic language with extensive use of imagery to some newly added thematic details.

The play sounds far more contemporary than its source, which set the story in 1720. For example, Cecilie and Horatio reminisce about the museum in the "castle of Paris," thus placing the action after 1793 when, in the wake of the Revolution, the Louvre became an art museum. Revolution, too, is more of a declared theme as rebellious Maroon activity is palpable in Andersen's play. Not only have Reybaud's French *épaves* become Andersen's Danish *Herreløse*, but there is also a newly added underground group called "The Revengers" ("Hævnerne"), and revolution seems to be as much in the air in Andersen's world as it was in Séjour's.

This revolutionary atmosphere is readily apparent in the revised character of the runaway slave "Paléme" (as Andersen renders his name). It is significantly Andersen's Paléme who tells Horatio about "The Revengers," the plotting ex-slaves who creep like snakes to a secret meeting at which Paléme preaches the gospel of freedom (*Friheds Evangelium*), which promises to bring about the end of white day and the beginning of the night of black rule (29).

> White day has carried the crown for too long;
> Soon black night will sit on his throne. (29)[40]

Paléme agrees with Horatio's prediction that this ascension of the night of revolt will be a bloody coronation, indeed, accompanied by murder and rape. Like the Maroons that Séjour's Georges ultimately joins, Paléme contemplates the killing of all whites:

> We will invite Hell itself to be our guest;
> Plantations all ablaze in celebration,
> The scarlet carpet, dyed with red blood,
> Our procession shall step on with bare feet.
> Into my master's chest I will plunge the knife,
> But first, I will violate what is sacred to him,
> If not, may God curse me like all others.
> Our call for freedom shall resound to Europe! (30)

The murderous call that links Andersen's Paléme more with the "brigands" in Séjour than with Reybaud's *épaves* does not, however, lead to any *action* in the play, merely to fantasies; and Paléme begins to reconsider his plan when Horatio asks him who would be enslaved if all whites were dead. Fearing that he might have to serve black masters, Paléme sketches the vision of a permanent rule by Mulattoes:

> Should there be a leader of blacks and whites,
> Then let him be of the middling color!
> The Mulatto must be chosen as king,
> Then nobody could complain! (31)

Horatio warns Paléme that there is no middle time, no dusk, in tropical countries. Paléme speaks to Horatio from Bastard to Bastard of the "same race, same kind" (31) and thanks Horatio again for saving his life when he found him, like Job, offering to kill an enemy Horatio chooses. Horatio shrewdly names his pride (his "master" in another sense) as such an enemy.

When, inspired by the rum from his coconut, Paléme dreams his revenge fantasies against his former master, he imagines him transformed into a tree, powerless though endowed with the sense of sight, forced to watch how Paléme kisses the plantation mistress's mouth and breasts (27).[41] A product of Paléme's magical imagination, this sadistic scene of taking revenge on the owner by taking possession of the owner's wife is a startling new element in the play, in which Paléme lays bare his uncontrolled revolutionary fantasies, his curses of whites, his lust for the swelling alabaster breasts of white women (33) as well for coal-black girls (34).[42] When one of Horatio's shots backstage wakes up Paléme he believes that his dream of revenge upon his master's wife seems to have come true: he is alone in the forest with the two white women whom he threatens to kiss on their rosy lips in order to pay back with "love" (*Kjærlighed*) for all the hatred and contempt he has received (41). In the scheme of the play, Paléme stands for the perversion of love brought about by the power relations of slavery. Paléme perverts love into lust and wants to take revenge upon the two unprotected white women in the forest. Fortunately Horatio comes to the rescue.

His uncontrolled sexual wishes make Paléme a more sharply drawn negative contrast figure for the virtuous Horatio, yet it is not without interest that Andersen also gave Paléme his own properties of a fairy-tale inventor:[43] his Puck-like magic, his fantasies of inversion, of revenge; his playing the part of pure freedom and wanting to save Horatio from the treachery of whites and, significantly, from marriage. Horatio, too, does not hate Paléme—far from it. Andersen thus seems to have taken a cliché of the eighteenth century, the dialectically related pair of the noble savage (who has been described as the darling of European literature) and the slave rebel (his much feared opposite number), and, while keeping it intact, also humanized, Andersenized, or at least made more interesting, one of the "bad" parts of this play.[44]

Interestingly, Eleonore *tells* her husband about this event (which she knows must spur his wrath). If Paléme marks an extreme that is even heightened above Reybaud's version, then the upstart La Rebelliere marks the opposite exaggeration. When La Rebelliere, full of jealousy, desires to humiliate, to whip, and to torture to death the Mulatto in front of Eleonore's eyes, this is a wish symmetrically opposite to that of Paléme: "Suffer, because I suffered for a phantom" (69/G 76). The white mistress seems to be a pawn in the power game between cruel master and rebellious slave. Yet in his jealous marital and racial blindness, which is intensified by Andersen, La Rebelliere still is only able to suspect a white man and hopes that Horatio will name the culprit under torture. This imaginary white man's, Eleonore's, and Horatio's suffering will be music in his ears: a snake arabesque (69). It is significant that both Paléme and La Rebelliere are men who do not know how to control their passions. Hence their social and sexual politics are similarly confused, and neither has much interest in culture. Yet whereas Paléme represents only a symbolic threat, Rebelliere is the sine qua non of the action of the play.

La Rebelliere also yells at slaves, calls them animals, and instantly complains that his Mulatto slave Sem took care of only himself and not his mule: the alliteration of *Muuldyr* and *Mulatten* (54) is used in order to call attention memorably to La Rebelliere's racism, evoking the popular etymology of the term Mulatto, and to drive home the criticism common later in such writers as Charles Chesnutt or Zora Neale Hurston. In La Rebelliere's view, Sem's brown hide (55) must be tanned because he thought of himself rather than the mule.

By contrast to the other men, Horatio is the natural nobleman and chivalric protector of women. Horatio is not only named after Shakespeare: he is a versatile Renaissance man among whose many properties is the knowledge of literature. Eleonore and Cecilie rightly admire Horatio's tasteful home furnishings, his way of life, and his manners. He is interested in botany and zoology, has a library that includes not only French poetry but also Shakespeare's *Hamlet* and *Macbeth*, and he owns paintings (including one of the benefactor Enambuk, who was like a "father" (15) to Horatio—a not so innocent phrasing that shall prove its deeper meaning later on). In turn Horatio was like his master's "shadow."[45] The sophisticated cosmopolitan traveler Horatio shares fond memories of France with Cecilie (the art galleries, Greek gods, Tuileries, Seine, Versailles, the "sanctuary" of Notre Dame—reminiscent of Hugo's *Hunchback of Notre Dame*). They even discover that Horatio once, at a soirée at Mme. de Polignac, heard Cecilie at age ten recite a poem of the Negro king's daughter (18), and Horatio now admits that he had composed it (19)—all of which is new in Andersen. Later we learn that the woman that is the subject of it was Horatio's mother, Biscuya.[46] The poem was absent from Reybaud, but it was also published by Andersen in a collection of his own poems under the title "Negerkongens Datter."[47] Horatio is a piece of "living Shakespeare" in a context that does not fully know how to appreciate him. Cecilie and Eleonore, however, discuss "our Mulatto" (22) admiringly, showing their differentiated openness to Romanticism. More than did Reybaud, Andersen uses the idealized figure of the Mulatto as the site for a discussion of genius, and some reviewers focused on the ideals of "nobility of the soul" and "love" that the romantic drama was seen to advocate.

The Mulatto theme is very specifically enacted, with reflections on the nature of black and white, the attitude of Creoles, and so forth, but it is also clustered with such general themes as romantic love vs. calculating coldness; spirit vs. form/body; entitlement of mind and valor vs. entitlement of inheritance. In this scheme of things, the handsome, Paris-educated Mulatto is a perfect human being, has nobility of soul, is well educated, yet retains Rousseauvian naturalness: in one word, he seems so eminently eligible that it is little wonder that two women would fall in love with him. To a lesser extent, Andersen also intensifies the figures of Eleonore and Cecilie. Whereas Eleonore's growing love for the Mulatto Horatio, despite her initial prejudices, is much more explicitly and vividly represented than it was by Reybaud, Cecilie's natural modesty and innocence are strengthened. In Andersen Cecilie expedites a letter to the imprisoned Horatio, whereas Reybaud let her go right into his cell. (On the other hand, in *Mulatten*, Cecilie does recognize the danger that comes from Paléme in the forest, in "Les Épaves" she did not.)

In its language and imagery Andersen's play takes the strongest departures from its prototype. For Andersen chose not only the form of a drama, but a drama written in rhymed verse, which is a highly stylized medium. The formalism of the rhymes often calls attention to itself. This is not only the case in the many couplets in which we hear *grønne Faner* ("green flags of palm leaves") rhyme with *Bananer* ("bananas"), or *hænge-matten* ("hammock") echo *Mulatten*, but even more so when the rhyme scheme alternates from a triple to a quadruple rhyme, followed by two couplets, or when regular patterns alternate with free rhymes. The effect of the intricate language and poetic diction is further enhanced by a very elaborate use of imagery that goes far beyond Reybaud. Thus when Cecilie imagines royal origins of Horatio's mother and recites the already mentioned romantic poem about the African king's daughter who has to endure the horrors of enslavement and middle passage, we are self-consciously reminded that the whole play is also a poem.

The differences between Reybaud and Andersen suggest the extent to which the Danish playwright put his own stamp on the French author's story. Yet both versions reach their climax in the dramatic scene of the slave sale that also provides the context for the presence of the *Code noir*. At the auction blacks are seen in "picturesque groupings" (107) and among them is Horatio, bareheaded and barefoot. One slave has just been sold for "400" (of an unnamed currency), when La Rebelliere announces the sale of Horatio, orders him to rise, and threatens to flog him. Horatio answers with his characteristic praise of spirit over the body:

> Free I am like my thoughts, free and proud!
> You can dominate my body, not my spirit!— (108)

La Rebelliere cannot believe what is happening, while Eleonore (as in Reybaud) is exuberant and mockingly reminds La Rebelliere of his threat to flog Horatio to death. At that moment, La Rebelliere invokes the law (it is the familiar *Code noir* provision—that was *not* used by Reybaud) that any slave who lifts his hand against a white man has to *die* by flogging— which the auctioneer reiterates, and which La Rebelliere triumphantly makes the occasion to repeat that Horatio will be whipped to death in front of Eleonore's eyes, whereupon she breaks all bonds between her and her husband.[48] Yet Cecilie intervenes with that other law that Reybaud, too, ascribed to the *Code noir*, in a move that has justly been termed a "legal deus ex machina":[49]

> And the law is: that when a free-born woman
> Of noble ancestry marries a slave,
> Then he is free; all punishment which was threatening him

Will be annulled, his crimes forgiven,
His chains are hung in the church's nave.
He is free! Free! (111–12)

And before Horatio has the chance to say anything she continues after the auctioneer has verified the law:

Let it be known, this man no longer is a slave,
No, he is my husband! The Countess of Ratél
Gives him her hand. He will never stay a slave
Whose soul is noble! The spirit always wins,
The soulless form is blown away like dust. (112)

Only then does she actually ask Horatio's technical consent with the question: "Say, do you want to be free?" which Horatio simply answers with the exclamation "Cecilie!" Eleonore (much more quickly than in Reybaud) gives her blessing, too, and the crowd cheers the new young masters of Ratél.

The adaptors and translators of Reybaud's tale and of Andersen's play were obviously startled by the conciseness of the resolution. Thus Antier and Decomberousse (who confusingly turn Reybaud's Cécile into their Éléonore) add Donatien's response: "Have I heard well? . . . She . . . she, my wife!," and the play ends, amid "Viva" shouts, as Donatien invokes the status to which he was almost reduced by Rebelière's scheming: "I was your slave!" to which Éléonore gives the answer: "And now you are my master! Come, your hand, sir." Le Petit's German adaptation of 1845, which follows Andersen closely, enlarged Cecilie's question to: "Say, do you want to be free—free by my side?" And the authorized German translation of *Mulatten* gives Horatio at least the chance to respond to all the changes with more than one word. He now says, "Free, and eternally faithful to you!" (G 125), and Eleonore's blessing is also lengthened from a "live well" (112) to "Love's pure sun may shine brightly upon you!" (G 125).[50]

Andersen's last scene certainly contains surprise moves, as the play ends even more abruptly than the novella. Again, the story ends with the Mulatto's freedom *and* his marriage; yet the law is given more lines in the final scene than is the titular hero. The suddenness of the last happy turnabout leaves many loose ends, however. Slavery, for example, is not abolished—in fact, Horatio is a slave owner—only Horatio's short-lived subjugation by a jealous husband and loathsome *parvenu* comes to an end. The slave who is sold on stage—on a pedestal made by a board on top of two caskets—*remains* a slave. Andersen, who "swallowed all the available books on Africa and America" when he wrote *Mulatten*, may have wished, as Marker argued, to express in this play his "perpetual preoccupation with the 'ugly duckling phenomenon,' his running apologia for the gifted but poor, persecuted, or 'different' individual, excluded from polite society but ultimately triumphant."[51] The affinities of a sensitive writer, transplanted (as Andersen was during his mediterranean journeys) into an overwhelming southern clime, to the figure of a darker double, are also apparent in Andersen's tale *Skyggen*/"The Shadow" (1847)—an eerie story which makes explicit references to the transformative power southern heat has upon skin color and to the shadow's desire to "purchase" his freedom from his owner, and which culminates in the inversion of the roles of man and shadow and of the man's execution to make way for the shadow.[52] Everybody hails Cecilie and Horatio as new *masters* (with *her* surname). La Rebelliere is never dethroned, and his future relationship to Eleonore, let alone to the Ratéls, is ambiguous.

Eleonore, the white Creole, is close to her husband's racist position: she believes at the beginning that the dark race is stupid and that his African descent defines Horatio negatively. Born in the New World, she is less sensitive than Cecilie—as can be seen from her marital choice of the coldhearted racist La Rebelliere. Yet she is open to Horatio's charm. Of course, there is no single bad quality in Horatio. In fact he is so attractive that he outshines by far the only white man who matters (the father, jealous husband, social climber, and vindictive slaveholder). The play and its sources thus seem to lean toward the "hybrid vigor" hypothesis, and certainly are at odds with the degeneracy and feebleness beliefs concerning "mixed bloods" that were just being formalized (and echoed in the play by La Rebelliere) when Andersen's play was shown.

Everybody loves Horatio: this is often the fate of the female Mulatto figure. In Boucicault's *Octoroon*, for example, Salem Scudder, the observant Yankee, says about Zoe: "When she goes along, she just leaves a streak of love behind her."[53] One could also say this about Horatio. In fact, there are several aspects of the play and some of its source that suggest an inversion of expected gender roles. After all, two women fall in love with a man; he is put on an auction block; a woman bids for him; and, like the estate, Horatio will carry the woman's name since he does not have a surname. In these respects, Horatio surely fills the slot customarily accorded to women. He is also a little like a mix of Eros and pure genius, the true avant-garde of mankind, and he is the son-figure par excellence. Hence he is open to, and—unlike Paléme—invites, family-romance construction. Eleonore and La Rebelliere are structurally parents (though childless), Cecilie and Horatio are structurally children (though parentless—or ignorant of their true parentage); African and European royalty are the family-romance ancestors. Paléme is structurally the Bastard. This makes for a strange myth of origins (especially if one remembers that Madame Reybaud's novella is the story that explains Zoe's fingernails which, in turn, verify the tale of her great-grandparents).

What must *not* happen in the play? Rape, of course, though it did occur in the past as part of slavery, and though Paléme is never contained and remains a threatening spirit, and adultery, though the possibility is strongly suggested and the Rebellieres' marriage is never reconciled. What may happen, however, is intermarriage in the double sense of class mésalliance and racial mixing. French noblewoman and heiress and dark Creole bastard (with noble blood) marry—bypassing the white Creole couple, who yet remain the symbolic parents.[54] What is overcome by that match of transcendent nature and art lovers is the asocial aversion and rebelliousness of a Paléme and the selfishness and materialism of La Rebelliere. And Eleonore's ability to enjoy Horatio's and Cecilie's happiness at the end suggests that she has moved toward a better understanding of Christian love.

The critic Johan Ludvig Heiberg, married to the actress Johanne Louise Heiberg (the Cecilie of the play), mocked *Mulatten* in his "apocalyptic comedy" *En sjæl efter Døden/*"A soul after death" (1840). In this satire, Mephistopheles explains hell to the soul as the place which one reaches on a macadamized road and where the theaters perform Andersen's *Mulatten* and *Moorish Maiden* as part of a steady repertoire. Andersen retaliated with the sketch of a nightmare in which the author finds himself in hell and sees that his plays are successful indeed amid the damned souls. However, when the devil puts on Heiberg's play "Fata morgana," the damned souls revolt: "Even hell can be made too hot, and everything must have its limits!"[55]

### From Patricide, Rebellion, and an Interracial Marriage to Paternalism, Restoration, and an Intraracial Match

Eugène Scribe's *Le Code noir: Opéra-comique en 3 actes*, first performed at the Comic Opera in Paris on 9 June 1842, is another adaptation of Reybaud's "Les Épaves," but it takes the by now very familiar materials in quite another direction.[56] Reybaud and Andersen constructed the Mulatto as the focal point of passion for two white women of different generational locations; by contrast Eugène Scribe (1791–1861), in making one relatively small but central substitution, alters this pattern significantly. An immensely popular dramatist, author of more than four hundred plays, and member of the Académie Française, Eugène Scribe may be best known for such perfect comedies as *Le Verre d'eau; ou, Les Effets et les causes* ("A Glass of Water; or, Effects and Causes") and the libretto for Giacomo Meyerbeer's opera *L'Africana*. His work is associated with the change from romantic to realistic theater, especially in the development of realistic prose in drama. He is considered one of the founders of social drama and social comedy. Like Séjour, Scribe was buried at Père-Lachaise.

In his adaptation of Reybaud's novella Scribe radically excised the freestanding and marriageable white woman (Reybaud's Cécile), giving some of her functions to Gabrielle (who is otherwise the partial equivalent of Éléonore) and others to the new figure Zoé. Whereas Cécile was Rebelière's ward, Gabrielle is the niece of Parquet Denambuc (Énambuc brought back to life with real plot presence), and, as was Éléonore, Gabrielle is married to the loathsome, jealous slaveholder and *Code noir*-enforcer Marquis de Feuquières (Rebelière in Reybaud). Gabrielle's attraction to Donatien is, however, much more ambiguous than was Éléonore's. Is it all a misunderstanding of the stupidly jealous husband? This is a legitimate question in Scribe's *Code noir*, whereas Reybaud and, even more emphatically, Andersen had left no doubt about the reality of the married woman's deep attraction to Donatien/Horatio. Feuquières furthermore is a man whom we witness making sexual advances to Zamba, the black woman who takes the place of Reybaud's Fémi—but who turns out to be really Donatien's mother Zabi, that is, Reybaud's Bécouya or Andersen's Biscuya.

Scribe's discarding of the part of Cécile leaves a free space that is taken by the slave woman Zoé (whose name may have come from Reybaud's frame narrative)[57] who now gets to marry Donatien at the auction scene, and he is the best and most desirable match for her, even though she counts both Denambuc and Palème (who plays a much-diminished role in Scribe's play) among her suitors. In other words, the triangular interracial romance that is resolved with an interracial marriage in Reybaud and Andersen is replaced by an intraracial match in Scribe after several interracial courtships. Is Scribe's thus the more conservative strategy?

Politically, the answer is probably yes, as the play celebrates the restoration of the old order symbolized by Denambuc's magnanimous aristocratic rule; in terms of racial politics, however, the answer may be different, since "race" is only of marginal significance for Scribe in constructing his version of the tale. Thus, for a long time we do not know Donatien's racial background and familial identity, and different matches are proposed in the course of the play without any mention of racial difference. Thus, whereas Reybaud and Andersen differentiated an unprejudiced Cécile from a racially biased Éléonore (who is given some strong racialist lines, as is, of course, Rebelière), the emotional household of Scribe's "comic opera" is that of love and lust, requited and unrequited; jealousy, founded or unfounded; and aristocratic generosity in substituting a father's for a suitor's emotions. Enslavement is part of this plot strategy of making available or not available a potential lover—but the play is not racialized. Slave *status* is strongly thematized as a possible marriage impediment, and raises the question to whom Donatien "belongs," which is what justifies the changed title *Code noir*, since law is more important for the marriage plot than "Mulatto" identity or the presence of *épaves*. Yet race seems to play no role in various matches that are contemplated in the course of the action. It is neither thematized in

Denambuc's pursuit of Zoé, nor in Zoé's love for Donatien. In Zamba's rebuffing of the lecherous advances by Feuquières, her status as a free person gives her a strength that she would not have had when she was still a slave. (Since Zamba later on will be revealed to be Donatien's mother Zabi, this sexual advance gives Feuquières an additional loathsome quality.) Palème belongs to Gabrielle as part of her dowry, as even Feuquières concedes (310), but he is a far cry from the Andersen rebel. Donatien goes through no racial identity crisis, but through status anxiety since his newfound family history makes him at first subject to be sold and enslaved, but finally he can be freed and married—ironically *because* his slave status is established: His slave mother and her master become known and that master also turns out to be the generous Ur-aristocrat Denambuc and not an upstart governor like Feuquières—who is the only character in the play to thematize race when he reveals himself to be a bigoted hypocrite who keeps racial etiquette by thinking it an offense to have a slave seated at table with a white person (resembling Reybaud's Éléonore in this respect) but, at the very same moment, has his eyes set on Zamba (309).

Again it is the familiar high point of the dramatic auction scene at which the *Code noir* moves into the foreground while it was mentioned only peripherally before, for example, in justifying the governor's taking possession of masterless slaves, among them Donatien (345). Feuquières opens the slave sale, at which Donatien is chained to his fellow slaves with iron links, following the formal terms of the *Code noir* (363). Having recognized that Zamba is really the slave woman Zabi, Feuquières declares void her purchase of Donatien, because she cannot buy a slave since she herself is one. Denambuc offers at first to purchase Donatien, but the jealous Feuquières refuses any offer, and now Scribe lets Denambuc invoke a paragraph of *Code noir* different from any of the other texts—so that it is now the aristocratic master who performs the act that was the young woman's Cécile's show of bravery in Reybaud and Andersen:

> According to the *Code noir*, which you know better than I do, the sale of a masterless slave is void if the master presents himself . . . and the master am I! (380)

As son of Denambuc's slave Zabi, Donatien is also Denambuc's slave, and his master is free to dispose of him. Good that he is, Denambuc chooses liberty for his slave, asking Gabrielle (who is as happy to make a contrary gesture toward her husband as was Éléonore) whether she would be kind enough set Zoé free so that Donatien could marry Zoé (on whom Denambuc had set his hopes though she loves Donatien). When the grateful Zoé, who looks at Denambuc as a tutelary God (*Dieu tutélaire*) asks him how to call her benefactor, he addresses both of them with patriarchal benevolence:

Call me your father,
For both of you, from now on, will be my children. (381)

By asking both Donatien and Zoé to call him "father" (in French *père* rhymes with *Dieu tutélaire*) the spiritual quality of this paternity is understood—though Denambuc is very likely literally Donatien's father (an issue Reybaud had strongly implied and Andersen had definitely resolved, but that remains unexplored, even unasked, in Scribe). Of course, everybody is happily headed for France at the end.

One can hardly imagine the French word for father pronounced in more extremely antithetical ways than it is at the end of Séjour's story and of Scribe's play. In Séjour *pè-re* is the last word of the father, interrupted by the process of being decapitated by the man to whom he establishes a paternal relationship only at the moment of his death; when Alfred asks for mercy "in the name of your father" a little earlier, this plea has a hollow ring, for from his childhood the name was withheld from Georges. In Scribe, a cheery, old-order pseudo-family has been constituted, and Enambuc's "Nommez-moi votre père" (381), in inviting both Zoé and Donatien to call him by the symbolic name "father," does not reveal the *specific* meaning of the word for Donatien. Enambuc's gesture does, however, make him live up to the exhortation of the *Code noir* "to govern . . . slaves as good fathers of family."[58]

Compared with the extremes of revolutionary oedipal patricide (Séjour) and lack of interest in finding the father while settling for aristocratic paternalism (Scribe), Reybaud and Andersen take intermediary positions. In Reybaud it was Cécile who asked Fémi at the end of her long tale about Horatio's mother, "Mais son père?" ("But his father?"). Fémi responds: "His father? There was only one white man on the plantation, and that was the count of Rethel, your uncle" (175). It is an answer that makes Cécile blush. In Andersen, the word "father" also was important, as Andersen makes less ambiguous Reybaud's story. Horatio was raised by Enambuk, but realizes only long after Enambuk has died that he was also his father:

He was my father! I am so deeply moved!
He showed himself often as strict as a master.
Oh, as a philanthropist he gave too much,
As a father — oh, as a father much too little! (86)

The father is represented by a portrait (in Séjour, Reybaud, and Andersen), and the identity of the father, suggested by the sack with the secret (in Séjour), the mark "R" (in Reybaud and Andersen), or by the Rethel coat of arms (in Scribe), also affects the question to whom the protagonist "belongs" (always in the double sense of the word). Perhaps it comes as little of a surprise that literary texts in which "the law" is thematized may also find the need to discuss "the name of the father."[59] Yet in the relationship of "law" and "father" there are significant differences. In Séjour, the father is identical with law in its most cruel and sadistic interpretation—*Code noir* as unambiguously Bad Law—which is why violence, not legal procedure, is the only possible resolution. In Reybaud and Andersen, the memory of the dead father and ruler of the island who symbolized the Good Law is threatened by the legal maneuvers of a parvenu governor who uses the *Code noir* as a stage for acting out his vile passions, so that the young niece of the dead father has to reestablish, on the day she comes of age, the rule of the Good Law through a courageous legal countermaneuver. The *Code noir* may thus be Bad Law or Good Law, and the realm of law is of supreme importance and makes all the difference for the pursuit of happiness. In Scribe, the highest-ranking official is the symbolic (and probably literal) father, who invokes the *Code noir* as Good Law against the inferior upstart to clarify slaves as property, only to set Donatien and Zoé free and give them to each other in marriage; the Good Law is not really in jeopardy, and nobody has to be concerned much about legal changes, as long as good aristocratic rulers continue to apply the law so selflessly—which, however, seems to be more definitely the case in France than in Martinique.

The name of the law is as variedly represented in these texts as is that of the father. In Séjour the *Code noir* is so much taken for granted that it does not even have to be named, let alone cited; Reybaud and Andersen name and cite it repeatedly and contradictorily; Scribe takes it so little for granted that he lets Donatien ask Marquis de Feuquières, of all people, for more information when he hears it named for the first time: "The *Code noir* . . . you say? . . . I've never heard it mentioned in France." To which Scribe lets Feuquières respond, for the benefit of the audience: "It is the collection of ordinances and regulations concerning Negroes and slaves. . . . Severe and inflexible laws!" (311). Thanks to Denambuc, however, this very inflexibility turns to Donatien's advantage. Incidentally, the *Code noir* comes up in the context of Donatien's request for a definition of the word *épave*—as it is the existence of masterless slaves in a slaveholding colony that would most call upon the fine points of law.

The shared and apparently marginal similarity of the realm of the law, represented in all four cases by paragraphs of the *Code noir*, brought up an impressive number of further similarities in the four texts published from 1837 to 1842, of which the enunciation of "father" was only one. For Reybaud, Andersen, and Scribe the hero's search for his origins includes his having to find his mother and his slavery past. Georges, Donatien, and Horatio are wounded. Other shared elements are revolutionary and antityrannical language, Maroon rebels, dramatic slave auction (and other sales), segregationist etiquette (inhibiting interracial dining), reaching adulthood, illegitimacy, marriage and freedom, inheritance, revenge, forest, cabin, plantation, town, African origins, West Indian setting, a storm, dawn—all of which appear in several, and some in all of the texts. Yet it is also apparent that despite using shared motifs and topoi the works have dramatically different properties, and the divergent uses of same motif may give each text a distinct valence. For example, the results of the search for origins are: The Mulatto is an orphan (Reybaud and Andersen); the Mulatto becomes an orphan when he kills his own father (Séjour); or the Mulatto finds his mother and at least the symbolic father (Scribe). In Scribe, the slogan of killing tyrants is once pronounced,[60] but justice is restored without need for violent political change; in Reybaud, rebellious action is threatened, but the threat is averted; in Andersen, revolution is fully articulated and remains in the air, but does not affect the central character; and in Séjour, revolution is first rejected and then accepted as a course of action by the protagonist. The search for similarities that is central to the thematic approach might thus also benefit from the simultaneous search for differences.

The last difference among the texts that I wish to mention is that of splitting the functions given to one character into two (or of merging different characters into one). This has already become clear in Scribe, who divides the functions given to Reybaud's Cécile between his Gabrielle and Zoé—but who reserves Cécile's most dramatic action for the resuscitated Denambuc (who is also a good double to Feuquières). Perhaps the doubling strategy is even more revealing in comparing Séjour with Reybaud and Andersen. Georges's function is split into the heir Donatien/Horatio—the idealized young son who wants the rule of Good Law, knowledge of his father, freedom, and a marriage—and the outlaw Palème, who envisions freedom as revenge in the form of a sadistic retribution wreaked upon the innocent master's wife. Thus considered, what Séjour renders as Georges's *action* resembles what is represented only as the *wish* of Paléme (especially Andersen's)—and this wish is deflected by the action of Horatio/Donatien. The presence of two figures who split a single character's functions in an earlier text may here serve a strategy of containment.

Naming the right paragraph of the *Code noir* could make the difference of life and death, of a happy marriage or a sale into slavery. This difference was also at the root of literary retellings of precursor stories, as writers—and the institution of literature as a whole—participated in the debate about the nature of interracial love and family relations against the background of colonialism and the slave trade. The following chapter traces certain literary recurrences in eighteenth- and nineteenth-century literary texts in which marriage and slave sale, familial loyalty and abandonment, have functioned as ideologically charged alternatives.

# Retellings: Mercenaries and Abolitionists

'T wan't the abolitionists; 't was the slaveholders and their friends that made a race of half-breeds all over the country; but, slavery or no slavery, they showed nature hadn't put any barriers between them,—and it seems to me an enough sight decenter and more respectable plan to marry fair and square than to sell your own children and the mother that bore them.

—Jim to Captain Coolidge in Anna E. Dickinson, *What Answer?* (1868)[1]

Sold me? sold me? sold—And you promised to give me my freedom!—
Promised me, for the sake of our little boy in Saint Louis!
What will you say to our boy, when he cries for me there in Saint Louis?

—Louisa in William Dean Howells, "The Pilot's Story" (1860)[2]

*"I dearly loved my master, son," she said.*
*"You should have hated him," I said.*
*"He gave me several sons," she said, "and because I loved my sons I learned to love their father though I hated him too."*
*"I too have become acquainted with ambivalence," I said. "That's why I'm here."*
*"What's that?"*
*"Nothing, a word that doesn't explain it. Why do you moan?"*
*"I moan this way 'cause he's dead," she said.*
*"Then tell me, who is that laughing upstairs?"*
*"Them's my sons. They glad."*
*"Yes, I can understand that too," I said.*

—Ralph Ellison, *Invisible Man* (1952)[3]

ydia Maria Child's "Joanna" (Fig. 27), published in 1834, in the Boston antislavery collection *The Oasis*, was an early example of abolitionist storytelling, and it has been considered the female-authored origin of miscegenation literature in the United States.[4] The tale may have defined the issues that were to remain in the foreground of aesthetic representation for a long time. Yet it was hardly an original story, and its sources had little to do with women's antislavery literature of the United States, as it derived from the account of a British mercenary's expedition to the colony that the Dutch had received in return for letting New Amsterdam become New York. For the purposes of thematic investigation, this relationship raises the question of "versions" and "subversions" of precursor texts. Are retellings a prerequisite for the emergence of something that can be called "theme"? How do texts signal a relationship with other texts? What happens when the precursor text is "corrected" and "revised" in the retelling? And, in turn, what are we to make of exact repetitions? Whereas the shared references to the *Code noir* in a narrowly defined period put into focus texts that were dramatic adaptations of a prose narrative, and yielded a repertoire of recurrences across genre boundaries, the pursuit of direct and indirect retellings that is the subject of the present chapter covers a much larger period and proceeds along the investigative thread of direct or implied literary allusions and citations. Even though thematic references to the realm of *literature* rather than to that of *law* are the subject here, the different ideological effects of thematically similar texts continue to be of concern, as will be the plot alternative of sale and marriage. Taking its point of departure from Child, this chapter will lead us back to some eighteenth-century narratives on which her text was founded and forward to about thirty years of thematic production that can be said to have come out of, or at least partly reacted to, Child's "Joanna."

Child (1802–80) acknowledged that she had excerpted her "Joanna" from John Gabriel Stedman's *Narrative of a Five Years Expedition Against the Revolted Negroes of Surinam* (1796), and the frontispiece of the *Oasis* is

**Figure 27** G. G. Smith,
*Joanna*, revised from an
engraving by T. Holloway (1834)

**Figure 28** T. Holloway,
*Joanna*, illustration for John
Stedman's *Narrative* (1796)

recognizable as a slightly chastened illustration of Joanna taken from Stedman (Fig. 28). The story puts together and adapts most of Stedman's report about the Mulatto woman Joanna whom he met, and who took care of him, in Surinam. Stedman had described Joanna at age fifteen, complete with a footnote explaining that "A Mulatto's between white and black":

> Rather more than middle Size—She was perfectly streight with the most elegant Shapes that can be view'd in nature moving her well-form'd limbs as when a Goddess walk'd—Her face was full of Native Modesty and the most distinguished Sweetness—Her Eyes as black as Ebony were large and full of expression, bespeaking the Goodness of her heart. With Cheeks through which glow'd/in spite of her olive Complexion/ a beautiful tinge of vermillion when gazed upon—her nose was perfectly well formed rather small, her lips a little prominent which when she spoke discovered two regular rows of pearls as white as Mountain Snow—her hair was a dark brown—next to black, forming a beauteous Globe of small ringlets, ornamented with flowers and Gold Spangles—round her neck her Arms and her ancles she wore Gold Chains rings and Medals—while a Shaul of finest indian Muslin the end of which was negligently thrown over her polished Shoulder gracefully covered part of her lovely bosom—a petticoat of richest Chints alone made out the rest bare headed and bare footed she shone with double lustre carrying in her delicate hand a bever hat the crown trim'd rown[d] with Silver.[5]

Stedman pulled out the whole arsenal of neo-Petrarcan description (ebony eyes, vermillion cheeks, teeth that are rows of snow-white pearls, and lovely bosom), adjusted for some racial features (olive complexion and nearly black hair forming a globe of small ringlets), as he directly appealed to the sense of sight by mentioning that she blushed "when gazed upon." The description also has a sentimental flavor and echoes, for example, Richardson's representation of Clarissa—at the moment that Lovelace takes her.[6] In its mix of highly conventional and new-sounding exotic language, Stedman's description yet achieves the sense that it refers to a specific individual, and Stedman accompanied his prose with the engraving by T. Holloway that follows the text closely and that Child's engraver made more modest.[7] This passage has been viewed as a mixed-race stereotype, but one could speak about this representation only in hindsight as "stereotypical" because elements of it were used—as if it were a mold—in many later descriptions of mixed-blood women. In Stedman's book, the plate by Perry entitled "Female Quadroon Slave of Surinam" (Price 243 and xxxix) that was modeled on Holloway's Joanna marks the direction from specific image to type.

According to Stedman, whose published version Child followed quite closely, he "married" Joanna (though the precise meaning of this term is not completely clear in the text) and they had a son, Johnny. However, when Stedman was sent back to Britain in 1777 he was unable to raise the money needed to secure Joanna's and Johnny's freedom. He learned in August 1783 that Joanna had died the preceding November. His son arrived with nearly two hundred pounds of inheritance from his mother, was educated at Devon, became a sailor and midshipman and, as Child adds, later "perished at sea, off the island of Jamaica" (104). Child follows, hence "repeats," Stedman's account, but she also offers several distancing comments on his story: for example, she says sarcastically:

> Should any fastidious readers be alarmed, I beg leave to assure them that the Abolitionists have no wish to induce any one to marry a mulatto, even should their lives be saved by such a one ten times. (65)

And she notes:

> His marriage was unquestionably a sincere tribute of respect to the delicacy and natural refinement of Joanna's character. Yet we find him often apologizing for feelings and conduct, which are more truly creditable to him than any of his exploits in Surinam; and he never calls her his *wife*.[8]

She adds with her characteristic irony:

> If he had any reluctance to acknowledge his love, his admiration and his gratitude in England, he is at least manly enough to be ashamed of confessing it.

On his attitude toward slavery and the trade, she comments:

> Captain Stedman appears to have been extremely kindhearted, and strongly prepossessed in favor of the African character. He was often made ill and wretched by the cruelties he witnessed;—(cruelties, which the imagination of the most "fanatical" Abolitionist could never have conceived;) he saved a negro slave from a dreadful whipping by restoring a dozen of china, which she had accidentally broken[9] —while fighting to support the tyranny of slave owners, he mourned over the horrors of slavery, and left a share of his own provisions, by stealth, in the woods, where he had seen a poor rebel, half starved negro concealed;—he was even unhappy for days, because he could not forget the reproachful look of a dying monkey, which he had shot in order to release the poor animal from lingering torments. Yet he conjured the English Abolitionists not to oppose the continuance of the Slave TRADE; lest Holland should make more money than England! Alas, for the inconsistency and selfishness of man! (104–5)

Child thus attempts to put Stedman to abolitionist use, precisely because he wasn't one. Stedman's *Narrative* is striking for its obvious love of massive literary allusions (ranging from Homer and Shakespeare to Phillis Wheatley and Ignatius Sancho) which ironically serve to authenticate, because they make familiar to readers, the novel autobiographical account that aims to portray a modern, sensitive character and idealize "nature" (with a remarkable interest in botany and zoology—

that may have been an inspiration to many later texts of interracial literature, such as Andersen's *Mulatten* or Mayne Reid's *The Quadroon*, in
which this scientific interest in nature is pronounced). The romantic
spirit of fresh experience and individual originality is thus presented and
contained in a very deeply engrained sense of linguistic conventionality
and tradition which Stedman constantly employs. For example, when
Stedman gives Joanna twenty guineas' worth of bridal presents, she
brings the articles back to the merchants and returns the gold to Stedman
with the words:

> "Your generous intentions toward me are sufficient, sir," said she: "allow
> me to say that I consider any superfluous expense on my account as a
> diminution of that good opinion, which I hope you now, and ever will,
> entertain concerning my disinterested disposition." (72/Price 101)

Stedman feels obliged to explain and praise not just her pure action in
defiance of "love of gain" but, quite absurdly, the stilted language in
which the narrator chose to cast her sentiments:

> Such was the language of a slave, who had simple nature only for her
> instructer. The purity of her sentiments requires no comments of mine; I
> respected them, and resolved to improve them by every care. (72)

Child rightly stresses that Stedman's is an interracial love-but-not-
quite-marriage story, and that he is inconsistent. What Child does not
mention, however, is that the tale is phrased in such a way as to retell,
adjust, and correct precursor stories. In fact, as we shall see, the desire to
represent his life in such terms as to set right a precursor tale may at
times outweigh Stedman's interest in basing his account on personal
experience.

Most especially, Stedman's *Narrative* functions as an answer and a
specific corrective to Richard Steele's *Spectator* essay on "Inkle and
Yarico," first published on 13 March 1711 and so immensely popular in
Europe that, apart from reprints and translations into such languages as
Russian, Swedish, Danish, Dutch, Hungarian, Italian, and Latin, forty-
five different literary versions in poetry, prose, and drama have been
identified in eighteenth-century English, German, and French literature
(Fig. 29), some of them casting Yarico as an African. "Inkle and Yarico" is
told by the frame narrator Arietta, who presents the story as a tale not
about slavery but about "the old topic of constancy in love" which, since
it is told by a woman, cannot follow the men's conventions in representing women as "unbecoming," for once the lion will start to paint we shall
no longer see only pictures of men killing lions.[10] Thomas Inkle is a
twenty-year-old Englishman devoted to "Love of gain" who, on an expedition to America in 1647, is surprised by natives but saved by the Indian
maiden Yarico, a "Person of Distinction":

***Figure 29*** J. M. Moreau and N. De
Launay, *Un Anglais de Barbade vend sa
Maîtresse* (1780)

After the first Surprize, they appeared mutually agreeable to each other. If
the *European* was highly charmed with the Limbs, Features, and wild
Graces of the Naked *American*; the *American* was no less taken with the
Dress, Complexion, and Shape of an *European*, covered from Head to
Foot. The *Indian* grew immediately enamoured of him, and consequently
solicitous for his Preservation: She therefore conveyed him to a Cave,
where she gave him a Delicious Repast of Fruits, and led him to a Stream
to slake his Thirst. In the midst of these good Offices, she would sometimes play with his Hair, and delight in the Opposition of its Colour to that
of her Fingers: then open his Bosome, then laugh at him for covering it.
She was, it seems, a Person of Distinction, for she every day came to him in
a different Dress, of the most beautiful Shells, Bugles, and Bredes. She
likewise brought him a great many Spoils, which her other Lovers had presented to her; so that his Cave was richly adorned with all the spotted Skins
of Beasts, and most Party-coloured Feathers of Fowls, which that World
afforded. To make his Confinement more tolerable, she would carry him
in the Dusk of the Evening, or by the favour of Moon-light, to unfrequent-
ed Groves and Solitudes, and shew him where to lye down in Safety, and
sleep amidst the Falls of Waters, and Melody of Nightingales.

After several months in which Inkle wishes he could take Yarico with
him to England, she discovers a ship, makes signals to it, and it stops,
picks up the pair, and takes them to Barbadoes where an immediate slave

market is always held upon the arrival of a ship (Fig. 30). The story ends abruptly:

> To be short, Mr. *Thomas Inkle*, now coming into *English* Territories, began seriously to reflect upon his loss of Time, and to weigh with himself how many Days Interest of his Mony he had lost during his Stay with *Yarico*. This Thought made the Young Man very pensive, and careful what Account he should be able to give his Friends of his Voyage. Upon which Considerations, the prudent and frugal young man sold *Yarico* to a *Barbadian* Merchant; notwithstanding that the poor Girl, to incline him to commiserate her Condition, told him that she was with Child by him: But he only made use of that Information, to rise his Demands upon the Purchaser.

This brief and simple moral tale represents slavery as the betrayal of a beloved, combining a mild antislavery sentiment with a critique of the merchant as a type. Yarico, too, is a type, a figure akin to Pocahontas or La Malinche: she is the benevolent, beautiful, and devoted native woman, to whom the European hero owes his life. Yet in Steele's contagiously presented version the idyllic romance by waterfalls and accompanied by the singing of (European) nightingales is short-lived. Although Yarico alerts Inkle to the arrival of a ship, she is cruelly sold by him; her pregnancy is not viewed by Inkle as the possible beginning of a foundational story or as a joyful sign of his impending fatherhood, but as an increase in her value as a commodity. The victory of "Love of gain" that the accountant-like Inkle achieves in the story contrasts sharply with the implied reader's expected sentimental counterreaction, for had not Inkle carried a bit far the maxim that time is money? A stingy man's calculating

***Figure 30*** Inkle and Yarico (1808)

***Figure 31*** Howard and Heath, Inkle
and Yarico (1808)

and merciless frugality is thus viewed critically and found wanting from
the point of view of a beautiful woman's natural generosity. London and
West Indies, city and country, metropolis and the colonial periphery,
unpitying concern with property and selfless love and natural nobility,
modern time and the timelessness of paradise, clash in the two figures of
a man and a woman—and it is hard to imagine a reader who could easily
side with the unsympathetic Inkle in this melodrama. His ironic characterization as prudent and frugal is calculated to make the reader wonder
about other abuses of mercantile virtues. The story raises a romantic
expectation only to dash it with the last sentences, starting with the
intentionally misleading phrase "to be short."[11] Indeed, far from continuing the tone of the preceding sentences in order to cut short toward a
conclusion, the last few lines radically shift gears as the romantic island
life appears in a new light to Inkle. At the same time, "Mr. Thomas
Inkle" is made the target of social satire that contrasts with the previous
idyllic descriptions, and goes further than his initial characterization as a
man whose "Prepossession toward his Interests" prevented the "natural
Impulses of his Passions" (Fig. 31).

Not only is the slave trade symbolically cast as the merchant's betrayal
of a fellow human being who deserves to be loved (yet is sold like "Oxen"
or "Horses"), but it also seems to require literally the sale of the mer-

chant's own progeny. In a very direct fashion, family is thus sacrificed to slavery, an antislavery point that would be scored again and again, culminating perhaps in *Uncle Tom's Cabin*.

### The Reverse of "Inkle and Yarico"

Stedman's narrative can be said to *subvert* the *Spectator*'s: Instead of acting as a mercantile traitor to his beloved, the hero and narrator casts himself as a human being who—against the prejudices of his peers—wants nothing more than to see his beloved (and, later, their son) free and together with him.[12] Whereas Inkle *sells* the pregnant Yarico in order to make money (considering all the time he has "wasted" by being with her), Stedman wishes to *buy* freedom for his Joanna. And while Inkle is rescued by Yarico, Stedman tries to save Joanna, and they do get "married." Stedman notes that a lady assured him that he "was censured by some, applauded by many, but she believed in her heart envied by all" (72). The narrator seems to expect the reader (or at least some readers) to object to his attachment to Joanna. It was Stedman's conscious engagement with such potential audience reactions that Child had criticized as needlessly apologizing for creditable feelings and conduct. Of course, Stedman may have sought approval by many precisely by thematizing his censure by some.

In his account, Stedman and Joanna enter a paradise of love consummated in a fittingly Edenic setting, rich with provisions, fruit, vegetables, and sheep. Again Child (who was the editor of *The Oasis*, in which her "Joanna" appeared) chose a regularized adaptation of Stedman's touching and exotic plate "Rural Retreat —The Cottage" for a vignette (Fig. 32). "Never were two people more completely happy," Stedman writes

**Figure 32** *Rural Retreat—The Cottage*, illustration for John Stedman's *Narrative* (1796)

(79), recognizing this time as the "golden age" of his expedition. Stedman makes the analogy of Stedman and Joanna to Adam and Eve explicit by incorporating a passage from Milton's *Paradise Lost* at this moment.[13] Yet problems are lurking in this interracial paradise, stemming from Stedman's military duties and Joanna's slave status, and from the many dangers to their health. The fact that she was expecting a child "redoubled" Stedman's distress: "The idea that my best friend, and my offspring must be slaves, was insupportable" (82). One more time Joanna (though pregnant at the time) nurses Stedman when he is so ill that he is considered dead.

Two weeks after she gives birth to a boy, Stedman happily presents Joanna with "a gold medal, which," he says, "my father had presented to my mother on the day of my birth" (87/Price 297). He thus recognizes himself as a link between his father and his son (to whom he also confers the name John Stedman), though this gift also signals an economic exchange and reminds the reader of the gold ornaments Joanna had received from her father—instead of her freedom. Stedman is particularly antagonistic to his friends' advice as far as the fates of their children from slave women are concerned. His messmates tell him, sounding like Iago: "Do as we, do, Stedman. . . . If our children are slaves, they are provided for; and if they die, what do we care? Keep your sighs in your bosom, and your money in your pocket, my boy" (85/Price 289). This, Stedman says, he only repeats in order to show how hurt and disgusted he was by such advice. He lacks sufficient funds, but he states that "no price would be too dear for one so excellent, provided I could pay it" (88). Stedman presents himself as a loving husband and caring father who is prevented—by the harshness of the legislation that inevitably enslaves children of slave women, and by the constraints imposed upon him by his limited funds—to act fully upon his moral impulses and purchase Joanna's freedom.

If the reader did not get the message that Stedman's story was a *subversion* of a prior story and its moral (rather than merely an account of an expedition based on a logbook), the narrator, upon two occasions, quite explicitly drives home that point. Having made up his mind to protect Joanna, Stedman chooses an ironic way of addressing the reader that Child renders as follows:

> Reader, let my youth and extreme sensibility plead my excuse. Yet surely my feelings will be forgiven, except by those few who approve of the *prudent* conduct of Mr. Inkle toward the unfortunate and much injured Yarico, at Barbadoes. (69/see Price 98)

This passage, with its explicit echo of the *Spectator*'s irony toward Inkle's understanding of the mercantile virtue of "prudence," suggests that Stedman counts on the reader's familiarity and moral agreement with Steele's parable of the colonial encounter as the betrayed trust of a love relationship; yet it also shows that the story was told in the hope that a less upsetting conclusion could be offered to the tale than the one in the well-known "Inkle and Yarico" story. The *Spectator* readers merely had to arrive at a critical laugh at Inkle for failing to live up to his responsibilities and using mercantile exchange value as a weak and shallow excuse for his abominable conduct; Stedman's readers had to be convinced that the narrator-hero should be commended for his love and family loyalty. No one needed to fear that Stedman might in any way repeat Inkle's action. Looked at another way, this mode of narration establishes Stedman's originality and probity precisely by invoking a familiar literary script that he does *not* follow.

Shortly before he has to leave for Britain, when he is finally granted freedom for his son, upon pledging his word of honor to the governor that his "dear boy, John Stedman . . . shall never, to the end of his life, become a charge to the Colony of Surinam" (99), Stedman describes his feelings:

> But so extravagant was my joy on this day, at *having acted a part the reverse of Inkle to Yarico*, that I was half frantic with pleasure. I made my will in favor of my boy, and appointed two of my friends his guardians during my absence. . . . (100; my emphasis)[14]

Stedman thus seems to experience the joy of the emancipation of his own son very directly in terms of a story, one that his experience fortunately subverts or "reverses," however. He does not repeat the "prudence" of an Inkle (whose attitude is, however, well represented among Stedman's messmates, fellow citizens, and, as he undoubtedly presumes, some of his readers), and, expecting and inviting controversy, he casts himself as a post-Inkle lover of a slave woman. His moral authenticity is described and made plausible by a focus on its defiance of the patterns of previous fiction.

If "Inkle and Yarico" is the representative liberal story on the theme of enslavement, then the reader's focus is on the inherent danger that the mercantile world may violate even the most sacred-seeming contracts in return for greater profits.[15] In representations of slavery in exchange systems, "sale" or "marriage" could function as moral alternatives between which a white partner in an interracial liaison could choose.[16] Stedman voices a more conservative view: a human being of some integrity can make better moral choices than Inkle, even in a slave-trading and -holding world. In Stedman's view, as rendered (but criticized) by Lydia Maria Child, slavery does not corrupt absolutely; it merely provides a temptation that can be shunned by a good soul.

Focusing on another detail of the 1790 manuscript, however, the reader might find Stedman directly echoing a popular opera adaptation of the "Inkle and Yarico" tale and thus see him reenacting a version of the tale despite all his denials. When he arrived in Surinam, on his first night in Paramaribo, Stedman describes himself sexually pursued and finally giving in to a "Masculine young *Negro-woman*, as black as Coal, holding a lighted *Tobacco pipe* in one hand, and a burning *Candle* in the other"—and when he describes her pulling off his shoes and stockings and kissing and pursuing him into his "sleeping apartment," he calls her "*wousky*." He thus alludes, as Richard and Sally Price note, to the black female character Wowski, who is Yarico's attendant with whom Inkle's servant Trudge forms the *buffo* pair in the popular opera version of *Inkle and Yarico* (1787) by George Colman the Younger (Fig. 33).[17] Yet whereas the opera's Trudge was faithful to Wowski, thus forming a comic contrast to the *Spectator*'s Inkle, and Colman brought the plot to a happy ending, Stedman uses the vulgar and in part racist comedy of the episode to create a foil for the idealization of his relationship with Joanna.

R. Cruikshank, Del.    G. W. Bonner, Sc.

TRUDGE AND WOWSKI: "COME, LET US DANCE AND SING"

*Figure 33*  R. Cruikshank, "Come, let us dance and sing" (1829), featuring Trudge and Wowski from George Colman's *Inkle and Yarico*

## "John Stedman" and John Stedman

Child, in her own antislavery trajectory, was suspicious of Stedman. Much though he built up his credentials out of the same sentimental materials that were to animate American abolitionist literature, she mistrusted his account. If anything, she was not suspicious enough. For, as we can now safely assert in hindsight and with the help of the critical edition of the manuscript of Stedman's *Narrative*, even the skeptical reader Child fell for a good part of Stedman's sentimentalized self-representation; she probably would have been surprised by the extent to which the historical figure John Stedman had invented himself as a romantic character, a process the editor of the first published version completed. The log of the years Captain John Stedman spent in Surinam, and the 1790 manuscript, differ significantly from the published account. From the following examples given by the Prices one has to conclude that Stedman's transformation of the Joanna episode was remarkable.

Stedman's log suggests very strongly that he met Joanna and another woman for the purpose of engaging in sexual activities, and that Joanna's mother offered a plaçage, or concubinage, for a price that caused some dispute. Thus Stedman's log for 22 February 1773 reads: "a negro woman offers me the use of her daughter, while here, for a sertain soom we dont agre about the price." On 11 April 1773 Stedman notes: "J——a, her mother, and Q—— mother come to close a bargain with me, we put it of for reasons I gave them." The difficulties in negotiating the arrangement known as "Surinam marriage" that gave a mercenary access to a mistress for the duration of his stay seem to have been ironed out a little later: on 12 April Stedman writes "B——e and J——a both breakfast with me, I call meself Mistire," and by 23 April 1773 the log states: "J——a comes to stay with me" (xxxii). It was Stedman's custom in his log to indicate sexual partners by abbreviations; in the manuscript he prepared for publication they are named, though described more discretely.[18] Instead of focusing on such episodes as taking "soop in my room with two mallato girls" (25 February 1773), Stedman had obviously decided to concentrate on an imaginatively conceived romance with "the beautifull Mulatto Maid Joanna" alone that changed her role as a sexual partner. The Prices summarize:

> There is no mention of her sleeping with Stedman (either alone or with "B——e") until well after they become good friends; the very telling scene in which her mother offers her to Stedman for a price is deleted wholesale; and in general, the early stages of their relationship are rephrased by Stedman to elevate Joanna from the role of a slave girl providing routine sexual services, as part of a commercial transaction, to the status of a pure and noble beauty . . . whom Stedman first began to worship from afar. (xxxiii)

> While his diaries depicted a society in which depersonalized sex
> between European men and slave women was pervasive and routine, his
> 1790 manuscript transformed Suriname into the exotic setting for a deeply
> romantic and appropriately tragic love affair. (xxxv)

Stedman and Joanna entered their "Surinam marriage" on 8 May
1773, yet the 1790 narrative stylizes the affair romantically as a modern,
European-style, reciprocated love-and-marriage plot. The published
narrative of 1796 finally speaks of a "decent wedding, at which many of
our respectable friends made their appearance, and at which I was as
happy as any bridegroom ever was" (ch. 5, 62; Price xcvn54), a passage
that Child revises a bit stylistically but reprints in her version. Though he
does not admit this in his chronology, it seems established that back in
England Stedman did marry a European woman in 1782, a few months
*before* Joanna died, "possibly from the effect of poison" (lxxxvii). The
Prices conclude: "In spite of his sentimentality about Joanna throughout
the 'Narrative'. . . , he seems to have decided well before her death to
keep her simply as a precious memory and not to seek to bring her to
Europe" (lxxxvii).[19] Still, the book ends with Stedman's happiness at
being reunited in Devon with his son Johnny.

The desire not to be another Inkle carried Stedman very far.[20] His
sympathy for the suffering of slaves was memorably expressed, and it was
captured by William Blake's engravings that, among others, illustrated
the book; in fact, Theotormon's inability to free his beloved Oothoon in
Blake's *Visions of the Daughters of Albion* may well have been inspired by
Stedman's Joanna narrative.[21] Yet Stedman's attitude toward slavery was
complicated, its representation strongly affected by the revisions: the
editor of the 1796 narrative made him sound like a more consistent
proslavery advocate than he was in the manuscript (lxii-lxiii), and his critical observations were toned down. For example, some references to the
beauty of African or Mulatto slaves and to their superior cleanliness were
deleted as were Stedman's unflattering remarks about the unattractive-
ness of European women in Surinam (lxiii and xcvn55); in one instance,
Stedman changed the description of Joanna "bathing with her
Companions" to let her appear "bathed in tears" instead.[22] By this
process the book became both more sentimental and more conservative,
but also perhaps more useful to Child.

What is the significance of such transformations, especially if we
remember that Child's work has been viewed as the origin of miscegenation literature in the United States, that Child returned to the materials
she culled from Stedman in her short story "The Quadroons" (1842) and
her novel *Romance of the Republic* (1867), and that the tale has been rewritten by other nineteenth-century writers, including Harriet Beecher
Stowe?[23] If we also remember Child as a promoter of Harriet Jacobs—
whom she edited—and an inspiration to William Wells Brown—who

incorporated her "Quadroons" into his novel *Clotel*—we can assume that the effect of Child's medium has been large.[24] Has American abolitionist writing remained tied to a subversion of a subversion? And what was it that was repeated, perhaps unconsciously, in this process?

Child did not mention in her framing comments that Stedman's story was a revision of "Inkle and Yarico," but it was precisely this implication of Stedman's narrative that the abolitionist Child had to oppose in her own right. She articulated her opposition, as we saw, in her frame narrative to Stedman's "Joanna," but also in her own works. It thus seems possible to read some of Child's literary œuvre as continuing the revising process that she had initiated in the "Joanna" tale of 1834.

## Lydia Maria Child's Revision of the Revision; or, From Yarico to Xarifa?

In her short story "The Quadroons" (originally published in 1842, and reprinted with a slightly altered ending in 1846), set in Sand-Hills, Georgia, Child retold Stedman's Surinam story not, as one might expect, by going back to the clear-cut moral allegory of the original "Inkle and Yarico," but by further developing the newer sentimental materials and details that had appeared in Stedman's narrative, yet turning them *against* what Child perceived to be Stedman's line of interpretation: Child's focus switched to the double family, in which the white *pater familias* has an illegitimate mixed and a legitimate white family, and he gives up the former in order to enjoy the latter. The two families interact since the worlds of metropolis and colony now coexist in the single space of Sand-Hills. If Inkle *sells* Yarico, and Stedman *"marries"* Joanna, then Child's white male hero Edward notably *fails to marry* his beloved half-caste woman Rosalie, and not merely because Georgia laws prohibit it. Edward ultimately, after ten years of living with Rosalie, and despite the fact that they have a beautiful daughter, Xarifa, marries someone else: it is Charlotte, a white woman with property. This partly opportunistic move makes Edward a weakling and a traitor, but it is only in further indirect consequence of his action that his own daughter is sold, violated, turns insane, and commits suicide. As Carolyn Karcher put it, Child embarked on the contradictory enterprise of employing the "conventions of romance" in order to "dispel readers' romantic illusions about slavery."[25]

If Steele's view of slavery was that it turns what should be tender ties into marketable commodities, and Stedman responded by focusing on the difficulties of undoing the slave status of a beloved (however imaginary his published account may have been in that respect), then Child showed slavery as a white man's literal betrayal of a beloved half-caste woman (whom he does *not* marry) and of their daughter (to whom he fails to convey the name of the father and the protection of a legitimate

family), by marrying another woman of "his own race." Xarifa is a quotation brought to life, for Child took the name from the ballad "The Bridal
of Andalla"[26]—a popular Spanish song that addresses the romantic
Moorish maiden with downcast, teary eyes, similar also to Stedman's
romanticized Joanna, "bathed in tears." Xarifa's complexion is "rich and
glowing as an autumnal leaf," and in mentioning that Xarifa's "young
cheek often mantled at the rude gaze of the young men" (63), Child's
narrator follows Stedman's detail of the cheeks that turn "vermillion
when gazed upon."

Child also connected the description of Xarifa's eye with the halftone
metaphor from printing techniques when she wrote:

> The iris of her large, dark eye had the melting, mezzotinto outline, which
> remains the last vestige of African ancestry, and gives that plaintive expres-
> sion, so often observed, and so appropriate to that docile and injured race.
> (63)

Child may not have been the first one to focus on the eye in that way, and
she certainly drew on Joanna's "Eyes as black as Ebony," "large and full
of expression," the Xarifa of the ballad whose tearful "eyes look down,"
and probably also on the conservative Joseph Holt Ingraham's *The
Quadroone* of 1841, which includes the already cited definition of the
word "Quadroon" (which would have been of interest to Child when she
was at work on "The Quadroons" of 1842) and which mentions the
Quadroons' "remarkable and undefinable expression of the eyes, which
always betrays their remote Ethiopian descent" (ix). Ingraham's interest
in the "expression of the eyes" as a racial sign may have been echoed by
abolitionists and other American writers through Child's good services.

Near the end of the same year in which Child published "The
Quadroons," for example, the young Walt Whitman in his novel
"Franklin Evans; or, The Inebriate. A Tale of the Times," described
Margaret, the Creole woman, in rather similar terms:

> She was of that luscious and fascinating appearance often seen in the south,
> where the slight tinge of the deep color, large, soft voluptuous eyes, and
> beautifully cut lips, set off a form of faultless proportions—and all is com-
> bined with a complexion just sufficiently removed from clear white, to
> make the spectator doubtful whether he is gazing on a brunette, or one
> who has indeed some hue of African blood in her veins. Margaret belonged
> to the latter class: and she only wanted an opportunity to show, that the
> fire of her race burnt with all its brightness in her bosom, though smoth-
> ered by the necessity of circumstance.[27]

Child, whose story is just as packed with literary allusions and quotations as was Stedman's, transformed the fable into a familiar sentimental
plot-line that focuses on the moral distinction between a mistress and a
wife.[28] In reading Child's description of Edward's and Rosalie's union,

one remembers the author's comment that Stedman never called Joanna his *wife*: "It was a marriage sanctioned by heaven, though unrecognised on earth" (62–63). By contrast, Edward's marriage to Charlotte is legitimate but secular, as it is based on expedience rather than on deep love. Child phrases the story as the contrast between interracial concubinage founded on love and intraracial marriage motivated by expedience (the latter an equivalent of Inkle's "Love of gain").

Child's literary code echoed Stedman's mix of high-flown literary allusions, sentimental strategies, and detailed botanical observations, blended further with the oriental flavor of Washington Irving's Spain and elements of Ingraham's New Orleans. Thus the cottage inhabited by Edward and Rosalie, "almost hidden by the trees," is blessed by very beautiful natural surroundings.[29] The natural paradise (that Child was to develop into the even more elaborate floral fantasy of *Romance of the Republic* that makes that New Orleans novel a botanist's delight) forms a sharp contrast to the moral tragedy of its human inhabitants, in a chain of events initiated by a fall from Eden brought about by *a man*, by Edward's infidelity to his "marriage sanctioned by heaven." Here is the moral turning point of the story:

> When Xarifa entered her ninth year, these uneasy feelings [that is, Rosalie's worries about Xarifa's future in the United States] found utterance in earnest solicitations that Edward would remove to France, or England. This request excited but little opposition, and was so attractive to his imagination, that he might have overcome all intervening obstacles had not "a change come o'er the spirit of his dream." He still loved Rosalie, but he was now twenty-eight years old, and, unconscious to himself, ambition had for some time been slowly gaining an ascendancy over his other feelings. (64)

Edward becomes patriotic and envisions a career in politics—"the arena where so much American strength is wasted," as the narrator comments (obliquely suggesting, perhaps, Child's disappointment in her own husband's disastrous political career);[30] he visits frequently the house of an important, popular, and wealthy man, whose daughter Charlotte seems to have a "timid preference" for him that excites his vanity. With a few lines Child suggests Edward's dissolute character: he succumbs to the temptations of political ambition and to his desire for "variety in love." It is the father and patriarch alone who is morally responsible and reprehensible—Charlotte would have shared that moral burden with him only if she had been flirtatious and actively erotic. And, of course, she knows nothing of her future husband's mistress and daughter. Furthermore, Edward is too ashamed to let Rosalie know of his impending marriage with Charlotte so that Rosalie has to confront him after hearing rumors. The beauty of the moonlit night at Sand-Hills and her memories of the many times Edward had "fondly twined" a passion flower's vine's "sacred blossoms with the glossy ringlets of her raven hair" (66)[31] cruelly contrast with the news she receives.

The results of Edward's betrayal are manifold. Rosalie refuses to remain the married man Edward's mistress when he proposes, in Child's words, that she "enter into a selfish league against the happiness of the innocent young bride" (67), and although she does not commit suicide only because she thinks of their daughter, Rosalie finally dies of grief. Edward finds his own death after he takes to drinking.

The death of both of her parents leaves Xarifa as the protagonist or, rather, the most prominent victim, of the latter part of the story. In this focus on the younger generation, Child was part of a construction of a brief symbolic narrative of American slavery that had been sketched by many authors of the nineteenth century. Between the publication of "Joanna" and that of "The Quadroons," for example, Captain Frederick Marryat had given the following account of slavery in his popular *Diary in America* (1839):

> A planter of good family (I shall not mention his name or the state in which it occurred, as he was not so much to blame as were the laws), connected himself with one of his own female slaves, who was nearly white; the fruits of this connection were two female slaves, very beautiful girls, who were sent to England to be educated.
>
> They were both grown up when their father died. At his death his affairs were found in a state of great disorder; in fact, there was not sufficient left to pay his creditors. Having brought up and educated these two girls and introduced them as his daughters, it quite slipped his memory that, having been born of a slave, and not manumitted, they were in reality slaves themselves. This fact was established after his decease; they were torn away from the affluence and refinement to which they had been accustomed, sold and purchased as slaves, and with the avowed intention of the purchaser to reap his profits from their prostitution!![32]

Tocqueville reported a similar story.[33] It is against the expectation of such critical vignettes of slavery that Child's tale continues. Child's Edward, too, never made a will. For a while Xarifa's fate is in the hand of Edward's widow, Charlotte; surprisingly, even though she ultimately finds out the truth about her husband's past association and progeny, Charlotte, who is described as a good, though fairly passionless, white woman throughout, continues the full child support of Xarifa.[34] Xarifa's teacher George Elliot, significantly an Englishman, falls in love with her. Now it turns out that Rosalie (who never knew about this) was the daughter of a slave, Angelique,[35] and Xarifa, as Angelique's granddaughter, is claimed by the creditors of the estate, reverts to the status of a slave and property, and is sold for the absolutely enormous sum of $5000 to an unnamed "wealthy profligate."[36]

Thus Child restores the motif of the sale from "Inkle and Yarico," yet in a different fashion and for a different purpose. George Elliot is in the position of the disempowered lover who cannot save his beloved from the sale; he is killed when he trusts a double-crossing slave in planning an escape plot for Xarifa. Toward the end of the story, Xarifa's purchaser is "weary of her obstinacy, as he pleased to term it; and threats took the place of persuasion" (76). Xarifa goes mad in that situation and commits suicide:

> That pure temple was desecrated; that loving heart was broken; and that beautiful head fractured against the wall in the frenzy of despair. Her master cursed the useless expense she had cost him; the slaves buried her; and no one wept at the grave of her who had been so carefully cherished, and so tenderly beloved. (76)

By creating a double story of a wife and a daughter, Child keeps the old motif of the exchange value of the woman intact, though she places increased emphasis on the *descendant* who is no longer, as in "Inkle and Yarico," Marryat, Tocqueville, or, though less so, in Stedman, merely a characterless function illustrative of the white father's guilt of omission or commission, but a central figure in her own right. On the other hand, even though her physical description, inspired by Stedman's Joanna, included what were to become clichés of Mulatto portraiture, Xarifa is not yet, it seems to me, a "Tragic Mulatto" (a term that I shall investigate in the next chapter), but rather someone whose slave origin (rather than whose "race") entangles her, as she may be claimed as property (rather than be identified as "nonwhite").[37]

In all versions, the dominant moral (or immoral) center of consciousness is the white man as lover and father, though in Child's narrative he dies halfway into the text and is then substituted by a good and a bad double: the responsible Englishman (!) and the wealthy American profligate.[38] Child's "Quadroons," in its retelling of "Inkle and Yarico" and Stedman's *Narrative*, may thus offer support to the feminist contention that the ban on intermarriages can be destructive of all family life (Child pleaded for an abrogation of the Massachusetts law), that legitimate and illegitimate female partners are equally innocent and good (if not equally beautiful), and that the source of the family conflict and collapse is solely located in the man and father. The maxim seems to be that all women stand to lose when they trust an irresolute man.[39] Charlotte is remarkably caring toward her husband's illegitimate daughter, though their bond of sisterhood is ultimately severed by the force of slavery.

"The Quadroons" may constitute a step away from Stedman, both toward a sharper political creed of opposing slavery (and alcohol) and toward a repetition and generalization of some of his specific descriptive details that were beginning to lend a "genre" feeling to the story, which reads more like an outline than a fully fleshed-out work of fiction. In fact, twenty-five years later when Child returned again to the matter of "The Quadroons" and expanded it into the full-length novel *A Romance of the*

*Republic* (1867), the details taken from Stedman appeared with the full force of clichés. The story of retellings, however, does not end with Child.

### Further Retellings: "The Quadroon's Story" and Inkle as Jefferson, Yarico as Sally Hemings

A few examples may suggest the directions that writers took after Lydia Maria Child's use and revision of Stedman's *Narrative*. In a chapter of *Uncle Tom's Cabin*, entitled—perhaps with a nod toward Child—"The Quadroon's Story"[40]—Harriet Beecher Stowe included the story of Cassy's life. In the description of Cassy, the eye, "her most remarkable feature," takes a very prominent part, "so large, so heavily black, over-shadowed by long lashes of equal darkness, and so wildly, mournfully despairing." In her "eye was a deep, settled night of anguish."[41] In the tale that Cassy tells Uncle Tom, elements of the stories of both Rosalie and Xarifa seem interwoven. Cassy grew up in luxury; but when she was fourteen her father died—of course, without having made a will. Entered on the inventory of her father's property and threatened to be sold, she falls in love with the handsome Henry, a young lawyer, who protects her but instead of marrying, *buys* her, a fact which Cassy reports to Uncle Tom very much in the manner of "Inkle and Yarico":

> I shall never forget that evening. I walked with him in the garden. I was lonesome and full of sorrow, and he was so kind and gentle to me; and he told me that he had seen me before I went to the convent, and that he had loved me a great while, and that he would be my friend and protector;—in short, though he didn't tell me, he had paid two thousand dollars for me, and I was his property. . . . (423)

Her buildup of a marriage plot is shockingly altered into a story of a purchase, and the phrasing "in short" that introduces the surprising change despite its promise to summarize only what preceded it echoes very precisely the turnabout in "Inkle and Yarico" that also introduced a story of a sale, only that Stowe (like Child) retells it from the point of view of the woman who is bought, whereas Steele had told the story of a man who sells the loyal and loving woman. Cassy confesses to Uncle Tom:

> I wanted only one thing—I did want him to *marry* me. I thought, if he loved me as he said he did, and if I was what he seemed to think I was, he would be willing to marry me and set me free. But he convinced me that it would be impossible; and he told me that, if we were only faithful to each other, it was marriage before God. (424)

But a marriage before God is not a real marriage, and Cassy joins Joanna and Rosalie in finding that out for herself. She nurses Henry through a yellow fever, and they have two beautiful children, a boy, also called

Henry, and a girl, little Elise. But the lawyer's cousin (whom Cassy dreads) introduces him to gambling and to another woman, and he *sells* Cassy and his children "to clear off his gambling debts, which stood in the way of his marrying as he wished" (424). In fact, he sells them to the very cousin who turns out to have always wanted to possess Cassy and to have instigated Henry's gambling and infatuation with the other woman only to get closer to his goal; he threatens to sell the children away if she does not behave "reasonably." Though she complies, he sells the children anyway, and she sees little Henry being taken away by slave-breakers, whereupon she takes a bowie knife, jumps upon him, and faints. A Captain Stuart takes care of Cassy later, and she has another son from him who looks like poor Henry. But her mind is made up:

> I would never again let a child live to grow up! I took the little fellow in my arms, when he was two weeks old, and kissed him, and cried over him; and then I gave him laudanum, and held him close to my bosom, while he slept to death. How I mourned and cried over it! and who ever dreamed that it was anything but a mistake, that had made me give it the laudanum? but it's one of the few things that I'm glad of, now. I am not sorry, to this day; he, at least, is out of pain. What better than death could I give him, poor child! (427)

Inspired perhaps by the same Cincinnati story that caught Toni Morrison's eye a century and a quarter later, and perhaps also by Elizabeth Barrett Browning's startling antislavery poem, "The Runaway Slave at Pilgrim's Point" (1848), Stowe retold the Yarico story in such a way that the betrayed mother could be represented committing infanticide.[42] This went far beyond Child. Another narrative, however, though it was partly inspired by Harriet Beecher Stowe, stayed much closer to "The Quadroons."

In 1853 William Wells Brown, a runaway slave, published—in London—the first novel written in English by a black author of the United States, *Clotel; or, The President's Daughter.* It is a novel that lifts the story of the Inkle and Yarico tradition to the level of a critical national allegory and makes an interracial romance in the world of slavery *the* story of American origins.[43] Following the never-verified stories that were circulating in Jefferson's lifetime and put into verse by Thomas Moore, Brown casts Thomas Jefferson in the role of the white patriarch who fails to recognize his slave mistress (here called Currer but modeled on the historical Sally Hemings), thus pointing out the paradox that the author of the Declaration of Independence (and, as we saw, of calculations on color classification) also may have authored unrecognized slave children; and Currer and her two daughters Clotel and Althesa are put up for sale right in the first chapter. Jefferson as a new Inkle lends support to the argument that Brown shares with Child: "the marriage relation, the oldest and most sacred institution given to man by his Creator, is unknown and unrecognised in the slave laws of the United States" (56). Even republican revolutionaries may sell their own children. As far as Jefferson is concerned, the historical and literary stories surrounding his relationship with Sally Hemings have been discussed more often than not in terms of whether or not the rumors could be verified. Yet as Nathan Huggins has suggested, "we will never get at a truth everyone will accept." Therefore, no matter whether or not the story is "*actually* true," it is "*symbolically* true," and the "Sally Hemings story ties a people to the founding of the nation, reinforcing birthright claims."[44]

After the provocative juxtaposition of republicanism and slavery in the founding generation, Brown's novel actually takes a deeper interest in the stories of the generations that follow the original interracial couple. His pastiche book, a mix of different (partly anachronistic) stories Brown put together from his own experience, hearsay, and from reading journalism and fiction, explicitly mentions his indebtedness to "Mrs. Child, of New York, . . . for part of a short story." This story is, in fact, "The Quadroons," and Brown incorporated large stretches of it, verbatim, into chapters four (tellingly entitled "The Quadroon's Home"), eight, and fifteen (the Coleridge epigraph of which also opened Child's story) of his novel, changing only the setting from Georgia to Virginia and the characters' names so that Rosalie becomes Clotel, Edward turns into Horatio Green, their daughter is named Mary rather than Xarifa, and Charlotte is now called Gertrude. The similarity of the prose to a plot summary that was already noticeable in "The Quadroons" is strengthened by the cuts Brown made in the story for *Clotel*.

To focus on one representative example, Jefferson's granddaughter Mary is described in the following way:

> As the child grew older, it more and more resembled its mother. The iris of her large dark eye had the melting mezzotinto, which remains the last vestige of African ancestry, and gives that plaintive expression, so often observed, and so appropriate to that docile and injured race. (80)

Child readers are likely to recognize this description instantly. What starts not just as similarity but as virtual and verbal identity with the precursor text[45]—even to the oddity of an African American speaking of "that" race— reaches a sharp and ideologically interesting point of divergence, however, as Brown wants to drive home a point different from Child's. Clotel (the old Rosalie) does *not* die of heartbreak, and although Horatio Green turns to drinking, he merely becomes weak (instead of passing away), succumbs to his wife's demands, and permits his father-in-law to arrange for the sale of Clotel and their daughter Mary (Child's Xarifa).

> The result was that Clotel was immediately sold to the slave-trader, Walker, who, a few years previous, had taken her mother and sister to the

far South. But, as if to make her husband drink of the cup of humiliation to its very dregs[46] Mrs. Green resolved to take his child under her own roof for a servant. Mary was, therefore, put to the meanest work that could be found, and although only ten years of age [the age matches the Child part of the story], she was often compelled to perform labour, which, under ordinary circumstances, would have been thought too hard for one much older. (143–44)

Quite obviously, Brown diverges from Child by casting the white wife no longer as an innocent victim who suffers together with the mixed-race mistress at the hands of a duplicitous husband's weakness and evil. Instead, Brown transforms Gertrude virtually into an embodiment of the evil stepmother from a fairy tale. She is a far cry from her prototype: whereas Child's Charlotte was a woman of high ethical principles who took good care of Xarifa, Brown's Gertrude turns her jealousy into a truly sadistic treatment of her husband's innocent daughter, the purpose of which seems to be not only to punish both but also to stress and strengthen the racial boundary between father and daughter in order to destroy their kinship tie in which Gertrude could have no part:

> The child was white, what should be done to make her look like other negroes, was the question Mrs. Green asked herself. At last she hit upon a plan: there was a garden at the back of the house over which Mrs. Green could look from her parlour window. Here the white slave-girl was put to work, without either bonnet or handkerchief upon her head. A hot sun poured its broiling rays on the naked face and neck of the girl, until she sank down in the corner of the garden, and was actually broiled to sleep. (153)[47]

The ideological effect of this change is twofold. On the one hand, there is no longer any bond of sisterhood between mistress and slave woman of the kind that Child's version posited;[48] on the other hand, the intensified focus on the *child* of a mixed couple and on that child's *racial* identity rather than only on slave origins brings the character closer to the figure customarily discussed as the Tragic Mulatto. For whereas Xarifa was victimized by a return to her grandmother's slave *status*, Mary is a despised outcast because she is a member of neither the black nor the white group. Gertrude and the black cook Dinah agree on this very point:

> "Dees white niggers always tink dey sef good as white folks. . . ."
>   "Yes, but we will teach them better; won't we Dinah?"
>   "Yes, I don't like dees mularter niggers, no how; dey always want to set dey sef up for something big." (153–54)[49]

Brown adds: "The cook was black, and was not without that prejudice which is to be found among the negroes, as well as among the whites of the Southern States" (154). Mary is thus turned by Brown into a positively conceived,[50] but racially defined Mulatto, while Mrs. Green has become a full-blown version of the evil jealous mistress and unjust stepmother—though she finally relents when she feels that her husband has lost interest in his own daughter. And Horatio Green? As Mary turns darker until she is "but little whiter than any other mulatto children running about the yard," she reminds her father, every time he sees her, "of the happy days he had spent with Clotel" (154)—who, however, though Brown seems to have forgotten it, had been described as "not darker than other white children" (80). Green now pleads to have Mary sent away, but his wife remains "determined to carry out her unfeeling and fiendish designs" upon "the granddaughter of Thomas Jefferson" (154). In Brown's version two generations of white patriarchs have become quite ineffectual: Jefferson left Currer in order to "fill a government appointment" in Washington (60), and Horatio Green, who had bought Clotel for $1500, succumbs to the white mistress who plays the role of the manipulative villain wreaking her "legitimate" vengeance upon the "illegitimate family."

In the further course of Brown's novel, Clotel dies jumping into the Potomac, "within plain sight of the President's house," pursued by slave catchers onto the Long Bridge, as she is trying to get back to Richmond and to her daughter. Mary, however, unlike Xarifa, does *not* die but falls in love with George, one of the Greens' slaves who participates in a slave rebellion, and helps him get out of prison by disguising herself and trading places with him.[51] At the end of the novel, Mary—who meanwhile married a Mr. Devenant out of gratitude and is now widowed—and George are surprisingly united in Dunkirk, get married, and continue living in Europe. Lifting the story again to the level of national allegory, Brown (who had omitted the topos of the blushing cheek from Child and Stedman) also turns the motif of "blushing" political when he concludes:

> We can but blush for our country's shame when we recall to mind the fact, that while George and Mary Green, and numbers of other fugitives from American slavery, can receive protection from any of the governments of Europe, they cannot return to their native land without becoming slaves. (243)

The transformation of the "Inkle and Yarico" story through Stedman's revision, and Child's influential revision of that revision, had "Americanized" some generally available motifs. The long afterlife of the materials brought into wide circulation by Steele and Stedman may be suggested by the fact that Wendell Phillips introduced Frederick Douglass's *Narrative* (1845) with the comment that the time had come when the lions write history. And when the playwright Franz Kratter tried to intrigue his Frankfurt audience with the exotic interracial love-and-marriage play *Die Sclavin in Surinam* (1804), he described the heroine in the dramatis personae as "wearing chains, rings, and medals on her neck, arms, and legs, a skirt of colorful chintz, a shawl of Indian muslin negligently thrown over her shoulder and partly covering her bosom; with curly hair flowing around head and shoulders in soft ringlets." Instead of continuing in this vein, Kratter simply added that one could find out more about the appearance of all characters in the play by looking at Stedman's engravings.[52]

## From the Slave South to the "Free" North

A later urban text makes its connection to Child and Brown known by a detail that comes out of the familiar descriptive convention of the eye. In the novel *The Garies and Their Friends* (1857), Frank Webb takes the outline of Child's "Quadroons" into yet another direction.[53] What, he seems to ask, if the interracial couple of the plantation owner/quadroon woman type were completely and honestly committed to each other and were prevented from marrying each other only by southern laws? What would they do in order to make sure that their children could never be enslaved? This is exactly the situation in which Mr. Clarence Garie and his common-law wife Emily find themselves at the beginning of the novel. They live in the most beautiful paradise of a Georgia plantation setting. In this *locus amoenus* live the Garies, not legally married, but referring to each other in private and public as husband and wife. They have a girl, Emily, and a boy, Clarence, and it is the *boy*'s eyes that are described with the detail that links Webb to Child (and Brown):

> The critically learned in such matters, knowing his parentage, might have imagined they could detect the evidence of his mother's race, by the slightly mezzo-tinto expression of his eyes, and the rather African fulness of his lips; but the casual observer would have passed him by without dreaming that a drop of negro blood coursed through his veins. (2–3)

Webb lets the narrator invoke "the critically learned" rather than permit himself to endorse the notion that the eyes really give evidence of racial origin, but the use of the word "mezzo-tinto" clearly places the novel into the orbit of the racialized type of eye-description that Lydia Maria Child and William Wells Brown had also used.

Again like the interracial couple in Child, the Garies contemplate moving to France or Italy, "some foreign country where there is no such thing as slavery" (55). But—tragically, as it shall turn out—Mr. Garie is too much of a democrat to live in a European monarchy, and although he is very southern and both of them know that there is much prejudice against colored people in the northern United States, they decide to move to Philadelphia in the free state of Pennsylvania.

As in Stedman's narrative, peers are invoked in order to suggest the high moral character of the man who takes his love and family seriously and who could never become like Inkle. One white acquaintance of the Garies, who thinks of Garie as "a soft-headed fool, led by the nose by a yaller wench," asks pointedly:

> "Why can't he act . . . like other men who happen to have half-white children—breed them up for the market, and sell them?" and he might have added, "as I do," for he was well known to have so acted by two or three of his own tawny offspring. (59)

The bulk of Webb's novel, however, leaves the prototype of the Child plot line far behind, as the Garies encounter not only the social world of successful colored people like the Ellises and Mr. Walters, but also the new, massive racism of a northern city. These elements are independent from any story of a man's recognition of his spouse and refusal to sell his children: Jim Crow trains, ministers who do not want to wed a white man to a black woman, school segregation, public discrimination at the polls and in restaurants, sensationalist press reporting, bribed policemen, and a fierce mob that, incited by the arch-villain George Stevens, brutally kills Mr. and Mrs. Garie. (Webb's representation of mob violence was based on the Philadelphia riots of 1843.) They are buried in a segregated graveyard, and their son and daughter are left unprotected. By lifting the plot line of the black-white couple out of the setting in a slaveholding state, Webb wrote an urban novel that questioned the dream of the free North several years before slavery was abolished.[54] In his critique of northern urban prejudice Webb followed the example of Gustave de Beaumont, whose *Marie* (1835) had pioneeringly represented the New York race riot of 1834, in which the Reverend Peter Williams was one target for the violence of the crowd because he had married a colored man to a white woman.[55] However, Webb also placed the source of all evil into the pettifogging attorney Stevens as the self-declared representative of the pure white and legitimate (that is, noninterracial) Garie line, even though Stevens is actually a poor-white déclassé relative (167), an upstart who violently hates the patriarch and finds racism a convenient form to bring about his familial revenge. Needless to say, he is also physiognomically repulsive with a parchment-like, cadaverous appearance (124), a stark contrast to the aristocratic Garie and even more to the handsome mixed-race characters.[56]

Interracial marriage is an institution that is opposed by real or prospective intraracial family members who could then be the "legitimate" ones, and tensions between the "legitimate" and the "illegitimate" branches are always possible. In the unfolding of the rewriting process that moved from "Inkle and Yarico" to *The Garies* one may notice a growing sense not only of the evil, irresponsibility, or cowardice of the mercantile would-be husband (Inkle or Stedman), but also—starting in this line up with Brown, the first anglophone African American writer to insert himself into this thematic—of the sadism and vindictiveness of the white family members, male and female, that is directed against the interracial couple, the descendants, and any memories of the alliance: all of this becomes the central plot propulsion of Webb's novel. *The Garies* therefore also functions (like Brown's *Clotel*) as an obvious corrective to the "women and sisters" theme that Child had helped to conventionalize for progressive abolitionist literature: "Let's blame the weak or hypocritical double-family patriarch and soft-pedal the differences between his two families (and especially between free and slave women)" could be generalized as the motto of some abolitionist fictionalizing on this matter. Brown seemed to say, but let's also focus on the clash between wife and mistress, between a stepmother and her husband's illegitimate daughter, if we want to capture the full allegorical meaning of the double families on the Jeffersonian model.[57] To this Webb adds a sharper turn—prophetic for the next century of interracial literature, as he proceeds with a slaveholding patriarch who is honestly willing to enter an interracial marriage in order to legitimate the family that the lurking "legitimate" ones, that the law, that common sense, that public opinion, that all institutions that matter consider illegitimate, even when sanctioned by marriage. This change deflects the story from the melodramatic core of the irresolute and unprincipled male who alone seems to have plot-propelling agency. The result of this alteration obviously necessitates going North where interracial life is (barely) legal, but where it is hard to find a minister who will perform the wedding, impossible for the mixed-race children to find a school in which they can stay once their background becomes known, and where the most violent social stratum easily allies itself with the cowardly, self-made "legitimate" family in order to annihilate the interracial couple and its descendants. By making this move, and by incorporating it into a novel that makes very good reading and follows a nineteenth-century urban coding (in the tradition of Sue and Dickens), Webb prophetically redirects attention from the sentimental fictions of slavery and southern patriarchy to racism and northern mob rule, while melodramatic villainy migrates from the patriarch to the upstart. Let Inkle marry Yarico, Stedman truly wed Joanna, Edward remain forever faithful to Rosalie—and see what happens to them in Philadelphia, in New York, in the Free North! Many other texts followed this line of argument, aimed at questioning some self-righteous abolitionist clichés, and one could pursue further retelling in numerous other works.

### Abolitionists "are too good for me": John William De Forest's "A Gentleman of an Old School"

That even the best-intentioned man may not be prepared for the social and legal obstacles that are awaiting him is also the theme of a remarkably subtle short story by John William De Forest, "A Gentleman of an

Old School" (1868), with which I would like to close this particular exploration.[58] De Forest represents in this short story the high ethos of a disappearing southern nobility, embodied by the hero, the old Charlestonian Vance Fosbrooke—to whom the phrasing of the title is explicitly applied—and his friend James Vane Hightower. Their values, their sense of honor, their impeccable code of conduct, their fierce insistence on independent judgment, and their imperviousness to the vulgarities of public opinion make them stand out against a new set of parvenus (551) in the years surrounding the Civil War.

The action starts in 1859 when Fosbrooke explains to Hightower that he has decided to do something about "those children—you know" (547). This phrase is repeated in the story, and it refers to Fosbrooke's four children from his alliance with a Quadroon woman that he entered when he purchased her some time after the death of his wife. His legitimate white son Robert is an idler and gambler, and Fosbrooke worries more about the future of his other children—Alfred, Flora, Louise, and Sophie—"who, without any miracle in the matter, were octoroons" as the narrator alludes to the Calculus of Color in a strangely humorous tone. The fiction that Fosbrooke is talking to his best friend also permits De Forest to introduce social and legal information as if the reader were already familiar with it. For Fosbrooke is concerned about how "these cursed laws of ours" (547) threaten to deprive his children of their birthright and endanger "this most illegal family, this family which had been formed and brought to its present condition in spite of commandments and enactments" (548). The delicacy of the subject forces him to confide to Hightower only in a whispering voice:

> By Jove! Hightower, it's a dem'd outrage,—one of the dem'dest outrages that I can conceive of. They are my property,—and I don't want to own them. I can't set them free. I can't leave them a penny. It's enough, Hightower, to make a man turn Yankee. (547–48)

The gentleman of the old school is presented with allusions to biblical patriarchs—Fosbrooke wears "shining raiment" and redirects Hightower's weakness for roast pig—and to American history—Fosbrooke is one year younger than his century, his cravat is called, in an allusion to the motto of the Spanish empire before the discovery of America, the "*ne plus ultra* of starching and ironing," and he is likened to the nation. But he is most certainly not Marryat's or Tocqueville's stock figure of the patriarch who forgets to make a will. In keeping with his character he gives his legal son a year to agree to a property division which would leave half to the other four children—a proposal which Robert rejects, forcing the father to resolve the problem by sacrificing himself and withdrawing all his assets, leaving only his house for Robert, and investing everything else in movable railroad bonds and secretly escaping by steamboat with his four other children to New York City. The high point of the first part of the story is reached when Fosbrooke tells his children after the boat has left South Carolina waters and they have come out of hiding that they are free. Here De Forest explicitly connects his story with the abolitionist argument that slaveholders withheld family names from their own mixed-race children:

> "God bless you, master!" was the reply, almost inaudible for tears. They did not call him father, and had never so called him in their lives, and had no thought of ever so calling him. There were no words of relationship in this family; there were no endearments, either in manner or speech; but there was strong affection and confidence. (553)

Whereas in Eugène Scribe's play *Le Code noir* the unrecognized benevolent father can ask to be called "father," De Forest lets the known father be called "master" by his children. Both writers are considered harbingers of realism, possibly because of the twist they gave to preexisting materials, and in both texts it is the father who confers freedom on the children, a theme that has a conservative valence. But De Forest's story continues. The second part of the story is set after the Civil War in New York, where Hightower goes to raise capital and encounters Fosbrooke—whose son Robert has died, whose Charleston house has been destroyed, and whose fortune has been lost in the war. Fosbrooke describes himself as a "tree without a leaf" (554), yet he takes Hightower home to a simple house above a milliner's and a barber shop on the West Side. "There, waiting around a still unserved dinner-table, were all 'those children—you know'" (554). Alfred has the barber shop, Louise and Sophie work as milliners, and Flora is married to a man "in costume evidently clerical, his mulatto face marked by education, respectability, and self-respect" (554).[59] In tears Fosbrooke—"noble, shall we call him?" the narrator asks—confesses to his old friend that he is living on the bounty of the children that he calls his "friends and benefactors." De Forest embeds in this scene his most dramatic swerve from the abolitionist tradition: not only has the father sacrificed himself but also he has been saved by his most illegal of families, embodying the good version of the southern patriarch who had so often been the target of antislavery literature. Not held together by the name of "family" they yet give the lie to the northern representation of southern fathers. And more than that: the southern aristocrat Fosbrooke puts northern abolitionists to shame and reveals their hypocrisy:

> "These are all my acquaintance," he resumed. "Hightower, I am not on speaking terms with a white person in this city. There is not an Abolitionist of them all who would call on me here, or receive me at his house. They are too good for me, because I have sought to rectify the mistake of a lifetime. They are too good for *them*,—too good for Flora there. Good Ged, Hightower! look at her. Good Ged! to think that in Charleston that woman had not a civil right, and here has not a social right! Hightower,

you and I, old South-Carolinians, we are not ashamed of them."
"God bless them!" said James Hightower. "Proud of them!" (555)

Fosbrooke's life does not make for a story that fits into a plot-line in which southern patriarchs have been typecast as villains. The man who sells his family had a firm place in sentimental antislavery literature from "Inkle and Yarico" to "The Quadroons" and *Clotel*, and abolitionists defined this man as southerner. A morally noble southern conservative gentleman who lives up as best he can to the responsibility he has toward has children, however, did not "fit," and, "A Gentleman from an Old School" suggests, such a man was no more welcome in the homes of northern abolitionists than were his mixed-race children. John Willam De Forest's conclusion is not that different from Frank Webb's (though De Forest does not introduce a villain like Stevens and blames upstarts and hypocritical abolitionists in a general fashion instead). The story ends sternly: when Hightower promises the dying Fosbrooke not to forget these his children, the clergyman asks the authorial question, "And is death a gain?," to which Fosbrooke can no longer respond, though the narrator ends the story with the answer *"Espérons!"*

The line from Child back to Stedman and "Inkle and Yarico" and forward to Brown, Stowe, Webb, and De Forest has constituted only one thread. In the historical development of interracial literature there have been many other such threads, retellings which accommodate the writer's particular personal, political, or historical relationship toward the material. Some retellings are explicitly declared as such in the texts: for example, Claire Goll's *Der Neger Jupiter raubt Europa* is a retelling of *Othello*, and predictably, allusions to *Othello* are widespread in interracial literature.[60] Other retellings are easily recognizable as direct responses to particular precursor texts. Victor Hugo's *Bug-Jargal* stands out as a text that has generated surprisingly many reactions; and the tradition from Hugo and Beaumont to antislavery literature of the United States deserves to be studied in great depth. In different ways both Charles Chesnutt's "Her Virginia Mammy" and Pauline Hopkins's "Talma Gordon" revise William Dean Howells's *An Imperative Duty*, Matt Crim's "Was It an Exceptional Case," and George Washington Cable's "Madame Delphine" and "'Tite Poulette," tales in which the hidden racial past of a white man's bride is the issue. Thomas Dixon, Jr.'s, *The Leopard's Spots* is a declared response to Stowe's *Uncle Tom's Cabin*.

Some texts may react to a whole set of texts, as Lafcadio Hearn's *Youma* may be reacting to the combined *Bug-Jargal* and *Ourika* tradition, and as Charles Johnson's *Oxherding Tale* and *Middle Passage* may constitute an ironic reflection on interracial literature from Frederick Douglass to Prosper Mérimée's *Tamango*.[61] Some authors rewrite, without necessarily thinking of a particular text to oppose, a plot element that has become implausible from the point of view of the writer's reexamination of the thematic constellation. Constance Fenimore Woolson's short story "Jeannette," for example, makes fun of the clichéd representation of a white suitor whose struggle to overcome his racial prejudices against a mixed-race beauty may make a writer lose sight of the woman's motivation. Woolson's focus on Jeannette's own love interest (not in her suitor) may constitute a conscious strategy of suggesting verisimilitude by ridiculing conventional expectations; other writers have offered variations on themes and motifs of existing stories without showing any awareness of their precursors at all.[62] In either case, the storyteller's attitude toward the material may often be characterized by the exclamation: "That's *not* the story!" In this sense most retellings are almost inevitably "subversions" of previous tales, if only to avoid becoming no longer plausible, or even faulty, replicas.

# Excursus on the "Tragic Mulatto"; or, The Fate of a Stereotype

Divided between conflicting attitudes, the poor mulatto finds added unhappiness in his interpreters.

—Sterling Brown

It will never do for a mind merely to live through its passions or its perceptions; it must discern recognizable objects, in which to centre its experience and its desires; it must choose names and signs for them, and these names and symbols, if they are to perform their function in memory and intercourse, must be tightly conventional. What could be more unseemly than a fault in grammar, or in many cases more laughable and disconcerting? Yet any solecism, if it were once stereotyped and made definitely significant, would become an idiom: it would become a good verbal mask.

—George Santayana, "The Tragic Mask" (1922)[1]

[A]ny disturbance of the stereotypes seems like an attack upon the foundations of the universe. It is an attack upon the foundations of *our* universe, and, where big things are at stake, we do not readily admit that there is any distinction between our universe and the universe.

—Walter Lippmann, "Stereotypes as Defense," *Public Opinion* (1922)[2]

[T]he white and not-white dichotomy,
the Afroamerican dilemma in the Arts—
the dialectic of
to be or not to be
a Negro.

—Melvin Tolson, *Harlem Gallery* (1965)[3]

*220*

Let us backtrack to the point at which Brown diverged from Child, a point that is all the more remarkable since it occurred in the context of a section that was a verbal repetition of the precursor tale. The child of an interracial couple may have become more interesting as the subject of fiction than either or both of his parents; and this is here also the expression of a racial interest. In "Inkle and Yarico," the child to be born is important only to the extent that it makes Inkle's betrayal more dramatic: in fact, there was no child at all yet in Steele's source, Ligon. In Stedman, the life of Johnny seems of marginal significance, so completely overshadowed by the relation of his parents that Mary Louise Pratt, in her reading of Stedman which focuses on Joanna's resistance to go to England, can ignore the fact that their son Johnny does go to Britain. The hour of a full representation of the next interracial generation had not yet come.

In Child's "Quadroons," Xarifa is more important, but she is also represented as an extension of her mother Rosalie whose fate hers completes. In fact, we saw that both mother and daughter were called "Quadroons," and that it was Rosalie whose fate more closely resembles that of the Spanish Xarifa, after whom her daughter was named. As in the case of Stedman, the mother's fate is more important than the child's. In the descriptions of mother and daughter racial features are included, perhaps even stressed. However, neither is, as of yet, a victim of racially conflicting bloodstreams, and again, it is primarily the issue of enslavement and that of "belonging" to a crude owner rather than to a chosen lover that matter.

In *Clotel*, however, Mary takes on a part that not only equals but surpasses that of her mother, Clotel, who is only the titular heroine of the novel. And as we saw, Brown surrounds Mary by circumstances in which it is not so much hereditary slavery as her interracial location that makes her vulnerable, and in which her skin color plays a central role. More than that, Brown's narrator also explicitly refers to "blood" (or, at least, consciousness of blood) in order to explain the mixed-race psyche when he comments:

> Aware of their blood connection with their owners, these mulattoes labour
> under the sense of their personal and social injuries; and tolerate, if they do
> not encourage in themselves, low and vindictive passions. (211)

This difference in racialization could also be drawn between a work by
the prolific Austrian writer Ignaz Franz Castelli (1781–1862) and one by
Dion Boucicault. Castelli's short story of 1848, "Die Verlassenschaft des
Pflanzers" ("The Planter's Legacy"), is a clichéd work focusing on Jenny
Makensie, a young woman who finds out after her financially bankrupt
father's death that she is part of the inventory and subject to being auctioned off and enslaved. Behind this development is the evil Plakson, the
most offensive white upstart in Alabama who, even though Jenny once
told him that she finds him loathsome, has been scheming to possess her
and who is now paying $20,000 for her, for the heroine turns out to be
the daughter of a Louisiana *slave* woman, and hence for sale. Yet she herself is never defined as mixed-race: she is not believed to have a complicated nature because of her divided heritage, physical appearance, or
other descent-based characteristics. In fact, Castelli's Jenny is barely
described, though she is called beautiful. For Castelli's narrator she is
merely a *junge Amerikanerin* ("young American woman") who encounters a difficult scheme devised by a villain. She sees no way out: it is either
"belonging" (in the double sense) to the loathsome Plakson or escaping
such a fate (while still rescuing her father's honor and legacy) by jumping
into the Alabama River from the "balcony" of the Montgomery estate.
The heroine chooses suicide after ascertaining that the purchase to
which she has agreed has really extinguished her father's debts—but it is,
if one may venture such a distinction, a suicide as a result of Jenny's decision to sacrifice herself for familial and social reasons, and certainly not a
death brought about by any racial self-division.[4] Jenny's fate may be
melodramatically sad, and the story certainly does not have any feeling of
great originality to it, but it does not yet constitute the full case of a
"Tragic Mulatto." Dion Boucicault's Zoe in *The Octoroon* (1859), however, was a different figure. To be true, Zoe shares with Castelli's Jenny the
fate of becoming part of an estate, and being auctioned off as a slave to a
truly revolting upstart—in one of the more spectacular nineteenth-century auction scenes, so memorable that Wilkie Collins and Charles
Fechter's *Black and White* (1869), a play first produced by Charles
Dickens, simply suggested that the "*Octoroon* costumes will suit very
well."[5] But Zoe is precisely the figure who has internalized her racial
condition as a central problem for herself, so that she invokes, as has
been variously cited, the curse of Ham, the calculus of her blood drops,
and her fingernails as a racial sign in order to define herself as "unclean."
One may say that she has "naturalized" her *slave status* as a *racial
condition*—a feeling absent in Castelli.

The shifts in focus from interracial (or mixed-status) founding couples to biracial descendants, from parents to their children, and from slavery to race, were central to the rise of the figures that have become known collectively as the "Tragic Mulatto." Since this term is used very widely, not always precisely, and often dismissively in critical and popular literature it may be helpful to review its origins and functions.

## The Six Elements of the "Tragic Mulatto" Complex

Sterling A. Brown appears to have been the first to call attention to the literary "stereotype" of the Tragic Mulatto in a systematic fashion, and to have named it (he sometimes also referred to the Tragic Octoroon or to the melodrama of the Octoroon). In 1933 he criticized the wild racial generalizations that he found in characterizations of Mulattoes, offered without scientific authority, yet with the consequence of setting certain *"idées fixes* in the mob mind." In 1937 he published two books in which the representation of "Negro characters" was central and in which he found many occasions to continue his argument; in 1941 he restated his findings in the context of World War II. And in 1966 he continued his reflections with another important essay. In these works, and in various other essays and reviews, Brown defined the concept of the "Tragic Mulatto," and it may be helpful to differentiate six central elements that went into his argument.

First, Brown's criticizes the Tragic Mulatto in literature as "a lost, woebegone abstraction" and finds it clichéd, unrealistic, nonindividual-ized, and unoriginal. Brown's aesthetic is explicitly tied to realism; and he likes to puncture sentimental conventions. Thus he points out that the slaves George and Caroline in W. W. Smith's *The Planter's Victim* (1855) "speak highflown drivel."[6] Again and again, texts are measured with the yardstick of originality and found wanting and weak if merely derived from conventions and not from "life." Brown's Tragic Mulatto stereo-type thus constitutes a case, not a unique one in thematic approaches, in which a representation is considered disconnected from reality or verisimilitude and anchored only in rhetorical precursors. Commenting specifically on the heroine of Boucicault's *Octoroon*, he quips: "Though unmarried, Zoe is the mother of a numerous brood (in drama and fiction)."[7]

Second, Brown regrets that the writers' focus on Tragic Mulattoes results in the avoidance of more serious social issues and the absence of statistically more representative characters. It is not only, however, the subversive all-black rebel that he misses; Brown deplores, for example, that often the "workaday life of the average slave, who, through fear, ignorance, loyalty or habit did not revolt, or run away, and who learned to accommodate himself so that the whippings and penalties would be less, is missing"[8] from antislavery literature; and he finds that some of his own contemporaries have "bourgeois standards" and are "concerned less with the unspectacular drama of the Negro middle class than with the melodrama of the octoroon."[9] "Bourgeois Realism" may be a misnomer, he thinks. Similarly, he believes that the problem of miscegenation, "generally stated romantically, was stressed above all other problems which were of graver moment to the Negro."[10] The Tragic Mulatto thus detracted from the whole picture, as it did not represent "the real gamut of Negro life and character."[11]

Third, Brown notes a significant gender division in the type: the male "mixed blood characters, merely because they were nearer white, were more intelligent and militant, and therefore more tragic in their enslavement" than their "pure" black counterparts, whereas the women were, like Camille in John T. Trowbridge's *Neighbor Jackwood* (1856), "jest dark enough to be ra'al purty," exceptionally beautiful but often doomed.[12] Proceeding historically, Brown notes that in literature of the 1920s and 1930s "'octoroon' has come to be a feminine noun in popular usage."[13]

Fourth, Brown repeatedly emphasizes the underlying racialism in certain abolitionist treatments of the theme: "The mulatto is a victim of a divided inheritance; from his white blood come his intellectual strivings, his unwillingness to be a slave; from his Negro blood come his baser emotional urges, his indolence, his savagery."[14] The Tragic Mulattoes' conflict was ultimately believed to be biological, generated by the "warring blood" that was believed to be coursing in their veins.

Fifth, he sees in white readers' racial prejudice much of the reason for the existence of the stereotype. For obvious racial reasons "rebellious and militant" men were "generally shown to be of mixed blood," and choosing Quadroon and Octoroon heroines represents to Brown "a concession, unconscious perhaps, to race snobbishness even among abolitionists."[15] White readers were interested in these characters because of their (nearly complete) whiteness.

> The Negro of unmixed blood is no theme for tragedy; rebellion and vindictiveness are to be expected only from the mulatto; the mulatto is victim of a divided inheritance and therefore miserable; he is a "man without a race" worshipping the whites and despised by them, despising and despised by Negroes, perplexed by his struggle to unite a white intellect with black sensuousness. The fate of the octoroon girl is intensified—the whole desire of her life is to find a white lover, and then go down, accompanied by slow music, to a tragic end. Her fate is so severe that in some works disclosure of "the single drop of midnight" in her veins makes her commit suicide.

For Brown, the recurring descriptions of the beauty of half-caste women, and the serious heroism and rebelliousness of men—both due to the infusion of white blood—were a form of race flattery:

The stereotype is very flattering to a race which, for all its self-assurance, seems to stand in great need of flattery. But merely looking at one of its particulars—that white blood means asceticism and Negro blood means unbridled lust—will reveal how flimsy the whole structure is. It is ingenious that mathematical computation of the amount of white blood in a mulatto's veins will explain his character. And it is a widely held belief. But it is nonsense, all the same.[16]

Brown also gives the following, often-cited explanation in his discussion of miscegenation in nineteenth- and twentieth-century American drama:

The audience was readier to sympathize with heroes and heroines nearer to themselves in appearance. The superiority wished upon the octoroons was easily attributed to the white blood coursing in their veins, and the white audience was thereby flattered. On the other hand, the unfailingly tragic outcomes supported the belief that mixture of the races was a curse.[17]

Sixth, Brown implies and occasionally states explicitly that white American writers were more likely to employ the stereotype of the Tragic Mulatto, though he also gives ample evidence of black writers who did so. The title of his essay, "Negro Character as Seen by White Authors," was especially likely to tempt later readers to assume that the subject at hand was an exclusively white invention and literary vehicle.[18]

These six elements constitute the Tragic Mulatto complex. Individually, some of them also applied to countless other texts in which nonoriginal descriptions of attractively conceived, gendered characters (the woman pretty, the man heroic) took more room than pressing social issues or more representative social types. However, the truly significant fourth, fifth, and sixth points make the Tragic Mulatto stereotype definably special. Conceived for white readers, these characters invite empathy because they are so much like whites and so little like blacks; the internal conflict they experience is explainable as a result of racial forces; therefore, no wonder white writers were far more eager to develop them.

Sterling Brown was a pioneer in the field of thematic studies now known as imagology; and his work has exerted a powerful influence on later studies of literary, visual, and cinematic representations of African Americans. Many subsequent interpretations of the Mulatto theme, of interracial literature, and of other topics have followed and extended Brown's line of argument and emphasized the warring blood imagery and the flattery to whites that certain texts, some of which were written by white authors, undoubtedly expressed.[19] The extent of Brown's influence can hardly be overstated.[20]

For example, Brown's famous thesis was echoed by Hugh Gloster, who deplored that the color bias in the representation of "white-Negro

hybrids" has kept many white writers "from painting the whole picture."[21] And many many other critics have followed suit, so much so that
today the phrase "Tragic Mulatto" has a very wide circulation, indeed.
To be sure, in the act of reiterating the argument, some readers set
slightly different accents, emphasized only one of Brown's points, or
offered critical corrections to another. Robert Bone found, for example,
that George Washington Cable, William Dean Howells, and Mark
Twain use Tragic Mulatto characters "for whom the reader's sympathies
are aroused less because they are colored than because they are nearly
white," but added that black writers also used the Tragic Mulatto
because this figure helped them "stress the 'irrational' nature of caste,
with the implication that the color bar should be lowered, at least for
descendants of the dominant race."[22] Bone thus nibbled at Brown's sixth
point, and suggested the possibility of reading the Tragic Mulatto as a
vehicle for the criticism of "race," though he focused on the theme of
special pleading for a Mulatto elite. Blyden Jackson, in his attempt to follow Sterling Brown's argument by quantifying it with statistics based on
Gloster's and Carl Milton Hughes's studies of the Negro novel, seriously
undermined the validity of Brown's sixth point. In the period from 1853
to 1940 Jackson finds that in 28 out of 78 of the novels written by African
Americans "the concept of the tragic mulatto is either at, or very close
to, stage center of the fiction."[23] By contrast, in black novels from 1940
to 1950 only three out of 35 used the stereotype, giving Jackson reason
to be hopeful. As Brown had, of course, also recognized, the Tragic
Mulatto was also at home in, and perhaps central to, black writing in the
United States before World War II. It was not just a white idiosyncrasy.

When Judith Berzon followed Brown, she was apparently unim-
pressed by Bone's and Jackson's arguments and reestablished the general
sense that the Tragic Mulatto was "usually a product of the white man's
imagination," even though she herself had found many black-authored
texts that used it.[24] Jacquelyn Y. McLendon's is among the dissertations
that were based on Brown's argument. As she explains it, she stresses the
unchanging nature of the stereotype (Brown's first point) and deplores
that "even though the mulatto image remained essentially the same for
nearly a century, criticism of the works of its creators seldom reflects
this fact."[25] Yet many individual works have also been read in the light
of Brown's thesis. For example, Richard Yarborough saw the Tragic
Mulatto in Frank Webb as a factor that "unfortunately encourages
Webb's weakest, most maudlin prose."[26] Charles Chesnutt has been so
much debated against the concept of the Tragic Mulatto that there is a
dispute over whether his work constitutes an embodiment of it, a variation upon it, or a profound critique of it. The Tragic Mulatto was also
clearly behind  Mary Louise Pratt's reading of Stedman, since Pratt
quotes parts of Stedman's description of Joanna, followed by "and so
on," as an illustration of the "conventional facial sketch of the non-

European love object" and sees in the transracial love stories with "these idealized half-European subalterns" merely attempts at neutralizing "concrete dimensions of slavery."[27]

Many readers have spun out the gender issue that was Brown's third point, and some have implied or stated that the name really applies more to women. Thus Ellen Peel thought that Kate Chopin's story "The Father of Désirée's Baby" used the Tragic Mulatto convention and reiterated some of Brown's main points, arguing that white readers are likely "to identify with the Tragic Mulatto, because she or he is typically raised as white and only later discovers the trace of blackness" and that the Tragic Mulatto idea "also suggests that mulattoes may be more tragic, more deserving of pity, than people of purely black ancestry." Peel thus reads Désirée as the good, appealing, vulnerable embodiment of the type, adding that "Tragic Mulattoes tend to be *mulattas*."[28] Anna Shannon Elfenbein goes a step further and focuses only on the female tragic Octoroon, rehearses the whole argument of the stereotype, yet maintains that it is sometimes difficult to determine whether the character's passivity "is the result of the spot of black blood or a reaction to the yielding femininity demanded of women in the period." According to Elfenbein, however, the sexism of the Tragic Mulatto has remained unrecognized. It manifests itself in the heroines' youth and beauty: "To be old or ugly for a woman in a sexist society was a tragedy that compelled little sympathy. To be black in a racist society likewise compelled little sympathy, but to be young, beautiful, ladylike, and only technically black was truly pathetic."[29] This line of argument implies, of course, that the "Tragic Mulatto" is likely to be a male-authored stereotype. Hortense J. Spillers undertook the following reflection on the subject.

> In an inventory of American ideas, the thematic of the "tragic mulatto/a" seems to disappear at the end of the nineteenth century. . . . A semantic marker, already fully occupied by a content and an expectation, America's "tragic mulatto" exists for others—and a particular male other—in an attribution of the illicit that designates the violent mingling and commingling of bloodlines that a simplified cultural patrimony wishes to deny. But in that very denial, the most dramatic and visible of admissions is evident.[30]

From its origin in teacher's education the "Tragic Mulatto" has not only come to be at home in the flourishing fields of cultural studies, gender studies, and postcolonial theory, but the stereotype has also moved from the context of the adjective "bourgeois" and a realist aesthetic yearning for the "whole picture," to sharing pages with such words as "subalterns," the "power of the phallus," "sexism," "discourse," "totalizing," and "hegemony." One wonders what Sterling Brown would have thought had he seen the description of the figure that looks white but is defined as black, and that he named Tragic Mulatto, as "the most abstract and artificial of *embodied* citizens, . . . occupying the gap between official codes of racial naming and scopic norms of bodily framing conventional to the law and to general cultural practices."[31] What has also been intensified over the years is the sense that the Tragic Mulatto is a determinist concept that can exert such power over writers that it has been hard, perhaps impossible, for them *not* to use it. By contrast, Brown still operated under the assumption that ideological representation was at least partly a matter of a writer's choice and skill.

However transformed it was in the process, the stereotype of the Tragic Mulatto certainly has become part of dominant critical vocabulary. Not only is it in a position of dominance in the profession of literature, but it also appears in mass media. It can now be cited as a "normal," unquestionable reference point in other contexts. When a fresh observation and a newly launched term become widely adopted in the course of the decades, the freshness of the initial observation tends to get lost under the wear and tear of repeated use, and the name becomes a cliché or, to use that other term that had its origin in the technology of printing—a stereotype. "Unmasking" fictional characters as embodiments of the stereotype of the Tragic Mulatto was a novel point when Brown made it sixty years ago. By now, the insistence on naming or otherwise invoking this stereotype may in itself have become a stereotype that could profit from some fresh investigation. It may also be helpful to ask such questions as: What *is* a stereotype? What, for Sterling Brown, was "realism"? and, Is the "Tragic Mulatto" *tragic*?

## "Stereotype" vs. "Realism"

In literary studies, the word "stereotype" "is commonly used pejoratively to apply to underdeveloped or 'flat' characters or caricatures recognizable in outline," Mary Anne Ferguson writes. "A flat character may serve as a contrast or foil to a more rounded one; character types used in comedy and satire make readers who recognize them feel superior and hence in a position to laugh." Lacking individuality and psychological depth, such "types" are quickly and recognizably sketched and given only a few memorable traits; hence such figures may be especially suited for minor parts. Yet behind even the most fully developed characters may lie stereotypes and generalizations that readers abstract from them. Therefore, she concludes: "The method by which the best literature communicates is to present specific characters in concrete circumstances; a reader is able to abstract from the specifics a generalization, a theme, which he sees as relevant to other specific situations."[32]

The word, derived from Didot and Herrmann's printing device of 1798, *stéréotype*, originally referred to "the method or process of printing in which a solid plate of type-metal, cast from a papier-mâché or plaster mold taken from the surface of a form or type, is used for printing," from which the meanings of something "continued or constantly repeated" and "an unvarying form or pattern; fixed or conventional expression, notion, character, mental pattern, etc., having no individuality, as though cast from a mold" was abstracted. The *Oxford English Dictionary* gives as first instance of the figurative use of the word an example of 1850. In its employment in literature this origin of the word would imply that a stereotype is constituted by repeated use. Thus C. Hugh Holman draws a line from the "metal duplication of a printing surface, cast from a mold" to its application to "commonly-held and oversimplified mental pictures or judgments of a person, a race, an issue, a kind of art, or anything." *Webster's* gives as its only illustration: "as, the Negro is too often portrayed as a *stereotype*."[33] The transition from the printing device to the constantly repeated, received notion—parallel to the word *cliché*—took place in the course of the nineteenth century; in the United States it was probably Walter Lippmann's work *Public Opinion* (1922) which gave very wide currency to the word denoting a helpfully simplifying, often necessary, though also potentially antidemocratic phenomenon that may inhibit enlightenment among masses of people. And it was especially in connection with ethnic groups that the word flourished. Alain Locke adopted the term famously in his manifesto *The New Negro* (1925), the motto of which might have been, "No more stereotypes!" In his introductory essay, Locke argued memorably that "in the mind of America the Negro has been more of a formula than a human being" and that, as a consequence, "his shadow, so to speak, has been more real to him than his personality." Locke explicitly and strategically used the word "stereotype" in order to name this state of affairs and to articulate his call to go beyond it:

> Through having had to appeal from the unjust stereotypes of his oppressors and traducers to those of his liberators, friends and benefactors he [the Negro] has had to subscribe to the traditional positions from which his case has been viewed. Little true social or self-understanding has or could come from such a situation.[34]

For Locke the "New Negro" was a matter of new internal definitions that would replace the old and false out-group images, not only of "aunties" and "uncles" but also of the "Colonel" and "George": "The popular melodrama has about played itself out, and it is time to scrap the fictions, garret the bogeys and settle down to a realistic facing of facts" (5). Locke's quest for truthful self-images was not only for fresh literary realism and against repetitive conventionality, but also for ethnic authenticity against debasing (or positive) ethnic out-images (or heterostereotypes). This connection, which operated in Sterling Brown's writing as well, gives the word "stereotype" a much more serious social and political sense than "flat character," literary "type," or "cliché." Moreover, clichés advanced from within a social group (autostereotypes) could sometimes serve as social correctives.

The meaning of the word "stereotype" got even more sinister during World War II, when social scientists in the United States involved in understanding and combating Fascism also paid increasing attention to "prejudice." Stereotyping Jews was part of the daily Nazi propaganda in preparation for the Holocaust. In 1941 Sterling Brown cosigned the introduction to *The Negro Caravan* which argued rather strongly: "It appears to be a literary truism that racial and minority groups are most often stereotyped by the majority. Today in Europe, conquered or threatened minorities receive substantially the same literary treatment that the Negro has received here for so many years."[35] Now Brown also drew a sharper distinction between white stereotypes and black litera-ture. The Tragic Mulatto moved into the ambience of the extremes of ethnic hatred. It was not a matter of lack of originality or unrealistic por-traiture, of sentimentalism or idealization—it was essentially a matter of racism, and it was dangerous.

Brown certainly had a point. One centerpiece of racism was, as we have already seen, the objection to interracial generation, and the Mulat-to sterility hypothesis was a weapon in the rise of racism that made all representations of Mulatto characters potentially a part of a serious ideo-logical struggle. By some racist creeds Mulattoes should not exist, and if they were shown feeble and moribund in fiction that would echo, help to validate, and spread the belief. Brown probably did not expect racists and segregationists to offer positive images of Mulattoes, but he was disap-pointed in finding abolitionists and liberals who incorporated racist doc-trine into their very descriptions, in the speeches made by characters, and in authorial or narrative comments. He gave many such instances in his work, and his followers have augmented our knowledge of the persis-tence of the "warring blood" accounts. I can therefore limit my argument to just three brief examples of one type of such comment that make the point:

1. Well, there is a pretty fair infusion of Anglo Saxon blood among our slaves, now. . . . There are plenty among them who have only enough of the African to give a sort of tropical warmth and fervor to our calculat-ing firmness and foresight.
2. The infusion of Anglo-Saxon with African blood has created an insur-rectionary feeling among the slaves of America hitherto unknown.
3. [W]e do not allow for the infusion of white blood, which became pretty generally distributed in the inferior black race during the existence of slavery. Some of this blood, too, was the best of the country.

In passages such as these—we might refer to them collectively as articulations of the topos of "blood infusion"—and in other cases in which a character's motivation is accounted for by racial biology, Brown's argument stands.[36] Yet Brown's third point hardly applies to all texts with representations of Mulatto characters; in fact, several of such texts and some of the authors who have been considered the originators of the Tragic Mulatto stereotype explicitly attacked the racialism that they have been believed to purvey. For example, although Richard Hildreth's Archy Moore has been considered "the first of a long line of tragic mulattoes cursed with a 'white' spirit in a 'colored' body,"[37] it is noteworthy that in the text of the novel when Archy Moore, now in New York, is recognized by his master, and a crowd of people gathers, he explicitly attacks any racially motivated preference for empathizing with light-skinned blacks:

> When they heard that I was seized as a fugitive slave, some of them appeared not a little outraged at the idea that a white man should be subject to such an indignity. They seemed to think that it was only the black, whom it was lawful to kidnap that way. Such indeed is the untiring artfulness of tyranny that it is ever nestling even in the bosoms of the free; and there is not one prejudice, the offspring as all prejudices are, of ignorance and self-conceit, of which it has not well learned how to avail itself. (223–24)

Hildreth was as circumspect as the twentieth-century critics of the "Tragic Mulatto." And Lydia Maria Child, who has also been honored as the inventor of the "Tragic Mulatto," commented in a letter:

> Mrs. G. seems to think it is a *very* hard case that the grand child of Lafayette should be a slave; and *white*, too! But for my part I should feel just as much sympathy for the grand child of Pompey, the wood-sawyer, and black as the ace of spades. That Washington, Lafayette, and *all* the heroes of the Revolution, left descendants among the slaves, is a matter of course. The *wise* construction of society makes such results inevitable. This is a precious world we live in. Above all things, do I long to get out of it.[38]

In Pauline Hopkins's novel *Contending Forces* (1900), another Tragic Mulatto site, Dora says explicitly:

> I am not unhappy, and I am a mulatto. I just enjoy my life, and I don't want to die before my time comes, either. There are lots of good things left on earth to be enjoyed even by mulattoes, and I want my share. (152)

What Brown has argued about "much Negro writing," that in "consciously revolting from the offending stereotypes" it "produces counter-stereotypes,"[39] may also be true for other writers who engage this directly with stereotypical expectations. Conversely, it is also true that black American and women writers participated in racialist discourse. (Two of the three "infusion" topos examples that I cited were taken from African

American texts; two of the three are also female-authored.[40]) What makes the situation even more complicated is the fact that, given the way in which "Mulatto identity" has often been considered as a (not representative) part of "black identity," mixed-race self-images have in many cases been "themed away"—as we saw in the case of Chesnutt's "The Wife of His Youth" and as the reception of Jean Toomer's work also suggests—making *any* representation of biracial characters appear to be "unrealistic" and potentially dangerous heterostereotypes.

Since Brown's third point was central to his argument, and powerfully connected to the notion of vicious ethnic stereotyping, it may be useful in future analyses to differentiate various possibilities of a pre-, non-, or antiracialist from a racialist description of beautiful women or heroic men who are also of mixed race. Léon-François Hoffmann has made just this distinction in eighteenth- and nineteenth-century French literature and made some points that appear to be more generally valid. From the racists, Hoffmann suggests, the Mulatto elicits even more repugnance than the Negro, for he is the living incarnation of the supreme danger: métissage, bastardy, degeneration into African savagery—hence they sometimes choose to depict Mulatto criminals. For white writers free of prejudices, the Mulatto could demonstrate that the black part of him was no impediment: such writers create heroes, often very white and able to pass, at times without even knowing about their own black origins. (Unintentionally, they may thereby at times seem to support the claims of white superiority.)[41]

And in her analysis of Mulatto characters in novels from four Latin American countries, Carol Anne Beane made a useful distinction between one way of writing that identifies the Mulatto with the *past* and another that associates him with the *future*. In the first, racially conservative version, the character is dependent upon his white ancestry for positive, and his black background for negative traits: the figure thus remains connected to the racial hierarchy in his makeup that often makes itself manifest in the "infusion" topos. In the second, progressive version, the Mulatto may show "the superiority of the racially mixed person," whose specific background is important only as promise for an innovative potential.[42] This last version is obviously akin to the "Hybrid vigor" hypothesis. Without following the belief in Mulatto superiority that is perhaps implied here, one could extend this distinction and speak of the Mulatto characters as the incarnation of a specific myth of origins (that may or may not be racist, but that is tied to different pasts) or as an embodiment of a vision of the future (that need not be a progressive view of a Mulatto utopia, as many racists have also used the Mulatto in order to describe degeneration, adulteration, and "mongrelization" as feared scenarios of a horrible future that must be avoided at all costs).

Since it is possible to think of stereotypical features in progressive literature, and of realism in racist writing, it may also be helpful to reexamine Brown's notion of "realism" (rarely shared by the contemporary critics who use the term "Tragic Mulatto") and his connection between Mulatto characters and flattery to white readers (his second and fourth points).

As it turns out, the very origin of the central, aesthetically defining term in Brown's argument points to a conservative antiabolitionist and segregationist, rather than a progressive, context. For it has not escaped critical attention that in developing his argument Brown drew on John Herbert Nelson,[43] a "Southern apologist and extreme racial conservative." Brown quotes him approvingly (without naming him), and it is worth reading Nelson more fully in order to understand the ideological position from which he launched his critique of antislavery poetry:

> In brief, the Africans of the Abolitionist poet were little more than white men with black skins—creatures devised by the versifiers, as Professor Wendell has it, in "the simple process of daubing their own faces with burnt cork." Not only were they assigned the psychology of the white man, but worse still, the psychology of a highly glorified white man. Although objections have been made to drawing distinctions between the negro and the European, undeniably there are wide differences between them. Men belonging to branches of the same race differ noticeably, and how much more men of separate races. Thus when we find the slave, here, always deporting himself as the white man writing of him might under the circumstances, we must not only pronounce the presentation inaccurate, but in addition deplore its subsequent influence upon fiction.[44]

It is not hard to discern that the literary figure of the Mulatto confused Nelson's notion of firm racial difference, because the biracial character was not recognizable by his "Negro psychology." How could a slave from a "separate race" deport himself like the "white man writing of him"? Nelson asks rhetorically. And in his discussion of fiction and drama, Nelson continues in a similar vein (and it is from the following passage that Brown quotes directly and endorsingly):

> Not content with this appeal to the chivalry of the reader, Abolitionists tried, by making many of their characters almost white, to work on racial feeling as well. This was a curious piece of inconsistency on their part, an indirect admission that a white man in chains was more pitiful to behold than the African similarly placed. Their most impassioned plea was in behalf of a person little resembling their swarthy protégés, the quadroon or octoroon.[45]

It is startling, but not without a certain cultural logic, that the nucleus of a widely cited argument that is typically made and has been reiterated in order to play down the significance of the literary portraiture of racially mixed characters in literature of the United States is a direct quote from an intellectual fellow-traveler of racial segregation.[46] Comparing Brown and Nelson, one notices their shared adherence to the ideal of "realistic" portraiture in evaluating black characters in literature, and though their political sense of what that would be differs dramatically, they could at least find a point of agreement in considering the Tragic Mulatto "unrealistic." It is not necessary for contemporary readers to join in this compromise.

### Beyond the "Tragic Mulatto": Challenge to "Race" and Potential for Tragic Art versus "Warring Blood Melodrama"

On the contrary, it is possible to see the outline of a less visible counter-tradition in which the Mulatto actually appears as a most upsetting and subversive character who illuminates the paradoxes of "race" in America, for the figure called "Tragic Mulatto" may also have constituted a powerful critique of the southern plantation tradition's benevolent description of slavery. This is probably why such a character still had to be denounced as "unrealistic" by apologists like Nelson. Alain Locke, so important in applying the notion of ethnic stereotypes to reading black American literature, may have been the first modern critic to stress this fundamentally critical potential of the Mulatto figure. Locke noted in 1926 that the southern tradition, embodied by such works as John Pendleton Kennedy's *Swallow Barn* (1832) or William Carruther's *The Cavaliers of Virginia* (1834), had "discreetly ignored . . . the really important figures of the régime" such as "the mulatto house servant concubine and her children." Therefore the "shadow of scandal" articulated by northern antislavery writers "darkened the high-lights of the whole régime and put the South on the defensive." And it is in this context that the creation of what Brown criticized as "Tragic Mulatto" literature appeared *subversive* to Locke:

> It is a very significant fact that between 1845 and 1855 there should have appeared nearly a score of plays and novels on the subject of the quadroon girl and her tragic mystery, culminating in William Wells Brown's bold exposé. . . . Southern romance was chilled to the marrow, and did not resume the genial sentimental approach to race characters for over a generation.[47]

Locke thus found those sections of *Clotel* most revolutionary and subversive that others were to dismiss as instances of the Tragic Mulatto stereotype. Locke's approach has also been followed by scholars who have called into question the argument concerning white flattery (Brown's fourth point). Jules Zanger, for example, who appears to have been the first to note Brown's reliance on Nelson, attacked the point of supposed racial snobbishness in Tragic Mulatto literature, and argued:

The very existence of the octoroon convicted the slaveholder of prostituting his slaves and of selling his children for profit. Thus, the choice of the octoroon rather than of the full-blooded black to dramatize the suffering of the slave not only emphasized the pathos of the slave's condition but, more importantly, emphasized the repeated pattern of guilt of the Southern slaveholder. The whiter the slave, the more undeniably was the slaveholder guilty of violating the terms of the stewardship which apologists postulated in justifying slavery.[48]

Daphne Patai and Murray Graeme MacNicoll write, speaking about novels which choose "white blacks" as protagonists in ostensibly antislavery and antiracist fiction, that

> it can be and usually is said that in their time they allowed the white reader to identify and hence sympathize with the protagonist's plight, thus breaking through a conditioned acceptance of the institution of slavery and the practice of discrimination as things that happen to "others," to people essentially unlike "oneself." Although this position is true as far as it goes, such a line of argument misses some of the deconstructive potentialities of the white-black character. . . .
>
> The white-black character in fiction . . . elevates the entire discussion to the level of social rather than biological constructs, for the absence of the characteristic "taint," as these novels show, does not automatically alter status or life options. Instead, by their very presence, which points to the arbitrariness of the dominant society's rationale for exclusion, such characters call attention to the real motive behind the attribution of inferiority to others: the protection of privilege, both material and physical.[49]

This line of argument also makes clearer why interest in "mixed race" has been rising just as there has been a steep incline in interpretations of race as a social construction. For read in this light, the literary representation of biracial characters, whatever their statistical relevance may have been, does not constitute an *avoidance* of more serious issues, but the most direct and head-on *engagement* with "race," perhaps the most troubling issue in the period from the French Revolution to World War II. Most especially, the representation of biracial characters was likely to call into question the hierarchically arranged system of racial dualism, and the formulaic dismissal of the "Tragic Mulatto" could help to protect beliefs in essential racial difference.

As Simone Vauthier writes, the Octoroon "disproves the myth of two discrete races separated by an 'impassable gulf'"—the very myth Boucicault's Zoe proclaims. Vauthier argues that "contrary to what is often thought it is not *merely* [the Mulatto's] whiteness, it is the *unidentifiable* remaining blackness in the whiteness" that calls into question the opposition between black and white and "the social structure insofar as it determines status according to race, i.e. color." The subversion embodied in literature may go even deeper, for "the place of the white individual within the race-based social scheme and hence his very identity are threatened by the mere existence of the white Negro":

> In order to tell what I am and what is my place in the pecking order I must be able to tell what you are and what is your place. The white Negro raises up fears of indifferentiation as he calls into question the whiteness of the white man. So both the reversal of fortune of the "tragic octoroon" and the rise of the militant octoroon signify, in fact, the destruction of the myth of a God-given and/or natural order in which one's place is supposedly fixed by racial differences. Both patterns are an invitation, tendered either in fear or chaos, or in serene acceptance of the new, to reconsider the definition of blackness and whiteness. . . .
>
> It follows also that interest in the white Negro may be read as an imaginary testing of boundaries. The white Negro represents a *cas limite*, the smallest difference that marks the point where the Other turns into the Same, and when the either/or disjunction is no longer operative.

"Concern with Mulatto characters," Vauthier argues, "may therefore imply awareness of the multiracial character of *American* society" which they spectacularly embody, of the United States, the land in which "there is no unmiscegenation."[50] Taking a similar direction, Glenn Cannon Arbery has stressed that in early abolitionist and some modern southern literature Tragic Mulatto characters are "Victims of Likeness" who are "forced into the role of victims" and who "suffer the whole weight of the social difference between the races." Yet he goes on to show that, contrary to what abolitionists may have thought, such a character "never becomes a victim, not even in their own fiction, because of his blackness alone." Arbery quotes René Girard for this purpose: "Despite what is said around us persecutors are never obsessed by difference but rather by its unutterable contrary, the lack of difference."[51] The Mulatto character who appeared to Nelson and to Brown as the outgrowth of abolitionist race prejudice presented for critics from Locke to Vauthier a most profound challenge to the idea of racial difference. In fact, one finds in this critical strain a plausible reason for Nelson's dismissal of the Mulatto for not being a "genuine black."

Another new approach that questions the Sterling Brown tradition on similar grounds was suggested by Hazel Carby, who sees the Mulatto figure as a vehicle of racial mediation:

> It is no historical accident that the mulatto figure occurs more frequently in Afro-American fiction at a time when the separation of the races was being institutionalized throughout the South. As a mediating device the mulatto had two narrative functions: it enabled an exploration of the social relations between the races, relations that were increasingly proscribed by Jim Crow laws, and it enabled an expression of the sexual relations between the races, since the mulatto was a product not only of proscribed consensual relations but of white sexual domination.[52]

One assumption of the "Tragic Mulatto" convention is that it was created because it mattered to *white* readers who loved the whiteness of the character's features. Carby and Ann duCille suggested that at least for some writers the audience primarily implied was black. Earlene Stetson made the broader claim that the "Tragic Mulatto" of nineteenth-century fiction sustains the "sexual fantasies and projections of both races in which all distinctive traits are merged into an expressionless type."[53] Indeed, one can only endorse her approach and wish that more investigations were undertaken that took the sexual dynamic of interracial relations more seriously. The way it has often been looked at, it would work something like this: the beauty ideal is white, hence abolitionists choose near-white characters who can therefore be as close as possible to the white ideal. (The critical counterposition could then lead scholars to pronounce their disapproval of the very existence of characters whose facial features bear the inscription of "white patriarchy," as one critic put it.) Yet when one remembers, for example, in Frank Webb's world, the contrast between the Garies's mixed-race beauty and Stevens's cadaverous white appearance, one wonders. And there is not infrequently in interracial literature a near-white heroine and her all-white double (sometimes they are half-siblings), and the racial logic—the whiter the more attractive—would thus dictate that the *white* heroine should get the prize (for example, a dashing young heir of an estate). The only problem is that the actual dynamic of the plots is often different. Child's mixed-race Rosalie is far more beautiful than the pure white Charlotte. Aurore in Mayne Reid's novel *The Quadroon* or Zoe and Boucicault's *Octoroon* are more attractive than white parallel characters and potential rivals, perhaps *because* of the unidentifiable remaining blackness that redeems the mixed-race characters from the fear of thinly bred (or incestuous since unmiscegenated, boringly legitimate since unadulterated) purity that characterizes Boucicault's Dora Sunnyside or even Reid's Creole Eugénie Besançon.[54] One can only conclude that Tragic Mulattoes and Octoroons may not have been interesting to their varied audiences because of their whiteness alone.

Yet even in cases in which they were, projection could be a more complicated process than has often been assumed. Looking at the Mulatta character as a projection of white women writers, Karen Sánchez-Eppler speculated that the figure may also have served to permit covert fantasies of interracial sex:

> The light skin of the mulatta names her white, yet her black ancestry keeps her union with the black hero from being labeled miscegenation. Through this figure the love of a white-skinned woman and a black-skinned man can be designated, and even endorsed, without being scandalous.[55]

Sánchez-Eppler's imaginative opening of the issue of identification obviously goes far beyond the simple way in which readers, writers, and characters have often been correlated according to racial background and gender. One wonders whether, read through this lens, some black-authored Tragic Mulatto fiction would support a corresponding speculation. For example, when Jean Fagan Yellin summarizes her findings that "when African-American writers dramatize a woman of mixed race, she is very different from the Tragic Mulatto; this woman embraces her black identity, lives in a black community, and chooses a black man," could not Sánchez-Eppler hypothesize that a similar fantasy is at work?[56]

In reading the literature on the Tragic Mulatto it is also striking to find that the text in front of us only rarely seems to fit the stereotype that it supposedly so rigidly and unchangingly and ineluctably embodies. Gerald Early pointed out that Zanger's typifying description does not even fit Cassy in *Archy Moore*, though Hildreth's novel was to some extent Zanger's model. William Andrews claimed that while Tragic Mulatta "qualities are applicable to Clotel, . . . they do not sum up her character." And whereas Sánchez-Eppler implies a white female abolitionist pattern that includes a marriage between a Mulatta and a black man, Yellin sees this as the distinctive pattern of black-authored fiction (which Dearborn elaborates as a rational marriage choice, for it supposedly reduces the possibility of incest), and Ratna Roy finds in one of her set of texts that "none of these quadroones ever think of uniting themselves in marriage to men other than pure white."[57] Simone Vauthier, in her most subtle reading of interracial literature, makes a distinction between the female Mulatto who is "recognized," affectively, at least, if not legally, and the male who is not given a father's name—though the pattern clearly does not apply to Cassy in Hildreth's *Archy Moore*, a novel she cites.[58]

If one correlated the various "typical" plot lines that have been offered as constituting *the* Tragic Mulatto, one would be surprised by the differences between one and the next version of the stereotype. And if one looks at the broad spectrum of literary production well into the twentieth century, the richness and variety of characters is remarkable. It is not a variety that easily divides by the authors' racial background. Brown's sixth point seems to have little validity. The empirical evidence for the differences is insufficient, and the paradox in the white writers/black writers approach is that it first criticizes characters who act on the basis of racial biology rather than of individual psychology and then turns around and assumes that writers write on the basis of their "race."[59] Ratna Roy, who found no sharp boundary between black and white versions of Mulatto themes, argued forcefully against the way in which the Mulatto character "has been grossly misunderstood and oversimplified by the literary critics" who "have used clichés like the 'tragic mulatto' and generalizations like the 'maladjusted mulatto' which are simplistic and erroneous. There is, in fact," she continues, "a wide variety in the fictional characterizations" of "near-whites" (as she calls them through-out).[60] Perhaps this variety might explain the attractiveness of working with "stereotypes" as this permits readers to concentrate on just a few texts but to make very large generalizations. It would seem that the field is wide open for new studies.

One issue that, to my knowledge, has not been fully investigated is that of historical origin: When and how did the Mulatto figure emerge? Sterling Brown explicitly stated that antislavery fiction "set up" the stereotype of the "tragic octoroon," though he also offered James Fenimore Cooper's Cora Munroe (from *The Last of the Mohicans*, hardly an antislavery novel) as its first emanation.[61] Earlene Stetson rightly pointed to origins "anterior to American literature" of the figure that took its peculiar resonance and form from the dynamics of the American cultural scene.[62] This raises the general question of when Mulattoes began to be important for literary representation. And the answer seems to be that after more or less isolated instances here and there, it is early in the nineteenth century that they become significant. Léon-François Hoffmann states that one finds relatively few Mulatto characters in French literature before 1815, but many after that date.

Generally, eighteenth-century interracial texts seem to focus more on black-white couplings: odes to a black Venus; the slave who falls in love with a white woman—not on the descendants of such unions. In the ver-sions where Yarico is black, the baby that she will deliver might become a "Tragic Mulatto" (in Brown's sense), but it is generally peripheral to the story. In stories of children of mixed couples, the Mulatto may simply play the same role that a black woman might also have played. When the literary focus is on the Mulattoes' background, it is their *slave* descent, not racial mixing, that commands attention. Slave descent on the mater-nal line means literally that through some vagaries of fortune one may be put up for sale.[63] Some stories up to Child and Castelli kept that interest dominant, and, as we saw, William Wells Brown in his novelistic rewrit-ing of Child, and Boucicault in his drama, move their story lines toward the "Tragic Mulatto" complex. This important change may be the result of numerous historical developments, such as the American and French Revolutions with their proliferating notions of the importance of youth, rebellion against the principle of descent embodied in aristocracy, turn-ing against origins on the model of Greek tragedy (Tom Paine), redoing Noah, or the Romantic fascination with youth and with descendants, the political topic of mixed-race people in the wake of the Haitian Revolution, the discussions of "race" as the period of African slavery was drawing to a close, and the growing scientific interest in the offspring of interracial unions.

These and other factors came together and may help to account for the rise of the representation of the Mulatto in literature and the arts, and at least as a double figure (often gendered). On the one hand is the

Mulatto as forward-looking prophet of the future (often a male rebel, defiant, not yet recognized for his promise) who denounces accident of birth and trammels of the past and is of a restless, tempestuous, rebellious, patricidal or fratricidal disposition; and on the other is the Mulatto as defined by descent, often a woman who, beautiful though she may be, is yet unable to give herself in marriage (first because of slave status and later because of discovery of racial background in a racist environment) and is thus sad, melancholy, resigned, self-sacrificing, or suicidal. As new characters they may have been coined by the new interest in the shaping force of history (Sir Walter Scott) as well as in the young rebel against old orders (Lord Byron), and they may have affinities with such classical roles as Antigone and Mary Magdalene or Orestes and Ishmael.

One early text that offers a fairly full and sustained development of both a male and a female Mulatto is Gustave de Beaumont's *Marie* (1835).[64] Whereas Tocqueville, in one of his vignettes (as we saw), located the tragedy of the interracial family drama still in the white *parent* who could not buy his quite characterless children's freedom, Beaumont's Marie and Georges are the new characters, more interesting (and appealing) than their white father, Mr. Nelson; they are shaped by a racial past of which they are brutally reminded by their society and even their own father so that they accept it as part of their own makeup. This has the effect of turning Marie into a melancholy woman, and Georges into a rebel. Both articulate their feelings directly in a chapter meaningfully entitled "The Revelation." Marie does so in a dialogue with her enlightened French suitor Ludovic:

> "My friend," she added in an almost solemn tone, "you understand nothing of my fate on earth; because my heart can love, you believe that I am worthy of love; because my brow is white, you think that I am pure. But no; my blood contains a stain which renders me unworthy of esteem or affection. Yes! my birth condemned me to the contempt of men."

And Georges explodes in anger at his unenlightened white American father, Mr. Nelson, who has the nerve to argue that most slaves "are better clothed, better fed, and happier" than the "free peasant of Europe."

> "Stop!" cried George violently (for at this moment his anger became stronger than his filial piety). "This talk is iniquitous and cruel! It is true that you take as much care of your Negroes as you do of your beasts of burden! Better, even, because a Negro brings in more for his master than a horse or a mule. When you beat your Negroes, I know, you do not kill them: a Negro is worth three hundred dollars. But don't boast about the humanity of the masters toward their slaves—the unthinking cruelty that kills is far better than the calculated cruelty that leaves one to suffer a horrible life! It is true that according to law a Negro is not a man; he is a chattel, a thing. Yes, but you will see that he is a thinking thing, an acting thing, that can hold a dagger! Inferior race! So you say! You have measured the

Negro brain and said 'There is no room in that narrow skull for anything but grief!' and you have condemned him to suffer eternally. You are mistaken; your measurements were wrong; in that brutish head there is a compartment that contains a powerful faculty, that of revenge—an implacable vengeance, horrible but intelligent."[65]

Marie has internalized "race"; Georges is turned into a rebel by the racism he encounters. Both deliver set speeches, though Beaumont's *Marie* may well be the first text in which both a male and a female mixed-race character are drawn in this way.[66] The representation of important Mulatto characters may thus go back to France (rather than to abolitionists in the United States), and it is therefore also possible that future discussions of the topic might speak of "representations of male and female mixed-race characters in the manner popularized by Beaumont's *Marie*" rather than of the "Tragic Mulatto."

The figure of the Mulatto as the ultimate marginal man was of immense importance in nineteenth-century Western literature. This character was a living challenge to the central contradiction of the New World, where the antiaristocratic promise of abandoning hereditary systems in favor of self-made men clashed with slavery and segregation, which reinstated a particularly sharp focus on the question of a character's ancestry. The mixed-race character represented a testing of boundaries and a quest for knowledge of origins. Conversely, dismissing or laughing off the boundary-challenging Mulatto characters—a tradition that reached the point in the wake of the 1960s when Mulatto characters became stock figures for comic relief—could help to stabilize a belief in separate races. Since the Mulatto character may deflect from the assumption that race is a matter of "either/or," denouncing the figure may have become a new consensus stereotype that helps to stabilize racial boundaries and may be functional in sustaining racial dualism.[67]

The critical wisdom of the past rested on a frequently reiterated line (adopted from a racial conservative but repeated by many liberal and radical critics) that the abolitionists chose Mulatto characters, "little resembling their swarthy protégés," because "a white man in chains was more pitiful to behold than the African similarly placed," which was an expression of racism. Yet biracial characters could also be anathema because their representation (indeed, their very existence) has always challenged, and still challenges, the notion that there is an obvious and easily definable boundary between black and white. This is as upsetting to a right-wing segregationist's as it is to a left-wing relativist's need for contained cultures—since mixed-race figures have so vividly illuminated the fact that—if such a boundary exists at all—human beings are eminently distinguished in being able to traverse it.

While some aspects of Brown's argument are certainly convincing even today, the very fact that the term "Tragic Mulatto" has become part of the dominant vocabulary in American literary studies and cultural discourse raises the possibility that the stereotype not only has helped to criticize an ideology of the past (notably that of active abolitionists in the age of slavery), but has also served as a vehicle of the ideological wish for a wholesale rejection of the representation of interracial life in literature. By dismissing as "Tragic Mulattoes" a good many characters who are "neither black nor white yet both" and by ridiculing the "conventions" of their representation in literature as "unrealistic" we may also silently, or not so silently, reinstate the legitimacy of two categories only, black and white. In other words, the term "Tragic Mulatto" may have come to such prominence in criticism and in the public realm not because it permits a better understanding of past ideologies, but because it supports, in the guise of subversive-seeming ideological criticism, the ideology of racial dualism and the resistance to interracial life that are still more prevalent in the United States than are calls for hybridity. In short, by saying "Tragic Mulatto" and thus devaluing much nineteenth-century interracial literature we may also be supporting racial essentialism, or advocating as "normal" a view of the world that divides people first of all into "black" and "white"—and hence ridicules intermediary categories as "unreal."

In closing, a few words are probably still needed concerning the use of the adjective "tragic." This word, though often used by literary scholars, has not suggested to many a relationship between abolitionist fiction and, for example, Aeschylus's *Eumenides* or Sophocles's *Oedipus at Colonus*. Neither does it appear to be connected to any theory of tragedy, be it Aristotle's or Hegel's. In Edith Pope's *Colcorton* (1944), the writer Johnson describes the condition of Jad (the mixed-race descendant) in the technical context of (and incompatible with) tragic theory:

> One-eighth of his blood does not match the colour of the rest. That may be a disability, like jangled nerves or a craving for drink. I don't think it is. He has a slight little body but he seems in amazing good health. He has the best, he has vigour, I'd swop disabilities with him any time. Jad's situation isn't tragic. Do you know the criterion for tragedy? A situation is tragic only when it's painful and can't be altered. If a situation is alterable and is not altered then the tragedy is phony. And Jad's can be changed by an overnight train trip, by removing him beyond the danger of detection. The whole world is open to him, except here.[68]

This may be another case of a character who is calling attention to a critical perception that does not fit him. What Edith Pope's character proposes as a solution is "passing," a subject that is intimately connected with the "Tragic Mulatto" who "looks white" but is "really black," and that we shall turn to in the next chapter.

The use of the term "Tragic Mulatto" in critical literature seems to carry the sense of violent action, sentimentality, and denouement in an unhappy ending ("accompanied by slow music, to a tragic end," as Brown put it). It is evocative of "heavy" emotions, tough confrontations between the recognizable forces of good and evil, innocence beleaguered by perfidious villainy, disastrous turns of the plot, the power of coincidence, and tears at the end. In short, the word stands for melodrama, a genre that numerous literary scholars have taken to be the opposite of tragedy. Perhaps it is useful to cite Robert Heilman, who specialized in distinguishing tragedy and melodrama:

> In melodrama, man is seen in his strength or in his weakness; in tragedy, in both his strength and his weakness at once. In melodrama, he is victorious or he is defeated; in tragedy he experiences defeat in victory, or victory in defeat. In melodrama, man is simply guilty or simply innocent; in tragedy, his guilt and his innocence coexist. In melodrama, man's will is broken, or it conquers; in tragedy, it is tempered in the suffering that comes with, or brings about, new knowledge.[69]

In this sense, some of the literary conventions that have been labeled "Tragic Mulatto" would seem to be more appropriately called melodramatic. In fact, as we have seen, Sterling Brown did speak of the "melodrama of the octoroon" as an alternative term; and Simone Vauthier rendered the term "Tragic Octoroon" as "octavonne pathétique" in French.

One conclusion to draw from this may be to suggest that it might be best perhaps if the Tragic Mulatto stereotype were renamed "Warring Blood Melodrama," in the understanding that the term be limited to texts (written by anybody) in which the racial composition of a flat, stenciled character (male or female) is expressly and deterministically made accountable for the character's psychology; in other words, if the term were limited to racist *Kitsch*, characterized by such rhetorical features as the "infusion" topos. It would then be helpful to criticize such passages as the following:

> Precieuse, becoming more restless each night that she slept alone, tossed about on her bed. The murmur of the river and the soft *slap-slap* of little waves against the boat seemed to keep time with the strong beat of her heart. Her dual inheritance was the violence of the elemental passions of her mother's people, and the imagination and the high-strung sensitive nerves of the white.[70]

This is clearly a case of slap-slap "Warring Blood Melodrama," but it seems quite unrelated to Richard Hildreth, Hans Christian Andersen, or Lydia Maria Child. Perhaps the image of the "Warring Blood Melodrama" has worked in the way in which stereotypes often do function—it has served as a mold that has been superimposed upon, and has usurped, the variety of other representations of mixed-race characters. Perhaps the "Warring Blood Melodrama" should also be called a "mirage" rather than an "image" to stress its illusory nature.[71] Free of this association, the many interesting and varied mixed-race characters in different literatures can be read without the impediment of having to make them conform to a stereotype that then forces us to discard them as "unrealistic."

In fact, these characters might even reveal a possibility of experiencing the "tragic" in the modern world. And this is the second conclusion at which one might arrive: perhaps the word "tragic" in "Tragic Mulatto" does deserve to be taken seriously. For it just might be that Aeschylus and Sophocles *did* have a bearing on interracial literature of the nineteenth and twentieth centuries with its Cassandras and Sphinxes, its choruses, and its repeated cries of "Never Was Born."[72] Sophocles's Antigone was caught in a paradoxical world in which secular law and divine justice were at odds. She speaks, for example, of daring a "crime of piety," whereas Creon is called a "breathing corpse." She defies her uncle Creon's edict and buries her brother Polyneices, thus valuing the claim of kinship more highly than the order of the polis. Creon, on the other hand, is all state and fails to see the obligations stemming from his family, including not only his niece Antigone but also his own son Haemon—who, with Antigone's sister Ismene, tries, in vain, to mediate between the colliding opponents. This was, for Hegel, the model case of dramatic collision in tragedy.

The themes of slavery and segregation provided an ideal occasion for a tragic vision in and of the New World. In the revived polis of republicanism there was a paradoxical emphasis on blood, in which characters could easily be caught. Human beings, often very close blood relatives, were—in the name of race—separated from each other as if they belonged to different species, so that some treated others as objects, articles, or things; living beings were "natally alienated," considered "socially dead." No wonder that the literature of American slavery, in that respect much like Greek tragedy, dwells on the paradox, the oxymoron. Family tragedies against the background of race relations have been popular with writers of the nineteenth and twentieth centuries, including black and white Americans. Many authors have used this theme as the subject for a tragic construction of the conflict between real blood ties of family relations and the social barriers of slavery and color line (often based on fake "blood" imagery).[73] The biracial heir, for example, may be denied his birthright and inheritance by his father and hence have to engage in a quest for recognition. Georges's momentary happiness in Séjour's "Le Mulâtre" at thinking that Alfred might know who Georges's father is, as he is already engaged unknowingly in the process of killing his father, constitutes a tragic point that makes the loss of Séjour's drama "L'Esclave" all the more saddening. In such moments the Greek themes of obscure origins and interfamilial strife have survived. The dramatic conflict of "family" and "race" may have continued the tragic tradition in the New World and in the modern age. It may well be that the now-ridiculed figure of the Tragic Mulatto was, in some cases, truly tragic.

In many cases literary Mulattoes were able to cross racial boundaries that were considered fixed, real, or even natural. This ability is what made them such ideal questioners of the status quo. It is also what led to the emergence of the popular literary theme of crossing lines. For, as Caleb Johnson put it in 1931, "[c]rossing the color line is so common an occurrence that the Negroes have their own well-understood word for it. They call it 'Passing.'"[74]

# Passing; or,
# Sacrificing a *Parvenu*

[I]f you should settle down here, you'll have to be either one thing or other—white or coloured. Either you must live exclusively amongst colored people, or go to the whites and remain with them. But to do the latter, you must bear in mind that it must never be known that you have a drop of African blood in your veins, or you would be shunned as if you were a pestilence; no matter how fair in complexion or how white you may be.

> —Mr. Ellis to Mr. Winston in Frank Webb, *The Garies and Their Friends* (1857)[1]

I am both white and Negro and look white. Why shouldn't I declare for the one that will bring me the greatest happiness, prosperity and respect?

> —Angela Murray in Jessie Fauset, *Plum Bun* (1929)[2]

[I]n America today there are one million of people who are neither white nor black and yet who are accepting, almost without protest, the discrimination laid down for those who are black.

> —"The Adventures of a Near-White" (1913)[3]

Mimi Daquin . . . grows up thinking of herself as neither white, not colored, but just human being.

> —Ernest Gruening, "Going White" (1926; on Walter White's novel *Flight*)[4]

P assing, an Americanism not listed in the first edition of the *Oxford English Dictionary*,[5] may refer to the crossing of any line that divides social groups. Everett Stonequist cites a great variety of cases, including Jews passing for Gentiles, Polish immigrants preferring to be German, Italians pretending to be Jewish, the Japanese Eta concealing their group identity to avoid discrimination, the Anglo-Indians passing as British, and the Cape Coloured as well as mixed bloods in the Caribbean and in Latin America moving into the white groups; one could add many other instances, such as Chinese Americans passing as Japanese Americans—and vice versa.[6] There was also some passing from white to black in the United States, for example, by musicians, by white partners in interracial marriages, white siblings and other persons connected by kinship to Afro-Americans, or by white individuals who wanted to reap affirmative action benefits.[7]

"Passing" is used most frequently, however, as if it were short for "passing for white," in the sense of "crossing over" the color line in the United States from the black to the white side. Thus the "Glossary of Negro Words and Phrases" to Carl Van Vechten's novel *Nigger Heaven* (1926) contains the entry *"passing*: i.e. passing for white."[8] Louis Wirth and Herbert Goldhamer see in passing "an attempt on the parts of Negroes to enter into the white community in a fashion that would otherwise be forbidden because of racial barriers."[9] Ratna Roy defines passing as "assimilating into white society by concealing one's antecedents."[10] And according to Joel Williamson, passing means "crossing the race line and winning acceptance as white in the white world."[11] *Webster's Dictionary* defines it as the "act of identifying oneself or accepting identification as a white person—used of a person having some Negro blood."

Though the camouflaging of aspects of one's identity is probably a human universal, racial passing is particularly a phenomenon of the nineteenth and the first half of the twentieth century. It thrived in modern social systems in which, as a primary condition, social and geographic mobility prevailed, especially in environments such as cities or crowds that provided anonymity to individuals, permitting them to resort to imaginative role-playing in their self-representation.[12] A second constitutive feature for "passing" was the widely shared social belief system, according to which certain descent characteristics, even invisible ones, were viewed as essential and more deeply defining than physical appearance, individual volition, and self-description, or social acceptance and economic success.[13] Perhaps most important, only a situation of sharp inequality between groups would create the need for the emergence of a socially significant number of cases of "passing." According to Stonequist's perceptive formulation, passing "signifies that the group conflict is so severe that the individual is compelled to resort to subterfuge." Therefore, "Passing is found in every race situation where the subordinate race is held in disesteem."[14] The social inequality that is one premise for the emergence of passing is also captured by Earlene Stetson's memorable definition: "'Passing' is, after all, passing oneself off as a human person with all the rights and privileges thereof."[15]

A person whose ancestors come from groups X and Y could theoretically live as an X, a Y, an XY, or assume another identity altogether. In the United States, for example, the child of Irish and Italian parents might be considered Irish, Italian, Irish Italian, Catholic ethnic, "simply American," or become, as by marriage, a voluntary member of another ethnic group. Yet some types of "Y" ancestry (often those colloquially associated in the United States with the term "race" rather than "ethnicity") deny a descendant the legitimate possibility of claiming certain other forms of ancestry (Xness, including even the identity of one parent, of three grandparents, of fifteen out of sixteen, or, in some cases, an even higher proportion of ancestors further removed) because—according to "The Calculus of Color"—the identity of the remaining part of the ancestry (Yness) may be considered so dominant that the individual might at any time be "discovered" to be "really" a Y. Mary Waters put the case forcefully when she wrote:

> Certain ancestries take precedence over others in the societal rules on descent and ancestry reckoning. If one believes one is part English and part German and identifies as German, one is not in danger of being accused of trying to "pass" as non-English and of being "redefined" English. . . . But if one were part African and part German, one's self-identification as German would be highly suspect and probably not accepted if one "looked" black according to the prevailing social norms.[16]

The needling description of Francesca Ercildoune by another character in Anna Dickinson's novel *What Answer?* (1868) gives full expression to this paradoxical racial identification:

> [H]ere's Miss Ercildoune, we'll say, one eighth negro, seven eighth Anglo-Saxon. You make that one eighth stronger than all the other seven eighths:

you make that little bit of negro master of all the lot of Anglo-Saxon. Now I have such a good opinion of my own race that if it were t'other way about, I'd think the one eighth Saxon strong enough to beat the seven eighths nigger.[17]

William Javier Nelson called the United States a "hypodescent" society in which children of a higher-caste and a lower-caste parent may be assigned the lower-parent status, a procedure derived from slavery.[18] In hypodescent societies Xness is seen not as an "ethnic option" (Mary Waters's useful term) for an XY, not as a legitimate parental or ancestral legacy, but merely as a "disguise." Since in biracial societies XY is not an option for identification either, Naomi Zack's precise formulation describes the limited range of possibilities. "Americans of mixed race can 'pass' for either black or white, although everyone expects them to try to 'be' black and many profess outrage if they present themselves as white (regardless of how many white kin they have)."[19] According to the rules of passing, an XY is considered, immutably and permanently, a Y who is therefore merely "passing for," "posing," or "masquerading as" what he or she is "not really": an X. Hence a person who passes—or, put differently, an XY who describes himself also as an X—is considered a "counterfeit" X, a "pseudo" X, a "phony" X, or an "impostor" who uses his skin as "camouflage."[20]

These social rules have sometimes sanctioned a moral condemnation of passing on the grounds that it is a form of deception, hence dishonest. Yet this only works as long as it is taken for granted that partial ancestry may have the power to become totally defining. This aspect of passing distinguishes it from true masquerades in which an identity choice need not at all connect with any part of the masked person's particular background. "Passing" can thus justly be described as a social invention, as a "fiction of law and custom" (Mark Twain) that makes one part of a person's ancestry real, essential, and defining, and other parts accidental, mask-like, and insignificant—which is strange in a republican society. It runs against the notion that ancestry (after all, an aristocratic concern) should not matter in a true democracy. And even if one cared about ancestry, it would seem to go against any principle of majority rule to let a distinct minority of ancestors "outvote" the others in a form of ancestor-counting that lacks symmetry.

This way of giving undue weight to only a part of the ancestry may be supported by an appeal to an honor code, according to which it is, of course, worthier for human beings to acknowledge what puts them at risk than what confers dominance to them.[21] Yet it is a form of defining identity on the basis of only partial ancestry (perhaps it is also modeled on the notion of aristocratic blood that in some cases gets canceled by any "impure" ancestry), which seems at particular odds with a social system that otherwise cherishes social mobility and espouses the right of individuals to make themselves anew by changing name, place, and fortune, and that has produced famous *parvenus* and confidence men.[22] The paradoxical coexistence of the cult of the social upstart as "self-made man" and the permanent racial identification and moral condemnation of the racial passer as "impostor" constitute the frame within which the phenomenon of passing took place.

In the era of passing, the notion also found support that one could "always tell" Ys by certain ineffaceable characteristics and visible or otherwise detectable signs such as their eyes, fingernails, or the babies that they or their descendants might generate, even generations later. Because this is, however, not empirically true, as we have seen, passing highlights an illusory sense of certainty in what is actually an area of social ambiguity and insecurity.

Stories of passing may appeal to modern readers' fascination with the undecidable, or they may indirectly offer the assurance of some firmness in at least *one* social identity—that based on racial ancestry—in a world of fluidity. This makes tales of "passing" allegories of modernization that may speak to people who move toward new identifications and may experience anxieties about giving up old localities, homes, families, and belief systems. In a generally mobile society, the world of "passing" suggests, against first appearances, an unchangeable hold of at least one origin and "community." One may therefore say that the term "passing" is a misnomer because it is used to describe those people who are *not* presumed to be able to pass legitimately from one class to another, but who are believed to remain identified by a part of their ancestry throughout their own lives and that—no matter whom they marry—they bequeath this identification to their descendants. Ironically, the language speaks only of those persons as "passing" who, it is believed, cannot really "pass," because they are assumed to have a firm and immutable identity. This is so despite the fact that, unlike in the case of many true "masquerades," what they are passing for may be intimately connected with parts—even the major part—of their real backgrounds.[23]

## Typologies of "Passing"

The experience of passing has been subjected to scrutiny by sociologists and other scholars and differentiated in various ways. The person who passes *voluntarily* (or by "conscious" and "deliberate" decision[24]) may be doing it for a variety of motives that push him out of one group and pull him into another: the possibility of economic advancement and benefits (opportunism); interracial courtship and marriage (love); escape from slavery, proscription, discrimination, and the restrictions that segregation imposed on black life (political reasons); the desire to get away from the hypocrisy, narrowness, and double standard of black life; and for many other motives such as curiosity, desire for kicks (an "occasional thrill"[25]), love of deception, preparation for political acts of subversion or revenge, and investigation of white criminal misconduct.[26] A person may also pass inadvertently, when being mistaken for white and failing to protest;[27] or involuntarily, because the individual may be too young to decide for himself (*The Garies and Their Friends*) or because it is arranged for him or her by others, known (*Subdued Southern Nobility, God's Step-children*) or "unknown to the person who is passing"[28] ("Tristan," *A Romance of the Republic*), for example, in stories of orphans, foundlings, or switched babies.[29]

Passing may be undertaken full-time, twenty-four hours a day, or it may be part-time or segmental, for job purposes on a daily basis (a form of commuting out of and back into the race), or for avoiding segregation in transportation, hotels, restaurants, theaters, clubs, and other places of entertainment. It may be permanent, at least by intention, for the duration of an individual's life; or it may be temporary or sporadic (though full-time) for a shorter or longer period of a person's life, for a single purpose or temporary scheme, such as escaping from slavery, finding and holding a job, completing a program of education, or simply while waiting for an advantageous moment to "come out."[30]

Passing may be arranged by a secretive individual alone; revealed to some confidants, siblings, family members, friends, or protectors and sponsors; or it may be done in the open, forcing others to pretend that they do not notice or know. According to Edward Byron Reuter, much passing "is more a matter of acceptance or indifference than of actual and successful concealment."[31] It may be undertaken collectively by several family members (Child's *Romance of the Republic*), siblings (Charles W. Chesnutt's *The House Behind the Cedars*), or friends, a couple, a whole family (in Edith Pope's *Colcorton*), a town, or even larger groups (George Schuyler's *Black No More*). And, with Ratna Roy, one may distinguish successful passing (Walter White, *Flight*, or Hallie F. Dickerman, *Stephen Kent* ) and the unsuccessful kind (Vera Caspary, *The White Girl*, and G. M. Shelby and S. G. Stoney, *Po' Buckra*).[32]

Passing may be experienced as a source of conflict or not.[33] Fear and "constant anxiety" of discovery may so much intensify the stress that a person who passes experiences that giving up the subterfuge may come as a relief.[34] "It is a great risk, and they live in almost daily fear of exposure."[35] Louis Wirth writes:

> For even though a person could not be identified by means of any physical marks as having Negro ancestry, there is always the possibility that someone who knew him as a Negro may discover his present mode of existence, or the possibility that he may have to account for his family and his early life. Even where the chance of such discovery is slight, there may be such constant anxiety and daily fear that the individual prefers to remain within the Negro community.[36]

And Mary Helen Washington makes similar observations about Nella Larsen's treatment of the specific anxieties of a woman who passes:

> She lives in terror of discovery—what if she has a child with a dark complexion, what if she runs into an old school friend, how does she listen placidly to racial slurs? And more, where does the woman who passes find the equanimity to live by the privileged status that is based on the oppression of her own people?[37]

Some who pass may feel like cowards, race traitors, or losers, or they may sense that they have made a bad deal. For example, in Rebecca Harding Davis's novel *Waiting for the Verdict* (1868), Dr. Broderip feels that he has "turned his back on blacks" and is "a cheat and a coward!" To the extent that passing may imply turning one's back on the (or at least, on one) group of one's origins, the criticism of it as unheroic, self-denying, and cowardly (and not just as opportunistic) becomes plausible. George De Vos stressed this point when he wrote:

> But passing is not simply a procedure used for direct social advantage; it also has expressive emotional meaning. . . .[P]eople often need to escape what is perceived to be a negative social self-identity. Most individuals who pass are in this sense prejudiced against their group of origin. Passing is used to escape as well from a way of feeling and acting which the individual perceives to be necessary or inescapable for his primary social group.[38]

In Pauline Hopkins's novel *Of One Blood* (1902–3), Reuel Briggs feels that he "played the coward's part in hiding his origin." And at the end of *The Autobiography of an Ex-Colored Man* (1912) the narrator similarly believes that he has been a "coward" and a "deserter."[39]

Some may also simply miss the familiar world of their pasts, their friends, and families. Thus in Nella Larsen's *Passing* (1929), Clare Kendry passes very successfully, to the point of being married to a white bigot who does not suspect her and calls her (rather endearingly) "Nig"; yet somehow Clare is drawn, as Nathan Huggins has observed, "as if by a magnet, to surreptitious trips into Harlem. . . . There is something essential to Negro life—the gaiety, the warmth that she misses in her white world."[40] Symbolically, this yearning for black life may stand for a yearning for the warmth of *life*, and "passing" may resemble the experience of death, or may at least be experienced as a form of *social* death. As the authors of *Deep South* (1941) put it:

> "passing" has the characteristics of sociological death and rebirth. The individual completely severs all relations with his past life and conceals himself from all who knew him, so that he is as completely removed from his former social relations as if he were actually dead. Once having left his past behind, he must then re-establish himself in a new life and in a new pattern of behavior. He must be a white, must act as a white, and must

become completely identified with the white group. He must be reborn as a new social personality.[41]

A recurring conflict stems from the need to keep the past a secret. This may force some characters to withhold public acknowledgment of their closest of kin and dearest friends when they are in the presence of their new white allies or spouses.[42] The coincidental encounter with a person who links a passing character to a (racially defined) past may be traumatic or necessitate betrayals, subterfuges, and lies. The setting is often a crowded public space (such as a street or a railroad station), is usually part of a (partly secretive or undeclared) interracial courtship, and at times forces the confrontation of a passing person's blood relations or closest friend with his or her white beloved. Fannie Barrier Williams summarized this aspect of passing in 1907:

> The actual experiences of many of these people in their efforts to live the double life into which they are forced, would furnish the most romantic kind of fiction. Parents and children, sisters and brothers of different complexions are often found openly living apart yet cherishing a secret and abiding love for each other, which may be exhibited only under cover and when free from the interfering forces of prejudice.[43]

Yet passing does not have to be as conflictual as is often assumed. Wirth stresses that the people who tell their stories are more likely to be the ones who suffered from the experience: "The successful and well-adjusted person who passes is not likely to be heard from." Passing may even lead an individual who succeeds in it to a feeling of elation and exultation, an experience of living as a spy who crosses a significant boundary and sees the world anew from a changed vantage point, heightened by the double consciousness of his subterfuge. Thus persons who pass may enjoy their roles as tricksters who play, as does the "ex-colored man," a "capital joke" on society, or who, as Langston Hughes puts it, "get a kick out of putting something over on the boss, who never dreams he's got a colored secretary."[44] John Calvert in Henry Downing's novel *The American Cavalryman* (1917) is content to be passing and looks at himself with amusement as one of the peculiar products of the "Bleachery" that is America.[45] Passing may lead to the higher insight of rising above and looking through the "veil" of the color line, to an experience of revelation, to seeing while not being seen—learning about the freemasonry of whiteness, surreptitiously joining an enemy camp for a while—like a Trojan horse.[46] The secretive way in which information was obtained could make passing a vivid reminder of the absurdity of racial divisions. People who cross the line,

> by reason of their fair skins, are able to gain information about what white people are doing and thinking that would surprise many of them. Often

have I gone into the South in my capacity of newspaper correspondent, and as a white man secured vast quantities of information on the race and other questions.

Thus writes the anonymous author of "White, but Black" in *Century Magazine* (1924/25), and the information that was often found was the truth about white people, including their prejudices. Jeana Woolley stated in 1994:

> In the environments I grew up in, because people thought I was white, nobody shielded any of their attitudes from me. So I see through the representations a lot of white people make about who they are and what they believe in. I watched that stuff the whole time I was growing up because they didn't know that I was there; they thought I was somebody else.[47]

And Adrian Piper suggests that the African American community keeps the secret of those who pass, in part because of the "vicarious enjoyment of watching one of our own infiltrate and achieve in a context largely defined by institutionalized attempts to exclude blacks from it."[48] In William Henry's novel *Out of Wedlock* (1931), Mary Tanner devises a scheme for her oldest children to pass in order to undermine racial prejudice. Her address to John and Eulelia stresses that they should not forget racial solidarity in their new lives as whites: "When you leave Galveston and become white people, temptation will be great for you to forget the struggling millions for whom you are now enlisting to fight. Let their cries be continually upon your hearts."[49] This motif of passing as a way toward helping all those blacks who could not pass is also present in other texts; it is, for example, what Angela Murray in Fauset's *Plum Bun* claims to be doing but later forgets to act upon consistently.

For reasons such as these, passing was often perceived not as race flattery but as a threat by whites. Elmer A. Carter describes the 1924 Virginia Act to Preserve Racial Integrity as an effort "to stem the tide of pseudo Caucasians who are storming the Anglo-Saxon ramparts."[50] The Act included a provision that made it a "felony to make a willfully false statement as to color," and Walter White reports that in 1926 he was threatened by the sheriff of Aiken, South Carolina, with an indictment for passing for white.[51]

By such categories—emphasizing volition, time, social, and individual contexts as well as effects—the ideal type providing the most intense experience of "passing" would be the individual who does it by volition, full-time, permanently, alone, secretly, successfully, but experiences intense psychological conflicts and generates considerable social tensions. Yet this is perhaps the rarest case both in social life[52] and in literary texts (the most prominent example being *The Autobiography of an Ex-Colored Man*); the majority was probably constituted by varying combinations of the less intense types, especially of the sporadic and segmental sorts. As has become apparent, the theme of passing links literary texts with sociology and investigative journalism. The historical origins of the literary theme of passing have been less obvious to readers and have remained relatively unexplored.[53]

## Passing for Free, Passing for White: The Emergence of a Literary Theme

The first American instances in which the word "passing" was used to signify "crossing the color line" would seem to have appeared in notices concerning runaway slaves, and the term "passing"—first for "free," and then for (its later part-synonym) "white"—may have entered American fiction through the citing of such bills.[54] One early—perhaps the first—literary example appears in Richard Hildreth's *The Slave; or, Memoirs of Archy Moore* (1836), which includes the full text of Charles Moore's advertisement for the return of the runaways Archy and Cassy, who are given very detailed descriptions:

### FIVE HUNDRED DOLLARS REWARD

Ran away from the subscriber, at Spring-Meadow, on Saturday evening last, two servants, Archy and Cassy, for whose apprehension the above award will be paid.

They are both very light colored. Of the two, Cassy is a shade the darker. Archy is about twenty-one years of age, five feet eleven inches high, and a stout muscular frame. . . . His hair is a light brown, and curls over his head; he has blue eyes and a high forehead. . . .

Cassy is about eighteen, five feet three inches, or thereabouts, and a handsome face and figure. She has long dark hair, and a bright black eye. When she smiles there is a dimple in her left cheek. She has a good voice, and can sing several songs. . . .

Whoever will return them to me, or lodge them in any jail, so that I can get them, shall be paid the above award; or one half for either separately.

CHARLES MOORE

Interestingly, the advertisement ends with the note: "I suspect they have taken the road to Baltimore, as Cassy formerly lived in that city. No doubt they will attempt to pass for white people."[55] This last sentence may be of historical significance in the emergence of the notion of "passing" as it was echoed in later texts. Captain Marryat cites a Virginia advertisement of 1838, offering a $50 reward for the recovery of the runaway George and describing this man in his twenties in the following way: "*Said boy* is in a manner *white*, would be passed by and taken for a white man. His *hair* is long and straight, like that of a white person. . . ."[56] In a chapter of *Uncle Tom's Cabin* that was first published in 1851, Harriet Beecher Stowe quotes the following advertisement concerning George Harris's escape from the Shelby plantation:

Ran away from the subscriber, my mulatto boy, George. Said George six feet in height, a very light mulatto, brown curly hair; is very intelligent, speaks handsomely, can read and write; will probably try to pass for a white man; is deeply scarred on his back and shoulders; has been branded in his right with the letter H.[57]

This may very well have been the most popular instance that inspired many other writers to use the phrase "pass for white," and citing runaway slave advertisements remained a common feature in literature about slavery.[58]

It would thus appear at first that "passing" entered American literature through social history. In the American imagination, however, passing may also have emerged through its connections with literature of masquerading and with traditional social satire upon the upstart; hence passing has not infrequently remained allied with such themes as the *parvenu*, cross-dressing, double, rebel and victim, or the motif that Ratna Roy has called the "Heartbroken Mother Left Behind."[59]

In the history of United States literature, there even seems to be a case in which a major character temporarily passes for black—before any characters passed for white. In his novel *The Spy* (1821), James Fenimore Cooper—who has been credited for having introduced the Mulatto to American fiction in *The Last of the Mohicans* (1826)[60]—had his white protagonist Henry Wharton, suspected of being a loyalist traitor, escape from imprisonment during the War of Independence by wearing an exaggerated black parchment mask and changing clothes with Caesar, the black servant (who, without a mask, but with some negative comment concerning the lip of the black mask, takes Henry's place in jail). The word "passing" is not used, but the tradition that master and man must change places for a season is specifically referred to; the disguise is described as resulting in a transformation "that would easily escape detection from any but an extraordinary observer," and Caesar calls the wig that imitates his hair "an excellent counterfeit."[61]

Passing as a literary theme may go back further than to the uses of the word or to the early literary adaptation of racial cross-dressing in the United States. One might say that it developed from the motif of the *parvenu* and the migrant as it combined with the age-old one of role-playing, of dressing up and acting as a member of another group—so well exemplified in *Thousand and One Nights*—thereby being able to see things that only the camouflage reveals; but this theme was affected in very deep and particular ways by racial caste.[62]

It is exactly as an upstart that the first character who can be said to be "passing" in the racial sense enters literature; he is the minor, unnamed figure (mentioned before) who appears three times in Victor Hugo's novel *Bug-Jargal* (1826). Captain Léopold d'Auverney, the narrator, writes about this man, a rich colonist whose "doubtful color" points to "suspicious" origins. In a discussion among white men about the effect of the Decree of 15 May 1791 that conferred political rights upon the free men of color of Santo Domingo, Léopold bluntly and in a loud voice warns this man that "they are saying things here which you, who have mixed blood (*sang mêlé*) in your veins would hardly like to hear."[63] The planter, clearly in the *parvenu* category as it is moving toward racial "passing," challenges Léopold, and they are both wounded. The rich man with the suspicious background presents himself as ostentatiously white another time when he warns the Governor against arming Mulattoes and has to pretend not to hear the question whether that means that he himself does not want to fight (64). Yet opportunistically he maintains this identity only as long as it is advantageous; at the height of the revolution, when he is in the hands of the black rebels, he changes his tune and now declares with some pathos that he is a Mulatto. His firm statements, "I am one of you" and "I have no glory or happiness except in belonging to the colored race," as well as all the proofs he offers, are considered insufficient, and he is ordered to take the racial loyalty test of proving his Mulatto identity by killing two white prisoners (149–52), one of them Léopold, who, however, unlike the other man, fortunately escapes this fate. The upstart reveals himself as an opportunist both ways, and a bad, unreliable, and unstable character, no matter what he may "really" be racially. Hugo thus seems to make aesthetic use of racial ambiguity in order to convey social and historical verisimilitude to the character of an opportunist in revolutionary times that he is sketching in *Bug-Jargal*. The character's "true" racial identity does not seem to concern Hugo very much.

In Gustave de Beaumont's novel *Marie; or, Slavery in the United States* (1835), "passing" is beginning to detach itself from "being a *parvenu*," while it is still understood in the context of the same forces of social mobility that brought about the swindler and the bigamist. The narrator Ludovic, in love with Marie, the daughter of Daniel Nelson, a descendant of the Puritans, and Theresa Spencer, a New Orleans Creole orphan[64] who turns out to have some African ancestry, slowly begins to learn the power of racial thinking in America: there is no escape, as race is the only *permanent* social category.

> Public opinion, ordinarily so indulgent to fortune-seekers who conceal their names and previous lives, is pitiless in its search for proofs of African descent. . . . There is but one crime, of which the guilty bear everywhere the penalty and the infamy; it is that of belonging to a family reputed to be of color.—Though the color may be effaced, the stigma remains. It seems as if men could guess it, when they could no longer see it. There is no asylum so secret, no retreat so secure as to conceal it.[65]

Beaumont's imaginative work of comparing and contrasting characters who leave a certain racial past behind and confidence men, bigamists, upwardly mobile types, and emigrants who escape from other pasts made the *parvenu*, often a negatively or satirically drawn character type, suitable in this case for serious, sentimental, and even tragic treatment. The predicament of a character who is believed to be forever and immutably shaped by his background is all the more serious as he finds himself in a society in which everybody else is permitted to keep migrating, moving, and changing.

The symbolic connection between the character who passes and the upstart has also been drawn *from the other side*, so to speak, in works of literature dedicated to the *parvenu*.[66] Henry James, for example, in order to make intelligible the upstart Gilbert Osmond, develops the following analogy in *The Portrait of a Lady* (1881):

> If he had English blood in his veins it had probably received some French and Italian commixture; he was one of those persons who, in the matter of race, may, as the phrase is, pass for anything.[67]

With his characteristic sense of irony, Charles Chesnutt in *The House Behind the Cedars* (1900) represented passing in terms of the immigration story: when John Walden who had been passing and experiencing loneliness, persuaded his sister Rena to accompany him in his adventure, "there was a measure of relief in having about him one who knew his past." The narrator explains:

> For he had always been, in a figurative sense, a naturalized foreigner in the world of opportunity, and Rena was one of his old compatriots, whom he was glad to welcome into the populous loneliness of his adopted country.[68]

And just as Beaumont and Chesnutt placed the character who passes into a context of migrant and *parvenu*, so William Graham Sumner was to describe the social type of the *parvenu* with the verb "pass," while also mentioning the emigrant:

> If a man passes from one class to another, his acts show the contrast between the mores in which he was bred and those in which he finds himself. The satirists have made much fun of the *parvenu* for centuries. His mistakes and misfortunes reveal the nature of the mores, their power over the individual, their pertinacity against later influences, the confusion in character produced by changing them, and the grip of habit which appears both in the persistence of old mores and the weakness of new ones. Every emigrant is forced to change his mores.[69]

Stonequist comments on Sumner's definition of the *parvenu* with the suggestion that "in a society of relatively open classes, where ancestors count less heavily in the balance sheet of the individual's present status, the *parvenu* is the rule instead of the exception." In a society that glorifies the "self-made man" and the passage "from log-cabin to White House" there are "strictly speaking no *parvenus*."[70]

Yet ethnic and racial groups that were, for a very long time, excluded from the term "American" on the grounds of their ancestry may very well constitute the kinds of groups from which a new type of exceptional upstart can emerge—the person who passes and is looked at as a transgressor who may evoke different emotions in the reader than any run-of-the mill *parvenu*.[71] In the whole portfolio of stories of social transformations that are available, black-white racial passing constitutes an exception in that it is condemned or even *punished* in societies that otherwise idealize, applaud, condone, or at least express amused ambivalence toward, mobility. One may thus look at the function of stories of passing as more than reflecting or representing social realities: they could be role models or models of intimidation, as readers seem to be invited to *sacrifice* the character who does what everyone else does—only is evaluated with a different set of rules. Perhaps the character who passes may function as a scapegoat sacrificed, as a victim of likeness[72] rather than of difference, on the altar of the very mobility which he so well embodies—but in the one area where mobility is not supposed to exist because racial determinism is believed to overrule it. To put it another way, one could say that in societies that maintain strong class boundaries, it is the figure of the upstart who is likely to be ridiculed and vilified; whereas in cultural arrangements that rest on a strong racial divide, intraracial upward mobility may be idealized while passing may be singled out for contempt and criminalization.

Beaumont's departure from Hugo, who had viewed the character who passes as just another opportunistic *parvenu*, was a remarkable case in point. Beaumont even called attention to the difference: we saw that Ludovic explicitly compares passing with other aspects of social mobility, but he concludes that the rules for "passing" are different than those for being a social climber, bigamist, emigrant, or urban migrant who may change his name and his identity. This becomes clear in Ludovic's reflections that the rich and the poor are "separated by no impassible barrier," and that oppression is tempered by the recognition that the poor may become rich and the rich poor: "But when the American crushes the black population beneath his contempt, he knows full well, that he can never have to undergo the fate of the Negro."[73] This "fate" follows the maxim that black can never become white.

In his story of the Nelson family, Beaumont develops two serious models of characters who pass. Whereas Marie identifies with her whiteness, and thinks that her blood bears a "taint" that makes her unworthy of Ludovic's affection, her brother Georges rebels against their white father's prejudices and articulates his pride in African origins. After a first discovery by an antagonist in New Orleans which results in Theresa's death, the Nelsons' attempts to live as a white family in Baltimore and, later, in New York succeed only temporarily; even then they always have to fear that one word from an enemy could ruin them. Yet while they keep their secret, they do tell Ludovic the truth.[74]

Significantly, Georges rejects as cowardly both emigration and individual passing, and he identifies himself firmly as a colored man in a New York theater where a play on Napoleon is shown to a crowd that resents the presence of nonwhites in the audience. Georges rejects the possibility of hiding behind a friendly and Quaker-like man's protective comment, "Why drive a man out in this way? Nothing in his appearance shows that he is of the black race. You say he is a man of color, but you have not proved it." Georges does not take this option, and the narrator continues: "Georges, whose long stifled wrath could no longer be restrained, cried, in a commanding voice, 'Yes!—I am a man of color!'"[75] If the deception often implied in passing is cowardly then Georges heroically blows his cover and takes the consequences bravely.

Beaumont gives a social explanation that anchors the phenomenon of racial passing in the world of *parvenus* while giving it a special tragic meaning; his opposition to slavery and segregation makes him draw the story of a family's passing very sympathetically. He connects it to an interracial love story,[76] yet he also adds a rebel figure who heroically refuses to reap any benefits from deception. For nearly a century after Beaumont's successful effort at reconceiving passing as a *serious* theme, comic or satirical representations receded.

In 1836, the cultural oxymoron "white slave" pointed Richard Hildreth into the direction of "passing" in imagining an individual who could be so described to play his "white" color against his "slave" status."[77] This is exactly what Archy Moore does in Hildreth's novel when he plans to escape together with his wife (and half-sister) Cassy: "Our complexions would not betray our servile condition; and we should find no great difficulty, we thought, in passing ourselves as free citizens of Virginia."[78] Thinking of the advertisements with the identifying descriptions (the thought which may have generated the phrasing in Hildreth's narrative), Archy decides to let Cassy dress up as a man and act as his younger brother—a common occurrence of combining racial passing, especially of the sporadic kind, with sexual cross-dressing, and one that was often written up after the legendary escape of William and Ellen Craft in 1848. In what may be a case of fiction preceding fact, Hildreth's novel of 1836 actually contained a fairly detailed plan for an action of the sort the Crafts were to realize only later.

> We finally determined to assume the character of persons travelling to the north to seek our fortunes; and we arranged that Cassy should adopt a man's dress, and accompany me in the character of a younger brother. The night on which we had left Spring-Meadow, I had brought away my best suit, one of the last gifts of poor master James, and such as would well enough enable me to play the part of a travelling Virginian. But I had neither hat nor shoes; nor any clothes whatever, that could properly serve as a disguise for Cassy. (48)

The choice of passing as siblings is quite ironic since Archy and Cassy actually *are* siblings, and the planned disguise, unlike in the case of the

Crafts, here turns out to be a plot impediment since it leads only to their being captured again, for the clothes dealer James Gordon is duplicitous. By contrast, the Crafts did succeed, and their narrative *Running a Thousand Miles for Freedom* (1860) vividly relates how, in order to make possible their escape from slavery, Ellen Craft dresses up as a white man; she is shown in her remarkable disguise on the frontispiece (Fig. 34). This intriguingly ambiguous engraving of an elegant person in a top hat who looks like a free white man but is actually a black slave woman was also sold separately for antislavery purposes.[79] It is an image that contrasted with her more customary appearance (Fig. 35). As has been noted, the narrator, her husband William, refers to her when she is cross-dressed with the pronoun "he."[80] In Lydia Maria Child's play "The Stars and Stripes" (1858), a dramatic version of the Crafts' tale, the term "passing" appears repeatedly. Thus the stage directions describe Ellen as a person "*who might pass for a white woman.*" William describes his escape plan to Ellen with the words: "I know where there is a suit of young massa's clothes, and I have no doubt they will fit you. You can pass for a white lad, and I will be your servant." Finally, he says to her during their escape: "So far, we have got along very well, thanks to your white face, and passing yourself for a slaveholder. . . . Your clothes are so worn and dusty, that you can hardly pass for the son of a rich slaveholder; but you may be taken for a poor white, emigrating with his only nigger."[81]

***Figure 34*** Ellen Craft, disguised as a white master (1860)

***Figure 35*** Ellen Craft, undisguised (1851)

While the theme of racial passing remained connected to others such as "*parvenu*," "cross-dresser," and "emigrant," it also assumed a somewhat different function once it moved to the foreground of literary representation.

### Passing as a Major Theme: Subversion, Practical Joke, or Cowardice? Frank Webb's *The Garies and Their Friends*

In Frank Webb's novel *The Garies and Their Friends* (1857) the theme of passing was fully developed in two rather detailed subplots, suggestive of the divergent ways in which the theme would increasingly come to be treated. The first concerns George Winston, who describes how he was taken for white by the New York socialites, the Van Cotes, to the point of being asked to escort their daughter Clara to church. This is an irony appreciated by Mr. Garie, who notes that Mr. Van Cote "prides himself on being able to detect evidences of the least drop of African blood in any one; and makes long speeches about the natural antipathy of the Anglo-Saxon to anything with a drop of negro blood in his veins."[82] For Mr. Garie, Winston's passing should even convince a Van Cote that, prevailing prejudice notwithstanding, "a man can be a gentleman even though he has African blood in his veins." The comic legacy of the theme has here been turned into social satire, not upon the character who passes, but upon the social pretense on which a condemnation of racial passing must rely. Mr. Garie appreciates George's story all the more since Mr. Van Cote, who has "a holy horror of everything approaching to amalgamation," was scandalized by Mr. Garie's relationship with Emily, who is partly of African origin. In the case of George Winston, "passing" is an act of spying and boundary defiance that dramatically illuminates the hypocrisy inherent in racism; it is a challenge of the status quo and helps to illustrate that even the worst racial bigots actually have no way of telling black from white. The story of a person who passes successfully may thus have the potential of subverting the notion of a "race instinct." When the colored carpenter Charles Ellis meets George and hears his story, he comments, "It is a great risk you run to be passing for white in that way." This first instance of "passing" in Webb's novel thus stressed the heroic, risk-taking side: George, who after all passes only temporarily and shares his secret with others who appreciate it, plays the subversive trickster and spy whose successful (if dangerous) activity undermines racial thinking and exposes its adherents to ridicule.[83]

Webb, however, also wrote a long section concerning the fate of Garie's son Clarence, who is, after the death of his parents (at the hands of a violent white mob in Philadelphia), placed in a New England boarding school and raised as white. Clarence, who does not himself choose the fate of passing, experiences intense conflicts:

> I can't be white and coloured at the same time; the two don't mingle, and I must consequently be one or the other. My education, habits, and ideas, all unfit me for associating with the latter; and I live in constant dread that something may occur to bring me out with the former. (323)

He falls in love with Anne Bates ("little Birdie"), a white girl whose family detests blacks, "constantly making them a subject of bitter jests" (325).[84] This constellation breeds conflicts. Clarence is afraid to tell his secret and afraid that it will come out. The stress on the subterfuge connects Webb with Beaumont, yet whereas Beaumont's interest in the secret of a passing family was predominantly social, Webb's is psychological. Thus the narrator gives a rather elaborate account of Clarence's agonizing over the bosom serpent of his deep secret that he is too weak to reveal to his white beloved:

> I dare not tell—I must shut this secret in my bosom, where it gnaws, gnaws, until it has almost eaten my heart away. Oh, I've thought of that [i.e., telling Birdie about his racially mixed background], time and again; it has kept me awake night after night, it haunts me at all hours; it is breaking down my health and strength—wearing my very life out of me; no escaped galley-slave ever felt more than I do, or lived in more constant fear of detection: and yet I must nourish this tormenting secret, and keep it growing in my breast until it has crowded out every honourable and manly feeling; and then, perhaps, after all my sufferings and sacrifice of candour and truth, out it will come at last, when I least expect or think of it. (324–25)

In addition, he feels like an accomplice to white racist joking, like a cowardly traitor to the memory of his mother: "I, miserable, contemptible, false-hearted knave, as I am, I—I—yes, I join them in their heartless jests, and wonder all the while my mother does not rise from her grave and *curse* me as I speak!" (325). Anne's own prejudices also are apparent when she reacts to a newspaper story about a man from New Orleans who married a "Quateron" woman. Clarence's suggestion that it must be love startles Anne: "'Love a colored woman! I cannot conceive it possible,' said she, with a look of disgust; 'there is something strange and unnatural about it'" (331). At this moment, Clarence (unlike Beaumont's Georges in the theater) simply cannot make himself say that he, too, is colored. When Anne's father finds out later about Clarence's background, he expels and humiliates him and prohibits any further contact with Anne. Little Birdie's true love for Clarence finally does prevail, however, and she goes to see him—but it is too late. He has just died of a broken heart (391). Webb's second story of passing is not a heroic tale of the challenge to racial boundaries, but a sad and sentimental love story of a poor and somewhat timid man.

Webb presented a full-fledged system of passing, one that many later treatments of the theme expanded upon and varied—often by stressing only one of Webb's two models of rebel and victim, or hero and coward, of passing as vehicle of social criticism and as representation of self-denial and sacrifice.[85] After its early nineteenth-century beginnings and its first major representation in the 1850s, the theme of passing flourished at the turn of the century, peaked in the interwar period, and has receded sharply since the 1960s. The following readings focus on a few selected texts which employed remarkable formal strategies or which offered particularly full thematic representations of passing.

### Passing and Literary Form: James Weldon Johnson, *The Autobiography of an Ex-Colored Man*, Boris Vian's "Vernon Sullivan" Novels, and Works in Other Genres

> I know that in writing the following pages I am divulging the great secret of my life, the secret which for some years I have guarded more carefully than any of my earthly possessions; and it is a curious study to me to analyse the motives which prompt me to do it. I feel that I am led by the same impulse which forces the un-found-out criminal to take somebody into his confidence, although he knows that the act is likely, even almost certain, to lead to his undoing.[86]

This is the dramatic opening of James Weldon Johnson's novel *The Autobiography of an Ex-Colored Man* (1912). What distinguishes it from many other novels about passing that were published in the intervening and subsequent years is that it represents a perfect *formal* answer to the theme of passing.[87] Written in the first person singular and published anonymously—as was Hildreth's first edition of *The Slave*—Johnson's book was a literary hoax that generated anxiety about its true author.

Johnson reports that many reviewers accepted his novel as "human document," and adds:

> I did get a certain pleasure out of anonymity, that no acknowledged book could have given me. The authorship of the book excited the curiosity of literate colored people, and there was speculation among them as to who the writer might be—to every such group some colored man who had married white, and so coincided with the main point on which the story turned, is known. I had the experience of listening to some of these discussions. I had a rarer experience, that of being introduced to and talking with one man who tacitly admitted to those present that he was the author of the book.[88]

The *Springfield Republican* did take Johnson's novel to be a true autobiographical document in the context of contemporary accounts of upward mobility and of ethnic assimilation: the reviewer compared the novel with Booker T. Washington's *Up from Slavery* and Mary Antin's *The Promised Land*, noting that *The Autobiography of an Ex-Colored Man* "is possessed of a certain element which may be termed either legitimate romance or legitimate tragedy and which is to be found in neither" Washington nor Antin.

> It does not sound the note of optimism nor is it constructive in the sense that both Dr. Washington's book and that of the young Jewish immigrant are constructive, but it is a story of intense human interest in the terms of fact and personal experience such as has been told before only in weakly imagined fiction.[89]

*Christian Work* fell for the hoax and described the author as "a white man with a fatal drop of negro blood in his veins." Confirmation of the fiction of authenticity could also come from sources that vehemently denied it: thus the *Nashville Tennessean* denounced the book as a lie and an "insult to Southern womanhood" since there was no such thing as "an ex-colored man." The rule was, "once a negro, always a negro."[90] By contrast Jessie Fauset, reviewing *The Autobiography of an Ex-Colored Man* for *The Crisis*, considered it a "fiction based on hard fact" and "the epitome of the race situation."[91]

The form of this purported autobiography in which true autobiographic and ironic and satiric impulses coalesced[92] thus supported the theme; and one may say that the form of the book constitutes in itself an act of passing. Johnson carefully chose to publish the novel as if it were a true autobiography, believed that it would fare better if readers did not know the author (and the fact that its true author could not have been the main character of the book), and suggested promoting the novel in a way that would stimulate the readers' curiosity by clouding the authorship in mystery.[93] As Richard Kostelanetz has put it, the book is "an achieved example of a totally fictional memoir whose first-person narrator is so intimate and honest with his readers that they would, unless warned otherwise, accept his words as authentic autobiography."[94]

Despite all narrative discontinuities in this picaresque account, the first-person narrator offers the reader a full confession of his racial background and putative life story yet consistently withholds the revelation of his name—even of his first name in a scene in which his beloved addresses him by it: "she called me by my Christian name" (209). The alternation of revelation and masking is further intensified by the narrator's self-characterization as a man who on the one hand feels compelled to tell his story, because, like a criminal in an Edgar Allan Poe story (3), he unconsciously wants to be found out, but who on the other hand stresses that he would do anything to assure that his children's identity will remain a secret (210).[95] The reader learns only that his birthplace was somewhere in Georgia and that he grew up in Connecticut; the names of most other figures are also withheld.

Ironically, Johnson uses the word "passing" to describe the narrator's introduction into the *black* world (39), a passage followed by an adaptation of W. E. B. Du Bois's famous formula of the double-consciousness.[96] Characteristic in this first-person singular narrative—Johnson knew Douglass's and Booker T. Washington's autobiographies and may also have drawn on Hildreth, on the genre of journalistic autobiographies of near-whites, and on other texts in addition to the stories of a friend that he identifies in *Along This Way* ("D——" = J. Douglas Wetmore)—is the complicated use of pronouns: "we" often refers to white Americans (e.g., 15), "they" may describe "Negroes" (55–56). He also speaks once of "my identity as a coloured man" (185)—but in a technical, not an existential sense. The narrator seems to suggest that the secretive dimension of passing can be linked with Anglo-Saxon hypocrisy, but also mentions the Negro's adaptive abilities—that the narrator amply displays by so readily blending into different social worlds and cultures and easily learning new musical styles and languages. Johnson's brother's suggestion for the title, "The Chameleon," would have been fully justified, as it describes the mimicry not only of the protagonist, but of the whole book.

The novel takes its point of departure from, but leaves behind, some sentimental features of nineteenth-century versions of the literature (by Brown, Webb, or Chesnutt), and Johnson reduced what were some of the central concerns of their stories to the "little tragedies" that only fringe the main narrative and make their appearances as short episodes rather than full-fledged accounts. For example, the story of his interracial parentage is briefly reviewed after the narrator has achieved a clearer perception of race by reading *Uncle Tom's Cabin*; his mother now reveals all to him: "she, the sewing girl of my father's mother; he, an impetuous young man home from college; I, the child of this unsanctioned love"

(42–43). She also explains that she and the narrator moved from Georgia to Connecticut because the father "was about to be married to a young lady of another great Southern family" (43). In his description of the Atlanta students the narrator very briefly rehearses the familiar description of the beauty of mixed blood (61–62), but Johnson also applies it in a novel fashion to the narrator's gaze *at himself in the mirror* in order to resolve the question of his racial identity:

> I had often heard people say to my mother: "What a pretty boy you have!" I was accustomed to hear remarks about my beauty; but now, for the first time, I became conscious of it and recognized it. I noticed the ivory whiteness of my skin, the beauty of my mouth, the size and liquid darkness of my eyes, and how the long, black lashes that fringed and shaded them produced an effect that was strangely fascinating even to me. I noticed the softness and glossiness of my dark hair that fell in waves over my temples, making my forehead appear whiter than it really was. How long I stood there gazing at my image I do not know. (17)

Johnson seems to transform the "typical" idealization of mixed-race beauty, from a gaze that is directed by a male observer (like Stedman) at the mixed-race female beloved, to a narcissistic and somewhat androgynous *self*-description by the narrator. (Again, the character who crosses the color line also subverts the certainties of sexual identity.) Johnson may thus be said to mobilize the by his time clichéd interest in only certain aspects of interracial life in order to describe a much greater variety of aspects of the "panorama" of black-and-white social life and to probe a greater psychological depth in his protagonist than had been customary in novels about passing. The mystery of passing serves as a vehicle to initiate the reader into what Johnson calls "the freemasonry" (xii, 74) of the race that has been "more or less a sphinx to the whites" (xii).

Foremost among the psychological elements he focuses upon is the narrator's ability to fit into many different social situations, to learn languages easily, and to account for dramatic changes with weak explanations. This is especially true for his embarking upon racial passing. When the narrator feels shame and fear upon witnessing a lynching, he takes a train to New York, and during the journey justifies his decision to pass by comparing passing to emigration: "I argued that to forsake one's race to better one's condition was no less worthy than to forsake one's country for the same purpose" (190). He further rationalizes his decision by claiming merely a passive role:

> I finally made up my mind that I would neither disclaim the black race nor claim the white race; but that I would change my name, raise a moustache, and let the world take me for what it would; that it was not necessary for me to go about with a label of inferiority pasted across my forehead. (190)

He does recognize that it was not opportunism but shame that drove him out of the Negro race. Nonetheless, he eagerly accepts the opportunities that result from this decision (and from his linguistic skills) and takes the *parvenu*'s excessive pleasure in money as a symbol of mobility:

> What an interesting and absorbing game is money-making! After each deposit at my savings-bank I used to sit and figure out, all over again, my principal and interest, and make calculations on what the increase would be in such and such a time. Out of this I derived a great deal of pleasure. . . . The day on which I was able to figure up a thousand dollars marked an epoch in my life. (195)

The narrator is able to offer excellent observations that drive home the irony in his situation and describe a part of the experience of passing that has been endorsed by other observers:

> The anomaly of my social position often appealed strongly to my sense of humour. I frequently smiled inwardly at some remark not altogether com-plimentary to people of colour; and more than once I felt like declaiming: "I am a coloured man. Do I not disprove the theory that one drop of Negro blood renders a man unfit?" Many a night when I returned to my room after an enjoyable evening, I laughed heartily over what struck me as the capital joke I was playing. (197)[97]

The story of his courtship and marriage to a beautiful white woman seems willfully shortened by Johnson, who puts the tale of their meeting, his confession, her hesitation, her declaration of love, their marriage, the birth of two children, and her death into the total space of about ten pages of the last chapter—that significantly starts with a declaration that is hardly fully explained:

> I have now reached that part of my narrative where I must be brief and touch only on important facts; therefore the reader must make up his mind to pardon skips and jumps and meagre details. (192)

Still, we do get the outline of the story that reveals much internal ten-sion in the ex-colored man who experiences the typical crisis situation associated with passing in which he has to deny his identity. An encounter of his white beloved and his black school friend Shiny takes place in the urban crowd in the Eden Musée, then a popular wax-work show with musical performances and a cinematograph, located on 23rd Street between Fifth and Sixth Avenues in New York City.[98] Fortunately for the ex-colored man the extreme delicacy of his old friend saves the situation so that no crisis ensues. When he recognizes Shiny he is nervous:

> My first impulse was to change my position at once. As quick as a flash I considered all the risks I might run in speaking to him, and most especially the delicate question of introducing him to her. I confess that in my embarrassment and confusion I felt small and mean. (202)

Yet to his great relief the recognition scene is handled well by Shiny who "seemed, at a glance, to divine my situation, and let drop no word that would have aroused suspicion as to the truth" (202). After his beloved has declared that she reciprocates his love and they get married he experiences a strange, unfounded dread that never leaves him: "I was in constant fear that she would discover in me some shortcomings which she would unconsciously attribute to my blood rather than to a failing of human nature" (210). At the ending of the novel, after the death of his wife in giving birth to their second child, he returns to the confessional tone of the beginning, though there remains always the contradiction between his wish to tell the truth and his readiness to suffer anything "to keep the brand from being placed upon" his children (210)—a tension that finds its formal expression in the anonymous publication of the book. In conclusion the narrator articulates his compounded sense of marginality, his guilt for racial betrayal and moral cowardice, and his belief that he has "sacrificed" his true talent by settling opportunistically for money-making rather than for producing interracial art:

> Sometimes it seems to me that I have never really been a Negro, that I have been only a privileged spectator of their inner life; at other times I feel that I have been a coward, a deserter, and I am possessed by a strange longing for my mother's people. (210)

At a meeting he hears Mark Twain, Booker T. Washington, and others speaking on behalf of racial progress, and recognize that they have "the eternal principle of right on their side":

> Beside them I feel small and selfish. I am an ordinarily successful white man who has made a little money. They are men who are making history and a race. I, too, might have taken part in a work so glorious.
>
> My love for my children makes me glad that I am what I am and keeps me from desiring to be otherwise; and yet, when I sometimes open a little box in which I still keep my fast yellowing manuscripts, the only tangible remnants of a vanished dream, a dead ambition, a sacrificed talent, I cannot repress the thought that, after all, I have chosen the lesser part, that I have sold my birthright for a mess of pottage. (211)[99]

The novel thus ends with a decidedly moralistic critique of passing as treason and cowardice: the ex-colored man has replicated Esau's opportunism in selling his birthright to the Jacob he could have been had he been more courageous. Passing means losing his opportunity of making history, as he also gives up his plans to create new American music out of the ingredients of his dual heritage.[100] He sacrifices to the bipolar world of race the artistic vitality that could come from interracial sources—the black and white keys of the piano, the merging of spirituals and New World symphonies, or the fusion of Frédéric Chopin and ragtime that the book represents as indicative of a larger utopian possibility.

There have probably been several other fiction writers who have drawn formal consequences from the theme of passing as Johnson did in creating texts that simulated the crossing of racial lines. One particularly interesting path was chosen by the French writer Boris Vian, who invented an American persona, a biracial, near-white man named Vernon Sullivan, under whose name he published some of his own novels as if they were "translations from the American." He had read Erskine Caldwell, James Cain, Raymond Chandler, and William Faulkner, translated Richard Wright's "Down by the Riverside," listened to a lot of black music, and was particularly inspired by an American magazine article on passing in creating his "alter Negro" (as Henri Magnan wrote in *Le Monde*). In the preface to the first novel he published, *J'irai cracher sur vos tombes* ("I Shall Spit on Your Graves," 1946), Vian explained that its supposed author, the "white Negro" Sullivan, "considers himself more as a black than a white, although he has passed the line." The publisher marketed the book under the slogan, "the novel that America did not dare to publish." The protagonist and narrator is Lee Anderson, who passes for white; after his brother Tom gets lynched for having had relations with a white woman, Lee decides to live as a white in the southern Buckton where he is completely unknown. Soon he socializes with the white girls and proposes marriage to the upper-crust Asquith sisters Jean and Lou (who hates blacks)—only to kill them both, in a desperate act of revenge for his brother. Hunted down by the police in a dramatic car chase, he dies (the ending is narrated in the third person). With its hard-boiled focus on race, jive talk (*parler le jive*), graphic sex, and violent crime, the novel became a French bestseller of which about half a million copies were printed. *Newsweek* authenticated Sullivan's existence, describing him as a twenty-six-year-old Negro from Chicago; in 1948, the Vendome Press in Paris even published an English translation of the novel (by Vian and Milton Rosenthal) as the supposed American original. On the strength of this success, Vian published a second Vernon Sullivan novel, *Les Morts ont tous la même peau* ("All Dead People Have the Same Skin," 1947), which is another novel about passing. Its narrator is Dan Parker, who believes he has passed successfully and is married to Sheïla, a white woman, when Richard, who identifies himself as his black brother, threatens to expose him to his wife and his employer (he is the bouncer in a New York cabaret). Dan kills his brother in cold blood, is drawn more deeply into crime, and hunted down by the police. Trapped, he learns that he is really white, that his wife is ready to betray him, that he has killed Richard for nothing, and he commits suicide by jumping out of a window; this novel also ends in the third person, as the photographer Max Klein takes a picture of Dan's corpse for *Life*.[101] Whether representing passing for white or passing for black, Vian seemed drawn to a shrill, misogynous account of racial violence in which siblings are also mysteriously prominent, set in a world of jazz, whisky, drugs, and film-noir existentialism. Passing is connected not to assimilation but to blood vengeance. The absurdity of racial lines and their violent consequences for the characters are placed into the foreground of the fictionalization of passing—while the novelist also clearly enjoyed the act of impersonating an American of mixed race and wrote a total of four novels and one novella under the name Vernon Sullivan. Literary hoaxes such as the anonymous publication of *The Autobiography of an Ex-Colored Man* and the invention of the author "Vernon Sullivan" suggest the possibilities of connecting the theme of passing to formal plays with truth-telling and authenticity, as James Weldon Johnson and Boris Vian play hide and seek with their readers' expectation of an authentic identity of the author—even in fictions that thematize the fluidity of lines of identification.

Except perhaps for the case of Boris Vian, the novels of passing are far more well known than are literary works about this theme in other genres. Yet there are interesting short stories and poems about passing, and, before moving on to representative longer fictions I would like to insert a brief discussion of two exemplary texts. Among the many short-story writers who have thematized passing, Langston Hughes stands out in having chosen the rare form of an epistolary story. In the "Dear Ma" letter that constitutes the text Hughes's "Passing" (1934), ostensibly written after perhaps the most ironic encounter requiring the passing man's denial of his identity, the letter writer apologizes to his own mother for not having greeted her in the street in downtown Chicago and praises her for her reaction: "You were great, though. Didn't give a sign that you even knew me, let alone I was your son. If I hadn't had the girl with me, Ma, we might have talked." Hughes's letter-writing son has to end this note because he is taking his "weakness" to the movies, but he still asks for Ma's opinion about her: "Isn't she sweet to look at, all blonde and blue-eyed?" He closes comfortingly:

> I will take a box at the Post Office for your mail. Anyhow, I'm glad there's nothing to stop letters from crossing the color-line. Even if we can't meet often, we can write, can't we, Ma?
> With love from your son,
>     JACK.[102]

Despite the humor and the irony, Hughes's story is also a moralistic critique of passing and represents the man who does it as a self-serving opportunist whose "crisis" is resolved by the ridiculous letter he writes to his mother, who literally falls into Ratna Roy's category of the "Heartbroken Mother Left Behind." Passing, once again, is viewed as cowardly treason of kin.

Countée Cullen's double poem, "Two Who Crossed a Line" (1925), may here stand for many other poetic treatments of passing. Both parts, "She Crosses" and "He Crosses," add up to a composite picture of going away but returning back home. "She Crosses" is seen from the point of view of a community ("we") that is "hurt" by the unnamed mixed race woman's departure.

> We envied her a while, who still
> Pursued the hated track;
> Then we forgot her name, until
> One day her shade came back. . . .

Yet the community also accepts her back, "no word asked," and her story has to be inferred from the "silence in her face" that only says, "seats were dear in the sun." The suggestion is that of a sad, thwarted interracial love story. In "He Crosses," the imagery suggests that it is also a sexual story that motivates the crossing of the angry young man who has "savage oats to sow" and wants to even a score.

> From every flower bed
> He passed, he plucked by threes and fours
> till wheels whirled in his head.

(These lines could have served as the epigraph to Boris Vian's *I Shall Spit on Your Graves*.) Yet the "anodyne" seems to work quickly, and

> With scornful grace, he bowed farewell
> And retraversed the line.[103]

Cullen's suggestive poems never explicitly mention race yet touch upon many of the issues that fiction writers would explore fully in novels of manners of the interwar period, as plots of passing now often came to include the feature of a return to a warm and accepting black community, at least as a wish if not as the act of retraversing the line.

### Passing in Three Modern Novels of Manners: Walter White's *Flight*, Jessie Fauset's *Plum Bun*, and Nella Larsen's *Passing*

The novel that goes furthest into the direction of presenting a truly courageous character who passes may be Walter White's *Flight* (1926). Mimi, the daughter of the proud New Orleans Catholic Creole Jean Daquin and named after *La Bohème*, is a "new woman" and eager reader of Walt Whitman and Romain Rolland who decides neither to have an abortion nor to marry Carl Hunter, the weak father of her child; she is also too proud to accept money from his folks. Mimi leads quite heterogeneous chapters of her life in Atlanta, where she witnesses the race riot in 1906 (61–76); in Philadelphia, where she cuts down to size a white employer who makes inappropriate sexual advances (165–68); and in Harlem, where she lives with an aunt and is part of the smart set until a gossip from Atlanta recognizes her. Mimi then passes for white, builds up a successful professional career as a seamstress and "French" dress designer for the New York house of Francine's, and marries the rich socialite Jimmie Forrester, who is also a white bigot and Ku Klux Klan sympathizer. She wants to tell Jimmie about her racial past and about her son Petit Jean, but Jimmie wants to hear nothing about her background. Yet the novel which had previously shown Mimi's Atlanta past catching up with her in Harlem does not reach the high point of a discovery scene in which Jimmie's prejudiced feelings would be directed against Mimi.[104] She is rather so moved, at the end of the novel, by seeing a black historical show with him in Harlem which distances her from her husband and reorients her toward her black roots that she simply decides to leave him:

> Calm peace filled her. She knew now why she had been ill at ease, restless, dissatisfied with the life which at first had seemed so happy a one.
>
> She knew too that Jimmie would not, could not understand. Should she try to tell him? No, she decided. It were better to leave his dreams and illusions undisturbed—he had little enough real happiness as it was. And his convictions, his prejudices were too deeply rooted, she was sure, to enable him to comprehend without pain and suffering. He had done all he could—it was not wholly his fault. . . . (300)

At sunrise she abandons her husband and her white life to reclaim her son (now a teenager raised as a white boy in Westchester County) and her blackness:

> "Free! Free! Free!" she whispered exultantly as with firm tread she went down the steps. "*Petit* Jean—my own people—and happiness!" was the song in her heart as she happily strode through the dawn, the rays of the morning sun dancing lightly upon the brilliant gold of her hair. . . . (300)

On this high note the novel ends. *Flight* is remarkable for carefully separating some of the motifs that are often clustered in tales of passing: thus Mimi is *not* tempted by the horror of the Atlanta riots to pass for white—an explicit antithesis to *The Autobiography of an Ex-Colored Man*; in posing as a young widow in order to account for her pregnancy and motherhood she practices deception long before embarking on racial passing; she is economically very successful and independent before the interracial marriage plot emerges, and is tied to a past not so much through being recognized as black but through being recognized as Mimi, because of her attachment to her child, and because of her desire for the aesthetic superiority and resilience of black American life that the Chinese intellectual Wu Hseh-Chuan points out to her: "I have been in your country many times and I feel that only your Negroes have successfully resisted mechanization—they yet can laugh and they can enjoy the benefits of the machine without being crushed by it. . . ." (282). This is compatible with the philosophy of Mimi's father, who sees in sleepy, calm, and placid New Orleans Creole culture the ideal synthesis between black and white.

Mimi similarly finds the idea of passing unattractive in a city where the most beautiful women "were not white—at least, they were not Anglo-Saxon." In fact, their often unrecognized black ancestry accounted for "a warmth, a delicate humanness, an attractiveness" not easily found outside of the Creole world (126). She deplores that in Atlanta "these coloured people with the gifts from God of laughter and song and creative instincts [. . .] are aping the white man—becoming a race of money-grubbers" (53–54). It therefore follows the logic of the novel[105] that Mimi realizes at the end of *Flight* what the black uptown world of Harlem really means to her:

> Gone were the morose, the worried, the unhappy, the untranquil faces she had been seeing downtown for years. Here there was light and spontaneous laughter, here there was real joyfulness in voices and eyes. Here was leisureliness, none of the hectic dashing after material things which brought little happiness when gained. (293)

In Walter White's fictional universe, passing works to detract from one of the vital sources of American civilization—the familiar warmth of black life; hence passing is deplorable for this reason alone, and not on the moral ground of its deception and opportunism, which are largely shared features of modern American life. It is this understanding that makes White develop the motif of the upstart that has been present in literature of passing since Hugo and Beaumont. At the fashion house of Francine's, White lets Mimi become a successful self-made woman in the company of other ethnic upstart women: Madame Francine herself really started as the Irish immigrant girl Margaret O'Donnell (230), and Mimi's friend Sylvia Smith grew up as Sylvia Bernstein on the Lower East Side in a Jewish immigrant family with seven children (218–20).[106] Though Mimi feels a sense of kinship to such women who are also "sailing under false colors" (218), she also finds herself thinking that Sylvia is ambitious, "just like a Jew"—and feeling embarrassed at having had this thought (219). But the novel does not only insert parallel upstart stories into the lives of Mimi, it explicitly phrases a critique of the ideology of the self-made (wo)man as "bunk" (206). The criticism is part of a broader questioning of Western materialism and hypocrisy from the point of view of an existentially vital black culture and of black laughter. Passing is therefore a mistake, not because it constitutes an act of supposedly aberrant dishonesty in a country of authentic identities, but because it signals the surrender of a potentially critical position to the all too pervasive ethos of money-grubbing.

Jessie Fauset's novel *Plum Bun* (1929) may well be the most comprehensive psycho-social novel on the theme.[107] As Fauset explores the inward and outward experience of her protagonist Angela Murray, she places her first of all into a family context in which sporadic and part-time passing had already occurred: her mother Mattie had done it frequently as a joke, a game, a lark, a pastime—though even this form of passing had compelled Angela's mother some times to disavow her husband Junius, most dramatically in the hospital. Whereas such writers as Webb, Chesnutt, or Johnson focus on the first passing generation in a family, Fauset (like Beaumont) represents the second generation. Angela's decision to pass for white is a departure from her mother's adventures only insofar as she decides to undertake it seriously and full time. She is thus different from her mother, while also following in her footsteps. To some extent she and her sister Virginia repeat the parts of their parents, with Virginia taking the father's role. Angela changes her name to Angèle Mory (94, 107) and experiences passing as an adventure (92) yielding subversive insights (58).

She moves from Philadelphia to New York and passes successfully; yet, like many characters who passed before her, she is forced to become complicit in racial oppression, first toward the colored girl Rachel Powell at Cooper Union, then when her white racist boyfriend Roger Fielding asks a waiter to make the colored guests at another table leave the restaurant, in order to protect Angela (whom he of course presumed to be white), and she has to be quiet. Even worse, Angela, in her crisis moment of self-denial, humiliatingly pretends not to recognize her own darker sister Virginia when she arrives at Pennsylvania Station in New York—in order not to make Roger suspicious (who by coincidence runs into Angela at the crowded station). Though Virginia has never been to New York and is looking forward to being met by her only sister on the date that Angela had suggested, she still has enough presence of mind to salvage the situation (as did Shiny in Johnson's novel) and to pretend that she has mixed up Angela with someone else. She asks, "I beg your pardon, but isn't this Mrs. Henrietta Jones?" (159), permitting Angela to say no and to escape from the potentially embarrassing situation with Roger—though leaving her sister to fend for herself.[108] By her denial and disavowal Angela literally sacrifices her darker sister Virginia to her white suitor Roger.

The motif of the sacrifice is explicitly articulated in Angela's description of "colour as the one god to whom you could sacrifice everything" (44), though she does recognize sheepishly that "no ambition, no pinnacle of safety" is "supposed to call for the sacrifice of a sister" (159). It is also present in the question that Anthony Cross (a telling name) asks her—who, it turns out, is passing in his own right, only he does it in order to restore justice.[109] Angela's passing is placed into a context that includes parallels with the successfully passing Jewish Miss Salting (107), with mésalliance (127-28), and with crossing the gender divide (88). Passing is furthermore connected by the narrator to social climbing (352). The secrecy and deception that passing requires is repeatedly made the touchstone of its condemnation; yet when Angela ultimately comes out, her ill-timed courage goes unrewarded.[110]

Nella Larsen's novel *Passing* (1929) is, as we have already seen, a virtual encyclopedia on the theme. The novel represents the relationship between a woman who passes, Clare Kendry, and a woman who does it only sporadically, Irene Westover Redfield;[111] and the narrator's comments about Irene's curiosity have already been cited:

> She wished to find out about this hazardous business of "passing," this breaking away from all that was familiar and friendly to take one's chance in another environment, not entirely strange, perhaps, but certainly not entirely friendly. What, for example, one did about background, how one accounted for oneself. And how one felt when one came into contact with other Negroes. But she couldn't. She was unable to think of a single question that in its context or its phrasing was not too frankly curious, if not actually impertinent.[112]

This passage seems to imply that the reader may be just as curious as Irene, and the narrator both explains passing ("this breaking away. . .") and keeps it mysterious, though Irene gets to ask some of her questions anyway. Larsen seems to invite social interests directly by referring to social texts such as antimiscegenation legislation and the Rhinelander case.[113] One of Irene Redfield's ambivalent statements also addresses the question of how blacks who do not pass react to those who do:

> It's funny about "passing." We disapprove of it and at the same time condone it. It excites our contempt and yet we rather admire it. We shy away from it with an odd kind of revulsion, but we protect it.[114]

Because the novel's attention is focused on two women, the eroticized gaze that is conventional when male-imagined narrators describe mixed-race women—and that James Weldon Johnson had reimagined as the narrator's gaze at himself—here is directed from a *female* center of consciousness toward the mysterious *woman* who passes permanently, and the (otherwise conventional) description therefore calls attention to itself. Startling is the focus on Clare's "dark, almost black eyes" (177); when Irene steals another glance, she finds them "strange, languorous" (178); and drawn more toward Clare she exclaims in her mind:

> [T]he eyes were magnificent! Dark, sometimes absolutely black, always luminous, and set in long, black lashes. Arresting eyes, slow and mesmeric, and with, for all their warmth, something withdrawn and secret about them.
>
> Ah! Surely! They were Negro eyes! Mysterious and concealing. And set in that ivory face under that bright hair, there was about them something exotic.
>
> Yes, Clare Kendry's loveliness was absolute, beyond challenge, thanks to those eyes which her grandmother and later her mother and father had given her.
>
> Into those eyes there came a smile and over Irene the sense of being petted and caressed. She smiled back. (191)

This passage makes the reader think of the first meaningful encounter of lovers' eyes, but we remember that it is Irene who is looking at Clare.[115]

In a conversation with Irene and Gertrude about children, Clare states that she does not think that she will have any more children (197), and Larsen seems to take for granted that the reader knows something about the fear of *Natus Æthiopus* and offers no further explanation (just as she does not explain the Rhinelander case). And when Clare tells Irene how she was taken in by her white aunts after her father died, but had to do all the housework and most of the washing for them, she sarcastically comments on their invoking the curse of Ham (188)—as we have seen earlier.

Irene, worried about being detected as temporarily passing, puts her concerns aside with the thought that "White people were so stupid about such things for all that they usually asserted that they were able to tell; and by the most ridiculous means." The first racial sign that she mentions are, of course, fingernails (178). The comprehensiveness of Larsen's coverage of all these topics is striking.

### Universal Passing: George Schuyler's *Black No More: Being an Account of the Strange and Wonderful Workings of Science in the Land of the Free, A.D. 1933–1940*

In its transformation from Hugo's representation of racial passing as an opportunistic gesture of an upstart to the serious vehicle of social criticism in Beaumont, "Passing" became, as we saw, a theme that invited serious, at times sentimental and at other times moralistic treatments, whether a psychological or a sociological focus prevailed. This is not to say that comedy (let alone irony) was absent from the fiction of passing, only that it was often employed to make a serious point—as in the case of Hughes's "Passing" with its stinging critique of the letter writer as a traitor to his own mother.

It is the merit of George S. Schuyler to have gone back to the origin of the *parvenu* theme and made passing look as much like a social folly as any other gesture of opportunism. His novel *Black No More* (1931) is a satire which makes it especially intriguing for thematic exploration, since satire by definition is "about" something that it has to misrepresent recognizably enough in order to deride it effectively.[116] Schuyler's text achieves its distinctive quality by making us laugh at human folly, especially greed and opportunism, as he uses the by 1931 quite conventional theme of "crossing the line" in order to stage comic effects in a world that is both referential and comically exaggerated. A whole array of characters are caricatures of contemporaries whom they serve to ridicule— which only works as long as they are both identifiable and made to seem ludicrous.

The general idea of the book is suggested by the dedication "to all Caucasians in the great republic who can trace their ancestry back ten generations and confidently assert that there are no Black leaves, twigs, limbs or branches on their family trees." One starting point for Schuyler is thus the premise that the United States of America is an interracial country, a fact that is not recognized or cherished by black or white. In a country where genealogy is both all-important and often unverifiable, and in which black and white work together, eat identical breakfasts, and live in the same towns, race distinctions can be nothing but hokum: seen this way one can say that in the United States it is the whole country that is "passing" for white. This makes racial etiquette a complete fiction and hoax, or, differently considered, an enormous business opportunity of which operators on both sides of the color line can take advantage. Schuyler ridicules the new and more mystical legal calculus of "blackness" and the eugenicist requirements of tracing ancestry and registering race in purity laws of the 1920s, makes fun of plastic surgery, satirizes advertising campaigns for self-improvement schemes, and shows how everyone is implicated in this absurd situation.

As his fictional vehicle he assumes the possibility of a general scheme of transforming all blacks into whites that Dr. Junius Crookman develops. It is a machine, a cross between dentist's seat and an electric chair, that makes unrecognizable whites out of paying black customers. Characteristic of the broad and double-edged humor of the book is the "Vanishing Mammy" song that makes fun of "America's premier black-faced troubadour" Al Jolson and the sentimental mammy cult of *The Jazz Singer* just as it deflates the fixtures of passing:

> Vanishing Mammy, Mammy! Mammy! of Mi—ine,
> You've been away, dear, such an awful long time
> You went away, Sweet Mammy! Mammy! one summer night
> I can't help thinkin', Mammy, that you went white. (148)

Schuyler uses the fiction of the machine that can turn black into white in order to make cultural bits that were floating about without his fictional device seem all the more ridiculous. He has thus created an aesthetic vehicle through which he can ironically comment on the conventions of interracial literature, including previous books on passing. He represents W. E. B. Du Bois as Dr. Shakespeare Agamemnon Beard, who

> talked at white banquets about "we of the black race" and admitted in books that he was part-French, part-Russian, part-Indian and part-Negro. He bitterly denounced the Nordics for debauching Negro women while taking care to hire comely yellow stenographers with weak resistance. (90)

Dr. Napoleon Wellington Jackson is easily recognizable as a caricature of James Weldon Johnson, who could

> speak to audiences of sex-starved matrons who yearned to help the Negro stand erect. During his leisure time, which was naturally considerable, he

wrote long and learned articles, bristling with references, for the more
intellectual magazines, in which he sought to prove conclusively that the
plantation shouts of Southern Negro peons were superior to any of
Beethoven's symphonies and that the city of Benin was the original site of
the Garden of Eden. (91)

Walter White appears under the name of Walter Williams, who, the
narrator says, "was known to be a Negro among his friends and acquain-
tances, but no one else would have suspected it" (95). A "tall, heavy-set
white man with pale blue eyes," he declares:

> I am very proud to be a Negro and always have been (his great-grandfa-
> ther, it seemed, had been a mulatto), and I'm willing to sacrifice for the
> uplift of my race. (94)

The race leader establishment is, of course, as worried about the Black
No More movement as are fanatic white racists and the producers of hair
straighteners and skin bleachers. The opposite experience of the "black"
who hears what whites think about other whites—familiar from the literature on passing—is taken to the extreme, at which the originally black
protagonist Max Disher has become the white man Matthew Fisher, so
white in fact that he turns into a white supremacist who marries Helen
Givens, the daughter of the Knights of Nordica wizard.[117] In the figure
of Dr. Samuel Buggerie, the statistician and author of such books as *The
Incidence of Psittacosis Among the Hiphopa Indians of the Mamazon Valley and
Its Relation to Life Insurance Rates in the United States* (197), Schuyler aims
at racialist social scientists and the eugenics movement, combining such
figures as Frederick Hoffman and Dr. W. A. Plecker, the Virginia statistician and lobbyist for the 1924 Virginia Act for the Preservation of
Racial Integrity.[118] Buggerie finds out "that over half the population has
no record of its ancestry beyond five generations" (177) and proceeds to
trace the arch-Anglo-Saxon Snobbcraft's ancestry to an English serving
maid and a black slave in the seventeenth century. Schuyler questioned
genealogy and race loyalty, the taboo on intermarriage and the legal definition of whiteness. His novel gave the repertoire of fiction on passing a
twist that has raised the stakes for further contributions to this tradition
very high indeed.

Yet even the sharp-tongued and irreverent Schuyler would articulate
the theme of "black warmth" in his novel on passing. *Black No More* sup-
poses on the one hand that all beliefs in races are weird fictions yet suggests on the other that there is something about black life that anybody
who had turned white would be likely to miss. Matthew Fisher recognizes this:

> There was something lacking in these ofay places of amusement or else
> there was something present that one didn't find in the black-and-tan

resorts in Harlem. The joy and abandon here was obviously forced. Patrons went to extremes to show each other they were having a wonderful time. It was all so strained and quite unlike anything to which he had been accustomed. The Negroes, it seemed to him, were much gayer, enjoyed themselves more deeply and yet they were much more restrained, actually more refined. Even their dancing was different. They followed the rhythm accurately, effortlessly and with easy grace; these lumbering couples, out of step half the time and working as strenuously as stevedores emptying the bowels of a freighter, were noisy, awkward, inelegant. At their best they were gymnastic where the Negroes were sensuous. He felt a momentary pang of mingled disgust, disillusionment and nostalgia.[119]

This aspect of the novel is reminiscent of the ending of Walter White's *Flight*, yet it is somewhat odd in the context of Schuyler's no-holds-barred approach to the topic.

Beneath Schuyler's spirited attack on the shibboleths of race relations is his fear that race thinking has inherently undemocratic and totalitarian implications, that unionization is inhibited by racism, and that it leads to mob violence and lynchings. Although there is little piety in this book, its sudden seriousness near the end is strongly connected to the broad attack on the holy cows of race relations, at the core of which Schuyler perceives the fanatical belief in essential black-white differences.[120] By creating a scenario of *universal passing*, Schuyler also responded to—and took to an extreme—the many speculations that circulated in the United States about the quantitative dimensions of passing; and the discussion of some real cases and some guesses about the extent of passing will conclude the chapter.

### How Widespread Was Passing in the United States?[121]

Many African Americans reported that they personally knew friends or relatives who have passed. A few cases have been noted by historians or elicited public discussion in the press. For example, in 1838 the fashionable French-accented confidence man Monsieur Dukay who charmed Memphis turned out to be no white sugar planter but a New Orleans Quadroon barber.[122] The Charleston grocer Thomas L. Grant passed after November 1909; the North Carolina journalist Alex Manley (whose 1898 editorial had been an element in the Wilmington riots) settled in Philadelphia and, for two years, worked as a white man while continuing his black family life.[123] In 1910 the wealthy Massachusetts plumber William Horton received a decree of annulment in the state supreme court after charging that his wife, Edith May Williams, who, before their marriage, had represented herself as being of Spanish descent, was really a Mulatto.[124] The Montclair (New Jersey) Construction Company owner, Columbia University graduate, and former member of the university's football team William E. Jackson publicly disclosed his background when he took a marriage license in order to get married to the white telephone operator Helen Burns in New York City in 1925,[125] and the Trinity College-trained Theophilus John Minton Syphax revealed his true identity only shortly before his death in 1948—after having lived for forty-five years as the white Wall Street lawyer T. John McKee.[126] The Harvard alumnus and Foreign Service officer Lawrence Dennis, an American supporter of Hitler who attended a Nazi party Nuremberg rally and was subject to a sedition trial in 1944, was discovered to have crossed the line from his colored parents and relatives in Atlanta.[127] Ernest Torregano, a wealthy San Francisco bankruptcy lawyer who died in 1954, had lived until 1911 as a colored entertainer in New Orleans.[128] How many such cases did exist?

"Five Million White Negroes," *Ebony* answered in 1948 and accompanied its sensationalist cover essay by Roi Ottley with a quiz, "Can you tell who on this page is Negro and who white?"—that asked readers to identify the race of a series of individuals portrayed in photographs that framed the first two pages of the article. The story was picked up by *Time*—with a quiz using a smaller sample of the same faces—but with an endorsement of *Ebony*'s numerical answer, which is among the highest guesses that have been offered.[129]

Ray Stannard Baker wrote in 1909 that no one, "of course, can estimate the number of men and women with Negro blood who have thus 'gone over to white'; but the number must be large."[130] An earlier excerpt from his study of the color line was also appropriately illustrated (Fig. 36). Reliable quantitative data do not exist, but Baker was one of the very few observers who drew the conclusion from this fact not to offer any figure. Most other writers have offered estimates that are, however, dramatically heterogeneous and range from hundreds to millions. For example, in "The Vanishing Mulatto" (1925), Charles S. Johnson inferred from census data that 355,000 blacks must have faded "into the great white multitude" between 1900 and 1920 (Fig. 37).[131] Based on similar data, E. W. Eckard assumed more modestly that there were 2600 cases per year nationally from 1920 to 1940.[132] Others who joined the guessing game include Carl Van Vechten (8000 p.a.), T. T. McKinney (10,000 p.a.), Walter White (12,000 p.a.), Burns Mantle (5000 to 20,000 p.a.), Harold Asbury (30,000 p.a.), and Roi Ottley (40,000 to 50,000 p.a.). William M. Kephart wisely drew the conclusion from the long debate that the "wide disparity in figures suggests the real answer, namely, *nobody knows*."[133] Passing was undoubtedly significant locally: New York City has already been cited; the Seventh Ward in New Orleans was known as the "Can't Tell Ward"; and in the 1920s a theater in Washington hired "a black doorman to spot and bounce intruders whose racial origins were undetectable to whites."[134] It was probably more fre-

*Figure 36* "SOME TYPICAL MULATTO GIRLS. *Showing how easily many Mulattoes may pass for whites*" (1908)

*Figure 37* Aaron Douglas, "The Vanishing Mulatto," *Opportunity* cover (1925)

quent in cities than in the country, though statistical computations to this effect rest on the same shaky foundation as all the other numbers given.[135] Kephart concludes that "any figure given must necessarily be little more than guesswork."[136]

Uncertainty has not kept writers from advancing speculations not only about the general figures but also about age and sex distribution among the population of people who pass. For example, Earnest Hooton expressed his belief that it is the younger rather than the older ones who pass;[137] according to Charles S. Johnson's "Vanishing Mulatto," while there were "1,018 black males per 1,000 females," there were "only 886 Mulatto males per 1,000 females," permitting the conclusion that men "travel more and are not so dependent as women on family connections." This sex-ratio approach, inspired by Hornell Hart, was based on the premise that men were more likely to pass than women, a notion shared explicitly by Reuter.[138] Though fictional literature often presented men as more successful at passing than women (for example, John as opposed to Rena Walden in Charles W. Chesnutt's *House Behind the Cedars*, or James Weldon Johnson's narrator compared with Larsen's and Fauset's—though not Walter White's—heroines), we have no evidence to support the belief that men have passed either at a greater rate or more successfully than women. Furthermore, and more devastatingly, Louis Wirth writes that "the sex ratio can give no indication of what the total amount of passing is unless one were to assume that females do not pass."[139] Caleb Johnson fancifully assumed the opposite, with equally little evidence:

> While there are no statistics to support the conclusion, there is strong reason for the belief that many more women than men cross the color line from Negro to white. This is partly due to the fact that sexual attraction is stronger between the light male and the darker female than in the opposite direction. It is a matter commented on by numerous scientific observers, who agree that the male Negro almost universally prefers a woman of his own color or darker, while the primitive sex-appeal of the octoroon girl is highly potent with the average young white male. Moreover, the social act of "passing" is easier for the girl than for the man.[140]

Joseph Washington has rightly reminded readers that "the knowledge of sex distribution of blacks who passed was even less adequate than the knowledge of the color distribution."[141] Whatever the numbers were, it is quite possible that the rate of passing among those who could do so was higher in literature than in real life.[142]

Though now relegated to a footnote in cultural history, the phenomenon of passing "unleashed tremendous anxiety and fear and fascination among whites" and became a "terrifying issue" to them.[143] From the 1850s to the 1930s, passing was also "the favorite theme in Negro fiction"[144] and became "a principal theme of American national consciousness until the end of World War II."[145] "From the 1920s to the 1940s, no book on Black people or race relations was complete without a section on passing."[146] Robert Farnsworth's assessment of Chesnutt's novel *House Behind the Cedars* is representative of the 1960s: he argued in 1969 that although this "was long Chesnutt's most popular novel . . . its concern with the problems of passing now seems historically dated."[147] Passing was swept aside in social history by the civil rights movement, and in literature by the combined successes of Zora Neale Hurston and Richard Wright, who no longer employed the theme.[148] Nathan Huggins summarized the situation perfectly in his essay "Passing Is Passé," arguing that the black revolution of the 1960s with its "insistence on race identity, race consciousness, race pride, and race beauty has made anachronistic the game of hide-and-seek, traditionally played by whites and blacks in America."[149] A generation later, as contemporary writers and artists may be returning to representations of racial passing,[150] the time may be ripe for case studies of known individuals who passed as well as for a full-fledged cultural investigation of the period in which "passing" was a significant feature.

# Incest and Miscegenation

The author [of the *Miscegenation* pamphlet] finds an emblem of his success in the blending of many to make the one new race, in the crowning of the dome above this Capitol with the *bronze statue* of Liberty! It is neither black nor white, but the intermediate miscegen, typifying the exquisite composite race which is to arise out of this war for abolition, and whose destiny is to rule the continent.

> —Mr. Samuel Sullivan Cox (D-Ohio) in Congress, 17 February 1864[1]

## Consanguinity or Miscegenation

Upon the dissolution by decree or sentence of nullity of any marriage that is prohibited on account of consanguinity between the parties, or of any marriage between a white person and a negro, the issue of the marriage shall be deemed to be illegitimate.

> —1911 *Nebraska Compiled Statutes*, chap. 25, sec. 31[2]

[I]ncest proper, and its metaphorical form as the violation of a minor (by someone "old enough to be her father," as the expression goes), even combines in some countries with its direct opposite, inter-racial sexual relations, an extreme form of exogamy, as the two most powerful inducements to horror and collective vengeance.

> —Claude Lévi-Strauss, *The Elementary Structures of Kinship* (1949)[3]

*—So it's the miscegenation, not the incest, which you cant bear.*
*Henry doesn't answer. . . .*

> —William Faulkner, *Absalom, Absalom!* (1936)[4]

W hat do incest and miscegenation have to do with each other? One of the most haunting scenes in American literature is probably Shrevlin McCannon and Quentin Compson's imaginative speculation, in William Faulkner's novel *Absalom, Absalom!* (1936), about what may really have happened in 1865 when Henry Sutpen killed Charles Bon at the gate of Sutpen's Hundred, an act no one else witnessed, but about which different stories circulate. Quentin and Shreve ultimately surmise that the white Henry must have killed his mixed-race half-brother in order to prevent Bon's marriage with Henry's white sister, Judith Sutpen, for the alliance would have constituted both brother-sister incest and miscegenation. Later Henry comes back to his father's house and secretly lives and ultimately dies there with his biracial sister Clytie. This dramatic and climactic reconstruction comes near the end of the novel, set in 1910, and shortly before Quentin commits suicide—as at least the contexts of the appended chronology and of Faulkner's novel *The Sound and the Fury* suggest. What seems beyond doubt, however, is that the whole house of Thomas Sutpen has collapsed.

Eric Sundquist has explored in depth the joining of incest and miscegenation in *Absalom, Absalom!* as a synthesis of the writer's concern with incest in *The Sound and the Fury* and miscegenation in *Light in August*. Wen-ching Ho stressed the fact that, before publishing *Light in August*, Faulkner had already written "two sketches, one novel, and eight stories in which miscegenation appears as a major or minor theme." In closely comparing the short story "Evangeline" (1931)—in which the outline of the triangle of Henry and Judith Sutpen and of Charles Bon is already at the center—with *Absalom, Absalom!*, Ho concludes that it is only in the novel that Bon also becomes the son of Thomas Sutpen, so that it is the incest theme (and not that of miscegenation) that Faulkner must have added in the process of writing the novel. By either account, however, it is the combination of the two themes that makes *Absalom, Absalom!* so remarkable. Both Sundquist and Ho note that the obsession with incest seems intimately connected with the fear of miscegenation.[5] Sundquist also pointed out in a later comment on Charles Chesnutt's story "The Dumb Witness" that there was a longstanding tradition of fusing the representation of incest and miscegenation.[6]

It is true indeed that many writers had thematized the intersection of miscegenation and incest long before Faulkner focused on it in *Absalom, Absalom!* The theme of incest has in fact had a fairly noticeable presence in the discussion of various recurrent elements in interracial literature. Incest appeared, for example, in myths of origins, was—as was miscegenation—one of the transgressions imputed to Ham, animated Jefferson's story of the merino ram that was told in order to establish a Calculus of Color, was palpable in the sibling-like love between Horatio and Cecilie in Andersen's *Mulatten* as well as in other interracial first-cousin pairs such as George and Zoe in Boucicault's *Octoroon* or Alfred and Jenni in Storm's "Von jenseit des Meeres," was one of the motives that could steer white lovers away from each other, and was presented as a possibility in other texts. It does not come as a surprise to recognize that incest is not a stranger to the thematic fields of interracial literature. There are, as we shall see, abundant instances of juxtapositions, comparisons, and conflations between incest and miscegenation, and there is much evidence for it in literature, law books, historical documents, and other sources, starting at least in the eighteenth century and extending to the twentieth.[7]

It is the case of a thematic cluster of two themes that, theoretically speaking, one perhaps might have expected to go their different ways. "Incest" derives from Latin *incestus* (*in-* + *castus*), or "impure, unchaste," and specifically applied to unchastity among "persons related within the degrees within which marriage is prohibited" (*Oxford English Dictionary*). The feminine form of Latin *castus* also became the Portuguese word *casta*, or "caste," a synonym for race and lineage, and for a "system of rigid social stratification characterized by hereditary status, endogamy, and social barriers sanctioned by custom, law, or religion." The word "miscegenation" was made up in 1863 (out of Latin *miscere*, "to mix," and *genus*, "race") by George Wakeman and David Goodman Croly in a political pamphlet published as part of a Democratic dirty trick in the Lincoln reelection campaign.[8] What was it that brought these two disparate terms together? I shall first present, in more or less chronological arrangement, the evidence for the clustering of the two themes in literature and other discourses, accompanied by some explanations that have been given for instances of their conjunction, then attempt to extend further some past speculations on the clustering of the two words and to differentiate significant ideological orientations that operated in making the analogy; finally, I shall return to *Absalom, Absalom!*.

# A Thematic Cluster in the Service of the Struggle Against Slavery: From *Jonathan Corncob* and *The Slave* to *Old Hepsy* and *Adela the Octoroon*

An early and remarkable instance can be found in the novel, published anonymously and for the author in London in 1787, entitled *Adventures of Jonathan Corncob, Loyal American Refugee*. One chapter of this work is entitled "The West-Indian way of white-washing, or rather the true way of washing the blackamoor white" and opens with the following episode, a multigenerational family story which is explicitly described in terms of repeated incest:

> My friend took me the following morning to the house of a planter from whom he had borrowed the mulatto girl. He was not at home, but we were, nevertheless, ushered into an apartment, at one end of which was sitting an old negress, smoking her pipe. Near her was an elderly mulatto woman; at a little distance was a female still less tawny of complexion, called in the country, as I believe, a mestee; and at the other end of the room I observed a yellow quadroon giving suck to a child, which, though a little sallow, was as white as the children in Europe generally are. I could not help remarking to the West-Indian this regular gradation of light and shade.
>
> "This," said he, "is the family of my friend, Mr. Winter; the three younger females and the child are the progeny of the old negress."
>
> "And who are the fathers?"
>
> "Mr. Winter himself is the father of them all," replied he: "when he was very young he had the mulatto woman by the negress; when the mulatto was twelve years old, he took her for his mistress, and had by her the mestee. At about the same age his intimacy with the mestee produced the quadroon, who had by him a few months ago the white child you see in her arms. This is what is called in this country washing a man's self white, and Mr. Winter has the credit of having washed himself white at a very early age, being at this time less than sixty years old."
>
> This complicated incest, and the coolness with which my friend spoke of it, made me begin to think it no wonder that Barbadoes was subject to hurricanes.[9]

This remarkable passage pushes to a bitingly satirical extreme the model of colonial family building—complete with a justified curse. One wonders whether this kind of story was the subtext of *any* classification system? Mr. Winter's story certainly resonates with Jefferson's tale of the ram and the ewe that had opened his attempt at conceiving race as a mathematical issue. *Jonathan Corncob* also offers a new possibility of reading Modesto Brocos's painting *Redenção de Cã* ("The Redemption of Ham," 1895, reproduced in Chapter Three) that shows only one white man with three generations of women. Sharp and startling satire such as the one here focused on the racial fantasy world of a self-made patriarch, the "father of them all," whose descendant-counting starts (as did some examples of the Calculus of Color) with himself as universal origin, was not the only mode in which miscegenation and incest merged in the eighteenth century.[10] In Thomas Southern's high-serious drama *Oroonoko; A Tragedy in Five Acts* (1796), Aphra Behn's famous story of 1688 was changed into an intermarriage plot, as Southern turned the heroine Imoinda white. The heroic African prince Oroonoko marries her and she expects a child, upon which he comments:

> She grew with child, and I grew happier still.
> O my Imoinda! But it could not last.
> Her fatal beauty reach'd my father's ears:
> He sent for her to court; where, cursed court,
> No woman comes, but for his am'rous use.
> He raging to possess her, she was forc'd
> To own herself my wife. The furious king
> Started at incest: but grown desperate,
> Not daring to enjoy what he desir'd,
> In mad revenge, which I could never learn,
> He poison'd her, or sent her far, far off,
> Far from my hopes ever to see her more.[11]

Here it is Oroonoko's *African* father who comes close to committing the interracial "incest" with his own son's white wife (who is pregnant), but, fortunately, the act is prevented.[12]

A literary example of both an attempted and a fully realized incest relationship is Richard Hildreth, *The Slave* (1836).[13] In fact, the representation of incest in this novel purporting to be a slave narrative led to some controversy that later editions of the novel incorporated into the prefatory matter. Thus Hildreth's introduction to the 1856 edition, entitled *Archy Moore, the White Slave; or, Memoirs of a Fugitive*, reports that the Pope placed the novel on the *Index Expurgatorius* (xxi) and also cites Lydia Maria Child's letter to the *Liberator* which concludes with the statement: "If I were a man, I would rather be the author of that work, than of anything ever published in America" (xiv). In her defense of the novel, Child explicitly endorsed the incest plot:

> Some are shocked because Archy Moore married his half sister; but it must be remembered that the author is not attempting to describe a beau ideal of human perfection; he is showing what a man of powerful character is likely to become under the degrading influence of slavery. It would be unnatural to suppose elevated purity of sentiment, or unimpaired moral strength, either in slaves or their masters. (xiv)[14]

Indeed, the novel's biracial narrator and protagonist Archy Moore does not only make veiled incestuously toned comments, such as the following one about his own mother: "I describe her more like a lover than a son" (8–9). More than that, the plot moves toward the threat of an interracial father-daughter incest that is deflected only to give way to a fully consummated sibling marriage. When his master and (unacknowledged) white father, Colonel Moore, prohibits the marriage with Moore's mixed-race daughter Cassy (who had also been the target of her father's own incestuous interracial advances), Archy speculates:

> One motive which occurred to me, I could not think of myself, with the slightest patience; and still less could I bear to shock and distress poor Cassy, by the mention of it [Moore's desire to make his natural daughter Cassy his concubine]. Another motive, which I thought might possibly have influenced colonel Moore, was less discreditable to him, and would have been flattering to the pride of both Cassy and myself [the fact that they are both Moore's natural children, and hence siblings]. But this, I could not mention, without leading to disclosures, which I did not see fit to make.
>
> Cassy knew herself to be colonel Moore's daughter; but early in our acquaintance, I had discovered that she had no idea, that I was his son. I have every reason to believe that Mrs. Moore was perfectly well informed as to both these particulars;—for they were of that sort, which seldom or never escape the eagerness of female curiosity, and more especially, the curiosity of a wife.
>
> Whatever she might know, she discovered in it no impediment to my marriage with Cassy. Nor did I;—for how could that same regard for the *decencies of life*—such is the soft phrase which justifies the most unnatural cruelty—that refused to acknowledge our paternity, or to recognize any relationship between us, pretend at the same time, and on the sole ground of relationship, to forbid our union? (48–49/1852: 38)

Archy Moore thus argues surprisingly and quite shockingly that sibling incest does not matter if, as in his and Cassy's case, the siblings' relationship is not openly acknowledged by their own father. An incestuous marriage can be entered into knowingly under such circumstances, since the "sole ground" of biological "relationship" is not sufficient to bar the union. But Archy does not tell Cassy about this in order to protect her delicate feelings.

Cassy, on the other hand, does invoke the incest taboo, and the reader is clearly supposed to share her indignation at the advances of her own father:

> In relating it, she blushed—she hesitated—she shuddered—her breathing became short and quick—she clung to me, as if some visible image of horror were present before her, and bringing her lips close to my ear, she exclaimed in a trembling and scarcely audible whisper—"Oh Archy!—and he my father!" (42)

In this passage, Hildreth adapts the language to the situation to create an effect of immediacy, an effect he intensifies when Cassy is, another time, harassed by Colonel Moore in the house of his concubine Ritty. A prolonged advance by the mean-spirited colonel comes to a climax:

> She told him that she was sick and wretched, and begged him to leave her. Instead of doing so, he threw his arms about her neck, and declared that her being sick was all imagination, for he had never seen her look half so handsome.
>
> She started up;—but he caught her in his arms, and dragged her towards the bed. Even at that terrible moment, her presence of mind did not forsake her. She exerted her strength, and succeeded in breaking away from his hateful embraces. Then summoning up all her energies, she looked him in the face, as well as her tears would allow her, and striving to command her voice, "Master,—Father!" she cried, "what is it you would have of your own daughter?"
>
> Colonel Moore staggered as if a bullet had struck him. A burning blush overspread his face; he would have spoken, but the words seemed to stick to his throat. This confusion was only for a moment. In an instant, he recovered his self-possession, and without taking any notice of her last appeal, he merely said, that if she were really sick, he did not wish to trouble her. With these words he unbolted the door, and walked out of the room. (129)

It would seem that Hildreth wanted to have it both ways. On the one hand he expected the heavily represented theme of incest (or, to be more specific, attempted father-daughter incest) to be so horribly shocking to his readers and characters that even the ogre about to perpetrate the deed recoils when Cassy *names* their relationship—which, entrapped in the language of slavery and lust, he has conveniently forgotten and cannot do, settling instead for a neutral excuse in making his exit. On the other hand, Archy rationalizes his own incest (or, more precisely, sibling incest) with a very weak and sophistic turn, and, even worse, he never lets his own wife and sister know the truth:

> But I knew that Cassy felt, rather than reasoned; and though born and bred a slave, she possessed great delicacy of feeling. Besides, she was a Methodist, and though as cheerful and gay hearted a girl as I ever knew, she was very devout in all the observances of her religion. I feared to put our mutual happiness in jeopardy; I was unwilling to harass Cassy, with what I esteemed unnecessary scruples. I had never told her the story of my parentage, and every day I grew less inclined to tell it. (39)

This is quite a different line of reasoning from indicting Colonel Moore! Archy Moore is apparently the hero, yet, quite like his father, the white patriarch and the novel's moral monster, Archy does not shrink back from incest and also cannot name his close affinity to Cassy. Unlike his father, however, Archy gets to consummate the incest with Cassy. He never reveals their sibling relationship to her or to their child Montgomery, and all kin terminology simply disappears in the course of

***Figure 38*** Colonel Moore, Archy, and Cassy in an illustration for Richard Hildreth, *The White Slave* (1852)

the narrative—so much so that when Archy holds up the healthy and vigorous Montgomery and his children as exemplary proof against the nonsensical myth of mixed-race sterility he never alludes to the fact that Montgomery was born of parents who are also half-siblings (405).

Marc Shell has argued that an ambivalence toward incest is inherent to Christianity: "The same (Christian) culture that inhibits the practice of incest also represents it as an ineradicable ideal."[15] Hildreth may be a case in point. Incest remains enough of a taboo (in the sense of the prohibition that makes the colonel blush, not in the sense of a sacred principle) for him to let Archy understand how upset Cassy might have been if he had told her the truth about their siblinghood, "harassing" her with "unnecessary scruples," as he puts it. Instead, he presents historical and political circumstances that cast the slaveholder's interracial father-daughter incest as the worst possible crime, but that make Archy's and Cassy's sibling incest understandable though it may not please delicate minds. Gerald Early wryly observes: "This may be, according to Hildreth, the trickle-down effect of Southern immorality; nonetheless it is still an unnecessarily prurient complication."[16] Early also calls attention to Colonel Moore's violent use of the whip[17] as a public extension of his touch and then focuses on the moment when Moore perversely demands that Cassy flog Archy. In this scene, accompanied by a plate in the 1852 edition (Fig. 38), Cassy throws down the whip that her father/master has given her

> as if the touch had stung her; and looking him full in the face, the tears, all the while, streaming from her eyes, she said in a tone firm, but full of entreaty, "Master, he is my husband!"

That word *husband*, seemed to kindle colonel Moore into a new fury, which totally destroyed his self-command. He struck Cassy to the ground, trampled on her with his feet, and snatching up the whip which she had thrown down, he laid it upon me with such violence, that the lash penetrated my flesh at every blow, and the blood ran trickling down my legs and stood in little puddles at my feet. (66)

Early summarizes the oddities of this "bizarre, Gothic picture":

Colonel Moore, the Southern planter, is assaulting two of his own children because they have married each other. But his outrage is not generated because the two children, as a result of the marriage, have committed incest but, [weirdly] enough, because the marriage thwarts his own incestuous desire for his daughter. Hildreth, in this scene, plays upon the fact that there is a thin line between the father who is disobeyed by a wilful daughter and the lover who is jilted.[18]

Early notes that Colonel Moore loses his self-control twice, triggered by the words "husband" and "father," and concludes that Hildreth here "conflates the taboo of miscegenation and the taboo of incest."[19]

One reviewer of Hildreth who was tempted to suspect that Lydia Maria Child had written *The Slave* reached the conclusion, however, that a *man* had to be its author. Perhaps alluding to this review, Child praised Hildreth with her comment that, if she were a *man*, she would have rather written *The Slave* than any other book published in the United States, and modern readers might take this as a comment on the fact that Child, as a *woman* writer, would of course be expressing herself in a different voice. Yet if this was the case, it did not affect her use of the clustering of incest and miscegenation. Having endorsed the incest plot of *Archy Moore*, she also adopted the motif of an attempted interracial father-daughter incest in *The Stars and Stripes: A Melo-Drama* (1858).[20] In Child's play, modeled on the Crafts' escape from slavery, Ellen tells William about being pursued by the master (in a way that is quite reminiscent of Hildreth):

When I am at the big house, sewing for missis, as sure as she goes out to ride, he comes into my room and asks me to sing, and tells me how pretty I am. And—and—I know by his ways that he don't mean any good. . . . Now massa says if I make him angry, he will sell *you* to the traders. (142–43)

William responds, "*clenching his fist*":

The old villain! and he knows all the while that you are his own daughter! (143)

In Child's novel *A Romance of the Republic* (1867) the intertwined and ingrown family story is balanced by the different races that go into the making of that family. When toward the end of the book Eulalia, the daughter of the older sister Rosa, and Alfred, the son of the younger sister Flora, seem to be moving closer toward each other, Flora reminds her husband that Eulalia's father "has a theory against the marriage of cousins." Her husband answers:

> So have I, . . . but nations and races have been pretty thoroughly mixed up in the ancestry of our children. What with African and French, Spanish, American, and German, I think the dangers of too close relationship are safely diminished. (432)

Flora and her husband agree that the "oddly mixed up" quality of the family members works as an antidote to the dangers of too close a marriage. Somewhat unusually, Child is here building up the family history of miscegenation as a healthy protection against the presumed consequences of incest, though the prescription is applied only to a first-cousin marriage.[21]

An anonymous review (perhaps written by John Greenleaf Whittier) of Mrs. C. W. [Mary Andrews] Denison's *Old Hepsy* (1858) appears to be making indirect comments on the incest plot that were somewhat less enthusiastic than Child's endorsement of Hildreth. Thus the review claims that the "main interest of the story turns on the fortunes and trials of a *white* slave girl, or one so nearly white and so related as to exhibit, in its worst features, the abominations of such a system." And after comparing the novel to Stowe's *Dred*, the reviewer states even more vaguely: "There are passages that address the feelings with a natural, simple pathos of human grief, though sometimes we meet also over-strained impulses of infuriated passion, that rather injure than aid the effect."[22]

Mary Denison's *Old Hepsy* is in many ways a remarkable exemplar of antislavery fiction. The three-generation family history, as is revealed near the end of the novel, has as its hidden center the past love affair of the white plantation daughter Amy Hollister (now Mrs. Kenneth) with the slave Fred Keene, who is also her half-brother, resulting in the hushed-up birth of a child, Lucina. Their affair started when Fred picked up Amy from a northern boarding school where she was known for her "recklessness and imprudence" and was "what is generally called a wild girl." Recognizing him as the playmate of their childhood, Amy exclaimed: "Why, Fred, is this you? You've grown so handsome I didn't know you!" (452). The narrator delicately reports the outline of the story in which Amy clearly plays the active role:

> The young man blushed, as he called to recollection their former intimacy. Miss Hollister had taught him to read and write while at her own childish studies. She had encouraged his precocious talents by helping him with her own books, and the facilities with which she was liberally endowed as the only daughter of a wealthy planter. He remembered her kindnesses gratefully, and could not but feel flattered with the abrupt and hearty compliment which she had just given him. She also admired his finely formed fig-

ure, his handsome features, and intellectual face and mien, and in school-girl fashion, without reflecting upon the consequences that might result by her encouragement of look and word—forgetting also the great distance in their comparative stations—entirely ignorant, besides, of his near relationship, fell in love with him, as the romantic phrase goes, and allowed herself to think too much of the elegant slave. (452–53)

The openly acknowledged interracial sexual attraction between white women and nonwhite men in *Old Hepsy* flies in the face of the commonly held belief that nineteenth-century literature did not represent a white woman loving a black man. That this may not have been true in works published in Latin, Russian, French, German, or Danish has already become apparent. But it is also a generalization that does not leave room for the English-language writer Denison (1826–1911) from Cambridge, Massachusetts, who published prolifically and sold more than a million copies of her works. Nina Baym suggested, and Simone Vauthier explicated in detail, how important *Old Hepsy* was in its fictionalization of slavery, Vauthier calling it a "milestone in the history of woman's liberation."[23]

The novel could also be read as yet another retelling of the familiar tale of the evil patriarch who sells his own children, for Amy Hollister's story marks the second generation of the plot which has one of its ultimate origins in the terrible ways of her father, Old Colonel Hollister. He "was widely and openly known as a man of immoral character and dissolute habits. He owned more slaves than any other holder in the country—possessed many who were very beautiful—and, report said, kept a secret harem" (453). No wonder that his sins are visited upon his children, for he not only made money "by the sale of his own children for the most revolting purposes" (453), but he also fathered Fred Keene with a French Mustee woman (the daughter of a rich white man who had married a slave); and the same Fred Keene becomes the father of the old Colonel's white daughter's child. More than that, Old Colonel Hollister also took possession of another beautiful Mustee woman (who had formed an attachment to Hollister's white son) and fathered with her the young man who calls himself Hollister and who, in the main part of *Old Hepsy*, is the suitor of young Amy Kenneth, Amy Hollister's white daughter from her marriage with the Philadelphia lawyer Everard Kenneth, and Old Colonel Hollister's granddaughter. And just like her mother, who loved a "white slave" (and like other young white women in the novel[24]), she finds herself attracted by one: her attention is focused upon Hollister (her mother's other half-brother), though she is also very ambivalent and contradictory. Hollister learns in the course of the novel that his own mother is a madwoman who has turned insane after Old Colonel Hollister's abuse,[25] so that the illegitimate young Hollister brings his own quest for vengeance as well as for redemption toward young Amy as a member of the legitimate family, driving him to a joint

Gothic *Liebestod* scenario, for he sees only in their deaths the fulfillment of his wish that they "meet somewhere as equals" (437). The house of Old Colonel Hollister lives on in the mixed-race descendants Fred Keene and Lucina (who had only one grandfather, the Colonel), and they go North at the end to fight against slavery.

Denison's intricate family saga with its recurrence of miscegenation and incest is stylized as representative. It is a national allegory of sorts, as the northerner Everard Kenneth marries the southern plantation daughter Amy Hollister and becomes a fiend when he finds out about his wife's scandalous past, taking revenge upon her mixed-race daughter Lucina. The central action of the novel is furthermore contextualized by the suggestion that there are other cases like it. Thus Keene answers Hollister's question whether he has known "a slave to aspire to the love of his mistress" not only by alluding to his own affair with Amy Hollister, but also by relating another case in which, "although the woman loved him, and she was a planter's daughter, he was murdered; and murdered by her father" (246). The interconnection of incest and miscegenation in the family story of slavery and freedom and of legitimacy and illegitimacy served Denison as a vehicle for criticizing the language of paternalism (that was used to justify slavery) by taking it literally in her novel.

As Vauthier argues, the plantation setting in which the unrecognized reality of miscegenation is represented can "create what it claims to be—a family order," though this creation is based on the disowning of the nonwhite family members who are thus "reduced to making up a loose shadow family." The noninclusion of the illegitimate family members in the official kinship system also leads with a certain logic to incest. *Old Hepsy* thus "dramatizes Southern ignorance of interracial incest while playing on the fascinated horror of incest in the American reader." While the novel does not "frown at miscegenation, *per se*," it shows how the failure to recognize it makes incest a more likely occurrence.[26]

In the antislavery novel by Hezekiah Lord Hosmer, *Adela, the Octoroon* (1860)—a novel that already caught Sterling Brown's attention—miscegenation is explicitly linked with interracial father-daughter incest that strengthens the novel's antipatriarchal pitch as it casts the Mississippi planter and politician George Tidbald as even more villainous than Simon Legree. Tidbald's character appears in sharp profile when he makes plans to sell the beautiful Mulatto woman Eunice to a terrible slave dealer who intends to take her to New Orleans, turning a deaf ear to her mother Agnes's plea that Tidbald reconsider. When her maternal feelings fail to touch him she goes a step further and asks her "good master":

> Can you for a few paltry dollars sell this child to prostitution? Are there no reasons—none, that will plead against it? Have you no upbraidings of conscience in the contemplation of an act so unnatural?

And when Tidbald asks her what she means, Agnes reminds him (and explains to the readers) that Eunice is, after all, Tidbald's own daughter:

That Eunice, whom you now propose to sell, is your own flesh and blood, master—your child—more willingly yours, as you know, and as God knows, than mine. And has not that natural tie which is supposed always to exist between parent and child, no voice to beseech the safety of Eunice?[27]

"Natural ties" mean little to Tidbald, and the cold-hearted father-master sells Eunice anyway. Prostitution was a common metaphor for slavery, especially after Wendell Phillips had spoken against the South as "one great brothel."[28] But Hosmer goes even further in representing Tidbald as a most thoroughly and luridly perverted version of the heartless Inkle. As Sterling Brown puts it, he is a "distinguished champion of southern rights, but seducer of his own slave daughter."[29] In fact, the planter later fathers a child with Crissy, another slave woman who is also his own daughter. When Crissy, sick of consumption, is nearing death she asks the character named Aunt Christmas (three-quarters of a century before Faulkner) to call for Tidbald one last time. At first Crissy only whispers how glad she is that he has come; but emboldened by the approach of death and encouraged by Aunt Christmas—who tells her, in tears, "why dont'ee tell him dat you knows it all?"—Crissy does use the word "fader" in addressing Tidbald, whose face had "fairly blenched under the gaze of Christmas." Christmas spells out the unnamable web of relationships, when she answers Tidbald's question what Crissy knows: "Dat you are her fader, and de fader of dis chile, and dat's what's killed her, mass'r." Tidbald gives the dying Crissy an "erring father"'s blessing, and

with her eyes fondly fixed upon him, the father and seducer, she drew her last breath without a struggle.

Tidbald gazed long and silently upon the victim of his unhallowed passions. He felt humbled—crushed. The fountain in his bosom was, for once, unsealed, and he wept long and bitterly over the dead body of the unfortunate girl.

Instructing Christmas to take good care of the little boy, though she believes he will soon follow the mother, Tidbald leaves the cabin full of (momentary) remorse and does not seek a "refuge" for the "wrong he committed" "among the incidental and permitted evils of slavery" (317–19). Hosmer's characters' tears were surely meant to be accompanied by those of his readers, and Kinney's assessment that "the shock value of miscegenation has been augmented by connecting it with incest" is rather an understated description of Hosmer's operatic temper.[30]

### From Scientism and Law to Progressive and Reactionary Fantasies

At an earlier point we looked at the Civil War letters from Louis Agassiz to the former abolitionist Dr. Samuel Gridley Howe as evidence for the scientist's support of the Mulatto sterility hypothesis. In fact, in the middle of his foundational argument for racism, triggered by the debate about the emancipation of slaves, Agassiz also made a revealing connection between miscegenation and incest. He wrote on 9 August 1863:

> Viewed from a high moral point of view the production of halfbreeds is as much a sin against nature, as incest in a civilized community is a sin against purity of character. And I have no doubt in my mind that the sense of abhorrence against slavery which has led to the agitation now culminating in our civil war, has been chiefly and unconsciously fostered by the recognition of our own type in the offspring of southern gentlemen, moving among us as negroes, which they are not. Far from presenting to me a natural solution of our difficulties, the idea of amalgamation is most repugnant to my feelings, I hold it to be a perversion of every natural sentiment.... Whenever it is practiced amalgamation among different races produces shades of population the social position of which never can be regular and settled. ... It is unnatural, as shown by their very constitution, their sickly physique and their impaired fecundity.

Agassiz was hardly alone among scholars in describing racial mixing (the word "miscegenation" was still to be coined a few months later) in terms of incest, though his interpretation of the motives for Civil War and the abolition of slavery may have been less than widely shared. Anticipating Agassiz, the supremacist Henry Hughes, who modeled his writing on Auguste Comte's positivism, had also attempted in his *Treatise on Sociology: Theoretical and Practical* (1852) to derive the following "laws" from social observation:

> Races must not be wronged. Hygienic progress is a right. It is a right, because a duty. But hygienic progress forbids ethnical regress. Morality therefore, which commands general progress, prohibits this special regress. The preservation and progress of a race, is a moral duty of the races. Degeneration is evil. It is a sin. That sin is extreme.
> Hybridism is heinous. Impurity of races is against the law of nature. Mulattoes are monsters. The law of nature is the law of God. The same law which forbids consanguineous amalgamation forbids ethnical amalgamation. Both are incestuous. Amalgamation is incest. [31]

In his comment on what he terms a "series of virtual nonsequiturs," David Lawrence Rodgers views Hughes as representative of "the hysteria that enveloped the discourse of slavery immediately before the Civil War" that would lead him to an "illogical and eventually ironic position." Rodgers generalizes:

> By conflating miscegenation—"ethnical amalgamation"—with incest—"consanguinous amalgamation"—Hughes transforms the hybrid or mulatto from someone who is considered "impure" because he combines qualities that are too different to mix successfully, according to the sanctions of nature and God, to someone whose "impurity" and transgressions lie in the blending of traits that are, by contrast, too much *alike*.[32]

In the context of Hughes's essay the claim that miscegenation was as unnatural as incest was made in order to support his view that co-sovereignty and political amalgamation between black and white (which inevitably leads to sexual amalgamation) must be prevented by a "warrantee" system of "ethnical segregation" in which one race would be sovereign, the other "sub-sovereign" to it—as wives are to their husbands.

On 24 March 1864, as Sidney Kaplan has shown, the somewhat hypocritical editor of the New York *World* attacked the pamphlet *Miscegenation* (which he had secretly coauthored) with the argument that if marriage between a white man and a black woman begetting his children was now recommended as "miscegenation," then the same "might be asked in relation to incest, or any other abomination which the *progressists* have not yet dubbed with a euphemistic name."[33] The field of law did not stand apart. Charles W. Chesnutt reported that the Mississippi law of 1880 prohibiting miscegenation called interracial marriages "incestuous and void."[34] Many other laws combined the prohibition of marriage by consanguinity and miscegenation. After science, social science, journalism, and law, let us go back to fiction.

Cirilo Villaverde's Cuban novel *Cecilia Valdés* (Fig. 39) appeared in New York in 1882.[35] Villaverde (1812–94), an advocate of the annexation of Cuba by the United States in 1848 but an ardent opponent of slavery, had to escape a death sentence in Cuba, found himself a political refugee on the Florida coast, and lived most of the second half of his

***Figure 39*** Frontispiece of *Cecilia Valdés* (1935)

life in New York City. (Had he published in English instead of Spanish, he would undoubtedly be known as an American immigrant author.) Whereas the earlier versions of *Cecilia Valdés* contain allusions to Cecilia's family resemblance to the Gamboas and Cecilia's mother's unexplained admonition to her daughter not to interact with the Gamboas, the 1882 novel brings together the titular heroine, the "little bronze virgin" (*la Virgencita de bronce*—an allusion to a nineteenth-century poem entitled "La Mulata" that praised the "bronze Venus" that is formed of different races as bronze is made out of different metals[36]), with Leonardo Gamboa, the spoiled young heir of a Spanish-born upstart, the slave trader and planter Cándido Gambao; Cándido is now also definitely identified as Cecilia's father, though this is not known either to her or to Leonardo. As was the case in Eugène Scribe's metaphor of paternalism that substituted for the recognition of paternity in *Le Code noir*, Cándido Gamboa also plays only the general paternal role of benefactor but not the specific one of father to his daughter Cecilia—which is what brings down the male line of his house in incest and fratricide. The reader finds out soon that Cecilia is Cándido's daughter and is thus aware of the truth of social gossip, of the paradoxes in Cecilia's interaction with the Gamboas, and of the double irony of the fact that the white woman destined to become Leonardo's bride mixes up Cecilia and one of Leonardo's legitimate sisters. Wishing to make Cecilia stop going out (unknowingly) with her own brother Leonardo, her grandmother Josefa asks her, "What would you do if your protector, your constant friend, the only help you had in the world, your father, so to speak, for he really is all that to us poor helpless women, advised you and forbade you to do a certain thing? What would you do? Would you disobey him?" (107–8).[37] In order to prevent the incestuous act of his children, Cándido has Cecilia even committed to a hospital from which Leonardo, however, frees her and sets her up in an apartment. Though Cecilia gives birth to a "very beautiful girl," Leonardo soon tires of his concubine and sister, finding her less attractive after childbirth and below him in social rank. Instigated by his mother, who has meanwhile also learned that her husband Cándido was the father of Cecilia, Leonardo leaves Cecilia in order to marry the planter's daughter Isabel Ilincheta. Cecilia incites her Mulatto friend José Dolores Pimienta to make sure that the wedding will not take place. Pimienta does not hear Cecilia's instructions to harm only the bride, and he stabs Leonardo to death on his wedding day. While the ending leaves open whether or not Pimienta gets caught, Cecilia Valdés is sentenced as an accomplice and committed for a year to the Paula hospital in which her lunatic mother Rosaria is also still confined.

Villaverde's family novel includes many fascinating themes. The *parvenu*'s wish for pseudo-aristocratically ennobled white descendants—Gamboa has a family tree drawn up in Spain in order to show that there is "not one drop of Jewish or Moorish blood in his ancestry" (82)—is off-set by the violent end of his only son.[38] The denial of a black family con-nection, from which four generations of mixed-race women have emerged and suffered, a denial which they have also internalized, is pre-cisely what sustains and destroys Gamboa's dream of nobility.[39] And the Creole plantation mistress, Doña Rosa Gamboa, is not an embodiment of marital loyalty and maternal strength but of a psychologically troubled attachment to her own son as a vehicle of getting back at her husband. Furthermore, Rosa displays a spiteful vindictiveness toward the black wet nurse María de Regla, who also gave milk to Cecilia Valdés. María fills the vacant role of a "capital M" Mother as if she were part of the revolu-tionary allegory of Fraternity; thus she tells the Gamboas' daughter Adela how she nursed both her and her own black daughter Dolores: "I placed you on my right and Dolores was on my left. But I fell asleep" (313). When Doña Rosa finds her like this, María is no longer permitted to nurse her own daughter Dolores; later María—whom Rosa also loathes as another of her husband's past affairs (64)—is sent away to another plantation. William Luis has argued that María de Regla's name "suggests both the Virgen María and the Cuban black Virgen de Regla" and offered the allegorical reading of her not only as the "symbolic mother" of Adela, Cecilia, and Dolores, but also as "the mother of the white, mulatto and black races that her daughters represent."[40] This uni-versal black mother is up against the white racial aristocratic pretense that rests on the denial of black membership in the family—the very denial that results in incest and fall of the house of Gamboa.

Another Latin American antislavery novel, *O Mulato* ("Mulatto," 1881) (Fig. 40) by the Brazilian Aluísio Azevedo (1857–1913), juxtaposed the young protagonist Dr. Raimundo José da Silva's expectation that it was "some close kinship" between himself and his admired Ana Rosa that made her father, the merchant Manoel Pescada, opposed to a possible marriage, and Manoel's revelation that it was the fact that Raimundo is "a colored man" and the "son of a slave woman." The Coimbra-educated and handsome Raimundo is also Manoel's nephew, hence Ana Rosa's cousin, but it is not Manoel's fear of incest but of miscegenation that motivates his prohibition of the match.[41] Manoel attempts to distinguish between his feelings—he views himself as Raimundo's friend and admir-er—and the social code by which he feels obliged to act:

> You surely see, my friend, that it's not for my own sake I denied you Ana Rosa's hand but for all these other reasons. My wife's family was always quite scrupulous in that regard, and all of Maranhão is like them. I agree it's a gross stupidity, I agree it's a silly bias. You can't imagine how deep the prejudice against mulattoes is around here! They'd never forgive me for such a marriage; besides, in order to carry it out, I'd have to break the promise I made to my mother-in-law not to give her granddaughter to anyone other than a proper white man, either Portuguese or the direct

**Figure 40** Illustration for Aluisio
Azevedo, *O Mulato* (1989)

descendant of Portuguese. You're a very worthy young man and quite deserving of esteem, but you were freed at your baptism, and everyone here is aware of it. (204)

Raimundo is shattered and embittered by finding out about his social identity as a "Mulatto" in this way. His inner voice tells him that "nature did not create captives" and that it is unjustifiable that he should be "punished and damned by the brothers of those very men who introduced slavery into Brazil" (205). Ana Rosa, too, feels only an additional attraction to Raimundo, "that of prohibition" (212), and they consummate their love just when Raimundo is expected to leave the province of Maranhão. When Ana Rosa, pregnant with Raimundo's child, attempts to escape with her "bastard cousin," however, Manoel and an evil priest conspire to have the Mulatto killed by the man whom Manoel wanted as a son-in-law and who does get Ana Rosa at the end.

In James Weldon Johnson's novel of passing, *The Autobiography of an Ex-Colored Man* (1912), interracial sibling incest is described as a possibility by the narrator. This takes place in a scene in the Paris opera that absorbs its theatrical quality from this setting; yet it is the audience that becomes the stage for the ex-colored man's interracial family drama. As the mixed-race protagonist suddenly recognizes his white father who happens to be sitting in the same row in the opera attending *Faust*; he also realizes that "the beautiful, tender girl" next to him, by whose presence he had been so deeply attracted before, must be his own (white) half-sister:

> At the end of act I I noticed that my neighbor on the left was a young girl. I cannot describe her either as to feature, or colour of her hair, or of her eyes; she was so young, so fair, so ethereal, that I felt to stare at her would be a violation; yet I was distinctly conscious of her beauty. During the intermission she spoke English in a low voice to a gentleman and a lady who sat in the seats to her left, addressing them as father and mother. . . . I occasionally stole a glance at her, and each time I did so my heart leaped into my throat. Once I glanced beyond to the gentleman who sat next to her. My glance immediately turned into a stare. Yes, there he was, unmistakably, my father! looking hardly a day older than when I had seen him some ten years before. What a strange coincidence! What should I say to him? What would he say to me? Before I had recovered from my first surprise, there came another shock in the realization that the beautiful, tender girl at my side was my sister. Then all the springs of affection in my heart, stopped since my mother's death, burst out in fresh and terrible torrents, and I could have fallen at her feet and worshipped her. . . . I knew that I could not speak, but I would have given a part of my life to touch her hand with mine and call her "sister." I sat through the opera until I could stand it no longer. I felt that I was suffocating. Valentine's love seemed like mockery, and I felt an almost uncontrollable impulse to rise up and scream to the audience: "Here, here in your very midst, is a tragedy, a real tragedy!" This impulse grew so strong that I became afraid of myself, and in the darkness of one of the scenes I stumbled out of the theatre. . . I finally took a car and went from café to café, and for one of the few times in my life drank myself into a stupor. (134–35)

This "little tragedy" is a self-contained short episode in the novel—not the full-fledged thematization that the possibility of sibling incest in a younger generation resulting from the secrecy of miscegenation of its elders inspired in other texts. Still, it suggests how the protagonist's desire for his white sister is linked with his wish to be recognized by his father. Incest thus remains a threat, a fortunately unrealized possibility, in the life of the nameless ex-colored man. As in other parts of the novel, here Johnson may also have isolated (though not excised from his work) some dramatic aspects of the tradition of interracial literature in order to make more room for other previously unrepresented aspects of black-white life. And the psychology of the protagonist continues along the familiar lines of his contradictory wish to follow the *impulse* to reveal himself publicly (that had been articulated at the opening of the novel with its nod toward the "Imp of the Perverse") and to guard his secret in the fear that its revelation could be dangerous to him.

In Pauline Hopkins's serialized novel "Of One Blood" (1902–1903) the mixed-race woman Dianthe Lusk first marries Reuel Briggs, whose secret biracial origin only his friend Aubrey Livingston knows. The reader presumes Aubrey to be white, and he himself believes the same.

Aubrey wants to possess Dianthe, and so he sends Reuel on an archeological journey to Africa, and then takes away Reuel's wife Dianthe after telling her that her husband Reuel has died. According to later revelations, however, all three protagonists turn out to be siblings. In Egypt the dying Jim Titus (who is also Aubrey's foster brother) unveils to Reuel the secret that Reuel and Dianthe are brother and sister, and that Aubrey is their white half-brother. Titus also warns Reuel of Aubrey's sinister schemings, adding the oracular command: "Return home as soon as possible and rescue your wife—your wife, and yet not your wife—for a man may not marry his sister" (585). Reuel is thunderstruck, "his mind . . . far away in America looking with brooding eyes into the past and gazing hopelessly into the future." Yet this reaction, if it was prompted by the revelation of his and Dianthe's incest, is channeled into a critique of the miscegenation in the family past, as the chapter ends with the narrative comment: "And Reuel cursed with a mighty curse the bond that bound him to the white race of his native land" (586).

Later on, even the "white" half-sibling Aubrey is identified as really of mixed race, since Aunt Hannah—who is also the grandmother of all three younger protagonists—according to her own testimony switched the (stillborn) baby of Livingston's white wife with that of his mistress (and Hannah's daughter) Mira, so that Aubrey is in reality Mira's youngest child. Thus Reuel, Dianthe, and Aubrey are not merely, as it seems at Jim Titus's disclosures, children of the same father, but also of the same mother. Aubrey is not the other children's white half-sibling, but their mixed-race full brother, and because of their Egyptian royal origins all of Mira's children carry a lotus-lily mark (728). This discovery toward the end of the novel forces readers to recognize that in the course of the installments of the serialized novel, Dianthe Lusk has first married one and then lived with another brother (whom she, too, had taken for white, only to learn now that the relationship was not a case of miscegenation but of incest). However, the three siblings' parents, Mira and Dr. Livingston, are also both children of old master Livingston—hence the parents' alliance constitutes both incest and miscegenation. This intensely incestuous situation gives the biblically universalist title "Of One Blood" (Acts 17:26) and its official interpretation as human descent from one common heavenly father (581, 807) another, secular meaning (584, 729).[42] When Aunt Hannah proclaims at the end of her revelation that all of Mira's children are "of one blood," Dianthe reacts to this recognition with the Oedipus-like shock at her double incest:

> Dianthe staggered as though buffeted in the face. Blindly, as if in some hideous trance, reeling and stumbling, she fell. Cold and white as marble, she lay in the old woman's arms, who thought her dead. "Better so," she cried, and then laughed aloud, then kissed the poor, drawn face. But she was not dead.
>
> Time passed. The girl could not speak. The sacrilege of what had been done was too horrible. Such havoc is wrought by evil deeds. The first

downward step of an individual or a nation, who can tell where it will end, through what dark and doleful shades of hell the soul must pass in travail?

The urgency of this question of the October 1903 issue of the *Colored American Magazine* in which the novel was serialized, seems to have receded a month later. For when Dianthe is dying of poison, her death-bed reunion with Reuel hardly has the valence of a sibling encounter:

> With one wild scream of joy she rushed forward, and Reuel Briggs clasped her in his arms.
>
> For a few brief moments, the wretched girl lived an age in heaven. The presence of that one beloved—this drop of joy sweetened all the bitter draught and made for her an eternity of compensation. With fond wild tenderness she gazed upon him, gazed in his anxious eyes until her own looked in his very soul, and stamped there all the story of her guilt and remorse. Then winding her cold arms around his neck, she laid her weary head upon his shoulder and silently as the night passed through the portals of the land of souls. (805)

At the end Aubrey's body is found floating in the Charles River, and the narrator suggests that he killed himself following the command of the Egyptian Ai. Reuel, now ruler in a hidden city in Egypt, still finds that "shadows of great sins darken his life," but the narrator does not return to the incest theme and ends instead with questions about the future of the United States.

This was also a topic of great interest to Thomas Dixon, Jr., best known as the writer on whose novel *The Clansman* (1905) D. W. Griffith's film *The Birth of a Nation* (1915) was based. For Dixon, "the future American" had to be "either an Anglo Saxon or a Mulatto"—and unlike Hopkins, he dreaded the latter possibility, advocating instead the large-scale colonization of African Americans in Liberia. He also wrote a novel in which he teases the reader with the possibility of interracial incest. In *The Sins of the Father* (1912), the Octoroon woman Cleo seduces the helpless Georgian Ku Klux Klan-oriented politician Major Dan Norton and has a daughter from the affair. Many years later, as part of an intricate revenge scheme engineered by Cleo, Norton's son Tom, born from his legitimate marital relation to a white woman who died as a result of Norton's affair with Cleo, falls in love with Helen (Cleo's and Norton's daughter, the reader is led to believe) and secretly marries her—as the father tries to stop them.[43] Tellingly, Norton—whose political work is connected with disfranchisement, segregation, and the forced settlement of black Americans in Africa—finds it "unthinkable" at first to acknowledge Helen to his son. He sets his hope on making a partial revelation only to Helen: "If he could tell the girl the truth and make her see that a marriage with Tom was utterly out of the question because her blood was stained with that of a negro, it might be possible to save himself the humiliation of the full confession of their relationship and of his bitter shame" (372). Norton thus wants to invoke miscegenation as a marriage impediment in order to preserve the more personal secret that his son's marriage to Helen would also be incestuous because they are siblings. Norton's revelation throws the pure Helen into a deep identity crisis that Dixon fleshes out with the racist exploitation of familiar motifs: she is horrified, looks at her fingernails, imagines having a cannibal as her ancestor and giving birth to a black baby (382–83). Heartbroken, she agrees to give up Tom. Tom, however, is not ready to break with Helen and simply cannot believe that she should be the daughter of an Octoroon. The father formally pronounces the interdict in Helen's presence: "I forbid you to ever see or speak to this girl again!" (395), and he amplifies: "in the name of the law—by all that's pure and holy, by the memory of the mother who bore you and the angels who guard the sanctity of every home, I forbid you!" (396). Yet the twenty-two-year-old Tom does not cave in to father or law; rebelliously he reminds his father sharply that he is of age and threatens violently to disregard the father's "prohibition" and leave the house together with Helen. Now father and son withdraw and discuss the matter alone, giving Dixon the opportunity to put into Dan Norton's mouth theories of white superiority and the need for segregation. Yet Tom points out his father's inconsistency in having let his son be nursed by Cleo, a black woman: "I grew at her breast" (404). Tom also questions his father's readiness to host Helen in his house and demands proof of her background. When he tells the father for the first time that they are already married, Major Norton finally reveals, reluctantly and too late, that Tom's alliance with Helen is also incestuous because they are siblings, victims of the sin of their father. Norton lets his son read a letter with the mother's dying words, "Rear our boy free from the curse!" (443), and explains what it was that his wife had to forgive him for. This moment of truth is devastating for Tom:

> "God in Heaven, let me keep my reason for just a moment!—So—you—are—Helen's—"
>
> The bowed head sank lower.
>
> "Father!"
>
> Tom reeled, and fell into a chair with a groan: "Lord have mercy on my lost soul!"
>
> Norton solemnly lifted his eyes: "God's full vengeance has fallen at last! You have married your own—"
>
> The boy sprang to his feet covering his face: "Don't! Don't! Helen doesn't know?"
>
> "No."
>
> "She mustn't!" he shivered, looking wildly at his father. "But why, why—oh, dear God, why didn't you kill me before I knew!" (446–47)

Neither father nor son can pronounce the word "sister," and in voiceless shame Tom agrees to let his father shoot him before Norton commits suicide himself. This is exactly what happens, only Tom survives and learns from Cleo's confession (what the black servant Andy has assumed all along) that Helen was not Cleo's daughter at all, but an adopted white girl used by Cleo to get her revenge on the Nortons, making Helen what Ratna Roy calls a "Mulatto-Proved-White" and her marriage to Tom a case of neither incest nor miscegenation. Tom now grimly dedicates himself to the extremist political causes of his father. The novel ends with the emphatic sentence: "But the thing which marks the Norton home with peculiar distinction is that since the night of his father's death, Tom has never allowed a negro to cross the threshold or enter its gates" (462). As James Kinney concludes, Dixon was extreme in his dramatization of the "conflict between white attraction to the mulatto and white revulsion at miscegenation," a conflict that is here violently resolved in favor of revulsion, and with the help of an incest scare and a father's suicide—all as a consequence of a secret miscegenation.[44]

In an imaginative reading of D. W. Griffith's *The Birth of a Nation* Michael Rogin calls attention to a scene in which he reads the miscegenation plot as if it were a veil thrown over an incest story.

[The radical congressional leader Austin] Stoneman is shown with his mulatto mistress [Lydia] and mulatto protégé [Silas Lynch, who will later become a sexual threat], as if they constituted a family. . . . [Stoneman's daughter] Elsie replaces Lydia in the next scene. Lynch stares at her and, after he leaves, she caresses her father. The sequence establishes a circuit of desire initiated by Lydia that runs from Lynch to Elsie to Stoneman. The camera also sets up the formula Stoneman to Lydia as Lynch wishes to be to Elsie. Drop out the two middle (shadow) terms, and Stoneman's wish is for his daughter. The blacks have been invented as a defense against what their invention allows to return, father/daughter incest.[45]

This is an interesting approach as it makes the scene literally visualize the intersecting desires for incest and miscegenation, expressed as an equation. There is one axis from Stoneman (modeled after Thaddeus Stevens) to Lydia and from Silas to Elsie, and another axis from Stoneman to his daughter. In fact, the latter line becomes clear only once the axis of miscegenation has been removed. "Drop out the two middle (shadow) terms, and Stoneman's wish is for his daughter," Rogin writes. In the work at hand, however, the axis of miscegenation is *not* taken away, so that the incest pattern never becomes active, not even as more fully articulated desire.

There is another work, however, to which Rogin's approach seems eminently applicable, as it presents less obliquely a constellation like the one he was seeking to find in Griffith's film. It was written by Hans Grimm (1875–1959) and was published in the years between the completion of Thomas Dixon's novel *The Clansman* and the release of the movie that was based on it. The novella "Wie Grete aufhörte ein Kind zu sein" ("How Grete Stopped Being a Child") was part of Grimm's popular collection entitled *Südafrikanische Novellen* (1913).[46] Set in 1903 in the German "protectorate" of Southwest Africa (now Namibia), it reaches back into the past before and after the Boer War. Its protagonist is the fourteen-year-old Grete, the daughter of Karl von Troyna—a man who has dropped the "von" since aristocracy does not mean much in the colonies. Her mother, the Scotswoman Mary, died after giving birth to a second child, also dead, leaving Grete alone with her father on the plantation Stylplaats before she goes off to a boarding school run by English Catholic nuns.

Troyna brings home with him, from one of his efforts at suppressing illegal arms trading across the border, the Hundasi Ellen, a pale brown mixed-race woman of a "wild beauty" (85), and her brother Alfred, "who strangely resembled his sister" (92). Troyna killed their father, a white weapons-smuggler, and he is warned by others of the duplicity of the Hundasi. Still, he gets more and more intimate with Ellen, up to the point of "almost forgetting" that he is a white man. And he is blind to Ellen and Alfred's scheming with revolutionary forces that threaten German colonial rule. When Grete comes back, now thirteen years old, a tomboy who loves to wear a Scottish kilt, the eighteen-year-old Alfred soon becomes more her friend and her social equal than her servant. Grete loves riding horses—male style—and enjoys being watched by her father (who had also written letters to her at school as if she were his twin sister, letters that made Grete blissful). She tells Ellen that she must have made a mistake in setting three plates for dinner, for servants do not eat with masters. When Ellen leaves, no dinner conversation gets going between the "two lonely white people." Grete also has to accept that she cannot have her old room back, the one next to her father's bedroom.

A year goes by in which Troyna is often gone. In the perception of others as well as of the narrator, Alfred now seems too close to Grete, and even she begins to look at him with a "soft haze in her eyes, blurring her awareness for the first time that he belonged to a different race from hers; and she also did not notice that his eyes became small and piercing in responding to her gaze and that his hands dared to grab her hesitatingly but greedily while playing, for these hands did not bother her any more" (107). Grete's fifteenth birthday is approaching, for which her father, who looks at her as if she were a "royal daughter of Europe" (105), promises to be present. But before he gets back, there are reports of a revolution, an *orlog*, many servants quit (not Ellen and Alfred, who are, of course, involved in the plot), and a shady character comes and asks Grete deviously for the key to their armory. Grete, who has the (Creole) mentality of a person born in the colonies, despises the drunk and dirty rebels, and when she sees twelve of them going by she is disgusted and thinks: "Such creatures should dare to raise their hands against whites? Such low beings should kill a man—well, like my father perhaps!" (113). She only wishes she were a boy.

Having come back from an upsetting visit to the Christian mission, she senses more and more of a threat in the air. Alfred first warns her against riding out alone and then contrasts the missionaries' language of universal brotherhood with the social distinctions the white settlers make: "When a white man takes a colored woman. . . . even one who is the daughter of a white man, the other whites avoid him and ride around his house. . . . And a white girl will never become the wife of a colored man, Ellen says" (119). Grete is surprised at how cool and calm she remains; fatigued after cleaning the house some more in preparation for the father's arrival, she withdraws to her mother's room. In the dark she prepares a pistol and two rifles in her father's bedroom. There is a sandstorm, rats are running on the canvas ceiling, and Grete keeps falling asleep and waking up.

In a heavy dream she sees herself as if she were part of another modified allegory of *fraternité*: her breasts are fountains of cool water and Alfred comes running to drink first at one and then at the other nipple. Fondling his hair, she says: "I thought you were a stranger and I liked you, but now, now I know that I am mother to you and you are my child!" (125). Briefly awaking, she wonders how a man could be the child of a child, and a Hundasi. Sinking back into her dream she turns around and sees her father—who was behind her—tightly embracing Ellen, and against Grete's protestations, Ellen starts talking. Grete wakes up again, and Ellen is still talking—really talking to Alfred in the kitchen. (The whole ending would be even more worrisome if Grete were dreaming what she hears.) "The child in the chamber learned her father's story the way no grown-up son must ever know it " (127), the narrator comments.

She also learns of the plot that the Hundasi siblings are planning to execute, including tying up Grete. Her first impulse is to run away on her fast horse, then she realizes that she alone can "save" her "poor Dad" (129). Looking like the ghost of Mary von Troyna, Grete opens the door to the kitchen and shoots Ellen with her father's Browning. The narrator comments that it was "as if one killed a wild cat in a narrow stable" (130). Soon Alfred comes, drunk, and approaches Grete, whose face showed "neither hatred nor love, nor even hardness, but infinite indifference" (130). She warns him not to come closer and tells him that she has heard everything and killed Ellen—but Alfred keeps moving toward her, grabbing her shirt. Thinking that she has never seen such an ugly face, she shoots him three times. Then she washes herself. An old loyal servant helps her carry the bodies outside, and they board up the plantation and take guard. Almost at daybreak the rebels come, but when they see Ellen and Alfred's bodies they believe the farm to be occupied by whites and they move on. In the morning three white riders appear, one of them Troyna. Grete tells her father what has happened. Later she changes, taking off her kilt—a man's piece of clothing—and putting on one of her mother's dresses. "Even the father was startled and barely recognized his daughter in the beautiful, pale, budding young woman" (133). He moans "Mary!" Grete keeps her firmness of character, but collapses and cries at Alfred's burial. The narrative ends with the report that the natives believed that the ghost of Mary von Troyna had come back and so they avoided the plantation, for "the revenge of the white woman lasts forever" (134).

This is a heavy colonialist tale, the racism of which makes obvious why Grimm was praised as an author by National Socialists, as Joachim Warmbold has shown. Grimm became best known as author of the fascist bestseller *Volk ohne Raum* (People without Space) that popularized the slogan *Blut und Boden* ("blood and soil"), which came closest to an official articulation of Nazi aesthetic. In the novella "How Grete Stopped Being a Child" the racist activism functions on the basis of a story line in which the white, "pure," and explicitly aristocratic father-daughter axis is crossed by the mixed, "impure" Hundasi sibling axis that is symbolically connected not only with revolution and deceptiveness, but also with the sexuality that remains hidden in the realm of purity. In the sense of Rogin's argument, there is a line of erotic tension that goes from Troyna to Ellen and from Alfred to Grete and back. But different from Griffith, Grimm actually *does* remove the axis of miscegenation, and does so with sharply drawn violence—leaving father and daughter (the "two lonely white people") reunited in a way that has an incestuous valence (though there is no representation of any incestuous act). Grete's dream reveals the erotic lure coming from Alfred and the imagery of social equality that her interest in a physical contact with the young man of mixed race brought about. This is what she sees looking forward, whereas the primal scene involving her father and Ellen is behind her. Both Ellen and Alfred are *obstacles* on the white dream road that connects her with her father. At the end, Grete has become a woman; she has saved her father and herself. Killing the look-alike siblings makes possible a white happy ending in which racial purity has been violently reestablished. Karl von Troyna is together with someone "of his own race" (also most literally in the sense of race as "generation"). The colonial order is rescued together with the fantasy of purity that may have at its core both the need for the violent purging of impurity and the regression to the incestuously toned realm of origins alone.

A maternal dress as a generational link to the daughter also appeared in Paul Green's short play *White Dresses: A Sorrow of First Love* (1920). At the end of the drama Granny McLean, an old Negro woman, reveals the secret in a mysterious little box that she has been hiding. Her granddaughter Mary McLean, who has been courted by the white man, and landlord's son, Hugh Morgan, and is refusing to marry the Negro Jim Matthews, learns that the white dress that Hugh sent her as a Christmas present is a repetition of the past. Granny says:

I's gwine tell you the secret of this little box. Your mammy said tell you if the time ever come, and it's come. And when I tells you, you'll see why you got to marry Jim. She went through sin and trouble that sent her to her death, and I's gwine save you. [GRANNY *opens the box and pulls out a wrinkled white dress, of a generation ago, yellowed with age.* JIM *looks on with open mouth.*] Listen here, poor baby, i's gwine tell you now. Nineteen years ago come this Christmas they was a white man given your mammy this here dress, and that white man is close kin to you, and he don't live far off neither. Gimme that other dress there on the bed.[47]

Granny puts both dresses into the fire and thus symbolically averts the interracial incest between Mary and Morgan, as she says to her granddaughter, "I knows your feelings, child, but you's got to smother 'em in, you's got to smother 'em in."

When Walter White solicited Charles W. Chesnutt's views of Ohio Senator Newton Baker, Chesnutt responded with a letter on 10 February 1932:

In a conversation not very long ago with Mr. Baker, as to a probable solution to the race question, I suggested the amalgamation of the races. . . . Mr. Baker said that was absurd, unthinkable, and he said it in a tone of voice and with a flash of the eye, which seemed to class it as akin to incest or sexual perversion.[48]

The suggestion of violence that Chesnutt captures here in a politician will concern us again. It is certainly of interest that Adolf Hitler, too, defined Aryan-Jewish alliances with the same term that is commonly used to describe incest. Wilhelm Reich in *The Mass Psychology of Fascism* (1933) developed the argument that race theorists

who are as old as imperialism itself, want to achieve racial purity in peoples whose interbreeding, as a result of the expansion of world economy, is so far advanced that racial purity can have a meaning only to a numbskull. . . . The race theory can be refuted only by exposing its irrational functions, of which there are essentially two: that of giving expression to certain *unconscious* and *emotional* currents prevalent in the nationalistically disposed man and of concealing certain psychic tendencies. . . . We are especially interested in the fact that Hitler speaks of "incest" when an Aryan interbreeds with a non-Aryan, whereas it is usually sexual intercourse among those who are related by blood that is designated as incest.

The word Hitler used, *Blutschande*, a translation of *sanguinis contumelia*, was easily applied to race because the rhetoric of race drew so heavily on "blood": hence *Blutschande* ("incest") and *Rassenschande* ("miscegenation") could be confused in Hitler's vocabulary, and in the language of National Socialism generally. Reich connected Hitler's unconscious confusion to the fascist splitting of "purity" and sexuality, resulting in the advocacy of a "male state organized on a homosexual basis."[49]

In 1933, Gilberto Freyre called attention to the intertwining of incest and miscegenation in Brazilian cultural history. Freyre cites a song by Eloi Pontes in the tradition of black-white love poetry, but with the difference that the black slave lover who addresses her "small white magician" also points out that "you call your poor black girl sister." From this instance Freyre proceeds to the general observation that relations between young masters in the mansions and the Mulatto girls in the shanties were often incestuous since it was very easily possible that the white son and the Mulatto daughter of the same father would love each other.[50]

Let me end this lineup with a widely noted literary example. In Ralph Ellison's *Invisible Man* (1952), the black sharecropper Jim Trueblood describes the interracial dream he had while committing incest with his daughter Mattie Lou. He sees himself in a big white bedroom where he has no business being; he cannot find the door again and he smells woman everywhere:

> Then I looks over in a corner and sees one of them tall grandfather clocks and I hears it strikin' and the glass door is openin' and a white lady is steppin' out of it. She got on a nightgown of soft white silky stuff and nothin' else, and she looks straight at me. . . . I tries to talk to her, and I tries to git away. But she's holdin' me and I'm scared to touch her 'cause she's white. Then I gits so scared that I throws her on the bed and tries to break her holt. That woman just seemed to sink out of sight, that there bed was so soft.[51]

When he wakes up intending to tell his wife about his "crazy dream" he realizes that he has been raping his own daughter:

> And there I am, lookin' straight in Mattie Lou's face and she's beatin' me and scratchin' and tremblin' and shakin' and cryin' all at the same time like she's havin' a fit. She's cryin', "Daddy, Daddy, oh Daddy," just like that. (59)

Although he wants to disentangle himself to keep from sinning he also wants to continue:

> Then I'm pullin' away and shushin' her to be quiet so's not to wake her Ma, when she grabs holt to me and holds tight. She didn't want me to go then—and to tell the honest-to-God truth I found out that I didn't want to go neither. . . . the more wringlin' and twistin' we done tryin' to git away, the more we wanted to stay. (60)

Valerie Smith stressed the parallels between Trueblood's transgressions of social taboos in his dream and in real life, where the sexual taboo he violates is "incest instead of miscegenation."[52] The scene ends when Trueblood's wife Kate wakes up and starts screaming, "Git up offa my chile!" and throwing things at him. The irony of the Trueblood narrative is compounded by the fact that he tells his tale to the white philan-thropist Mr. Norton, whose devotion to the cause of racial uplift may be linked to an unacknowledged incestuous desire for his own late daughter about whom he speaks (as Valerie Smith also noted) more like a bereaved lover than a father.[53]

In his conflation of incest and miscegenation in the Trueblood episode, Ellison also suggests the dimension of unequal power relation that is inherent in father-daughter incest, and the violence that often accompanies it, by representing it as a rape, a point made by Ann DuCille.[54] Though some readers have elevated this father-daughter incest in the name of purity or pseudo-aristocratic lineage, the rape vic-tim is hardly a mere "vessel" for a pure line of descent. As W. Arens has also noted, there *is* a difference between "royal incest" which is "best understood in most instances as a symbolic performance," and "incest in our society," which "entails actual sexual behavior and, sometimes, reproduction."[55]

### "Too Close" and "Too Far"? From Hildreth to Hitler

In many literary texts, the themes of interracial unions and of incestuous relationships are intertwined, ranging from projections and fantasies of the two taboos to representations of the transgressive acts, and from passing allusions to plot-constitutive centrality. Many more examples could undoubtedly be found for this surprising cluster.[56] But how do we make sense of it? The juxtaposition, combination, and conflation of incest and miscegenation is a topic that has, of course, been noticed and commented on by very good readers of single texts or authors, but it is not a thematic cluster that has often been analyzed more broadly and comparatively—despite its pervasiveness. Still, some individual readings have yielded interesting findings that may have broader applicability.

From the perception of a symmetrical opposition between incest (a form of exaggerated endogamy, or forming a union with someone "too close") and miscegenation (a socially censured version of exogamy, or uniting with someone "too far") proceeds an approach that attempts to understand the cluster in the terms of anthropology.[57] Among critics who have pursued the issue in this way is Richard King, who in examin-ing southern literature finds that "the historically specific taboo underly-ing the Southern family romance is the taboo against miscegenation, the inverse of the incest taboo." When both taboos get violated together, a patriarchally defined culture seems to "collapse back into nature." Because of their analogous threats to the order of the South the "two taboos come to be identified."[58] Paradoxically King thus finds in interra-cial relations the key to "Southern family romance," yet his definition limits its traumatic effects to whites. He explicitly states that for black southerners "the Southern family romance was hardly problematic. It could be and was rejected out of hand. Their great theme was the attempt (literally) to escape the white South which had historically oppressed their people" (8). To be sure, the migration narrative has been an important feature of the African American imagination. Yet one only has to think of Ellison's Trueblood episode in order to see that the conflation of incest and miscegenation could matter to blacks as it did to whites. Even Richard Wright's titles (*Native Son* or *Black Boy*) suggest the significance of family romancing for him, although King may have been thinking of Wright in his generalization about black literature. Furthermore, the cluster has not been limited to southern writers of the United States. King's approach is nonetheless interesting. He invokes Claude Lévi-Strauss and attempts to make structural anthropology useful to the investigation of a theme. His findings suggest a mythic or archetypal structure that makes itself manifest in texts, though his key witness Lévi-Strauss had also warned readers that exogamy and endogamy "could appear symmetrical only from a formal point of view."[59] Can this be *the* explanation for the examples we have looked at? Some literary texts may indeed adhere to the mythic mode, and others may not. For it is startling that proslavery thinkers, racial conservatives, and fascists on the one hand as well as racial liberals and antislavery writers on the other have felt impelled to blur the boundaries between incest and miscegenation, as the examples have ranged from Hildreth to Hitler. And incest has also often been invoked in discussions and in the actual legislation of interracial marriage bans. Could all these authors, all these texts, be caught in the throes of a powerful discourse that has an anthropological origin, a symmetrical deep structure, and speaks through all of them? Perhaps it is futile to look for a single motive underlying the cluster. In fact, a single motive may be no more behind a cluster than it is behind a theme, and different, contradictory interests may coalesce in a cluster as they may in a theme. What I would therefore like to explore further are the heterogeneous ideological motives that may have inspired different conflations of incest and miscegenation.

There would seem to be at least three different ideological explanations for the perhaps surprising frequency with which connections between incest and miscegenation have been made in politically heterogeneous contexts: a "pragmatic" state-interventionist, a "realistic" abolitionist-liberal, and a "paranoid" proslavery-racialist-fascist trajectory. And what may be the oddest finding is that while the two latter, opposing camps start from an emphatic acceptance of the incest *taboo*, both also come close at moments to articulating an overt or covert acceptance of the *deed* of incest.

The confusions may start with the terms themselves. It was not only Hitler who mixed them up, but the English term "intermarriage" has also been used to denote "incestuous marriage," a practice which was widespread enough for Robert K. Merton to observe and attempt to explain it:

> Incestous marriages are often termed *inter*marriage. This would appear to be an instance of the rhetorical fallacy of catachresis, in which one term is wrongly put for another. Its source is possibly the following. In lay language, the term intermarriage commonly denotes those marriages which *deviate* from *endogamous* norms. This attribute of *non-conformity and group disapproval* has come to be the identifying characteristic of intermarriage. Hence, incestuous marriage—surely at the polar extreme from inter-(group) marriage—which is also commonly *condemned*, comes mistakenly to be assimilated to the category of intermarriage, which is interpreted as tabooed marriage.[60]

In order to avoid confusion, Merton advises scholars to drop this usage "from the sociological if not the folk lexicon."

The identification of incest and miscegenation may be misleading for social analysis, but it was a common strategy for the field of law, and the easiest instances to understand—exactly in Merton's terms—may be the legal ones. Many laws since Deuteronomy have regulated various degrees of incest proscriptions, and this fact permitted a simple and legitimate-sounding insertion of antimiscegenation legislation in or near the paragraphs governing incest. Occasionally this might lead to a spillover from one language to the other—such as the heading to the 1911 Nebraska statute of "Consanguinity or Miscegenation" (that served here as an epigraph), or the 1880 Mississippi code reported by Charles Chesnutt according to which interracial marriages are paradoxically deemed "incestuous and void." Perhaps the origin for the usage reported and deplored by Merton that incestuous marriage is called "intermarriage" lies in the perceived parallelism that comes from the condemnation that both incest and miscegenation may summon as "deviations." Yet the intervention of the state's right into the most private of contracts that would seem to lie in the domain of individual liberty, interfering in interracial marital choice, also found a useful precedent and a convenient legitimation in the analogy with the incest prohibition. An article in the constitution of Mississippi, repealed in 1987, also decreed that "the marriage of a white person with a Negro or mulatto, or person who shall have one-eighth or more of Negro blood, shall be unlawful and void," and the statute provided the same punishment as for "marriage within the prohibited degrees of consanguinity or affinity."[61] This comes close to the "catachresis" of making incest and miscegenation the same in the eyes of the law, and the wording was hardly unique, as the 1928 *Revised Statutes of State of Arizona* also stipulated in remarkable parallelism—and with more prohibitions on either side:

The marriage of persons of Caucasian blood, or their descendants, with Negroes, Mongolians or Indians, and their descendants, shall be null and void. The marriage between parents and children, including grandparents and grandchildren of every degree, between brothers and sisters, of the one-half as well as of the whole blood, and between uncles and nieces, aunts and nephews, and between first cousins are incestuous and void.[62]

Eva Saks rightly speaks of the "typical association of miscegenation and incest" and finds that "state criminal codes . . . usually listed miscegenation next to incest as two crimes of 'blood.'"[63] From the point of view of law, the symmetry is not in the act but in the prohibitions of it, as Merton argued. It was convenient for legislators to use the incest provisions as an instrument: thus they did enact intermarriage bans that would not just take effect after a certain date but that would *eo ipso* make existing marriages null and void, and the laws could not be circumvented by marriages contracted in other states.

The association of miscegenation bans with those laws prohibiting incest gave social rules that were instituted by local white majority votes a "natural" and universal ring. The powerful ally of the incest taboo helped to enact and enforce these laws and to keep them on the books against political opposition. This was apparent in some debates about proposed changes to the existing antimiscegenation legislation. For example, when Hannah Arendt argued in 1958 that the best way to end segregation in the United States was not by integrating schools, restaurants, and hotels, but by repealing the laws prohibiting miscegenation (which were an interference in the private affairs of citizens), she had a hard time getting her views published and generated a venomous debate in the course of which she was called a champion of "equality in the bedroom." The liberal journal that finally consented to publish her article in 1959 also included an editorial disclaimer and two rebuttals, one of which took Arendt to task for her views on the ground that "the logic of her position would require her to argue . . . that incest [was also a] purely private [matter]."[64] This critic of Hannah Arendt followed the pragmatic logic that the state had the right to legislate certain restrictions, and the case of incest was the model for that of miscegenation. The example also suggests, however, that the parallel between incest and miscegenation is hardly neutral and has the ability to emotionalize debates, as the discussion about the wisdom of legal provisions that constitute "politically enforced endogamy" (Margaret Mead) is put under the spell of the horror of incest—according to Emile Durkheim, due to the human fear of shedding the blood of "blood" relatives, whether by murder, defloration, or childbirth.[65] At this moment the "pragmatic" fusion of incest and miscegenation does rub shoulders with the "mythic" view.

The liberal-antislavery hypothesis starts with the "realistic" argument according to which unrecognized miscegenation may lead to (unknowingly committed) incest. Simone Vauthier, whose perceptive analysis of Denison's *Old Hepsy* (1858) has already been reviewed, argues more generally that in interracial literature the white father often fails

> to transmit with his surname what Jacques Lacan calls the-Name-of-the-Father, i.e. the universal Law that prohibits incest. . . . Instead he forbids the White Woman *en masse* thus setting a (fairly) clear but extensive and artificial boundary while discounting the normal universal barrier. (90)[66]

This increases the likelihood of incest between his illegitimate and legitimate offspring. The slave may combine "aspiration to his master's daughter, i.e. his half-sister, and yearning for social justice" (90–91). According to Vauthier,

> No social group offered a more suitable setting for the staging of "realistic" incestuous dramas, since, if bastardy is a common enough phenomenon, in no modern society has the *silence* of the Father been to the same extent a factor in the development and structuration of the social organism. (91)

A society that excludes a part of its population from naming generates chaos, Vauthier argues. The establishment of a racial demarcation line in the name of "blood" thus simultaneously destabilizes the kinship system. By placing an emphasis solely on the barrier against miscegenation, incest is made a real possibility. Nina Baym has also commented perceptively on *Old Hepsy*: "Given the dispersal of white blood through the slave population, Denison shows, any act of miscegenation is likely to be an act of incest."[67]

This line of argument opens the possibility of reading the representation of miscegenation as incest as a "realistic" strategy, made likely by a social system in which paternity is an "explosive secret," as Doris Sommer put it in her discussion of Cirilo Villaverde's novel *Cecilia Valdés*:

> The family might not be quite so threatened by extramarital affairs, on which the men look with indulgence, were it not for the secrecy imposed by the conflicting code of bourgeois marriage contracts. It is secrecy that puts Leonardo at risk of incest. He will not be guilty with Adela because their relationship is clear; but Cecilia's parentage is an explosive secret, a debilitating blindspot where the rule of masters' privilege (double-)crosses modern family ties. . . .
>
> The fine divide between exogamy and incest goes unattended, largely because of a certain reluctance to attend to the information slaves command.[68]

In a similar vein, Lorna Williams takes Don Cándido's "withholding his name from" Cecilia "and thus symbolically expelling her from his family" as the necessary premise for the tragic action of *Cecilia Valdés*:

Cecilia's ignorance of her own origin causes the Oedipus theme . . . to become explicit in Villaverde's novel. In a manner reminiscent of Sophocles' hero, Villaverde's protagonist fails to recognize a relative, and therefore she violates sacred familial bonds by engaging in sexual relations with a blood relative and bringing about his violent death. Moreover, Cecilia meets her tragic end precisely because of the steps she takes to avoid the fate that was determined for her.[69]

The resulting catastrophe is also precisely what her father and her grand-mother wanted to prevent; but all is futile, given the secrecy surrounding the identity of her father that drives Cecilia Valdés toward sibling incest with the logic of Sophoclean tragedy.[70]

If "mixed race" is not descended from "white" but only from "black" ancestors, this constitutes a weakening or severing of interracial kinship ties and may lead to a higher possibility of incest. In other words, for liberal writers the critical representation of miscegenation as incest provides a perfect occasion to bring home the denial of kinship that is inherent in a biracial organization of the world and present also in the *mestizaje* setting of Villaverde's Cuba.[71]

Perhaps this danger is all the more present since interracial alliances are often perceived to be the opposite of, or the antidote to, closely endogamous ones, so that in literary texts in which a white lover chooses a mixed race beloved over a pure white rival there is often a sense that a feeling of incestuousness attaches itself to endogamy. John Dollard, too, gives as one of the reasons why white men seek interracial sexual contacts: "Boredom with the legitimate object or unconscious fear of the incestuously toned white woman may redirect genuine sexual desire to Negro women."[72] Whereas miscegenation might look like a safe way of avoiding incest, it often turns out to *be* incest in liberal antislavery writing. The very fact that an interracial relationship can still also be described as incestuous suggests that there is a deeper collision between the system of maternal descent that sustains hereditary slavery and the patriarchal belief that kinship is established through the father. And for the antislavery and antisegregationist writers this collision provided a crack in the system of racial domination into which they could drive a wedge.

Incest is horrifying, and the fact that miscegenation takes place outside of legal sanctions makes this terrible event more likely. The worst of evils, however, lies in the white, slaveholding patriarch who knowingly wants to, or actually does, commit incest with his own nonwhite daughter, and this specter has been drawn vividly in the examples we examined from *Jonathan Corncob* to *Adela, the Octoroon*. "Race" gives a threadbare excuse for failing to acknowledge interracial paternal descent; thus Colonel Moore makes Cassy available as an object of incest by not calling her "daughter," yet he blushes when she reminds him of the relationship—which indicates that Moore believes in paternal descent more than in the kinship logic of slavery, upon which he yet acts. The tyrannical patriarch who does not stop short of incest signals the chaotic perversion of the whole system he embodies, putting his unacknowledged children into a problematic position as victims and possible rebels and setting into motion a chain of events that may end in the downfall of the house when the illegitimate and the legitimate families encounter each other. There seems nothing magical or mythical in the connection between miscegenation and incest for antislavery and progressive authors. Or is there?

For there was another countervailing element in the liberal-antislavery literature as well that does bring back incest as a justifiable action, perhaps even as the "ineradicable ideal" of which Marc Shell speaks. This is obliquely the case in the many first-cousin intermarriages in liberal texts and the specific justification of an alliance of close relatives if they are of different or mixed race background in Child. It is also present in *Old Hepsy*, for example in Fred Keene's alliance with his half-sister Amy Hollister, or in Hollister's combined Romeo-and-Juliet and Othello-and-Desdemona love for his niece Amy Kenneth. Yet while Denison's incestuous affairs are rather fatal, incest is fully presented as a viable and justifiable possibility in Hildreth, who comes close to endorsing, if not actually extolling, Archy's knowingly committed brother-sister incest with Cassy. Like Denison's Lucina, like Cecilia Valdés's and Leonardo Gamboa's daughter, and like all three Livingston children in Hopkins's "Of One Blood," Hildreth's Montgomery also has only one grandfather, an evil white patriarch who has initiated a cycle of sins. But Archy, Cassy, and Montgomery Moore may look forward to a happy family future. Perhaps as a legacy of romanticism or as a consequence of a revolutionary sentiment, sibling incest is positively charged—a feeling which runs counter to the horror of incest, most especially father-daughter incest, that is also invoked in the liberal narratives. The maxim that incest is terrible if committed by tyrants and fathers is offset by the principle that antipatriarchal incest, especially sibling incest of the tyrant's own children, can be defended and may be justified or even extolled.

Marc Shell made the point that "universalist liberal ideology which would enlarge the particular siblinghood to include all humankind, compels all people either to marry within the same siblinghood or not to marry. The liberal maxim 'All men are brothers' requires a lifting of the incest taboo in much the same way as the racialist rule 'Marry only your brother.'"[73] To the universalist the ideal of *fraternité* applies to the "human race" and makes all human beings siblings. This position suggests also that there is really no such thing as miscegenation, only a form of universal incest that is weakened, however, by being so universal. Sibling incest can thus be represented as the victory of revolutionary *fraternité* over the tyrannical father.

The proslavery-fascist position is a sinister illustration of the principle that the same theme—or the same cluster of themes—can serve completely different ends. Whereas the legislator moved miscegenation into the vicinity of incest for "pragmatic" reasons, and the liberal often did so in order to show "realistically" the consequences of the illicit sexual relations that came along with slavery, the proslavery radicals had another agenda entirely.

In racist scenarios, miscegenation takes a central part in the imagination. As has already been suggested, the idea of a taboo of "miscegenation" may be needed in order to constitute a sense of "race." One possible definition of "race" is that it emerges when people of group X, as proof of their "purity," forbid their daughters and sisters to marry people from group Y. As Robert Merton put it:

> [i]t appears that notable increases in group consciousness and solidarity involve a tightening of endogamous prescriptions. The Nazi taboo on interracial and interreligious marriage is a case in point.[74]

More generally, "intercaste marriage may be viewed as a catalyst which activates and intensifies group consciousness."[75] Condemning it with the power of the incest taboo would thus seem to build group consciousness in a powerfully emotional way. Henry Hughes's remarkable formulation stated it explicitly. Viewed as incest, interracial sexual alliances may be considered a perversion of nature, the violation of a primary cultural taboo—resulting in degenerate offspring, sterility, feebleness, effeminacy.

From such premises "incest" suggested itself to the racist radicals as the perfect metaphor for expressing their horror. They summoned the specter of incest in order to make miscegenation seem "unnatural" and "repulsive." Hence miscegenation *was* incest for Henry Hughes and Adolf Hitler, not because they were thinking of the arrangement of legal proscriptions or because they were confused by the structural symmetry of what was "too close" and "too far"—let alone because they were worried that unacknowledged miscegenation might lead to incest—but because miscegenation is the true horror to any radical ethnocentrist, and incest is the metaphor through which this horror can be (partly) expressed, for there is a general, widely shared sense of *that* taboo. The paradoxical equation, "amalgamation is incest," was set up not in the hope of discovering a human law, but in order to make hybridism seem as "heinous" as incest. So far their approach still had much in common with that of the lawmakers generally, and was probably somewhat indebted, too, to the antipatriarchal side of abolitionist writing.

But perhaps in retaliation against the abolitionist and liberal portrayals of slaveholders as incestuous perverts and operators of family harems, the texts by reactionary radicals, unlike those of the laws, dwelled on the gory details of the same themes of incest and miscegenation in depth. In fact, some of the most paranoid writing at the turn of the century may be characterized as a belated rebuttal of abolitionist melodrama—with the means of the same genre. (One only has to remember *The Leopard's Spots*, Thomas Dixon's continuation of *Uncle Tom's Cabin*.) Alain Locke noticed not only that the antislavery camp's focus on the Quadroon girl and her tragic mystery had chilled southern romance to the marrow but also how the melodramatic stereotypes that were at times employed by the antislavery authors backfired in lending more verisimilitude to the southern version of the Negro after the Civil War and the obsession with the "problem of miscegenation."[76] But the venom that the antislavery writers had aimed at their caricatures of incestuous, slaveholding, tyrannical patriarchs was redirected by the proslavery radicals against *any* form of miscegenation as treason to the race. The race radicals liked to imagine miscegenation—especially sexual relations between white women and nonwhite men, and, to a lesser extent, the legalization of any interracial relationship—as the unthinkable horror of horrors. "UNTHINKABLE" was the word echoing from Durham's *Call of the South* and Dixon's *Sins of the Father* in Baker's reply to Charles Chesnutt for the ultimate taboo. And an anonymous Ku Klux Klan poet put it similarly, with the white sister in focus, in (not) speaking about interracial rape.

> The unspeakable crimes, the shame, the anguish—that befel [*sic*]
> > The only sister of our race.
> > A thing too horrible to tell.
> When families sacrificing their land for a song would steal away to some distant state to spend the remainder of their days in obscurity, with the dark story locked in their own breasts.[77]

The incestuous undertone is audible, as is the high emotion at stake in the family's sacrifice to keep secret the tale that cannot be told. "No death is quick enough, no grave is deep and silent enough for such monstrosities," Hans Grimm wrote, pondering the possibility that a white woman would have intercourse with a black man, thus "betraying the honor of the whole race." Perhaps it is suggestive of the power of the taboo—that makes speaking about it as much of a violation as acting against it—that this passage was deleted from later editions of Grimm's works.[78]

Even not speaking about it was not a safeguard against thinking about it, and this ambivalence is the reason why I have used the term "paranoid" to describe this particular disposition toward miscegenation and incest. Declaring miscegenation "unthinkable" does not mean that one cannot see it on top of the Capitol of the United States (see this chapter's epigraph) or in a children's book such as *The Rabbits' Wedding*. Finding it as horrifying as incest does not mean that one cannot be haunted by it continuously and drawn to it helplessly—as in Grete's dream of Alfred and her father, or in Klan leader Major Norton's inability to resist the feline Cleo's seduction. It is not farfetched to see in such scenes the attempts at resolving ambivalence, at feeling attracted and overwhelmed, hence like a victim who also begins to feel entitled to end the "repulsive" spectacle violently. What incest and miscegenation have in common for the paranoid trajectory is that they are reminders of repressed, forbidden motives.

Yet on another level, this is quite contradictory to an impulse toward the exaggeration of endogamy that always tends to push the right-wing radical close to a pro-incest position that can be heard in the background. If opposition to miscegenation was advanced with the force of the incest taboo, this could also cover up a secret or not-so-secret incest wish. After all, the notion of racial "purity" has an incestuous valence and is based on a program for the future ("no more miscegenation" as a racist slogan) rather than on the past and on accurate history or even genealogy. And it is a future in which, in the presumed absence of interracial exogamy, only intraracial endogamy is imagined to prevail as an ideal. To the racist, only his own "whole race" seems kin (precisely by virtue of not being related to at least one other "less pure" or "lower" race that any concept of racial purity requires); hence any woman of a man's own race may be called "sister," as did the KKK poet, and yet she may also be married to him. This position implies that since miscegenation must be avoided at all cost, incest (racially enlarged) becomes an ideal almost by necessity.

Max Weber in his reflections on "'race' membership" draws a development from the "undiminished patriarchal powers" which once enabled the father to "grant equal rights to his children from slaves." As these powers were curtailed with the "monopolistic closure"

> of political, status or other groups and with the monopolization of marriage opportunities, these tendencies restricted the *connubium* of the offspring from a permanent sexual union within the given political, religious, economic and status group. This also produced a high incidence of inbreeding. The "endogamy" of a group is probably everywhere a secondary product of such tendencies, if we define it not merely as the fact that a permanent sexual union occurs primarily on the basis of joint membership in some association, but as a process of social action in which only endogamous children are accepted as full members. . . . "Pure" anthropological types are often a secondary consequence of such closure.[79]

For Weber, the whole notion of "purity"—so central for racial thinking—is connected to restricted *connubium*, producing a "high incidence of inbreeding." Looked at in another way, incest—real or symbolic—may be a *prerequisite* for anything like "racial purity" or "race" to emerge.[80] Hence racial fantasies may on the first level express horror at miscegenation as if it were incest, but on a second level reveal a deep and necessary yearning for incest.

This yearning may find further fuel in the pseudo-aristocratic prerogative of race thinking: kings and dukes did it, so why don't we pool our precious blood? Fear of miscegenation serves as the exhortation to violence and retribution, as a most powerful bonding device for the group. "Fathers, save us from nigger husbands," was the young women's slogan at a mid-nineteenth century Democratic Party parade in Indiana,[81] and "Would you like your sister to marry one?" was a perhaps more polite but equally emotional question.[82] Such statements seem to be addressed to the fathers and brothers, but they might as well be asking, "Would you like your sister to *marry*?" and expressing these cries differently as "Fathers, save us from *husbands*." The presence of the words "nigger" or "one"—really the "shadow" terms in Vauthier's and Rogin's sense—reveals how deeply the fear of interracial alliances may be anchored not in the prohibition of, but in the wish for, incest. Lévi-Strauss writes: "The prohibition of incest is less a rule prohibiting marriage with the mother, sister or daughter, than a rule obliging the mother, sister or daughter to be given to others"—and this is what may be so difficult.[83] Viewed this way, race and the strong articulation of miscegenation may put a veil over—*and simultaneously permit*—incest fantasies. Mr. Norton's response to the Trueblood episode stems from his incest-toned relationship to his daughter, and, conversely, Trueblood's dream literally presents the "white" woman as the "screen" behind which there is really his own "black" daughter and, perhaps, his fantasy of a pure royal "Trueblood" line. Grimm (read in the manner of Rogin's interpretation of Griffith) presents a mixed-race pair that stands between a white father and a white daughter, and this "royal" white daughter becomes the avenging white woman who kills not only her father's mistress (and thus "saves" him, tearing him violently from a possible intermarriage by shooting the untrustworthy object of his nonincestuous desire) but also the young man to whom Grete has felt quite attracted. The racial purity that is established with the "two lonely white people" at the end rests on avoiding and violently recanting miscegenation, but not necessarily on saying no to incest. The master daughter (*Herrentochter*) has become a woman by sacrificing her father's and her own love interests and can now put on her mother's clothes (the very gesture that was defined as incestuous repetition in Paul Green). She obviously comes to resemble her mother, but in using his guns on Ellen and Alfred she is also very much like her father, who previously killed Ellen's and Alfred's white father. The fantasy of racial purity may thus rely on first denouncing miscegenation as incest and then obliquely accepting at least the symbolic possibility of (or wish for) incest once the threat of miscegenation has been violently eliminated. Thus the restricted universalism of racism makes all whites brothers and sisters while denouncing interracial alliance with blacks in the sharpest terms, and (symbolic) incest would be the only logical consequence. Thus, as Marc Shell argues, the racialist rule is to "marry only your brother."

There may be no single "discourse of incest and miscegenation" that keeps speakers in thrall, and legislators, liberals, and fascists may have tried to accomplish rather different things when they put miscegenation into heterogeneous relationships with incest. But how about Faulkner? Can his use of miscegenation and incest in *Absalom, Absalom!* be linked with these trajectories?[84]

## William Faulkner's *Absalom, Absalom!*

Offering the "mythic" approach, J. Hillis Miller suggests an analogy between Faulkner's theme and the language of anthropology. He invokes Edmund Leach (rather than Lévi-Strauss), arrives at the conclusion that the symmetrical avoidance of "too much sameness, in one direction, or too much difference, in the other" is at stake, and regards Faulkner's novel as a thematization (he calls it dramatization) of the familiar maxim:

> Too much sameness is incest, the same mating with the same. Incest is a pollution of the bloodline through an excess of purification. The narcissistic perversity of incestuous desire is brilliantly dramatized in Henry's love for his sister Judith. . . .
>
> Too much difference is miscegenation, the same mating with the wholly different, introducing so much difference into the community that the bloodline is hopelessly contaminated, the community in danger of ceasing to be itself. . . . If too much sameness is bad, too much difference is even worse. As *Absalom, Absalom!* indicates, the violence of the taboo against miscegenation is even more compelling, more absolute and finely drawn, than the taboo against incest. An eighth, a sixteenth, a thirty-secondth [*sic*], even the tiniest soupçon of black blood makes someone a forbidden partner for lawful marriage intended to produce children who can be assimilated into the white community.[85]

Miller sees in that "double prohibition" "an impossible contradictory taboo" under which southern history has had to struggle, and he views Faulkner's novel not only as the thematic illustration of this maxim but also as a formalization of it:

> The analogy between the failure of a design in life and the failure of narration may be expressed as a ratio: incest is to performative narration as miscegenation is to constative narration. If Thomas Sutpen and his children are caught between incest and miscegenation, between his desire to be entirely self-sufficient and the taboo against that, on the one hand, and the need to appropriate the unlike and the taboo against that, on the other, narration is undone by the impossibility of being either purely performative or purely constative. (165)

Miller explains:

> If in one direction a storyteller tries to stick to the facts (the constative effort), and ends by inventing them (the performative element), in the other

direction if a storyteller tries to invent a purely fictional story, wholly cut off from life, if he tries to absorb life into a perfect narrative design, he always ends by referring to life and to history, since the words he must use are after all referential. (167)

In Miller's terms, *Absalom, Absalom!* might be seen as steering a difficult middle course between performative/incest and constative/miscegenation *in narration*, yet that also means that the grounds have been shifted from a discussion of incest and miscegenation as a puzzling thematic cluster to a weighing of referentiality in literature.

Indeed, in *Absalom, Absalom!* the form of the narration, refracted by Miss Rosa Coldfield, by Quentin's father, Mr. Compson, by Quentin and Shreve, as well as by a narrator and an appended genealogy and chronology, is of supreme importance—even to the extent that it alone can legitimate, or make questionable, the statement that Charles Bon's marriage to Judith Sutpen would have constituted miscegenation and incest. From Aby Warburg to Erwin Panofsky, thematically oriented art historians who work iconographically and iconologically have noted that mediocre works may be best suited to thematic analysis because they follow the code that operates in them most closely. It is possible to argue that the same might apply to literary texts: it is thus difficult to insert snippets from *Absalom, Absalom!* as "evidence" in motif-and-theme line-ups because Faulkner's work alters the thematic trajectories and is thus not easily reduceable to exemplify it. Looked at in another way this might also mean that a thematic approach could provide comparative evidence for aesthetic evaluation: the more a text resists becoming an "instance" of preexisting themes or motifs, the more it is likely to be aesthetically innovative—also in establishing new codes upon which later writers may (or may not) draw. Thematic studies may thus be especially suited to include works of great aesthetic merit and innovative power as well as examples from "bad" and conventional literature and from other, nonliterary discourses, and establish a relationship between them. The maxim is probably true that some great literary works transcend thematic approaches, but then again thematic comparisons provide one backdrop against which great works that depart from the "conventional mold" can be understood more fully, the nature of their innovation be measured more specifically. Because of its formal accomplishment and its revision of inherited themes, *Absalom, Absalom!* may have worked like a funnel in gathering up past themes and their clusters from interracial family sagas with miscegenation and fratricide and making them available in a new narrative form to later writers ranging from Toni Morrison to Latin American magical realists and to postmodern authors in the Western world.

In *Absalom, Absalom!* the presence or absence of the thematic cluster of incest and miscegenation is entirely dependent upon the novel's form.[86]

How are the themes built up in the novel so as to shed light on why Henry Sutpen killed Charles Bon in order to prevent Bon's marriage to Henry's sister Judith? The reader of the novel *Absalom, Absalom!* knows that the superimposition of incest and miscegenation is by no means the only attempt at making sense of the killing. Mr. Compson suggests that the central problem was that Bon had a previous child from a mistress. For Mr. Compson then, the motive for the Greek-themed family tragedy that he constructs lies neither in incest nor in miscegenation, but in Bon's intended bigamy that Sutpen must have wanted to block after finding out about Bon's mistress and son. When Mr. Compson calls Bon "at least an intending bigamist even if not an out and out blackguard, and on whose dead body four years later Judith was to find the photograph of the other woman and the child" (110) it is noteworthy that he does not at first speak of Bon's mistress as "Octoroon."[87] A few pages later, however, the marriage to "that other" woman is contrasted against "this one with a white woman" (116).

Thus "race" comes in, but it concerns at first—and for a considerable length of time—not Bon's "being" but his "doing." It is Bon's forever nameless "octoroon mistress" that evokes the speculation:

> She must have seen him in fact with exactly the same eyes that Henry saw him with. And it would be hard to say to which of them he appeared the more splendid—to the one with hope, even though unconscious, of making the image hers through possession; to the other with the knowledge, even though subconscious to the desire, of the insurmountable barrier which the similarity of gender hopelessly intervened. (117)

The gaze presumed to be interracial resembles the forbidden same-sex glance ("Because Henry loved Bon" (110)), and it intensifies the ingrown quality of the Sutpen children in Mr. Compson's speculation:

> No engagement, no courtship even: he and Judith saw one another three times in two years, for a total period of twelve days, counting the time which Ellen consumed; they parted without even saying goodbye. And yet, four years later, Henry had to kill Bon to keep them from marrying. So it must have been Henry who seduced Judith, not Bon. (122)

The conventional country boy Henry has fallen in love with the sophisticated amoral city-slicker Charles and wants his sister Judith to marry the man *he* loves. Then what was it that made Henry kill Charles? Mr. Compson's (certainly "performative") narrative constantly revises itself and suggests that the fact of "that other woman," the "existence of the eighth part negro mistress and the sixteenth part negro son" (123), was insufficient:

> It would not be the mistress or even the child, not even the negro mistress and even less the child because of that fact, since Henry and Judith had grown up with a negro half sister of their own; not the mistress to Henry,

certainly not the nigger mistress to a youth with Henry's background, a young man grown up and living in a milieu where the other sex is separated into three sharp divisions, separated (two of them) by a chasm which could be crossed but one time and in but one direction—ladies, women, females—the virgins whom gentlemen someday married, the courtesans to whom they went while on sabbaticals to the cities, the slave girls and women upon whom that first caste rested and to whom in certain cases it doubtless owed the very fact of its virginity. (135)

Judith and Henry's familiarity with Clytie would not make Bon's conduct so exceptionally reprehensible as to justify violence, and Mr. Compson uses the occasion to offer the view of the grander social scheme in which the differentiated ways of making "vessels" (see also 148) out of women are controlled by men. If it is not Bon's act, his conduct as such, it must be the fact that he *married* the Octoroon woman that marked his offense. Although "the morganatic ceremony . . . was as much a part of a wealthy young New Orleansian's social and fashionable equipment as his dancing slippers" (123–24), this pseudo-aristocratic arrangement would still irk the less worldly Henry: "No: it would be the ceremony, a ceremony entered into, to be sure, with a negro, yet still a ceremony; this is what Bon doubtless thought" (136). The next revision, now casting Bon definitely as a white man, is an imaginary response by Bon to Henry's putative charge that he had married a "bought woman. A whore" (142); Charles rejects the term—"Not whore. Dont say that" (142)—and offers more of the larger view: "Not whores. And not whores because of us, the thousand. We—the thousand, the white men—made them, created and produced them; we even made the laws which declare that one eighth of a specified kind of blood shall outweigh seven eighth of another kind. I admit that" (142).

At this stage the reader is made to believe by the way in which the narrative proceeds that the question to be pondered is whether it was the miscegenation between Bon and the Octoroon mistress or the fact that he solemnized the relationship in a "ceremony" that mattered more to Henry, and it is resolved in a third way that it was "not the two ceremonies but the two women; not the fact that Bon's intention was to commit bigamy but that it was apparently to make his (Henry's) sister a sort of junior partner in a harem" (147). Hence Henry asks Charles to renounce the other woman and dissolve his first marriage; and Charles's provocative refusal to comply is what leads to the killing.[88] Charles Bon thus seems to be the embodiment of the southern profligate with New Orleans manners who will not accept the rules of monogamy—a familiar figure from the abolitionist imagination.

Rosa's narrative contributes little more than her remembered statement, "*my nephew had just murdered his sister's fiancé*" (168), so that the significant revisions of the novel take place in the inventive swirl of Quentin and Shreve's active ruminations about the story—so active that

Faulkner lets Quentin and Shreve be syntactically present with Henry and Charles at Sutpen's Hundred in 1865 ("the four of them") while they are imagining the past in their Harvard room half a century later. But are they the modern detectives who unravel the mystery and find the "chemical formula" (124) that makes things happen in the past, or do they project what they wish to find onto the sources and come up with a story that makes the South, as Shreve puts it, "better than Ben Hur" (271)?

Given that the Quentin Compson of *The Sound and the Fury*—whose most pressing question could be paraphrased as "Would you like your sister to marry?"—was haunted by incest fantasies, it is remarkable that Quentin and Shreve in *Absalom, Absalom!* first add the factor of incest to the story by imagining that Thomas Sutpen suddenly recognized that Charles Bon was his son—at the moment at which Henry brings Charles home for the first time and Sutpen "looked up and saw the face he believed he had paid off and discharged twenty-eight years ago" (331). Shreve articulates his own fantasy of sibling incest, believing that "the gods condone and practise these" couplings (404). It is strange that they cite Mr. Compson's opinion that Sutpen "probably named him himself. Charles Bon. Charles Good" (331) as evidence for the paternity, although Mr. Compson had not only not spoken of Charles as Sutpen's son but had constructed the problem in such a way as to make this not even a remote possibility; furthermore, the unrecognized Sutpen son Charles carries his mother's surname Bon rather than a surname invented by the father. Still, from this moment on, it is the issue of incest that keeps Quentin and Shreve's story line going breathlessly as they imagine the theme from all sides. They picture Judith's possible reaction to Bon's kiss—"maybe afterward just looking at him with a kind of peaceful and blank surprise at the fact that your sweetheart apparently kissed you the first time like your brother would—provided of course that your brother ever thought of, could be brought to, kissing you on the mouth" (412). They imagine Bon's wish to be recognized, even in the most minimal way, by his father, his puzzling out "whatever it was his mother had been or done" (413)—whatever "tainted" her (and therefore also Bon's) blood that could have justified Sutpen's repudiation of her—and they settle on Bon's contemplation and ultimate readiness to commit incest with his sister Judith (407) in the futile hope of provoking a reaction from his father as well as from Henry, who has to respond to the new development that it was his own brother who was going to marry his sister, a continued and difficult rationalization of agreeing to break the taboo that is so deeply engrained in his provincial Methodist socialization.

The new factor of incest is logically connected to the pseudo-aristocratic hubris of the founder Thomas Sutpen, who had said "Let there be Sutpen's Hundred" in the same manner in which the God of Genesis had said "Let there be light." The Virginian who experienced a social slight when he was young and went to the West Indies in order to get rich finds slaveholding an important instrument in establishing his upstart royalty. Sutpen also "just told Grandfather how he had put his first wife aside like eleventh and twelfth century kings did: 'I found that she was not and could never be, through no fault of her own, adjunctive or incremental to the design which I had in mind, so I provided for her and put her aside—' . . . 'So I went to the West Indies'" (300). If the divine logic of kings was good enough for his father, it is good enough for Henry, who rationalizes the possible incest between his siblings Charles and Judith as a sign of their aristocracy, crying: "But kings have done it! Even dukes! There was that Lorraine duke named John something that married his sister. The Pope excommunicated him but it didn't hurt. It didn't hurt! They were still husband and wife. They were still alive. They still loved!" (427), and, again: "But that Lorraine duke did it! There must have been lots in the world who have done it that people dont know about, that maybe they suffered for it and died for it and are in hell now for it. But they did it and it dont matter now; even the ones we do know about are just names now and it dont matter now" (428).

Much later, more than a hundred pages after the first revelation of Bon's identity as Sutpen's son, comes the second speculative reconstruction, as Quentin and Shreve surmise that Sutpen (never acknowledging Bon's existence in the least) talked with Henry and said that the marriage had to be stopped because of Bon's mother's *race*: "*He must not marry her, Henry. His mother's father told me that her mother had been a Spanish woman. I believed him; it was not until after he was born that I found out that his mother was part negro*" (443). This hypothetical revelation, near the end of the novel, is what leads up to its famous lines about incest and miscegenation; it alone is what explains things to Quentin and Shreve (the narrator at times mildly condoning their assumptions as "probably right," and the chronology and genealogy endorsing it—with some contradictions). The whole story of the fall of the house of Sutpen—in 1934 Faulkner wanted to entitle the novel-in-progress "DARK HOUSE or something of that nature"[89]—thus becomes plausible to them. Suzanne Jones explains convincingly that the weighing first of incest and then of miscegenation adds a clearer understanding of Henry's motivation to the novel:

> While Henry's love for Bon is so great that he can use another code to sanction incest, his love is not strong enough to overcome the most stringent taboo in Southern society—miscegenation. . . . Once Henry begins to view Bon as black, he can no longer regard him as a brother. In deciding to kill Bon, Henry makes a social choice, not a personal one.[90]

In Quentin and Shreve's version, Henry could tolerate Charles Bon as husband of his sister even though they are all siblings, but he cannot accept the idea that his sister would commit miscegenation, and kills Bon to save her. *Absalom, Absalom!* thus suggests that the power of the fear of miscegenation could exceed by far that of the incest taboo. For the perspective of the patriarch Sutpen, this event marks the end of his design of planting a family that, Quentin and Shreve think, he must have anticipated with dread, for

> even though he knew that Bon and Judith had never laid eyes on one another, he must have felt and heard the design—house, position, posterity and all—come down like it had been built out of smoke, making no sound, creating no rush of displaced air and not even leaving any debris. And he not calling it retribution, no sins of the father come home to roost; not even calling it bad luck, but just a mistake. (333)

In the resolution of the conjunction of incest and miscegenation, Sutpen's house comes down as did Old Colonel Hollister's in Denison's *Old Hepsy*—and in both cases continues in the unacknowledged mixed-race descendants. Faulkner specifically revises Dixon's *Sins of the Father* (Faulkner echoes Dixon's title) for whom it was the (false) news of incest, not the (equally false) suggestion of miscegenation that persuaded Tom Norton that his secret marriage to Helen was wrong and demanded the joint sacrificial suicide of the two seduced white men, Tom and his father, as retribution. For Faulkner, the contemplation of Henry's motives laid bare the stronger social force of the taboo on miscegenation, and the form of storytelling enhances this critique; the focus on Bon shows Faulkner's use of the liberal-realistic mode that operates on the premise that it was Sutpen's failure to recognize Bon, both at his birth and at the time of crisis, that once set inevitably into motion now completes the downfall of the house of Sutpen.

Faulkner created a form in *Absalom, Absalom!* that makes the cluster of incest and miscegenation both a plausible element in understanding the Sutpen family saga and the expression of a particular narrative desire that two young men who are very close, even homoerotically attached to each other, bring to the story: neither of them was a witness, Shreve is the Canadian outsider to Quentin's southern romancing, and yet they construct a fable that makes sense out of many details that would otherwise remain unexplained (even though many contradictions remain). Through his formal strategy Faulkner was able to disentangle the cluster of miscegenation and incest (that was present, as we saw, even in the false expectation that Charles Etienne de Saint Valery Bon was Sutpen's son and grandson generated with Clytie). By introducing one element at a time, and including even such willfully misleading elements as Bon's statements to Henry of "we the white men," Faulkner weighs the force of incest and miscegenation, both separately and in tandem. This way the novel plays with the "mythical" approach and the expectation of symmetry (promised by the famous lines, *"it's the miscegenation, not the incest, which you cant bear,"* that Quentin and Shreve let Henry say to Bon), while showing in Henry's reaction the violence generated by the violation of the miscegenation taboo that is far in excess of that of the incest taboo. As "*Henry looks at the pistol*," panting and trembling, his voice "*is the suffused and suffocating inbreath itself*." His last effort to claim Bon as brother is rebuked, and violence can take its course.

—*You are my brother.*
—*No, I'm not. I'm the nigger that's going to sleep with your sister. Unless you stop me, Henry.* (446)

This is the emotional center of gravity of the novel, yet it also needs to be remembered that neither Mr. Compson nor Miss Rosa had noticed anything like incest and miscegenation behind this central event.

By leaving plot contradictions in suspension and by focusing on the process of storytelling as much as on the tales that result from that process, Faulkner both accommodates and calls attention to the reader's wishes for familiar and even lurid stories, for the theater, for Ben Hur, for the chemical formulae that make something happen with the contradictory and often inconclusive fragments of the past. The novel gives the readers a tale and then asks, almost clinically, what would change in it if the elements of first incest and then miscegenation were added to it. The result is a family saga of sorts in which the liberal reader is satisfied and may find in the fratricide of the second generation a powerful critique of Sutpen as a racially biased and male-obsessed founding father, whereas the reactionary may find most plausible Henry's inability to tolerate miscegenation for his sister. Yet Faulkner also asks a pervasive question that might raise some doubt in his readers' minds as to whether the wonderful story line they wish to find in a mythic place called "South" might not be the result of very complex desires that may have remained unexamined in the tradition from abolitionist to segregationist exaggerations. The question is whether it is not male homosexual attraction that has been a hidden player on the stage of incest and miscegenation. The homoerotic axis of the novel extends from Sutpen's naked fights with his "wild negroes," witnessed by his white daughter Judith as if it were a primal scene, to Charles's "seduction" of Henry and the double entendre of Charles's taunt "unless you stop me." The axis reaches its culminating point, however, in the encounter between Quentin and Shreve, out of whose obvious attraction for each other the reconstruction of incest and miscegenation in the house of Sutpen is made possible and is fleshed out, so that even their joint depiction of Judith's supposed surprise that Bon kissed her "like your brother would—provided of course that your brother ever thought of, could be brought to, kissing you on the mouth" (412) seems to resonate with their own late-night, demiclad, college-roommate interaction.[91] The ideal of *fraternité* is thereby taken to a point that may have been implied but has rarely been explicit in Faulkner's precursors. His recognition of how the "abstraction" of "the Negro" and the fantasies of "race" have served as the screen for all sorts of repressed desires has been rendered in a form in which themes, especially deep and politically volatile themes, become understandable not as natural givens but as the consequence of narrative structures and the partial points of view that may underlie these structures.

*Absalom, Absalom!* offers many other thematic connections for the reader interested in "uniting texts."[92] Faulkner's novel may be the text for which not only this chapter but this whole study might be considered an extended footnote. In the background of *Absalom, Absalom!*, with its allusions to Genesis, there is an interracial island paradise in Haiti, where Thomas Sutpen, an upstart with a sense of bookkeeping, finally "repudiates" his nonwhite wife and their son Charles behind—reenacting "Inkle and Yarico" and their numerous successors. Such origins come to haunt the (nonexistent) town tellingly called "Jefferson" by Faulkner, and with a white founding father whose first name is Thomas and who is more interested in the "design" than in acknowledging his own offspring. The plan and the building of Sutpen's Hundred show, starting with its name, a predilection for a mathematical approach to life and an obsession with fractions reminiscent of the Calculus of Color. Frederick Karl has interestingly focused on the stream of "nonverbal, mathematical" narrative in *Absalom, Absalom!*. Thus, as Quentin and Shreve surmise, Sutpen repudiates his first wife because of a small "fractional part of her which is not Spanish, but Negro":

> That diluted part, that fraction, dooms her son, Bon, when he seeks acceptance as a Sutpen. That same Bon marries an octoroon, 1/8 Negro, and has a son who is that fraction of Negro that derives from 1/8 Negro plus whatever fraction of Negro Bon is, if indeed he is. Further, Sutpen has Clytie by a Negro slave, which makes her 1/2 Negro; she is also, 1/2-sister to Henry and Judith, and, we may forget, 1/2-sister to Bon, but a much greater fraction of black than he is. At issue when Bon wants to marry Judith is less that they are 1/2-siblings than that diluted fraction of Negro blood.[93]

As Karl concludes, "the life and death of the characters depend on fractions," and it is, "ultimately, fractions that destroy Sutpen's grand design" (219). The language of the ledger combines the critique of bookkeeping with a satire on a mathematical language that hides moral issues behind the measurement of economic value:

> *Say 1860, 20 years. Increase 200% times intrinsic val. yearly plus liquid assets plus credit earned. Approx'te val. 1860, 100,000. Query: bigamy threat, yes or No. Possible No. Incest threat: Credible Yes* and the hand going back before it put down the period, lining out the *credible,* writing in *Certain,* underlining it. (387)

Faulkner's critique of the mix of pedantry and arrogance culminates in Sutpen's inability to recognize any moral failing, searching instead for his "mistake" with legal advice.

The novel also offers sharp comments on the popular etymology of

"Mulatto," on the motif of mixed-race effeminacy, and on the curse of Ham, especially in passages on Bon's son Charles Etienne, "the boy with his light bones and womanish hands struggling with what anonymous avatar of intractable Mule, whatever tragic and barren clown was his bound fellow and complement beneath his first father's curse" (250). Revealing the false appropriation of biblical patriarchalism by slave-owners, Faulkner simply inserts a made-up biblical quote on Abraham and his generations: "Praise the Lord, I have raised about me sons to bear the burden of mine iniquities and persecutions; yea, perhaps even to restore my flocks and herds from the hand of the ravisher: that I might rest mine eyes upon my goods and chattels, upon the generations of them and of my descendants increased an hundred fold as my soul goeth out from me" (406). He describes not Charles Etienne's skin, but the mass-produced shapeless denim overall jumper that replaces his earlier Lord Fauntleroy outfit, as "that burlesque uniform and regalia of the tragic burlesque of the sons of Ham" (246) and "the uniform . . . of his ancient curse" (256). Mr. Compson imagines how Wash Jones's belief in the curse of Ham was a futile hope connected to Wash's poor-white class position, from which it would seem to Wash, however, "that this world where niggers, that the Bible said had been created and cursed by God to be brute and vassal to all men of white skin, were better found and housed and even clothed than he and his granddaughter—that this world . . . was just a dream" and the Book's statement that "all men were created in the image of God" and "the same in God's eyes anyway" might be more real (352). Most remarkable is Faulkner's bold alteration of Ham's crime as he describes Bon "not even thinking *I am looking upon my mother naked* since if hating was nakedness, she had worn it long enough now for it to do the office of clothing like they say that modesty can do, does—" (383). This observation is connected to both the possibility that Bon's mother, with the help of the lawyer, is using her son as a vehicle of revenge and Bon's wish to know from his father "*what it was my mother did that justified his action toward her and me*" (408)—speculations which lead not to anything she did but to her "race," hence connecting again to the curse of Ham. Faulkner shows how Bon's mother's blackness may have functioned as the equivalent of a moral stain to Sutpen.

*Absalom, Absalom!* has been read as a reaction to the Tragic Mulatto stereotype. Thadious Davis argued that Bon's son Charles Etienne evolves out of the "rather conventional" literary image of the free Mulatto who, "envisioned as searcher, occupies the tragic 'no-place' in southern life."[94] Faulkner does represent other Mulatto figures who are never recognized by their father such as Clytie, a hidden center of the novel. And Bon's mistress is described by Mr. Compson as "a woman with a face like a tragic magnolia" (141). Yet *Absalom, Absalom!* may also be the most fully realized modern tragedy in which slavery and race have become central. This is suggested by the novel's adaptation of the bibli-

cal incest and fratricide story of King David's children, Amnon, Absalom, and Tamar (2 Samuel:13–19) to Sutpen's Judith, Henry, and
Charles Bon; it is also apparent from Faulkner's countless allusions to
Greek tragedy—from his use of the family structure of Oedipus and two
fratricidal sons, Eteocles and Polyneices, and two daughters, Antigone
and Ismene, to the named and not only ironic connections with the cast
of the *Oresteia*: Cassandra, Clytie, and Agamemnon, from the *Oresteia*'s
most pressing issue of who is the parent, what is kinship, in a world in
which "race" makes a line that separates husband from wife, father from
son and daughter, brother from brother, and sister from sister.[95] The
failed recognitions, the desperate quests for recognition, and the denials
of bonds set up the mechanism for the collapse of the house, and of Sutpen's design. In this respect, Faulkner is again responding to expectations as he offers, through Mr. Compson's (incomplete) view, an interpretation of the story of Sutpen as a tragedy. What Quentin and Shreve
add to Mr. Compson's narrative, however, is what makes it a modern
tragedy in which race has become a central force.

When Quentin and Shreve imagine Bon's wish to be recognized, they
think of a letter in which he begs Sutpen for an acknowledgment.
Settling even for a nonverbal sign, Bon proposes that Sutpen send him a
finger nail paring:

> *Maybe he will write it then. He would just have to write "I am your father. Burn
> this" and I would do it. Or if not that, a sheet of scrap paper with the one word
> "Charles" in his hand, and I would know what he meant and he would not even
> have to ask me to burn it. Or a lock of his hair or a paring from his finger nail and
> I would know them because I believe now that I have known what his hair and his
> finger nails would look like all my life, could choose that lock and that paring out of
> a thousand.* (407–8)

What Bon wishes for is, of course, a sign not of race (in the way in which
Faulkner had mentioned fingernails as a racial sign in his story "Elly")
but of "the name of the father," in its most diminished form that still
would stop Charles and the incest plot.

In the part of the narrative that focuses on Charles Etienne, passing is
explicitly thematized. Judith "would have made a monk, a celibate, of
him perhaps yet not a eunuch, who may not have permitted him to pass
himself for a foreigner, yet who certainly would not have driven him to
consort with negroes" (251).

The novel is a continuous form of retelling not only of the Sutpen
story by Rosa, Mr. Compson, Quentin, and Shreve, or of miscegenation
in "Evangeline" and *Light in August*, and incest in *The Sound and the Fury*,
but of the tradition of interracial literature. Yet whereas some other texts
have supplied "instances," *Absalom, Absalom!* "talks back" to the thematic
traditions of interracial literature, calls attention to its narrative conven-

tions by juxtaposing them against each other, and plays with thematic expectations that stem from precursor texts.

After Quentin and Shreve have reached their conclusions, Shreve points out sharply to Quentin that the Sutpen line continues in Charles Etienne's child Jim Bond, "and so in a few thousand years, I who regard you will also have sprung from the loins of African kings" (471). Storytelling and inventing create kinship and a sense of a culture, of a place. The ending of "their" Sutpen saga suggests to the Canadian a particularly "Southern" story line so that he asks Quentin pointedly: "Why do you hate the South?" Quentin answers:

> "I dont hate it," Quentin said, quickly, at once, immediately; "I dont hate it," he said. *I dont hate it* he thought, panting in the cold air, the iron New England dark: *I dont. I dont! I dont hate it! I dont hate it!* (471)

By locating the hypothetical reconstruction of the deep drama of the Sutpen family in the cold Harvard winter, Faulkner may be evoking the historical roots of "Southern" fictions of incest and miscegenation in New England abolitionism. Quentin's vehement denial is what ends the novel that thereby both makes a connection with the resolution of a narrative and a place and at the same time questions that connection.

# Endings

Many are the comedies and many are the tragedies which these artificial lines of demarcation have created.

—Walter White, "The Paradox of Color" (1925)[1]

Let's go to Paris! Where things like that are understood. We'll raise the child there. We'll keep her in Europe all her life. We'll stay in Europe. She won't have to be American-white or American-black. She'll be cosmopolitan—a woman of the world. We'll do that, Paul, you and I. I'll do it gladly, Paul, gladly.

—Mary Nile to Paul Grimm, in Samson Raphaelson, *White Man* (1935)[2]

Will the future come? It seems that we may almost ask this question, when we see such terrible shadow.

—Victor Hugo[3]

Zoe marries her white suitor and first cousin George—Zoe dies by her own hand. How shall the story of *The Octoroon* end? In interracial literature, this was also a question often tied up with *where* a story ends. Any closure given to a text implies that an alternative resolution to the problems at hand has been denied, overruled, or buried; hence it is not surprising that interracial literature has displayed a good amount of self-consciousness and some ambivalence about where and how the plot lines could be brought to a conclusion. As this book, too, is coming to an end, I would like to consider two recurring patterns of closure in the literature examined, the wish for "A World Elsewhere," whether or not it is realized, and the rewriting process that often results in "Alternative Endings."

As has been suggested on the preceding pages, one can imagine infinite tellings and retellings of the many plot lines of interracial literature and the many variations on certain themes. In pondering the fact that there are a thousand variants of *Cinderella* tales Barbara Herrnstein Smith questioned the very *existence* of a "thematic plane" in texts and concluded: "All of these stories are in some respects similar and in some respects dissimilar. The incidence, nature, and degrees of resemblance and disparity are so diverse, however, that they allow just about every conceivable type of causal relation among the stories, including none at all."[4] To some extent this observation might also apply to the themes of interracial literature.

Yet one may also distinguish two basic alternative modes of conceptualizing the diverse themes, either as a "tragic" impossibility or as a "comic" plot that ends happily and often with a marriage (many times a happy interracial marriage). Versions in the tragic mode tend to have endings in irresolvable conflicts and often in death—frequently violent death inflicted by others, suicide, or heartbreak—and those in the comic mode are likely to end with the reign of law, a marriage (often in "a world elsewhere"), and the realization, or at least the promise, of a descent line that will continue the story into the future.

## A World Elsewhere

In Edith Pope's *Colcorton* (1944), the writer Johnson (who, we remember, has discovered Abby Clanghearne's racial family secret) speaks to Abby about the future of her nephew Jad. It is the context in which he rejects the idea that Jad's situation can rightly be termed tragic, for there is nothing inevitable or unchangeable about it.

> Jad's can be changed by an overnight train trip, by removing him beyond the danger of detection. The whole world is open to him, except here. And when he's grown, should he be discriminated against in the north let him go to France, or to Russia or England or Spain. This is the only country where such prejudice exists. (306)

According to *Colcorton* a plot is not "tragic" if a simple change of venue can bring it to a happier conclusion. In that sense "race tragedy" is not really tragic as long as the protagonists can reach a place elsewhere in which the racial code does not apply. Put differently, the age of emigration to desirable places elsewhere replaces the sense of exile as banishment and punishment and marks the end of tragedy. And Johnson offers a comprehensive vision of a better world elsewhere as a happy alternative to a tragic America—that cannot be considered truly tragic because of the existence of modern means of transportation. Raimundo, the protagonist of Azevedo's *O Mulato*, a charming man with large possessions, a law degree from Coimbra University, and a fine reputation in Switzerland and Germany, realizes that it is only the provincialism of northern Brazil that reduces him to the status of "the son of a slave woman" and makes impossible his marriage to Ana Rosa. Once away from here, he would no longer be somebody who was merely "freed at baptism" (209). Yet he is caught and killed by the machinations of his uncle and an evil priest, unable to carry out his plan to take Ana Rosa away with him. In *O Mulato*, the "world elsewhere" might be anywhere from Rio de Janeiro to Lisbon, but it is defined only as being "away from" the province of Maranhão, where Raimundo is trapped.

For literature of slavery in the United States, especially after the Fugitive Slave Act of 1850, the British Dominion of Canada was often the closest and most logical haven of freedom, for example at the ending of Lydia Maria Child's play *The Stars and Stripes*. Surprisingly often it is also the Old World that gets specifically styled as the place where the color-line-crossed lovers could be united without encountering the kind of opposition they have to face in the New. The classic "European theme" takes young Americans to the continent with a history, with manners, and with a difficult web of social relations into which the heirs of the New World no longer fit very easily, and the traditional "European theme" is commonly employed to juxtapose the ways of the Old and the New Worlds. The interracial variant of the theme that

might in many cases be called the "European Dream" has the very specific function of contrasting white American and Creole hostility to racial
mixing and to black achievements (one has only to think of Reybaud's
Rebelière) with a somewhat idealized representation of European open-
mindedness (Reybaud's Cécile). "Europe" often becomes something like
an asylum for mixed couples and their descendants. Hence, for black-
white couples or biracial individuals, going to Europe appears to be the
most frequently used plot alternative to that of finding unhappiness or
death in the New World. For the race-divided lovers of the New World,
the European Dream seems to be the realization of the wish, "Let's get
away from it all," a migratory logic that here exhorts interracial protagonists to go—*east.*

The tradition of exoticism would seem to have stipulated a different
resolution: in "Inkle and Yarico," in Stedman, or in Tennyson's
"Locksley Hall," the utopian idyll is possible only in a colony, on an
island, as far away from Europe as possible—though the dramatic adaptation of Stedman's book by Franz Kratter lets "Stedmann" take his
beloved to Europe, marriage, and a happy ending. Close vicinity to the
motherland and its modern mercantile values changes the white person's
mind, bringing out most notably quite a brutal side in Inkle. In Cooper's
*Spy* (1821), too, there is a long discussion directed against the European
Dream. Doctor Sitgreaves argues, over Colonel Wellmere's objections
to American slavery, that "every nation of civilised Europe does, or has
held their fellow-creatures in this kind of *duresse*," including Great
Britain:

> It was her children, her ships, and her laws, that first introduced the prac-
> tice into these states; and on her institutions the judgment must fall. There
> is not a foot of ground belonging to England, in which a negro would be
> useful, that has not its slave. England herself has none, but England is
> overflowing with physical force, a part of which she is obliged to maintain
> in the shape of paupers. The same is true of France, and most other
> European countries. (148–49)

The "motherlands" are hypocritical, even when they may appear "toler-
ant" at times. Yet when in the course of the first half of the nineteenth
century, fueled by the abolition of slavery by Britain in 1833, and by most
other European powers by 1848, the United States, Brazil, and the
Spanish colony of Cuba became increasingly isolated as slaveholding
powers, the notion won broader acceptance that "Europe" meant the
absence of American-style slavery and race prejudice. This rhetorical
strategy may also have helped to make attacks on slavery less local,
more cosmopolitan, and hence more persuasive. It also deflected from
the notion that whites had a biologically inbred race-instinct, since
European whites seemed to lack it.

Richard Hildreth's 1852 edition of his famous novel, now entitled *The*

*White Slave*, was representative. The book ends with a strong exhortation against the last vestiges of slavery—and a praise of "free England":

> Take courage, then, and do as I did. Throw off the chains! and stop not there; others are also to be freed. It seems a doubtful thing; but courage, trust, and perseverance . . . will do it. I am old, and may not live to see it; but my five grandchildren, born, thank God, in free England, surely will. (407–8)

Hildreth consciously played on the historical irony that three-quarters of a century after the Declaration of Independence it is birth in the old motherland that conveys freedom to Archy and Cassy's grandchildren.

In Lydia Maria Child's "The Quadroons," going to France or England (64) with their daughter Xarifa was the fondest wish of Rosalie, whose white lover Edward, however, marries the white woman Charlotte and stays in Georgia. After Rosalie's death, Edward thinks "what a pleasant thing it would be, if English freedom from prejudice should lead him to offer legal protection to his graceful and winning child" (72). The horrifying resolution of the plot is thus due to the fact of its American setting.

William Wells Brown's *Clotel* (1853) reunited George and Mary Green in Europe; and for Brown, England constituted the realized utopian ideal of freedom. As Christopher Mulvey argues, however, this may have meant both measuring England unrealistically against the yardstick of the American Fugitive Slave Act while ignoring British colonial policy toward India or Africa, and criticizing American racism while sharing British anti-Semitism.[5]

In Charles Kingsley's novel *Two Years Ago* (1857), it was again England and also Italy where refuge could be found; in Frank Webb's *The Garies and Their Friends* (1857), as we saw, France and Italy are mentioned as possibly better alternatives to Georgia and the trap of free Philadelphia. Italy was also the world elsewhere for Hubert Warner and Helen Dupré at the end of Mary Pike's novel *Caste* (1856):

> By the shores of the tideless sea, beneath the purple skies of Italy, Hubert Warner has made his home with the bride he won so dearly; and never has he regretted that for her sake he relinquished his father's house and his native land. . . .
>
> Happy in each other and their children, they seldom care to leave their grove-embowered villa; but old friends now and then find them out in their seclusion, and a gradually-widening circle of congenial and cultivated families are ever ready to welcome them when they visit the neighboring city. . . .
>
> They see few Americans, and seldom refer to the land they have left; partly because then only does a frown gather on Hubert's brow, and a deep sadness, not unmixed with stronger and harsher feelings, overspread the features of Colonel Bell, and partly because, like all persons really content-

ed and absorbed with their surroundings and occupations, they live in the present, and the past does not often intrude itself upon their thoughts.[6]

Here the ending promises what sounds very much like an American ideal that has come true in an Italian setting—a suburban location in a circle of families, in which the past has been forgotten and the fact of their emigration does not become a source of regret, though the wish for a better America is written on Hubert's brow. If American slavery was often the touchstone for this positive thematization of Europe, the wish for a happier world elsewhere did not come to an end with the period of New World slavery.

William Dean Howells's *An Imperative Duty* (1891) also ends in Italy, as the idealized site for the interracial couple's future life, and explicitly for reasons of race rather than of slavery. Howells's choice of Italy as the ideal location has the advantage that Dr. Olney's mixed-race bride Rhoda Aldgate blends right in:

> [A]s yet their secret remains their own. They are settled at Rome, after a brief experiment of a narrower field of practice at Florence; and the most fanciful of Olney's compatriot patients does not dream that his wife ought to suffer shame from her. She is thought to look so very Italian that you would really take her for an Italian.[7]

In Lydia Maria Child's *Romance of the Republic* (1867), it is again the lure of Italy that makes the difference, whereas in texts from Theodor Storm's "Von jenseit des Meeres" (1865) and in William Gardner Smith's *The Last of the Conquerors* (1948), it is Germany that provides the interracial haven.

As we have seen, in Reybaud, Andersen, and Scribe it is France that symbolizes the ideal world of freedom from slavery and aristocratic harmony—as opposed to Creole upstart hypocrisy in the colonies. France also appears, at least in the subjunctive, as a better alternative to Frances E. W. Harper's Iola Leroy, who explains to her bridegroom that she never blames her white father for shielding her from her racial identity, for she knows that he did it for the best:

> Had he lived he would have taken us to France, where I should have had a life of careless ease and pleasure. But now my life has a much grander significance than it would have had under such conditions. Fearful as the awakening was, it was better than to have slept through life. (274)

In Samson Raphaelson's play *White Man* (1935), the love story between Paul Grimm, who passes, and his later wife Mary Nile develops in the Old World (the settings include a Mediterranean cruise and Paris), but goes to pieces in New York. Therefore Mary entreats her husband at one point to go back to France.[8] The narrative by an anonymous light-skinned black woman, partly published in Everett Stonequist's *Marginal*

*Man* (1937), also idealizes going to Paris as the dream of the mixed-race person:

> I often feel that I belong to no race. I sometimes feel that even members of my own race would rather not be in my company because I "look like white." . . . I frequently engage in daydreams. In my daydreams, I plan to go to some foreign country where it won't make any difference whether I am white or black. I often think that I'd like to live in France.

Stonequist adds the clarifying footnote: "France is almost a Mecca for the marginal Negro."[9]

The theme of the "World Elsewhere," or of the European Dream, has affinities to the theme of "passing" though no deception is necessary to break through the color bar there. This is not due to the amazing open-mindedness of Europeans, but it is possible because the Old World lent itself to such migratory projections, since the racial fault lines in Europe have been (or at least were in the nineteenth and early twentieth centuries) somewhat different from the major fault line of the New World. An American descendant of black Africans was *not* a Jew, not a Gypsy, not a Moor, not an Algerian, and was present only in small numbers. Howells's Rhoda Aldgate "really" would be taken for Italian. Furthermore, a mixed-race individual whose non-European racial background was imperceptible could be regarded by the grid of class relations that has been so important to Europeans—so that a doctor's wife, the Sorbonne-trained husband of a countess, other respectable members of the upper and middle classes, and even an artist with charm and social graces would hardly have to have their fingernails examined. It "would have taken a Yankee's glance" to do that—as we saw Paul Bourget's *Cosmopolis* argue, representing Lincoln Maitland as unprejudiced since he was raised in England rather than the United States. And, of course, Europeans liked to view themselves as open-minded, unlike Creoles.

This does not mean that interracial literature describes freestanding blacks as easily marriageable in the European context. To be sure, in the feudal world where some form of aristocratic rule was still in place, there were many stories of interracial loves and marriages. From the Tsar-arranged interracial marriage of Puškin's Ibrahim and Natasha to the happy ending in France for Reybaud's Cécile and Donatien, there are many examples, and it is tempting to juxtapose the matter-of-fact representation of an interracial marriage in an illuminated fifteenth-century manuscript (Fig. 41) and the palpable tension of the racially bifurcated marriage scene in Eugene O'Neill's *All God's Chillun Got Wings* (Fig. 42). Juan Latino, the historical protagonist of Don Diego Ximénez de Enciso, *Comedia famosa de Juan Latino* (1652), set a high standard for the possible social acceptance of the interracial love story in a comedy plot, even though it involved the relationship between a black man and a white woman.[10]

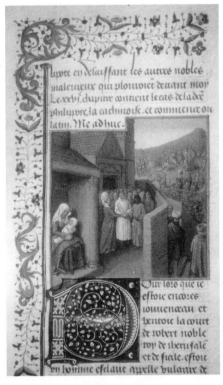

***Figure 41***   Jean Fouquet, Marriage of
Philippa of Catania to Raymond de
Campagne (1458)

***Figure 42***   Paul Robeson and Flora Robson in Eugene O'Neill,
*All God's Chillun Got Wings*, London production (1933)

Yet there was also the opposite tendency, present already among the aristocracy, but especially strongly developed in the more and more dominant mercantile and bourgeois worlds, to cast a black-white relationship not as legitimate but as adulterous, or the freestanding black person (even a very beautiful black woman) in Europe as an impossible match. Some of Masuccio's cruel tales in the *Novellino* (1475), organized around such themes as "events caused by jealousy," or "the defective female sex," are examples of the jealous fantasies that also inform so much of the interracial life of *Thousand and One Nights*, starting with the frame narrative of "King Sharyar and His Brother," in which the figure of the black slave as lover of a married woman serves to magnify the humiliation experienced by the white husband. The power of such story lines helped to create the ready association of interracial love stories with adultery tales.[11]

There was also another thematic recurrence that suggested less than European easiness with interracial love stories. It is the motif of the beautiful African woman who simply is not considered marriageable in Europe because she is black. One could take the verdict of the provincial parents of the protagonist of Maupassant's "Boitelle" (1889) as motto, "If only she were not so black . . . " (Fig. 43). The ironist Maupassant, however, told his tale in order to question the maxim that one should obey one's parents in choosing a spouse and to make fun of the destructive capabilities of provincialism in the case of Antoine Boitelle, who was too

***Figure 43*** Illustration for Guy de Maupassant, "Boitelle" (1889)

obedient to insist on his alliance with the (unnamed) black woman whom he had met in his days as a soldier at the Café des Colonies at Le Havre. Whereas his love was fed by exoticism as well as by the recognition that her ideals were the same as those of women in his country—"thrift, work, religion, and good manners"—and whereas the black woman who had been abandoned by an American captain had inherited some money from an oyster woman who had adopted her, Boitelle's peasant parents only respond to her blackness: "It is a pity she is so black, but there, she really is too black."[12] Antoine listens to his parents and, though he ultimately marries another woman and fathers fourteen children with her, he becomes a listless sewage worker.

Probably the once most famous and widely celebrated—though by now largely forgotten—European tale of a beautiful African woman who cannot get married in France was the immensely popular novella *Ourika*[13] (1824) by Madame Claire Lechat de Duras (1778–1829). A sentimental marvel, the book which was first published privately and then went through many editions started an international cult, was rapidly translated into Italian, German, Spanish, and English, elicited royal comment by Louis XVIII and artistic endorsement by Goethe, and inspired the writing of a sequel, a parody, several elegies, and numerous instant dramatizations. *Ourika* was also made a theme of other arts, as one of the poetic versions was set to music, and the heroine of the novella was also transformed into widely reproduced visual image based on a painting by François Gérard (Fig. 44). Like Goethe's *Sorrows of Young Werther*, Duras's *Ourika* was even celebrated in clothing styles and hairdos, and a reviewer of a dramatic adaptation noticed Ourika bonnets and kerchiefs among the Vienna audience and mentioned that Parisians were eating Ourika cutlets and biscuits.[14]

The sad tale of *Ourika* is the story of the absence of an interracial match and its programmatic impossibility. Ourika, the sensitive, intelligent, and beautiful young Senegalese captive is raised and educated in France at Mme. de Beauval's estate, where she is happy and feels part of the family until she overhears a conversation about her in which another countess describes the sadness and hopelessness of Ourika's situation, for while she has all the qualities a refined young lady might desire—education, good taste, and charm—she will never find a husband in France because of the color of her skin. Ourika is thunderstruck, sees her life in a new light, and, resigned to accept her fate, now identifies more closely with Charles, the grandson of Mme. de Beauval, who is like a brother to her. Believing that she has somewhat overcome the sad side effects of her problematic social position as an ineligible foreigner, Ourika is traumatized when, after Charles has married another woman, the same countess says maliciously that it is quite apparent that Ourika has madly fallen in love with Charles. "Poor" Ourika (*pauvre* is her standard epithet) had been quite unaware of her emotions, renounces them, becomes a nun

***Figure 44***   Alfred Johannot's steel
engraving of François Gérard, *Ourika*
(1824)

(the stage in which she was often portrayed and elegized), and ultimately
dies of heartbreak. The contrast between Ourika's capacity for refined
emotions and the cruelty of the external world gives the novella its life;
and the high points are the representations of Ourika's interiority. After
the second discovery, for example, she exclaims:

> Great God! thou dost bear witness that I rejoiced in the happiness of
> Charles: but why, why hast thou laden pour Ourika with life? Why was I
> not suffered to perish on board the negro bark, or upon my mother's
> bosom? Why did not the sands of my own Africa receive me, and release
> poor Ourika from the burden of existence? The world—what need has it
> of Ourika? Why is she condemned to live? That she may live alone, for
> ever alone, for ever a stranger to love! Oh my God, suffer it not to be! Take
> away poor Ourika from the earth! There are none to feel her loss. Her
> life—is it not solitude?[15]

The popularity of this tale in its many emanations may be the result of
contradictory ideological tendencies, as its tear-jerking strategy could be
read both as an affirmation of essential racial difference and as a critique
of the faultiness of human judgment that is based not the content of a
person's character but on the color of her skin. The conservatives might
believe that Ourika would have been better off as a slave, without the
benefits of French education, but in the company of her own kinfolk.

The liberals might be drawn to read the novella biographically as an oblique expression of Madame Duras's deep love for Chateaubriand which made her thematize unrequited love by creating "objective" obstacles of class or race in her fictions. Thus her *Édouard* focuses on the difficulties of class mésalliance as *Ourika* does on the obstacle of race. Behind both novellas, however, there might shimmer the hope for a better world in which love may yet conquer all. And everybody could cry.

Set in the 1790s, with explicit references to the Haitian and French Revolutions, the tale might also seem the logical outcome of *fraternité*, of making blacks part of an allegorical French family in which, consequently, the choice is that between the symbolic sibling love of Ourika and Charles (evoking again the combined fears of incest and miscegenation[16]), and Ourika's celibacy (the plot alternative chosen). In Mélesville and Carmouche's dramatic adaptation, for example, a vaudeville of Amazons gives voice to Christian universalism, comforting Ourika with the observation that there is Someone (in the sky) who never forgets the unhappy ones: "Negroes or whites, what matters origin,/ All pure hearts are equal in front of Him."[17] Yet all the same, Mme. de Beauval's brother Franville (tellingly, a Creole) states that there is a "natural order" of racial difference that one must not upset with impunity, an order which may be seen in the botanical analogy of a flower that simply cannot grow far from the soil of its homeland—hence Mélesville and Carmouche send the transplanted and therefore heartbroken Ourika back to Africa, her "natural" world elsewhere, at the end of their play, though it is hard to imagine a new love interest emerging beyond the final image of Ourika, engulfed in her pain.

Whether *Ourika* was viewed as egalitarian critique of prejudice or as proof of the incompatibility of races, whether the heroine was worshipped as the cultural embodiment of everything that was desirable in a woman or pitied in the image of her as a melancholy nun, whether she was seen as an artist with a fuller, more utopian vision than that of the shallow and notoriously gossipy French society or as a hopeless victim of unnatural uprooting—the immense popularity of the *Ourika* cult does suggest that the image of France, or Europe, as interracial haven was hardly an unproblematic reality but the subject of some cultural debate. It was more an expression of the hope for a better world "there" than a realistic depiction of a "here." In fact, in the different versions of this tale the heroine's fate seems dependent on whether she leaves for Africa (meaning survival) or stays in Europe (signifying death)—and this was a difference that elicited contemporary comment. For example, when Ignaz Franz Castelli adapted *Urika, die Negerinn* ("Urika the Negress") for a presentation at the most prestigious Burgtheater at Vienna, in 1824, removing the revolutionary context of the novella, a reviewer commented ironically that "the Parisian audience, familiar with the tale of this pious and spirited black woman, had to be indebted to the playwright for having managed to keep her alive, although the narrator of the novella had not succeeded in doing so."[18] The reviewer might have added that this was accomplished only by taking the heroine elsewhere, as her ship is seen leaving France at the end of the play.

## Alternative Endings

The migratory logic of *"there* it could work, and *here* it's so doomed" may have helped to generate a broader plot ambiguity and to bring into the open a widespread ambivalence in the literature as far as plot resolution and closure were concerned. Does the forbidden couple marry, overcome all obstacles, and live happily ever after (the solution of "there")? Or are the lovers overcome by fatal forces that engulf them and pull them—or at least one of them—down (the logic of "here")? The cultural ambivalence surrounding this basic situation has generated ambivalent formal responses.

It was not uncommon for both versions of the same plot to emerge, simultaneously or successively, as has already become apparent in the case of *Ourika*. The themes of interracial literature seem to belong to the category of topics that have generated a particular ambivalence toward endings in writers and critics. This found its formal expression in many alternative treatments of the same story as tragedy and as comedy. We may thus find the same plot developed in both directions (by the same author or by different writers), inviting comparisons of the versions; occasionally such different versions invoke explicit structural, cultural, national, or historical differences in order to justify the change.

To return, for example, to the famous story of "Inkle and Yarico" (1711), the sentimental tale of the English merchant who sells his pregnant beloved and savior Yarico, this was a story rewritten and adapted so many times that the various versions have been made the subject of monograph. There was, for example, an explicitly black-white version, perhaps written by a woman, that appeared in the *London Magazine* (1734) and described the reaction of the *"negro virgin"* Yarico to the English Inkle in such lines as: *"His face like polish'd marble did appear;/ His silken robe, and long-curl'd flaxen hair/ Amaz'd the nymph."* She saves him from her own tribe of cannibals (*"The savage race their trembling flesh devour/ Off'ring oblations to th'infernal power"*). Yet the change in a leading character's race did not lead to a substantially different conclusion:

> He thrust her from him with remorseless hand,
> For her condition rais'd his first demand.
> Pleas'd with success he chearfully returns,
> While hapless Yarico in bondage mourns.
> The merchants all the prudent youth admire,
> That could, so young, a trading soul acquire.[19]

However, the popular opera version, *Inkle and Yarico* (1787) by George Colman the Younger, did give its viewers a comedy. After Inkle offers Yarico for sale to the Barbadian governor—who is, in fact, Yarico's father—she quickly gets married to the young Captain Campley, whereas Inkle apologizes and puts the blame on education:

> Ill founded precept too long has steeled my breast—but still 'tis vulnerable—this trial was too much—Nature, 'gainst habit combating within me, has penetrated to my heart; a heart, I own, long callous to the feelings of sensibility; but now it bleeds—and bleeds for my poor Yarico. Oh, let me clasp her to it, while 'tis glowing, and mingle tears of love and penitence.[20]

Yarico forgives him, and the play ends with the dance of Yarico's black maid Wowski and Inkle's white servant Trudge, who have been faithful to each other: "Come, let us dance and sing/ While all Barbadoes bells shall ring." This ending with the strange marriage to a substituted groom has obviously changed the theme dramatically. However faulty and unconvincing the resolution may seem, it does give the theme a "happy ending."

Five years after Colman's transformation of *Inkle and Yarico*, an alteration of another famous interracial plot line inspired a writer engaged in revising a famous work to offer some general reflections on the need for changes and the addition of what he called "dénoûement heureux"— happy ending. In 1792 J. F. Ducis adapted *Othello* for the Parisian stage and claimed in the *avertissement*[21] that, unlike the English, the French— even at the height of the Revolution, as Jan Kott has remarked[22]—would not tolerate the violent Shakespearean ending. Ducis made the threshold for the limits of pity and fear explicitly dependent on "national character." He believed that whereas for the English it might be acceptable to see Othello push a pillow again and again on Desdemona's mouth until she suffocates, the French spectators would never tolerate this. "A tragic poet is therefore forced to conform to the character of the nation to which he presents his works." This is an "unquestionable truth" for Ducis, and in order to please his French audience, he offered the change—happily, it was quite "easily made," as he points out—of substituting a happy ending (*dénoûement heureux*) that seemed more appropriate to the nature and morality of the theme. However, Ducis printed both the original and his alternative conclusions, thus leaving theater directors the choice of presenting a violent or a happy ending. Perhaps Ducis's wonderful strategy of publishing a multiple-choice text would make a model for a whole possible anthology of interracial literature with alternative endings. It is fascinating that the argument was made in the wake of the French Revolution, and that it again associated a different ending with a different place—though the places had become the "national characters" believed to correspond to nation states, an issue to which I shall return. The rewriting of a Shakespearean tragedy with an audience-inspired happy ending was not the only instance of an interesting alternation between versions of stories about black-white couples.

Another example was the stark ending of the brilliant novella "Die Verlobung in St. Domingo" ("The Engagement in Santo Domingo," 1811) by Heinrich von Kleist (1777–1811). Reviewing Kleist's tale, Wilhelm Grimm commented that whereas "the main scene in which the omnipotence of love cuts across all deceptions and lies of a young misguided girl's heart and lifts her noble nature out of its suppression to the highest pinnacle of freedom," one might "wish for a less terrible ending; for it is almost too ghastly to evoke a truly tragic feeling; in the rapid annihilation of the two lovers, however, there is a little softening."[23] It is remarkable that Kleist even changed the name of the Swiss protagonist from Gustav to August as he approached the violent climax.[24] The novella's denouement hinges on the problem of *trust* in the setting of a political upheaval that makes duplicity and deception necessary. In 1803, during the Haitian revolution, Gustav von Ried, who had lost his first fiancée in the reign of terror in Strasbourg, seeks refuge on the Guillaume de Villeneuve estate which is now controlled by the African Congo Hoango and his mistress, the Mulatto woman Babekan, who uses her fifteen-year-old, light-skinned daughter Toni as deceptive bait for white fugitives who are killed whenever Congo Hoango returns. However, Gustav and Toni fall in love, and Toni saves not only Gustav but also the larger group of Swiss relatives with whom he was traveling and who were hiding nearby. In order to be able to carry out her plan, Toni has to mislead her suspicious mother and Congo Hoango, and she has to tie up Gustav on his bed without being able to explain her scheme to him. At the risk of her own life, she warns Herr Strömli, his sons, and Gustav's other relatives and leads them to the estate, where they overpower Congo Hoango and Babekan and free Gustav (now called August). But when Toni enters the room, he angrily takes a pistol and kills her, then kicks her body away from him, calling her a whore. Herr Strömli and his sons explain, horrified, that they all owe their safety to Toni, whose dying words to Gustav are, "you should not have mistrusted me." Recognizing his error and failing in his frantic efforts to revive Toni, Gustav puts a pistol into his mouth and kills himself, his skull bespattering the wall in bits and fragments. The relatives bury Toni and Gustav together, and put up a monument for them upon their escape to Switzerland via Port au Prince.

Paul Heyse (1830–1914)—known to readers of interracial literature as the author of a poetic "Urica" (1851)—expressed high praise for Kleist's novella while noting that he remained unconvinced "that it necessarily had to develop the way it did" and that "the ending, especially, must appear arbitrary" since the past of the heroine "according to the view of the artist himself does not require a tragic termination."[25] Heyse thus echoed Wilhelm Grimm, who had also hoped for a "less terrible end-

***Figure 45*** Edmund Brüning,
illustration for Theodor Körner,
"Toni" (ca. 1900)

ing." The pivotal moment in which tragic and comic possibilities begin
to diverge is the point at which Toni ties up Gustav in order to make possible the rescue plan. Why does she not whisper a few explanatory words
into his ears, a close reader wondered.[26] "Gustav" would not have
become "August," and the ending could have been a true "engagement,"
indeed.

This is exactly what happened when Kleist's novella was transformed
into a comedy in Theodor Körner's *Toni* (1812), for Körner does take his
point of comic departure by changing the crucial moment in the way in
which some of Kleist's readers had wanted to see it changed. Körner's
Toni (Fig. 45) is permitted to find the opportunity to tell Gustav what
she is doing: "God is benevolent! Wear your chains/And trust in God;
love shall save you!"—before exiting rapidly.[27] These words make all the
difference when Gustav, bound and guarded by one of Hoango's men, is
tempted to doubt his beloved but realizes that she could not have lied to
him (251). He still has to lie through a terrifying speech by Hoango, who
announces the imminent death of all whites—"for where there are still
whites, there are still slaves" (252)—but just as the news of the arrival of
the whites prompts Hoango to transform his program into action by
attempting to stab Gustav, Toni arrives with the pistol and shoots
Hoango to death. Gustav compliments himself for having trusted her,
"the heroic girl," and believed in her love (the exact parallel to Toni's

dying words in Kleist). Toni is also praised by Strömly as an "angel," but when she is sharply condemned and disowned by her mother Babeckan, who escapes, after accusing her daughter of committing treason with the white "Franks," Toni is moved to bitter tears, which Strömly explains to Gustav as the "pain with which she is burying her mother" (253). In the last scene Toni connects her fate with Gustav's, and Strömly joins their hands with the concluding ceremonial lines:

> Say it aloud and through all times
> Your grandchildren might sing it after you!
> God is merciful, that was the motto;
> And brave love has won the victory. (254)

Körner's ending resolves the issues of the novella by promising not only the protagonists' survival but also the emergence of a long descent line—making Toni and Gustav a foundational couple. Yet Toni's mother, who is unassimilable to the world of the white Franks, simply has to be discarded, "buried" with some tears. Finally, Toni's act of rescuing Gustav by shooting Hoango makes her appear as a more active and excessive Pocahontas (or Yarico) figure who has redefined herself in relationship to her white beloved—even to the extent of killing the symbolic father figure of her socialization. The comedy is achieved only by valuing intermarriage infinitely more highly than filial loyalty,[28] the right of the younger generation over that of the elders, and, above all, the right of the white bridegroom to "lead" his mixed-blood bride "into the magic land of love"—which might not be synonymous with Switzerland to most Haitians.

If Kleist's tragic vision makes readers wish for the few words that could have changed the course of action, Körner's comic vision lets theatergoers have this wish—but at the expense of turning Toni into an unpunished traitor to the only world that has been hers so far, and the play has to gloss over this flaw by rushing toward its resolution in little more than a page from Toni's deadly shot to Strömly's benediction (so that Hoango's corpse must literally still be on the stage on which the engagement takes place). Thomas Mann commented on Kleist's novella and Körner's play and found that "Kleist's choice of plot was clearly dictated by his taste for the horrible, and wholly in keeping with that taste is his treatment of the climactic event of the story." Mann was surprised that Körner's Toni, "shallow and sentimental, appealed greatly to Goethe who had taken no notice whatever of Kleist's story. He even gave a public reading of Körner's adaptation at the Weimar court and drew sketches of a Negro hut to be used in the same stage set during production. It is most annoying, and at the same time quite comical, to see a man of Goethe's stature bestow his favor time and again on rank mediocrity."[29] Mann's opposition between Kleist's "horrible" and Körner's "sentimental" versions suggests the presence of contrasting excesses operating in these artists' strategies—despite their obvious difference in aesthetic accomplishment.

Georg Lukács also took this aesthetic difference for granted when he tried to push toward a more general observation based on the difference between Kleist's tragic novella and his "mediocre contemporary" Körner's bad "comedy with a 'happy ending'": "Körner could lift the action almost without change from Kleist's novella, only having to remove and to make shallower the psychology of mistrust in order to arrive at a comedy." Lukács perceives in this close kinship of tragic and happy endings the more general problem that in the modern period "the tragic and the comic have ceased to be objective categories of reality, and increasingly become subjective points of view for explaining phenomena of life."[30] In Lukács's view, the rise of individualism makes comedy and tragedy more easily interchangeable and makes alternative endings easy to bring about: it requires, as Ducis had already recognized, only very minor alterations to bring about a major about-face. For Lukács this signaled a modern crisis of genres and of representation in general; for Ducis's viewer-friendly approach it meant increased options for different national audiences; and for many writers this state of affairs made all the easier the wish to redo their own works, be it because they remembered an initial ambivalence in the creative process, because they had afterthoughts after the work had become an object, or because they wished to revise their work in view of imagined or real audience pressure.

One writer who agonized about the ending of a work of his was Theodor Storm. In his novella "Von jenseit des Meeres" (1865) he made Jenni, the beautiful mixed-race woman from the West Indies who comes to Germany, the author of a poem Storm also published, under his own name, with only a small alteration that makes the speaker an orphan rather than a homeless child. Storm's correspondence reveals how satisfied he was with the main part of the novella, yet how he thought of changing the ending which provided for a happy interracial alliance. In a letter of 16 February 1865 Storm wrote to Theodor Fontane:

> My novella "From beyond the sea" is, I believe, a good piece of work, the main scene seems to me almost of the first order, only the ending should be changed, as it does not exhaust the tragic conflict. A scream must sound across directly from her. Have something in my head already.[31]

In another letter written to to Ivan Turgenev on 9 December 1866, Storm enclosed a copy of the novella and wondered whether Turgenev, should he get to read the story at all, might "miss the tragic ending," as did Storm himself: "I wanted to revise, but—you may know this, perhaps, I was impotent, and let the matter go by in apathetic laziness, until it was too late and the printed book lay in front of me."[32] In his answer on 20

January 1867 Turgenev praised the poetic tenderness of the work and the character of Jenni but agreed that the novella might have been better as a tragedy: "A tragic conclusion of your narrative I might also have wished for perhaps—from the aesthetic-misanthropic point of view, that is.—The young souls, however, will savor it more the way it is—and one must take them into consideration, too."[33] Turgenev thus discussed Storm's ambivalence toward the ending of the novella in terms of appealing either to an implied popular, younger audience or to a more aesthetically refined, older, and more misanthropic reader. Storm did change the ending in a very minor way when he published his collected novellas, but he never attempted to—and left no manuscripts that would—draw out the fuller tragic potential that he sensed in his story.[34]

Turgenev's distinction between young souls and aesthetic misanthropes is an attempt at correlating certain types of literary endings with the expectations of social groups, and Turgenev made the *age* cohort a decisive social factor. In his review of Rebecca Harding Davis's and comment on Anna Dickinson's interracial novels Henry James stressed *gender*, as he implied that female authorship and readership had something to do with making these texts plausible.[35] In numerous examples cited in this study, texts have been read for the *racial* backgrounds of their authors and implied audiences. Other exchanges took place around the issue whether a happy union between black and white might not be too much for certain *nationally* defined audiences to "tolerate," and alternative endings have often been linked to what Ducis already called "national character." Different endings could thus be taken as the expressions of distinct national audiences and, by extension, as an indication of national differences. Thus Ducis was concerned about the sensibilities of a national theater audience (the French) for whom the final violence and murder in *Othello* might be too much. More recently, Sander Gilman described a little-known German drama of 1775 by Ernst Lorenz Michael Rathelf, *Die Mohrinn zu Hamburg* ("The Mooress at Hamburg"), and compared it with the French play of 1787 by Jean-Baptiste Radet and Pierre-Yon Barré, *La Négresse; ou, Le Pouvoir de la reconnaissance* ("The Negress; or, The Power of Recognition"). The German tragedy of a triangular dilemma ends with the black woman's suicide; the farcical French comedy, however, with a parentally sanctioned intermarriage. Gilman concludes: "For Radet and Barr[é] interracial marriage is not an insurmountable obstacle. Rathelf's German audience would not have allowed a miscegenous relationship."[36] The different trajectories of two plays in which the representation of interracial unions is possible—they have little else in common—are here viewed as evidence of a national audience's presumed acceptance of, or aversion to, intermarriage.

Yet would we not need more far-reaching empirical evidence to substantiate such generalizations? As we have seen, in *Le Code noir* (1842),

Eugène Scribe's adaptation of Madame Reybaud's novella "Les Épaves" (1838) differed dramatically from its model, whereas Hans Christian Andersen followed it closely. In other words, there was intra-French difference and Franco-Danish similarity on the question of whether or not the story should end with an interracial marriage. As we saw, there were also happy and sad versions of "Inkle and Yarico," all published in England. And how may ambivalence be settled along national lines if even the same author could agonize about, and alter, endings?[37]

The most fully documented case of an author who wrote, published, and produced a play with two endings may be that of Dion Boucicault's *Octoroon* (1859)—my final example here—and again, it is enmeshed in "national" differences. It is the case of the titular heroine Zoe who dies in the "American" version by taking poison in order to escape being raped by the evil upstart and overseer M'Closky. In the "English" versions of the play, however, she survives and gets to marry the man of her choice, her white first cousin George Peyton, a cosmopolitan who has recently returned from Paris, "that siren city." (Her precursor Aurora in Mayne Reid's novel *The Quadroon* ended up marrying the English narrator Rutherford.) What Ducis noticed about his *Othello*, and what Lukács observed about Kleist and Körner, is also true about Boucicault: it took relatively little work—a few changed lines in the printed version or a single short additional act in the play as it was produced in London in 1861 were all that was needed to turn the tragedy into a comedy. Why did Zoe inevitably die in America, but not always in England?—this has been the question. Can the ending indeed be associated with a "national character"? Robert Hogan argued on aesthetic grounds that the tragic ending was stronger, more logical, and serious.[38] Sidney Kaplan reported that American audiences also yearned for a better than tragic conclusion. For example, when *The Octoroon* played in Portland, Maine, in 1860, an ardent abolitionist leaped over the footlights at the very moment at which Zoe was about to take the poison and shouted: "Hold! Zoe, hold! I command the Underground Railway! Fly, fly with me, and I will place you in safety in Queen Victoria's dominion, and God have mercy on whoever interferes."[39] The theatergoer who may have been confusing text and context thus suggested the familiar method of arriving at a happier plot resolution by changing the place of action from the United States to Canada as the place elsewhere. And John Degen showed that other American audiences, too, wanted a happy ending.

It was the Irish American author Boucicault who much preferred the original, serious conclusion and stood by it for nearly two years. Boucicault originally was committed to view in the horrors of Zoe's situation "what he considered a modern tragedy."[40] The New York *Tribune* granted that Boucicault had chosen the right subject for a tragedy in the New World: "The main element of tragedy . . . is inseparable from hereditary social distinctions," hence an American tragedy had to be "connected with the sole remaining hereditary privilege in this country—Slavery" and could be "fierce as ten furies, terrible as hell."[41] The London *Times* also attested to Boucicault a tragic vision: "Mr. Boucicault saw in the peculiar position of the coloured race across the Atlantic the basis for as sharp a tragic collision as might be exhibited in some legend of antiquity."[42]

When the play opened in London in 1861, however, Boucicault experienced more than two weeks of apparently intense pressure by the audience supported by the press.[43] The London *Times* critic reported the audience's dissatisfaction with Zoe's "unfortunate end":

> Several of the audience refused to understand why George could not marry his devoted "Yellow Girl" in one of the many happy States where Louisiana law does not prevail. . . . To this feeling alone can we ascribe the few sounds of disapprobation which followed the descent of the curtain last night, and contrasted so strongly with the enthusiastic applause that had accompanied the first four acts.[44]

Boucicault still justified the "tragic" version as the only authentic one in a letter he wrote the *Times* on the same day, which starts with an exoneration of the slaveholding South from the charge (presented in *Uncle Tom's Cabin*) of excessive ill-treatment and corporeal punishment of the slaves; yet, Boucicault proceeds to argue,

> there are features in slavery far more objectionable than any of those hitherto held up to human execration, by the side of which physical suffering appears as a vulgar detail. Some of these features are, for the first time, boldly exhibited in *The Octoroon*. The audience hailed with every mark of enthusiasm the sunny views of negro life; they were pleased with the happy relations existing between the slaves and the family of which they were dependents; they enjoyed the heartiness with which these slaves were sold, and cheered the planters who bought them.
>
> But, when the Octoroon girl was purchased by the ruffianly overseer to become his paramour, her suicide, to preserve her purity provoked no sympathy whatever. Yet, a few years ago, the same public, in the same theatre, witnessed with deep emotion the death of Uncle Tom under the lash, and accepted the tableau of the poor old negro, his shirt stained with the blood from his lacerated back, crawling across the stage, and dying in slow torture.
>
> In the death of the Octoroon lies the moral and teaching of the whole work. Had this girl been saved, and the drama brought to a happy end, the horrors of her position, irremediable from the very nature of the institution of slavery, would subside into the condition of a temporary annoyance.
>
> While I admit most fully the truth of your statement that the public was disappointed with the termination of the play, and would have been pleased with a happier issue, I feel strangely bewildered at such a change of

feeling. Has public sentiment in this country veered so diametrically on this subject, and is it possible that this straw indicates that the feeling of the English people is taking another course?[45]

With this comment in the London *Times* Boucicault appears to join those critics who connect a "national" audience orientation to different endings. In fact, however, Boucicault may here call something "the feeling of the English people" that he could also imagine writing himself. For a few weeks later, he caved in and he did write a new fifth act. The Adelphi theater advertised Boucicault's change of heart: "In obedience to the universal request that the Slave Girl in the Octoroon should be saved, . . . Mr. Boucicault has altered the drama and brought the story to a happy conclusion."

Was his tragic vision forgotten when Boucicault had to deal with "popular demand"? Degen argued that there were signs in Boucicault's press announcement as well as in the way in which he wrote the new fifth act that he gave in only reluctantly and with some irony. Thus the playwright was obviously quite sarcastic about the audience's desire for a changed ending, overdoing the melodrama, and not only promising a happy lawful union between Zoe and George "in another land"[46] but also bringing even the minor characters Scudder and Dora Sunnyside to a happy union that is quite surprising from the logic of the play, as Scudder previously thought that the rich and good-looking Dora was "a little too thoroughbred—too much of the greyhound" and believed that Zoe has "won this race agin the white, anyhow; it's too late now to start her pedigree" (22). It was as if Boucicault had said, You want a marriage?—I'll give you *two* of them! The curious fact remains, however, that he did make the concession, and that a different version printed in England (ascribed to Boucicault by Degen, who argued that this version was produced neither in England nor in America) also ends with a happy *fourth* act (only minimally altered from the tragic version). The "English" conclusions may thus be merely a historical coincidence rather than an indication of national differences in audience expectations.

Boucicault's sea change offered much opportunity for witticism, and *Punch* writers commented on the issue most fully. Tom Taylor composed a poem upon the alteration of *The Octoroon*, which puts the following lines in Boucicault's mouth:

> Tragic necessity, good-bye—
> And manners change your tune.
> The public voice I'll ratify—
> My pretty *Zoe* shall not die—
> I'll save the *Octoroon*.[47]

How attuned contemporary reviewers were to the cultural meaning of the double ending can be inferred from the anonymous column "Our

***Figure 46***   Zoe and overseer, *Punch* (1861)

Dramatic Correspondent" in *Punch*, signed simply "ONE WHO PAYS" (Fig. 46):

> As far as attractiveness is generally concerned, the *Octoroon* is certainly improved by being altered. Of course there are some people who find fault with the amendment, and who suggest that as tastes differ, and some play-goers delight in being made extremely miserable, the heroine should try to please both sorts of her admirers, by killing herself one night and marrying the next. This would give relief to the monotony of acting the same drama every evening throughout a lengthened run, and would have the advantage that all who felt dissatisfied with either way of ending might repeat their visit and applaud the other. Were SHAKESPEARE living now to write "sensation" dramas, he might, to please the public, make *Othello* kill *Iago* three nights in the week instead of venting his blind wrath upon the virtuous *Desdemona*.[48]

This sarcastic suggestion of alternating tragic and comic performances hints once again at the structural ambivalence in plot lines that are brought to a forced closure at a price: each resolution rests on the denial of another possibility that is being eliminated by the choice made. Authors and audiences often seem to be keenly aware that by accepting one version of a story they may be suppressing another one.

In the age of interactive literature and electronic texts, perhaps inter-racial literature will—or has already begun to—take up and transform the modest proposals made by Ducis and "ONE WHO PAYS"; free the issue from pandering to market forces or national character; make the question of the plot resolution, a question that has been so heavily charged when racial themes were present or perceived—and so brilliantly transformed by Faulkner's *Abalom, Absalom!*—part of the formal structuring of texts; and produce works in which the relativization of "tragedy" and "comedy" that Lukács observed may become an aesthetic possibility in imagining a world of neither, nor, and yet both.

# A Chronology of
# Interracial Literature

| | |
|---|---|
| 5th century B.C.? | Cleobulus. Riddle. |
| A.D. 2nd century | Calpurnius Flaccus. "Natus Æthiopus." |
| A.D. 3rd/4th century | Heliodorus. *Æthiopica*. |
| ca. 900 | *The Book of the Thousand Nights and One Night* emerges (present form ca. 16th/17th c.): esp. "The Story of King Sharyar and His Brother," "The Story of the Eunuch Buhkayt," "The Man of Al Yemen and His Six Slave Girls," and "The Story of the Ensorcelled Prince." |
| 1197–1210 | Wolfram von Eschenbach. *Parzival*. Trans. Jessie Weston (episode of Gachmuret, Belakane and their son Feirefiz, esp. in book I). |
| 1212–18 | Wolfram von Eschenbach. *Willehalm*. |
| 1475 | Masuccio Salernitano. *Il Novellino*. Esp. XXII (story of wife who runs away to Africa with her slave), XXIV (deceived lover), XXV (Geronima). |
| 1566 | Giovanbattista Giraldi Cinthio. *Heccatommithi*. Venezia (seventh novella of third decade is source of *Othello*). |
| 1578 | George Best. "A true discourse on the three Voyages of Discovery, for the finding of a passage to Cathay," in Hakluyt's *Voyages*. |
| 1595 | First British use of word "Mulatto" cited in *Oxford English Dictionary*. |
| 1558–1612 | François Beroalde de Verville. "Le Moyen de Parvenir." |
| 1604 | William Shakespeare. *Othello* (performed in 1605, published in 1622). |
| 1605 | Garcilaso de la Vega. *Historia de la Florida*. |
| 1608 | Antonio Marin Ocete. *Antigüedad y excelencias de Granada* (with remarks on Juan Latino). |

| | |
|---|---|
| 1614 | Marino. "Black you are, but beautiful, o pretty monster . . . " (sonnet). |
| 1613 | Lope de Vega. *La Dama Boba* (finished in ms. 28 April; with scene about Juan Latino). |
| 1633 | George Herbert (1583–1633). "The Blackamoor and Her Loves" (poem). |
| 1646 | Thomas Browne. "Of the Blackness of *Negroes.*" Chapter X of *Pseudodoxia*. |
| 1652 | Don Diego Ximénez de Enciso. *Comedia famosa de Juan Latino*. Ed. Eduardo Juliá Martínez. |
| 1657 | Richard Ligon. *A True and Exact History of the Island of Barbados* (a source of "Inkle and Yarico"). |
| 1657 | Christopher Marlowe. *Lust's Dominion; or, The Lascivious Queen*. |
| 1657 | Eldred Revett. "The fair Nymph scorning a black Boy courting her," "The Inversion," "One Enamour'd on a *Black-moor*," and "A black Nymph scorning a fair Boy Courting her." In *Select Poems: Humane and Divine*, ed. Donald M. Friedman. |
| 1658 | John Cleveland. "A Faire Nimph scorning a Black Boy Courting her." In *The Poems of John Cleveland*, ed. Brian Morris and Eleanor Withington. |
| 1665 | Edward Lord Herbert of Cherbury. "The Brown Beauty," "Sonnet of Black Beauty," "To Mistress Diana Cecil," and "Another Sonnet to Black it self." In *The Poems of Herbert of Cherbury*, ed. G. C. Moore Smith. |
| 1668 | Henry Neville. *The Isle of Pines*. Reprinted in *Shorter Novels: Seventeenth Century*, ed. Philip Henderson. |
| 1678 | A.O. Exquemelin [Hendrik Barentzoon Smeeks]. *De Americaensche Zee-Roovers Behelsende een Pertinent Verhaelvan alle de Roverye En Ommenselÿcke Vreetheeden die de Engelsche en Franse Roovers Tegens de Spanyaerden in America Gepleeght Hebben*. Amsterdam: Jan ten Hoorn (English translation: John Esquemeling, *The Buccaneers of America*). |
| 1688 | Aphra Behn. *Oroonoko: The History of the Royal Slave*. |
| 1692 | Use of "Malatta" in Samuel Sewall's diary (10 October). |
| 1696 | Thomas Southern. *Oroonoko; A Tragedy in Five Acts*. Cited from ed. with intro. by Mrs. Inchbald (Imoinda has become white). |
| 1698 | William Walker. *Victorious Love* (tragedy published by the 19-year-old son of a wealthy Barbadoes planter and produced at Drury Lane in June). |

| | |
|---|---|
| 1698 | William Walsh. *Oroonoko.* |
| 1700 | Samuel Sewall. *The Selling of Joseph* (special condemnation for those who wanted to "connive at the Fornication of their Slaves"). |
| 1702 | Report in Académie royale. |
| 1711 | Richard Steele. "Inkle and Yarico" (*Spectator*, 13 March). (Yarico is Indian in this original; became black in some versions of the cult that followed; trans. German 1713, French 1714, Swedish 1734, Danish 1742, Russian 1759). |
| 1720 | W. P. *The Jamaica Lady*. Reprinted in *Four Before Richardson: Selected English Novels, 1720–1727*, ed. William H. McBurney (picaresque erotic novel contains interesting story of Holmesia and her exploits). |
| 1722 | Jean-Baptiste Labat. *Nouveau voyage aux isles de l'Amérique, contenant l'histoire naturelle de ces pays, l'origine, les moeurs, la religion & le gouvernement, des habitans anciens & modernes, les guerres & les evenements singuliers qui y sont arrivéz pendant le sejour que l'auteur y a fait.* |
| 1728 | William Pattison. "Yarico to Inkle, an Epistle." |
| 1732 | "The Cameleon Lover." Poem in *Charleston Gazette*, 11 March. |
| 1732 | John Whaley. "To a Gentleman in Love with a Negro Woman" and "On a Young Lady Weeping at Oroonoko." |
| 1734 | Anon. "The Story of *Inkle* and *Yarico*. From the 11th *Spectator*." *London Magazine; or, Gentleman's Monthly Intelligencer* III (May 1734): 257–58 (earliest poetic version makes Yarico a Negro virgin). |
| 1740 | Madame de * * * [Villeneuve; Gabrielle Suzanne Barbot]. *La Jeune Américaine et les contes marins* (first version of "La Belle et la Bête"). |
| 1740 | Padre Joseph Gumilla. *El Orinoco ilustrado, y defendido, historia natural, civil, y geographica de este gran rio, y des sus caudalosas vertientes . . .* (de Pauw cites vol. II, 147–48; Alvar: use of *ochavón*). |
| 1743–47 | Thomas Astley. *A New General Collection of Voyages and Travels*, 4 vols. |
| 1745 | Antoine de Laplace. Translation of Aphra Behn's *Oroonoko* (1688). |
| 1746 | Christian Fürchtegott Gellert. "Inkle und Yariko." In *Fabeln und Erzählungen.* |
| 1749 | Don Jorge Juan and Don Antonio de Ulloa. *Noticias secretas de America* (partly trans. *Discourse and Political Reflections on the Kingdoms of Peru*, 1978). *Voyage au Pérou* (de Pauw cites tome I, liv. v, ch. 5, p. 228). |

| | |
|---|---|
| 1753 | Stephen Duck, *Avaro to Amanda* (Inkle/Yarico version). |
| 1755 | [Diderot et al.]. *Encyclopédie; ou, Dictionnaire Raisonné.* Vol. 5 (*Esclave*). |
| 1757 | Madame Leprince de Beaumont, "La Belle et la Bête" (new, shorter version of Villeneuve's tale of 1740). |
| 1764 | G. Mailhol. *Le Philosophe nègre.* |
| 1765 | [Diderot et al.]. *Encyclopédie; ou, Dictionnaire Raisonné.* Vol. 11 ("*Esclave*," "*Nègre*," "*Nègres*" with "*Code noir*"). |
| 1767 | Edward Jerningham. *Yarico to Inkle, an Epistle.* |
| 1770 | C[ornelius] de P[auw]. *Recherches philosophiques sur les américains; ou, Mémoires interessants pour servir à l'histoire de l'espèce humaine.* 2 vols. |
| 1773 | Thomas Day and John Bicknell. "The Dying Negro" (black slave in love with a white woman). |
| 1774 | [Edward Long]. *The History of Jamaica; Or, General Survey of the Ancient and Modern State of the Island: With Reflections on Its Situation, Settlements, Inhabitants, Climate, Products, Commerce, Laws, and Government.* 3 vols. |
| 1775 | Ernst Lorenz Michael Rathelf. *Die Mohrinn zu Hamburg* (play; a variation on Gellert's "Die beiden Schwarzen"?). |
| 1776 | Buffon, *De l'homme*; esp. *Suppléments* à l'article "Mulets." |
| 1777 | Buffon, *Additions* to *Variétés dans l'espèce humaine.* |
| 1778 | James de la Cour. "In Laudem Æthiopissae." |
| 1779 | Carl Franz Guolfinger. *Die Negersklaven* (play). |
| 1780 | Pierre Louis Moreau de Maupertuis, *La Vénus physique.* |
| 1782–86 | Karl August Musäus. "Melechsala." In *Volksmärchen der Deutschen* . |
| 1785 | Immanuel Kant. "Bestimmung des Begriffs einer Menschenrace." In *Gesammelte Schriften*, Akademie-Ausgabe, VIII. |
| 1787 | *Adventures of Jonathan Corncob, Loyal American Refugee. Written by Himself,* esp. ch. 13, "The West-Indian way of whitewashing, or rather the true way of washing the blackamoor white. Jonathan begins to lose his good opinion of Barbadoes." |
| 1787 | [Jean-Baptiste] Radet, and [Pierre-Yon] Barré. *La Négresse; ou, Le Pouvoir de la reconnaissance* ("The Negress, or the Power of Recognition"). Paris: Brunet. |

| | |
|---|---|
| 1787 | Bernardin de Saint-Pierre. *Paul et Virginie* (no mixed couple, but very influential on exoticism). |
| 1788 | Hannah More. "The Slave Trade." |
| 1789 | J. Lavallée. *Le Nègre comme il y a peu de Blancs.* |
| 1789 | Lecointe-Marsillac. *Le More-Lack.* |
| 1790 | Baron de Wimpffen. *St.-Domingue.* |
| 1791 | C[harles] W[ilson] Peale. "ACCOUNT of a Person born a NEGRO, or a very DARK MULATTOE, who afterwards became WHITE." *Universal Asylum and Columbian Magazine* 7.6 (Dec.): 409–10 (the Henry Moss case). |
| 1792 | Hugh Henry Brackenridge. *Modern Chivalry: Containing the Adventures of Captain John Farrago, and Teague O'Regan, His Servant.* Vol. II (ridicules interest in Moss). |
| 1795 | Charles-Antoine Guillaume Pigault-Lebrun. *Le Blanc et le noir.* |
| 1796 | Jacques Grasset de Saint Sauveur. *Hortense; ou, La Jolie courtisane. Sa vie libertine, à Paris, et ses aventures tragiques avec le nègre Zéphire dans les déserts de l'Amérique.* |
| 1796 | August von Kotzebue. *Die Negersklaven* (The Negro Slaves). |
| 1796 | [Henry Moss]. "A Great Curiosity." In Benjamin Rush, "Commonplace Book," broadside pasted in with entry for 27 July. |
| 1796 | Captain John Stedman. *Narrative of a Five Years Expedition against the Revolted Negroes of Surinam, in Guiana, on the Wild Coast of South America, from the year 1772 to 1777: elucidating the History of that Country, and describing its Productions, viz. Quadrupeds, Birds, Fishes, Reptiles, Trees, Shrubs, Fruits and Roots; with an Account of the Indians of Guiana and Negroes of Guinea.* Transcribed from 1790 manuscript, ed. Richard and Sally Price (see also Child 1834 for the "Joanna" narrative). |
| 1797 | M.[édéric] L.[ouis] É.[lie] Moreau de Saint-Méry. *Déscription topographique, physique, civile, politique et historique de a partie française de l'isle Saint-Domingue.* 2 vols. |
| 1797 | J. B. Picquenard. *Adonis, anecdote coloniale* (rapes and sadism in Haitian Revolution). |
| 1789 | J. B. Picquenard. *Adonis; ou, Le Bon nègre.* |
| 1800 | J. B. Picquenard. *Zoflora; ou, La Bonne negresse.* |
| 1801 | Maria Edgeworth. *Belinda* (Juba subplot). |

| | |
|---|---|
| 1803 | *La Mulâtre comme il y a beaucoup de Blanches, ouvrage pouvant faire suite au Nègre comme il a peu de Blancs.* 2 vols. |
| 1804 | Franz Kratter. *Die Sclavin in Surinam.* |
| 1806 | Ch. de Cornillon. *Odes, suivies d'une lettre sur l'esclavage des Nègres* (contains an ode to a quadroon woman Angelique by this proslavery poet). |
| 1806 | Thomas Moore. *Odes and Epistles* (incl. poem "To Thomas Hume, Esq. M. D."). |
| 1808 | [Miss (Mary?) Hassal]. *Secret History; or, The Horrors of St. Domingo in a Series of Letters, Written by a Lady at Cape François, to Colonel Burr* (as titles promise, and with strong focus on erotic and violent occurrences: e.g., 18–19, 145–53, 169–72). |
| 1810 ff | Johann Friedrich Ernst Albrecht. *Scenen der Liebe aus Amerikas heißen Zonen.* |
| 1810 | Maria Edgeworth. *Belinda* (revised ed. in *Tales and Novels*); see also her letter to Mrs. Barbaud of 1810 (the Juba intermarriage subplot suppressed at the advice of author's father). |
| 1811 | Heinrich von Kleist. *Die Verlobung in St. Domingo.* |
| 1812 | Theodor Körner. *Toni: Ein Drama in drei Aufzügen* (Gilman; a dramatization of Kleist 1811). |
| 1814 | William D[i]mond, Esq. *The Ethiop.* Composed for the Piano Forte by R. Taylor. |
| 1815 | Thomas Jefferson. Letter to Francis Gray (4 March). |
| 1819 | Charles de Rémuzat. *L'Insurrection de Saint-Domingue* (*L'Habitation de Saint-Domingue*), 5-act drama. |
| 1820 | Victor Hugo. *Bug-Jargal* (text written in 1818; first version). |
| 1821 | James Madison. "Jonathan Bull and Mary Bull: An Inedited Manuscript." Printed for Presentation by J. C. M'Guire. ("Written but not published at the period of the Missouri question, 1821.") |
| 1822 | *Mœurs des trois couleurs aux Antilles.* |
| 1822 | Horace de Saint-Aubin [Honoré de Balzac]. *Le Nègre: mélodrame en trois actes* (unpublished ms., rejected by Théâtre de la Gaîté; published in 1930). |
| 1824 | Mme. [Claire de Kersaint] la duchesse de [Durfort-] Duras. *Ourika* (English trans. by [George Wallis Haven]). |
| 1824 | Mélesville [Anne Honoré Joseph de Duveyrier] and [Pierre Frédéric (or Frédéric?) Adolphe] Carmouche. *Ourika; ou, La Petite Négresse.* Drame en un acte, mêlée des couplets. |

| 1824 | Mme. Adèle Huvey Daminois. *Lydie; ou, La Créole.* 4 vols. Leterrier. |
|---|---|
| 1824 | Mme. Augustine Dudon. *La Nouvelle Ourika; ou, Les Avantages se l'éducation* (about the natural child of a quarteronne.) |
| 1824 | J. T. Merle and F. de Courcy. *Ourika; ou, L'Orpheline africaine.* |
| 1824 | Victor Vignon Rétif de la Bretonne. *Og* (parody of *Ourika*). |
| 1825 | Gaspard de Pons. "Ourika l'Africaine." *Inspirations poétiques*, reprinted in *Adieux poétiques*, vol. 2, pp. 41–46. |
| 1825 | Ulric Guttinger. *Ourika.* |
| 1825 | François Gérard. *Ourika* (a painting). |
| 1826 | François-René de Chateaubriand. *Les Natchez.* |
| 1826 | James Fenimore Cooper. *The Last of the Mohicans: A Narrative of 1757.* |
| 1826 | Ignaz Franz Castelli. *Urika, die Negerinn.* In *Dramatisches Sträußchen* 11: 133–78. |
| 1826 | Mme. Ballent and J. Quantin. *La Négresse* (*Ourika*-inspired). |
| 1826 | Victor Hugo. *Bug-Jargal.* Both versions reprinted in *Bug Jargal; ou, La Révolution haïtienne*, ed. Roger Toumson. |
| 1826 | Christopher E. Lefroy, ed. *Outalissi: A Tale of Dutch Guiana* (*Ourika* influenced). |
| 1827/28 | Aleksandr Sergeevič Puškin. *Arap Petra Velikogo* ("The Blackamoor of Peter the Great"). |
| 1829 | Prosper Mérimée. *Tamango.* |
| 1829 | David Walker. *Appeal.* |
| 1830/31 | Édouard Corbière. "Petite histoire d'un Mulâtre en France." *Le Navigateur*, 28–35. |
| 1832 | Charles Castellan. "La Mulâtresse." *Les Palmiers*, 137–38. |
| 1832 | Édouard Corbière. "Le Bamboula." *Le Cabinet de lecture*, 4 Sept. |
| 1833 | [Charles James Cannon]. *Oran the Outcast; or, A Season in New York.* |
| 1833 | Victor Charlier and Eugène Chapus. "Le Dernier des Tarquins," "L'Épave," "Jean-Pol," "M. de Cluvigny." In *Titime, histoires de l'autre monde.* |
| 1834 | Lydia Maria Child. "Joanna." In *The Oasis* (story of slave woman Joanna, derived from Stedman 1796), 65–105. |

| | |
|---|---|
| 1834 | Édouard Corbière. "Le Mariage blanc et noir." *Le Cabinet de lecture*, 14 July. |
| 1834 | Édouard Corbière. *Le Négrier, aventures de mer*. |
| 1834 | David M. Reese. *A Brief Review of the First Annual Report of the American Anti-Slavery Society* (pamphlet). |
| 1834 | David Ruggles. *The "Extinguisher" Extinguished! or David M. Reese, M.D. "Used Up"* (pamphlet). |
| 1834 | Antony Thouret. *Toussaint le Mulâtre*. |
| 1835 | Gustave de Beaumont. *Marie; ou, L'Esclavage aux Etats-Unis, tableau de mœurs américaines*. Transl. and ed. Barbara Chapman, *Marie; or, Slavery in the United States*. |
| 1835 | Oliver Bolokitten [Jerome B. Holgate]. *A Sojourn in the City of Amalgamation in the Year of Our Lord, 19——*. |
| 1835 | Louis de Maynard de Queilhe. *Outre-mer*. |
| 1835 | Alexis de Tocqueville. *Democracy in America*, esp. vol. I, ch. xviii. |
| 1836 | John Quincy Adams. "The Character of Desdemona." *American Monthly Magazine* 1: 209–17. |
| 1836 | [Richard Hildreth]. *The Slave; or, Memoirs of Archy Moore*. |
| 1837 | Alfred Maillant et Legoyt. *L'Esclave Andréa*, drama in 5 acts. |
| 1837 | Victor Séjour. "Mœurs coloniales: le Mulâtre." *Revue des Colonies* (March 1837): 376–92; reprinted with introduction by David O'Connell, *Revue de Louisiane* 1.2 (Winter 1972): 60–75 (see 1858). |
| 1838 | Madame Charles [Henriette Etienne Fanny] Reybaud. "Les Épaves." *Revue de Paris* (Feb.); reprinted in *Valdepeiras* (Paris: Hachette, 1864). |
| 1839 | Alexis Decomberousse et Benjamin Antier. *Le Marché de Saint-Pierre*, mélodrama in 5 acts (dramatization of Reybaud 1838, produced Théâtre de Gaîté, 20 July 1839). |
| 1839 | Paul Foucher et Laurencin [Paul-Aimé Chapelle]. *Maria: drame en 2 actes;* reprinted in *Magasin théatral* 24. |
| 1839 | Frederick Marryat. *A Diary in America*, esp. vol. III: 56–58. |
| 1839 | Cirilo Villaverde. *Cecilia Valdés* (first version of part 1). |
| 1840 | Hans Christian Andersen. *Mulatten: originalt romantisk Drama i Fem Akter* (inspired by Reybaud 1838). |

| | |
|---|---|
| 1840 | Eugène Chapus. "L'Amour d'une Créole." *Babel: publication de la société des gens de lettres* II, 37–76. |
| 1840 | Lamartine. *La Marseillaise noire*. |
| 1840 | Harriet Martineau. *The Hour and the Man*. |
| 1841 | Lydia Maria Child. "Annette Gray." *Anti-Slavery Standard*, 22 July. |
| 1841 | Gertrudis Gómez de Avellaneda. *Sab*. |
| 1841 | [Joseph Holt Ingraham]. *The Quadroone; or, St. Michael's Day*. |
| 1841 | William Gilmore Simms. "Caloya; or, The Loves of the Driver." *The Magnolia* 3 (May, June, July): 222–29, 264–73, 317–24. |
| 1842 | Lydia Maria Child. "The Quadroons." *Liberty Bell*; reprinted in *Fact and Fiction*. |
| 1842 | Henry Wadsworth Longfellow. "The Quadroon Girl." |
| 1842 | Sarmiento. "El Oro, ó Dios nos assista!" 5 May. |
| 1842 | Eugène Scribe. *Le Code noir*, opéra-comique in 3 acts (dramatization of Reybaud 1838); in *Œuvres complètes: opéras comiques*, 277–382. |
| 1842 | William Gilmore Simms. *Beauchampe; or, The Kentucky Tragedy. A Tale of Passion*. 2 vols. (Kinney) (sequel to *Charlemont; or, The Pride of the Village: A Tale of Kentucky*). |
| 1842 | Alfred Lord Tennyson. "Locksley Hall." |
| 1842 | Walt Whitman. *Franklin Evans; or, The Inebriate. A Tale of the Times*. In *New World* II (no. 10, Extra Series, Nov.) (1846 version significantly changed). |
| 1843 | Alexandre Dumas (père). *Georges*. |
| 1843 | J. C. Nott. "The Mulatto a Hybrid—Probable Extermination of the Two Races If the Whites and Blacks Are Allowed to Intermarry." *American Journal of Medical Sciences* 66 (July): 252–56. |
| 1843 | Eugène Sue. *Les Mystères de Paris*. Reprinted in 1851. Esp. ch. xxi-xxii. |
| 1845 | *Horatio der Mulatt; romantisches Drama in fünf Aufzügen*. Nach H.C. Andersen frei bearbeitet von Le Petit. |
| 1845 | Frederick Douglass. *The Narrative of Frederick Douglass, an American Slave*. |
| 1845 | Margaret Fuller. Letter to Ellis and Louisa Loring, 22 Aug. |
| 1845 | Armand Lanusse, ed. *Les Cenelles*. |

| | |
|---|---|
| 1846 | Anicet Bourgeois and Philippe Dumanoir. *Le Docteur noir*, drama in 7 acts [Porte Saint-Martin, 20 July 1846]. *The Black Doctor: A Drama in Five Acts*. Trans. I. V. Bridgeman and adapted by publisher (first performed Paris 30 Junly [*sic*] 1846; as played at the Royal Victoria Theatre, 13 Nov. 1846) (5 acts). *The Black Doctor*. Adapted for the English stage by Ira Aldridge. 1847 [4 acts]. |
| 1846 | [Howard Meeks]. *The Fanatic; or, The Perils of Peter Pliant, the Poor Pedagogue*. |
| 1846 | [Howard Meeks]. *Winona; or, The Brown Maid of the South* (no copy known). |
| 1847 | Charlotte Brontë. *Jane Eyre*. |
| 1847 | Paul Féval. *Le Mendiant noir*. |
| 1848 | William Henry Brisbane. "Amanda: A Tale for the Times." Serialized in *National Era*, 23 March 1848: 48; 30 March: 52; and 6 April: 56; published as book *Amanda: A Tale for the Times*. |
| 1848 | Elizabeth Barrett Browning. "The Runaway Slave at Pilgrim's Point" (poem). |
| 1848 | I[gnaz Vincent] F[ranz] Castelli. "Die Verlassenschaft des Pflanzers." *Erzählungen* Bd. 4 (*Sämmtliche Werke* Bd. 8). |
| 1848 | Henry Senior. *Charles Vernon*. |
| 1848 | Michael William Balfe. *Der Mulatte: Romantische Oper*. |
| 1849 | Mrs. Emma D. E. Nevitt Southworth. *Retribution; or, The Vale of Shadows. A Tale of Passion*. |
| 1849 | Albert W. Sumner. *The Sea Lark; or, The Quadroon of Louisiana. A Thrilling Tale of Land and Sea*. |
| 1850 | Alphonse de Lamartine. *Toussaint-Louverture*, drama in 5 acts [Porte Saint-Martin, 14 Jan.]. |
| 1850 | Daniel Whitney. *Warren: A Tragedy in Five Acts Designated to Illustrate the Protection Which the Federal Union Extends to Citizens of Massachusetts*. |
| 1851 | Barbey d'Aurevilly. *Une vieille maîtresse*, reedited with a preface by Paul Morand. |
| 1852 | Paul Heyse. "Urica" (written in November). In *Novellen in Versen* I (*Gesammelte Werke* 2): 1–29. |
| 1852 | [Richard Hildreth]. *The White Slave; or, Memoirs of a Fugitive* (chapters 37–59 added; see 1836, 1856). |
| 1852 | Harriet Beecher Stowe. *Uncle Tom's Cabin; or, Life Among the Lowly*. Esp. ch. xxxiv, "The Quadroon's Story." |
| 1853 | William G. Allen. *American Prejudice Against Color* (Allen, the professor of Greek and German at Central |

College, had just married one of his white students, causing a scandal).

| | |
|---|---|
| 1853 | William Wells Brown. *Clotel; or, The President's Daughter.* |
| 1853 | M. J. McIntosh. *The Lofty and the Lowly; or, Good in All and None All-Good.* 2 vols. |
| 1853 | Pocahontas [Emily C. Pearson]. *Cousin Franck's Household; or, Scenes in the Old Dominion.* |
| 1853 | Theodore Poesche and Charles Goepp. *The New Rome; or, The United States of the World.* |
| 1853 | [R.] Max Radiguet [or Max-Radiguet?]. "Un bamboula à la Martinique." *La France maritime.* 2e éd. IV: 334–36 [or 355?]. |
| 1854 | *El Mulato: periódico politico, literario y de costumbres* (includes serialized novel "El Negro martir"). |
| 1854 | Mary Langdon [Mrs. Mary H. Pike]. *Ida May: A Story of Things Actual and Possible.* |
| 1855 | Elizabeth D. Livermore. *Zoe; or, The Quadroon's Triumph: A Tale for the Times.* |
| 1855 | W. W. Smith. *The Planter's Victim* (Brown (identical with *The Yankee Slave Driver, 1859*); Zanger). |
| 1856 | Paul Creyton [John Townsend Trowbridge]. *Neighbor Jackwood.* |
| 1856 | Richard Hildreth. *Archy Moore, the White Slave; or, Memoirs of a Fugitive. With a New Introduction* (see 1836, 1852). |
| 1856 | Frederick Law Olmstead. *A Journey in the Seaboard Slave States* (description of alliances between upperclass white men and Quadroon women). |
| 1856 | James S. Peacocke. *The Creole Orphans; or, Lights and Shadows of Southern Life. A Tale of Louisiana.* |
| 1856 | Mayne Reid. *The Quadroon; or, A Lover's Adventures in Louisiana*; cited from *The Quadroon; or, Adventures in the Far West.* |
| 1856 | Sidney A. Story, Jr. [Mary Pike]. *Caste: A Story of Republican Equality.* |
| 1856 | Harriet Beecher Stowe. *Dred: A Tale of the Great Dismal Swamp.* |
| 1856 | George Vashon, *Autographs of Freedom*, esp. poems "Vincent Ogé" and "A Life Day." |
| 1857 | Harriet Hamline Bigelow. *The Curse Entailed.* |
| 1857 | Van Buren Denslow. *Owned and Disowned; or, The Chattel Child.* |
| 1857 | [Mattie Griffiths]. *Autobiography of a Female Slave.* |

| | |
|---|---|
| 1857 | Charles Kingsley. *Two Years Ago* (Girouard, about doctor and subplot "Elsie"; Marie, "La Cordifiamma" in ch. 9, "Am I Not a Woman and a Sister?"). |
| 1857 | J.[ohn] T.[ownsend] Trowbridge. *Neighbor Jackwood: A Domestic Drama in Five Acts* (produced 16 March, 1857). |
| 1857 | Frank J. Webb. *The Garies and Their Friends.* |
| 1858 | "The Quadroon's Revenge." *National Anti-Slavery Standard* 19 (Sept./Oct.). |
| 1858 | William Wells Brown. *The Escape; or, A Leap for Freedom.* |
| 1858 | Lydia Maria Child. "The Stars and Stripes: A Melodrama." In *The Liberty Bell.* |
| 1858 | Mrs. C. W. [Mary (Andrews)] Denison. *Old Hepsy* (reviewed in *National Era*, 8 April). |
| 1858 | Frances H. McDougall. *Shamah in Pursuit of Freedom; or, The Branded Hand.* |
| 1858 | Victor Séjour. "The Brown Overcoat." |
| 1858 | Dr. C. Testut. *Le Vieux Salomon* (written 1858; published in 1872; French plantation novel). |
| 1859 | Dion Boucicault. *The Octoroon; or, Life in Louisiana. A Play in Five Acts.* |
| 1859 | Martin R. Delany. *Blake; or, The Huts of America.* In *Anglo-African Magazine* (Jan.–July). |
| 1859 | Frances Ellen Watkins Harper. "Two Offers." *The Anglo-African Magazine* I, 9 and 10 (Sept.–Oct.): 288–91, 311–13. |
| 1859 | William White Smith. *The Yankee Slave Driver; or, The Black and White Rivals.* |
| 1859 | Mrs. H. E. Wilson. *Our Nig; or, Sketches from the Life of a Free Black in a Two-Story White House, North. Showing That Slavery's Shadows Fall Even There.* |
| 1859/60 | Mattie Griffiths. "Madge Vertner." 38 chapters serialized in *National Anti-Slavery Standard* 20–21 (30 July 1859–5 May 1860). |
| 1860 | *Running a Thousand Miles for Freedom; or, The Escape of William and Ellen Craft from Slavery.* |
| 1860 | [Mrs. G. M. Flanders]. *The Ebony Idol.* |
| 1860 | J. Davis Harris. "A Summer on the Borders of the Caribbean Sea." In Howard H. Bell, *Black Separatism and the Caribbean.* |
| 1860 | H. S. Hosmer. *Adela, the Octoroon.* |
| 1860 | William Dean Howells. "The Pilot's Story." *Atlantic Monthly* (Oct.). |

| | |
|---|---|
| 1860 | William Henry Peck. *The Moctoroon*. Performed in New York by Christy's Minstrels at Niblo's Concert Saloon, 23 Jan. |
| 1861 | Charles Baudelaire. *Les Fleurs du mal*. "Sed non satiata" (26 & 27). |
| 1861 | Linda Brent [Harriet Jacobs]. *Incidents in the Life of a Slave Girl*. |
| 1861 | Rev. H[iram] Mattison. *Louisa Picquet, the Octoroon Slave and Concubine: A Tale of Southern Slave Life*. |
| 1861 | M. T. S. [Mary] Putnam. *Tragedy of Success* and *Tragedy of Errors*. |
| 1861 | Mrs. Metta Victoria Victor. *Maum Guinea, and Her Plantation "Children"; or, Holiday-Week on a Louisiana Estate: A Slave Romance*. |
| 1862 | "The Deserter." *Harper's Weekly* 6 (14 June, 1862): 37–38. |
| 1862 | "In Western Missouri." *Harper's Weekly* 6 (1 March, 1862): 138–39. |
| 1862 | S. C. Blackwell. "Fugitives at the West." *Continental Monthly* 1 (May 1862): 584–91. |
| 1862[?] | Miss M[ary] E. Braddon. *The Octoroon*, n.d. (1896 is Harvard library acquisition date; Rogers II: 331 dates it 1862; Braddon originally serialized "The Octoroon; or, The Lily of Louisiana" in *The Halfpenny Journal* sometime between 1861 and 1865, shortly after the publication, and at the peak of the publicity, of Boucicault's *Octoroon*; plagiarized from Boucicault and Reid). |
| 1862 | Edmund Kirke [James Roberts Gilmore]. *Among the Pines; or, South in Secession-Time* (vol. 1 of trilogy). |
| 1862 | Nora Perry. "Clotilde and the Contraband." *Harper's Monthly* 24 (May 1862): 764–71. |
| 1862 | M. T. S. [Mary] Putnam. *Tragedy of Success*. |
| 1863 | Louis Agassiz's letters to Dr. Howe. |
| 1863 | [Louisa May Alcott]. "The Brothers." *Atlantic Monthly* 12 (Nov. 1863): 584–95. |
| 1863 | Louisa May Alcott. "M.L." |
| [1863] | [David Goodman Croly and George Wakeman]. *Miscegenation: The Theory of the Blending of the Races Applied to the American White and Negro* (appeared in 1863 but with 1864 imprimatur; see Kaplan, "Miscegenation," 277). |
| 1863 | [James Roberts Gilmore]. *My Southern Friends* (Kinney) (vol. 2 of trilogy). |
| 1864 | "Buried Alive." *Harper's Weekly* 8 (7 May, 1864): 302. |

| | |
|---|---|
| 1864 | "The Devil's Frying Pan." *Harper's Weekly* 8 (7 May, 1864): 294–95. |
| 1864 | "The Revenge of the Goddess." *Harper's Weekly* 8 (24 Sept., 1864): 622–23. |
| 1864 | "Why It Could Not Be." *Harper's Weekly* 8 (25 June, 1864): 406–7. |
| 1864 | James H. Hackett, *Notes and Comments upon Certain Plays and Actors of Shakespeare, With Criticisms and Correspondence.* Pp. 217–28, also 229 and the reprint of "Desdemona," 234–49. |
| 1864 | Edmund Kirke [James Roberts Gilmore]. *Down in Tennessee, and Back by Way of Richmond* (vol. 3 of trilogy). |
| 1864 | Epes Sargent. *Peculiar: A Tale of the Great Transition.* |
| 1864 | L. Seaman, Ll.D. *What Miscegenation Is! and What we are to expect now that Mr. Lincoln is re-elected.* |
| 1864 | George Boyer Vashon. "A Life-Day" (126-line poem, in sections "Morning," "Noon," and "Night," tells story of marriage between white southerner and slave woman, that ends with his death and the family's reenslavement). |
| 1865 | Helen Pierson. "Chip." *Harper's Monthly* 31 (July 1865): 254–58. |
| 1865 | Elizabeth Stoddard. *Two Men.* |
| 1865 | Theodor Storm. "Von jenseit des Meeres." *Westermanns Illustrierte Deutsche Monatshefte,* Jan. 1865 (written in 1863/64; book publication 1867). |
| 1866 | D. R. Castleton. "The St. Leons." *Harper's Monthly* 33 (Aug. 1866): 373–84. |
| 1866 | W. H. Palmer. "A Woman." *Galaxy* 2 (Nov. 1866): 413–23. |
| 1866 | de Roosmalen. *Le Nègre. Le Mulatre. Plaidoyers dramatiques en faveur des hommes de couleur, présentés sous la forme de comédies.* |
| 1866 | M. Schele De Vere. "The Freedman's Story." *Harper's Monthly* 33 (Oct. 1866): 647–57. |
| 1867 | Lorenzo D. Blackson. *The Rise and Progress of the Kingdom of Light and Darkness.* |
| 1867 | Lydia Maria Child. *A Romance of the Republic.* |
| 1867 | James Schönberg. *Oscar the Half Blood: A Sensational Play in a Prologue and Four Acts.* Performed at Wood's Theatre, New York, 27 March; pub. Dick's Standard Plays #474. |
| 1867 | Edward Spencer. "Tristan: A Story." *Galaxy* 3.1 (1 Jan.): 5–23; 3.2 (15 Jan.): 117–40; 3.3 (1 Feb.): 229–39. |

| | |
|---|---|
| 1868 | Rebecca Harding Davis. *Waiting for the Verdict.* |
| 1868 | John William De Forest. "A Gentleman of an Old School." *Atlantic Monthly* 21 (May 1868): 546–55. |
| 1868 | Anna E. Dickinson. *What Answer?* |
| 1869 | Louisa May Alcott. "An Hour" and "My Contraband." In *Camp and Fireside Stories.* |
| 1869 | Wilkie Collins and Charles Fechter. *Black and White. A Drama in Three Acts* (first produced by Charles Dickens). |
| 1869 | John Hay. "The Foster-Brothers." *Harper's Monthly* 39 (Sept. 1869): 535–44. |
| 1870 | Freeman S. Bowley. "A Dark Night on Picket." *Overland Monthly* 5 (July 1870): 31–37. |
| 1870 | T[heoda] F[oster] B[ush]. "Clara's Choice." *New National Era* 1 (24 March, 1870): 4. |
| 1870 | Maria Louise Pool. "Told by an Octoroon." *Galaxy* 10 (Dec. 1870): 827–38. |
| 1871 | *The Sisters of Orleans: A Tale of Race and Social Conflict.* |
| 1871 | Thomas Detter. *Nellie Brown; or, The Jealous Wife, With Other Sketches.* Esp. short story "Octoroon Slave of Cuba" (119–42) and sketch "My Trip to Baltimore" (143–48). |
| 1872 | Alice Dutton. "The Castleworth Tragedy." *Atlantic Monthly* 29 (Feb. 1872): 197–209. |
| 1874 | George Washington Cable. "'Tite Poulette." *Scribner's* (Oct.). |
| 1874 | Henry Churton [Albion W. Tourgée]. *Toinette: A Novel.* |
| 1874 | Constance Fenimore Woolson. "Jeannette." *Scribner's Monthly* 9 (Dec. 1874): 232–43. |
| 1875 | Bernardo Guimarães. *A Escrava Isaura* (Brazilian antislavery novel; French translation: *L'esclave Isaura*, 1986). |
| 1876 | Mme. van den Bussche [Marie Emery]. *Les Nègres de la Louisiane; scènes américaines.* 5ème éd. |
| 1877 | Sarah A. Dorsey. *Panola: A Tale of Louisiana.* |
| 1879 | George Washington Cable. *Old Creole Days.* |
| 1879/80 | George Washington Cable. *The Grandissimes: A Story of Creole Life*; first in *Scribner's*, Nov. 1879–Oct. 1880. |
| 1880 | Joaquim Maria Achado de Assis. *Memorie postume di Braz Cubas.* |
| 1880 | Sherwood Bonner. "Volcanic Interlude." |
| 1880 | Albion W. Tourgée. *Bricks Without Straw.* |

| | |
|---|---|
| 1881 | Aluísio [Tancredo Gonçalves de] Azevedo. *O Mulato*. Translations: *El Mulato*, versión castellana de Jesús de Amber; *Der Mulatte*, trans. into German by Michael O. Güsten, 1964; *Mulatto*, trans. by Murray Graeme MacNicholl, ed. Daphne Patai, 1990. |
| 1881 | George Washington Cable. *Madame Delphine* (first published in *Scribner's*, May, June, July). |
| 1881 | Pierre Loti. *Le Roman d'un Spahi*. |
| 1881 | Dr. Alfred Mercier. *L'Habitation St. Ybars* (Louisiana novel). |
| 1881 | Albion W. Tourgée. *A Royal Gentleman* (reprint of Churton, 1874). |
| 1882 | *Subdued Southern Nobility: A Southern Ideal. By One of the Nobility*. |
| 1882 | Bartley Campbell. "The White Slave" (play holograph; printed 1909). |
| 1882 | Cirilo Villaverde. *Cecilia Valdés; o La Loma del Ángel. Novela de costumbres cubanas* (critical ed., 1953). Trans. Mariano J. Lorente, *The Quadroon; or, Cecilia Valdes. A Romance of Old Havana*, 1935. |
| 1883 | Albion W. Tourgée. *Hot Plowshares: A Novel*. |
| 1884 | *The Shadow of the War: A Story of the South in Reconstruction Times*. |
| 1884 | L. V. Denance. *La Famille de Martel le planteur: épisode de la révolution de Saint-Domingue*. |
| 1884 | Joel Chandler Harris. "Where's Duncan?" (see also 1891). |
| 1884 | Frederic Allison Tupper. *Moonshine: A Story of the Reconstruction Period*. |
| 1885 | *Le Planteur de la Guyane ou les Nègres chrétiens*. Trans. and reprod. from the German, by P.-C. [F.-C.] Gérard. |
| 1885 | Henry W. Grady. "In Plain Black and White." *Century* 29.7 (1885): 909–17 (a response to "The Freedman's Case in Equity"). |
| 1886 | Jules-Berlioz d'Auriac. *La Guerre noire: souvenirs de Saint-Domingue*. |
| 1886 | Margaret Holmes Bates. *The Chamber Over the Gate*. |
| 1886 | James H. W. Howard. *Bond and Free: A True Tale of Slave Times*. |
| 1886 | Grace Elizabeth King. "Bonne Maman." *Harper's* (July). |
| 1886 | Grace Elizabeth King. "Monsieur Motte." *New Princeton Review* (Jan.). |

| | |
|---|---|
| 1887 | R. T. Buckner. *Towards the Gulf: A Romance of Louisiana.* |
| 1887 | Mary Peabody Mann. *Juanita: A Romance of Cuba Fifty Years Ago.* |
| 1887 | Giuseppe Verdi. *Otello.* |
| 1888/89 | George Washington Cable. "Attalie Brouillard," "The Haunted House on Royal Street," and "Salome Müller, the White Slave." In *Strange True Stories of Louisiana* (first published in *Scribner's*, Nov. 1888–Oct. 1889). |
| 1888 | James Edwin Campbell. "The Pariah's Love." *AME Church Review* 5 (April 1889): 370–74. |
| 1888 | Lizzie M. Elwyn. *Millie; the Quadroon* (drama). |
| 1888 | Grace Elizabeth King. *Monsieur Motte* (first part is the story first pub. in 1886). |
| 1889 | Charles W. Chesnutt. "What Is a White Man?" *Independent*, 30 May. |
| 1889 | Anatole France. *Balthasar.* |
| 1889 | William N. Harben. *White Marie.* |
| 1889 | Guy de Maupassant. "Boitelle." In *La main gauche.* Reprinted in *Contes et nouvelles* II, ed. Louis Forestier. |
| 1890 | *Miss Breckenridge: A Daughter of Dixie.* |
| 1890 | Lafcadio Hearn. *Two Years in the French West Indies* (a perfect companion piece to *Youma*). |
| 1890 | Lafcadio Hearn. *Youma.* |
| 1890 | Grace Elizabeth King. *Monsieur Motte.* |
| 1890 | Albion W. Tourgée. *Pactolus Prime.* |
| 1891 | Joel Chandler Harris. "Where's Duncan?" In *Balaam and His Master and Other Sketches and Stories.* |
| 1891 | William Dean Howells. *An Imperative Duty.* |
| 1892 | George Washington Cable. "A West Indian Slave Insurrection." *Scribner's Magazine* 12.6 (Dec. 1892): 709–20, also included in *The Flower of the Chapdelaines*, 1918. |
| 1892 | Matt Crim. "Was It an Exceptional Case?" (first pub. 1891). In *In Beaver Cove and Elsewhere.* |
| 1892 | Frederick Douglass. *The Life and Times of Frederick Douglass.* |
| 1892 | Mrs. Frances E. W. Harper. *Iola Leroy; or, Shadows Uplifted.* |
| 1892 | Marietta Holley. *Samantha on the Race Problem* (see also 1894). |

| | |
|---|---|
| 1893 | George Washington Cable. *Old Creole Days*. Includes "'Tite Poulette." |
| 1893 | Kate Chopin. "The Father of Désirée's Baby." *Vogue*. |
| 1893 | Sara B. Groenvelt. "Otille the Quadroone: A Tragedy in Five Acts." Typescript, Library of Congress. |
| 1893 | Richard Malcolm Johnston. "Ishmael." *Lippincott's* 52: 359–66. |
| 1893 | Grace Elizabeth King. *Balcony Stories*. Reprinted in 1914, esp. "The Little Convent Girl." |
| 1894 | "Josiah Allen's Wife" [Marietta Holley]. *Samantha Among the Colored Folks: "My Ideas on the Race Problem."* |
| 1894 | Kate Chopin. *Bayou Folk*. Including "Desirée's Baby," first pub. in 1893. |
| 1894 | John Mercer Langston. *From the Virginia Plantation to the National Capitol*; esp. ch. 1. |
| 1894 | Mark Twain. *Pudd'nhead Wilson: A Tale* (cited from *Pudd'nhead Wilson and Those Extraordinary Twins*, ed. Sidney E. Berger, 1980). |
| 1894 | Amelia E. Johnson. *The Hazeley Family*. |
| 1894 | Thomas Nelson Page. In "How Andrew Carried the Precinct." *Pastime Stories* (Mencke). |
| 1894 | Sanda [Walter Stowers and William Anderson]. *Appointed*. |
| 1895 | P[aul?] Bourget. *Cosmopolis*; story of Napoléon Chapron, 191–96. |
| 1895 | James Edwin Campbell. "A Love Dream" and "The Pariah." In *Echoes . . . From the Cabin and Elsewhere*. |
| 1895 | Alice I. Jones. *Beatrice of Bayou Têche*. |
| 1895 | Bliss Perry. *The Plated City*. |
| 1895 | Albert Ross [pseud.]. *A Black Adonis*. |
| 1896 | George Washington Cable. *Madame Delphine* (also in *In Old Creole Days*, but here with new preface). |
| 1896 | Carlos Malheiro Dias. *A Mulata. Romance*. Reprinted in 1975. |
| 1896 | J. McHenry Jones. *Hearts of Gold: A Novel*. |
| 1896 | Opie Read. *My Young Master*. |
| 1897 | G. de Raulin [de Gustave Joseph Henri Landrieu]. *Owanga, amours exotiques*. |
| 1898 | Mary Johnston. *Prisoners of Hope: A Tale of Colonial Virginia*. |
| 1898 | Thomas Nelson Page. *Red Rock: A Chronicle of Reconstruction*. |

| | |
|---|---|
| 1899 | Charles W. Chesnutt. *The Wife of His Youth.* |
| 1899 | Sutton Griggs. *Imperium in Imperio.* |
| 1900 | Gertrude Atherton. *Senator North.* |
| 1900 | Charles W. Chesnutt. *The House Behind the Cedars.* |
| 1900 | Pauline E. Hopkins. *Contending Forces: A Romance Illustrative of Negro Life.* |
| 1900 | Pauline Hopkins. "General Washington: A Christmas Story." *Colored American Magazine* 2 (Nov. 1900): 95–104. |
| 1900 | Pauline E. Hopkins. "Talma Gordon." *Colored American Magazine* 1.5 (Oct. 1900): 271–90. |
| 1900 | Jack Thorne [David Bryant Fulton]. *Hanover; or, The Persecution of the Lowly: A Story of the Wilmington Massacre.* |
| 1901 | Charles W. Chesnutt. *The Marrow of Tradition.* |
| 1901 | Payne Erskine. *When the Gates Lift Up Their Heads: A Story of the Seventies.* |
| 1901 | Sutton E. Griggs. *Overshadowed.* |
| 1901 | Pauline E. Hopkins. "A Dash for Liberty." *Colored American Magazine* 3.4 (Aug. 1901): 243–47. |
| 1901 | Belle Kearney. *A Slaveholder's Daughter: An Autobiography.* |
| 1901 | Wm. C. Townsend. *Love and Liberty* (novel). |
| 1901 | Albery A. Whitman. *An Idyl of the South: An Epic Poem in Two Parts* (derived from Vashon 1856?). |
| 1901/2 | Sarah A. Allen [Pauline E. Hopkins]. "Hagar's Daughter: A Story of Southern Caste Prejudice." *Colored American Magazine* beginning 3.1 (March 1901): 337ff, 24–34, 117–28, 185–95, 262–72, 343–53, 425–35; 4 (1902): 23–33, 113–24, 188–200, 281–91. |
| 1902 | Sarah A. Allen [Pauline E. Hopkins]. "The Test of Manhood (A Christmas Story)." *Colored American Magazine* 4.6 (Dec.): 113–20. |
| 1902 | James D. Corrothers. *The Black Cat Club.* |
| 1902 | Thomas Dixon, Jr. *The Leopard's Spots: A Romance of the White Man's Burden—1865–1910.* |
| 1902 | Paul Laurence Dunbar. *The Sport of the Gods.* |
| 1902 | I. Dwight Fairfield. "A Modern Othello" (poem). *Colored American Magazine* (Dec.): 125–27. |
| 1902 | Charles H. Fowler. *Historical Romance of the American Negro.* |
| 1902 | Sutton E. Griggs. *Unfettered.* |

| | |
|---|---|
| 1902 | Joel Chandler Harris. *Gabriel Tolliver: A Story of Reconstruction*. |
| 1902 | [Pauline Hopkins]. "Winona: A Tale of Negro Life in the South and Southwest." *Colored American Magazine* 5 (May 1902–Oct. 1902). |
| 1902 | G. Langhorne Pryor. *Neither Bond nor Free (A Plea)*. |
| 1902 | Hugues Rebell. *Les Nuits chaudes du Cap Français*. Reprinted with a preface by d'Auriant and an afterword by Hubert Juin. |
| 1902 | Ruth D. Todd. "The Octoroon's Revenge." *Colored American Magazine* 4[?]: 291–95. |
| 1902/3 | Pauline Hopkins. "Of One Blood; Or, The Hidden Self." *Colored American Magazine* (Nov. 1902–Nov. 1903). |
| 1903 | Cyrus T. Brady. *A Doctor of Philosophy* (novel; Rogers, *Sex and Race*, III: 330). |
| 1903 | Mrs. M. Louise Burgess-Ware. "Bernice the Octoroon." *Colored American Magazine* (Aug. 1903): 607–61; (Sept. 1903): 652–57. |
| 1903 | W. E. B. Du Bois. *The Souls of Black Folk* (esp. "The Coming of John"). |
| 1903 | Marius-Ary Leblond. *Le Zézère, amours de Blancs et de Noirs*. |
| 1903 | Theodore E. D. Nash. *Love and Vengeance*. |
| 1904 | Edward A. Johnson. *Light Ahead for the Negro*. |
| 1904 | Frank Norris. *The Octopus: A Story of California*. |
| 1905 | Norah Davis. *The Northerner*. |
| 1905 | Thomas Dixon, Jr. *The Clansman: A Historical Romance of the Ku Klux Klan*. |
| 1905 | Thomas Dixon, Jr. "The Clansman: An American Drama. From the Material of His Two Novels 'The Leopard's Spots' and 'The Clansman.'" Typescript, Harvard Theater Collection. |
| 1905 | Sutton E. Griggs. *The Hindered Hand; or, The Reign of the Repressionist*. |
| 1906 | Thomas Dixon, Jr. "Why I Wrote 'The Clansman.'" *Theatre* 6 (Jan. 1906): 20–22. |
| 1906 | George Marion McClellan. *Old Greenbottom Inn and Other Stories*. |
| 1907 | Mary Evelyn [Moore] Davis. *The Price of Silence*. |
| 1907 | Thomas Dixon, Jr. *The Traitor: A Story of the Fall of the Invisible Empire*. |

| | |
|---|---|
| 1907 | James E. McGirt. "In Love and War." In *The Triumphs of Ephraim.* |
| 1907 | Fannie Barrier Williams. "Perils of the White Negro." *Colored American Magazine* 13 (Dec.): 421–23. |
| 1908 | Margaret Deland. "A Black Drop." In *R.J.'s Mother, and Some Other People.* |
| 1908 | Margaret Deland. "The Black Drop." Serial in *Collier's Weekly,* beginning May 2. |
| 1908 | Robert Lee Durham. *The Call of the South.* |
| 1908 | Sutton E. Griggs. *Pointing the Way.* |
| 1909 | John Wesley Grant. *Out of the Darkness; or, Diabolism and Destiny.* |
| 1909 | [Walter Hines Page]. *The Southerner: A Novel: Being the Autobiography of Nicholas Worth.* |
| 1909 | Gertrude Stein. *Three Lives.* |
| 1910 | Edward Sheldon. *The Nigger: An American Play in Three Acts.* |
| 1910 | Robert Lewis Waring. *As We See It.* |
| 1910 | Ulysses G. Weatherly. "Race and Marriage." *American Journal of Sociology* 15.4 (Jan. 1910): 433–53. |
| 1911 | Alexander Corkey. *The Testing Fire.* |
| 1911 | W. E. B. Du Bois. *The Quest of the Silver Fleece.* |
| 1911 | William E. Waston. *Christophe.* |
| 1912 | Joseph S[eamon] Cotter. *Negro Tales,* esp. "Rodney" (23–34) and "Tesney, the Deceived" (35–49). |
| 1912 | Thomas Dixon. *The Sins of the Father: A Romance of the South.* |
| 1912 | James Weldon Johnson. *The Autobiography of an Ex-Colored Man.* |
| 1912 | Yorke Jones. *The Climbers.* |
| 1913 | Ellen Glasgow. *Virginia,* esp. book 2, ch. 9: "The Problem of the South." |
| 1913 | Hans Grimm. *Südafrikanische Novellen.* |
| 1913 | Oscar Micheaux. *The Conquest: A Story of a Negro Pioneer,* ch. 25, "The Scotch Girl." |
| 1914 | Thomas Pearce Bailey. *Race Orthodoxy in the South.* Reprinted in 1972. |
| 1914 | George Washington Cable. *Gideon's Band: A Tale of the Mississippi.* |
| 1915 | William M. Ashby. *Redder Blood.* |
| 1915 | Dorothy Canfield [Fisher]. *The Bent Twig.* |

| 1915 | F. Grant Gilmore. *"The Problem": A Military Novel.* |
|------|-----|
| 1915 | Oscar Micheaux. *The Forged Note: A Romance of the Darker Races.* |
| 1915 | Otis M. Shackleford. *Lillian Simmons; or, The Conflict of Sections.* |
| 1915 | Thomas H. B. Walker. *J. Johnson; or, The Unknown Man: An Answer to Mrs. Thomas Dixon's "Sins of the Fathers."* |
| 1916 | Don Marquis. "Mulatto." *Harper's* (April 1916). |
| 1917 | Clayton Adams [Charles Henry Holmes]. *Ethiopia, the Land of Promise: A Book With a Purpose.* |
| 1917 | Henry F. Downing. *The American Cavalryman: A Liberian Romance.* |
| 1917 | George W. Ellis. *The Leopard's Claw.* |
| 1917 | Sarah L. Fleming. *Hope's Highway.* |
| 1917 | Oscar Micheaux. *The Homesteader* (rewritten in 1941). |
| 1917 | Joel Augustus Rogers. *From "Superman" to Man.* |
| 1918 | George Washington Cable. *The Flower of the Chapdelaines* (includes "A West Indian Slave Insurrection," first published in 1892). |
| 1918 | George Washington Cable. *Lovers of Louisiana.* |
| 1918 | Joseph Cotter, Jr. "The Mulatto to His Critics." In *The Band of Gideon,* 5; also reprinted in *Negro Poets and Their Poems* (1923), ed. Robert Kerlin. |
| 1918 | Edwin Byron Reuter. *The Mulatto in the United States, Including a Study of the Role of Mixed-Blood Races Throughout the World.* |
| 1918 | Carter G. Woodson. "The Beginnings of Miscegenation of the Whites and Blacks." *Journal of Negro History* 3.4: 335–53. |
| 1919 | Herman Dreer. *The Immediate Jewel of His Soul.* |
| 1919 | Robert A. Tracy. *The Sword of Nemesis.* |
| 1920 | W. E. B. Du Bois. *Darkwater,* esp. "The Comet" and "The Damnation of Women." |
| 1920 | Paul Green. *White Dresses: A Sorrow of First Love.* |
| 1920 | William McFee. *Captain Macedoine's Daughter.* |
| 1920 | Mary White Ovington. *The Shadow.* |
| 1920 | Stella George [Stern] Perry. *Palmetto: The Romance of a Louisiana Girl.* |
| 1920 | Zara Wright. *Black and White Tangled Threads* and sequel, *Kenneth.* |

| | |
|---|---|
| 1921 | John Bennett. *Madame Margot: A Grotesque Legend of Old Charleston.* |
| 1922 | Georgia Douglas Johnson. "The Octoroon." In *Bronze: A Book of Verse.* |
| 1922 | William Pickens. *The Vengeance of the Gods and Other Stories of Real American Color Line Life*, title story only (11–86) (invites comparison with *Pudd'nhead Wilson*). |
| 1922 | T. S. Stribling. *Birthright.* |
| 1923 | Waldo Frank. *Holiday.* |
| 1923 | Ottie B. Graham. "Holiday." *Crisis* 26.1 (May): 12–7. |
| 1923 | Gertrude Sanborn. *Veiled Aristocrats.* |
| 1923 | Jean Toomer. *Cane.* See also his "Withered Skin of Berries." |
| 1924 | John T. Dorsey. *The Lion of Judah.* |
| 1924 | Jessie Fauset. *There Is Confusion.* |
| 1924 | Ronald Firbank. *Prancing Nigger.* Intro. Carl Van Vechten. |
| 1924 | Joshua Henry Jones. *By Sanction of Law.* |
| 1924 | Vara A. Majette. *White Blood.* |
| 1924 | Leonard Merrick. *The Quaint Companions.* |
| 1924 | Sarah Gertrude Millin. *God's Step-Children.* |
| 1924 | Eugene O'Neill. "All God's Chillun Got Wings." *American Mercury* 1.2 (Feb. 1924): 129–48. |
| 1924 | Walter White. *The Fire in the Flint.* |
| 1925 | Countée Cullen. "Near White." *Color*, 11. |
| 1925 | Rudolph Fisher. "High Yaller." *The Crisis* 30–31: 281–86; 33–38. |
| 1925 | David Garnett. *The Sailor's Return.* |
| 1925 | Langston Hughes. "Cross." In *The Weary Blues.* |
| 1925 | Georgia Douglas Johnson. "The Riddle." In *The New Negro*, ed. Alain Locke. |
| 1925 | Harry F. Liscomb. *The Prince of Washington Square.* |
| 1925 | Claude McKay. "The Mulatto." *Bookman* 72 (Sept. 1925): 67. |
| 1925 | Joan Sutherland. *Challenge.* |
| 1926 | Barry Benefield. *Short Turns*, esp. story, "Simply Sugar Pie" (219–34). |
| 1926 | Maxwell Bodenheim. *Ninth Avenue* (Brown: intermarriage plot evocative of O'Neill). |
| 1926 | Joshua A. Brockett. *Zipporah, the Maid of Midian.* |

| | |
|---|---|
| 1926 | Caroline Bond Day. "The Pink Hat." *Opportunity* (Dec.): 379–80. |
| 1926 | Arthur H. Estabrook and Ivan E. McDougle. *Mongrel Virginians: The Win Tribe* (nonfiction: small group of "Indian-negro-white crosses"). |
| 1926 | Edna Ferber. *Show Boat.* |
| 1926 | Claire [Liliane] Goll. *Der Neger Jupiter raubt Europa* (reviewed under the title *Le Nègre Jupiter enlève Europa* "The Negro Jupiter Ravishes Europe" by Cullen in 1929). |
| 1926 | Paul Green. "The End of the Row." In *Lonesome Road.* |
| 1926 | Myrtle A. Smith Livingston. "For Unborn Children." *The Crisis* 32.3 (July 1926): 122–25; play won third prize in *Crisis* contest of 1925. |
| 1926 | Joan Sutherland. *Challenge.* |
| 1926 | Walter White. *Flight.* |
| 1927 | Countée Cullen. *The Ballad of the Brown Girl: An Old Ballad Retold.* |
| 1927 | Paul Green. *The Field God* and *In Abraham's Bosom.* |
| 1927 | Langston Hughes. "Mulatto" and "Red Silk Stockings." In *Fine Clothes to the Jew.* |
| 1927 | Zora Neale Hurston. "The First One." In *Plays of Negro Life,* eds. Alain Locke and Montgomery Gregory. |
| 1927 | Grace Lumpkin. "White Man." |
| 1927 | Julia Peterkin. *Black April.* |
| 1927 | Elizabeth Madox Roberts. *My Heart and My Flesh.* |
| 1927 | Evelyn Scott. *Migrations.* |
| 1927 | Lucy White. "The Bird Child." In *Plays of Negro Life,* eds. Alain Locke and Montgomery Gregory. |
| 1928 | *Confessions of a Negro Preacher.* |
| 1928 | Rudolph Fisher. *The Walls of Jericho.* |
| 1928 | Isa Glenn. *A Short History of Julia.* |
| 1928 | Paul Green. "The Goodbye." In *In the Valley, and Other Carolina Plays.* |
| 1928 | Marcet and Emanuel Haldeman-Julius. *Violence: A Story of Today's South.* |
| 1928 | Roland E. Hartley and Caroline Power. "Madame Delphine." In *Short Plays from Great Stories,* eds. Hartley and Power (based on George Washington Cable). |
| 1928 | Leslie Pinckney Hill. *Toussaint L'Ouverture.* |
| 1928 ms | Langston Hughes. "Mulatto: A Tragedy of the Deep South" (first produced in 1935). |

| | |
|---|---|
| 1928 | Georgia Douglas Johnson. "Blue Blood." In *Fifty More Contemporary One-Act Plays*, ed. Frank Shay. |
| 1928 | Nella Larsen. *Quicksand.* |
| 1928 | Enrique López Albújar. *Matalaché: novela retaguardista.* |
| 1928 | Robert E. Park. "Human Migration and the Marginal Man." *American Journal of Sociology* 33: 881–93. |
| 1928 | Edward Larocque Tinker. *Toucoutou.* |
| 1929 | Roark Bradford. *This Side of Jordan.* |
| 1929 | Vera Caspary. *The White Girl.* |
| 1929 | Albert E.[vander] Coleman. *The Romantic Adventures of Rosy, the Octoroon: With Some Account of the Persecution of the Southern Negroes During the Reconstruction Period.* |
| 1929 | Narena Easterling. *Broken Lights: A Novel.* |
| 1929 | Jessie Fauset. *Plum Bun.* |
| 1929 | Lafcadio Hearn. "The Original Bras Coupé." In *Essays on American Literature.* |
| 1929 | DuBose Heyward. *Mamba's Daughters.* |
| 1929 | Nella Larsen. *Passing.* |
| 1929 | Evelyn Scott. *The Wave.* |
| 1929 | Howard Snyder. *Earth Born: A Novel of the Plantation.* |
| 1929 | Wallace Thurman. *The Blacker the Berry.* |
| 1929 | Evans Wall. *The No-Nation Girl.* |
| 1930 | Gilmore Millen. *Sweet Man.* |
| 1930 | Gertrude Shelby and Samuel G. Stoney. *Po' Buckra.* |
| 1931 | R. Hernekin Baptist. *Four Handsome Negresses: The Record of a Voyage.* |
| 1931 | Jessie Fauset. *The Chinaberry Tree.* |
| 1931 | William S. Henry. *Out of Wedlock.* |
| 1931 | DuBose Heyward. *Brass Ankle.* |
| 1931 | Alin Laubreaux. *Mulatto Johnny.* Trans. from the French by Coley Taylor. |
| 1931 | Robert E. Park. "Mentality of Racial Hybrids." *American Journal of Sociology* 36: 534–51. |
| 1931 | Arturo Uslar Pietri. *Las Lanzas coloradas.* |
| 1931 | George Schuyler. *Black No More: Being an Account of the Strange and Wonderful Workings of Science in the Land of the Free, A.D. 1933–40.* |
| 1931 | T. S. Stribling. *The Forge.* |
| 1932 | "Geoffrey Barnes" [James Whittaker]. *Dark Lustre.* |
| 1932 | Countée Cullen. *One Way to Heaven.* |

| 1932 | William Faulkner. *Light in August.* |
|---|---|
| 1932 | Roy Flannagan. *Amber Satyr.* |
| 1932 | Welbourn Kelley. *Inchin' Along.* |
| 1932 | Claude McKay. "Near-White." In *Gingertown,* 72–104. |
| 1932 | Donna McKay. *A Gentleman in a Black Skin.* |
| 1932 | Julia Peterkin. *Bright Skin.* |
| 1932 | T. S. Stribling. *The Store.* |
| 1932 | Evans Wall. *Love Fetish.* |
| 1933 | Sterling A. Brown. "Negro Character as Seen by White Authors." *Journal of Negro Education* 2 (April 1933): 179–203 (includes discussion of "Tragic Mulatto"). |
| 1933 | Jessie Fauset. *Comedy, American Style.* |
| 1933 | E. Franklin Frazier. "Children in Black and Mulatto Families." *American Journal of Sociology* 39.1 (July 1933): 12–29. |
| 1933 | John H. Hill. *Princess Malah.* |
| 1933 | Fannie Hurst. *Imitation of Life.* |
| 1933 | George Milburn. *No More Trumpets,* esp. "White Meat." |
| 1934 | Randolph Edmonds. *Six Plays for a Negro Theatre,* esp. "Breeders" (83–101). |
| 1934 | Emily Hahn. *Naked Foot.* |
| 1934 | Langston Hughes. *The Ways of White Folks.* |
| 1934 | William March. *Come in at the Door.* |
| 1934 | T. S. Stribling. *Unfinished Cathedral* (last part of trilogy; see 1931, 1932). |
| 1934 | Clement Wood. *Deep River.* |
| 1935 | Hallie F[erron] Dickerman. *Stephen Kent.* |
| 1935 | Georgia Douglas Johnson. "William and Ellen Craft." In: *Negro History in Thirteen Plays,* eds. Willis Richardson and May Miller. |
| 1935 | Grace Lumpkin. *A Sign for Cain.* |
| 1935 | May Miller. "Christophe's Daughters." In *Negro History in Thirteen Plays,* eds. Willis Richardson and May Miller. |
| 1935 | Willis Richardson. "The Elder Dumas." In *Negro History in Thirteen Plays,* eds. Willis Richardson and May Miller. |
| 1935 | Samson Raphaelson. "White Man." In *Accent on Youth and White Man.* |

| 1935 | Elizabeth Madox Roberts. *Deep, Dark River*. |
| 1935 | Robert Rylee. *Deep Dark River*. |
| 1936 | Edwin R. Embree. *Brown America: The Story of a New Race*. |
| 1936 | William Faulkner. *Absalom, Absalom!*. |
| 1936 | Langston Hughes. *Mulatto* (produced). |
| 1936 | O'Wendell Shaw. *Greater Need Below*. |
| 1936 | Marie Stanley. *Gulf Stream*. |
| 1937 | Marjorie Hill Allee. *The Great Tradition*. |
| 1937 | Sterling A. Brown. *Negro Poetry and Drama* and *The Negro in American Fiction*. |
| 1937 | Rómulo Gallegos. *Pobre negro*. In *Obras completas*. |
| 1937 | George Washington Lee. *River George*. |
| 1937 | Lyle Saxon. *Children of Strangers*. |
| 1937 | Everett Stonequist. *The Marginal Man* (contains some unpublished life stories). |
| 1938 | William [E. B.] Du Bois. *Haiti*. In *Federal Theatre Plays*, ed. Pierre de Rohan. |
| 1938 | Mercedes Gilbert. *Aunt Sara's Wooden God*. |
| 1938 | Julian R. Meade. *The Back Door*. |
| 1938 | Pauli Murray. "Mulatto's Dilemma." *Opportunity* 16 (June 1938): 180. |
| 1938 | Henry Nemours Nunez. *Chien Negre*. |
| 1938 | Alfredo Parejo Díaz Conseco. *Baldomera: tragedia del cholo americano*. |
| 1938 | Allen Tate. *The Fathers*. |
| 1938 | Robb White. *Run Masked*. |
| 1939 | Thomas Dixon, Jr. *The Flaming Sword*. |
| 1939 | Artie Shaw. "Octoroon." Recorded June 5 on Victor Bluebird 10319 (composed by Harry Warren). |
| 1939 | Waters E. Turpin. *O Canaan!*. |
| 1940 | Willa Cather. *Saphira and the Slave Girl*. |
| 1940 | John M. Lee. *Counter-Clockwise*. |
| 1940 | George S. Schuyler. "Who Is 'Negro'? Who Is 'White'?" *Common Ground* 1 (Autumn 1940): 53–56. |
| 1942 | William Faulkner. *Go Down, Moses*. |
| 1942 | Frances Parkinson Keyes. *Crescent Carnival*. |
| 1942 | J[oel] A. Rogers. *Sex and Race: A History of White, Negro, and Indian Miscegenation in the Two Americas*. 3 vols. |
| 1942 | Marguerite Steen. *The Sun Is My Undoing*. |

| | |
|---|---|
| 1942 | Richard Wright. "Black Confession" (with Mulatto episode that did not appear in *Black Boy*); ms. |
| 1944 | Henrietta Buckmaster. *Deep River*. |
| 1944 | Martha Gellhorn. *Liana*. |
| 1944 | Edith Pope. *Colcorton*. |
| 1944 | Lillian Smith. *Strange Fruit*. |
| 1945 | Gwendolyn Brooks. *A Street in Bronzeville*; esp. "The Ballad of Pearl May Lee" (42–45). |
| 1945 | Mark Harris. *Trumpet to the World*. |
| 1945 | Chester Himes. *If He Hollers Let Him Go*. |
| 1945 | Philip Yordan. *Anna Lucasta*. |
| 1946 | Donald Joseph. *Straw in the Wind*. |
| 1946 | Edward Kimbrough. *Night Fire*. |
| 1946 | "Vernon Sullivan" [Boris Vian]. *J'irai cracher sur vos tombes* ("I Shall Spit on Your Graves"). |
| 1946 | Cid Ricketts Summer. *Quality*. |
| 1946 | Mrs. Cid Rickette Sumner. *Quality*. |
| 1946 | Judith Wright. "Half-Caste Girl." Australian; included in Sandra Gilbert and Susan Gubar, *The Norton Anthology of Literature by Women: The Tradition in English*. |
| 1946 | Frank Yerby. *The Foxes of Harrow*. |
| 1947 | Mario Castelnuovo-Tedesco (1895–1968; Italian composer). *The Octoroon Ball* op. 136. |
| 1947 | Chester Himes. *Lonely Crusade*. |
| 1947 | Sinclair Lewis. *Kingsblood Royal*. |
| 1947 | Emil Ludwig. *Othello*. Trans. Franz von Hildebrand (a novelization of Giraldi's novella). |
| 1947 | Oscar Micheaux. *The Masquerade* (version of Chesnutt's *The House Behind the Cedars* (1900)). |
| 1947 | "Vernon Sullivan" [Boris Vian]. *Les Morts ont tous la même peau* ("All Dead People Have the Same Skin"). |
| 1947 | Will Thomas [William Smith]. *God Is for White Folks*. |
| 1947 | William Lindsay White. *Lost Boundaries*. |
| 1947 | Frank Yerby. *The Vixens*. |
| 1948 | Peter Abrahams. *The Path of Thunder*. |
| 1948 | William Faulkner. *Intruder in the Dust*. |
| 1948 | Georges Fouret. *La Négresse blonde*. |
| 1948 | John Hewlett. *Harlem Story*. |
| 1948 | Ross Lockridge, Jr. *Raintree County*. |
| 1948 | William Gardner Smith. *The Last of the Conquerors*. |

| | |
|---|---|
| 1948 | Dorothy West. *The Living Is Easy.* |
| 1948 | David Westheimer. *Summer on the Water.* |
| 1949 | Barbara Anderson. *Southbound.* |
| 1949 | Erskine Caldwell. *Place Called Esterville.* |
| 1949 | Frances Gaither. *Double Muscadine.* |
| 1949 | Bucklin Moon. *Without Magnolias.* |
| 1949 | Alberto Moravia. "Il Negro e il vecchio dalla roncola." In *L'amore coniugale.* (English: "The Negro and the Old Man with the Scythe.") |
| 1949 | Willard Savoy. *Alien Land.* |
| 1949 | Lillian Smith. *Killers of the Dream.* |
| 1950 | Elizabeth Boatwright Coker. *Daughters of Strangers.* |
| 1950 | Ramón Díaz Sanchez. *Cumboto.* |
| 1950 | Sarah Gertrude Millin. *King of the Bastards.* |
| 1950 | J. Saunders Redding. *Stranger and Alone.* |
| 1952 | Lonnie Coleman. *Clara.* |
| 1952 | Dorothy Lee Dickens. *Black on the Rainbow.* |
| 1952 | Ralph Ellison. *Invisible Man.* |
| 1952 | Alex Gaby. *To End the Night.* |
| 1952 | Ian Gordon. *The Night Thorn.* |
| 1952 | Langston Hughes. "African Morning" and "Who's Passing for Who?" (short stories). In *Laughing to Keep From Crying.* |
| 1953 | Mouloud Feraoun. *La Terre a le sang.* |
| 1953 | Shirley Ann Grau. *The Black Prince and Other Stories,* esp. "Miss Yellow Eyes." |
| 1953 | Alan Paton. *Too Late the Phalarope.* |
| 1953 | Ann Petry. *The Narrows.* |
| 1954 | Hamilton Basso. *The View from Pompey's Head.* |
| 1954 | Chester Himes. *The Third Generation.* |
| 1954 | William Gardner Smith. *South Street.* |
| 1954 | Charles Smythwick, Jr. *False Measure: A Satirical Novel of the Lives and Objectives of Upper Middle-Class Negroes.* |
| 1954 | Charles Tarter. *Family of Destiny.* |
| 1954 | Elizabeth West Wallace. *Scandal at Daybreak.* |
| 1955 | Noel Clad. *White Barrier.* |
| 1955 | Lonnie Coleman. *The Southern Lady.* |
| 1955 | Chester Himes. *The Primitive.* |
| 1955 | Arnold Krieger. *Geliebt, gejagt und unvergessen.* |
| 1955 | Reba Lee. *I Passed for White.* |

| | |
|---|---|
| 1955 | Robert Penn Warren. *Band of Angels.* |
| 1956 | Yacine Kateb. *Nedjma.* |
| 1956 | Pauli Murray. *Proud Shoes: The Story of an American Family.* |
| 1956 | Sembène Ousmane. *Le Docker noir.* |
| 1956 | Ferdinand Oyono. *Une vie de boy.* |
| 1956 | Elizabeth Spencer. *The Voice at the Back Door.* |
| 1957 | Peter S. Feibleman. *A Place Without Twilight.* |
| 1957 | Kyle Onstott. *Mandingo.* |
| 1957 | Sembène Ousmane. *O pays, mon beau peuple!* |
| 1957 | Herbert Simmons. *Corner Bay.* |
| 1958 | Fay Liddle Coolidge. *Black Is White.* |
| 1958 | Muriel Spark. "The Black Madonna." In *The Go-Away Bird and Other Stories.* |
| 1959 | Jacques Stephen Alexis. *L'Espace d'un cillement.* |
| 1959 | Hannah Arendt. "Reflections on Little Rock." *Dissent* 6.1 (Winter 1959): 45–56 (emphasizes importance of right to intermarriage). |
| 1959 | Hamilton Basso. *The Light Infantry.* |
| 1959 | Leon R. Harris. *Run, Zebra, Run!* |
| 1959 | Herbert D. Kastle. *Camera.* |
| 1960 | Jenn Lawrie. *The Marriage of Gor: The True Account of a White Girl's Life With a Black Man.* |
| 1960 | Ferdinand Oyono. *Chemin d'Europe.* |
| 1961 | Henry L. Anderson. *No Use Cryin'.* |
| 1961 | [René] Etiemble. *Blason d'un corps.* |
| 1961 | Athol Fugard. *The Blood Knot.* |
| 1961 | Chester Himes. *Pinktoes.* |
| 1961 | Cheikh Hamidou Kane. *L'Aventure ambiguë.* |
| 1961 | M. B. Longman. *The Power of Black.* |
| 1962 | James Baldwin. *Another Country.* |
| 1962 | Robert Gover. *One Hundred Dollar Misunderstanding.* |
| 1962 | Willard Motley. "The Almost White Boy." In *Soon, One Morning: New Writing by American Negroes, 1940–1962,* ed. Herbert Hill. |
| 1963 | Miguel Angel Asturias. *Mulata de Tal.* |
| 1963 | Guy des Cars. *Sang d'Afrique.* Vol. 1: *L'Africain;* vol. 2: *L'Amoureuse.* |
| 1963 | William Gardner Smith. *The Stone Face* (set in Paris; black American and Polish actress). |
| 1964 | Robert Boles. *The People One Knows.* |

| | |
|---|---|
| 1964 | Robert Gover. *Here Goes Kitten* (sequel to Gover 1962). |
| 1964 | Shirley Ann Grau. *The Keeper of the House.* |
| 1964 | Lorraine Hansberry. *The Sign in Sidney Brustein's Window.* |
| 1964 | Adrienne Kennedy. *Funnyhouse of a Negro.* |
| 1964 | LeRoi Jones. *Dutchman* and *The Slave.* |
| 1964 | Sembène Ousmane. *L'Harmattan.* |
| 1964 | Anna Seghers. "Die Hochzeit von Haiti" (story; see 1976 collection). |
| 1965 | Alston Anderson. *All God's Children.* |
| 1965 | William Melvin Kelley. *A Drop of Patience.* |
| 1965 | Adrienne Kennedy. *The Owl Answers.* |
| 1965 | Roi Ottley. *White Marble Lady.* |
| 1965 | Sembène Ousmane. *Le Mandat précéd' de Véhi Ciosane.* |
| 1966 | Adrienne Kennedy. *A Rat's Mass.* |
| 1966 | Jean Rhys. *Wide Sargasso Sea.* |
| 1966 | Margaret Walker. *Jubilee.* |
| 1967 | Erskine Caldwell. *The Weather Shelter.* |
| 1967 | Ernest Gaines. *Of Love and Dust.* |
| 1967 | Frank Hercules. *I Want a Black Doll.* |
| 1967 | William Bradford Huie. *The Klansman.* |
| 1967 | LeRoi Jones. *Tales,* esp. "Going Down Slow." |
| 1967 | William Melvin Kelley. *dem.* |
| 1967 | John Oliver Killens. *'Sippi* (story of Carrie Wakefield, a wealthy plantation owner's daughter and Charley Chaney, son of a field hand). |
| 1967 | Simone and André Schwarz-Bart. *Un plat de porc aux bananes vertes.* |
| 1968 | James Baldwin. *Tell Me How Long the Train's Been Gone.* |
| 1968 | Ernest Gaines. *Bloodline.* |
| 1968 | Robert Gover. *J C Saves* (sequel to Gover 1962 and 1964). |
| 1969 | Cecil Brown. *The Life and Loves of Mr. Jiveass Nigger.* |
| 1969 | Thérèse Kuoh-Moukouri. *Rencontres essentielles.* |
| 1969 | Clarence Major. *The Night Visitors.* |
| 1969 | Frank Yerby. *Speak Now.* |
| 1970 | "I Am Curious (Black)!" *Superman's Girl Friend Lois Lane* #106. D.C. Comics (November). Script: Robert Kanigher. |

| | |
|---|---|
| 1970 | Hal Bennett. *Lord of the Dark Places.* |
| 1970 | George Cain. *Blueschild Baby.* |
| 1970 | Norman Daniels. *Slave Rebellion.* |
| 1970 | William Melvin Kelley. *Dunfords Travels Everywhere.* |
| 1971 | Ernest J. Gaines. *The Autobiography of Miss Jane Pittman.* |
| 1971 | John Oliver Killens. *The Cotillion; or, One Good Bull Is Half the Herd.* |
| 1972 | Ayi Kwei Armah. *Why Are We So Blest?* |
| 1972 | Mbella Sonne Dipoko. *Black & White in Love.* |
| 1972 | André Schwarz-Bart. *La Mulâtresse Solitude.* Trans. Ralph Manheim, *A Woman Named Solitude.* |
| 1972 | Alice Walker. *Meridian.* |
| 1972 | John A. Williams. *Captain Blackman.* |
| 1973 | Leon Forrest. *There Is a Tree More Ancient Than Eden* (see 1977, 1983). |
| 1973 | Bessie Head. *A Question of Power.* |
| 1974 | Calvin Hernton. *Scarecrow.* |
| 1974 | Jean Gilmore Rushing. *Mary Dove.* |
| 1975 | Gayl Jones. *Corregidora.* |
| 1976 | Nuruddin Farah. *A Naked Needle.* |
| 1976 | Anna Seghers. *Die Hochzeit von Haiti: Karibische Geschichten*, esp. title story, orig. pub. 1964. |
| 1976 | Margaret Walker. *Meridian.* |
| 1976 | John A. Williams. *The Junior Bachelor Society.* |
| 1977 | Mariama Bâ. *Une si longue lettre.* |
| 1977 | Maurice Deneuzière. *Louisiane* (Prix Alexandre Dumas). |
| 1977 | Leon Forrest. *The Bloodworth Orphans.* |
| 1977 | Barbara Ferry Johnson. *Delta Blood.* |
| 1979 | Barbara Chase-Riboud. *Sally Hemings.* |
| 1979 | Cyrus Colter. *Night Studies.* |
| 1979 | Maurice Deneuzière. *Fausse Rivière.* |
| 1980 | Fanny Howe. *The White Slave.* |
| 1981 | Mariama Bâ. *Un chant écarlate.* |
| 1981 | Maurice Deneuzière. *Bagatelle.* |
| 1981 | Maurice Deneuzière. *Un chien de saison.* |
| 1982 | Francis Bebey. *Le Fils d'Agatha Moudio.* |
| 1982 | Rita Mae Brown. *Southern Discomfort.* |

| | |
|---|---|
| 1982 | Charles Johnson. *Oxherding Tale.* |
| 1983 | Mongo Beti. *Les Deux mères de Guillaume Ismael Dzewatama futur camionneur.* |
| 1983 | Leon Forrest. *Two Wings to Veil My Face* (see 1973, 1977). |
| 1983 | Wilson Harris. *The Womb of Space: The Cross-Cultural Imagination.* |
| 1984 | Mongo Beti. *La Revanche de Guillaume Ismael Dzewatama.* |
| 1984 | Hans Christoph Buch. *Die Hochzeit von Port-au-Prince.* |
| 1984 | Michele Cliff. *Abeng: A Novel.* |
| 1984 | Yvonne R. de Miranda. *A Mulata Ana Lúcia.* |
| 1984 | William Plomer. *The South African Autobiography.* |
| 1984 | William Plomer. *Turbott Wolfe* (intro. Laurens van der Pot). |
| 1985 | Maurice Deneuzière. *Les Trois-chènes.* |
| 1985 | Lore Segal. *Her First American.* |
| 1985 | John Edgar Wideman. *The Homewood Trilogy: Damballah, Hiding Place, Sent for You Yesterday.* |
| 1986 | Anne Garréta. *Sphinx.* |
| 1986 | Katharina Oguntoye, May Opitz, and Dagmar Schultz, eds. *Farbe bekennen: Afro-deutsche Frauen auf den Spuren ihrer Geschichte.* |
| 1987 | Maurice Deneuzière. *L'Adieu au sud.* |
| 1987 | Nicolás Guillén. "Mulata" (High Brown). *Callaloo* 10. 2 (1987): 174–75. |
| 1987 | Sally Morgan. *My Place.* |
| 1988 | Valerie Belgrave. *Ti Marie.* |
| 1988 | Abdoulaye Sadji. *Nini: mulâtresse du Sénégal.* |
| 1988 | Joseph Thomson. *An African Romance.* |
| 1988 | Tom Vidal. *Schwarzer Zucker.* |
| 1989 | Rachel Countryman. "A Little Bit White." Germantown Friends School *Studies in Education* 56 (Winter): 8–15. |
| 1989 | Rolf Lasa. *Schwarze Haut, weiße Haut.* |
| 1989 | Mark Mathabane. *Kaffir Boy in America: An Encounter with Apartheid.* |
| 1990 | Bodo Kirchhoff. *Infanta.* |
| 1991 | Karin Burschik. *Yves: eine afrikanische Liebe.* |
| 1991 | Marien Ndaye. *En famille.* |
| 1992 | Eva Demski. *Afra: Ein Roman in fünf Bildern.* |

1992      Christa Karrer. *Liebesgeschichten? Schweizerinnen und Asylbewerber.*

1992      Mark Mathabane and Gail Mathabane. *Love in Black and White: The Triumph of Love over Prejudice and Taboo.*

1992      Chima Oji. *Unter die Deutschen gefallen.*

1992      Jane Ray. *The Story of the Creation.*

1992      Barry Unsworth. *Sacred Hunger.*

1993      Barbara Faith. *This Above All.*

1993      Alex Haley (and David Stevens). *Queen: The Story of an American Family.*

1993      Adolf Muschg. *Der Rote Ritter* (a modern Parzival).

1994      John Gregory Brown. *Decorations in a Ruined Cemetery.*

1994      Anita Richmond Bunkley. *Black Gold.*

1994      Carol Camper, ed. *Miscegenation Blues: Voices of Mixed Race Women.*

1994      Barbara Chase-Riboud. *The President's Daughter* (sequel to *Sally Hemings,* 1979).

1994      Rita Dove. *The Darker Face of the Earth: A Verse Play in Fourteen Scenes.*

1994      Lise Funderburg. *Black, White, Other: Biracial Americans Talk About Race and Identity.*

1994      Shirlee Taylor Haizlip. *The Sweeter the Juice: A Family Memoir in Black and White.*

1994      John Updike. *Brazil.*

1996      *Love Across the Color Line: The Letters of Alice Hanley to Channing Lewis,* eds. Helen Lefkowitz Horowitz and Kathy Peiss.

1996      James McBride. *The Color of Water: A Black Man's Tribute to His White Mother.*

1996      Scott Minerbrook. *Divided to the Vein: A Journey into Race and Family.*

# Prohibitions of Interracial Marriage and Cohabitation

| | |
|---|---|
| 1514 | Spanish law of 19 October explicitly permits intermarriage with Indians; permission of intermarriages reenacted in 1515 and 1556; intermarriage with blacks neither encouraged nor prohibited. |
| 1527 | Spanish royal decree of 11 May recommends that male slaves ought to marry female slaves as much as possible: "with marriage and their love for wives and children and orderly married life they will become more calm and much sin and trouble will be avoided." |
| 1541 | Another Spanish decree for the colonies recommends that black men be married to black women since reportedly Negro slaves kept "great numbers of Indian women, some of them voluntarily, others against their wishes." |
| 1630 | 1 Laws of Virginia 146; Hugh Davis in Jamestown ordered whipped for "abusing himself to the dishonor of God and the shame of Christians by defiling his body in lying with a Negro" (Higginbotham and Kopytoff note that "we cannot tell the gender of the Negro" and speculate that the "extremely strong language may have reflected the Council's revulsion at a homosexual relationship"). |
| 1638 | Ordinance of the Director and Council of New Netherland prohibits adulterous intercourse between whites and heathens, blacks or other persons, upon threat of exemplary punishment of the white party. |
| 1640 | 1 Laws of Virginia 552; "Robert Sweat is to do penance in church according to the law of England, for getting a negro woman with child, and the woman to be soundly whipped." |
| 1649 | "William Watts and Mary (Mr. Cornelius Lloyds negro woman) are ordered each of them to doe penance by standing in a white sheete with a white Rodd in their hands in the Chapell of Elizabeth River in the face of the congregation on the next sabbath day that the minister shall make penince service and the said Watts to pay the court charges" (Virginia case). |
| 1661 | Maryland act condemns free-born English women who intermarry with Negro slaves: "whatsoever free-born woman shall intermarry |

with any slave, shall serve the master of such slave during the life of her husband; all the issues of such free-born women, so married, shall be slaves as their fathers were." (According to Reuter, 78, children are condemned to 30-year slavery. Twenty years later amended to promise freedom to women and children if owner's permission was secured.)

1662    First Virginia laws against intermarriage and against interracial sex: "if any christian shall committ ffornication with a negro man or woman, hee or shee soe offending shall pay double the ffines imposed by the former act [which set fines for fornication at 500 pounds of tobacco]."

1677    Pennsylvania law.

1678    Political council of Cape colony prohibits marriages between Dutch *burghers* and freed slaves; reaffirmed by edict in 1685.

1681    Maryland statute threatens punishment of any master who "instigated or merely allowed marriage between his white female servants and Black male slaves."

1685    Dutch Cape law prohibits marriage between white men and slave women; some legal unions of white men with free women of color continued to take place, but with decreasing frequency.

1685    Article 9 of *Code noir* of Louis XIV threatens those men who live in concubinage with a (Negro) slave woman with the high fine of 2000 livres (pounds of sugar). Penalty could be avoided if the man so charged was unmarried and married the slave woman, which also legitimated any earlier offspring.

1686    *Code noir* permits intermarriage between white men and slave women, but penalizes cohabitation.

1691    Virginia law against "abominable mixture and spurious issue": penalty for intermarriage is permanent removal from the dominion; white mothers of an illegitimate child by a Negro or Mulatto have to pay 15 pounds sterling and the child becomes a servant until age 30; 3 Laws of Va. 86, 87; reenacted in 1696 (3 Laws of Va. 140) and 1705 (3 Laws of Va. 252, 453); punishment: banishment of white partner, minister who performs marriage has to pay 10,000 pounds of tobacco.

1692    Acts of Maryland 76.

1705    Virginia penalty for ministers performing intermarriages: 10,000 pounds of tobacco.

1705    Massachusetts "Act for the Better Preventing of a Spurious and Mixt Issue" bans interracial fornication and marriage by statute. Section 1 prohibits fornication of "any negro or molatto man" "with an English woman, or a woman of any other Christian nation within this province," punishable by whipping of both partners, the selling of the man out of the province within six months (after continuous imprisonment), and pressing the woman into servitude if she is unable to maintain a child. Section 2 bans fornication of "any

Englishman, or man of another Christian nation within this province" "with a negro, or molatto woman," punishable by whipping of only the man, who also shall pay a fine of five pounds and, if applicable, child support, and by the selling of the woman out of the province. Section 4 prohibits the contracting of matrimony between one of "her majesty's English or Scottish subjects, [or] of any other Christian nation within this province" and "any negro or molatto," threatening persons authorized who solemnize such a marriage with a fine of 50 pounds. Samuel Sewall polemicizes, without success, against the Act.

| 1715 | Laws of Maryland, ch. 44, sec. 25, providing for forced servitude of white women who had sexual relationships with black men. |
| 1715 | North Carolina prohibits interracial marriage. |
| 1717 | 3 Statutes at Large of South Carolina, no. 383, at 20. |
| 1721 | Delaware intermarriage ban. |
| 1724 | French edict (of March) by Louis XV bans intermarriages between whites and blacks (but not whites and Indians) in Louisiana; this special *Code noir* for Louisiana also prohibits whites "or freeborn or freed blacks" to live in concubinage with slaves; article 6 says: "Défendons à nos sujets blancs, de l'un et de l'autre sexe, de contracter mariage avec les Noirs, à paine de punition et d'amende arbitraire; et à tous curés, prêtres ou missionaires, séculiers ou réguliers, et même aux aumôniers de vaissaix de les marier." ("We forbid our white subjects of either sex to contract marriage with blacks, under threat of punishment and fines; and forbid all clerics, priests, or missionaries, lay or ordained, and even ships' chaplains, to marry them.") |
| 1725 | Pennsylvania forbids interracial marriage and cohabitation. |
| 1728 | Maryland extends law to prohibit intermarriage and cohabitation between free mulatto women and black slaves; and subjects Negro women who have bastard children by white men to the same penalties as white women and Negro men. |
| 1738 | Declaration prohibits the marriage of a slave while in France, openly ignored by Church. |
| 1741 | 1 Laws of North Carolina, ch. 35, sec. 15, at 157. |
| 1748 | 5 Laws of Virginia 548. |
| 1753 | 6 Laws of Virginia 111, 325, 361. |
| 1769 | 8 Laws of Virginia 358. |
| 1771 | Viceroy of Portuguese Brazil orders degradation of an Amerindian chief, who, "disregarding the signal honours which he had received from the Crown, had sunk so low as to marry a Negress, staining his blood with this alliance." |
| 1778 | 5 April: "Order of the Council of State forbidding all marriages between whites and blacks in France, on penalty of being expelled at once to the colonies." |

| | |
|---|---|
| 1778 | Spanish marriage regulation of 1776, requiring parental consent for couples under twenty-five (in order to prevent unequal alliances), is extended to overseas possessions with proviso that it is not to be applied to "Mulattoes, Negroes, Coyotes and other Castas and similar races." |
| 1780 | Pennsylvania repeals its law of 1725. |
| 1786 | Virginia bill, drafted by Thomas Jefferson, revises colonial marriage law, omitting reference to ecclesiastical authority but reenacting the following: "A marriage between a person of free condition and a slave, or between a white person and a negro, or between a white person and a mulatto, shall be null." |
| 1786 | 22 June: Massachusetts reenacts the colonial law, "That no person by this Act authorized to marry, shall join in marriage any white person with any Negro, Indian or Mulatto, on penalty of the sum of *fifty pounds.* . . ; and that all such marriages shall be absolutely null and void." |
| 1800–1900 | "During the nineteenth century, as many as thirty-eight [U.S.] states prohibited interracial marriages." |
| 1805 | Spanish royal decree requires that persons of "pure blood" obtain permission of the viceroy or the audiencia in order to marry "elements of Negro and Mulatto origin." |
| 1808 | Louisiana Civil Code 1808, page 24, article 8: "Free persons and slaves are incapable of contracting marriage together; the celebration of such marriages is forbidden, and the marriage is void; it is the same with respect to the marriages contracted by free white persons with free people of color." |
| 1819 | First reported U.S. (postcolonial) case. |
| 1819 | *Midway v. Needham,* 16 Mass. 157, upheld the validity of a marriage between a Mulatto man and a white woman, both domiciled in Massachusetts, "although celebrated in Rhode Island in order to avoid the Massachusetts law." |
| 1825 | Louisiana Civil Code continues the prohibition of marriage between slaves, free persons of color, and whites. |
| 1837 | 5 June: Texas act provides "It shall not be lawful for any person of Caucasian blood or their descendants to intermarry with Africans or the descendants of Africans." |
| 1839 | 20 March: Lydia Maria Child petitions the Massachusetts House of Representatives to abolish antiamalgamation legislation. |
| 1841 | 19 January: Massachusetts House of Representatives petition by Wm. E. Channing and 42 other Bostonians to repeal intermarriage ban. |
| 1841 | Rhode Island repeals its law banning intermarriage. |
| 1841 | Pennsylvania bill passed in the House but defeated in the Senate. |
| 1843 | Massachusetts repeals law. |

| | |
|---|---|
| 1849 | Virginia Code, ch. 109, sec. 1, at 471 makes "any marriage between a white person and a Negro absolutely void without further legal process" (Higginbotham and Kopytoff 2007n, stress that before then children of mixed marriages were not illegitimate). |
| 1861 | Ohio law forbids intermarriage between a person of pure white blood and one having a visible admixture of African blood. |
| 1869 | *Scott v. Georgia*, 39 Ga. rep. 321, 324 (1869): "The amalgamation of the races is not only unnatural, but is always productive of deplorable results. Our daily observation shows us, that the off-spring of these unnatural connections are generally sickly and effeminate, and that they are inferior in physical development and strength, to the full-blood of either race. It is sometimes urged that such marriages should be encouraged, for the purpose of elevating the inferior race. The reply is, that such connections never elevate the inferior race to the position of the superior, but they bring down the superior to that of the inferior. They are productive of evil, and evil only, without any corresponding good." |
| 1869 | Missouri supreme court approves a miscegenation law because "mixed marriages cannot possibly have any progeny and such a fact sufficiently justifies those laws which forbid intermarriage of blacks and whites." |
| 1871 | *State v. Gibson*, 36 Indiana 389, 404, citing with approval: "The natural law which forbids their [black and white] intermarriage and that social amalgamation which leads to a corruption of races, is as clearly divine as that which imparted to them different natures." |
| 1871 | Tennessee: *Doc. Lonas v. State*, 50 Tenn. 287, 310–11: "The laws of civilization demand that the races be kept apart in this country. The progress of either does not depend upon an admixture of blood. A sound philanthropy, looking to the public peace and the happiness of both races, would regard any effort to intermerge the individuality of the races as a calamity full of the saddest and gloomiest portent to the generations that are to come after us." |
| 1877 | Alabama supreme court, in *Green v. State*, 58 Ala. 190, 195, asserts state's right to enforce intermarriage bans: "Manifestly, it is for the peace and happiness of the black race, as well as of the white, that such laws should exist. And surely there can not be any tyranny or injustice in requiring both alike, to form this union with those of their own race only, whom God hath joined together by indelible peculiarities, which declare that He has made the two races distinct." |
| 1877 | In the Virginia case of *McPherson v. Commonwealth*, 69 Va. 292, Judge Moncure decided that Rowena McPherson was permitted to marry a white man because "less than one-fourth of her blood is negro blood. If it be but one drop less, she is not a negro." |
| 1877 | Colorado passes the following laws only for the part settled by the United States (not valid in the part of Colorado settled by Mexico): |

"All marriages between Negroes and mulattoes of either sex and white persons are declared absolutely void. . . . provided that nothing in this section shall be construed as to prevent people living in that portion of the State acquired from Mexico from marrying according to the custom of that country." Penalties: "Fine of not less than fifty nor more than five hundred dollars, or imprisonment for not less than three months, nor more than two years." Chapter 63, 1736, sec. 2, and 1737, sec. 3.

1878    Virginia supreme court, in *Kinney v. Commonwealth*, 71 Va. 858, 869, considers it the state's duty to protect the moral welfare of both races and ban miscegenation: "The purity of public morals, the moral and physical development of both races, and the highest advancement of our cherished southern civilization, under which two distinct races are to work out and accomplish the destiny to which the Almighty has assigned them on this continent—all require that they should be kept distinct and separate, and that connections and alliances so unnatural that God and nature seem to forbid them, should be prohibited by positive law, and be subject to no evasion."

1880    Mississippi code bans intermarriage, declaring it to be "incestuous and void." Statute provides the same punishment as for incest. Section 3244: "any party thereto, on conviction, shall be punished as for a marriage within the degrees prohibited by the last two sections."

1881    Alabama supreme court, in *Pace v. State*, 69 Ala. 231, 232, upholds a statute more severely punishing adultery when it is interracial and stresses the hazardous effects of racial mixing: "Its result may be the amalgamation of the two races, producing a mongrel population and a degraded civilization, the prevention of which is dictated by a sound public policy affecting the highest interests of society and government."

1881    Florida act provides twelve months' imprisonment and a maximum fine of $500 for a Negro and a white person of opposite sex who occupy the same room habitually. Penalty for violation of intermarriage prohibition is prison up to ten years and a maximum fine of $500; for clergymen, priests, or public officials who solemnize such a union, it is prison up to one year and a fine up to $1000.

1882    U.S. Supreme Court rules the Alabama Code's harsher punishment of interracial fornication constitutional in *Pace v. Alabama*, 106 U.S. 583—on the grounds that both black and white get punished more severely for interracial than for intraracial fornication: "The two sections of the code cited are entirely consistent. The one prescribes, generally, a punishment for an offense committed between persons of different sexes; the other prescribes a punishment for an offence which can only be committed where the two sexes are of different races. There is in neither section any discrimination against either race. Sect. 4184 equally includes the offence when the persons of the two sexes are both white and when they are both black. Sect. 4189 applies the same punishment to both offenders, the white and the black. Indeed, the offence against which this latter section is aimed cannot be committed without involving the persons of both races in the same punishment. Whatever discrimination is made in the punishment prescribed in the two sections is directed against the offence designated and not against the person of any particular color or race. The punishment of each offending person, whether white or black, is the same."

1883    Maine and Michigan laws repealed.

1883    Missouri: *State v. Jackson*, Mo. 175, 179: "It is stated as a well authenticated fact that if the issue of a black man and a white woman, and a white man and a black woman, intermarry, they cannot possibly have any progeny, and such a fact sufficiently justifies those laws which forbid the intermarriage of blacks and whites, laying out of view other sufficient grounds for such enactments."

1883    Constitution of North Carolina, art. 14, sec. 8: "All marriages between a white person and a Negro, or between a white person and a person of Negro descent to the third generation inclusive, are hereby forever prohibited."

1886    New Mexico repeals its law.

1887    Ohio legislature repeals all laws establishing or permitting distinctions of color, including intermarriage bans.

1888    U.S. Supreme Court, in *Maynard v. Hill*, 125 U.S. 190 (not an intermarriage case), decides that marriages are not contracts in the sense of those constitutionally protected.

1889    Georgia II Code, sec. 2422: "The marriage relation between white persons and persons of African descent is forever prohibited, and such marriage shall be null and void."

1890    Constitution of Mississippi, art. 14, sec. 263: "The marriage of a white person with a negro or mulatto, or person who shall have one-eighth or more of negro blood, shall be unlawful and void."

1890    Federal District Court of Southern Georgia determines, in *State v. Tutty*, 41 Fed. 753, that Georgia laws forever prohibiting marriage between whites and persons of African descent cannot be circumvented by contracting a marriage in another state.

1891    Colorado: Mill's Annotated Statutes, secs. 1320–2989: "All marriages between Negroes or Mulattoes, of either sex, and white persons are declared to be absolutely void."

1892    State Constitution of Florida, art. 16, sec. 24: "All marriages between a white person and a negro, or between a white person and a person of negro descent to the fourth generation, inclusive, are hereby forever prohibited."

1893    Kentucky Statutes, sec. 2097, prohibits and declares void marriage "between a white person and a negro or mulatto"; intermarriages from other states are not recognized; no property rights come from such a marriage.

1895    The Constitution of South Carolina, art. 3, sec. 33: "The marriage of a white person with a negro or mulatto, or person who shall have one-eighth or more of negro blood, shall be unlawful and void."

1895    Georgia, II Code, sec. 2422: "The marriage relation between white persons and persons of African descent is forever prohibited, and such marriage shall be null and void."

1896    Constitution of Tennessee, art. 11, sec. 14: "The intermarriage of white persons with negroes, mulattoes, or persons of mixed blood, descended from a negro to the third generation, inclusive, or their living together as man and wife in this State is prohibited. The legislature shall enforce this section by appropriate legislation."

1897    Transvaal passes law no. 2—1897, "Wet tot tegengaan van de ontucht," immorality legislation against extramarital intercourse between consenting white women and black men (defined to include all members of indigenous and colored races of South Africa as well as Coolies, Arabs, and Malays). Penalties for the white woman (in cases other than rape) were up to five years' imprisonment or expulsion from the republic; for black men, six years of hard labor and up to 50 lashes. This law and its amendments (no. 46—1903, "Immorality Ordinance," and no. 16—1908, "Criminal Law Amendment Act") provided the models for other South African laws, including the 1927 "Immorality Act."

1897    Transvaal law no. 3—1897 regulating marriages of coloured people, "Wet regelnde de huwelijken van kleurlingen," which specified only the possibility that colored people marry other colored people, whereas the previous marriage law of 1871 was only for whites; colored marriages contracted before 1897 were legalized with ordinance no. 29—1903.

1898    Utah Revised Statutes, sec. 1184: "Marriage is prohibited and declared void: between a negro and a white person" and "between a Mongolian and a white person."

1901    Alabama State Constitution (amended), sec. 102: "The legislature shall never pass any law to authorize or legalize any marriage between any white person and a negro, or a descendant of a negro."

1901    Arizona Revised Statutes, sec. 3092: "All Marriages of persons of Caucasian blood, or their descendants, with Negroes, Mongolians or Indians, and their descendants, shall be null and void" (followed by incest ban).

1902    Oregon: Bellinger and Cotton Code, sec. 5217: "What marriages are void. 3. When either of the parties is a white person and the other negro, or Mongolian or a person of one-fourth or more of negro or Mongolian blood." Sec. 1999: "Hereafter it shall not be lawful within this state for any white person, male or female, to intermarry with any negro, Chinese, or any person having one-fourth or more negro, Chinese or Kanaka blood, or any person having more than one-half Indian blood, . . . . and all such marriages, or attempted marriages, shall be absolutely null and void."

1902     Cape Colony law no. 36–1902, "Betting Houses, Gaming Houses, and Brothels Suppression Act," prohibits voluntary sexual relations for the purpose of gain between white women and Africans ("aboriginal natives"); the maximum punishment for women is two years' imprisonment at hard labor (sec. 24), for procuring up to five years at hard labor, and for male procurers additionally up to 25 beatings (secs. 35 and 36). In the House of Assembly debates of 1902 (pp. 438 and 486ff) the law was advocated by Mr. Graham as a protection of women, and by Mr. Merriman as a device in the interest of white and black in order to prevent riots of the kind that were familiar from the southern United States. (Prostitution and procuring were only punishable when they were interracial. Unlike in the model of this law from Transvaal, the black men in these cases were not subjected to punishment. The law did not affect white men and black prostitutes or white women and colored men.)

1903     The British colonies in what was to become South Africa enacted laws similar to but going beyond that of the Cape Colony.

Natal: No. 31-1903, "Criminal Law Amendment Act," prohibits indecent relations between white women and colored persons (sec. 16); colored were defined in the "Vagrancy Law" 15-1869 as "Hottentots, coolies, bushmen, Lascars, and members of the so-called kaffer population."

Orange Free State: No. 11—1903, "Suppression of Brothels and Immorality Act," sec. 14–16.

Transvaal: No. 46-1903, "Immorality Ordinance," similar to Natal, but with harsher punishment and with a very broad definition of "native" as including natives of the indigenous or colored races of Africa, Asia, or St. Helena; in addition Transvaal had no provisions for (though also no direct ban of) intermarriages since 1897.

1903     Rhodesian "Immorality and Indecency Suppression Act" (by Cecil Rhodes's British South African Company) makes illegal and punishable sexual relations between a white woman and a black man (but not those between a white man and a black woman).

1904     Arkansas, Kerby's Statues, sec. 5174: "All marriages of white persons with Negroes or Mulattoes are declared to be illegal and void."

1906     *Kerr's Code of California*, vol. 2, part 3, paragraph 60: "All marriages of white persons with negroes, mongolians, or mulattoes are illegal and void."

1906     Missouri Statutes, ch. 50, sec. 4312: "All marriages between white persons and mongolians, are prohibited and declared absolutely void, and this prohibition shall apply to illegitimate as well as legitimate children and relatives." Sec. 2174: "No person having one-eighth part or more of negro blood shall be permitted to marry any white person, nor shall any white person be permitted to marry any negro or person having one-eighth part or more of negro blood; and every person who shall knowingly marry in violation of the provisions of this section shall, upon conviction, be punished by imprisonment in the penitentiary for two years, or by fine of not less than one hundred dollars, or by imprisonment in the county jail not less than three months, or by both such fine and imprisonment; and the jury trying any such case may determine the proportion of negro blood in any party to such marriage from the appearance of such person."

1906 Texas Criminal Statutes, art. 346: "If any white person and negro shall knowingly intermarry with each other within this state, or, having so intermarried, in or out of the state, shall continue to live together as man and wife within this state, they shall be punished by confinement in the penitentiary for a term not less than two or more than five years."

1906 West Virginia Code, sec. 2917: "Void marriages: 1. All marriages between a white person and a negro."

1908 Natal Native Affairs Committee publishes report in which desirability of intermarriage ban is discussed (but not formally proposed); the report invoked Herbert Spencer's condemnation of intermarriage on the ground that it leads to incalculably chaotic character traits in the second generation.

1908 Indiana statutes make void marriage between a white person and one of one-eighth or more of Negro blood.

1908 Louisiana Act 87 makes "concubinage between a person of the Caucasian race and a person of the negro race a felony, fixing the punishment therefore and defining what shall constitute the concubinage"; penalty imprisonment of one month to one year with or without hard labor.

In the same year the Louisiana Supreme Court in *State v. Treadaway* (126 La. 1908) acquits Treadaway of miscegenation charge "because his companion was an octoroon, and an octoroon was not 'a person of the negro blood or black race.'" This, the court argues, is because "[t]here are no negroes who are not persons of color; but there are persons of color who are not negroes" (see 1910 for Louisiana's legislative response).

Louisiana Civil Code, art. 94, prohibits and voids marriage between white persons and persons of color.

1909 Montana statutes passed declaring marriages between whites and persons of whole or part Negro blood or Chinese or Japanese null and void.

1909 North Dakota makes marriage of white state residents with persons of one-eighth or more Negro blood unlawful and void, punishable by prison of up to ten years and/or a fine of up to two thousand dollars.

1910      Louisiana legislature, in act 206, House bill no. 220, amends inter-racial concubinage prohibition to extend to any "person of the col-ored or black race."

1910      Natal case of *Biscombe and Bissesseur v. Rex*: The white woman Bis-combe was acquitted of miscegenation charges for her relation with the Indian man Bissesseur because the court determined that "coolies" was not a racial term but included class features: for exam-ple, a barrister of Indian parentage was not a "coolie" and Bissesseur was a "free" Indian and hence not a "coolie."

1910      North Carolina case of *Ferrall v. Ferrall* turns down a husband's request to evade a property settlement and alimony on the grounds that his wife was "negro within the prohibited degree": "Years ago the plaintiff married a wife who, if she had any strain of negro blood whatever, was so white he did not suspect it until recently. . . . Now . . . he seeks to get rid of her . . . in a method that will not only deprive her of any support while he lives by alimony, or by dower after his death, but which would consign her to the association of the colored race which he so affects to despise. . . . The law may not permit him thus to bastardize his own children."

1910      Oklahoma Revised Laws, sec. 3894: "The marriage of any person of African descent, as defined by the constitution of this State to any person not of African descent to any person of African descent, shall be unlawful and is hereby prohibited within this State." The state constitution, art. 23, sec. 11, defines races as follows: "Wher-ever in this Constitution and laws of the State the word or words 'colored' or 'colored race,' 'negro' or 'negro race' are used the same shall be construed to mean or apply to all persons of African descent. The term 'white race' shall include all other persons."

1911      Nebraska Compiled Statutes, ch. 25, sec. 31, Consanguinity or Miscegenation: "Upon the dissolution by decree or sentence of nullity of any marriage that is prohibited on account of consanguin-ity between the parties, or of any marriage between a white person and a negro, the issue of the marriage shall be deemed to be illegiti-mate."

1912      Nevada Revised Laws, sec. 6517: "If any white person with any per-son shall live and cohabit with any black person, mulatto, Indian, or any person of the Malay or brown race or of the Mongolian or yel-low race, in a state of fornication, such person so offending shall, on conviction thereof, be fined in any sum not exceeding five hundred dollars, and not less than one hundred dollars, or be imprisoned in the county jail not less than six months or more than one year, or both."

1912      17 January: Ban of racial intermarriages in German Samoa.

1912      8 May: German *Reichstag* defeats proposal to ban intermarriage in colonies and resolves (202 to 133 votes) that Bundesrat enact legis-lation securing the validity of marriages between whites and natives in German colonies and regulating the rights of illegitimate children; sponsors: Zentrum, supported by Social Democrats.

1913     Nebraska Laws, ch. 72, sec. 5302. Void marriages: "First—when one party is a white person and the other is possessed of one-eighth or more negro, Japanese or Chinese blood."

1913     South Dakota Compiled Laws, ch. 166, sec. 1: "The intermarriage or illicit cohabitation of any persons belonging to the African, Corean, Malayan or Mongolian race, with any person of the opposite sex, belonging to the Caucasian or white race, is hereby prohibited, and any person who shall hereafter enter into any such marriage, or who shall indulge in any such illicit cohabitation shall be deemed guilty of a felony and upon conviction thereof shall be punished by a fine of not exceeding ten years or both such fine and imprisonment."

1913     South African *Assaults on Women Committee*, p. 36, criticizes 1902 "Brothels Suppression Act" for not including sexual relations between white men and native women.

1915     Michigan Compiled Laws, sections 5700–5703 makes intermarriages expressly valid.

1915     28 U.S. states have statutes prohibiting interracial marriages or cohabitation; ten among them have constitutional prohibitions.

1919     Idaho law (amended 1921) declares marriage between whites and Mongolians, Negroes, or Mulattoes to be illegal and void; penalty for cohabitation is imprisonment up to six months and a maximum fine of $300.

1920     Statutes of Louisiana, act 220, prohibits marriage between persons of Indian race and of colored or black race; act 230 forbids cohabitation between Negroes and Indians.

1920     Wyoming Compiled Statutes prohibit marriage of a white and a Negro, Mulatto, Mongolian, or Malay.

1921     Georgia act makes felonious and void the intermarriage of whites and persons with an ascertainable trace of African, West Indian, Asiatic Indian, or Mongolian blood. Provisions for detecting such blood could not be enforced for lack of appropriations.

1921     Montana Revised Codes, sec. 5700, declares null and void the marriage between a white person and a Negro or a person with some part of Negro blood.

1923     Public Acts of Michigan, no. 7, declares intermarriages legal.

1923     Oklahoma Supreme Court, in *Blake v. Sessions*, declares void the marriage between a man of 3/4 Indian and 1/4 Negro blood and a woman with 3/4 Indian and 1/4 white blood (reason: 1910 Oklahoma Laws, sec. 1677, prohibits marriages between persons of African descent and persons of non-African descent).

1924     27 February: Virginia Senate passes 23 to 4 the "Act to Preserve Racial Integrity," requiring racial ancestry certificate for all citizens born before 14 June 1912 and sharpening previous intermarriage bans: "It shall be unlawful for any white person in this state to marry any save a white person, or a person with no other admixture of blood than white and American Indian. For the purpose of this act, the term 'white person' shall apply only to the person who has no trace whatsoever of any blood other than Caucasian; but persons who have one-sixteenth or less of the blood of the American Indian and have no other non-caucasic blood shall be deeemed to be white" (previously persons of less than one-quarter Negro blood did not count as Negroes).

1927    South African Union House of Assembly (under Hertzog government) passes "Immorality Act," no. 5—1927, which bans all extramarital interracial sexual relations between Europeans and Africans. "Illicit carnal intercourse" is defined as an "offence" punishable with prison up to five years for men and up to four years for women. In the *House of Assembly Debates* 1926, p. 36, and 1927, pp. 37ff., the minister of justice Tielman Roos defended the proposed act as protecting the native women of South Africa, and, second, in order to teach the populace that intercourse between Europeans and natives was not a thing to be taken lightly. From 1928 to 1938 about 550 Europeans (among them 75 women) and 600 natives (among them 510 women) were punished.

1927    Georgia passes law requiring citizens to provide information on racial antecedents.

1930    Virginia requires persons to provide racial genealogy.

1934    South West Africa enacts "Immorality Proclamation," no. 19-1934, modeled on South Africa's 1927 "Immorality Act."

1935    15 September: "Nürnberger Gesetze" prohibit interracial sex and marriage between "Aryans" and "Jews" in Nazi Germany; "Gesetz zum Schutz des deutschen Blutes und der deutschen Ehre" and "Reichsbürgergesetz," *Reichsgesetzblatt* 1146.

1936/37    Proposals for union-wide bans of interracial marriages are introduced to South African House of Assembly by Major Roberts and General Pienaar but defeated; the minister of the interior, Jan H. Hofmeyr, strongly opposed the proposals. A Mixed Marriage Commission is formed.

1938    17 November: "Provvedimenti per la difesa della razza italiana," *Reggio Decreto Legge* no. 1728 in fascist Italy: "Il matrimonio del cittadino italiano di razza ariana con persona appartenente ad altra razza è proibito."

1945    End of World War II; racial legislation in Italy and Germany annulled.

1948    California supreme court case of *Perez v. Sharp*, 32 Cal. 2d 711, 198 P. 2d 17, declares state miscegenation laws unconstitutional.

1949    South African Union passes "Prohibition of Mixed Marriages Act" which makes intermarriage between Europeans and all non-Europeans illegal.

1950        South African Union amends 1927 "Immorality Act" to extend it to "Coloureds"; sexual intercourse or even "immoral or indecent acts" between whites and *all* nonwhite groups prohibited; maximum punishment of seven years of hard labor, corporal punishment for men; only exceptions are couples legally married before 1949 Act. "Sexual relations between persons of African, Coloured, and Asiatic origin are not forbidden by law." According to Wauthier, *Literature and Thought of Modern Africa*, 181, the official number of those found guilty from the enactment to June 1964 exceeded 5000: "*Europeans*: men 2,614, women 118; *Africans*: men 119, women 1,208; *Coloureds*: men 76, women 1,072; *Asians* (mainly of Indian origin): men 17, women 28."

1950        Intermarriage prohibited in 30 of 48 U.S. states (same figure for 1944; by the 1967 Supreme Court ruling, 13 states had repealed their laws).

1951        Oregon repeals interdiction.

1953        Montana terminates prohibition.

1955        North Dakota laws voided.

1955        In *Naim v. Naim*, 197 Va. 80, 87 S.E. 2d 749, Virginia supreme court sustains miscegenation statute; state's legislative purpose was "to preserve the racial integrity of its citizens" and to prevent "the corruption of blood," "the obliteration of racial pride," and the creation of "a mongrel breed of citizens."

1957        South Dakota and Colorado repeal laws.

1959        Louisiana supreme court upholds the state's miscegenation law, arguing that the state could protect the children from such marriages from "a feeling of inferiority as to their status in the community that may affect their hearts and minds in a way unlikely ever to be undone" (Zabel, 121 notes that this was a sarcastic verbal echo of the Supreme Court's 1954 school integration ruling in *Brown v. Board of Education*).

1959        California, Idaho, and Nevada repeal ban.

1961        Rhodesian "Immorality and Indecency Suppression Act" of 1903 abrogated.

1962        Arizona law repealed.

1963        Nebraska and Utah revoke intermarriage prohibitions.

1964        In *McLaughlin et al. v. Florida*, U.S. Supreme Court strikes down Florida criminal statute 798.05, which prohibits an "unmarried interracial couple from habitually living in and occupying the same room in the nighttime" with a penalty of jail up to one year and a fine up to $500; ruling explicitly overturns *Pace v. Alabama* (1882). Court avoids the intermarriage issue as it rejects Florida's argument in support of the interracial cohabitation ban "without reaching the question of the validity of the State's prohibition against interracial marriage. . . . For even if we posit the constitutionality of the ban against the marriage of a Negro and a white, it does not follow that the cohabitation law is not to be subjected to independent examination under the Fourteenth Amendment."

1965    Wyoming laws removed.

1966    19 U.S. states (17 in the South) have intermarriage proscriptions.

1967    12 June: *Loving v. Virginia.* U.S. Supreme Court rules (9 to 0) that antimiscegenation laws are unconstitutional within the equal protection clause of the Fourteenth Amendment. Chief Justice Warren: "There can be no question that Virginia's miscegenation statutes rest solely upon distinctions drawn according to race. . . . Marriage is one of 'the basic civil rights of man,' fundamental to our very existence and survival. . . . To deny this fundamental freedom on so unsupportable a basis as the racial classifications embodied in these statutes, classifications so directly subversive of the principle of equality at the heart of the Fourteenth Amendment, is surely to deprive all the State's citizens of liberty without due process of law. The Fourteenth Amendment requires that freedom of choice to marry not be restricted by invidious racial discriminations. Under our Constitution, the freedom to marry or not marry, a person of another race resides with the individual and cannot be infringed by the State." The case was that of the white construction worker Richard Loving and his Negro wife Mildred Jeter, who had married in the District of Columbia and then returned to Virginia. Decision affected Virginia and the following sixteen states with statutes or constitutions outlawing interracial marriage: Alabama, Arkansas, Delaware, Florida, Georgia, Kentucky, Louisiana, Mississippi, Missouri, North Carolina, Oklahoma, South Carolina, Tennessee, Texas, and West Virginia. Maryland had initiated a repeal of the law.

1968    South African parliament votes to consider null and void any interracial marriage, solemnized abroad, between white South Africans and nonwhites.

1977    Limited Constitutional Convention eliminates prohibition of interracial marriages from Tennessee Constitution by resolving unanimously that "Article XI, of the Constitution is hereby amended by deleting therefrom in its entirety Section 14 prohibiting interracial marriages."

1978    31 March: Tennessee proclaims repeal of the 1896 constitution's art. 11, sec. 14, prohibiting racial intermarriage after narrow approval of electorate with 199,742 against 191,745 votes.

1985    15 April: Home Affairs Minister Frederik W. de Klerk announces that South African government accepts recommendation from three-chamber parliamentary committee to overturn the 1949 "Prohibition of Mixed Marriages Act," the "Immorality Act," and other legislation prohibiting interracial sex or marriage. In the five preceding years, 918 people had been prosecuted for violations of these laws.

1987        4 December: Mississippi Secretary of State proclaims that section 263 of 1890 constitution, prohibiting interracial marriage, is deleted based upon House Concurrent Resolution #13 (Laws 1987, ch. 672) and ratification by the electorate on November 3.

# Notes

## Epigraphs

1. Ch. 20, "Topsy," *Three Novels* (New York: Library of America, 1982), 280–81. Shortened citations refer to the Selected Bibliography, pp. 523–560, in this book.

2. (1857; rpt. New York: Arno Press, 1969), 323.

3. *A Tale of Race and Social Conflict* (New York: Putnam, 1871), 14.

4. "[Fils d'un Blanc et d'une Noire sont] ni blancs ni noirs, ni Français ni Africains, ni frisés ni plats. Le malheur est qu'ils soient tout de même quelque chose." Albert Londres, *Terre d'ébène: La traite des Noirs* (Paris: Albin Michel, 1929), 70. Cited in Ada Martinkus-Zemp, *Le Blanc et le Noir: essai d'une description de la vision du Noir par le Blanc dans la littérature française de l'entre-deux-guerres* (Paris: A.-G. Nizet, 1975), 167.

5. *Saturday Review of Literature* (11 Oct. 1947): 52. See Hortense Spillers's brief theming of the "shadow" in Frances Harper and Faulkner in her suggestive "Notes on an Alternative Model—Neither/Nor," 181–83.

6. *Sex and Science Fiction Writing in the East Village, 1957–1965* (New York: Arbor House, 1988), 52. Delany may here be particularly thinking of Jean Toomer's aphorism: "I am of no particular race. I am of the human race, a man at large in the human world, preparing a new race" and "I am neither male nor female nor in-between. I am of sex, with male differentiations." *Essentials: Definitions and Aphorisms* (Chicago: privately printed, 1931), xxiv.

## Introduction

1. The "interracial" focus here is on black-white relations, historically the most significant ethnic difference in the United States, though interesting findings could be made in the investigation of many other racial frontiers. I was inspired to adopt the word from uses in scholarship and literature of the first half of the twentieth century, for example, G. Spiller, *Papers on Inter-Racial Problems* (London: P. S. King & Son, 1911), the "National Interracial Conference" reported by W. E. B. Du Bois in the *Crisis* 36 (Feb. 1929): 47, 69–70, or the poem "Interracial" (1943) by Georgia Douglas Johnson (JWJ, Shelf ZAN, Johnson, Georgia Douglas, folder 5, Beinecke Library, Yale University).

2. Williamson, *Crucible of Race*, 522. B. Fields, 117, argued: "If race lives on

today, it does not live on because we have inherited it from our forebears of the seventeenth century or the eighteenth or the nineteenth, but because we continue to create it today."

3. See, for example, Danielle Williams's statement in Lise Funderburg, *Black, White, Other: Biracial Americans Talk About Race and Identity* (New York: William Morrow, 1994), 48, in response to being called "biracial," that the word "Mulatto" "means only black and white." Rachel Countryman, "A Little Bit White," Germantown Friends School *Studies in Education* 56 (Winter 1989): 8–15, here 9–10, finds the word "biracial" "less offensive, but . . . also less descriptive" than "Mulatto": "Someone who is Arab and Sudanese is also biracial."

4. Immanuel Kant's definition of "race" as one of four skin colors within a unified mankind that had one origin rested on the observation that biracial children by necessity come out somewhere between their parents' skin colors. "Bestimmung des Begriffs einer Menschenrace" (1785), in *Gesammelte Schriften*, Akademie-Ausgabe, VIII (Berlin & Leipzig: de Gruyter, 1923), 89–106.

5. Definitions of "race" may, in fact, rest on bans of certain forms of exogamy: "The practice of endogamy is the most significant social control in any caste situation," write Davis, Gardner, and Gardner in *Deep South*, 24. B. Fields, 107, contemplated a Maryland law of 1664 and argued: "*Race* does not explain that law. Rather, the law shows society in the act of inventing race."

6. See, for example, Langston Hughes's fictional account of the fate of Roy Williams and Miss Reese in the story "Home" in *The Ways of White Folks* (1934; rpt. New York: Vintage Books, 1971), 32–48; or Richard Wright's strong evocation of the terror in that situation, both in "The Ethics of Living Jim Crow" (1940), most easily available as the preface to *Uncle Tom's Children* (New York: Harper & Row, 1965), esp. 11–12, and the end of the book "Fear" in *Native Son* (1940; rpt. New York: Harper & Row, 1966), 83–85, where Bigger Thomas's presence in Mary Dalton's bedroom constitutes an inherently Gothic plot element that directly leads to the killing. See also the representations of the Scottsboro boys and the continuing debate about the meaning of the Emmett Till case, for example in the contributions by Jeffrey Melnick and Katrin Schwenk to *The Black Columbiad* (Cambridge: Harvard Univ. Press, 1994), 298–324.

7. Howard Schuman, Charlotte Steeh, and Lawrence Bobo, *Racial Attitudes in America: Trends and Interpretations* (Cambridge: Harvard Univ. Press, 1985), 82–83, show a range from about 20% in 1962 to a peak of near 50% in 1974. In the North the rate is much higher, starting at between 40 and 50% and peaking above 80% in 1978.

8. Mangum, 237, referring to Mississippi Code Ann. par. 1103 (1930).

9. When Hannah Arendt, for example, argued in her essay "Reflections on Little Rock" (1959) that intermarriage bans should be removed, she had a hard time publishing it; when it finally appeared in *Dissent*, she was reminded by her critics that what the oppressed seek is "not the right to be accepted as brother-in-law but as brother" (63) and was called an "ardent champion" of intermarriage. Sidney Hook expressed deep shock at Arendt's proposal and felt that she gave "priority to agitation for equality in the bedroom rather than to equality in education," a phrasing that Arendt, in a further response, repeated in disbelief. See my essay "Of Mules and Mares in a Land of Difference; or, Quadrupeds All?," *American Quarterly* 42.2 (June 1990): 167–90.

10. *The Annotated Lolita*, ed. Alfred Appel, Jr. (New York: McGraw, 1970), 316.

11. Ford, "The [Miscegenation] Theme in *Pudd'nhead Wilson*," 13.

12. Henry Louis Gates, Jr., "Introduction" to Harriet Wilson, *Our Nig* (1859; rpt. New York: Random House, 1983), xxviii. Claude Julien stressed that this book was not exceptional for its theme but for handling it without a focus on the external obstacles to an interracial couple. For discussions of interracial marriage fiction in the pre–Civil War United States, see, for example, the section "Marriage" in Roy, 19–24, or Baym, 268–71.

13. Sánchez-Eppler, 244.

14. Kinney, 30. The author also claimed specifically that Harriet Wilson's autobiographical work supposedly introduced the motif of "a willing relationship between a white woman and a black man," a motif he believes only black American writers thematized before World War I (100). This comment suggests that the part of the interracial tradition thematizing consensual relations and marriage between a black man and a white woman that extends from *Othello* and Don Diego Ximénez de Enciso's *Comedia famosa de Juan Latino*, Thomas Southern's adaptation of *Oroonoko* and John Cleveland's "A Faire Nimph scorning a Black Boy Courting her," to Fanny Reybaud's "Les Épaves," Hans Christian Andersen's *Mulatten*, Gertrudis Gómez de Avellaneda's *Sab*, and C. W. [Mary] Denison's *Old Hepsy*, is so widely unfamiliar as to escape even the attention of professionals specializing in interracial literature.

15. O'Neill wrote "Go fuck yourself!" to the Grand Kleagle of the Georgia Ku Klux Klan; see Joel Pfister, *Staging Depth: Eugene O'Neill and the Politics of Psychological Discourse* (Chapel Hill and London: Univ. of North Carolina Press, 1995), 123. The Production Code of the Motion Picture Producers and Directors of America, Inc. (1930–34) ruled that "Miscegenation (sex relation between the white and black races) is forbidden." See Ella Shohat, "Ethnicities-in-Relation: Toward a Multicultural Reading of American Cinema," in *Unspeakable Images: Ethnicity and the American Cinema*, ed. Lester D. Friedman (Urbana and Chicago: Univ. of Illinois Press, 1991), 215–50, here 233. Eleanor Blau, "Do Scarlett and Rhett Discover Love Anew? A Sequel Reveals All," *New York Times* (25 Sept. 1991), C15 and 17, quote from C17. In April 1939, Cyril Clemens, then president of the International Mark Twain Society, asked Du Bois for advice in finding an appropriate colored publisher for a young "colored boy who has written a very readable novel." Du Bois answered on 31 May 1939: "With regard to the young man's novel of which you spoke, I beg to say that almost any of the reputable publishers will be glad to consider a novel on a Negro theme. They may be afraid of it if it is too radical or if it has too much miscegenation; but there is a good chance today of publishing such books" (Papers of W. E. B. Du Bois, reel 50, exp. 359, courtesy Shelley Fisher Fishkin).

16. See Maria Edgeworth, *Belinda* (1801; rpt. London: Everyman, 1993), xxv, 206–10, 243–44. Samuel Henry Romilly, *Romilly-Edgeworth Letters 1813–1818* (London: Murray, 1936), 87; Dykes, 140. On Edgeworth's relationship to her father as a background to *Belinda* see Elizabeth Kowaleski-Wallace, *Their Fathers' Daughters: Hannah More, Maria Edgeworth and Patriarchal Complicity* (New York: Oxford Univ. Press, 1991), 95–138, which makes no reference to the Juba subplot.

17. *Retrospect* (London and New York, 1838) I, 141; Dykes, 145 adds: "Miss Martineau was doubtless unaware of the fact that in England the same prejudice arose in some circles to such an extent that Mrs. Edgeworth changed the name from 'Juba' to 'Jackson.'"

18. Roy, 15–19. This formula has also invited many retellings: for example, George Washington Cable, responding to the letter by a reader, retold "'Tite Poulette" in "Madame Delphine." See Clark, "Cable," 607. In theatrical performance and early cinema the nonwhite partner in interracial romance situations was customarily portrayed by a white actor or actress.

19. Zack, 146, citing *Dust Tracks on a Road* (1942; rpt. Urbana and Chicago: Univ. of Illinois Press, 1984), 235–37. Jacquelyn Y. McLendon, "The Myth of the Mulatto Psyche: A Study of the Works of Jessie Fauset and Nella Larsen" (Ph.D. diss., Case Western Reserve University, 1986), has shown how important Hurston was in changing the interracial focus of previous novelists and replacing it by a black focus.

20. Zack, 146-47. Focusing on critics of Jean Toomer, Hutchinson, 228, has similarly criticized that "a discourse that allows no room for a 'biracial' text (except by defining it as 'black') is part of the *same discursive system* that denies the identity of the person who defines himself or herself as both black and white (or, in Langston Hughes's phrase, as 'neither white nor black')."

21. Both are quoted, among many other examples, in the excellent essay by Edelstein, 182 and 185.

22. (New York: Neale Publishing, 1914), 42. The terms for a black-white encounter on terms of sexual equality have often been subjected to some linguistic camouflage so that "social equality" in authors less candid than Bailey could become the term that veiled "interracial marriage." Fredrickson, *Black Image in the White Mind*, 297–98, gives a brief characterization of some of Bailey's views which included the rule, "let the lowest white man count more than the highest negro." L. Friedman, 99–100, takes Bailey's position as central for his thesis and stresses Bailey's insistence on white supremacy. Bailey may have been alerted to Tennyson's lines by the *Miscegenation* pamphlet of 1863 which quoted them (35; see also 54).

23. This is unlike, for example, Henry W. Grady, who claimed an "ineradicable and positive" instinct "that will keep the races apart" in his attack on George Washington Cable, "In Plain Black and White," *Century* 29.7 (1885): 909–17, here 912. As L. Friedman, 116 and 111, shows, Cable found himself arguing in a way meant, perhaps, to reassure the racialists that Reconstruction "produced no general intermingling" of the races, that there were "ordinary natural preferences of like for like," and that "[d]issimilar races are not inclined to mix spontaneously." See Cable, *The Negro Question*, ed. Arlin Turner (Garden City, N.Y.: Doubleday, 1958), 145; however, there Cable also addresses the issue of a "race instinct" critically (86).

24. *The Poems of Tennyson*, ed. Christopher Ricks (London: Longmans, 1969), 688–99, here 697–98. *Selections from Tennyson* (London: Leopold B. Hill, n.d.), however, omits the lines cited from its slightly abridged rendition of "Locksley Hall."

25. Bailey's ideas were undoubtedly shared by a few writers—many of whom published in the period from the turn of the century to the 1930s—who used their stories and novels precisely to polemicize *against* what they, however, still chose to represent, however paranoid such representations may have been. See, for example, Gertrude Atherton, Thomas Dixon, Robert Lee Durham, Hans Grimm, or Sarah Gertrude Millin.

26. Arens, 3–5, has similarly noted that many discussions of incest are, in fact, discussions of the incest *taboo*.

27. *Quicksand and Passing*, ed. Deborah McDowell (1929; rpt. New Brunswick, N.J.: Rutgers University Press, 1986), 39. Further references to this edition will be given parenthetically.

28. Previous thematic researches into various national literatures and periods have proved extremely valuable. The studies by Mencke and Berzon deserve special mention; the plot summaries in Kinney are particularly helpful for an analysis of selected novels from the United States; those given by Hoffmann are the best for French literature; Sommer is superb for Latin American writing; Marotti is useful for that of Brazil, Gilman for German literature, and Shyllon, Sypher, Barker, and Dabydeen for Britain. Sterling Brown, Jules Zanger, and Ratna Roy have successfully generalized certain *typical* plot lines of Mulatto fiction in the United States.

29. The original is at the Musée Carnavalet in Paris. A related 1774 allegory of nature and Charles Cordier's *Fraternité* were also reproduced in *The Image of the Black in Western Art*, 4.1 illus. 18 and 159. For the U.S. stamp, see Barth Healey, "Stamp for Bastille Day Reverses the Tricolor," *New York Times* (5 June 1989), A4. The Postal Service claimed that the figures were "redrawn in bas-relief to resemble statues, and in silver to stand out against the colored panels," all "without any thought of race."

30. I am aware of Naomi Zack's and Diana Williams's justified hesitation to develop a new "interracial" category, yet cannot resist the temptation to explore a tradition that subverts black/white thinking and confronts "mixed-race" alienation (141–47). Yet this is done not in order to invite "belonging" but in order to support Zack's contention that black and white racial identifications do not make sense. See also Simone Brooks's comment: "We have enough races as it is. Don't try to put me in one category on its own, thank you very much," in Funderburg, *Black, White, Other*, 320.

31. Since the issue (or the possibility) of descendants seems so intricately connected with the "interracial" cluster I am exploring here, the focus is exclusively on heterosexual couples and family structures. The homosexual and homosocial dimension of interracial literature, pioneeringly explored by Leslie Fiedler in *Love and Death*, would also make a good subject for further comparative investigations.

32. For a thoughtful critique of some contemporary uses of Gramsci's term "hegemony," see T. Jackson Lears, "The Concept of Cultural Hegemony: Problems and Possibilities," *American Historical Review* 90.3 (June 1985): 567–93.

33. Spillers, 166: "To understand, then, the American invention of the mulatto, a term imported from the European lexis, is to understand more completely, I feel, the false opposition of cultural traits that converge on the binary distribution of 'black' and 'white.'"

34. Diana Irene Williams, "New Orleans in the Age of Plessy v. Ferguson: Interracial Unions and the Politics of Caste" (Senior thesis, Harvard University, March 1995), 3. Pierre-André Taguieff used the term "mixophobie" in his "Doctrines de la race et hantise du métissage: fragments d'une histoire de la mixophobie savante," *Nouvelle Revue d'Ethnopsychiatrie* 17 (1991): 53–100; the English abstract translates the term as "crossphobia," the Spanish as "misofobia."

35. Sylvia Lyons Render, *The Short Fiction of Charles W. Chesnutt* (Washington, D.C.: Howard Univ. Press, 1974), 45–48, offers a brief survey of Chesnutt's general themes. William L. Andrews, "Charles Waddell Chesnutt: An Essay in Bibliography," *Resources for American Literary Study* (Spring 1976): 10–12, summarizes the secondary literature on the story.

36. *The Wife of His Youth and Other Stories of the Color Line* (1899; rpt. Ann Arbor: Univ. of Michigan Press, 1969), 7.

37. William Dean Howells, "Mr. Charles W. Chesnutt's Stories," *Atlantic Monthly* 85 (May 1900): 699–700, 701. For later "Mulatto" theming, see Robert A. Smith, "A Pioneer Black Writer and the Problems of Discrimination and Miscegenation," *Costerus* 9 (1973): 182.

38. *Bookman* (Feb. 1900): 597–98. Though written from a different political point of view, her argument that Ryder thinks too much of whiteness curiously anticipates the theming of the story done since the 1960s.

39. Hugh M. Gloster, *Negro Voices in American Fiction* (New York: Russell and Russell, 1965), 36.

40. *American Literature: The Makers and the Making*, vol. 2 (New York: St. Martin's Press, 1973), 1745.

41. Bone, *Down Home*, 99. "But Chesnutt is concerned more broadly with relations between the black elite and the black masses. In 'The Wife of His Youth' he celebrates the values of group solidarity, *noblesse oblige*, and a loyalty that is unwilling to betray its own."

42. Ibid. This phrasing was echoed by Alessandro Portelli's section title, "Un nero volontario," in "La Linea del colore: Introduzione a Charles W. Chesnutt," in *La Sposa della giovinezza* (Venezia: Marsilio, 1991), 14.

43. William Andrews, *The Literary Career of Charles W. Chesnutt* (Baton Rouge and London: Louisiana State Univ. Press, 1980), 115–16.

44. Sylvia Lyons Render, *Charles W. Chesnutt* (Boston: Twayne, 1980), 134.

45. Sundquist, *To Wake the Nations*, 299–300.

46. Ibid., 299, following Bone, *Down Home*, 98–99.

47. See *The Poems of Tennyson*, ed. Christopher Ricks (London: Longmans, 1969), 503–4. All further references to Tennyson's poems come from this critical edition.

48. Jerome Buckley, *Tennyson: The Growth of a Poet* (Cambridge: Harvard Univ. Press, 1960), suggestively discussed several of Tennyson's poems in terms of the conflict between past and present. Chesnutt renders the theme of women's devotion and fidelity (and men's likeliness to lack such virtues) in a phrasing repeated in the story. Thus Ryder says: "But perhaps the quality which most distinguishes woman is her fidelity and devotion to those she loves. History is full of examples, but has recorded none more striking than one which only to-day came under my notice" (96; see also 98).

49. Tennyson commented:

I was thinking of Shakespeare's Cleopatra: "Think of me/That am with Phoebus' amorous pinches black" (*Antony and Cleopatra* I v 28). Millais has made a mulatto of her in his illustration. I know perfectly well that she was a Greek. "Swarthy" merely means sunburnt. I should not have spoken of her breast as "polished silver" if I had not known her as a white woman. Read "sunburnt" if you like it better. (*Poems*, 447n127)

50. This allusion connects the motif of the aristocratic blue veins (after which the Groveland society is named) with the award for bringing back a beloved who is feared to be dead.

51. In her novel about racial passing, *Waiting for the Verdict* (New York: Sheldon, 1868), 285, Rebecca Harding Davis had used the same Tennyson lines.

52. 23 Sept. 1898; cited in Michael Flusche, "On the Color Line: Charles Waddell Chesnutt," *North Carolina Historical Review* 53.1 (Jan. 1976): 1–24; here 2n7.

53. "'The Desired State of Feeling': Charles Waddell Chesnutt and Afro-American Literary Tradition," *Durham University Journal* 66 (March 1974): 167.

54. Chesnutt also wrote to his publisher Houghton Mifflin in 1899 that "the backbone of the volume is not a character, like Uncle Julius in *The Conjure Woman*, but a subject, as indicated in the title—*The Color Line.*" Cited in Bone, *Down Home*, 94.

55. For Chesnutt's skepticism, see "The Future American" (*Boston Evening Transcript*, 18 and 25 Aug. and 1 Sept. 1900), reprinted in *Theories of Ethnicity: A Classical Reader*, ed. Werner Sollors (Basingstoke: Macmillan, 1996), 17–33. See also "What Is a White Man?," *Independent* (30 May 1899).

56. Hutchinson, "Jean Toomer," 226–50, traces the racial theming of Toomer with results similar to the ones suggested here, and refers to the change in the census forms. The *Encyclopedia of Southern Culture*, eds. Charles Reagan Wilson and William Ferris (Chapel Hill: Univ. of North Carolina Press, 1989), places the entry on "Miscegenation" in the larger section on "Black Life." See also Nell Irvin Painter's argument in "Of *Lily*, Linda Brent, and Freud: A Non-Exceptionalist Approach to Race, Class, and Gender in the Slave South," *Georgia Historical Quarterly* 76.2 (Summer 1992): 241–59, here 242, that for scholars of the South, "master-slave sex was a problem for the slaves, not the master" and that "interracial, interclass sexuality has been relegated to Afro-Americans alone."

57. For a more detailed survey of the field, see my collection *The Return of Thematic Criticism* (Cambridge: Harvard Univ. Press, 1993). I shall make repeated reference to various parts of it without, each time, giving a more detailed citation.

58. Such issues as time structure, narrative technique, repetitions of sounds and words, or three-part organization of the tale have elicited little commentary. Perhaps the most formalist approaches have been Howells, "Mr. Charles W. Chestnutt's Stories," 699–701, and Lorne Fienberg, "Charles W. Chesnutt's *The Wife of His Youth:* The Unveiling of the Black Storyteller," *American Transcendental Quarterly n.s.* 4.3 (Sept. 1990): 219–37. Carl Van Vechten called attention to Chesnutt's "ironic realism" and referred to him three times in a review of *The New Negro*, "Uncle Tom's Mansion," *New York Herald Tribune Books* (20 Dec. 1925): 5–7, here 6.

59. Claude Bremond, "Concept and Theme," in Sollors, ed., *Return*, 58.

60. Menachem Brinker, "Theme and Interpretation," in ibid., 21–37.

61. Bremond, "Concept and Theme," 54.

62. The card was reproduced in *Katzen lassen grüßen: Ein Postkarten-Bilderbuch . . . aus der Sammlung Stefan Moses* (Hamburg: Rasch und Röhrig, 1989), n.p.

63. Hurston used the white mare fable in "Why the Negro Won't Buy Communism" (1951) and told readers of the *American Legion Magazine* (June 1951):

14–15, 55–60, that Communists, in order to "mount their world rule on Black American backs," had taken for a blueprint "an ancient and long-discarded folk piece. The analogy of the 'white mare.' It got to be said during the Reconstruction that the highest ambition of every Negro man was to have a white woman."

64. Hurston, "Court Order Can't Make Races Mix," an open letter to the anti-integrationist *Orlando Sentinel* published on 11 Aug. 1955, quoted from a microfilm copy provided by R. B. Murray in the Orange County Library System. The *Sentinel* had a circulation of approximately 100,000 in the 1950s.

65. George A. Woods, "Pictures for Fun, Fact and Fancy," *New York Times Book Review* (8 June 1958): 42; also cited in "The Rabbit Wedding," *New York Times* (24 May 1959): IV: 2. Rod Nordell, "Pictures to Read," *Christian Science Monitor* (8 May 1958): 15, praised the "misty, dreamy brush" that has "painted the two little rabbits, one black and one white, with all the soft, defenseless charm of babyhood." He also noted the "brief text, kept simple and happy" and the "heart-stealing water-color illustrations" that "are spread generously over giant pages."

66. 197 Va. 80, 87 S.E. 2d 749. See Zabel, 120; *Loving*, 7; and the chronology of bans. The Tennysonian meaning of "fair" was overwhelmed by a racial reading.

67. Cited in "'Rabbits' Wedding' Banned: Black Bunny Marries White," *Atlanta Constitution* (22 May 1959): 12.

68. "Hush Puppies," *Orlando Sentinel* (18 May 1959): 8–B, partly cited in "The Rabbit Wedding," *New York Times* (24 May 1959): IV: 2 and in "Of Rabbits & Races," *Time* (1 June 1959): 19. Balch presented the full text of the book as self-evident support of his contention.

69. Cited in "'The Rabbits' Wedding' Should Be Burned," *Birmingham Post-Herald* (23 May 1959); 1.

70. "Of Rabbits & Races," *Time* (1 June 1959): 19.

71. "'Rabbits' Wedding' Banned: Black Bunny Marries White," *Atlanta Constitution* (22 May 1959): 12. In "White Rabbit Married Black One—Book Banned From Open Shelves," *Birmingham Post-Herald* (22 May 1959): 26, Reed is quoted as saying, "we have not lost our integrity" and defended her decision to "stop peddling the book" by referring to the charge of the Montgomery *Home News* that Williams's book was "promoting integration."

72. *Birmingham Post-Herald* (23 May 1959): 1. See also "'Rabbit' Book Burning Urged," *Orlando Sentinel* (23 May 1959): 1–A.

73. *New York Times* (22 May 1959): 29; *Time* (1 June 1959): 19. See also Zabel in Wilkinson 123.

74. Rita Levy, "All About Rabbits" (letter), *Orlando Sentinel* (25 May 1959): 9–A.

75. The press release has been reconstructed here from the excerpts published in the *New York Times* (22 May 1959): 29, and *Time* (1 June 1959): 19. Garth Williams, his publisher, and the Alabama Library system did not respond to inquiries.

76. It would be interesting to compare *The Rabbits' Wedding* with Ruth McEnery Stuart's "Little Mother Quackalina" (1898). Also, by contrast with Garth Williams's *Rabbits' Wedding*, his roughly contemporary, similar-looking rabbits in *Baby Farm Animals* (New York: Golden Press, 1959) and his illustra-

tions for Margaret Wise Brown's *Home for a Bunny* (New York: Golden Books, 1961) do not show another black-white contrast.

77. Nilli Diengott, "Thematics: Generating or Theming a Text?," *Orbis Litterarum* 43 (1988): 95–107; Ekkehard Kaemmerling, ed., *Ikonographie und Ikonologie: Theorien, Entwicklung, Probleme* (Köln: DuMont, 1991), 188.

78. See Shell, *Children of the Earth*, 142–43.

79. Brinker, "Theme and Interpretation," 21. I am here adapting Brinker's argument, example, and wording to the case of Larsen.

80. Ibid., 292; see also xxii. The distinction is useful in clarifying the New Critics' relationship to thematic criticism: their readings of texts—except in those few modernist works in which form has become the central or even the exclusive theme—included thematic elements, most notably, the search for "thematic unity," though usually in a single text. In Trousson's terms, they were doing thematics, but they sometimes polemicized against thematology. The present study attempts to do both thematics and thematology. See also Nancy Armstrong's argument in ibid., 45, that "what we call 'form' is simply the dominant theme of a given moment."

81. See Hugo Dyserinck, "Zum Problem der 'Images' und 'Mirages' und ihrer Untersuchungen im Rahmen der Vergleichenden Literaturwissenschaft," *Arcadia* 1 (1966): 107–20.

82. See Sander Gilman, "Theme and the 'Kernel of Truth," in Sollors, ed., *Return*, 294–96.

83. See Dyserinck, *Komparatistik: Eine Einführung*, 2nd ed. (Bonn: Bouvier, 1981). Many of Dyserinck's *desiderata* for a comparative thematological analysis—that it concern as great as possible a number of national literatures in order to permit comparisons and contrasts (112), that it permit the study of literary cross-connections (120), that it yield auto- and hetero-images and help to analyze such images present in literary criticism, too (127–33), and that it pay attention to translations (133–42)—can be met by the investigation of "interracial literature." René Wellek and Austin Warren, *Theory of Literature*, 3rd ed. (New York: Harper, 1956), 260, famously criticized thematology for lacking a "real coherence or dialectic."

84. See Robert Merton, "Insiders and Outsiders: A Chapter in the Sociology of Knowledge" (1972), reprinted in Sollors, ed., *Theories of Ethnicity*, 325–69.

85. In "'Topoi' of Realism: The Metamorphosis of Color," in Sollors, ed., *Return*, 212, Orlando deplores "the idealist aversion to acknowledging the importance of constants of any kind." On the topos of "neither . . . nor" that implies a "double exclusion," see Roland Barthes, "La Critique Ni-Ni," *Mythologies* (1957; rpt. Paris: Seuil, [1970]), 144–46.

86. One is tempted to say that interracial literature as a whole is still largely "invisible." See Larene LaSonde's comment, "We *are* Ralph Ellison's invisible men," in Lise Fundenburg's anthology of statements by biracial Americans, *Black, White, Other*, 336.

87. Brinker, "Theme and Interpretation," 30–31. Holger Klein, in the special thematological issue of *New Comparison* 6 (1988) calls attention to the links between intertextuality and thematics (2–3) and argues that literary scholarship "does well to look at altogether different kinds of discourse" (6). Nella Larsen directly invites the intertextual reading of such social texts as antimiscegenation

legislation and the Rhinelander case, a widely debated New York legal case of 1924/25 in which a rich young heir sued for annulment of his marriage on the grounds that his wife had hidden her racial background from him. See Mark J. Madigan, "Miscegenation and 'The Dicta of Race and Class': The Rhinelander Case and Nella Larsen's *Passing*," *Modern Fiction Studies* 36.4 (Winter 1990): 523–29; and Jamie L. Wacks, "Reading Race, Rhetoric, and the Female Body: The Rhinelander Case and 1920s American Culture" (Senior Thesis, Harvard University, 1995).

## Chapter One. Origins; or, Paradise Dawning

1. Toumson, 187–88. All further references will be to this edition, which reprints both versions of Hugo's novel and many relevant critical materials. English transl. *Jargal*, 44. As Toumson, 77, has pointed out, this formulation foreshadows Victor Hugo's interpretation of Othello: "Now, who is Othello? He is the night. A huge fatal figure. The night loves the day. Blackness loves aurora. The African worships the white."

2. *The Colored American Magazine* 1.5 (Oct. 1900): 273.

3. *Encyclopedia of Social Sciences* 2 (1937): 17; a similar statement appears in Reuter's *Race Mixture*, 28. See also Robert Park's "Human Migration and the Marginal Man" (1928), reprinted in *Theories of Ethnicity: A Classical Reader*, ed. Werner Sollors (Basingstoke: Macmillan, 1996), 156–67.

4. "Textualité et stéréotypes: Of African Queens and Afro-American Princes and Princesses: Miscgenation in *Old Hepsy*," in *Regards sur la littérature noire américaine*, ed. Michel Fabre (Paris: Publications du conseil scientifique de la Sorbonne Nouvelle—Paris III, 1980), 88.

5. Curt Stern, "The Biology of the Negro," *Scientific American* 191 (1954): 80. The absence of any snakes is also noticeable in this garden. The panel that is now on display in the city museum of Calw was once dated about 1710; it is now being interpreted as one of four allegorical representations of the mineral, vegetable, and animal realms, and dated 1770–80 by Peter Hartwig Graepel, "Allegorische Darstellung der drei Naturreiche in einer Apothekenmaterialkammer des 18. Jahrhunderts," *Deutsche Apothekerzeitung* 120.23 (5 June 1980): 1056–58. According to Graepel, the painting of paradise "shows men and animals of different continents: Here a standing black woman is talking with a seated white man, by which the painter probably wanted to show that in paradise there was as of yet no distinction among the various races" (1057); Graepel adds the cautious footnote that "the white figure's sex is not identifiable with certainty, though one can assume that the painter aimed at representing a man and a woman" (1058n7).

6. (New Haven: College & University Press, 1965), 132–33. See Emory Elliott, *Revolutionary Writers: Literature and Authority in the New Republic, 1725–1810* (New York, London: Oxford Univ. Press, 1986), 183–84, and Mencke, 36.

7. See Henri Petter's perceptive discussion in *The Early American Novel* (n.p.: Ohio State Univ. Press, 1971), 126–36, here 136.

8. *Family Fiction* (25 Dec. 1886), reprinted in *The Uncollected Short Fiction of Charles W. Chesnutt*, ed. Sylvia Lyons Render (Washington, D.C.: Howard Univ. Press), 178–79.

9. See Joseph Gärtner, *De fructibus et seminibus plantarum* (1788–91); Carl

Friedrich von Gärtner, *Versuche und Beobachtungen über die Bastarderzeugung im Pflanzenreich* (1849); and (the Gärtners' friend) Joseph Gottlieb Kölreuter, *Vorläufige Nachricht von einigen das Geschlecht der Pflanzen betreffenden Versuchen und Beobachtungen* (1761–66); all are discussed and the Darwin and Mendel references given in Graepel, *Die Gärtner-Gedenkstätte im Museum der Stadt Calw* (Calw: Kleine Reihe des Museums, vol. 3, 1991).

10. Jordan, *White Over Black*, 525. One could, however, also contrast such interracial beginning of a relatively equal couple with paranoid racial fantasies such as that of Charles Carroll, who, in *The Tempter of Eve* (St. Louis: Adamic Publishing, 1902), 403, represented the snake in paradise as a Negro woman. The full text is reproduced in John David Smith, ed., *Anti-Black Thought, 1863–1925*, vol. 6: *The Biblical and "Scientific" Defense of Slavery: Religion and "The Negro Problem,"* pt. 2 (New York and London: Garland, 1993).

11. (1992; rpt. New York: Dutton's Children's Book, 1993), n.p.

12. Patricia Dooley, *School Library Journal* 39 (Jan. 1993): 90; cited in *Book Review Digest* (1993): 182. An image combined of illustrations of this book was also published as a separate greeting card by Roger la Borde, 87 Kingsgate Road, London. Another indication of the changing times may be the difference between Alex Haley's first novel, *Roots*, and his last novel, *Queen*.

13. See Doris Sommer, *Foundational Fictions: The National Romances of Latin America* (1991; Berkeley, Los Angeles, London: Univ. of California Press, 1993).

14. Museo etnológico de Madrid, reproduced in Alvar, 19 and in Isidoro Moreno Navarro, *Los Cuadros del Mestizaje Americano: Estudio Antropológico del Mestizaje* (Madrid: José Porrua Turanzas, 1973), appendix; Caroline Bond Day, *A Study of Some Negro-White Families in the United States* (1932). See also Ilona Katzew, ed., *New World Orders: Casta Painting and Colonial Latin America* (New York: Americas Society, 1996).

15. This may be true for liberal plot lines such as Sinclair Lewis's *Kingsblood Royal* (1947), in which the protagonist Neil Kingsblood inadvertently traces back his ancestry to the black Xavier Pic and his Chippewa wife, as well as for reactionary ones like Robert Lee Durham's *Call of the South* (1908), in which the union of Guinea Gumbo's daughter Cindy and the German immigrant Schmidt is the mythic beginning, though in both of these novels the African ancestry is the significant one. On the "capital A" ancestor, see David M. Schneider, *American Kinship: A Cultural Account*, (Chicago: Univ. of Chicago Press, 1980), 67–68.

16. *The Greek Anthology* V, trans. W. R. Paton (Loeb Classical Library, London: Heinemann; New York: Putnam's, 1918), 76–77.

17. Cleobulus's choice of making days and nights undifferentiated siblings in the same family is a departure from more widespread myths that portray black nights as women and white days as men, thus adding a male-female polarity to a black-white contrast. *Harvard Magazine* (Jan.-Feb. 1989): 50, offered the following translation which could mystify anyone who believes that gender might be connected to progeny: "Twelve sons, the father glories in,/ Plus sixty daughters to each son,/ Half of them black, half white,/ And all immortal, yet they die."

18. *Iliad* 11:1f and *Odyssey* 5:1ff. There are more than a hundred mentions in Homer.

19. *Amores* 1.8.3–4. See Frank M. Snowden, *Blacks in Antiquity* (Cambridge, Mass.: Belknap Press of Harvard Univ. Press, 1970), 151–53, and 308–9 for this and many further references.

20. Vergil, *Aeneis* 1: 489; Heliodorus 118.

21. *Odyssey* 4: 187ff.

22. Ovid, *Metamorphoses*, 13: 620–22.

23. For example, Æthiopian Memnon, #23, Pergamon-Museum Berlin. When William Stanley Roscoe wrote his "Ode to May" in order to celebrate the end of the slave trade in 1807, he invoked Memnon as a representatively African figure:

> Nile lifts his dark Egyptian head,
> While golden songs, and rapturous fire
> Flash from Memnon's ancient lyre.

Roscoe, *Poems* (London: William Pickering, 1834), 100; also cited in Dykes, 49. For confusions about Memnon's lute or lyre, see Robin C. Dix, "The Harps of Memnon and Aeolus: A Study in the Propagation of an Error," *Modern Philology* 85.3 (Feb. 1988): 288–93, with poetic examples from Akenside, Coleridge, Keats, and Tennyson.

24. Chapter 12, *Colored American Magazine* (March 1903): 342.

25. Roscher, 1264. A comparative study of aubades, undertaken in this context, might yield interesting results.

26. This may be the deep cultural reason why a writer like Jean Toomer in *Cane* (1923) would be so attracted to twilight imagery when claiming the territory between black and white—or why Du Bois chose the title *Dusk of Dawn* (1940). Such interracial stories as Victor Séjour's "Le Mulâtre" (1837) begin with dawn.

27. "Essay on the Causes of different Colours of People in different Climates," Royal Society, *Philosophical Transactions* 1744 (London: C. R. Baldwin, 1809), 9: 65; referred to in Jordan 247.

28. John Winthrop to Ezra Stiles, Cambridge, 19 July 1759, in *Letters and Papers of Ezra Stiles*, ed. Isabel M. Calder (New Haven, 1933), 5–6; partly cited in Jordan, 248. Kant's effort at theorizing about race also falls into this category: in 1785, he stated that one could not determine what the original color of mankind might have been.

29. In other versions, the color of the original couple was black. In Brackenridge's already cited novel *Modern Chivalry*, the Guinea Negro Cuff surprises the gentlemanly discussants of the origins of races in what is a parody of Benjamin Franklin's American Philosophical Society with a speech that culminates in the statement:

> Now, shentima, I say, dat de first man was de black a man, and de first woman de black a woman; an get two tree children; de rain vasha dese, and de snow pleach, and de coula come brown, yella, coppa coula, and, at de last, quite fite; and de hair long; an da fal out vid van anoda; and van cash by de nose, an pull; so de nose come lang, sharp nose. (131)

The tale, "Why the Negro Is Black," included in Joel Chandler Harris, *Uncle Remus: His Songs and Sayings* (London: Routledge, n.d.), ch. 33, pp. 165–67, also proceeds from the assumption of an original blackness. Uncle Remus explains this to a little white boy who had noticed that the old man's palms were as white as his own.

30. Melville J. Herskovits, *Man and His Works: The Science of Cultural Anthro-*

*pology* (New York: Knopf, 1952), 68–69, drawn from unpublished research in the Cherokee Indians of the Great Smoky Mountains undertaken by Dr. F. M. Olbrechts of Brussels, Belgium. Herskovits discusses this myth as an example of the most usual form of gentle ethnocentrism among people, in a chapter devoted to "The Problems of Cultural Relativism." The tale does not seem to be included in *Eastern Cherokee Folktales: Reconstructed from the Field Notes of Frans M. Olbrechts,* eds. Jack Frederick Kilpatrick and Anna Gritts Kilpatrick, Smithsonian Institution, Bureau of American Ethnology Bulletin 196 (Washington, D.C.: Government Printing Office, 1966), though this collection, 443, prints a rather different tale of origins, entitled "The Whites, the Indians, and the Negroes." See also Bitterli, *Die "Wilden,"* 344.

31. Ovid turns Phaëthon into Apollo's son.

32. "Sanguine tunc credunt in corpora summa vocato/Æthiopum populos nigrum traxisse colorem." *Metamorphosen,* ed. Erich Rösch (München: Heimeran, 1964), 56; *Metamorphoses* 2: 235–36; trans. Rolfe Humphries (Bloomington and London: Indiana Univ. Press, 1955), 35. Samuel Sewall wrote in 1700: "Black Men are the Posterity of *Cush*: Who time out of mind have been distinguished by their Colour. And for want of the true, *Ovid* assigns a fabulous cause of it." *The Selling of Joseph: A Memorial* (1700; rpt., with notes by Sidney Kaplan, Amherst: Univ. of Massachusetts Press, 1969), 13–14. Le Cat, *Traité* (1765), 5–23, discusses Ovid's Phaëthon and other classical and modern theories of the origins of human difference. See Jordan, 11, who also cites a poem based on Ovid.

33. *Fabulae,* 152A, 154.

34. Browne, "Of the Blackness of *Negroes*" (ch. 10 of *Pseudodoxia* (1646)), in *The Works of Sir Thomas Browne,* ed. Charles Sayle (London: Grant Richards, 1904), II: 368–85, here 370–71, reviewed all sorts of ancient and modern objections to the climate theory and noted the absence of such tincture in tropical Asia or America, and even in some latitudes in Africa. He continues modestly that having cast doubt upon the sun as "the Author of this Blackness, how, and when this tincture first began is yet a Riddle, and positively to determine, it surpasseth my presumption" (375).

35. This does not mean, however, that it was no longer adopted. See Jordan, 13–20, 140–252. John Stedman, *Narrative,* in Price, 303, for example, sided with the climate theory.

36. Gernot Rotter, *Die Stellung des Negers in der islamisch-arabischen Gesellschaft bis zum XVI. Jahrhundert* (Bonn, 1967), 140.

37. Ibid., citing Ibn Sa'd's *Ṭabaqāt,* I.1, 11, line 21f.

38. Ibid., 140–41, citing Abū Dā'ūd, *Sunan,* Sunna, 16, and several other sources.

39. Marcel Griaule, *Schwarze Genesis—ein afrikanischer Schöpfungsbericht* (Freiburg: Herder, 1970), excerpted in Frederik Hettmann, ed., *Die Göttin der Morgenröte: Schöpfungsmythen aus aller Welt* (Frankfurt: Fischer, 1988), 94.

40. Pierre Louis Moreau de Maupertuis, *La Vénus physique* (Geneva, 1780) 118ff; cited in Bitterli, 353.

41. This is a theory similar to the one Labat refuted; de Pauw, 177, describes it more precisely in order to ridicule it: "la première femelle du genre humain avoit des ovaires, & qu'elle renfermoit dans ces ovaires des œufs blancs & des œufs noirs, d'oû naquirent les Allemands, les Suèdois, & tous les peuples blancs

d'une part, & tous les peuples Nègres de l'autre" (the first female human had ovaries, and in these ovaries she held white eggs and black eggs, from which were born the Germans, the Swedes, and all the white people on one hand, and all the black people on the other).

42. By contrast, race-thinking almost *requires* an opposition to such dialectic perception. In kinship terms racialism leans toward the fantasy of cloning—or to denials of actual kinship if it implies that a racial boundary is being crossed.

43. *Parzival, a Knightly Epic*, trans. Jessie Weston (London: D. Nutt, 1894), 31.

44. (1742 ed.), II: 189. On Labat see Hermann Hofer in Koebner and Pickerodt, 138; Bitterli, *Die "Wilden,"* 250–53. Kant, 1785, similarly saw the very fact that interracial progeny tended to be between their mothers and fathers as central for his definition of "race."

45. The discussion was undertaken another time, with similar results, in the twentieth century: see the report by Julian Herman Lewis, *The Biology of the Negro* (Chicago: Univ. of Chicago Press, 1942), 47:

> Analysis of the inheritance of skin color has been made even more difficult by the fact that none of the factors for black (or the absence of black) appears to possess the quality of dominance, in spite of many opinions to the contrary. Data . . . give little or no evidence that the average color of children taken in large numbers is nearer the color of one parent than of the other. The dark children in a family are not predominantly of any one sex, nor does it make any difference in the distribution of color in children if the father or mother is darker.

46. Louisiana followed the patrilineal system. See Johnston, *Race Relations*, 230. See also B. Fields, 107, for a discussion of patrilineage in slave status in Maryland in 1664.

47. Michèle Duchet, "Du noir au blanc, ou la cinquième génération," in Poliakov, 187; citing G. de Bory, *Essai sur la population des colonies à sucre*, in *Mémoires sur l'dministration de la Marine et des Colonies* (1776; rpt., Paris, 1789), 57.

48. F. James Davis, *Who Is Black? One Nation's Definition* (University Park: Pennsylvania State Univ. Press, 1991), 144.

49. See Shell, *Children*, 3–5.

50. See, e.g. Lillian Smith, "Three Ghost Stories," in *Killers of the Dream* (1949; rpt., Garden City, N.Y.: Doubleday Anchor, 1963), 97–119; and, very perceptively, Simone Vauthier and Susan Fraiman.

51. William Byrd II to Charles, Earle of Orrery, 5 July 1726, in "Virginia Council Journals, 1726–1753," *Virginia Magazine of History and Biography* 32 (1924): 27; cited and discussed as an example of "thoroughgoing *patriarchalism*" in Rhys Isaac, *The Transformation of Virginia, 1740–1790* (Chapel Hill: Univ. of North Carolina Press, 1982), 39–40. See also Michael Zuckerman, "William Byrd's Family," *Perspectives in American History* 12 (1979): 253–311. [Edward Long] *The History of Jamaica...*, 3 vols. (London: T. Lowndes, 1774), 2:217, writes that the planter wants to be the slaves' "common friend and father. His authority over them is like that of an antient patriarch."

52. Mary Boykin Chesnut, *A Diary From Dixie*, ed. Ben Ames Williams (Cambridge: Harvard Univ. Press, 1980), 21–22; see also 122. It is important to recognize that what separates Chesnut from Byrd was a dramatic historical

change in the perception of slavery. See Isaac, *Transformation of Virginia*, 308–10.

53. A detailed, excellent discussion of the picture can be found in James D. Birchfield, Albert Boime, and William J. Hennessey, *Thomas Satterwhite Noble 1835–1907* (Lexington: Univ. of Kentucky Art Museum, 1988), 61–68. J. Wilson, 92–93, follows Boime's reading but adds that Noble "apparently failed to seriously question his society's underlying assumptions about race. The formal language of *The Price of Blood* naturalizes the gulf between white father and brown son."

54. Getman, 126.

55. *Wirtschaft und Gesellschaft: Grundriß der verstehenden Soziologie*, ed. Johannes Winckelmann (Tübingen: J.C.B. Mohr, 1956), 234–35. Trans. Ephraim Fischoff et al. Guenther Roth and Claus Wittich, "Ethnic Groups," in Sollors, ed., *Theories of Ethnicity*, 52–54.

56. Evans, 20, citing Marc Henri Piault, "Captifs du pouvoir et pouvoir des captifs," in Claude Meillassoux, ed., *L'esclavage en Afrique précoloniale* (Paris, 1975), 333.

57. Hence the evidence Getman cites can also be read as a constraint, keeping masters from legalizing interracial sexual alliances. Furthermore, Getman 129 cites a 1681 Maryland statute stipulating that "any master who instigated or merely allowed marriage between his white female servants and Black male slaves was fined."

58. Edward Spencer's fascinatingly overwritten Gothic novella "Tristan" (1867) hinges on the diabolic revenge that the legitimate wife of a rich southerner plans and carries out against her husband's illegitimate son from a Quadroon woman—while the son believes that the white woman is his mother.

59. See Wilhelm Weisschedel's discussion of early Hegel in *Die philosophische Hintertreppe: 34 große Philosophen in Alltag und Denken* (1966; rpt., München: Deutscher Taschenbuch Verlag, 1986), 209–21. See Lise Funderburg's comment: "It takes two people to create a biracial child: a mother and a father." *Black, White, Other*, 25.

60. See Shell, 199n3. For striking examples in interracial literature—apart from the motif of switched babies—see, for example, Denison, *Old Hepsy* (1858), or Chesnutt, "Her Virginia Mammy" (1899).

61. *The Anthropological Treatises*, trans. Thomas Bendyshe (London: Longman, 1865), 216.

62. See, for example, Dr. James Parsons, "Of the White Negro Shown Before the R[oyal] S[ociety]," *Philosophical Transactions* 12 (London: Baldwin, 1809), 190–94, here 191, on the case of a white woman in York whose child was "entirely black, and in every particular of colour and features resembling the father": "This was thought a very singular case, because people naturally expect the issue of such a marriage would be tawny: which is indeed the usual effect produced by the congress of black and white persons."

## Chapter Two. *Natus Æthiopus/Natus Albus*

1. Justin Kaplan, *Mr. Clemens and Mark Twain.* (London: Cape, 1967), 149, citing *Mark Twain–Howells Letters*, 1:10–11.

2. Ed. McDowell, 168.

3. "The Drama of Racial Intermarriage," in *Region, Race, and Reconstruction:*

*Essays in Honor of C. Vann Woodward*, eds. J. Morgan Kousser and James M. McPherson (New York, Oxford: Oxford Univ. Press, 1982), 192, citing New York *Tribune* (26 Jan. 1929).

4. Curtis Wilkie, "33 Days That Defined a Candidate," *Boston Globe Magazine* (22 July 1992): 12. Presidential candidate Clinton at a closed-door meeting with Chicago Democrats, in an "attempt to put down one persistent rumor," as he answered "uncomfortable questions by quietly acknowledging he had been involved in extramarital affairs."

5. The discussion draws on the pioneering work by Frank W. Snowden, Jr., *Blacks in Antiquity* (Cambridge, Mass.: Belknap Press of Harvard Univ. Press, 1970), 167–95, and Lloyd A. Thompson, *Romans and Blacks* (Norman and London: Univ. of Oklahoma Press, 1989), 62–85. The materials were first put together by J. A. Rogers. Lawrence E. Tenzer, *A Completely New Look at Interracial Sexuality: Public Opinion and Select Commentaries* (Manahawkin, N.J.: Scholars' Publishing House, 1990), also gives a detailed survey. For "wonder," see Antigonus, *Mirabilia* 112 (122). See also the reaction to Feirefiz as "wonder" in Wolfram's *Parzival*. Atavism was also referred to as reversion to type or to black skin color; Durham, as we shall see, called it "recession."

6. *De generatione animalium* 1.18.722a. In *The Works of Aristotle*, vol. 5. Eds. J. A. Smith and W. D. Ross, trans. Arthur Platt (1912; rpt., Oxford: Clarendon Press, 1972), 722a. See also Aristotle, *Historia animalium* 7.6.586a, trans. Richard Cresswell (London: Henry G. Bohn, 1862), 188: "[C]hildren resemble their parents or their grandparents, and sometimes they resemble neither. This is handed down for many generations; as in Sicily, a woman cohabited with an Ethiopian, her daughter was not black, but her daughter's child was so." See also Aristophanes, *Historia animalium epitome* 2.272.

7. *Oxford English Dictionary*. An 1833 instance in the *OED* names Duchesne as the one who coined the term.

8. *Love Poems of Ovid* (New York: Mentor, 1964), 51. *Amores* 1.13.21–36; see Snowden, *Blacks in Antiquity*, 153.

9. *De sera numinis vindicta* 21 (563). *On the Delay of the Divine Justice*, trans. Andrew P. Peabody (Boston: Little, Brown, 1885), 58.

10. *Epigrammaton Libri* VI. 39. ed. W. Heraeus, corr. Iacob Borovskij (Leipzig: Teubner, 1902), 136.

11. Sixth satire, 594–601. Scholia ad S. VI. 594–601, *Iuvenalem vetustora*, ed. Paul Wessner (1931; rpt., Stuttgart: Teubner, 1967), 113.

12. Translated by Jessica Weiss. *Declamationes* II, ed. Georg Lehnert (Leipzig: Teubner, 1903), 2–3.

13. Pliny's *Natural History*, trans. John Bostock and H. T. Riley, vol. 2 (London: Henry Bohn, 1855), 145–46. See *Naturalis Historiae* VII. 12. 51, ed. Carolus Mayhoff (1909; rpt., Stuttgart: Teubner, 1967), 18. *The Historie of the World. Commonly Called, The Natural Histories of C. Plinius Secundus*, trans. Philemon Holland (London: Adam Islip, 1601), 161, reads: "The example is notable, and yet undoubted true, of one *Nicæus*, a famous wrestler of Constantinople, who having to his mother a woman begotten adulterie by an Æthyopian, and yet with white skine, nothing different from other women of that countrey, was himself blacke, and resembled his grandsire, the Æthyopian abovesaid." On the changed interest in Pliny after the discovery of the New World, see Anthony Pagden, *European Encounters With the New World: From Renaissance to Romanticism* (London and New Haven: Yale Univ. Press, 1993), 54–68.

14. *Naturalis Historiae* VII. 12. 52.

15. "Of the Blackness of *Negroes*," 375, invoking Hippocrates, Heliodorus, and the biblical story of Jacob's cattle, i.e. Laban's flocks (Genesis 30:31–43). The notion was also ascribed to Hippocrates by Augustine, who explained a case of *Natus Æthiopus* by the mother's intent viewing of a picture at the time of conception. See *Questiones in Genesis* 93 (*Corpus Christianorum Series Latina* 33.35); also cited in Tenzer. For some interesting nonracial examples of maternal impression, see Johann Caspar Lavater, "The Effects of the Imagination on the Human Form," *Essays on Physiognomy; for the Promotion of the Knowledge and the Love of Mankind*, 2nd ed., vol. 3 (London: Whittingham, 1804), 156–62.

16. 4:8; 119. See also Thomas Browne, "Of the Blackness of *Negroes*" (ch. 10 of *Pseudodoxia* (1646), in *The Works of Sir Thomas Browne*, ed. Charles Sayle (London: Grant Richards, 1904), II:375–76, and Quintilian and Jerome, cited in Snowden, 194.

17. One case reported by Parsons partly resembles Pliny's wording. It concerns a white woman in London who was married to a black man and gave birth to a daughter, "as fair a child to look at as any born of white parents." The husband's suspicions could be allayed by the presence of black skin on the child's right buttock and thigh. Parsons, "Of the White Negro shown before the R[oyal] S[ociety]," *Philosophical Transactions* 12 (London: Baldwin, 1809), 191.

18. Ibid., 192.

19. II, 216.

20. O. S. Fowler, *Hereditary Descent: Its Laws and Facts, Illustrated and Applied to the Improvement of Mankind* (New York, 1843), 34–35; quoted by Tenzer, 112–13.

21. A similar (or perhaps the same) case was interpreted by the *Charlottesville Jeffersonian*, however, as a warning to legislators not to "make those tainted with Negro blood white men and women." Quoting a note by William F. Van Amringe, the paper writes, as excerpted in *Frederick Douglass' Paper* (10 Feb. 1854):

> "Black Heir.—This unfortunate circumstance happened recently in ——
> —. A gentleman of high respectability married a beautiful girl, whose first
> child was a negro. [. . .] The fidelity of the wife was beyond suspicion"; but,
> on "investigation, it was discovered that her grandfather, or great grandfa-
> ther was a negro."

22. A classic Enlightenment refutation of maternal impression appears in Immanuel Kant's "Bestimmung des Begriffs einer Menschenrace" (1785), 97. Kant argues against opening the door to even a single superstition in a reasoned argument but also worries that, given the far range of human imagination, there would be no limits to the appearance of children formed by "maternal impression" rather than on the model of their parents. See also Bitterli, *Die "Wilden,"* 346. According to Tenzer, 113–14, the Dutch doctor Hermann Boerhaave's report included in the appropriately entitled work *The Wonders of the Little World* (1774) claimed that a "Princess was delivered of a black daughter, by only seeing, for the first time, a blackmoor whilst she was pregnant."

23. François Beroalde de Verville, *Le Moyen de Parvenir* (Paris: Charles Gosselin, 1841), 159–60. The figure of the devil is called *l'autre*. See also Rogers, *Sex and Race*, I: 261.

24. *Watkins v. Carlton*, in Helen Tunnicliff Catterall, *Judicial Cases Concerning*

*American Slavery and the Negro* (1926–37; rpt., New York: Negro Universities Press, 1968), 1: 196, followed by the note: "Among the hundred millions of whites in Europe, there is no authenticated instance of the produce of the white race being other than white, where there was no possibility of access between a black and a white." See also 2: 136 (the ruling in an 1849 paternity case that "if the child, when born, should prove to be black, the defendant had no redress in a Court of law") and 4: 370 (an 1816 case from Hudson, N.Y., in which Adam Heydon was deemed the father of William Heydon, though the child was born black and both Adam Heydon and his wife Catreen Race were "white persons"); partly cited in Tenzer, 115. See also Rogers, *Sex and Race*, III: 225. For a discussion of Virginia cases, see Higginbotham and Kopytoff, 1997–2000, who also point out that such cases sometimes revealed the uncertainty of the courts in determining that a child was "white" or "mulatto."

25. Rogers, *From "Superman" to Man*, 91, lets his characters on a train discuss the question at length.

26. Only parts of the untitled manuscript fragment were published in Puškin's lifetime; and the title comes from the editors of *Sovremennik* in which the whole manuscript appeared in 1837. For a perceptive and detailed discussion of Puškin's text as a historical novel, see Walter Schamschula, *Der russische historische Roman vom Klassizismus bis zur Romantik* (Meisenheim: Anton Hain, 1961), Frankfurter Abhandlungen zur Slavistik 3, 129–43. See also Vladimir Nabokov's stunning "Appendix," in *Eugene Onegin: A Novel in Verse*, trans. Nabokov, Bollingen Series 72 (Pantheon, 1964), and Jurij Striedter, *Dichtung und Geschichte bei Pushkin* (Konstanz: Universitätsverlag, 1977), 33–47.

27. (Rpt., Boston: Beacon Press, 1987), 85.

28. "A Matter of Principle," *Wife*, 109. Chesnutt's story is retold at great detail in Carl Van Vechten's novel *Nigger Heaven*.

29. Afro-American media regularly celebrate Puškin as a race hero; see, for example, J. A. Rogers, "Pushkin 'Made' Russian Literature," *Norfolk Journal and Guide* (25 May 1929), sec. 2, 1, which is full of praise of the writer and mentions that Hannibal had been captured in Africa and sold to a Russian officer at Constantinople but that when he died he left "several estates, 1500 slaves and seven children." On the other hand the *Random House Encyclopedia* on Infodesk (1990) makes no mention of Puškin's partial African ancestry, and in a critique of "Afrocentricity, Multiculturalism, and *Black Athena*," Robert W. Wallace, *Caribana* 3 (1992–93): 45–53, here 46, even lists Puškin in a lineup of great figures from Jesus to Beethoven who have been falsely claimed as blacks. In Felicity Barringer, "Soviet Vigils Held Widely for Pushkin," *New York Times* (15 Feb. 1987): 7, an article that was aimed at explaining to U.S. readers Puškin's popularity in his homeland, the only mention of his racial background was made in an anonymous comment:

> "He was hot-tempered, you know, he had that Ethiopian blood," said a Muscovite, referring to the poet's great-grandfather and his penchant for duels (six) and love affairs (many). In fact, these personal affinities seem to appeal to Russians as much as his literary strength.

Not surprisingly, the Golden Legacy comic book *The Life of Alexander Pushkin* (Seattle: Baylor Publishing, 1983), which has a longish genealogical section, makes no mention of the love affair with Countess D.—but it also fails to represent Ibrahim's marriage.

30. Paul Debreczeny, "Introduction" to Alexander Pushkin, *Complete Prose Fiction* (Stanford: Stanford Univ. Press, 1983), 3. Quotations from Debreczeny's translation will be given parenthetically in the text. Occasionally it was compared with the English versions in *The Poems, Prose, and Plays of Alexander Pushkin*, trans. T. Keane (New York: Modern Library, 1936), 745–86, and *The Complete Prose Tales of Alexander Sergeyevitch Pushkin*, trans. Gillon R. Aitken (New York: Norton, 1966), 1–42. The Russian editions consulted are A. S. Puškin, *Polnoye Sobranye Sochineniy* 8.I and 8.II (Isdatel'stvo Akademiy Nauk SSSR, 1948), and *Kapitanskaya Dočka. Proza* (Moskva: Chudozhestvennaya Literatura, 1987), 5–34.

31. In Russian, Ibragim. For the liberties Puškin took with his historical sources see Debreczeny, 495n4; Schamschula, *Der russische historische*, and Nabokov. See also Allison Blakely, 50–57.

32. The Russian word is *cudo*," literally, "wonder." Aitken translates it as "freak," Keane as "curiosity," and Debreczeny as "some strange phenomenon."

33. Most particularly, he is not at all built up as a "legitimate" *white* point of view from which the interracial adultery could receive a racial meaning. If the story of Countess D. was, indeed, Pushkin's invention, this would stress its function as a symmetrical counterweight to the (somewhat more historically based) plot that was to follow.

34. Gudrun Ziegler, *Alexander S. Puschkin* (Hamburg: Rowohlt, 1979), 91. As Debreczeny, 498n39, also says, there is no manuscript by Puškin that indicates an outline for the ending. The diary of Puškin's friend A. Vul'f for 16 Sept. 1827 is thus the only source. It reads: "The central intrigue in this novel, as Pushkin says, will be the infidelity of the blackamoor's wife, who will give birth to a white baby and will be banished to a convent for it."

35. See Schamschula, *Der russische historische*, 133, and Striedter, 34–38.

36. 73. Thompson used Pliny in order to represent the modern view and express his suspicion that—Pliny's belief in atavism notwithstanding—the case may well have been an adultery case after all.

37. Thompson, 76–77.

38. See by contrast, José Antonio Villareal, *Pocho* (Garden City, N.Y.: Doubleday, 1959), 123, with the account of a racialized socialization that suggests "a white horse is the best horse there is."

39. Thompson, 77–78, citing *PL* LXIV.30,56,79, 132–33, 145–46 [Boethius]; cf. *PG* LXIV.1279–82 [Meletius]; *PG* XXVIII.54 [Athanasius]; *CSEL* XXVIII I.78 [Augustine], Aug., *De civ. dei* XVI 8; Courtès, in *Image*, II.1, 11–14. See also Thompson, 122: "The monk Meletius, in his work *De natura hominis*, attributes the diversity of human complexion to the Creator's loving care. Athanasius, like many a modern social psychologist, philosophically distinguishes 'the proper' in humankind (the essential defining attributes of rationality and mortal and immortal natures) from the 'subordinate' or 'non-essential' (colour, morphology, height, weight, and so on), which are due to 'accidents'. Boethius similarly proclaims . . . that it is only the non-essential or accidental quality *nigritudo* that creates the category *Aethiops*. Augustine in like manner proclaims that all people, of whatever colours and shapes, trace their origin to a single human form: 'Man was made one,' and 'there are not several species of men as there are species of herbs, trees, fishes, birds, serpents, wild beasts, and grazing animals.'"

40. Thompson, 78.

41. The phrase "white negro" was also used to describe an albino; and John Stedman still used it in this sense in 1796; see his *Narrative*, in Price, 512.

Equiano's phrasing resembles that of the somewhat "preternatural" "White Negro" case reported by Parsons. Parsons's longer description of the *Natus Albus* case in Virginia, however, adheres to the "classical" understanding of "species" independent of genealogy.

42. Still, there have undoubtedly been many modern American cases resembling the classical view. Higginbotham and Kopytoff, 1980–81, for example, called attention to the 1847 Virginia case of *Dean v. Commonwealth*, which reports a legal "lightening" over the generations and which concerned the issue whether two witnesses were incompetent to testify in a criminal case because they were Mulattoes:

> [F]rom the testimony it appeared certainly, that they had less than one fourth of negro blood. Their grandfather, David Ross, who was spoken of as a respectable man, though probably a mulatto, was a soldier in the revolution and died in the service. The evidence as to the grandmother was contradictory: though she was probably white, the mother was so certainly.

Higginbotham stresses that the "grandfather would have been incompetent to testify because he was a mulatto, but the grandchildren were not. [ . . . ] Thus in mid-nineteenth century Virginia, mulatto parents and grandparents could have children and grandchildren who were legally white. That became impossible only in the twentieth century, when any trace of Negro blood would disqualify a person from being considered white under the law."

43. Thompson, 122, citing *CSEL* XXVIII 1.78.

44. *Howell v. Netherland*, Jefferson 90, Va. 1770, citing Virginia act of 1705, ch. 49, sec. 18; quoted in Getman, 125.

45. Michèle Duchet, in Poliakov, 185, citing *Instructions pour la Martinique*: "on ne saurait mettre trop de distance entre le deux espèces."

46. *Oxford English Dictionary*, "Species" II.7.

47. As Robert K. Barnhart, *The Barnhart Dictionary of Etymology* ([Bronx, N.Y.:] H. W. Wilson, 1988), 1042, summarizes the *OED* findings, the word "species," originally "appearance," was a classification in logic until 1398, was first recorded in the sense of "a distinct kind or sort" in 1561 (*OED* II.9); and only in 1608 was the first instance of the sense "in biology of a group of animals or plants that have common characteristics" (*OED* II.10).

48. Cited from a 1796 review of Blumenbach in Barker, 169.

49. "Bestimmung des Begriffs einer Menschenrace," 102. Kant also emphasized, 95, that the mixed race would perpetuate itself if limited to its own kind in further generations, but would revert to one of the parental races in a few generations if it were limited to that in its further procreation.

50. [Edward Long], *The History of Jamaica*, 3 vols. (London: T. Lowndes, 1774), 2:336, 335. See the discussions by Jordan, 484–85, 491–95, and Barker, 41–58. Long's comment, that "it seems extraordinary, that two Mulattos, having intercourse together, should be unable to continue their species" (an imaginary assertion that should have grave consequences, as we shall see later), suggests that in applying the term to Mulattoes he also still used "species" close to the sense of "complexion" and thus to the classical "aspect." Bernard Romans, *A Concise Natural History of East and West Florida*, vol. I (New York, 1775), 111, speaks of the

"Negro species," but adds, "like all others of the different species and varieties of the human genus," suggesting some fluidity.

51. Cited from *An Account of the Regular Gradation in Man, and in Different Animals and Vegetables, and From the Former to the Latter*, 129, in Barker, 170.

52. Stories of *Natus Æthiopus* thus moved toward the topos of "Never Was Born," the biracial child that should not have been.

53. Unlike class distinctions, racial divisions were therefore "natural." Fredrickson, *Black Image*, 91, citing James Kirke Paulding, *Slavery in the United States* (New York, 1836), 270–71.

54. See Anthony Pagden, "Razzismo e colonialismo europeo: Una indagine storica," in *Il Razzismo e le sue storie*, ed. Girolamo Imbruglia (Napoli: Edizioni Scientifiche Italiane, 1992), 178–81. See also Hoffmann, *Le Nègre romantique*, 125–27.

55. J. C. Nott, "The Mulatto a Hybrid—Probable Extermination of the Two Races If the Whites and Blacks Are Allowed to Intermarry," *American Journal of Medical Sciences* 66 (July 1843): 252–56, here 254. In the midst of his argument for the vanishing Mulatto he adds a footnote: "I would here remark, that there is a mixed race in New Orleans and Mobile, of French and Spanish blood with the negro, which presents a very different appearance from the chalky Mulattoes of the Atlantic States. They have a redder skin than the latter, are more robust, healthy, and superior in every respect. My remarks are meant to apply particularly to the Anglo-Saxon cross" (255n).

56. From *Two Lectures on the Natural History of the Caucasian and Negro Races* (Mobile: Dade and Thompson, 1844), reprinted in Faust, 212; also cited in Stanton, 69.

57. See the example of 1785 cited in the *Oxford English Dictionary* II.8c. See also ibid., the excerpt from Lane's translation of *Thousand Nights and One Night* I.30: "It is believed . . . that the difference between them and the Jinn and Sheytáns is a difference of species."

58. Since "essential" was once applied only to those qualities that define human nature, one could also argue that the modern essentialist notion of "race" gave human subcategories the space that was once taken by "man's immortal soul."

59. Josiah C. Nott and George R. Gliddon, *Types of Mankind; or, Ethnological Researches* (Philadelphia: Lippincott; London: Trübner, 1854), 405; also cited in Mencke, 43, who summarizes that Nott believed "races were separated by essential rather than accidental differences." Nott and Gliddon, 409–10, also accepted the possibility that certain types of mankind were headed toward extinction.

60. Ibid., 375. From this definition arose the need for Nott and Gliddon to side with polygenism and to argue explicitly against St. Paul's universalism of Acts 17. They find on the one hand that this would imply much troubling incest at the beginning of mankind and, on the other hand, that Paul "knew nothing of the existence of races or nations beyond the circumference of the Roman Empire" (409).

61. Nott, "The Mulatto a Hybrid," 255. The formulation admits at least to a difficulty in detecting color. The courts would be busy once physical appearance became an "accidental,"—or, as a Washington, D.C., court ruled in *Wall v. Oyster* (1910), the "sense of sight is but one avenue for the conveyance of information

upon the subject of racial identity to the mind of the investigator." See C. S. Wheatley, "Who Is a 'Colored' Person?," *Law Notes* 35 (July 1931): 68–70, here 69.

62. *On the Origin of Species* (Cambridge: Harvard Univ. Press, 1964), 245–78 (ch. 8). In *The Descent of Man* (1871; new ed., New York: Appleton, 1888), I. vii, 173, Darwin applied the "mongrel" metaphor to humans and spoke of an "immense mongrel population of Negroes and Portuguese" that the naturalist could find in Brazil.

63. *Random House Encyclopedia* for Macintosh (1990).

64. According to Hoffmann, *Nègre*, 126.

65. Aristotle, *The Works of Aristotle*, vol. 5, eds. J. A. Smith and W. D. Ross, trans. Arthur Platt (1912; rpt., Oxford: Clarendon Press, 1972), 722a; the editor is invoking William Lawrence, *Lectures on Physiology, Zoology and the Natural History of Man* (London: Benhow, 1822), 260, 261. See also Karl Pearson's review of the case of the woman in Elis in his "Note on the Skin-Colour of the Crosses Between Negro and White," *Biometrika* 6 (1908–9): 348–53, here, 350–51; and Julian Herman Lewis's account of the mythical nature of the "idea of 'reversion to black'" in *The Biology of the Negro* (Chicago: Univ. of Chicago Press, 1942), 47–48. In their edition of Pliny's *Natural History*, vol. 2 (London: Henry Bohn, 1855), 146n, John Bostock and H. T. Riley criticize the geographic discrepancy in Aristotle's tale from Elis/Sicily and suggest another adultery story: "If we are really to believe that his complexion was that of an Æthiopian, it is much more probable that his mother may have had connection with a negro."

66. See, for example, Du Bose Heyward's play *Brass Ankle* (New York: Farrar and Rinehart, 1931), which shows, according to Hilda Josephine Lawson, *The Negro in American Drama*, (Urbana, Ill.: 1939), the "[t]ragic consequences of the birth of a brown child to a woman who is unaware that she has colored blood."

The *Natus Æthiopus* theme has also been themed into texts where it is not overtly present, for example, Chesnutt's story "The Wife of His Youth." Following a speculative leap undertaken by Alice Walker, Sundquist, *To Wake*, 299, argued that "Ryder's black wife is too old to bear children, and his declaration that 'our fate lies between absorption by the white race and extinction in the black' . . . therefore does not present to him quite the moral dilemma that it appears to be." This foreshadowing follows another comment on Ryder's hypothetical reflections on his possible descendants: "By her coincidental appearance upon the scene, Ryder's wife, Liza Jane, interrupts his idyllic visions of increased assimilation of European standards and upward progress through a further lightening of his children's dark skin." Since "The Wife of His Youth" contains no comments on Ryder's children—apart from Ryder's general statement, "we must do the best we can for ourselves and those who are to follow us"—such theming may be a form of reading the story for a motif that is present in many other texts.

It is not difficult to recognize inversion at work in Cecil Brown's novel *The Life and Love of Mr. Jiveass Nigger* (1969; rpt. Greenwich, Conn.: Fawcett Crest, 1971), 135–36: "I have nightmares about having a white baby. I keep thinking about how white it will be." See also Frank Yerby, *Speak Now* (1969), 218, discussed by Little, 304. Itabari Njeri, "Sushi and Grits," in Early, ed., *Lure and Loathing* (1993), 15–16, reports how a "biscuit-brown woman revealed that she'd spent the past twenty years of her life in mortal fear that her vanilla-ice-cream-colored child would hate her, reject her because. . . . She hoped that her next baby would be *black-black-black*."

67. (Boston: L.C. Page, 1908), 383–84. The following excerpts come from 384 and 385.

68. Ibid., 186. This passage is also quoted and discussed by Berzon and Mencke. Parts of the speech are reminiscent of Bailey's *Race Orthodoxy*, but the core comes close to suggesting genocide, as Rutledge proposes "to take measures to restrict the increase of the negro race and let it die out like the Indian" (182–83). The publisher used the *Louisville Courier-Journal*'s wish that Rutledge's speech should be "printed in a pamphlet by itself and given world-wide distribution" in advertisements.

69. This scene is based on President Roosevelt's widely debated White House luncheon with Booker T. Washington in 1901, though Durham's "Dr. Woods" appears to be modeled on Du Bois. It is, in Durham's world, Phillips's lunch date that paves the path toward Helen's interracial marriage. See the comments on the Roosevelt episode in Arna Bontemps and Jack Conroy, *Anyplace But Here* (orig. 1945 as *They Seek a City*; New York: Hill and Wang, 1966), 156, and the doggerel popular at the time:

> *The Statue of Liberty hung her head;*
> *Columbia dropped in a swoon,*
> *The American eagle drooped and died,*
> *When Teddy dined with the coon.*

70. See Charles W. Chesnutt's report of 1932 on an Ohio senator's similar reaction—"absurd, unthinkable"—to the idea that "amalgamation of the races" might be a "solution to the race question," cited in full in Chapter Ten.

71. Durham, *Call*, 397, 437. Similar sentiments are expressed in Thomas Dixon's novel *The Sins of the Father: A Romance of the South* (New York: D. Appleton, 1912), 382–83 and 402–5, though the birth of a black baby is only imagined there.

72. The Harvard theme seems intertwined with interracial literature: see Dixon's *The Leopard's Spots* and Hopkins's *Of One Blood* for early examples; there is also Quentin Compson in *Absalom, Absalom!*

73. Louis Wirth and Herbert Goldhamer, "The Hybrid and the Problems of Miscegenation," in *Characteristics of the American Negro*, ed. Otto Klineberg (New York: Harper and Row, 1944), cite the following story from Edward M. East, *Heredity and Human Affairs* (1927; rpt., New York: Scribner's, 1929), 99–100:

A favourite short-story plot with which melodramatic artists seek to harrow the feelings of their readers is one where the distinguished scion of an aristocratic family marries the beautiful girl with tell-tale shadows on the half-moons of her nails, and in due time is presented with a coal-black son. It is a good framework, and carries a thrill. . . . The most casual examination of the genetic formulae . . . demonstrates its absurdity. If there ever was a basis for the plot in real life, the explanation lies in a fracture of the seventh commandment, or in a tinge of negro blood in the aristocrat as dark as that in his wife.

Wirth comments: "It should be pointed out in this connection that while two parties with Negro blood may very occasionally have an offspring with somewhat more negroid features than themselves, it is not possible for a white person and a person with some Negro ancestry to have an offspring more Negroid than the partner with Negro blood." Wirth is cited in Gunnar Myrdal, *An American Dilemma* (New York: Harper, 1944), 1209, though Myrdal adds that there is "at least one biologist, however, who takes the opposite view, and says the 'black baby' can happen, and occasionally does happen." Citing Julian S. Huxley and A. C. Haddon, *We Europeans* (1935), 82, Myrdal reports: "In some extreme cases, the offspring of a cross between a white man and a half-breed coloured woman have been fair and almost black respectively." Yet Huxley did not want this to be taken as unquestionable in a letter to Myrdal of December 1941. Myrdal concludes: "The controversy is not very important practically, since if a dark-skinned baby can be born to a light mulatto and a white person, this happens so extremely rarely that one is still justified in branding as a myth the popular belief that it occurs." Myrdal gives the discussion an absurd conclusion: "Finally, it should be said that it may be that the 'black baby' is not given a chance to appear, since belief in the myth might encourage the use of contraceptives in white-mulatto relations." We seem to have come full circle to Juvenal's quip that abortions kept the number of *Natus Æthiopus* cases small.

74. (14 Jan. 1893): 70–71, 74, followed by "The Lover of Mentine." All references are to this version of the story.

75. See the *Sturm und Drang* tradition from Heinrich Leopold Wagner, "Die Kindermörderin" (1776) and, most famously, Goethe's *Faust* to Richard Hildreth's *Archy Moore* (2:51), Elizabeth Barrett Browning's poem "The Runaway Slave at Pilgrim Point" (1848), Cassy's story in *Uncle Tom's Cabin* (1852), and Toni Morrison's *Beloved* (1987), connecting the image of an innocent unwed mother whose child was fathered by a man of a higher class or caste and infanticide, often near water.

Peel argues for the possibility that Désirée and her baby are alive at the end of the story.

76. Jon Erickson, "Fairytale Features in Kate Chopin's 'Désirée's Baby': A Study in Genre Cross-Reference," in *Modes of Narrative: Approaches to American, Canadian and British Fiction*, eds. Reingard M. Nischik and Barbara Korte (Würzburg: Könighausen & Neumann, 1990), 57–67, here 63–64. This essay is an excellent thematic exploration of the story in the context of such fairy-tale motifs as the wished-for child, the banished wife or maiden, the changeling, and child substitution. Inspired by Bakhtin, Erickson argues that the story is a case of genre dialogue, and that the second ending "follows from the fact that traditional fairytale conventions are used in a short story that ends tragically. Without the second ending the use of such conventions and the expectations they raise would be simply an irrelevancy, and the story would not evoke the interest that it does" (64).

77. "Delineation of Life and Character," in *Literary History of the United States*, ed. Robert E. Spiller et al. (1946; rpt., New York: Macmillan, 1964), 859. Wolff, 125, and Peel, 232, have argued that "we should cease analyzing the surprise ending and look elsewhere"—though Erickson's analysis made this demand seem premature. Robert D. Arner, "Pride and Prejudice: Kate Chopin's 'Désirée's Baby,'" *Mississippi Quarterly* 25 (1972): 132, praises the ending, and

Larzer Ziff and Per Seyersted compare the ending that depends on a twist with Maupassant.

78. Elfenbein, 127, in a general theming of Désirée's powerlessness as a woman, asserts: "The presumption of her infidelity would be sufficient to end the marriage, whereas the proof of his infidelity would be insufficient. If he is white and she is black, he may cast her out or relegate her to the status of La Blanche and make a house slave of their son." The failure to think of adultery is in marked contrast to the common practice in Virginia—reported by Higginbotham and Kopytoff, 1998—according to which

> when a couple classified as white produced a child whose racial identity was uncertain, the wife was suspected of having committed adultery with a Negro or mulatto man. Another possible explanation was that either the husband or the wife or both were in fact of mixed Negro-white ancestry, though legally white (if the proportion of Negro ancestry were small enough), or passing as white. Mixed-race parents would, on occasion, produce a child who looked more mulatto when they did not. That possibility was not explored. It may have not have occurred to white Virginians, or it may have been suppressed. It may have been more disturbing to them than the attribution of adultery to the women, for it called into question the idea of clear racial classifications, an idea that was central to the maintenance of slave society in Virginia.

79. "The Father of Désirée's Baby" has been considered by Frisby, 157, Chopin's only story dealing with "the profound tragedy of miscegenation." One might add that the only interracial marriage that was knowingly celebrated was that between Armand's white father and Creole mother, and it was entered into in the past and consummated in Europe by a couple that is dead at the beginning of the story. Neither Armand nor Désirée could be expected to knowingly marry a "black" person; hence Elfenbein, 126, speaks of "inadvertent miscegenation" in the story.

80. One could compare Chopin's story, for example, with Richard Wright's short story "Long Black Song" (1938), in which the black husband Silas finds out that his wife Sarah has made love to a white traveling salesman. Silas launches a tirade and throws Sarah, her daughter, and her belongings out of the shack. Or one could compare the reaction to a spouse's infidelity with that to the surprising revelation of the spouse's racial background—for example in William Ashby's *Redder Blood* (1915), 178, where Wanda says this to Adrian when she finds out about his "black blood": "You deceived me. Acid-like you ate into my pure soul, knowing all the time that you were black as midnight. Let me wipe away your kisses, let me tear my flesh from my frame." One can see the cumulative effect of interracial adultery stories such as the frame narrative of *Thousand Nights and One Night* or of novellas 22 and 24 in Masuccio's *Novellino* (1476). Such versions of an interracial family story can be used to legitimate violence, even murder. In interracial marriage annulment cases such as the 1924/25 Rhinelander case in New York City, the issue of "race deception" played a part similar to infidelity.

81. Long, *History of Jamaica*, 2: 327. See also Vandermonde's *Essai sur la manière de perfectionner l'espèce humaine* (1756), cited by Duchet in Poliakov, 183, for a different use of "adultérés" in interracial mingling. The *OED* cites seven-

teenth-century instances of "adulterated" in the now obsolete sense of "defiled by adultery" and of "corrupted by admixture of a baser ingredient."

82. Before going to the bayou, she also takes "her" child. Chopin is not consistent in the pronoun use, however, and refers also to "their child" when Armand accuses her of not being white.

83. The last sentence appears only in the first edition of the story.

84. Wolff, 128; see also Elfenbein, 131.

85. See Puškin, for example. In Joseph Holt Ingraham, *The Quadroone; or, St. Michael's Day* (1841), II: 187, the quadroon Ninine, mistress of the Marquis de la Caronde, tries to poison her lover's infant child, then kills the mother. Later she finds the child and compares him to her own: "The two boys were wonderfully like each other, both bearing their father's looks. . . . Suddenly this resemblance suggested a thought upon which she immediately acted." The plan is, of course, to switch them. Often a substitute for killing, switching similar-looking but different-race babies was a popular motif in interracial literature. See, for example, James S. Peacocke's *The Creole Orphans; or, Lights and Shadows of Southern Life: A Tale of Louisiana* (1856), the anonymous *Sisters of Orleans* (1871), *Millie the Quadroon* (1888), Mark Twain's *Pudd'nhead Wilson* (1894), or Pickens's *Vengeance of the Gods* (1922). Elfenbein, 130, believes that Désirée may also have noticed the "family resemblance" of the two children.

86. See Arner, "Pride and Prejudice," 133; and Peel, 229. Frisby, 159, writes of the "perfect retribution" that is "achieved when Aubigny is forced to live under the curse which he has imposed on others."

87. See also the discussion on fingernails in Chapter Five. In this strategy of representation, Chopin makes the child's race more open to question than Armand's assessment would permit. One thinks of the difficulty some courts had in making racial determinations: Higginbotham and Kopytoff, 1997–1998, for example, report a Virginia case of 1814 in which a husband was granted a provisional divorce, "provided that it shall be found by the verdict of a jury, upon . . trial . . . that the child of said Peggy Jones is not the child of said Richard Jones, but is the offspring of some man of colour." No trial followed, so that Higginbotham and Kopytoff hypothesize that the "Jones child probably looked white enough so that there was some question as to whether Richard Jones might not be the father after all." Similarly, one could say that the baby's race in Chopin is subject to debate, all the more so since its "blackness" is not described. Critics have been tempted to supply what Chopin's narrator withheld. Thus Richard Potter, "Negroes in the Fiction of Kate Chopin," *Louisiana History* 12.1 (1971): 49, finds that "recessive Negro traits begin to appear in the baby." Ellen Peel summarizes that the baby "looks partly black" (224) and that the child's "darkness" might be an instance of "poetic justice, the return of the oppressed" for Armand (228). Elfenbein, 130, stresses that Désirée is "the last to perceive the racial characteristics that become more pronounced as the baby's features develop."

88. It is against this backdrop that the story's elaborate color symbolism works so well. As Cynthia Griffin Wolff writes, highlighting "Chopin's ironic perception of the tenuous quality of [racial] distinctions": "None of the 'blacks' is referred to as actually dark-skinned" (128–29).

89. The status of an orphan intensifies namelessness, and in one crucial sentence the story anticipates Charles W. Chesnutt's "Her Virginia Mammy"

(which is much more critical of a character's desire not to be black): "He was reminded that she was nameless. What did it matter about a name when he could give her one of the oldest and proudest in Louisiana?"

90. Berzon, 102, writes that Désirée is "in actuality a white woman." Peel, 233, however, pursues the possibility that Désirée "may be black" and finds that this would mitigate some of the story's racism, yet concludes that "the impossibility of knowing her race reveals the fragility of meaning more than Armand's knowable race does."

91. 63. Potter, 49, also finds Armand's tragedy "in his own ignorance and, more significantly, in his own prejudice against the Negro race. So strong is this antipathy that it destroys the things he most loves. So strong is this prejudice that it destroys his capacity to love. The final irony is that it is he himself whom he hates."

92. Emily Toth, "Kate Chopin and Literary Convention: 'Désirée's Baby,'" *Southern Studies* 20.3 (Summer 1981): 207, suggests the possibility of a reading that would stress a "deterministic unfolding of Armand's character" and concludes: "Ultimately we do not know where [Chopin] stands on the connection between racial inheritance and character."

93. Pauline E. Hopkins, "Talma Gordon," *Colored American Magazine* 1.5 (Oct. 1900): 271–90. Page references to this text will be given parenthetically.

94. The passage is cited as an epigraph at the beginning of Chapter One, 31.

95. Cameron's confession is yet another story within the story, and Dr. Thornton says in response to the revelation, "Had I the pen of a Dumas I could not paint Cameron as he told his story" (289).

96. The novel will be discussed again in Chapter Nine, on "Passing." To my knowledge, Schuyler's novel has not received much critical attention, and when it was reprinted in 1971 it was introduced by what amounts to a diatribe against the author.

97. Schuyler had previously reported the press reaction to the white fears of cases of *Natus Æthiopus* and quoted what purports to be a segment from the Tallahassee *Announcer* on the consequences of the flight to whiteness by the process that Matthew also underwent:

> Day by day we see the color line which we have so laboriously established being rapidly destroyed. There would not be so much cause for alarm in this were it not for the fact that this vitiligo is not hereditary. In other words, THE OFFSPRING OF THESE WHITENED NEGROES WILL BE NEGROES! This means that your daughter, having married a supposed white man, may find herself with a black baby! (50)

98. Schuyler also played with the adultery implication of *Natus Æthiopus* when he comments on frequent press reports about white women giving birth to black babies with the statement that the blame "in the public mind always rested on the shoulders of the father, or rather, of the husband" (117).

99. By comparison, a modern and very subtle *Natus Æthiopus* tale like Muriel Spark's "The Black Madonna" (1958) would seem to fall behind Schuyler, as that story, set near Liverpool, reestablishes the contexts of possible atavism and suspected adultery—even though Spark's narrator very effectively exposes the hypocrisy of Raymond and Lou Parker, the childless couple who befriend two Jamaicans, Henry Pierce and Oxford St. John, and pray to the Black Madonna for

a child but who cannot accept as their own the dark child to whom Lou gives birth. In contrast to the narrative's spirit of Catholic universalism, Raymond proclaims: "Mind you, if it was anyone else's child I would think it was all right. It's just the thought of it being mine, and people thinking it isn't." Hence putting up their own daughter (whom they have named "Dawn") for adoption seems to them the "*right* thing," though not the "*good* thing," to do under the circumstances. Muriel Spark, "The Black Madonna," in *The Go-Away Bird and Other Stories* (Philadelphia and New York: Lippincott, 1958), reprinted in *Stories in Black and White*, ed. Eva H. Kissin (Philadelphia and New York: Lippincott, 1970), 230–53, here 252, 253.

100. "The Father of Désirée's Baby" is interesting in this respect, for although Armand's mother wrote only about being "cursed with the brand of slavery," the story never thematizes the possibility of enslavement but focuses instead on the question of which of the parents is "not white."

101. The original conjunction could mean either "and" or "but." See Snowden, *Blacks in Antiquity*, 198, and Charles B. Copher, "Three Thousand Years of Biblical Interpretaion With Reference to Black Peoples," in *African American Religious Studies: An Interdisciplinary Anthology*, ed. Gayraud S. Wilmore (Durham and London: Duke Univ. Press, 1989), 105–39, here 109.

102. The name of their child Manasseh was adopted by a Chicago biracial association that operated from 1892 to 1932. See Spickard, 333. Rebecca Harding Davis, *Waiting for the Verdict* (1868), 298, lets her protagonist Dr. Broderip, who is passing, voice Joseph's question.

103. This notion was present not only in the last sentence of "The Father of Désirée's Baby" but also in the advice that Senator North (in Gertrude Atherton's eponymous novel of 1900) gives to Betty Madison concerning her dark half-sister Harriet: "If she wishes to marry, you must tell the man the truth, if she will not. Don't hesitate on that a moment. Her children are likely to be coal-black. That African blood seems to have a curse on it, and the curse is usually visited on the unoffending" (86–87).

### Chapter Three. The Curse of Ham

1. (Rpt., Harmondsworth: Penguin, 1983), 120.

2. (Evanston and Chicago: Northwestern Univ. Press, 1970), 512–13.

3. "XI," *Harlem Gallery* (New York: Twayne, 1965), 83.

4. *Le Plaisir du texte* (Paris: Editions du Seuil, 1973), 20; trans. Richard Miller, *The Pleasure of the Text* (New York: Hill and Wang, 1975). Cited in Peter Brooks, *Body Work: Objects of Desire in Modern Narrative* (Cambridge and London: Harvard Univ. Press, 1993), 15 and 104. Brooks adds: "Barthes may suggest here that the attention to female nudity is something of a coverup for the more deeply feared nudity, though this would seem to run counter to the Freudian scenarios of castration. The question of the ultimately most scandalous nudity seems to me undecidable" (291n24).

5. It is possible to look at this play as a text in isolation, or to look at it in the immediate cultural context of its author, first publication, reception, and so forth. It is also possible—and this is what I would like to do here—to explore its theme cross-culturally. I shall briefly return to this play later.

The fact that there is no biblical sanction for this story of the origin of black skin color is mentioned as often as it is forgotten. The studies by Don Cameron Allen, Raoul Allier, Ron Bartour, Urs Bitterli, Charles B. Copher, Jean Devisse, William McKee Evans, George Fredrickson, Ephraim Isaac, Winthrop Jordan, Bernard Lewis, Albert Perbal, Thomas Virgil Peterson, Gernot Rotter, H. Shelton Smith, and others have made it possible to account more fully for the historical unfolding of the curse of Ham.

6. The passage has inspired famous visual representations from the San Marco mosaics to Michelangelo's Sistine Chapel; see Otto Demus et al., *The Mosaics of San Marco in Venice* (Chicago and London: Univ. of Chicago Press, 1984). Compare also twelfth to thirteenth-century mosaics in Monreale, Palermo, depicting the malediction of Ham. Other visual representations are in the 4th-century Priscilla catacomb, in el-Baghaouat (Egypt), in a Lateran sarcophagus of the third century, in another sarcophagus at Treviri, in the mosaics of the mausoleum of Centcelles in the province of Tarragona, in the miniatures of the *Pentateuch* of Ashburnham, and on Roman and Vatican coins, the 11th–12th-century Benedictine monastery Millstatt Genesis (now in the Kärntner Landesarchiv, Klagenfurt), on the glass windows of the cathedral at Chartres (1235–40), the 13th-century Codex Vindobonensis, the 14th-century choir chair carvings in the cathedral at Cologne, the British Library codex Or Ms 2884, fol. 8v.a; French tapestry of 1570. Compare the representation of Noah in Bernardo Luini, Milano, Brera; relief by Baccio Bandinelli, Florence, National Museum. For literature on curse of Ham in visual arts, see J. Fink, "Noah der Gerechte in der frühchristlichen Kunst," *Beihefte zum Archiv für Kunstgeschichte* 4 (Köln, 1955); L. Budde, "Die rettende Arche Noah," *Pantheon* 18 (1960); Hanna Hohl, *Die Darstellung der Sintflut*, Dissertation, Tübingen, 1967; Erich Lessing, *Die Arche Noah in Bildern* (Zürich: Fritz Molden, 1968); Engelbert Kirschbaum, S.J., *Lexikon der christlichen Ikonographie*, v. 4 (Rom, Freiburg, Basel, Wien: Herder, 1972), 611–19; and Peter Franke, "Bemerkungen zur frühchristlichen Noe-Ikonographie," *Rivista di archeologia cristiana* 49.1–4 (1973): 171–82.

7. John Calvin, *Commentaries on the First Book of Moses Called Genesis*, trans. John King, vol. I (Grand Rapids, Mich.: Wm. B. Eerdmans, n.d.), 306. For Ambrose, see Jean Devisse, *The Image of the Black in Western Art: From the Early Christian Era to the "Age of Discovery,"* series ed. Ladislas Bugner, vol. 2.1, trans. William Granger Ryan (Menil Foundation; distr. Harvard Univ. Press, 1979), 55. Gerhard von Rad, *Genesis: A Commentary*, rev. ed. (Philadelphia: Westminster Press, 1972), 137–40. U. Cassuto, *A Commentary on the Book of Genesis*, vol. 2 (1949; Eng. trans. Israel Abrahams, Jerusalem: Magnes Press, 1964), 141–70. Claus Westermann, *Genesis*, vol. I: *Genesis, 1–11* (Neukirchen-Vluyn, 1974), 656–57. See Ron Bartour, "'Cursed be Canaan, a Servant of Servants shall he be unto his Brethren': American Views on 'Biblical Slavery,' 1835–1865: A Comparative Study," *Slavery and Abolition* 4.1 (May 1983): 41–55, an excellent analysis of how pro- and antislavery exegesis paralleled—and even led indirectly to new scholarly questions in—serious biblical scholarship.

8. Gernot Rotter, *Die Stellung des Negers in der islamisch-arabischen Gesellschaft bis zum XVI. Jahrhundert*, Dissertation (Bonn, 1967), 145. Rotter mentions Ibn Isḥāq's version in al-Ṭabarī as the Arabic text closest to the biblical story, though Noah's intoxication is omitted.

9. In the contemporary Monreale mosaic, the scene of Ham pointing to his father's nakedness that his brothers cover (also from the gaze of the viewer) is accompanied by the comment: "hic ostendit Cam verenda patri ebríí fribus." Westermann, *Genesis*, 652, stresses that drunkenness was not considered a transgression in antiquity, and that the naming of Noah in Genesis 5:29 as the one who "shall comfort us concerning our work and toil of our hands" [an answer to Genesis 3:17] permits the interpretation that the cultivation of wine grapes is viewed as progress over agriculture.

10. Ramban [Nachmanides], *Commentary on the Torah: Genesis*, trans. Charles B. Chavel (New York: Shilo Publishing, 1971), 142–43. Nachmanides also suggests the reading "unto all men" (in the sense of Zechariah 8:10) or "his father's brothers" (as in Genesis 14:14), and he refers to Ibn Ezra's interpretation of "brethren" as "his father's children" (i.e., Canaan's brothers Cush, Mizraim, and Phut); see also Bartour, "Cursed be Canaan," 47.

11. Thomas Newton, *Dissertations on the Prophecies, Which Have Remarkably Been Fulfilled, and at This Time Are Fulfilling in the World* (Northampton, Mass.: William Butler, 1746), 10–11, invoking Vatablus, some copies of the Septuagint, a Mr. Green from Cambridge, and Augustin Calmet's *Dictionary of the Holy Bible* (1722–28). Newton regards the fact that many hundreds of "poor negroes . . . every year are sold and bought like beasts in the market from one quarter of the world to do the work of beasts in another" as evidence of the "execution of the sentence upon *Ham* as well as upon *Canaan*." Cited in Thomas Virgil Peterson, *Ham and Japheth: The Mythic World of Whites in the Antebellum South* (Metuchen, N.J., and London: Scarecrow Press, 1978), 43.

12. Josephus, *Antiquities of the Jews*, 1, vi.3 (1.142), in *Complete Works*, based on Havercamp's translation (New York: Bigelow, Brown, n.d.), I: 25–26. This reading was also invoked in 1729 in Ralph Sandiford's *Brief Examination of the Practice of the Times* (rpt., New York: Arno Press, 1969), 4, in order to oppose the biblical legitimation of the slave trade: "Neither can those Negroes be proved, by any Genealogy, the Seed of *Ham*, whom *Noah* Cursed not, saith *Josephus*, as being too nigh of Blood. But *Noah*'s Curse on *Canaan* the youngest Son of *Ham*, is thought a suitable original for the Negro Trade: But the Curse is not so extensive." Ephraim Isaac, "Concept biblique et rabbinique de la malediction de Noe" and "Biblical and Rabbinic Understanding of the Curse of Noah," *SIDIC: Service international de documentation judéo-chretienne* 11.2 (1978): 16–35, here 23, reports the syllogism proposed by some rabbis "that since God had already bestowed a blessing upon Noah and his sons (Gen. 9:1), and that a blessing could not be retracted or a curse be substituted in its stead, Noah put the curse on his grandson."

13. Cassuto, *A Commentary*, 154–55, distinguishes three attempts made to regularize the passage: the sin is transferred from father to son; the reference is declared to be really to the father; or the transgression was somehow Canaan's. See also the entries on "Ham," "Canaan," and "Canaan, Curse of" in the *Encyclopaedia Judaica* 5 and 7 (Jerusalem, 1971); Menaham M. Kasher, *Encyclopedia of Biblical Interpretation: A Millennial Anthology* (New York: American Biblical Encyclopedia Society, 1955), 2: 66–75; Samson Raphael Hirsch, *Commentary on the Pentateuch*, trans. Isaac Levi (London, 1960), 193.

14. Samuel Bochart, *Phaleg, Canaan, et Hierozoicon*, 3rd ed. (Lugduni Batavorum: Apud Cornelium Boutesteyn & Jordanum Luchtmans; Trajecti ad

Rhenum: Apud Guilielmum vande Water, 1692), 5–12 (book I, chs. 1 and 2). Bochart did not draw a parallel to Hyginus's version of Phaëthon.

15. *De Civitate Dei* XVI: 2; cited in Isaac, "Concept biblique," 22n2. Isaac also mentions that Augustine compares Ham with Cain.

16. *Historiae ecclesiasticae Francorum libri decem* I, 9, cited in Jean Devisse's contribution to *The Image of the Black in Western Art*, ed. Ladislas Bugner, vol. 2.1 (Menil Foundation; distributed by Harvard Univ. Press, 1979), 55–57. Devisse calls attention to Ambrose, Tertullian, Rabanus Maurus, and Bede, as well as to the cultural significance of genealogical tables; Winthrop D. Jordan, *White Over Black: American Attitudes Toward the Negro, 1550–1812* (1968; Baltimore: Penguin Books, 1969), 17–18, also notes that Jerome and St. Augustine referred to the curse in relationship to slavery; William McKee Evans, "From the Land of Canaan to the Land of Guinea: The Strange Career of the 'Sons of Ham,'" *American Historical Review* 85.1 (Feb. 1980): 15–43, stresses that genealogies may reveal more about "existing power relationships" than about "actual origins and kinships of peoples" (33).

17. Beda, *Hexaemeron* ii and Rabanus Maurus, *Commentarium in Genesim* II, ix. See Devisse, 221.

18. *Bible moralisée: Codex Vindobonensis 2554 der Österreichischen Nationalbibliothek*, reprinted in toto, ed. Reiner Hausherr; trans (from French) Hans-Walter Stark (Graz: Akademische Druck– und Verlagsanstalt, 1992), 7 = fol. *3v (Gen. 9), 52. Giuseppe Schirò, *Monreale: City of the Golden Temple* (Palermo: Edizioni Mistretta, 1990), 61, offers the following comment: "Ham symbolizes the sacrilegious unbelievers, who scorn and ridicule the nakedness to which the Word subjected itself out of love in order to redeem His creature." The wine in the mosaic replicates the snake in paradise (Schiró, 50–51); Shem and Japheth are shown bearded, whereas Ham is beardless (which marks a physical distinction between the brothers); and the scene is located on the right side of the nave, under the parts of the story of the creation in which living creatures "of all kinds emerged from the waters" to form diverse animals and the creation of man (Schiró, 27–28, 71). In Swedenborgian doctrine sons of Ham are "all those who are scientifically skilled in the knowledge of faith, and have no charity." See *A Dictionary of Correspondences, Representatives, and Significatives, Derived from the Word of the Lord, extracted from the work of Emanuel Swedenborg*, 5th ed. (Boston: T. H. Carter and Sons, 1868), 160. Erich Lessing, *Die Arche Noah*, 112, describes Noah as the prototype (*Urbild*) of Christ, deprived of his robe and humiliated, on his way to Golgotha.

19. See Alexander Perrig, "Erdrandsiedler," in Koebner and Pickerodt, 46–47 and 73, illus. 4. The "T-O" map from the Newberry Library copy is also reproduced in Stephen Greenblatt, *Marvelous Possessions: The Wonder of the New World* (Chicago: Univ. of Chicago Press, 1991), opp. 82, illus. 1. In 1995 the Bible Lands Museum in Jerusalem opened its exhibits with an introductory gallery that traced geography to the sons of Noah.

20. One problem was posed by the inhabitants of the New World. The Calvinist Jean de Léry in his *Histoire d'un voyage fait en la terre du Bresil* (1578), for example, thought of the Brazilian Tupinamba Indians as cursed descendants of Ham. See Anthony Pagden, *European Encounters With the New World: From Renaissance to Romanticism* (New Haven and London: Yale Univ. Press, 1993), 42–43.

21. This legend of the "Samothean Celts" is related in Rodger Cunningham, *Apples on the Flood: The Southern Mountain Experience* (Knoxville: Univ. of Tennessee Press, 1987), 6; see also 83 and 127. Samuel Taylor Coleridge, entry 4384 (Jan. 1818), *Notebooks 1808–1819*, by contrast believed the ancient Celts originated "in an intermixture of the descendants of Shem with those of Ham and Canaan." An Irish mark of Cain also occurs in Hamilton Basso's novel about racial passing, *The View From Pompey's Head* (Garden City, N.Y.: Doubleday, 1954), 173.

22. I am here following Lessing, 102. See also Henry Adams, *Mont-Saint-Michel and Chartres* (1904; rpt., Boston and New York: Houghton Mifflin, 1913), 180.

23. Ruskin, *Diaries* I, 187; cited in *John Ruskin: An Arts Council Exhibition 1983* (Sheffield: Mappin Art Gallery; Liverpool: Walker Art Gallery; Kendal: Abbot Hall Art Gallery; Oxford: Museum of Modern Art), 53. The sculpture has been ascribed to Filippo Calendario, who was sentenced to death in 1355 and who had been influenced by Pisano or the Lombard artists (Matteo Raverti?). See W. Wolters, *La Scultura veneziana gotica* (Venezia, 1976), and Giulio Lorenzetti, *Venice and Its Lagoon: Historical-Artistic Guide*, trans. John Guthrie (1926; rpt., Trieste: Edizioni Lint, 1985), 239.

24. I have not found a *visual* representation of the curse of Ham which shows a change in skin color. Only Josiah Priest's illustrator of 1845 drew Noah's family along strict racial lines—but did not actually represent the curse (73). Other passages concerning the mark of Cain (Gen. 4:15), Cush (Gen. 10:6–9), Ethiopia (Psalms 68:31), Egypt as "the land of Ham" (Psalms 105:23, 27 and 106:22) and sinful doings (Lev. 18:3), or concerning the Ethiopian's skin and the leopard's spots (Jeremiah 13:23) were sometimes inserted into the interpretation of Genesis 9; Le Cat and Thomas Browne suggested the alternative explanation of Laban's flocks (Gen. 30:31–43) in support of the "maternal impression" theory: *Traité de la couleur de la peau humaine* (Amsterdam, 1765), 19, also cited in Shelby T. McCloy, *The Negro in France* (Lexington: Univ. of Kentucky Press, 1961), 40; Browne, "Of the Blackness of *Negroes*," 375.

25. Augustin Calmet's *Dictionary of the Holy Bible* (1722–28) translates the name "Ham" as "burnt," "swarthy," and "black"; James Hastings's *Dictionary of the Bible* (1899) suggests that "Ham" is a version of the Egyptian name of Egypt, "kem," its meaning akin to Arabic "ahamm," that is black. Yet if these etymologies of "Ham" (that are no longer favored, as "Ham" is correlated to "heat" (*calor*) by most exegetes) account for the general application of the curse on Canaan to blacks, this was not universally recognized, not even in texts that attempted to make the curse stick specifically to Africans. Most notable is the infrequency of references to Cush—who is African in Jewish, Christian, and Muslim texts—in stories of the curse on Ham. In a story of a generational decline, Ambrose identified Ham with *calor*, Canaan with *commotio* and *inquietudo*, and Nimrod with *confusio*. Other etymologies applied to the biblical passage include "self-submission" or "kneebender" for Canaan, "name" for Shem, "gentle" or "consoled" for Noah, and "enlarge" for Japheth—telling names indeed.

26. John Herbert Nelson, a southern conservative, may have been the first to write in *The Negro Character in American Literature* (1926), 8, of the "trite explanation (. . . from rabbinical lore) of the origin of the black race through Ham." Later Raoul Allier, Albert Perbal, Winthrop Jordan, Thomas Gossett, Edith

Sanders, Martin Steins, Urs Bitterli, David Brion Davis, Thomas Virgil Peterson, Gernot Rotter, and William McKee Evans—as well as Louis Farrakhan and Tony Martin—commented on the curse of Ham in Jewish texts.

27. I. Epstein et al., trans., *The Babylonian Talmud*, 35 vols. (London, 1935–60), *Sanhedrin*, II (London, 1935), 745. Invoking B. Sanhedrin 72a–b, 108b; B. Pesahim 113b; Tanhuma Buber Gen. 49–50; Tanhuma Noah 13, 15; and Gen. Rab. 341, Robert Graves and Raphael Patai, *Hebrew Myths: The Book of Genesis* (Garden City, N.Y.: Doubleday, 1964), 121, relate an undated, composite, and highly problematic version according to which Noah said to Ham: "since you have disabled me from doing ugly things in the blackness of night, Canaan's children shall be born ugly and black! Moreover, because you twisted your head around to see my nakedness, your grandchildren's hair shall be twisted into kinks, and their eyes red; again, because your lips jested at my misfortune, theirs shall swell; and because you neglected my nakedness, they shall go naked, and their male members shall be shamefully elongated." This passage highlights the worrisome side of thematic approaches, as it abstracts and pastes together from many different sources a new version that, as such, never existed before. As a consequence of this decontextualized, linguistically not always accurate procedure, later readers have been able to misuse this excerpt as if it were evidence for their contention that the racialization of the curse on Ham was a particularly Jewish myth.

28. H. Freedman and Maurice Simon, trans., *Midrash Rabbah*, 10 vols. (London, 1931), I: 293.

29. Harry Sperling and Maurice Simon, trans., *The Zohar*, 5 vols. (London, 1931), I, 246–47.

30. *De Noe*, Corpus Scriptorum Ecclesiasticorum Latinorum 32.1.485ff., esp. 490–92; cited by Devisse, 55–57.

31. Max Grünbaum, 86; [Paul de] Lagarde, ed., 86, 30 fg., 87, 10 fg. Bernard Lewis, *Race and Slavery in the Middle East*, pp. 123–25, writes: "The earliest explicit reference to blackness as part of the curse inflicted on Ham for his offense against his father would appear to be a passage in the Bible commentary ascribed to the Syrian church father Saint Ephrem of Nisibis, according to whom Noah said: 'Accursed be Canaan, and may God make his face black,' whereupon the face of both Canaan and Ham became black. . . . This passage occurs in a late Arabic translation of some passages in Saint Ephrem's writings, and there may therefore be some question about its authenticity. No Syriac original for this passage has so far come to light; and the story may well be a later interpolation in the Arabic version, reflecting the current notions of that time" (124). Devisse, 56, writes about the geneaological tradition connecting the blacks with Ham that "Byzantium may have invented and certainly promulgated it."

32. Isidore, *Etymologiae* 7.6.19–22, cited in Devisse 221n175. Rodericus, *De Rebus Hispaniae*, in *Opera*, facsimile of 1793 edition, ed. Ma. Desamparados Cabanes Pecourt (Valencia, 1968), 6. As we shall see, Azurara cites "Don Roderic" (as well as Josephus) in order to buttress his racial reading of the curse of Ham. See also Tertullian (160–220), *De Spectaculis* III, trans. T. R. Glover (Cambridge: Harvard Univ. Press; London: Heinemann, 1977), 240, 241.

33. Devisse, 142–43, reproduces the illustration. Devisse also points out that a great number of Christian texts appeared from the earliest period on with such titles as *Book of Generations* or *Genealogical Book*. Derived from Genesis, these

works attempted to clarify, often confusingly, the different descent lines leading from Noah to various populations on earth. According to von Rad, *Genesis*, 137–40, the curse of Ham constitutes a later interpolation in the text between flood and genealogical tables; von Rad also stresses that the postdiluvian geneaologies are not to be read literally as signaling family relations; he furthermore mentions that the use of the name "Shem" to stand for Israel is so unusual as to make its occurrence in Genesis 9 unique in the Old Testament. David Brion Davis in *The Antislavery Vanguard: New Essays on Abolitionists*, ed. Martin Duberman (Princeton: Princeton Univ. Press, 1965), 5n, writes that the substitution of "the name of Ham as the father of Canaan, in an effort to harmonize the narrative with the later table of nations" had the accidental side effect that Negroes, who were early associated with Ham, were stigmatized with the curse of Canaan.

34. Rotter, 142–45, describes and distinguishes two basic types of Muslim genealogical tables. For the controversy see, for example, Rotter, 25, 75–78, 145–52, vs. B. Lewis, 9, 123–26.

35. *The Koran* (Qu'rān), trans. E. H. Palmer, intr. R. A. Nicholson (1900; rpt., Oxford and London: Oxford Univ. Press, 1928), 11:44ff.

36. Mas'udi, *Les Prairies d'or*, trans. Barbier de Meynard and Pavet de Courteille, ed. Charles Pellat (Paris: Centre national de la recherche scientifique, 1962), # 66, vol. I, 32.

37. Evans, 27, and Rotter, 146–47. Evans, 25, also notes that the *Koran* does not yet equate "slave" with "Negro."

38. Rotter, 147, writing on genealogies, contrasts the nonracial description of peoples that von Rad saw in Genesis with the "purely racial division according to external criteria" in Arabic-Islamic genealogies.

39. *Tanwīr*, 5a; cited in Rotter, 150.

40. Ibn Qutayba, *Ma'ārif*, 13; cited in Rotter, 146; B. Lewis, 124, cites this text as the first Islamic version in which Noah's curse consists of blackness though not servitude. Lewis, 125, also mentions that the South Arabian Wahb, on whom Ibn Qutayba drew, may have been a convert to Islam from Judaism or Christianity (the latter option favored by Lewis).

41. Al-Ṭabarī, *The History of al-Ṭabarī (Ta'rīkh a rusul wa'l-mulūk)*, vol. 2, trans. William M. Brinner (Albany: State Univ. of New York Press, 1987), 21 (section 223). This passage was cited somewhat differently by Evans, 33, who seems to translate from Rotter's German excerpts, 147, and who omits the negative reference to the descendants of Japheth.

42. *L'Abrégé des Merveilles*, trans. from Arabic by B. Carra de Vaux, ms. Bibliothèque nationale 1898, *Actes de la société philologique* 26 (1897): 99–101; cited in Devisse 221n179.

43. Ibn Ḵhaldūn, *Muḳaddima* 1.3, in Cuoq 359; Eng. trans. Devisse, 221 n179. Compare Franz Rosental's partly differing translation of *The Muqaddimah*, ed. N. J. Dawood (Princeton: Bollingen Series, Princeton Univ. Press, 1967), 59–60.

44. Aḥmad Bābā, *Mi'rāğ*, f. 5b–6a, cited in Rotter, 152. See also B. Lewis, 125. Rotter, 183, also argues that after the 13th century there was no more criticism of interracial marriages (which had always been and continued to be frequent) in Arab literature; and from the fifteenth century on, many writings expressed an explicit praise of it. Rotter explains that after the 10th century

maternal genealogy became unimportant in the Arab world; therefore mixed off-spring was easily incorporated on equal terms.

45. *The Book of the Thousand Nights and One Night*, trans. Richard F. Burton (London: priv. pub., n.d.), 4: 250. This translation was largely lifted from John Payne's almost totally identical text. Burton endorses this passage with one of his startling footnotes that goes a long way to illuminating the political uses to which the curse of Ham was put: "Here we have the naked legend of the negro's origin; one of those nursery tales in which the ignorant of Christendom still believe. But the deduction from the fable and the testimony to the negro's lack of intelli-gence, though unpleasant to our ignorant negrophiles, are factual and satisfacto-ry." See C. Knipp, "The *Arabian Nights* in England: Galland's Translation and Its Successors," *Journal of Arabic Literature* 5 (1974): 44–54; esp. 45; and Wiebke Walther, *Tausend und eine Nacht: Eine Einführung* (München und Zürich: Artemis, 1987), 28–53.

46. Despite its references to the Koran, the "authority of devout men" refers to the Noah story from Genesis rather than from the Koran.

47. Evans, 33, 42; Thomas Gossett, *Race: The History of an Idea in America*, 5. J. R. Willis, *Slaves and Slavery in Muslim Africa* vol. 1 (London, 1985), 8. Jordan, 18. B. Lewis, 123–26. See David Goldenberg on this issue.

Louis Farrakhan claimed that Harold Brackman's 1977 dissertation had proved that "the rabbis who compiled the Talmud" had "'invented' racism by concocting the so-called 'Ham myth.'" This prompted Brackman to write a letter to the *New York Times* (14 Feb. 1993, A16) in which he argued (following Ephraim Isaac and David Brion Davis) that the curse on Ham and Canaan was never believed to extend to Cush, who was viewed as the ancestor of African peo-ples south of Egypt. Tony Martin, *The Jewish Onslaught: Despatches from the Wellesley Battlefront* (Dover, Mass.: Majority Press, 1993), also cites "Harold D. Brackman of California's Jewish Simon Wiesenthal Center" (33) who is said to have written in his dissertation "that the Babylonian Talmud was the first source to read a Negrophobic content into the episode" of Noah's curse on Canaan (34). Brackman also said to cite two 3rd-century Jewish sages: "Rab maintained that [Ham] had unmanned Noah, while Samuel claimed that he had buggered him as well." Martin then quotes Brackman on the issue of blackness:

> The more important version of the myth, however, ingeniously ties in the origins of blackness—and of other, real or imagined Negroid traits—with Noah's curse itself. According to it, Ham is told by his outraged father that, because you have abused me in the darkness of the night, your chil-dren shall be born black and ugly; because you have twisted your head to cause me embarrassment, they shall have kinky hair and red eyes; because your lips jested at my exposure, theirs shall swell; and because you neglect-ed my nakedness, they shall go naked with their shamefully elongated male members exposed for all to see. (34–35)

The source given is Harold D. Brackman, "The Ebb and Flow of Conflict: A History of Black-Jewish Relations Through 1900" (Ph.D. diss., UCLA, 1977), 80, 81. The more well-known source for this passage is probably Graves and Patai, *Hebrew Myths*, 121, cited earlier. On this issue, see Ephraim Isaac, "Gene-sis, Judaism, and the 'Sons of Ham,'" *Slavery and Abolition* 1 (1980): 3–17, and

"Biblical" (1978): 16–35, an explicit and detailed polemic against the "Jewish-origins" claim advanced by Edith Sanders in "The Hamitic Hypothesis: Its Origins and Functions in Time Perspective," *Journal of African History* 10 (1969): 521–32. In such instances one recognizes the value of Urs Bitterli's insight that the study of racial history is beset by the twin dangers of excessive self-accusation and exoneration (Bitterli, *Die "Wilden,"* 7).

48. Evans, 34. Evans, 34n61, also cites the late 13th-century work *The Mirror of Justices*, ed. William Joseph Whitaker (London, 1895), 77, which argued that "serfage, according to some, comes from the curse which Noah pronounced against Canaan, the son of his son Ham, and against his issue."

49. For example, Gilbert Génebrand, professor of Hebrew at the Collège de France, explained the Talmudic interpretation of the curse of Ham in his *Chronographiae libri quatuor* and defended it against the climate theory; cited in Raoul Allier, *Une enigme troublante: la race Nègre et la malediction du Cham* (Paris: Société des Missions Évangéliques, no. 26 of Les Cahiers Missionaires, 1930), 16, and discussed in Don Cameron Allen, *The Legend of Noah: Renaissance Rationalism in Arts, Science, and Letters* (Urbana: Univ. of Illinois Press, 1963), 119, who refers to "Genebrardus, a Benedictine monk." In *The Truth of the Gospel* (Eng. trans. 1751), Abbé le Pluche writes that among the Mahometan Arabs whatever precedes *Abraham* is utterly confused and dark (I:19), though he cites a number of Arab sources, but also invokes Deucalion in his discussion of Noah (I: 58–59), and speaks of the dispersion of Japheth, Ham (or Cham), and Shem (I: 78) in a neutral manner, stressing the unity of human origins (I: 91). Thomas Newton, in his already cited *Dissertations on the Prophecies* (1759; rpt., Northampton: William Butler, 1796), quotes an Arabic version of Genesis and a new emended translation from the Hebrew in order to make African slavery understandable as the fulfillment of a prophecy. Augustin Calmet's *Dictionnaire* (1720), Eng. *Dictionary of the Holy Bible*, ed. Charles Taylor (Boston: Crocker and Brewster, 1832), 476, explicitly mentions a Muslim source, the Rozit ul Suffa, in discussing the descendants of Ham's nine sons; and Allier, *Une enigme*, 19, also mentions that in the French edition of 1845, Calmet refers to the "Tharak-Thabari" (that is, al-Tabari's *Ta'rikh*). John Fletcher, in his proslavery *Essays on Slavery, in Easy Lessons: Compiled into Eight Studies, and Subdivided into Short Lessons for the Convenience of Readers* (Natchez, Miss.: Jackson Warner, 1852), about which more later, quotes the *Zohar* (448) by way of Sale's *Koran* (437). See Peterson, *Ham and Japheth*, 43, who cites some of these sources and who reprints an anonymous pamphlet of 1860, *African Servitude*, which mentions, 147, "the Arabic translation" of the name Ham, and quotes, 156, Calmet's *Dictionary* to the effect that "Eastern writers maintain that all the blacks descended from Ham and Canaan."

50. There is a running dispute among etymologists about the origin of the term "race." Leo Spitzer, "Wortgeschichtliches," *Zeitschrift für romanische Philologie* 53.3–4 (July 1933); 300–301, *Essays in Historical Semantics* (New York, 1948), 147–69, and *American Journal of Philology* 52 (1941): 129–43, advocated a development from Latin *ratio* to *razza*. Benvenuto Terracini, *Nueva revista de filología hispánica* 5 (1951): 424–30, offered some critical comments on Spitzer. Gianfranco Contini, "I piú antichi esempi di 'Razza,'" *Studi di Filologia Italiana* 17 (1959): 319–27, and Francesco Sabatini, "Conferme per l'etimologia di *razza* dal francese antico *haraz*," *Studi di Filologia Italiana* 20 (1962): 365–82, found very early evidence for the origin of "race" in horse-breeding language from the Old

French word for horse-breeding *haraz* to Italian *razza* in a case of 1362, or even 1267. G. Merk, *Travaux de Linguistique et de Littérature*, pub. by Centre de Philologie at de Littératures Romanes de l'Université de Strasbourg VII, 1 (1969), 177–88, viewed French *race* as "le produit d'une contamination sémantique et phonétique de *generatio* avec *ratio* et, secondairement, avec *natio*." (The biblical phrase "generation of vipers" is rendered as "race de vipères" in French.) Diderot's *Encyclopédie* defined "race" as "Extraction, lignée, lignage, ce que se dit des ascendans que des descendans d'une même famille," and we just saw Le Cat referring to "Caïn . . . & sa race" in the sense of descendants and racial group. As Rosario Coluccia, "Ancora sull'etimologia di 'razza': Discussione chiusa o aperta?," *Studi di Filologia Italiana* 30 (1972): 325–30, argues, more research and more evidence are needed. See also Walther von Wartburg, "Rasse," *Französisches etymologisches Wörterbuch* vol. 10 (Basel: R. G. Zbinden, 1962), 111–18.

51. Browne, "Of the Blackness," 379–80. See also Le Cat, 5–6, 10.

52. Verena Stolcke, "Invaded Women: Gender, Race, and Class in the Formation of Colonial Society," in *Women, "Race," and Writing in the Early Modern Period*, eds. Margo Hendricks and Patricia Parker (London and New York: Routledge, 1994), 272–86, here 276–77. See also Adriano Prospero, "Tra natura e culturua: Dall'intolleranza religiosa alla discriminazione per sangue," in *Il Razzismo e le sue storie*, ed. Girolamo Imbruglia (Napoli: Edizioni Scientifiche Italiane, 1992), 113–29.

53. *The Chronicle of the Discovery and Conquest of Guinea*, trans. Charles Raymond Beazley and Edgar Prestage (London, 1896; rpt., New York: Burt Franklin, n.d.), I: ch. xvi, 54. He continues, "as wrote the Archbishop Don Roderic of Toledo, and Josephus in his book on the *Antiquities of the Jews*, and Walter [whom I have not been able to identify], with other authors who have spoken of the generations of Noah, from the time of his going out of the Ark." I am following the description of Azurara by Bitterli, *Die "Wilden,"* 24; see also "Biblische Abstammungstheorien," ibid., 339–43. Bitterli notes that Azurara, though he is very learned, does not seem to know the Bible well. Evans, 38–39, also cites Azurara. David Brion Davis, *Slavery and Human Progress* (New York and Oxford: Oxford Univ. Press, 1984), 86–87, 337n144, has argued that the Hamitic myth played only a minor role in justifying slavery until the late eighteenth century.

54. This was not the only time that the curse that Cain received from God after killing his own brother Abel (Gen. 4:11) would be conflated with Noah's malediction of Canaan, though the Portuguese manuscript's "Caym" may also simply be a misspelling of "Cam." See Gomes Eanes da Zurara, *Crónica de Guiné*, segundo ms. de Paris, ed. José de Bragança (Lisboa: Bibioteca Histórica, n.d.), ch. 16.

55. Zurara's manuscript uses the word *geeraçōes* (once spelled *geeraçooĕs*, and both printed as *gerações*), for "generations of Noah" as well as for "races of the world." This is still thirty years before the word *raça* was first listed in the Portuguese etymological dictionary: Jose Pedro Machado, *Dicionario etimologico da lingua portuguesa*, 3rd ed. (Lisboa: Livros Horizonte, 1977), gives the following instance from 1473: "non de pouco convertidas nun infeitas da mala raça de mouros o judios"—an instance that goes well with Verena Stolcke's argument about the importance of "conversos" for the rise of the concept of "race." Of course, the advocates of the theory that "race" derives from old French *haraz*—

rather than *generatio, radix,* or *ratio*—invoke much earlier evidence. See Sabatini, "Conferme," 367.

56. Allier, *Une enigme,* 10. Las Casas, *In Defense of the Indians: The Defense of the Most Reverend Lord, Don Fray Bartolomé de Las Casas, of the Order of the Preachers, Late Bishop of Chiapa, Against the Prosecutors and Slanderers of the Peoples of the New World Discovered Across the Seas,* trans. and ed. Stafford Poole (DeKalb: Northern Illinois Univ. Press, 1974), 110. He attacks a view according to which human beings only fulfill scripture when they commit a political injustice. In the King James version Genesis 41:45 reads: "And Pharaoh called Joseph's name Zaphnathpaaneah; and he gave him to wife Asenath the daughter of Potipherah priest of On." Jordan, 19, reports the interesting vacillation of Peter Heyleyn. The 1621 *Microcosmus* edition ignores the curse of Ham; the 1627 version calls it a "foolish tale"; and the *Cosmographiae* of 1666 partially endorses it.

57. Zedler cited in Alexander Perrig, "Erdrandsiedler," in Koebner, *Die andere Welt,* 47. Calmet, *Fragments,* ed. Charles Taylor (London: W. Stratford, 1801), 37, cited in Peterson, *Ham and Japheth,* 44.

58. Best, "A true discourse of the three Voyages of discovery, for the finding of a passage to Cathaya . . . " (1578), in Richard Hakluyt, *Voyages,* 8 vols. (London and New York: Dent and Dutton, 1927), 5: 182.

59. Richard Jobson, *The Golden Trade: Or, a Discovery of the River Gambra, and the Golden Trade of the Aethiopians* (1623; ed. Charles G. Kingsley, Teignmouth, Devonshire, 1904), 65–66; also cited by Jordan, 19. Jean-Louis Hannemann, a Dutch Protestant doctor and theologian, wrote *Curiosum Scrutinium nigritudinis posterorum Cham, i.e. Æthiopum* (Kiel [?], 1677), invoking Luther; cited in Allier, *Une enigme,* 14; Jean Pechlin, also a Dutch Protestant, from Leyden, set out to refute Hannemann in the same year, in *De Habitu at Colore Æthiopum* (1677), cited in Perbal, "La Race nègre et la malédiction de Cham," *Revue de l'Université d'Ottawa* 10.2 (April–June, 1940): 144–77, here 159–60, and Allier, *Une enigme,* 12–14. Thomas Herbert, *Some Years Travels into Divers Parts of Africa, and Asia the Great, Describing More Particularly the Empires of Persia and Industan. . . ,* 4th ed. (London, 1677), 16. *Relation universelle de l'Afrique ancienne et moderne* (1688), a plagiarized work, opens with a frontispiece depicting an allegorical African woman with the inscription "Je déscens de Cham"; cited in Roger Mercier, *L'Afrique noire dans la littérature française. Les Premières images (XVIIe et XVIIIe siècles)* (Dakar: Université de Dakar, 1962), 36, who also mentions that Leo Africanus and Marmol had already used this motif. William Byrd to Earl of Egmont, Va., 12 July 1736, cited in "Colonel William Byrd on Slavery," *American Historical Review* 1 (1895–96): 88–89.

60. Hugh Jones, *The Present State of Virginia* (1724; rpt., New York: Joseph Sabin, 1865), 6. Jones believed that the Indians were descended from Shem, whereas Joseph Gumilla thought that both Africans and Indians were in Ham's lineage; see *Histoire naturelle, civile et géographique de l'Orenoque* (Avignon: Desaint & Saillant, 1758), I, 178. He also found Noah's curse verified in the modern world (I, 180).

61. [Edwin Clifford Holland], *A Refutation of the Calumnies Circulated Against the Southern and Western States* (Charleston: A. E. Miller, 1822), 41; cited in Peterson, *Ham and Japheth,* 45. Samuel Cartwright, "The Education, Labor, and Wealth of the South," in *Cotton Is King, and Pro-Slavery Arguments,* ed. E. N. Elliott (Augusta, Ga.: Pritchard, Abbot & Loomis, 1860), 882–84, also identifies

whites with Japheth and blacks with Canaan, permitting him to argue that the slaveholding South is the best embodiment of American civilization, since "founded upon revealed truth and nature's laws" it "puts the negro in his natural position, that of subordination to the white man. . . . What are called the free States have provided no place for the poor negro."

62. Stolcke, "Invaded Women," 277–78. James Weldon Johnson's narrator in *The Autobiography of an Ex-Colored Man* (1912; rpt., New York: Hill and Wang, 1960) sarcastically comments: "Have a white skin, and all things else may be added unto you" (155). He calls it a "paraphrase," and it undoubtedly alludes to Luke 12:31, "But rather seek ye the kingdom of God; and all these things shall be added unto you." See also an early 20th-century comment by a Southern Coloured Woman: "Everything is forgiven in the South but color" (*Life Stories of Undistinguished Americans as Told by Themselves*, Hamilton Holt, ed. (New York: Routledge, 1990), 224). Comments on race as a form of white aristocracy are frequent. Friedrich Alexander von Humboldt, *Versuch über den politischen Zustand des Königreichs Neu-Spanien*, vol. 1 (Tübingen: Cotta, 1809), 193, observed the aristocratic sense among whites as a constitutive feature of the American continent when he wrote: "In a country dominated by whites, families of whom it is assumed that they who are least intermingled with Negro or Mulatto blood are those most highly honored; just as it is considered a kind of nobility in Spain to be descended neither from Jews nor Moors." Humboldt, who also gives a terminological essay on racial crossing, adds that a barefoot white man who mounts a horse believes to belong to the aristocracy of the land, and that their color even generates a sense of equality among whites: thus a common man may address one high above him with the phrase, "Do you believe that you are whiter than I am?" Perhaps this substitution of "whiteness" for "nobility" accounts for the frequent connections between themes of race and of aristocracy, for example in Beaumont's novel *Marie*, 62, when George says: "A white skin is the mark of nobility." Josiah Clark Nott dreamed of a classless white race, placing all whites above blacks: "*nature's noblemen* . . . often spring from the families of the backwoodsmen, or the sturdy mechanic" (Fredrickson, *Black Image*, 75). C. Eric Lincoln, "The Du Boisian Dubiety and the American Dilemma," in Early, *Lure and Loathing*, 200, summarizes the utility of the motif turned into a pseudo-aristocratic descent myth. "During the slave era," he writes, "it was strategic to effective slave management to convince as many slaves as possible that by some implausible sleight of history they were the 'sons of Ham' and cursed by God to be perpetual hewers of wood and drawers of water for the sons of Athelstan." See also *Kingsblood Royal*, the very title of which suggests such a relationship.

63. Boucicault, *The Octoroon*, 16; Braddon, *The Octoroon*, 68.

64. *The Price of the Ticket* (New York: St. Martin's Press, 1985), 347.

65. *Encyclopaedia Judaica* 7 (Jerusalem, 1971), "Ham"—which also contains an illustration; Cassuto, *A Commentary*, 152, mentions that this epic suggests that the Canaanites included, among the precepts of how a son has to behave toward a father, the duty of taking him by the hands and carrying him when he is filled with wine. See *Stories from Ancient Canaan*, ed. and trans. Michael David Coogan (Philadelphia: Westminster Press, 1978), 27–47; esp. 33–34:

> and there will be a son in his house,
> an heir inside his palace,

> [. . . .]
> to hold your hand when you are drunk,
> support you when you are full of wine;
> to patch your roof when it leaks,
> wash your clothes when they are dirty.

By contrast, Robert Graves and Raphael Patai, *Hebrew Myths: The Book of Genesis* (Garden City, N.Y.: Doubleday, 1964), 118, stress the connection of Noah, Deucalion—whose name means "new wine sailor" (deuco-halieus)—and Dionysus.

66. Stephen M. Vail, *The Bible Against Slavery* (New Hampshire: Hadley, 1864), 14; cited in Bartour, "Cursed be Canaan," 43.

67. Josiah Priest, *Slavery, as It Relates to the Negro, or African Race. . .* (Albany, New York: C. Van Benthuysen & Co., 1845), 76; cited in Bartour, 43. Priest, 79, also believed that the curse "against Ham and his race was not sent out on the account of that *one* sin only. But as the deed was heinous, and withal was in unison with his *whole* life, character, and constitutional make *prior* to that deed, the curse which had slumbered long was let loose upon him and his posterity, as a general thing, placing them under the ban of slavery, on account of his and their foreseen characters." Jerome B. Holgate, *Noachidæ: or, Noah, and His Descendants* (Buffalo: Breed, Butler, and Co., 1860), 155, thought that "a lurid smile played upon [Ham's] visage." See Elise Lemire, "Making Miscegenation," on the genealogist Holgate, who, as "Bolokitten," authored the racist fantasy *A Sojourn in the City of Amalgamation* (1835).

68. Rotter, 145. Of course, the representation of Noah washing also avoids showing his drunkenness.

69. The confusion of Ham and Canaan in the passage also played itself out in the slavery debate, with supporters of the institution arguing that Canaan must have committed the sin, that he was already black before Noah's drunkenness, or that Ham and Canaan together had ridiculed Noah. See Bartour, "Cursed be Canaan," 43.

70. *Babylonian Talmud*: Sanhedrin II, 645. We must remember Bernard Lewis's comment, 123, however, that "smitten" does not necessarily mean "turned black."

71. Rotter, 145.

72. *Midrash Rabbah*, I, 239. As always, the problem lies with the conjunction "and." In addition, Isaac, *Slaves*, 84–85, stresses that "not all manuscripts agree on the reading of the phrase" and that some give Noah's response as: "Therefore, I shall curse your fourth son."

73. Reported by Isaac, "Biblical," 23; this enhances the symmetry of transgression and retaliation.

74. Best, "A true discourse," 182; partly cited in Marienstras, 228n41, Jordan, 40–41, and discussed in Greenblatt, 113–18.

75. *The Five Books of Moses* with *Haphtaroth*, ed. A. Cohen (London: Soncino Press, 1956), 47. Other views are described in Graves and Patai, *Hebrew Myths*, 120–124.

76. Baldwin writes in his first novel, *Go Tell It on the Mountain* (1953; rpt., New York: Dell-Laurel, 1985):

Yes, he had sinned: one morning, alone, in the dirty bathroom, in the square, dirt-gray cupboard room that was filled with the stink of his father. Sometimes, leaning over the cracked, "tattle-tale gray" bathtub, he scrubbed his father's back; and looked, as the accursed son of Noah had looked, on his father's hideous nakedness. (197)

Baldwin's use of the motif in his novel *Go Tell It on the Mountain* was analyzed by Shirley S. Allen, "The Ironic Voice In Baldwin's *Go Tell It On The Mountain*," in *James Baldwin: A Critical Evaluation*, ed. Therman B. O'Daniel (Washington, D.C.: Howard Univ. Press, 1977), 30–37, here 36:

The voice comes from within John, expressing his own wishes, and its main attack is against any belief in this religion, which it attempts to discredit by associating it with "niggers" and by ridiculing the Bible's story of Noah's curse on Ham (194, 197). The voice, then, is the voice of unbelief within John, which Baldwin describes as predominant in his state of mind before his conversion.

Ralph Ellison, in "The World and the Jug" (1963–64), in *Shadow and Act* (1964; rpt., New York: Vintage Books, 1972), 109, writes about Irving Howe that

in his zeal to champion [Richard] Wright, it is as though he felt necessary to stage a modern version of the Biblical myth of Noah, Ham, Shem and Japheth (based originally, I'm told, on a castration ritual), with first Baldwin and then Ellison acting out the impious role of Ham: Baldwin by calling attention to Noah-Wright's artistic nakedness in his famous essays, "Everybody's Protest Novel" (1949) and "Many Thousands Gone" (1951); Ellison by rejecting "narrow naturalism" as a fictional method.

77. Isaac, "Biblical," 23.

78. Graves and Patai, *Hebrew Myths*, 121; they relate the story to the five Greek sons—among them Cronus, who was later unmanned by his son Zeus, and Hyperion, the father of Helios (sun), Selene (moon), and Eos (dawn)—who conspired against their father Uranus (122). Castration was also the context for the elaborate version of the curse cited earlier. Frederick W. Bassett, "Noah's Nakedness and the Curse of Canaan: A Case of Incest?," *Vetus Testamentum* 21.2 (April 1971): 232–37, relates an opinion, clearly derived from Graves and Patai, according to which "Ham's little son Canaan unmanned Noah by mischievously looping a cord about his genitals and drawing it tight. Ham's guilt in these accounts lies in the fact that he entered the tent, saw what had happened, and smilingly told his brothers" (233).

79. *Noah and the Ark* (Las Colinas, Tex.: Monument Press, 1992), e.g., 49: "Noah did nothing to stop sex from taking place inside his tent, with him as the recipient of at least one phallic advance, as he made no protestation about such an activity until his other sons became privy to what happened, and attempted to cover up the buggery."

80. *Zedlers Universallexikon*, vol. 5 (Halle und Leipzig, 1733); see also Bitterli, 341.

81. Priest, *Slavery, as It Relates to the Negro*, 33, 152. Mentioned by Fredrickson, *Black Image*, 60–61, and Peterson, *Ham and Japheth*, 79. Jacques Derrida, in *D'un ton apocalyptique adopté naguère en philosophie* (Paris: Galilée, 1983), 15–16,

also made the connection between Genesis and Leviticus—in a different context. For a discussion of more widely made connections between Genesis 9 and Leviticus 25: 44–46, see Bartour, "Cursed be Canaan," 48–51.

82. Priest, *Slavery, as It Relates to the Negro*, 73 (picture 7 in the book).

83. Bassett, "Noah's Nakedness," 235.

84. Fletcher, *Studies on Slavery*, 249, 445, 446; partly cited in Peterson, *Ham and Japheth*, 79, and Allen, *Legend of Noah*, 131, and H. Shelton Smith, 131. Fletcher specifically cites Arab sources, including i, 369 of the Koran, according to Sale's translation (437–38; 444). Newton also cites "Sale's Prelim. Disc. to the Koran, i, 30–31 and 2–3," and draws on Josephus, *Antiquities*, i.6. Fletcher may have been influenced by Brackenridge's *Modern Chivalry*, even though that book's spirit is contrary to Fletcher's: Brackenridge's narrator had asked, "How at the flood? when Noah, his first wife, his three sons, and their wives, eight persons, only were saved? It is but giving some of the sons Negro wenches for their wives, and you have the matter all right" (133).

85. *A Letter of Inquiry to Ministers of the Gospel of All Denominations on Slavery* (Hanover, N.H., 1860), 5–6; cited in H. Shelton Smith, 131. Lord also suspected an "unnatural crime" revealing the "obscene" nature of Ham: see Peterson, *Ham and Japheth*, 78.

86. *Jefferson Davis, Constitutionalist: His Letters, Papers and Speeches*, ed. Dunbar Rowland (Jackson, Miss., 1923), IV, 231. Cited in George Fredrickson, *The Black Image in the White Mind: The Debate on Afro-American Character and Destiny, 1817–1914* (1971; rpt., New York: Harper Torchbooks, 1972), 89. Davis may have drawn on Samuel A. Cartwright, a Louisiana doctor and slavery advocate; he also parallels Ham and Cain: "Cain, for the commission of the first great crime, was driven from the face of Adam, no longer the fit associate of those who were created to exercise dominion over the earth, he found in the Land of Nod those to whom his crime degraded him to an equality."

87. Cited in Shell, 218n92. One wonders whether this bird imagery is a response to, or was responded to by, Wolfram's *Parzival*.

88. Thornton Stringfellow, "A Brief Examination of Scripture Testimony on the Institution of Slavery" (1841), in Faust, 140. See also Peterson, *Ham and Japheth*, 78.

89. Charles Carroll, *"The Negro a Beast," or, "In the Image of God"* (St. Louis: American Book and Bible House, 1900), 76–80. Edward Atkinson in the *North American Review* 181.2 (Aug. 1905): 202, called this "pernicious" work "the most sacrilegious book ever issued from the press in this country." See also Ho, 69n69, citing I. A. Newby, *Jim Crow's Defense: Anti-Negro Thought in America, 1900–1930* (Baton Rouge: Louisiana State Univ. Press, 1965), and Fredrickson, *Black Image*, 277. Williamson, *Crucible*, 119, mentions that Carroll was a black man; Sundquist, *To Wake the Nations*, 395, states that Carroll was a Mulatto.

90. Racist craziness culminated in Monsignor Augouard's letter of 15 Feb. 1881, *28 Années au Congo* (Poitiers: Société française d'imprimerie, n.d.), I, 229; cited in Perbal, 169. Augouard's letter of 4 July 1878 explicitly endorsed the story of Ham's malediction (I, 77). See also Wauthier, *Literature and Thought of Modern Africa*, 212–13. Joseph Glanvill had derived the apes from Ham in *Scepsis Scientifica*, cited by Allen, 119.

91. The mosaics at Montreale, for example, include the representation of the Tower of Babel and, as the high point in the Presbytery, the Pentecost.

92. Wauthier, *Literature and Thought of Modern Africa*, 209, citing Jean Marc Ela from *Présence Africaine* anthology, *Personnalité africaine et Catholicisme* (Paris, Présence Africaine, 1963).

93. Reproduced in Raymond Sayers, *The Negro in Brazilian Literature* (New York: Hispanic Institute in the United States, 1956), opp. 218. In the years prior to his Brazilian success at the II Exposição Geral de Belas-Artes the Spanish-born painter had studied with the Ingres student Lehmann and with Ernest Hébert in Paris. See Carlos Cavalcanti, *Dicionario brasilieiro de artistas plásticos*, vol. 1 (Brasilia: Instituto Nacional do Livro, 1973), 297–98. According to Lilia Moritz Schwarcz, *O Espetáculo das Raças: Cientistas, Instituições a Questão Racial no Brasil, 1870–1930* (São Paulo: Companhia Das Letras, 1993), 11–12, Brocos's painting was accompanied by the explanation: "Le nègre passant au blanc, à la troisième génération, par l'effet du croisement des races."

94. Patrick Girard, "Le Mulâtre littéraire," in Poliakov, 211, speaking about a similar idea in the novel *Georges* (1843) by Alexandre Dumas.

95. Daniel Aaron, "The 'Inky Curse': Miscegenation in the White Literary Imagination," *Social Science Information* 22.1 (1983): 169–190; here 170.

96. Among the authors who, while criticizing the notion of the curse of Ham, undoubtedly contributed greatly to popularizing it were leading abolitionists. In her *Anti-Slavery Catechism* (Newburyport: Charles Whipple, 1836), 16–17, for example, Lydia Maria Child alluded to and ridiculed white genealogy "since the flood." And Harriet Beecher Stowe's *Uncle Tom's Cabin*, ch. xii, represents a discussion with a clergyman who invokes Genesis in defense of slavery. The subsequent rebuttal includes the quoting of the New Testament's "All things whatsoever that men should do unto you, do ye even unto them," with the speaker's comment, "I suppose, . . . *that* is scripture, as much as 'Cursed be Canaan'" (New York: Library of America, 1982), 151–52. John Greenleaf Whittier's once famous poem "Ichabod" criticizes the late Webster as if he were Noah seen from the point of view of Shem and Japheth.

97. "Of the Blackness of Negroes," chap. X of *Pseudodoxia* (1646), *The Works of Sir Thomas Browne*, ed. Charles Sayle (London: Grant Richards, 1904), ii, 380. Jordan, 201, mentions that the idea was used often by "antislavery advocates for purposes of refutation."

98. Ephraim Isaac, "Genesis," *Slavery and Abolition* 1.1 (1980): 3–4. Bishop Alfred G. Dunston, Jr., *The Black Man in the Old Testament and Its World* (Philadelphia: Dorrance, 1974), 51–53.

99. Samuel Sewall, *The Selling of Joseph* (1700; reprinted with notes by Sidney Kaplan, Amherst: Univ. of Massachusetts Press, 1969), 12–14. Charles W. Gordon, *Select Sermons* (New York, 1887), 305–6. John W. Tyndall, *The Origins of the Black Man* (St. Louis: Metropolitan Correspondence Bible College Department, 1927), 15–20. Elihu Coleman, *A Testimony Against That Anti-Christian Practice of Making Slaves of Men* (1733; rpt., New Bedford, 1825), 16–17; Ralph Sandiford, *A Brief Examination of the Practice of the Times* (1729; rpt., New York: Arno Press, 1969), 4. De Pauw, I, 176, arguing against Abbé Le Pluche, an anonymous *Essai sur la population du nouveau continent*, Labat, and Gumilla. John Woolman, "Some Considerations on the Keeping of Negroes," in *Journal and Essays of John Woolman*, Angela Mott Gummere, ed. (New York: Macmillan, 1922), 355, cited in H. Shelton Smith, 28. Kant also argued against the curse of Ham; see Bitterli, *Die "Wilden,"* 346.

100. Dimšqī's *Nuḫba* (or al-Dimashqī's *Nukhbat*), Hopkins, 212; see also Grünbaum, *Neue Beiträge*, 87.

101. "Essay on the Causes of different Colours of People in different Climates," Royal Society, *Philosophical Transactions* 1744 (London: C. R. Baldwin, 1809), vol. 9: 65; cited in Jordan, 247.

102. Browne, "Of the Blackness of Negroes," 383–84; partly cited or discussed in Jordan, 19; Bitterli, *Die "Wilden,"* 465n69; and Mercier, *L'Afrique*, 70; Barker, 45, stresses bias even in Browne's plea for relativism. Le Cat, 7, made a similar argument.

103. Brackenridge, *Modern Chivalry, Containing the Adventures of Captain John Farrago and Teague O'Reagan, His Servant* (New Haven: College & Univ. Press, 1965), 132. Brackenridge, too, connects the Cain story with that of Canaan when he writes: "Some have conjectured, that a black complexion, frizzled hair, a flat nose, and bandy legs, were the mark set on Cain, for the murder of his brother Abel. But, as the deluge drowned the whole world, and only one family was saved, the blacks must have all perished. . . ." Another writer to confuse Cain and Canaan is Rebecca Harding Davis, who in her novel *Waiting for the Verdict* (1868), 323, lets Dr. Broderip say: "I am Cainan. . . . Cainan; a servant in the tents of my brethren."

104. Rotter, 148–49.

105. There are many other examples. See, for example, Phillis Wheatley's "On Being Brought from Africa to America" (1768), in *The Poems of Phillis Wheatley*, ed. Julian D. Mason (Chapel Hill and London: Univ. of North Carolina Press, 1989), 53. Or see the black Congregational minister and ex-slave James W. C. Pennington, who argued in 1841 that though blacks were descended from Ham, they were not related to Canaan; hence he encouraged slaveowners to go out and find the true Canaanites; *A Text Book of the Origin and History, &c., of the Colored People* (Hartford: L. Skinner, 1841), 9–13, cited in Peterson, *Ham and Japheth*, 46–47. For other examples, see Charles B. Copher, "Three Thousand Years of Biblical Interpretation with Reference to Black Peoples," in *African American Religious Studies: An Interdisciplinary Anthology*, ed. Gayraud S. Wilmore (Durham and London: Duke Univ. Press, 1989), 121–23.

106. David Walker, *Appeal in Four Articles* (1829; rpt., New York: Arno Press, 1969), 71–72. See Brackenridge's use of the popular phrase, discussed in Henri Petter, *Early American Novel* (Columbus: Ohio State Univ. Press, 1971), 136.

107. *Narrative of the Life of Frederick Douglass, an American Slave: Written by Himself* (1845; rpt., New York: Modern Library, 1984), 20–21. In Lydia Maria Child's novel *A Romance of the Republic* (1867; rpt., Miami: Mnemosyne, 1969), 322–23, the abolitionist Bright argues similarly that "if there were an estate of Ham's left unsettled, I reckoned it would puzzle the 'cutest lawyer to hunt up the rightful heirs," to which Blumenthal adds, "especially when they've become so mixed up that they advertise runaway negroes with sandy hair, blue eyes, and ruddy complexion."

108. Alexander Crummell, "The Negro Race Not Under a Curse: An Examination of Genesis ix.25" (1850, 1852; rev. 1862), *The Future of Africa* (rpt., New York: Negro Universities Press, 1969), 325–54; here 351–54. I am grateful to Wilson Moses for calling my attention to this text.

109. Edward Wilmot Blyden, "Noah's Malediction," *Liberia's Offering* (New York, 1862), 31–42; reprinted in *Slavery and Abolition* 1.1 (May 1980): 18–24; here 21, 22, and 23n3.

110.  Chesnutt, *Family Fiction* (25 Dec. 1886); reprinted in Sylvia Lyons Render, ed., *The Uncollected Short Fiction of Charles W. Chesnutt* (Washington, D.C.: Howard Univ. Press, 1981), 178–79. Chesnutt used the curse on Ham another time with succinct irony in his novel *The Marrow of Tradition* (1901; rpt., Ann Arbor: Univ. of Michigan Press, 1970), 39. There is a longstanding tradition of comic stories derived from the flood from folklore to Bill Cosby's Noah routines and the parodistic use of the theme in Julian Barnes, *A History of the World in 10 1/2 Chapters.* (1989; New York: Vintage, 1990), 23ff. Mark Twain, who in *Pudd'nhead Wilson* (1894; rpt., New York: Penguin, 1981), 119, had given Tom Driscoll (who had just discovered his racial origin) the line "that the curse of Ham was upon him," did not miss the occasion. In "Letters from the Earth" (1909), in *Collected Tales, Sketches, Speeches, & Essays 1891–1910* (New York: Library of America, 1992), 906–10, he complained about the flies in the ark that gave Shem hookworm and also affected Ham.

111.  Hurston, "The First One: A Play in One Act," in *Ebony and Topaz*, ed. Charles S. Johnson (1927; rpt., Freeport, N.Y.: Books for Libraries Press, 1971), 53–57; Robert Hemenway, *Zora Neale Hurston: A Literary Biography* (Urbana: Univ. of Illinois Press, 1977), 68: "a biblical account of the Ham legend . . . comic in its presentation of Ham's curse as a product of the shrewishness in Shem and Japheth's wives." Leo Hamalian and James V. Hatch, who reprinted the play in the anthology *The Roots of African American Drama: An Anthology of Earlys Plays, 1858–1938* (Detroit: Wayne State Univ. Press, 1991), 186–203, argued similarly. And Deborah McDowell, in her preface to Hurston's *Moses, Man of the Mountain* (1939; rpt., New York: Harper, 1991), viii, supported these readings when she stated that "*The First One* mocked the myth of Ham, seized by proslavery advocates as the biblical justification of chattel slavery in the United States." To my knowledge only Freda Scott Giles, writing in *MELUS* 17.4 (Winter 1991–92): 144, has acknowledged that in "The First One," Hurston "plays both into and against stereotypes in her tale of Noah and Ham."

Hurston's version may, of course, go back to a slave legend of the kind the dialect poet Irwin Russell drew on in his *Christmas in the Quarters*, in which, as Sterling Brown, *Negro Poetry and Drama*, 89, writes, "how Ham, lonely on the ark for music, invented the banjo and strung it with hairs from the tail of a possum (since then hairless)." Cf. Deborah McDowell's annotation of Nella Larsen, *Passing* (1929; reprinted with *Quicksand*, New Brunswick, N.J.: Rutgers Univ. Press, 1986), 245: "In the Creation legends of black slaves, in punishment for laughing at his father's nakedness, Ham and his descendants will be 'hewers of wood and drawers of water' and known by their dark skin." See also Marguerite Yourcenar, *Fleuve profond, sombre rivière: Les "Negro Spirituals," commentaires et traductions* (Paris: Gallimard, 1964), 36–37.

112.  Pauline E. Hopkins, *A Primer of Facts* (Cambridge: P. E. Hopkins, Publishers, 1905), 6–10, argues that original man was red; that, of Noah's three sons, Shem was the color of Noah, Ham was black, and Japheth was white; and that, with the scattering of their descendants after the Tower of Babel, "God's design in the creation of races was accomplished, because it roused in the people a desire for race affinity, and also to people the remotest parts of the earth" (6). "Of the three sons, the history of the second, Ham, is fraught with more interest than that of either of the others" (10). See also Hopkins's novel "Of One Blood," *Colored American Magazine* 6, nos. I–II (Nov., Dec. 1902; Jan.–Nov. 1903) ch. 12, p. 342.

113. The decline of the power of theology also had another effect on stories of the curse of Ham: heretics and bohemians began to adopt him as a positively redefined rebel-hero and model—similar to the way in which a cursed biblical figure like Cain was chosen by artists like Byron and Baudelaire. When Rimbaud, for example, wrote in the section "Mauvais sang" (bad blood) of "Une saison en Enfer" ("A Season in Hell," 1873), "J'entre au vrai royaume des enfants de Cham," he hoped to find a primitive land without hypocrisy in Africa—different from France's "false Negroes." Rimbaud, *Œuvres*, ed. Suzanne Bernard (Paris: Garnier, 1960), 217, 460. Perhaps the most comprehensive recasting of the descendants of Noah was undertaken by Gérard de Nerval's "Histoire de la reine du matin et de Soliman, prince des génies" (1850), in which the genies of the fire keep intersecting with biblical genealogy so that a son of the genie Tubal-Kaïn secretly fathers Cush with Ham's wife, an event Nerval annotates with a reference to Abbot Villars, *Conte de Gabalis*. See Luca Pietromarchi, ed. *Storia della regina del mattino e di solimano, principe dei geni* (Venezia: Marsilio, 1992), 21–22 and 192.

114. Cited in H. Shelton Smith, 130. In Mattie Griffiths's anonymously published *Autobiography of a Female Slave* (1857; rpt., Miami: Mnemosyne, 1969), 80, the curse of Ham is explicitly cited in order to legitimate slavery: "Old perversions and misinterpretations of portions of the Bible, such as the story of Hagar, and the curse pronounced upon Ham, were adduced by Miss Jane and Miss Tildy in a tone of triumph."

115. Bartour, "Cursed be Canaan," 47–48.

116. Blyden, 24n3.

117. To the example of Baldwin one could also add numerous others. Rayford W. Logan, for example, reported in 1927 the following comments made by a Texan during a train trip: "How can a darky make any progress? The curse of Ham is upon him. A 'nigger' won't ever be nothing but a 'nigger.'" From "The Confessions of an Unwilling Nordic," reprinted in Sollors, ed., *Blacks at Harvard* (New York: New York Univ. Press, 1993), 273. In Nella Larsen's novel *Passing* (1929), ed. Deborah McDowell (New Brunswick, N.J.: Rutgers Univ. Press, 1986), 158–59, Clare tells Irene Redfield how she was taken in by her white aunts after her father died, but had to do all the housework and most of the washing for them. Sarcastically, Clare comments that the aunts may have thought that this was in keeping with God's intentions toward the sons and daughters of Ham: "I remember the aunts telling me that that old drunkard had cursed Ham and his sons for all time."

118. In Faust, 215. Nott also wrote to Morton, on 27 Oct. 1845: "I do not think the Negroes are descendants of Ham."

119. The accounts of human unity and difference could be carefully negotiated, and not necessarily be placed into the service of racial hierarchies, as Barker has shown in the case of Lord Kames. Kames believed in "original difference," yet also "that God created a single pair of the human species." He resolved the problem by assuming that God intervened at the time of the Tower of Babel (Barker, 53, citing Curtin, 42–43). See also Tzvetan Todorov's excellent discussion of the issue of unity and difference in *On Human Diversity: Nationalism, Racism, and Exoticism in French Thought*.

120. See the classic discussion by William Stanton, *The Leopard's Spots*, esp.

73–121, the section on Nott, who was settling on polygenesis, but was still drawn to lengthy reconciliations with Genesis.

121. Fredrickson, *Black Image*, 87–88, citing "Unity of the Human Race Disproved by the Hebrew Bible," *DeBow's Review* 29 (Aug. 1860): 129–30, 134; Fredrickson stresses that Cartwright was not considered a crackpot and that he influenced Jefferson Davis—though Davis's account may also have come from another source. See also Matthew Estes, *A Defence of Negro Slavery, as It Exists in the United States* (Montgomery: Press of the "Alabama Journal," 1846), 65–66, who quotes from *Southern Quarterly Review*, Oct. 1842, "Canaan Identified with the Ethiopian," "which has commonly been ascribed to the pen of Dr. S. A. Cartwright, of Natchez, Miss." and represents Cartwright's older position.

122. Carroll, *"The Negro a Beast,"* 76–79, 80. The book's elaborate title page includes the boldfaced statement "The Negro not the Son of Ham," followed by the explanation "Neither can be proven by the Bible, and the argument of the theologian who would claim such, melts to mist before the thunderous and convincing arguments of this masterful book." Like Cartwright, Carroll also thought that it must have been a Negro who had been the actual tempter of Eve and that Cain had a wife who was a Negro. Carroll, 141–50, 197ff, 290–92, partly cited in Fredrickson, *Black Image*.

## Chapter Four. The Calculus of Color

1. *Opportunity* 3.34 (Oct. 1925): 291 (editorial).

2. *Georgetown Law Review* 77.6 (Aug. 1989): 1967–2029, here 1976.

3. 102, 191.

4. Cited in Myrdal, 113 (who places the reference in vol. 2, p. 555—where I cannot find it); also cited in Ho, 209.

5. Here is a mathematician's comment on the algebra of this piece:

> The only relevant quantity (relevant to the author of this piece, I mean) in this simple-minded calculation is the "percentage" of "negro blood." The "Mendelian" assumption here is that the offspring of two parents will have the average of the "percentages" of the parents. So, the offspring of a *pure* negro and a *pure white* will be *half-blood*, etc. There is also the "cut-off": any person in whose veins a percentage of negro blood strictly smaller than 25% flows is to be considered "to all intents and purposes" *white*. Impressive, how much arithmetic the author manages to squeeze out of this.
>
> A curiosity in the "algebra" is that the author separates, by distinct letters, the various generations' contributions of white blood to an individual, but devotes only a single letter ("lower case," of course) to the entire negro blood bank of antecedent generations' contributions. Another curiosity is that he feels compelled to use "letters" at all.

Letter by Barry Mazur to author, 29 Nov. 1991.

6. This problem came up in some legal cases in which the argument was advanced that racial definition by generation would require the "proof" that the ancestor from whom one counted was a "full-blooded" Negro. See Daniel Sharfstein's discussion of *Ferrall v. Ferrall*, a case in which the issue was whether the legal definition of race by generation would require proof that the ancestors from

whom one counts were "full-blooded." (Senior thesis, Harvard University, 1994).

7. *A Jean Toomer Reader: Selected Unpublished Writings*, ed. Frederik L. Rusch (New York and Oxford: Oxford Univ. Press, 1993), 107–8.

8. See Ernst Rudin's provocative argument in "New Mestizos: Traces of the Quincentenary Miracle in Old World Spanish and New World English Texts," forthcoming in *Cultural Difference and the Literary Text: Pluralism and the Limits of Authenticity in North American Literatures*, ed. Winfried Siemerling and Katrin Schwenk (Iowa City: Univ. of Iowa Press, 1996). Rudin reviews such recent authors as Gloria Anzaldúa and Ana Castillo and reminds *mestizaje* enthusiasts that the terminological distinctions into all the "castas" of interracial generations "served to reinforce white superiority . . . and implied the discrimination of all other groups." Homi Bhaba has repeatedly offered the term "hybridity" as a positive word. Diana Irene Williams has stressed in "Jean Toomer's Art and Ideology: Echoes of Eugenics," *Harvard College Forum* 9 (Spring 1995): 1–12, the affinities between the position that would idealize a racially mixed "aristocracy" and that old racialist one of cherishing only "pure races." Toomer, she writes, "differed from American eugenicists in that he saw the key to cultural superiority not in racial *purity* but in racial *mixture*" (2).

9. (1742 ed.), II: 189–90.

10. Museo Etnológico de Madrid, reproduced in Manuel Alvar, *Léxico del Mestizaje en Hispanoamérica* (Madrid: Ediciones Cultura Hispánica, Instituto de Cooperación Iberoamericana, 1987), 19. This painting presents a particularly detailed domestic scene.

11. Museo Etnográfico Trocadero reproduced in Alvar, *Léxico del Mestizaje*, 32. See also Navarro, *Los Cuadros del Mestizaje Americano* and Ilona Katzew, *New World Orders.*

12. Wilson, 90.

13. Shell, *Children*, 210–11n149. Shell also concedes that these "nonuniversalist, intermediating terms and the gradations of political rights that they seem to require are disconcerting to those who would insist, in unmediated and idealist fashion, on the equal creation of all men."

14. Cited in Hoffmann, *Le Nègre*, 127. Virey may either be drawing on Long's system of 1774 or on Long's sources. See [Edward Long], *The History of Jamaica . . .*, 3 vols. (London, T. Lowndes, 1774), 2: ch. 13. According to Alvar, Virey also was influenced by Humboldt. Don Jorge Juan and Don Antonio de Ulloa (1749) also relate a terminology by generation consisting of Mulatto, Tercerones, and Quarterones (291).

15. This is hardly a critique in hindsight. When Alexander von Humboldt had to explain the term *saltatras* in his book on Cuba, *Versuch über den politischen Zustand des Königreichs Neu-Spanien* (1809), 193, he felt inspired to develop a scathing critique of white pseudo-aristocracy in the New World.

16. Long, *History of Jamaica*, 2: xiii, 260–61. Hensley C. Woodbridge, "Glossary of Names Used in Colonial Latin America for Crosses Among Indians, Negroes, and Whites," *Journal of the Washington Academy of Sciences* 38.11 (15 Nov. 1948): 353–62, with a bibliography; here 360, invoking Gumilla. Woodbridge also quotes Saco's literalization of the term as "throw back." In Virey, this principle is not applied consistently. The term *saltoatrás* also appears in Cirilo Villaverde's novel *Cecilia Valdés* (1882), 162; Eng. trans., 221, briefly discussed in Chapter Ten.

17. Humboldt, I: 193–94. Humboldt noted that among the families who are suspected of having mixed blood it had become customary to ask for a court declaration that they may consider themselves white, and he mentioned that the popular expression for this process was "coloring oneself white."

18. Eds. Richard and Sally Price, 399. See Jordan, 175n. I shall return to Stedman in Chapter Seven.

19. "Du noir au blanc ou la cinquième génération," in Poliakov, 177–90, esp. 178–81. De Pauw's reversible generational model from black to white and from white to black and Buffon's 1777 additions to the *Variétés* are at the center of Duchet's reflections. Duchet errs in asserting (180, invoking J. Roger) that such schemes generally implied the predominant generative function of the father: Labat, for example, was interested in racial mixing precisely because it illuminated for him the equal participation of father and mother in determining their progeny; Blumenbach writes about interracial parentage in a gender-neutral way; and Moreau de Saint-Méry offers charts that originate with a white man and a Negro woman as well as with a Negro man and a white woman.

20. The French terms in the original are: "le *sacatra*, le *griffe*, le *marabout*, le *mulâtre*, le *quarteron*, le *métis*, le *mamelouc*, le *quarteronné*, le *Sang-mêlé*" (172n).

21. I have not been able to find such a system in Benjamin Franklin.

22. Moreau, 93. Hoffmann, 127, mentions that the word *sang-mêlé* has been documented since 1772. The cutoff point varied considerably among different attempts at regularizing interracial genealogies. Long, *History of Jamaica*, 2: 260, for example, devises a five-generation scheme (Negroe-Mulatta-Terceron-Quateron-Quinteron) at the end of which whiteness is reestablished, though he adds that Jamaican laws "permit all, that are above three degrees removed in lineal descent from the Negro ancestor, to vote at elections, and enjoy all the privileges and immunities of his majesty's white subjects of the island" (261). Humboldt, II, 192–94, relates a four-generation plan, omitting only the category "Terceron," to reach the category "white." De Pauw, I: 180–81, also assumes that it takes four generations from white to black and from black to white, but he uses the term "Octavon" instead of "Quinteron."

23. Moreau, 93. The only other instance I have found of the racial fraction $\frac{1}{512}$ is George Findlay's pamphlet *Miscegenation: A Study of the Biological Sources of Inheritance of the South African European Population* (Pretoria: Pretoria News and Printing Works, 1936), 19, which traces ancestry nine generations back to Van Riebeck's landing in order to argue that of the 2.5 million "children of Europeans" at least 1.1 million have partly African ancestry.

24. *The Negro Question*, (New York: C. Scribner's Sons, 1990), 54.

25. Vauthier, "Textualité et stéréotypes," 88–89. The Virginia Racial Integrity Law of 1924 applied the term "white person" "only to the person who has no trace whatsoever of any blood other than Caucasian"—though the law adds: "but persons who have one-sixteenth or less of the blood of the American Indian and have no other non-caucasic blood shall be deemed to be white persons." The text of the law is reprinted in Arthur H. Estabrook and Ivan McDougle, *Mongrel Virginians: The Win Tribe* (Baltimore: Williams & Wilkins, 1926), 204.

26. Hoffmann, *Nègre romantique*, 230.

27. *The Octoroon; or, Life in Louisiana* (1859; rpt., Upper Saddle River, N.J.: Literature House, 1970), 16–17 (act II). The metaphoric world on which such statements rest constructs race in analogy to animal breeding and to aristocratic

descent; thus Josiah Nott argued in 1844 (fifteen years before *The Octoroon*) that "no horse has ever been the progenitor of successful runners, who has been *known to have one drop* of impure blood in his veins." Nott was also struck by the family likeness in "portraits of the Bourbon family." See "The Natural History of the Caucasian and Negro Races," in Faust, 227. For an earlier example of the type of statement Zoe makes, see Marie in Gustave de Beaumont, *Marie; ou, L'Esclavage aux états-unis* (1835; Eng. trans. Barbara Chapman, Stanford: Stanford Univ. Press, 1958), 66, cited below.

28. Hoffmann, *Nègre romantique*, 127. See also 231, on the "byzantine" terminologies.

29. *Race and Mixed Race* (Philadelphia: Temple Univ. Press, 1993), 5. The schema might look more "logical," perhaps, if one considers the possibility that "whiteness" may have been established on the model of aristocracy rather than on the model of a genealogical family tree.

30. *Southwestern Journal of Anthropology* 26.1 (Spring 1970): 1–14. For a study of the Mexican terminology, see G. Aguirre Beltrán, "Races in 17th Century Mexico," *Phylon* 6 (1945): 211–18. See also Woodbridge.

31. Harris, 12.

32. Without doubt a semantic system such as the Brazilian one that Harris studied creates much confusion about the nature of social domination in its blurring of lines; yet, as Sidney Mintz has suggested in a personal communication in 1992, the system may actually resemble that of naming relatives: racial naming in countries like Brazil may, in fact, not rest on precise genealogical principles but on a "species" recognition in the classical sense, i.e., on appearance, in relationship to the speaker, too, who perceives it and puts it into the context of his own perceived color—all of which results in much flexibility and fluidity in racial naming. United States racial dualism is rarely considered progressive from a Latin American perspective.

33. Verena Stolcke, "Invaded Women," 272–86, here 280; Mörner, 57.

34. Pierre L. van den Berghe reports it in *Race and Racism: A Comparative Perspective* (New York: Wiley, 1967), 10, and explains that a rich Negro may be seen as lighter than an equally dark poor Negro.

35. Alvar, 17, 114, 119, citing *The Florida of the Inca*, f. 53r, *a* and *b*. See also his section "New names for various racial groups" in *Royal Commentaries of the Incas, And General History of Peru*, trans. Harold V. Livermore (Austin and London: University of Texas Press, 1966), pt. 1, bk. 9, ch. 31, pp. 606–8. For a discussion of Garcilaso's reception in the eighteenth century see Duchet, *Anthropologie et Histoire au siècle des lumières: Buffon, Voltaire, Rousseau, Helvétius, Diderot* (Paris: Maspéro, 1971), 102–3.

Blumenbach, *Treatises*, 215n4, cites Garcilaso and suggests that the word *Creole* "originated with the Ethiopian slaves transported in the sixteenth century to the mines in America, who first of all called their own children who were born there, *Criollos* and *Criollas*: this name was afterwards borrowed from the Spaniards, and imposed on their children born in the new world." Alvar, 113–19, stresses that the Spanish term *criollo* denotes both "American of European descent" and "born in America of racially mixed descent." José Juan Arrom, 23, formulates that "if all those of European origin born in America are Creoles, not all Creoles are necessarily of pure European origins." See also Ingraham, *The Quadroone*, ix; Reid, *Quadroon*, 446n; White, *Flight*, 40; and Ann Petry, *The Narrows*, 179, for varied uses of the word "Creole."

36. See Mörner, 57.

37. Blumenbach, 216–18, may have been the first to present a comparative conspectus of the different terminologies.

38. In Virginia, for example, Negroes and Mulattoes were explicitly considered the same in the eyes of the law for the first time only in 1860, and only in 1920 did the U.S. census abolish a racially mixed category. See W. A. S., and Higginbotham and Kopytoff, 1976–77, who write: "The fact that some people were classified as mulatto rather than Negro seems to have been simply a recognition of their visible differences," and add: "After the Civil War, a single term, 'colored,' was often used for both Negroes and mulattos in legal writing." The 1860 statute is Virginia Code, ch. 103, sec. 9: "The word 'negro' in any other section of this, or in any future statutes, shall be construed to mean mulatto as well as negro." Jordan, 175, summarized such developments by the terse statement that the "English settlers on the continent borrowed one Spanish word to describe all mixtures of black and white."

39. According to a 1994 communication from Roderick Harrison at the United States Census Bureau, a biracial self-categorization is still unavailable, so that Americans who classify themselves as both black and white are counted as black, though a growing number of respondents uses the term "other." On the 9.8 million who identified themselves as "other race" to the census in 1990, see Gabrielle Sandor, "The 'Other' Americans," *American Demographics* 16.6 (June 1994): 36–40; and Lawrence Wright, "One Drop of Blood," *New Yorker* 70.22 (25 July 1994): 46–55, an essay that generated a lively debate; see, for example, "Blood Not So Simple," *New Yorker* (5 Sept. 1994): 8–10. The issue has also become important in public school registration. See also George Hutchinson, "Jean Toomer and American Racial Discourse," *Texas Studies in Language and Literature* 35.2 (Summer 1993): 229.

40. *Pudd'nhead Wilson* and *Those Extraordinary Twins*, ed. Sidney E. Berger (New York and London: W. W. Norton, 1980), 8–9, ch. 2. The phrase "as white as anybody" also appears in a popular account of Jefferson's slave Sally Hemings. See Hamilton W. Pierson, *Jefferson at Monticello. The Private Life of Thomas Jefferson. From Entirely New Materials* (New York, 1862), 110: Jefferson "freed one girl some years before he died, and there was a great deal of talk about it. She was nearly as white as anybody, and very beautiful. People said he freed her because she was his own daughter. She was not his daughter." Cited in William Edward Farrison, *William Wells Brown* (Chicago: Univ. of Chicago Press, 1969), 212.

41. Alvar, 119, and *Grand Larousse de la langue française*, ed. Louis Gailbert, René Lagane, and Georges Niobey (Paris: Larousse, 1977). French "Quarteron" is documented in Œxmelin (1678) and Labat (1722). Thomas Jefferson, responding to Buffon, used the word "Quarteron" in 1793. See his *Writings* IX: 276, listed in William Craigie and James A. Hulbert, *Dictionary of American English* (Chicago: Univ. of Chicago Press, 1938–44).

42. In other words, Ingraham's transparent purpose is the same as that of the scientific writers with a better background in algebra: to draw a line between black and white that might run beyond recognition by sight, beyond "appearance."

43. George Washington Cable, *Old Creole Days*, 46, and Ratna Roy, "The Marginal Man," have used the word "Quadroone" to identify females.

The term "Quadroon" was problematic to some critical intellectuals. Thus Charles W. Chesnutt pointed out that law books in the United States used the term occasionally, but never defined it. In his own work, Chesnutt showed an ambivalence toward using the term that is nowhere more apparent than in the story "Her Virginia Mammy"—itself a response to a tradition of fiction from Child's "Quadroons" to Cable's *Old Creole Days* and Howells's *An Imperative Duty*. In "Her Virginia Mammy" (published in 1899), Chesnutt describes Mrs. Harper, the mother who denies her maternity in order to let her daughter have happiness with a white spouse, as "a little woman, of clear olive complexion, regular features, and a face almost a perfect oval." This is the way it was published; in the manuscript of the story, however, he originally continued: "—an embodiment in fact of the best quadroon type, common in sub-tropical climates and not uncommon in the United States." He crossed out this phrase and replaced it by "except as time had marred its outline."

44. Joseph Gumilla, *El Orinoco Ilustrado*, 1745 edition cited by Alvar, 182; de Pauw, I:150, 180–81, and 200; and Buffon, *Additions* to *Variétés dans l'espèce humaine*, both cited by Michèle Duchet, "Du noir au blanc, ou la cinquième génération," in Poliakov, 178. Alvar cites Joseph Gumilla, Orinoco ilustr. (1745), I: 83, for his term "ochavón" (182). Moreau de Saint-Méry uses the alternative term "métif" (98) to designate the offspring of a white and a quadroon. Chesnutt, "What is a White Man?," 6, reports that the term octoroon is not used at all in law books of the United States.

45. *The House Behind the Cedars* (1900; rpt., Athens and London: Univ. of Georgia Press, 1988), 171–72.

46. According to the *Diccionario de la Lengua Espanola* (Madrid: Real Academia Espanola, 1970) and Carlos Moore in lectures in the 1980s. In a personal communication, Manuel Alvar, who does *not* cite this Arabic etymology in his *Lexico*, expressed the opinion that it was not a very likely origin of "Mulatto." As Alvar richly documents, the word "mulato" appears in Bernal Días del Castillo (c. 1568) and in Garcilaso, who uses the term as one that would have been familiar to Spanish readers in order to name the children of Indians and blacks.

47. E. L. McAdam, Jr., and George Milne, eds., *Samuel Johnson's Dictionary: A Modern Selection* (New York: Pantheon, 1964), 257.

48. *American Journal of Medical Sciences* 66 (July 1843): 254. For another use of "horse" and "ass," see Nott in Faust, 220.

49. Cited in Kenneth R. Manning, "Race, Science, and Identity," in Early, *Lure and Loathing*, 330. Wodsalek conceded that "unfortunately the mulatto is fertile."

50. (Trans. Boston, 1894), 194.

51. Woodbridge, 359. Hence the term *Pardo* is used as a substitute.

52. Spillers, 165–87, continues that "mulatto/a" denotes "a special category of thingness that isolates and overdetermines the human character to which it points." However, there have been undoubtedly many instances in which African Americans would describe themselves by the term "Mulatto." And there have also been racial conservatives who objected to the term; see, for example, Donald R. Morris, "South Africa: The Politics of Racial Terminology," *Political Communication* 9.2 (April–June 1992): 111–22, for an account that the word "mixed race" and "mulatto" as they are employed by the American media (but not "coloured") were considered "offensive" by South Africans because they implied miscegenation existed in South Africa.

53. *Callaloo* (Spring 1989); cited in Reginald McKnight, "Confessions of a Wannabe Negro," in Early, *Lure and Loathing*, 1993, 103.

54. 332–33. Pierre also reports himself saying, "[W]ell, this isn't something I should be ashamed of, this is something I should be proud of because of my parents, even though they had a lot of problems, and they went through a lot of changes."

55. The *OED* also defines the noun "hybrid" as "the offspring of two animals or plants of different species, or (less strictly) varieties; a half-breed, cross-breed, or mongrel," and gives racial instances from 1630 to 1878. It was applied to human crossings only in the modern period, as it came into use in the seventeenth century; see Alvar, 120. Isidore, *Origines* XII, 1, 61, cited in Minton Warren's brief, informative essay, "On the Etymology of the Hybrid (Lat. Hybrida)," *American Journal of Philology* 5.4 (1884): 501–2.

56. Anthony J. Barker, *The African Link: British Attitudes to the Negro in the Era of the Atlantic Slave Trade, 1550–1817* (London: Frank Cass, 1978), 52.

57. Long, *History of Jamaica*, vol. 2, book II, ch. xii, 333, 335–36. See Bitterli, *Die "Wilden,"* 329–30; Miller, 21; Curtin, 43–44; Davis, *Problem of Slavery in Western Culture* (Ithaca: Cornell Univ. Press, 1966), 459; Jordan, 491–96.

58. The recurrence of the motif "Never Was Born" in interracial literature is thus linked to the ideological argument against racial mixing.

59. In Chapter Two, from Barker, 170.

60. See Nott, "The Mulatto a Hybrid," and Stanton, 66.

61. Fredrickson, *Black Image*, 75–66.

62. "Amalgamation," *De Bow's Review* 29 (July 1860): 13, 2, 3–4. See also Fredrickson, 89. Samuel Cartwright, "Slavery in the Light of Ethnology," in *Cotton is King, and Pro-Slavery Arguments*, ed. E. N. Elliott (Augusta, Ga.: Pritchard, Abbot and Loomis, 1860), 712, views "hybridism" as the "most prolific source" of the "degeneration" that is albinoism.

63. Stanton, 189. See also Stephen Jay Gould, *The Mismeasure of Man* (New York: W.W. Norton, 1981), 48–50. Letters are cited from manuscripts in Houghton Library.

64. He made an interesting slip—seven years after Harriet Beecher Stowe published her novel *Dred: A Tale of the Great Dismal Swamp*—when he described the prospect of continued racial mixing as "dredful" (11 Aug. 1863). *Dred* was also directly cited in the *Miscegenation* pamphlet of 1863.

65. See my discussion in Chapter Ten, "Incest and Miscegenation."

66. Kaplan, "Miscegenation Issue," 297n, who also notes the strong response to such theories by the *Anglo-African*.

67. S. G. Howe, *The Refugees From Slavery in Canada West, Report to the Freedmen's Inquiry Commission* (Boston, 1864), 18, 26, 33; cited and discussed by Fredrickson, *Black Image*, 160–64.

68. *Congressional Globe* (17 Feb. 1864), 709; cited in Kaplan, "Miscegenation Issue," 296. The speech was directed against Croly's and Wakeman's *Miscegenation* pamphlet. See also "Caucasian" [William H. Campbell], *Anthropology for the People* (Richmond: Everett Waddey, 1891), 268–69, cited in Mencke, 125:

> It is a well-known fact in the Southern United States . . . that the mulatto and his progeny are more feeble than either of the parent stock, and much

more predisposed to certain diseases, as consumption and scrofulous affec-
tions. . . . A race of hybrids cannot perpetuate themselves; they die out
under the law of hybridity and reversion. . . . Nature avenges the unnatural
crime by excision.

69. Gould, *Investigations in the Military and Anthropological Statistics of American Soldiers* (New York: For the U.S. Sanitary Commission by Hurd and
Houghton, 1869), 319; and J. H. Baxter, *Statistics, Medical and Anthropological, of
the Provost-Marshall-General's Bureau* . . . , 2 vols. (Washington, D.C.: Government Printing Office, 1875), 394, 403, 285. Cited and discussed in Mencke,
39–40. Mencke speaks of the Civil War as a watershed in anthropometric studies.

70. *The Neighbor: The Natural History of Human Contacts* (Boston and New
York: Houghton, Mifflin, 1904), 161–62; partly cited in Mencke, 56 and 91n51.
Shaler, 161, endorses the "general belief" that "hybrids of blacks and whites are
less prolific and more liable to diseases than the pure bloods of either stock, but
also that they seldom live so long."

71. *Race Traits and Tendencies of the American Negro, Publications of the American Economic Association* 11.1–3 (New York: Macmillan, for the American Economic Association, 1896), 184.

72. Hugh Williamson, cited in Jordan, 495. Barker, 48, also shows Long's
plagiarisms; notes the flagrant contradiction between species/race distinctions
and racist theories of origins in man/monkey mating (158); criticizes Jordan
(55–56); argues that in the period through 1807, "theoretical racialism remained
a minority attitude" (159); and suggests that, because of Long's sharp criticism of
the slave trade and of the white planters' widespread use of Mulatto mistresses—
censuring them for "goatish embraces"—his work, "for all its racialism, came to
be used far more by abolitionists than by pro-slavery writers" (162).

73. Lionel W. Lyde, "Climatic Control of Skin-Colour," in *Papers on Inter-
Racial Problems*, ed. G. Spiller (London: P. S. King & Son, 1911), 104–12, here
112.

74. Moreau, 1: 90. English adaptation rather than translation cited in James
T. Holly and J. Dennis Harris, *Black Separatism and the Caribbean*, ed. and intro.
by Howard H. Bell (1860; rpt., Ann Arbor: Univ. of Michigan Press, 1970),
179–80: Moreau's last sentence does not appear in the English version. Moreau's
discussion takes place in the context of his classification system with ten categories in between black and white. For Moreau, 96, the Mulatto also marks the
proportional mean between the extremes of black and white—as he had for
Long.

75. Holly and Harris, *Black Separatism*, 179, 180–81. He invokes the 1850–51
researches of a Halle University professor of zoology, Hermann Burmeister, and
quotes an anonymous Philadelphia merchant who had spent 15 or 20 years in the
Caribbean. The essay was reprinted as an appendix to J. Dennis Harris's *A Summer on the Borders of the Caribbean Sea* (1860; reprinted in Holly and Harris, *Black
Separatism*). See also Kaplan, "Miscegenation Issue," 297n.

76. Cited and discussed in Fredrickson, *Black Image*, 120.

77. C. G. Parsons, M.D., *Inside Slavery; or, A Tour Among the Planters*
(Boston, 1855), 65–66; cited and discussed in Fredrickson, *Black Image*, 121.

78. Moncure Daniel Conway, *Testimonies Concerning Slavery* (London, 1864),
73–77. Cited and discussed in Fredrickson, *Black Image*, 121–22.

79. A brief discussion of this debate can be found in Wirth and Goldhamer, 326–29. Summarizing the debate in his article on "Amalgamation" for the *Encyclopdædia of the Social Sciences*, ed. Seligman, vol. 2 (1937), 16–17, E. B. Reuter writes: "The Darwinian belief that race crossing leads to increased vitality and the opposed belief that it results in sterility and racial degeneration appear, in the light of modern knowledge, to be equally unfounded." And Melville Herskovits extended this view in his entry on "Race Mixture," vol. 13: 43: "Neither these claims nor their opposites have been satisfactorily established by objective investigation; furthermore the same assertions may be matched by similar statements applied to inbred populations of 'pure' racial stock." In his essay "The Ancestry of Genius," *Atlantic Monthly* 71 (1893): 383–89, Havelock Ellis reviews the question by investigating the ancestry of five English poets (Tennyson, Browning, Swinburne, Rossetti, and Morris) and finds cross-breeding conducive to artistic sensibility: "Wherever the races have remained comparatively pure we seldom find any fine flowering of genius" (389). Of special interest to the present book is Ellis's discussion of Browning, whose father married

> Margaret Tittle, a Creole, born in the West Indies. The poet himself, it may be added, was in early life of "olive" complexion, and liable to be mistaken for an Italian. In after life he became lighter. (385)

Ellis concludes:

> If the Browning race had consciously conspired to make a cumulative series of trials in the effects of cross-breeding, they could not have been more successful. (385)

80. "The Question of Amalgamation," *Douglass' Monthly* 3.7 (Dec. 1860): 371–72. The letter by a Mr. Coonley ("whatever doubts his *name* might suggest," Douglass quips) reads as follows:

> I desire to ask you a few questions on the subject of Mongrels—"concrete men"—such as for instance Frederick Douglass, Wm Wells Brown, &c., &c. 1st. Does not the amalgamation of Negro and White produce in all things (physical stamina included,) an inferior race? 2d. Is it possible to perfectly hybridize the two species? In the Mulatto is not the union incomplete, or do the two bloods perfectly blend? Can a Mulatto ever get above "halfness"?

The editor of the *Herald of Progress* had answered in agreement that sperms by males and females of any nation will not perfectly blend, and that the most harmonious conjunction comes from the same general type of species (using the word in the modern sense, and also saying "hybrid" instead of the questioner's "mongrel"). The editor did not believe black and white extreme opposites, thus permitting their offspring to be "considerably perfect, both physically and mentally." "Amalgamation, therefore, cannot be practiced with impunity." Taking issue with the scientist "nonsense" of the answer and the implications of the "halfness" of the questioner, Douglass challenged the questioner to "suggest the time when, the place where, and the things to be done by a white '*whole*' man, and a mulatto '*half*' man":

> How long does a "*whole*" man live? well said; we have seen several mulat-

toes over an hundred years old, and doing well. How many *"whole"* white men did you ever see who were over two hundred years?

Douglass concludes with a brief remark concerning the "impertinence of calling us by name." His ironic questioning of the half and whole rhetoric prefigures that of *Pudd'nhead Wilson*.

81. Hildreth, 405.

82. Typically, however, the literature engaged the question *formally* rather than by direct thematic assertion. For example, Baudelaire's line "la froide majesté de la femme stérile" might refer to this clichéd context rather than to a poetic idiosyncrasy—though there is no explicit allusion to the debate there.

83. *Georges; or, The Isle of France*, trans. Alfred Allinson, in *The Novels of Alexandre Dumas*, vol. 24 (London: Methuen, n.d. [1903]), 11; see also the later description of Georges, 30. See the edition edited by Léon-François Hoffmann, *Georges* (Paris: Gallimard, 1974), 54 and 104–5. Patrick Girard, "Le Mulâtre littéraire," in Poliakov, 191–213, gives an interesting reading of Dumas's novel against the French debate about Mulattoes as reflected in such entries in the *Encyclopédie* as "Métissage" and "Race." Girard, 209, concludes that *Georges* was the "literary transcription of that debate."

84. *Peculiar: A Tale of the Great Transition* (New York: Carleton, 1864), 149.

85. *Pudd'nhead Wilson*, ed. Sidney Berger, 8.

86. McKay, *Gingertown*, 95–96; see also Berzon, 25.

87. Fannie Hurst, *Imitation of Life* (New York: Harper and Brothers, 1933), 300, 302; Grant, *The Conquest of a Continent; or, The Expansion of Races in America* (New York: Scribner's, 1933), 288–89. See Dearborn, 152. In Atherton's novel *Senator North* (1900), Harriet tells her white half-sister: "I shall have no children. I vowed long ago that the curse I had been forced to inherit should not poison another generation."

88. *Heredity of Skin Color in Negro-White Crosses* (Washington, D.C.: Carnegie Institution, 1913). Publications of the Carnegie Institution of Washington #188.

89. J. David Smith, *The Eugenic Assault on America: Scenes in Red, White, and Black* (Fairfax, Va.: George Mason Univ. Press, 1993), 79, calls Davenport one of the "deans" of the American eugenicists; Daniel J. Kevles, *In the Name of Eugenics: Genetics and the Uses of Human Heredity* (1985; Berkeley and Los Angeles: Univ. of California Press, 1986), 44–54, portrays Davenport and his well-funded institute.

90. Davenport, 2. The description in the passive voice makes it somewhat ambiguous whose skin was thus exposed. Another ambiguity was created by Caleb Johnson, 542, according to whose summary of Davenport's method in testing skin color "the arm or some other part not usually subjected to the action of the sun was exposed."

91. This effect is further enhanced by Julian Herman Lewis's account of an improved method that used "mechanical means to rotate the disks at a uniform and constant speed" and his summary of critiques that Davenport's approach later received by such scholars as Todd and Herskovits, who "pointed out the errors incident to the use of the color-top in measuring skin color" because the "red disk used was not pure spectral red," but "contained 59 per cent black, which should be subtracted from the red readings and added to the black ones." Lewis, *The Biology of the Negro* (Chicago: Univ. of Chicago Press, 1942), 31, 45.

92. On some tensions between Davenport and Plecker, see J. D. Smith,

86–88; Washington, 121, states that "Davenport made an important contribution to our knowledge about the black-white genetic combinations." Washington, 110–11, also suggests that Davenport "unwittingly popularized certain terms for mixed blooded blacks" such as Quadroon and Octoroon.

93. Day, 10. Also reproduced in Wirth and Goldhamer, 321. On 9 May 1928 Du Bois wrote Day that he tried to complete the questionnaire repeatedly but feared that he must have misunderstood it at first.

94. "The *Metis*, or Half-Breeds, of Brazil," in *Papers on Inter-Racial Problems*, ed. G. Spiller (London: P. S. King & Son, 1911), 377–82, here 377.

95. See, for example, Ulysses Weatherly in the *American Journal of Sociology* of 1910; for William Faulkner and Sherwood Anderson, see Joseph Blotner, *Faulkner: A Biography* (New York: Random House, 1974), 1: 498–99.

96. Boas cited in Klineberg, 327. Robert E. Park, "Human Migration and the Marginal Man" (1928), in *Theories of Ethnicity*, ed. Sollors, 156–67. E. Franklin Frazier, "Children in Black and Mulatto Families," *American Journal of Sociology* 39 (July 1933): 12–29; see the discussion of Williamson in *New People*, 123. Davenport cited in Klineberg, 327; Wirth in Klineberg, 328.

97. Melville J. Herskovits, "Race Mixture," *Encyclopedia of the Social Sciences*, ed. Seligman, 13, 42–43.

98. Cited in Kaplan, "The Octoroon," 556.

99. Wirth and Goldhamer in Klineberg, 323.

100. Barbara Chase-Riboud, *Sally Hemings* (1979; rpt., New York: Avon, 1980), 18–20.

101. *The Writings of Thomas Jefferson*, XIV, ed. Andrew A. Lipscomb and Albert Ellery Bergh (Washington: Jefferson Memorial Association, 1903), 267–71.

## Chapter Five. Fingernails as a Racial Sign

1. Le Cat, 91.

2. The presentation of this chapter was inspired by Francesco Orlando's contribution to *The Return of Thematic Criticism*.

3. Eugène Sue, *Les Mystères de Paris* (1843; rpt., Paris: Marpon et Flammarion, 1879), I: 154; ch. xxi; Eng. based on anon. trans. (New York: Peter Fenelon Collier and Son, 1900), 175.

4. Dion Boucicault, *The Octoroon* (1859; rpt., Upper Saddle River, N.J.: Literature House, 1970), 16–17.

5. Theodor Storm, "Von jenseit des Meeres" (1865); reprinted in *Gedichte, Novellen, 1848–1867*, ed. Dieter Lohmeier (Frankfurt: Deutscher Klassiker Verlag, 1987), 655.

6. Ibid., 675.

7. Rudyard Kipling, "Kidnapped" (1887), in *Plain Tales from the Hills*, ed. H. R. Woudhuysen, intro. David Trotter (Harmondsworth and New York: Penguin, 1987), 134.

8. MS. Twain, Box 37 DV 128 no. 4, "The Man With Negro Blood," cited by Arthur G. Pettit, in *Pudd'nhead Wilson and Those Extraordinary Twins*, ed. Sidney E. Berger (New York and London: W. W. Norton, 1980), 347; *Pudd'nhead Wilson*, 70. See Shelley Fisher Fishkin, "False Starts, Fragments and Fumbles: Mark Twain's Unpublished Writing on Race," *Essays in Arts and Sciences* 20 (Oct. 1991): 17–31, as well as her *Was Huck Black? Mark Twain and African American*

*Voices* (New York and Oxford: Oxford Univ. Press, 1993), 182n21. There is a 20th-century folk superstition that Mickey Mouse always wears gloves for a racial reason. Compare Maxine Hong Kingston, *Tripmaster Monkey: His Fake Book* (New York: Knopf, 1989), 80.

9. Gertrude Atherton, *Senator North* (New York and London: John Lane, 1900), 94–95.

10. *The Sins of the Father: A Romance of the South* (New York: D. Appleton, 1912), 382.

11. Dorothy Canfield, *The Bent Twig* (New York: Henry Holt, 1915), 72.

12. *The Vengeance of the Gods and Three Other Stories of Real American Color Line Life* (Philadelphia: A.M.E. Book Concerne, 1922), 23.

13. William Faulkner, *Collected Stories* (New York: Random House, n.d.), 222, 218.

14. Fannie Hurst, *Imitation of Life* (New York and London: Harper, 1933), 143.

15. Frank Yerby, *The Foxes of Harrow* (New York: Dial Press, 1946), 268.

16. While single instances of the telltale fingernails have caught the attention of such astute interpreters as Arthur G. Pettit and David Trotter, I am not aware of any secondary literature that investigates the materials comparatively or that looks at them as a motif.

17. See Joachim Schulze, "Geschichte oder Systematik? Zu einem Problem der Themen- und Motivgeschichte," *Arcadia* 10.1 (1975): 76–82.

18. Kate Chopin, "The Father of Désirée's Baby," *Vogue* (14 Jan. 1893): 70.

19. Ross Lockridge, Jr., *Raintree County* (Boston: Houghton Mifflin, 1948), 488. See also the brief mention of fingernails on the first page of "Vernon Sullivan" (Boris Vian), *J'irai cracher sur vos tombes* (1946; rpt., Paris: La Trompinette, n.d.), [11].

20. For example, does the suggestion that a (not represented) black-white interracial rape has taken place in Allen Tate's novel *The Fathers* (New York: Putnam's, 1938) find support in preceding southern gothic-racist codes of imagining it as a "bestial" attack, leaving claw marks as a clue, and thus ideologically substituting animal claws for human fingernails? (In 1788 the West Indian proslavery writer John Kemeys had referred to a cargo of Africans "whose hands had little or no balls to the thumbs" and "whose nails were more of the claw kind than otherwise." Cited in Barker, 158.) Compare Tate's *Fathers*, 226, and Dixon's *Clansman* (1905; rpt., New York: Triangle Books, 1941), 304.

21. Claude McKay, *A Long Way From Home* (1937; rpt., New York: Harcourt, Brace & World, 1970), 110–11. Perhaps it deserves mention that, with the exception of Frank Yerby, all Afro-American authors who have, to my knowledge, used the motif of the fingernails as a racial sign have done so in order to question the existence of such a mark. In addition to the texts discussed here, this is also the case in Nella Larsen's novel *Passing* (1929), ed. McDowell, 150, in which the protagonist Irene Redfield reflects in an interior monologue that white people asserted that they "were able to tell; and by the most ridiculous means, finger-nails, palms of hands, shapes of ears, teeth, and other equally silly rot. . . . Never, when she was alone, had they even remotely seemed to suspect that she was a Negro."

22. Frances Parkinson Keyes, *Crescent Carnival* (New York: Franklin Watts, 1942), 253.

23. *The Sins of the Father: A Romance of the South* (New York: D. Appleton, 1912), 382. This fact is revealed at the end of the novel, 456–60, when Dr. Williams with his medically trained eyes successfully prompts Cleo to confess her lie.

24. Edith Pope, *Colcorton* (New York: Charles Scribner's, 1944), 151, 286, 203.

25. Chester Himes, *If He Hollers Let Him Go* (1945; rpt., New York: New American Library, n.d.), 155–56.

26. Sinclair Lewis, *Kingsblood Royal* (New York: Random House, 1947), 70, 72, 73.

27. Robert Penn Warren, *Band of Angels* (New York: Random House, 1955), 78.

28. Miss M. E. Braddon, *The Octoroon* (New York: Optimus Printing, Golden Gem Library, n.d.), 6. Braddon originally serialized "The Octoroon; or, The Lily of Louisiana" in *The Halfpenny Journal* sometime between 1861 and 1865, shortly after the publication, and at the peak of the publicity, of Boucicault's *Octoroon.*

29. P. Bourget, *Cosmopolis* (New York: Amblard & Meyer Frères, 1895), 195, 196.

30. George Aberigh-Mackay's *Twenty-One Days in India: Being the Tour of Sir Ali Baba, K. C. B.* (1881; 6th ed., London and Calcutta: Thacker, 1898), 119; Trotter called attention to this text and to the identification of the observer in his introduction to Kipling's *Plain Tales from the Hills*, ed. H. R. Woudhuysen, intro. Daniel Troffer (Harmondsworth and London: Penguin, 1987), 20.

31. Storm, however, contemplated an alternate, "tragic" resolution of his story, too, that is discussed in "Endings."

32. Atherton, *Senator North*, 95.

33. Claude Bremond, "Concept and Theme," in Sollors, *Return of Thematic Criticism*, 46–59, has reflected on this relationship of variations to a thematic formation.

34. Schulze, "Geschichte oder Systematik?," 77.

35. In order to pursue this line of questioning we must be prepared to relate the literary series with more nonliterary texts. The fingernail motif, in contrast with such timeless and universal motifs as the full moon or the parting of lovers, seems eminently historical, culturally specific, and constructed; hence it invites such a procedure all the more. See Thomas Pavel, "Thematics and Historical Evidence," in Sollors, *Return of Thematic Criticism*, 121–45. See also the Berkeley student parody issue *Misrepresentations*, which argues the availability of a certain discourse to a New Historicist professor because it appears in the student's diary.

36. Mme. Charles Reybaud, *Valdepeiras* (1839; rpt., Paris: Hachette, 1864), 185.

37. Victor Hugo, *Bug-Jargal*, 2nd ed. (1826; rpt., ed. Roger Toumson, Fort-de-France: Editions Emile Désormeaux, 1979), 307 (ch. xxxiv); anon. Eng. trans. (Boston: Little, Brown, 1898), 149–50. For an earlier translation, see Charles Edwin Wilbour, *Jargal* (New York: Carleton, 1846), 192.

38. Hugo, *Bug-Jargal*, 307; Eng. trans. Charles Edwin Wilbour, *Jargal*, 192. Eugène Sue later explains the term *sang-mêlé* in a similar footnote, *Mystères de Paris* (Paris: C. Gosselin, 1843–44), I, 153.

39. For interesting observations on the rise of circumstantial evidence, or on

"clues" as opposed to confessions, see Ernst Bloch, "Philosophische Ansicht des Detektivromans," *Verfremdungen* I (Frankfurt: Suhrkamp, 1962), 37–63, esp. 38–39.

40. Médéric-Louis-Élie Moreau de St. Méry, *Description topographique, physique, civile, politique et historique de la partie française de l'Isle Saint-Domingue* (1797; rpt., Paris: Société Française d'Histoire d'Outre-Mer, 1984), 97. He includes a range from 56 to 70 white parts and, correspondingly, 58 to 72 black parts under the category "Mulâtre."

41. Hugo, *Bug-Jargal*, 172n, Eng. trans. Wilbour, 27n. Hoffmann, *Le Nègre*, 127, points out that the term *Sang-mêlé* is documented only since 1772.

42. Such scientistic authentication of racializing strategies would seem to support Tzvetan Todorov's worries about scientism. See his *On Human Diversity*, 12–23, 157–70, and 389–90. Phrasings like "it is said," however, sound like *Thousand Nights and One Night*.

43. Moreau de Saint-Méry, 73.

44. Marcello Malpighi, "Epistolae Anatomicae," *Opera Omnia* (1686; rpt., Hildesheim and New York: Georg Olms, 1975), 21–32. Malpighi gave a detailed description of nails (24) and was also among the pioneers in showing scientific interest in finger prints (28). See Eugene Block, *Fingerprinting: Magic Weapon Against Crime* (New York: David McKay, 1969), 4.

45. "Diverses observations anatomiques," published in *Histoire de l'Académie Royale des Sciences: Année MDCCII* (Paris: Charles-Étienne Hochereau, 1720), 24–32; here 32. M. Littré demonstrated to the society that the reticular membrane that in itself is black as charcoal seemed to be only as dark as soot when seen through the epidermis.

46. The Rouen surgeon Le Cat's *Traité de la couleur . . .* 91–92, reasons that the root of the nails opens a kind of door to the nerves, and that there is an equivalence of fingernails and male genital, though he selects the scrotum as the locus of the sign. Whereas the Academy report had pointed out that girls had *only* the fingernail mark, and several scholars agreed, Bernard Romans, *A Concise and Natural History of East and West Florida*, vol. I (New York, 1775), 111, held that "on the moment of birth in both sexes the exterior part of generatio[n] will shew, whether the person will be black, yellow, brown, red or any other color," and he makes no mention of fingernails. In 1745 the Jesuit Padre Joseph Gumilla, *El Orinoco ilustrado, y defendido . . .* (Madrid: Manuel Fernandez, 1745), I: 82, referred to the report to the French Academy in order to substantiate his own claim that children of Negroes may be born and remain white for some days but always have a black spot at the end of their nails. He also found a round mark on the back of the spine that he believed to be the equivalent identifier of Indians. On that issue, see Julian Herman Lewis, "Sacral Pigment Spots," in *The Biology of the Negro* (Chicago: Univ. of Chicago Press, 1942), 48–51.

Moreau draws on, cites, and argues with Buffon, Labat, Le Cat, and de Pauw; de Pauw, in turn, quotes Labat, Le Cat, and Gumilla; both Buffon and Gumilla invoke the Academy report of 1702; and Buffon also argues with de Pauw and cites Le Cat. Hence there is an intertextual trail of footnotes linking Hugo and Moreau to the anatomic discourse of 1702. Most of these texts also contain various genealogical nomenclature of racial mixing, though none as elaborate as Moreau's.

47. Buffon, *Natural History, General and Particular* (1749–88), Smellie transl., III: 200–201. Buffon's "On the Varieties of the Human Species" [1785] directly draws on the report to the Academy of 1702.

48. Ibid., 217.

49. Labat, *Nouveau voyage aux Isles de l'Amérique . . .* (Paris: Delespine, 1742), II: 188–89 and marginal comment.

50. An anonymous reviewer in the *Critical Review* of 1760, 82, for example, states "that the children of the Negroes come out white from their mother's womb, like ours, and have no blackness at all, except about their privities, and a small black circle about their nails, next to the flesh; that of the rest of their bodies being contracted gradually after the birth, in twenty-four hours by some, and by others in a week, more or less." See Winthrop Jordan, 248–49, citing Le Cat, Romans, Buffon and Stedman. Compare de Pauw, 183. For a modern view, see Lewis, *The Biology of the Negro*, 37.

51. It is this distinction, of course, that mattered most in the United States. See Higginbotham and Kopytoff, 1977, who argue that "the important dividing line was the white/mulatto boundary, not the mulatto/black boundary."

52. In *Frederick Douglass's Paper* (10 Feb. 1854) a news item from the *Charlottesville Jeffersonian* is cited that questioned the rule that individuals who are four generations away from any black ancestry be considered white: in a lecture delivered by the Philadelphian P. A. Browne in the Capitol of Virginia he asked, "What kind of white is thus 'manufactured out of black and white'?" and answered that "this last has black and curly hair, nails dark and ill shaped,—feet badly formed, and much of the Negro propensities."

53. In the introduction to *Finger Prints* (London and New York: Macmillan, 1892), 17–18, Francis Galton deplores that his "great expectation" that fingerprints could be used as a racial clue had been "falsified." See also Michael Rogin, "Francis Galton and Mark Twain" and Susan Gillman, "Sure Identifiers," both in Gillman and Robinson, esp. 78–80 and 97–100; and Sundquist, *To Wake the Nations*, 251–52. However, Galton, expecting that the marks *ought* to work as racial signs, adds the qualification that in Negro prints the "width of the ridges seems more uniform, their intervals more regular, and their courses more parallel than with us. In short, they give an idea of greater simplicity, due to causes that I have not yet succeeded in submitting to the test of measurement" (196). Lewis, *Biology of the Negro*, 60–61, reports the failures by Hepburn and Schlaginhaufen to discover racial differences in fingerprints, but notes Wilder's finding that "while no single type of formula occurred exclusively in one race, there still was one that predominated in each race"—which he called the "Negro formula" and the "white formula." And Earnest Albert Hooton, *Up From the Ape* (New York: Macmillan, 1947), 523–30, relates research suggesting that fingerprints may possibly reveal racial affinities but considers the results inconclusive and contradictory; he does not mention nails. In discussions of fingerprints and race one should remember, however, that long before Galton's interest was awakened in the possibilities of using fingerprints as racial identification, interest in fingerprints had been articulated by Nehemiah Grew in 1684, Marcellus Malpighi in 1686, Thomas Bewick in 1822, and other 19th-century figures such as Johann Evangelist Parkinji, William James Herschel, and Henry Faulds, not to mention much earlier knowledge, and cultural uses, of fingerprints in ancient China, in

Japan, and among American Indians in Nova Scotia. See Block, *Fingerprinting: Magic Weapon Against Crime* (New York: David McKay, 1969), 1–9. Blumenbach, in Barker, 169, cited above in Chapter One, "Origins."

54. For a suggestive discussion of the function of the servant's hand in the process of shaping sexuality around the motif of labor, see Bruce Robbins, *The Servant's Hand: English Fiction From Below* (New York: Columbia Univ. Press, 1986), esp. ix–x and 20–23.

55. Elizabeth Madox Roberts, *My Heart and My Flesh*, 50; this is written as if alluding to the fingernail motif without being specific about its signs while amplifying its associations with the psychology of disgust. See also Roberts, 38, 39.

56. Gustave Flaubert, *Madame Bovary*, édition nouvelle établie par la Société des Études littéraires françaises (Paris: Club de l'honnête homme, 1971), 62 (i.e., part 1, ch. 2); Eng. trans. from *Best-Known Works of Gustave Flaubert* (New York: Blue Ribbon Books, 1904), 9. Twelve other instances of "ongle" and "ongles" are listed in Charles Carlut, Pierre H. Dubé, and J. Raymond Dugan, *A Concordance to Flaubert's Madame Bovary* (New York and London: Garland, 1978), 157.

57. Etiemble, *Blason d'un corps: récit* (Paris: Gallimard, 1961), 55. For an extensive contemporary use of fingernail descriptions, and especially of nail-biting in erotic contexts, see also Samuel R. Delany, *The Motion of Light in Water: Sex and Science Fiction Writing in the East Village, 1957–1965* (New York: Arbor House, 1988), e.g., 134, 154, 290.

58. The chain of associations proceeds from "onychophage" via "inicophage" and "inique aux fages" to "eunuque aux fages" (54–55).

59. Etiemble, *Blason d'un corps*, 65. In William Melvin Kelley's novel *A Drop of Patience* (Garden City, N.Y.: Doubleday, 1965), 182, the blind, black jazz musician Ludlow Washington notices, when his white lover Ragan squeezes his hand: "Her smooth fingernails were colder than the rest of her hand." In Billy Wilder's comedy *Kiss Me, Stupid* (1964), Polly (played by Kim Novak) feels that the bad men of her life had small half-moons on their fingernails, whereas in good men they are big.

60. Newbell Niles Puckett, *The Magic and Folk Beliefs of the Southern Negro* (1926; rpt., New York: Dover Press, 1969), 457–58. In André Schwarz-Bart's novel *La Mulâtresse solitude* (Paris: Éditions du Seuil, 1972), 56, the fingernails are used to make a sign that signals color: "Then the light moved and the child saw the old man put down his fingernail on the black skin of his forearm in a gesture that she had seen dozens of times in the course of her short life. It was the *color sign*, which for the whites, blacks, and mulattoes of the du Parc plantation summed up all things here below." *A Woman Named Solitude*, trans. Ralph Manheim (New York: Atheneum, 1973), 64–65. This "color sign" may be related to the kind of claims reported by Lewis, *Biology of the Negro*, 38, "that pure strains of the colored races will not show a red mark on the skin when the fingernail is drawn over the chest with pressure, but if there is any intermixture with whites at all the redding will be distinct and of some duration and in proportion to the amount of intermixture."

61. Riccardo Di Segni reports the *Acharè Moth*'s interpretation (II 79 a, b), according to which the growth of nails (and hair) is a residue of the impurity the snake introduced following Eve's sin; he also develops an interesting connection between the motif of the fingernail and the veil (as in Exodus 33: 23). See Riccardo Di Segni, *Le Unghie di Adama: studi di antropologia ebraica* (Napoli: Guida editori, 1981), 154, 159. Job 37:7 has also been connected with finger marks: "He

sealeth up the hand of every man; that all men may know his work." See Block, *Fingerprinting*, 1.

62. Chesnutt, "The Future American," in *Theories of Ethnicity: A Classical Reader* (Houndmills: Macmillan, 1996), 24. Samuel Monash, "Normal Pigmentation in the Nails of the Negro," *Archives of Dermatology and Syphilology* 25 (1932): 876–81, here 877, 881. Davenport and Day do not discuss fingernails in their sections on physiological signs in racially mixed families; Lewis, "Pigmentation of the Nails," in *Biology of the Negro*, 55–57, draws on Monash and concludes:

> This occurrence has also been offered as a "giveaway" of colored descent in very fair people, but it is probably another accompaniment of heavy cutaneous pigmentation and can be found in dark people generally if sought for without regard to race. (55)

Edward M. East, *Heredity and Human Affairs* (New York: 1929), 99–100 (cited by Wirth and Goldhamer, 329) questions the melodramatic story "where the distinguished scion of an aristocratic family marries the beautiful girl with tell-tale shadows on the half-moons of her nails."

63. Cited in Norman L. Willey, "Exotic Elements in Storm and Sealsfield," *Germanic Review* 13 (1939): 31. This reply puts the fingernail motif into a special category, pretending to refer to "nature" (in the human body that, by the reference to the "moons," seems related to a cosmic order), but in fact referring to cultural beliefs expressed in certain texts for two and a half centuries.

64. Johnny Otis, *Listen to the Lambs* (New York: Norton, 1968), 29–30; cited in Burton W. Peretti, *The Creation of Jazz: Music, Race, and Culture in Urban America* (Urbana and Chicago: Univ. of Illinois Press, 1992), 194.

65. Milton A. Smith, "America's Most Sensational Mixed Marriage," *Tan Confessions* 2.2 (Dec. 1951): 22–78, here 24. The issue to be deliberated was whether or not Alice Jones could have deceived her husband Leonard "Kip" Rhinelander about her racial identity, justifying an annulment of their young marriage (without a financial settlement). See Jamie Wacks, "Reading Race, Rhetoric, and the Female Body: The Rhinelander Case and 1920s American Culture" (Senior thesis, Harvard University, 1995), 35.

66. In Lise Funderburg, *Black, White, Other: Biracial Americans Talk About Race and Identity* (New York: William Morrow, 1994), 288.

### Chapter Six. *Code Noir* and Literature

1. George Washington Cable, ch. xii of "Madame Delphine" (1879), in *Old Creole Days* (New York: Scribner's, 1893), 61–62, a passage in which the calculus of color is also criticized; cf. chs. 28 and 29 of *The Grandissimes* (1880; rpt., New York: Hill and Wang, 1957), 180–81. See Philip Butcher, *George Washington Cable* (New York: Twayne, 1962), 53, 58, and Alice Hall Petry, "'Dey's Quadroons': Love versus the Code Noir in *Madame Delphine*," in *A Genius in His Way: The Art of Cable's* Old Creole Days (London and Toronto: Associated Univ. Presses, 1988), 24–48.

2. "Esclave," *Encyclopédie, ou Dictionnaire Raisonné*, ed. Diderot et al. (Neufchastel: Faulche, 1765), 11, 942. In the entry "Negre," 5, 83, the article is cited as sec. 33 of the *Code noir* in a slight variation, e.g. *effusion de sang*.

3. See *Le Code noir; ou, Recueil des reglements rendus jusqu'à présent* (Paris: Prault, 1767; rpt., Basse-Terre and Fort-de-France, 1980); Riddell; and Mathé

Allain, *"Not Worth a Straw": French Colonial Policy and the Early Years of Louisiana* (Lafayette: Center for Louisiana Studies, 1988), 60, 79–83.

4. Michel Fabre, *From Harlem to Paris: Black American Writers in France, 1840–1980* (Urbana and Chicago: Univ. of Illinois Press, 1991), 14–16; and Era Brisbane Young, "An Examination of Selected Dramas for the Theater of Victor Séjour Including Works of Social Protest" (Ph.D. diss., New York University, 1979), 17, who invokes the records of St. Louis Cathedral. David O'Connell, "Victor Séjour: ecrivain Américain de langue française," *Revue de Louisiane* 1.2 (Winter 1972): 60–61, renders the mother's name Cloïsa-Philippe Ferrand. See also Edward Larocque Tinker, *Les Ecrits de langue française en Louisiana au XIXe siècle* (Paris: Librairie Ancienne Honoré, 1932), 427–28.

5. *Creole Voices: Poems in French by Free Men of Color First Published in 1845*, ed. Edward Maceo Coleman (Washington, D.C.: Associated Publishers, 1945), 105–8. The original publication carried an epigraph by Victor Hugo, whom Séjour knew. David O'Connell, *Revue de Louisiane* 1.2 (Winter 1972): 60–75, here 61, describes Séjour as a life-long Bonapartist who knew Napoleon III and wrote two plays in collaboration with M. Mocquard, the emperor's private secretary.

6. *Douglass' Monthly* 3.12 (May 1861): 461, reported that Séjour was affected by a French life of John Brown, prefaced by "Victor Hugo's famous letter, . . . that he is preparing it for the stage." O'Connell, 61, mentions that Séjour fell out of fashion in Paris after the fall of Napoleon in 1870.

7. First published under the heading "Mœurs coloniales" ("colonial manners") and under the subtitle "Esquisse" in the *Revue des colonies* 3.9 (March 1837): 376–92, the story was reprinted with a brief introduction by O'Connell, *Revue de Louisiane I*, 60–75. An English translation of "Le Mulâtre" by Andrea Lee is scheduled for publication in *The First Longfellow Institute Anthology* (1997), and some of the English excerpts have been drawn from that translation. Séjour is the subject of Young's dissertation, and there are very good discussions of him in Hoffmann, *Le Nègre romantique*, 234–35, and in Fabre, *La Rive noire*, 14–16. James V. Hatch and Ted Shine, eds., *Black Theater, U.S.A.: Forty-Five Plays by Black Americans, 1847–1974* (New York: Free Press, 1974), 25–33, reprint the play "The Brown Overcoat." *The Norton Anthology of African American Literature*, eds. Henry Louis Gates, Jr., and Nellie Y. McKay (New York and London: W. W. Norton, 1997), 286–99, also includes Séjour's short story in an English translation by Philip Barnard. Frances Ellen Watkins Harper's "The Two Offers," considered to be the first African American short story, was first published 22 years later in the *Anglo-African Magazine* I. 9 and 10 (Sept.–Oct. 1859): 288–91.

8. This is vaguely reminiscent of chapter 11 of Hildreth's *White Slave*, published the year before, though Hildreth has the whipping planter double up as *father* of the two slaves who are not only siblings but also married to each other. See Chapter Ten, "Miscegenation and Incest." Alexandre Dumas's novel *Georges* (1843) gives his protagonist the same name as Séjour did and also has a character named "Laïza." Two years before Séjour, Beaumont portrayed an explosive rebel Georges in *Marie*, who may in some respects have served as a model for Séjour.

9. See E. B. Young, 92, 166, and 168; Hoffmann, *Le Nègre*, 234; and Riddell, 324.

10. Vauthier, "Textualité et stéréotypes," 90–91.

11. This point was made by E. B. Young, 95. As early as 1833, Charles James Cannon published the little-known novel *Oran, the Outcast; or, A Season in New York*, in which the confrontation between the mixed-race titular hero and his white father who does not publicly recognize him is central. See Vauthier, "(Non-)famille romanesque." In the anglophone part of the African American tradition, however, it was only Charles Chesnutt who, half a century later, attempted a similarly mythic, but less violently resolved, family construction in his short story "The Sheriff's Children" (1899). And when, nearly a century after Séjour, Claude McKay and Langston Hughes revisited the full implications of the narrative Séjour had devised, both of them used his title "The Mulatto" for their poetic and dramatic visions. McKay, in his sonnet "The Mulatto," *Bookman* 72 (Sept. 1925), 67, seems especially close to the spirit of Séjour as the poem's speaker opposes the white man, his cruel father, with a hatred that "only kin can feel for kin," and concludes startlingly: "Into my father's heart to plunge the knife/ To gain the utmost freedom that is life." Langston Hughes's poem and play "Mulatto" continued this trajectory by giving a more Freudian valence to the Oedipus Robert, whose shout—"The white man's dead. My father's dead"—sounds like the incantation "The witch is dead." It is possible, however, that in its representation of the master engaged in rape and an infuriatingly inhumane application of the most cruel law, "Le Mulâtre" went further than did Séjour's 20th-century successors. This is also true when one compares Séjour with the sketches of an interracial patricide story that Mark Twain composed and that Susan Gillman discusses in "The Mulatto, Tragic or Triumphant? The Nineteenth-Century American Race Melodrama," in *The Culture of Sentiment: Race, Gender, and Sentimentality in 19th Century America*, ed. Shirley Samuels (New York and Oxford: Oxford Univ. Press, 1992), 221–43.

12. Reybaud's novella *Mademoiselle de Malepeire*, for example, the sentimental mésalliance tale of the noble titular heroine who falls in love with a man her father describes simply as a "peasant," appeared in 1856 in the Hachette series "bibliothèque des chemins de fer." The catalogue of books in the Hachette railway series that is appended to Reybaud's *Mademoiselle de Malepeire* includes not only guide books and volumes of anecdotes but also several authors and works that are of interest here: one notices Pushkin, Maria Edgeworth, Eugène Chapus, and Mayne Reid as well as Mme. Duras's *Ourika*, Hildreth's *L'Esclave blanc*, or Stowe's *La Case de l'Oncle Tom*. *Mademoiselle de Malepeire* was translated into German by Paul Heyse (ca. 1873), who was also the author of a German *Urica*.

13. *Valdepeiras* (Paris: Hachette, 1864). Further references to this text will be given parenthetically, though occasionally the text from the *Revue de Paris* 50 (Feb. 1838): 37–101, will also be cited with the abbreviation RP followed by the page number.

14. His perfect hospitality, coupled by a generous dinner invitation, is reminiscent of that with which Beast treated Beauty in the story to which Reybaud may be alluding here and later. Hoffmann, *Le Nègre*, 238–42, provides a context for the description of Donatien in the romanticization of Mulatto descriptions in French literature of the period.

15. This may be another echo of Beast's polite abstention from commensuality with his guest.

16. The narrator thus juxtaposes a natural aristocracy of genius that may

coincide with true aristocratic lineage against the racial blood mythology of white upstarts who place themselves, in imitation of old aristocracies, above those who have nonwhite "blood" in their veins.

17. Another echo of "La Belle et la bête."

18. 142. This is an odd phrase given that the narrative fiction is that Zoe, another Creole woman, is telling this tale of her grandfather's.

19. Literally, an *épave* is a "wreck": the term refers to a Black or Mulatto who belongs to nobody, but who also does not posses free papers, and who can thus be seized and sold by the government. Hoffmann, *Le Nègre*, 232, cites Victor Charlier and Eugène Chapus, "L'Épave," in *Titime, histoire de l'autre monde* (Paris: Renduel, 1833). In *Le Code noir* (1842), Eugène Scribe lets a character define *épave* as a slave without an owner (311). Baudelaire was to use the word in a title of a poem in *Fleurs du mal*. The issue of being enslaveable unless proven free was also important in Charles Ball's narrative of 1836, *Slavery in the United States*, a text Mark Twain used in his *Connecticut Yankee*. The word *épave* is often differentiated from *marron*, English "Maroon," who is, like Palème, a runaway slave in hiding. Hoffmann, in his notes to Dumas's novel *Georges*, 483, explains the term and its probable origin in the Spanish word *cimarron*, used to apply to animals who have been domesticated but return to a savage state.

20. As in wordplays on "belonging," this is a common pun on erotic dependence, only here it is paradoxically articulated by a man who literally faces enslavement. In Azevedo's novel *O Mulato* (1881) it is the white Ana Rosa who declares to her beloved Raimundo whose slave origins form a marriage impediment: "I'm a slave who weeps at your feet! . . . I'm yours! Here you have me, my master. Love me!" (242)

21. The case, also known (after the lawyers) as *Lestaing v. Hutteau*, is described at some detail in McCloy, *Negro in France*, 44–45.

22. Cf. *Bug-Jargal!*: this casts Palème in the role of the somewhat supernatural romantic rebel and may be suggestive of a splitting of the complex rebel figure into a good, marriageable and an evil, insurrectionary character.

23. Reybaud distinguishes "Indian" and "Caribbean" (*Caraibe*), and the context of the story implies that Bécoya is partly of African origin, as such references as the one to the "drop of black blood" (123) suggest.

24. The contrast sounds like the abolitionist juxtaposition of spire and auction block, though sharper than any other contrast of this sort was the Fourth of July in Beaumont's *Marie*.

25. Eugène Scribe, *Œvres complètes: opéras comiques* (Paris: E. Dentu, 1879), 370, lets three characters ask the question "qui pourra le sauver?" in unison at the equivalent moment of his play.

26. In the original magazine version of 1838 the passage reads *femme libre* ("free woman") (RP 101).

27. I have not found this precise rule, though sec. 9 of the *Code noir*, 33–34, reprinted in the entry "Negre" in the *Encyclopédie*, 82–83, prohibits concubinage under severe penalties that are, however, suspended "if the master wishes to marry his slave according to the rites observed by the Church, by which act the slave is free, and her children become free and legitimate." ("Cet article [providing penalties for concubinage] n'a point lieu, si le maître veut épouser dans les formes observeés par l'église, son esclave, qui par ce moyen est affranchie, & ses enfans rendus libres & légitimes.") And sec. 7 of the 1716 *Code noir*, 176 (reprint-

ed in "Esclave," 943), cites the provision that slaves who marry with the consent of their masters in France become free. Reybaud might also have been thinking of sec. 13 of the *Code noir*, 35–36, which stipulates that if a male slave marries a free woman, their *children*, male or female, shall be as free as the mother. Riddell refers to no specific rule involving the marriage of slaves and noblemen, and neither does McCloy, *Negro in France*, who mentions the Order of the Council of State of 5 April 1778 "forbidding all marriages between whites and blacks in France" (49), though he also reports the case of the Negro Alexis in Cassis, Provence, who was permitted to take his French wife's family name (53). Reybaud came from Provence.

28. Matthews, reprinted in *Massachusetts Review* 27.2 (Summer 1986): 169–91; here 182. Three years after Matthews's address, the New Orleans writer Ruth McEnery Stuart published "Little Mother Quackalina: Story of a Duck Farm" in the volume *Solomon Crow's Christmas Pocket and Other Tales* (1898), a parody of the "Ugly Duckling" that offers a broad critique of white-black relations at the turn of the century. See Frisby, 128–31. A century after Matthews, however, the London nursery school teacher Anne Douglas was reported to have refused telling "The Ugly Duckling" to her pupils because she viewed it as a tale that incites racism; see *Repubblica* (29 May 1995): 15.

29. *The Life and Times of Frederick Douglass: Written by Himself* (1892; rpt., Secaucus, N.J.: Citadel Press, 1983), 245. Allusions to Andersen are common in African American and interracial literature. See, for example, Zora Neale Hurston, *Dust Tracks on a Road* (1942; rpt., Urbana and Chicago: Univ. of Illinois Press, 1984), 54; Ann Petry, *The Narrows* (1953; rpt., Boston: Beacon Press, 1988), 155 ("The Snow Queen"), and Abbie Crunch's ironic reference to "The Ugly Duchess," 233. Guy Rose, *My Love, My Love; or, The Peasant Girl* (New York: H. Holt, 1990), used Andersen's tale of the little mermaid.

30. Frederick J. Marker, *Hans Christian Andersen and the Romantic Theatre: A Study of the Stage Practices in the Prenaturalistic Scandinavian Theatre* (Toronto: Univ. of Toronto Press, 1971), 37, invoking a diary entry after the failure of *The Bird in the Pear-Tree*. The subsequent discussion of the backgrounds of the Danish stage follows Marker's excellent account closely.

31. *Mulatten: Originalt romantisk Drama i fem Akter* was published separately in 1840 (2nd ed., Kjøbenhavn: C. A. Reitzel) and was included under the title *Der Mulatte: Romantisches Drama in fünf Acten* in volume 24 of the first collection of Andersen's works, *Gesammelte Werke*, published in German, without a translator's name, but edited by the author (Leipzig: Carl B. Lorck, 1847). *Mulatten* appeared in few if any of Andersen's later collected works. The play was, according to Andersen, translated into Swedish, too, but I have not found an English translation or adaptation of the play. The citations follow the second Danish edition of 1840, and the English quotes are based on a draft translation by Jesper Sørensen of 1987 that was checked against the Danish original of 1840 and compared with the German version of 1847 (occasionally cited with a G).

32. Marker, 30.

33. Ibid., 50; *The Story of My Life* (trans. New York: Hurd and Houghton; Cambridge: Riverside Press, 1876), 149–50, 196. Further references to this edition under *SML*.

34. It is not inconceivable that Andersen thought of his own initials when he changed the protagonist's name to Horatio: "H.C." Horatio/Cecile. The

detailed and very informative essay by Bo Grønbech, "Om 'Mulatten' og dens franske forlæg," *Anderseniana*, ser. 3, vol. 3 (1978–79): 43–60, here 49, stresses that the name "Horatio" should have been "Horace" in French Martinique.

35. *SML*, 151. Interestingly, however, Andersen did not set the auction on a Sunday, thus taking back the critique of the church implied in Reybaud.

36. *Fædrelandet* 70 (16 Feb. 1840): 435–40, esp. 438–39, a scholarly review that compared Andersen and Reybaud at length. See also P. Høybye, "H. C. Andersen og Frankrig," *Anderseniana*, ser. 2, 11 (1951–4): 146–47; and Grønbech, "Om 'Mulatten,'" 57–58.

37. *SML*, 153–54. Grønbech, "Om 'Mulatten,'" 58.

38. Of the four reviews cited in Birger Frank Nielsen, *H. C. Andersen Bibliografi: Digterens Danske Værker, 1822–1875* (København: Hagerup, 1942), 100, the Royal Danish Library in Copenhagen and H. C. Andersens Hus Odense kindly sent me *Fædrelandet* 70 (16 Feb. 1840): 435–40; *Kjøbenhavns Morgenblad* 6 (9 Feb. 1840): 24; and *Portefeuillen for 1840*, 1. Bind, 7. Hæfte (16 Feb. 1840): 161–67. The review by P. L. Møller in *Berlingske Tidende Søndagsblad* 10 (8 March 1840) could not be copied. In addition, Niels Oxenvad provided me with the review in *Kjøbenhavnsposten* (4 Feb. 1840): 135–36, and with notices for performances of the play in 1868 and 1873.

39. *SML*, 151–52. Marker, 50, mentions that of the first eleven performances five were sold out. A very brief discussion can be found in P. M. Mitchell, *A History of Danish Literature* (Copenhagen: Gyldendal, 1957), 151–52. Mentioning that Andersen's acclaim as a playwright rested on *Mulatten*, Mitchell calls it a "melodramatic work," reminiscent of "the pathos of *Uncle Tom's Cabin*," in which Andersen "portrays the evils of slavery, and pleads for the rights of man." Yet though Andersen voiced "the political liberalism of the day" and received some positive attention, Mitchell finds that it "drags for the modern reader; and the plot seems very unlikely indeed." The Casino Theatre in Copenhagen revived *Mulatten* in 1868 and 1873.

40. This is an inversion of Wolfgang Amadeus Mozart and Emanuel Schikaneder's *Zauberflöte* (*Magic Flute*) (1791), II:xxx: "Die Strahlen der Sonne vertreiben die Nacht"—which ends the power of both the queen of the night and the Moor Monostatos.

41. The authorized German translation of the play, 34, changes this line dramatically by forcing the master to watch how Paléme kisses his own (Paléme's) wife.

42. Paléme is also the lusting upstart who is often portrayed by a lower-class white character, like M'Closkey in Boucicault's *Octoroon*. In fact, he may be considered the symmetrical opposite of M. de la Rebeliere.

43. The word tellingly used is *Eventyr* (27); *Märchen* (G 33).

44. For provocative comments on the interrelationship of noble savage and black Spartacus see Hermann Hofer, "Befreien französische Autoren des 18. Jahrhunderts die schwarzen Rebellen und die Sklaven aus ihren Ketten? oder Versuch darüber, wie man den Guten Wilden zur Strecke bringt," in Koebner and Pickerodt, 137–70.

45. "Schatten," G 16. See Andersen's story *Skyggen* ("The Shadow," 1847). Combining functions of the double and that of the light differentiation, the motif of the shadow is prominent in interracial literature. See, for example, Victor Hugo, Anna Dickinson, Melville's "Benito Cereno," Cable's *Grandissimes* (318),

Hopkins's *Contending Forces* (152, 334), or Seghers, *Hochzeit von Haiti* (16). See also Adalbert von Chamisso's *Peter Schlemihls wundersame Geschichte*; Georg Simmel's comments on jealousy in "The Stranger," repr. in *Theories of Ethnicity*, 40–41; and the entry on "Shadow" in Horst S. and Ingrid Daemmrich, *Themes and Motifs in Western Literature: A Handbook* (Tübingen: Francke, 1987), 232–33.

46. As Grønbech, 49, suggests, Andersen changed the Mulatto's mother from a "Caraïbe" woman to the daughter of an African king. He thus made Horatio's African connection more explicit and his origins more aristocratic.

47. *Mulatten*, 11–12. Cf. H. C. Andersen, *Kjendte og glemte Digte, 1823–1867* (Copenhagen: C. A. Reitzel, 1867), 299. Similarly, Theodor Storm published the poem that he ascribed to the Mulatto woman Jenni in "Von jenseit des Meeres" (1864) also under his own name, and with the title "Waisenkind" (Orphan child).

48. It is true that Andersen follows Reybaud closely in the application of the *Code noir*, yet it deserves mention that the threat of death is another intensification of Reybaud's milder, or less specific threat, of twenty-nine lashes.

49. Marker, 50.

50. Benjamin Antier et Alexis Decomberousse, *Le Marché de Saint-Pierre* (Paris: Marchant, 1839), 33–35. Le Petit, *Horatio, der Mulatt; romantisches Drama in fünf Aufzügen* (1845).

51. Marker, 50. Erling Nielsen also interprets *Mulatten* as one version of Andersen's own persistent pariah feeling (palpable also in "The Ugly Duckling" or "The Little Mermaid"), projected here upon the racially mixed protagonist of his play (but *not* on La Rebelliere).

52. See Andersen, *Skyggen* ("The Shadow" 1847), *Fairy Tales*, trans. Reginald Spink (London: Everyman's, 1992), 302–15, that begins in a southern country where "people are turned the colour of mahogany"; Erling Nielsen, *Hans Christian Andersen*, trans. Thyra Dohrenburg (Hamburg: Rowohlt, 1958), 25, 84, 88; *H. C. Andersens Briefwechsel mit Sr. Königlichen Hoheit, dem Grossherzog Carl Alexander von Sachsen-Weimar-Eisenach und anderen Zeitgenossen*, ed. Emil Jonas (Leipzig: Wilhelm Friedrich, n.d.), 230–31.

53. *The Octoroon*, 5.

54. This structure invites comparison with the father-son drama of Pigault-Lebrun's *Le Blanc et le noir* (1795), in which oedipal conflict centers on attitudes toward slavery.

55. Nielsen, *Andersen*, 92. Johan Ludvig Heiberg's "En sjael efter Døden. En apocalyptisk Comedie" was first published in *Nye Digte* (1840), and included in *Udvalgte Digtninger* (Kjøbenhavn og Kristiana: Gyldendalske Boghandel, Nordisk Forlag, 1905), 3–69; esp. 30, 40–41; see Andersen, *A Poet's Bazaar* (1842).

56. Cited from Scribe, *Œuvres complètes*, 277–382.

57. Zoe, meaning life, or being, was a popular name for characters in 19th-century exoticist contexts. It appeared, for example, in William Dimond, *The Ethiop* (1814); Mélesville, *Zoé; ou, L'Amant prêté*; Elizabeth D. Livermore, *Zoe; or, The Quadroon's Triumph: A Tale for the Times* (1855); and Dion Boucicault, *The Octoroon; or, Life in Louisiana* (1859).

58. Allain, "Not Worth Straw," 81.

59. Compare Jacques Lacan, "On a Question Preliminary to Any Possible Treatment of Psychosis" (1955–56), in *Écrits: A Selection*, trans. Alan Sheridan (New York and London: W. W. Norton, 1977), 218; and Vauthier, "Textualité,"

90–91. Richard Hildreth's Archy Moore also had raised the topic of the slave's surname in 1836; when General Carter chides him for his impertinence in claiming a double name and tells hims: "Let me beg leave to request of you, Mr Archy Moore, to be satisfied with calling yourself Archy, the next time I inquire your name," Archy reflects: "I had taken the name of Moore, since leaving Spring-Meadow; an assumption not uncommon in Virginia, and which is there thought harmless enough. But the South Carolinians, who of all the Americans, seem to have carried the theory and practice of tyranny to the highest perfection, are jealous of every thing that may seem in any respect, to raise their slaves above the level of their dogs and horses" (172). On naming, see also Albion Tourgée, *Bricks Without Straw*, Chesnutt, "Her Virginia Mammy," and Adrienne Kennedy, "The Owl Answers."

60. By Zamba; Scribe, 320.

## Chapter Seven. Retellings: Mercenaries and Abolitionists

1. (Boston: Fields, Osgood, 1869), 195. See also the interesting reviews of the novel by Henry James, "Injurious Works and Injurious Criticism," *Nation* (29 Oct. 1868), and by William Dean Howells, *Atlantic Monthly* (Jan. 1869).

2. *Atlantic Monthly* 6, no. 35 (Sept. 1860): 323–25.

3. *Invisible Man* (1952; rpt., New York: Vintage Books, 1972), 10.

4. *The Oasis*, ed. L. Maria Child (Boston: Benjamin C. Bacon, 1834), 65–105, illustrations on 64 and 93. Further references to this story will be given parenthetically. I shall follow Child's edition and occasionally compare, and ultimately focus on, Stedman's manuscript version of 1790, published in *Narrative of a Five Years Expedition Against the Revolted Negroes of Surinam*, ed. Richard and Sally Price (Baltimore and London: Johns Hopkins Univ. Press, 1988). The relevant passages in the Prices' edition appear on 42–43, 87–90, 97–98, 100, 101, 117, 139, 154, 158, 161, 166, 175–76, 248–49, 253, 259–62, 270–72, 276–77, 289, 291, 293, 297, and 599–600. References to this edition will be with the identifier "Price." Jean Fagan Yellin, *Women and Sisters*, 71 and 197n50, briefly discusses "Joanna" and, invoking Leslie Fiedler, claims Child's pioneering role in miscegenation literature.

5. 1790 manuscript version, Price, 87–88.

6. See Lovelace to John Belford, Esq. (Letter 225): "And there, in the anguish of her soul, her streaming eyes lifted up to my face with supplicating softness, hands folded, dishevelled hair; for her night head-dress having fallen off her in her struggling, her charming tresses fell down in naturally shining ringlets, as if officious to conceal the dazzling beauties of her neck and shoulders; her lovely bosom too heaving with sighs, and broken sobs, as if to aid her quivering lips in pleading for her. . . ." Samuel Richardson, *Clarissa; or, The History of a Young Lady* (1747–48; rpt., London: Penguin, 1985), 725.

7. Child also omitted the fact that Joanna's shawl "gracefully covered part of her lovely bosom" in the text.

8. He does, however, not only call her "my mulatto," (e.g., 76) but also speaks of "my boy" (87) and "my little family" (91).

9. The reference to the slave's broken china may come from generic sentimental writing that resembled texts published before Stedman, for example, in William Hill Brown, *The Power of Sympathy* (1789), ed. William S. Osborne

(New Haven, Conn.: College & Univ. Press, 1970), 85–86, letter 46. Whereas Harrington is merely a sympathetic (though self-centered) observer who makes sentimental proclamations, Stedman actively intervenes (with money) and saves the slave from being punished.

10. The theming of the tale as one about "women's constancy" makes it possible to regard Reybaud's "Les Épaves" and Chesnutt's "The Wife of His Youth"—with the same declared theme—also as retellings of "Inkle and Yarico." The *Spectator* text is reprinted, without the frame narrative, in L. M. Price, *Inkle and Yarico Album*, 5–7.

11. The phrase "in short" also occurs in Cassy's tale in *Uncle Tom's Cabin*, and again in the change from romantic to financial discourse. Stowe also owned volumes of the *Spectator* in her personal library, and tried out its style before writing *Uncle Tom's Cabin*. See Joan Hedrick, *Harriet Beecher Stowe: A Life* (New York and Oxford: Oxford Univ. Press, 1994), 24, 141.

12. This self-humanization may be all the more important to Stedman since his book is otherwise concerned with the brutal military subjugation of Blacks: thus the frontispiece shows Stedman in a hunter's pose, leaning on his rifle and pointing down at the body of a black man.

13. Price, 260. The passage—in which Stedman's scribe sadly rendered "nuptial bed" as "ruptial"—is from *Paradise Lost* 4.708ff. See also Price, xxxiii–xxxv.

14. The 1790 manuscript is similar: "So Great indeed was my Joy this day at having Acted the Counter part of *Incle & Yarico* that I become like one Frantic with Pleasure" (Price, 599).

15. The powerful line taken by "Inkle and Yarico" stimulated much writing that aligned hypocritical immorality and limitless profit-mongering and saw their combination most fully realized in the slave trade. See, for example, the captain in Prosper Mérimée's novella "Tamango" or Heinrich Heine's poem "Das Sklavenschiff" which ends with the Dutch slaver whose cargo has been dying at an alarming rate praying to God to save the remaining slaves' lives, for he must have three hundred live ones in order not to have his deal ruined. Hoffmann, 234, also cites the play by Mélesville and R. de Beauvoir, *Le Chevalier de Saint-Georges* (1840) for the Inkle and Yarico motif.

16. This connection is apparent in the many slave sales that precede (or make difficult or impossible) marriage plots: for example, in Andersen's *Mulatten*, Mayne Reid's *Quadroon*, Boucicault's *Octoroon*, or in Cassy's tale in Stowe's *Uncle Tom's Cabin*.

17. Price, 42–43 and 632, and L. M. Price, *Inkle and Yarico Album*, 43–48. In this racist episode Stedman also employs the phrase "to be short."

18. The corresponding parts of his 1790 narrative make it more than likely that "J——a" is none other than "Joanna," though he does no longer mention a "B——e" in the narrative.

19. Child argued perceptively: "Perhaps Joanna, with her quick discernment of strong affection, perceived that he would be ashamed of her in Europe, and therefore heroically sacrificed her own happiness" (104)—which is, in fact, very close to one of the reasons that Stedman lets Joanna voice at their parting, namely that "she had rather be among the first of her own class in America, than a disgrace to [Stedman] in Europe" (101). By contrast, Mary Louise Pratt's interesting reading, "From Narina to Joanna," in *Imperial Eyes: Travel Writing and*

*Transculturation* (1992; rpt., London and New York: Routledge, 1993), 90–107, here 101, strongly emphasizes Joanna's agency in rejecting "European culture and the invitation to assimilate." For Pratt, who mentions the connection to "Inkle and Yarico" but not to Child, this reading turns Stedman's Joanna into an antiassimilationist heroine, an independent figure who, unlike Pocahontas or Phillis Wheatley, "does not want to be schooled, wear shoes, meet the King of England."

20. There is always the possibility to read Stedman as an author who denies his Inkle-ness so much because he recognizes himself in it: after all, he buys the freedom of the male slave Quaaco (a turn of events Leslie Fiedler might appreciate)—though in Europe he gives him as a present to a Countess; and while he argues that it was because of Joanna's virtue that she did not go to England with him, the fact remains that—quite like Inkle—Stedman ends up going back to Europe and leaving behind a slave woman who has mothered his child.

21. Price, xlii; David V. Erdman, "Blake's Vision of Slavery," *Journal of the Warburg and Courtauld Institutes* 15.3–4 (July–Dec. 1952): 242–52, here 245; see also Erdman, *Blake: Prophet Against Empire* (Princeton: Princeton Univ. Press, 1977), 229. Ronald Paulson, *Representations of Revolution 1789–1820* (New Haven and London: Yale Univ. Press, 1983), 93–94, reviews such possible sources as Aphra Behn's *Oronooko* (1678) and "Inkle and Yarico" only to conclude that Blake's "immediate model was Stedman's narrative *and* his personal knowledge of Stedman." Steven Vine, "'That Mild Beam': Enlightenment and Enslavement in William Blake's *Visions of the Daughters of Albion*," in *The Discourse of Slavery: Aphra Behn to Toni Morrison*, eds. Carl Plasa and Betty J. Ring (New York: Routledge, 1994), 40–63, extends this approach without taking into consideration, however, the findings on the construction of "Stedman" reported by the Prices.

22. Price, 97–98. The Prices also mention the amazing substitution of the rebel Negroes' "humanity" by the word "hurry" when Stedman gives the reason why the danger of a massacre was over (lxiii; 154 vs. I:103, ch. 8).

23. The Prices list twenty-five versions of Stedman and the Joanna tale, among them Franz Kratter's play; the prose versions "Joanna, or the Female Slave" (published in Edinburgh and Dublin, 1824) and "Narrative of Joanna; and Emancipated Slave, of Surinam" (Boston: Isaac Knapp, 1838); the loose adaptations by Eugène Sue in *Les Aventures de Hercule Hardi* (1840) and by Herman J. de Ridder in *Een levensteeken op een dodenveld* (1857). They also mention David Dabydeen's collection of poetry *Slave Song* (1984).

24. This effect also extends to Child's own later writings, among them "Slavery's Pleasant Homes," in *Liberty Bell* (Boston: Anti-Slavery Fair, 1843), 147–60. For a fascinating discussion of this story, see Jennifer Fleischner, "Mothers and Sisters: The Family Romance of Antislavery Women Writers," in *Feminist Nightmares: Women at Odds. Feminism and the Problem of Sisterhood*, eds. Susan Ostrov Weisser and Jennifer Fleischner (New York and London: New York Univ. Press, 1994), 125–41.

25. Carolyn L. Karcher, *The First Woman in the Republic: A Cultural Biography of Lydia Maria Child* (London and Durham: Duke Univ. Press, 1994), 335–36. "The Quadroons" will be quoted from L. Maria Child, *Fact and Fiction* (New York: C. S. Francis, 1846), in which the last paragraph that appeared in the *Liberty Bell* version of 1842 is missing. These three final sentences are: "Reader, do you complain that I have written fiction? Believe me, scenes like this are no infre-

quent occurrence at the South. The world does not afford such materials for tragic romance, as the history of the Quadroons."

26. For Diane Roberts, *The Myth of Aunt Jemima: Representations of Race and Region* (New York: Routledge, 1994), 137, the name Xarifa "evokes the harem," a comment that would apply to such works as Séjour's "Le Mulâtre" with its allusion to Alfred as Sultan of the Antilles, to Denison's *Old Hepsy* (1858), 453, where Old Colonel Hollister is rumored to have kept "a secret harem," or to Faulkner's *Absalom, Absalom!* (1936), 147, where Bon is suspected of wanting to make Judith a "junior partner in a harem." Yet Child says specifically that the name comes from a Spanish ballad, "and its Moorish origin was most appropriate to one so emphatically 'a child of the sun'" (63). *A Romance of the Republic* (1867), a more grandiose retelling of the story, includes a casual mention of Washington Irving's *Alhambra* and the singing of "the Moorish ballad of 'Xarifa,' which . . . always brought a picture of Rosabella [the character equivalent to Rosalie in "The Quadroons," but who now has a sister Flora who is singing here] before her eyes" (275). In the English-speaking world it was J. G. Lockhart, *Ancient Spanish Ballads, Historical and Romantic* (London: Blackwell, 1823), who helped to popularize the genre, and Lockhart's translation of "The Bridal of Andalla," 129–31, was also included in the section on "Moorish ballads" in Henry Wadsworth Longfellow's *Poets and Poetry of Europe* (Philadelphia: Carey and Hart, 1845), 651.

27. First published in the *New World*, II, no. 10, Extra Series (Nov. 1842): 1–31. This edition is reprinted and compared critically to later editions, especially the serialization in the *Brooklyn Eagle* of 16–30 Nov. 1846, in Walt Whitman, *The Early Poems and the Fiction*, ed. Thomas L. Brasher (New York: New York Univ. Press, 1963), 204.

28. See, for example, *The Power of Sympathy*, and especially *Charlotte Temple*, to which Child may also be alluding in her choice of the wife's name.

29. As in Stedman, the beauty of nature parallels a natural relationship, not easily sanctioned by society. The *locus amoenus* is thus a topos in interracial literature. See also Chesnutt's later use of it in his *House Behind the Cedars*.

30. See the descriptions of David Lee Child in Deborah Pickman Clifford, *Crusader for Freedom: A Life of Lydia Maria Child* (Boston: Beacon Press, 1992), passim. Edward's interest in politics also parallels Inkle's concern for bookkeeping.

31. Starting with Richardson's *Clarissa*, there have probably been many more "ringlets" in descriptions of women. Still, these "ringlets" also evoke Joanna's "beauteous Globe of small ringlets" and the phrasing in "Inkle and Yarico." And "long black ringlets" also appears, for example, Pauline Hopkins, "A Dash for Liberty," *Colored American Magazine* 3.4 (May 1901): 246.

32. *A Diary in America, With Remarks on Its Institutions* (New York: Colyer, 1839), 192. The white father who dies intestate, bringing his children—most especially daughters—in danger of being sold may be considered a topos of interracial literature, including writers from Ignaz Franz Castelli to Robert Penn Warren. As Brown, *The Negro in American Fiction*, 46, pointed out: "Too often the kindly disposed master dies suddenly, without having chance to fulfill his promises of freedom."

George Washington Cable gave this topos a new spin in his amusing story "Attalie Brouillard," in *Strange True Stories of Louisiana* (New York: Charles Scribner, 1889), 233–60: when Attalie's white friend John Bull suddenly dies, her other friend Camille Ducour impersonates John Bull in a darkened room and dictates, as if he were dying, his last will and testament to the legally required witnesses—making Attalie and himself beneficiaries.

33. "The Three Races of America," in *Democracy in America* (1835, 1840), trans. Henry Reeve, ed. Phillips Bradley (New York: Knopf, 1951), 1: 380.

34. In this respect, Child's Charlotte resembles Stedman's Mrs. D. B., who had a "peculiar tenderness" (69) toward Joanna—who was, however, *not* Mr. D. B.'s illegitimate daughter.

35. This constitutes another parallel to Stedman's Joanna, who was the daughter of Cery. There was a famous ode to a quadroon woman Angélique published in 1806 by the proslavery poet Charles de Cornillon: *Odes, suivies d'une lettre sur l'esclavage des nègres* (Paris: Samson, 1806); see Hoffmann, *Le Nègre*, 138.

36. In Child's story "Annette Gray," published in *The Anti-Slavery Standard* (22 July 1841), the titular heroine is also sold to "the most notorious old profligate in the city!"

37. Yellin claims that Child had invented the tragic mulatto, although Yellin's own earlier account explicitly and convincingly went back to the works of Hildreth and Beaumont.

38. It is ironic that American abolitionists, especially after 1833, felt compelled to portray Englishmen as more understanding in issues of race, while often modeling their bad "American" characters on the Englishmen of precursor texts.

39. See Karcher, *First Woman*, 336, who points out the paradox that "a code of gentility that did not protect slave women against rape or white women against their husbands' philandering must govern fictional treatment of sexuality." In her plot summary of "The Quadroons," Yellin omits any reference to Edward's white wife; it is not only Edward's "white patriarchy" or Rosalie's "black blood" that prevents her from becoming his wife, but also the existence of a white rival aiming for legitimacy (though the figure of Charlotte may complicate the critic's task of presenting a bond between antislavery and feminist sentiment).

40. The term "Quadroon" came into wider literary use in the mid-nineteenth century. See, for example, Longfellow's poem "The Quadroon Girl" (1842) and Mayne Reid's popular novel *The Quadroon* (1856).

41. *Uncle Tom's Cabin; or, Life Among the Lowly*, in *Three Novels* (New York: Library of America, 1982), 409.

42. The motivation of Cassy's child-killing is remarkably different from Browning's—see *The Poetical Works of Elizabeth Barrett Browning*, intro. Ruth M. Adams, Cambridge ed. (Boston: Houghton Mifflin, 1974)—yet seems closer to Morrison's in *Beloved*.

43. Brown mentions his international connections very explicitly in the "Narrative of the Life and Escape of William Wells Brown," that serves as an introduction to *Clotel*. For example, Brown reports that when he addressed the Peace Congress in Paris in 1850 he was "very warmly greeted by Victor Hugo" and that he attended a soirée given by Alexis de Tocqueville (spelled "Tocquerelle"). In the novel Brown incorporates the story of Salome Miller/Müller (ch. xiv), based on a New Orleans newspaper accounts of 1845/46; this was a tale that would receive further elaboration by Cable in *Strange True Stories of Louisiana* (1888–89), 145–91.

44. Huggins, *Revelations*, 277. Huggins follows up his discussion with the

interesting general comment: "Legitimizing myths and myths of national origins are commonly set in illicit sexual unions."

45. Brown's text includes, word for word, Child's description of nature—rendering only Child's "unity" as "amity"—and of Xarifa's/Mary's appearance. This was mentioned by William Edward Farrison, *William Wells Brown: Author and Reformer* (Chicago and London: Univ. of Chicago Press, 1969), 224. See Yellin, *Intricate Knot,* 172–73, for a cogent comparison of Child's short story and Brown's novel and for discussions of Brown's later rewritings of *Clotel;* and Kristin Herzog, *Women, Ethnics, and Exotics: Images of Power in Mid-Nineteenth-Century American Fiction* (Knoxville: Univ. of Tennessee Press, 1983), 134–35.

46. Brown may be echoing Sterne on slavery as cited, for example, in Hildreth's *Archy Moore,* when the narrator looks at a volume of Sterne's *Sentimental Journey* with the frontispiece of "a prisoner chained in a dungeon, and underneath, by way of motto, Sterne's celebrated exclamation, 'Disguise thyself as thou wilt, still Slavery, still thou art a bitter draught, and though thousands have been made to drink thee, none the less bitter on that account!'" (254). One of Longfellow's best-known antislavery poems, "Slave in the Dismal Swamp," also begins with the Sternian exclamation "Slavery is a bitter draught." The expression alludes to Christ's agony (Matthew 26:42, Mark 14:37, John 18:11).

47. Brown may have drawn on experience or on slave narratives for this episode. For example, Bourne's *Picture of Slavery* (1838), 145, told the story of a seven-year-old white boy who was kidnapped and enslaved: "He was tattooed, painted, and tanned. Every other method was also adopted which wickedness could devise, to change the exterior appearance of the unfortunate creature, into one uniform dark tinge." In Harriet Hamline Bigelow's novel *The Curse Entailed* (1857) the foundling Judy is forbidden to "wear a bonnet, wash her face, or comb her hair" and is sent out "on hot sunny days, into the open air or field," which the nursemaid Margaret interprets as an expression of the owner William La Rux's desire "to make de sweet little t'ing look like a nigger" (307). Similarly, in Harriet E. Wilson's *Our Nig; or, Sketches from the Life of a Free Black* (1859), the narrator describes Frado's treatment at the Bellmont house:

> At home, no matter how powerful the heat when sent to rake hay or guard the grazing herd, she was never permitted to shield her skin from the sun.... Mrs. Bellmont was determined the sun should have full power to darken the shade which nature had first bestowed upon her as best befitting. (39)

William Wells Brown returned to this theme in *My Southern Home; or, The South and Its People* (1880; rpt., New York: Negro Universities Press, 1969), 4–6. Here Billy, "a quadroon of eight or nine years," is put to garden work that "roasts" him by Mrs. Gaines, the mistress of the mansion, after a visitor expressed his belief that Billy is white and looks like Mr. Gaines. Lydia Maria Child had also taken on the subject of a white child who is kidnapped, blackened, and whose hair is made curly by a peddler so that he can sell her into slavery together with her black playmate, in "Mary French and Susan Easton," *Juvenile Miscellany,* 3rd series, 6 (May 1834): 186–202, discussed by Karcher, *First Woman,* 165–70, and Sánchez-Eppler, 236.

48. It is interesting that Brown, in his later versions of *Clotelle,* strongly

revised this characterization in order, as duCille, 155n17, put it, "to unindict the wronged wife." As duCille also noted, this change brought the later versions of the novel closer to Child's "Quadroons." By contrast, Kinney, 89–91, focuses on the hatred and sexual jealousy that Mrs. Miller feels toward Isabella and Clotelle, and calls attention to Brown's possible use of Walt Whitman's novel *Franklin Evans* (1842) for the motif of the destruction of an interracial marriage by a white woman as a rival. Stedman, too, graphically depicted Mrs. Stolkers's outrageous cruelties, committed out of jealousy against female slaves, Price, 340–41. For an astounding array of acts of violence toward beautiful female slaves supposedly committed by plantation mistresses in Brazil, see Gilberto Freyre's fourth chapter of *The Mansions and the Shanties* (orig. 1933).

49. This conversation may echo the words of the other Dinah in *Uncle Tom's Cabin* (1852).

50. In Brown's drama "The Escape," too, the operative literary code defines the standard English-speaking Mulattoes Glen and Melinda as serious and heroic, and casts blacks as *buffo* types who provide comic relief in dialect. Brown's runaway slave song in III.ii invited comparison with Child's *Stars and Stripes*, 134.

51. See the discussion of Cooper's *Spy* in Chapter Nine on "Passing."

52. *Die Sclavin in Surinam* (Frankfurt: Esslinger, 1804), [4].

53. Frank J. Webb. *The Garies and Their Friends* (1857; rpt., New York: Arno Press, 1969). Richard Yarborough. "Ideology and Black Characterization in the Early Afro-American Novel" (ms., University of California, Los Angeles, 1988), ch. 2, p. 55, seems to have been the first to note that there are "hints in the early chapters . . . that Webb may have read Brown's *Clotel* or else some of the same sources Brown used."

54. Alain Locke, "American Literary Tradition and the Negro," *Modern Quarterly* 3.3 (May–July 1916): 215–22, here 219, was among the few critics who recognized Webb's achievement when he wrote that "with its narrative of a sophisticated and cultured group of free Negroes," *The Garies* "was in its day a bold departure from prevailing conventions."

55. Beaumont, *Marie*, ch. 13, and appendix L, 248.

56. In Hopkins's *Contending Forces* it is again the constellation of the evil upstart Pollock who lusts after the mistress Grace Montfort and foments a racist revenge scheme—only he is not initially a part of the legitimate family. The type of the evil overseer may thus have developed out of the poor, pure white relative who uses racism in order to bring down the patriarch who is more open toward interracialism.

57. Perhaps the most extreme, breathtakingly morbid, and wonderfully over-written representation of the evil white stepmother who destroys her husband's illegitimate half-caste son is Edward Spencer's virtually unknown, suspenseful, and thoroughly decadent novella "Tristan" (1867)—which also has a strong homoerotic valence.

58. Published anonymously in *Atlantic Monthly* 21 (May 1868): 546–55.

59. Jan Cohn, "The Negro Character in Northern Magazine Fiction of the 1860's," *New England Quarterly* 43.4 (Dec. 1970): 572–92, here 581–82, argues that De Forest's "sincere dismay at race prejudice is somewhat undercut by his descriptions of the octoroon children. They are all light-colored, good-looking, and intelligent enough to be barbers and milliners, but they have no higher, more dangerous, aspirations, and remain hard-working, pious, and grateful to their

white father. . . . these are early pictures of the near-white Negro whose virtues find him a niche, not too high, in the white world." This reading ignores the references to pride and self-respect, the fact that Flora is married to a clergyman, and misses much of the tone of the tale.

60. See, for example, Walt Whitman's "Franklin Evans" (1842, 1846), motto of ch. 17; Mrs. G. M. Flanders, *The Ebony Idol* (1860), motto of ch. 13; Balzac's "Le Nègre" (1822) makes George, the Negro of the title, much like Iago rather than Othello; George makes M. de Gerval jealous of his wife Emilie (another Othello allusion). The elegy by Gustave de Pons, "Ourika l'Africaine" (1825), has Ourika declaim: "Le sang d'Othello bout toujours dans mes veins" (Hoffmann, *Le Nègre*, 225). Mélesville and Carmouche's *Ourika* also refers to Charles ironically as a "petit Othello." See also Denison's *Old Hepsy* (1858), 246–47; Thomas Dixon, Jr., *The Leopard's Spots* (1902), 89; Oscar Micheaux, *The Conquest* (1913), 154; Sinclair Lewis, *Kingsblood Royal* (1947), 140; Ann Petry, *The Narrows* (1954), 479; Peter Abrahams, *Tell Freedom*; William Melvin Kelley, *A Drop of Patience* (1965); Emil Ludwig, *Othello* (1946); and the telling handkerchiefs in Henry, *Out of Wedlock*, 25, and in Richard Wright, "Long Black Song" (1938).

61. I agree with Jonathan Little's argument, advanced in his dissertation and in his essay, "Charles Johnson's Revolutionary 'Oxherding Tale,'" *Studies in American Fiction* 19.2 (Autumn 1991): 141–51, that Charles Johnson's work constitutes a new departure in interracial representation. In the genre of modernist drama, Adrienne Kennedy's work may constitute a similar achievement.

62. For example, the substitution of Pliny's *Natus Æthiopus* motif in which adultery was suspected by Kate Chopin's choice of making the mother's race only suspect in "The Father of Désirée's Baby," or Durham's use of the phrase "call of the blood" in the sense of the knocking of the "race instinct," whereas for Azevedo the phrase "call of the blood" referred to libido and not to any descent claims.

## Chapter Eight. Excursus on the "Tragic Mulatto"

1. *Soliloquies in England and Later Soliloquies* (New York: Scribner's, 1922), 134–35; reprinted in *Tragedy: Vision and Form*, ed. Robert W. Corrigan, 2nd ed. (New York: Harper & Row, 1981), 75.

2. (rpt., New York: Macmillan, 1950), 95–96.

3. "Chi," in *Harlem Gallery* (New York: Twayne, 1965), 146.

4. I. F. Castelli, "Die Verlassenschaft des Pflanzers," in *Erzählungen*, vol. 4: *Sämmtliche Werke*, vol. 8 (Wien: Mayer & Compagnie, 1848), 85–110. Paul Foucher and Laurencin's drama *Maria* (1839) may constitute a transition between the two modes: when "Lucy Dolsey" confesses to her suitor Albert de Prével, in the climactic seventh scene of act two, that she is really the slave woman Maria, Albert reacts with a body movement to the fact that she is the daughter of a Mulatto woman from Cayenne and a European father, but he responds more strongly and with anger when she describes how her past slave status included working under the brutal hand of an overseer. Lucy/Maria's supplication to Albert inspired the engraver to produce the frontispiece.

5. *Black and White: A Drama in Three Acts* (New York: DeWitt, n.d.), 4.

6. *Negro in American Fiction*, 43.

7. *Negro Poetry and Drama*, 110.

8. *Negro in American Fiction*, 46.

9. Ibid., 139, 141, on Jessie Fauset, on whom he also comments critically that she "records a class in order to praise a race" (142).

10. "The Negro in Drama," in *Negro Poetry and Drama*, 113.

11. *Negro in American Fiction*, 46. This feature is tied to Brown's insistence upon realism, and the combined force of his aesthetic is also palpable when he criticizes Zora Neale Hurston's *Mules and Men* (1935), though some tales of hers "are a delight to read," because "there seem to be omissions" and the "picture is too pastoral." *Negro in American Fiction*, 160–61.

12. *Negro Poetry and Drama*, 109; *Negro in American Fiction*, 43.

13. "Negro Character as Seen by White Authors," 160.

14. Ibid.

15. *Negro in American Fiction*, 45.

16. "Negro Character as Seen by White Authors," 161–62.

17. "The Negro in Drama," in *Negro Poetry and Drama*, 113. See also Brown's "A Century of Negro Portraiture," in *Black and White in American Culture*, eds. Jules Chametzky and Sidney Kaplan (Amherst: Univ. of Massachusetts Press, 1969), 339, with the argument that antislavery authors used the Tragic Mulatto in "an attempt to win readers' sympathies by presenting central characters who were physically very like the readers."

18. The strongest assertion of racial difference in representation was made in 1941, when Brown cosigned the introduction to *The Negro Caravan: Writings by American Negroes*, eds. Sterling A. Brown, Arthur P. Davis, and Ulysses Lee (1941; rpt., New York: Arno Press, 1970), 5–6:

> In the literature of American Negroes, these favorite stereotypes do not often appear. The self-effacing black mammy, the obsequious major-domo, the naïve folk, and the exotic primitive, to name instances, are seen from a different point of view and are presented with a different stress. This is not the same as denial of the existence of Negroes who resemble and serve as bases for the stereotyping. But Negro writers feel justly that these stereotypes have received far more attention than their importance in the total picture warrants, and that, being stereotypes, they are superficial, resulting from memory more than from observation and understanding. Negro authors write of their kinsfolk, their friends, the people with whom they rub shoulders daily. They find it hard to believe that these characters are as simplified as much literature has made them. And they know so many types of Negroes who have never found places in the books.

In "A Century" (first published in 1966), however, Brown regretted how some contemporary "Negro authors have turned the story around; now after restless searching, [the female Tragic Mulatto] finds peace only after returning to her own people"—which, Brown states, makes the figure just as much of a "lost, unhappy, woebegone abstraction" as the Tragic Mulatto had been in white writing (340).

19. This is also the finding in intellectual enterprises independent of Brown. For example, Bitterli, *Die "Wilden,"* 359, writes that the interest shown by Europeans in the figure of the Mulatto woman was not a sign of the absence of prejudice but, on the contrary, a demonstration of European egocentrism. Bitterli invokes Roger Bastide, *Le Prochain et le lointain* (Paris, 1970). See also David W. Levy, "Racial Stereotypes in Antislavery Fiction," *Phylon* 31 (1970): 265–79, an

informative essay which focuses on the distinction between the representation of black and mixed-race characters but does not draw on Brown.

20. Brown was used by numerous pioneering critics in the field, including Berzon, Bone, Bullock, Gloster, Jackson, Kinney, Mencke, and Starke (who sees the figure as one of the oldest archetypes in American fiction). Many later writers have extended his argument without citing him directly. For a good historical account of imagological work before and after Brown, see Seymour L. Gross, "Introduction: Stereotype to Archetype: The Negro in American Literary Criticism," *Images of the Negro in American Literature*, ed. Gross and John Edward Hardy (Chicago: Univ. of Chicago Press, 1966), 1–26.

21. Gloster, 17. In the thematic category of "miscegenation," however, Gloster differed somewhat from Brown.

22. Bone, *The Negro Novel*, 23.

23. "A Golden Mean for the Negro Novel," *College Language Association Journal* 3.2 (Dec. 1959): 81–87, here, 82. Jackson, 84–85, continues with a specifically pointed critique of Fauset's work, since "Miss Fauset" alone is responsible for having written four of ten works in the Harlem Renaissance "in which the concept of the tragic mulatto appears." Her error is summarized as follows: "She is moving, as it were, from the top down, pretending, really, that her Negroes are actually upper-class people who do the middle class a favor by identifying themselves with it" (85).

24. Berzon, 99. Yellin, *Women and Sisters*, 197n52, asserts that black writers presented a different tragic mulatto. Carolyn Karcher, *The First Woman in the Republic: A Cultural Biography of Lydia Maria Child* (London and Durham: Duke Univ. Press, 1994), 336, views both Rosalie and Xarifa as prototypes of the Tragic Mulatto and cites Cassy's tale in *Uncle Tom's Cabin* as wells as Brown's *Clotel* among the stories that were generated by it.

25. Jacqueline Y. McLendon, "The Myth of the Mulatto Psyche: A Study of the Works of Jessie Fauset and Nella Larsen" (Ph.D. diss., Case Western Reserve, 1986), 7–8.

26. Richard Yarborough, "Ideology and Black Characterization in the Early Afro-American Novel" (ms., University of California, Los Angeles, 1988), ch. 2, p. 62.

27. Pratt, 100.

28. Ellen Peel, 230, 231. Yet would not Armand be a better candidate for the "Tragic Mulatto" in the terms of Peel's reading of the story?

29. Elfenbein, 3, 5.

30. "Notes on an Alternative Model—Neither/Nor," 165, 167.

31. Lauren Berlant, "National Brands/National Body: *Imitation of Life*," in Hortense Spillers, ed., *Comparative American Identities* (New York and London: Routledge, 1991), 113; cited in Diana Roberts, *The Myth of Aunt Jemima: Representations of Race and Region* (London and New York: Routledge, 1994), 158.

32. Mary Anne Ferguson, "Identifying the Stereotypes," *Images of Women in Literature* (Boston: Houghton Mifflin, 1973), 6

33. *OED*; C. Hugh Holman, *A Handbook of Literature*, 3rd ed. (New York: Odyssey Press, 1972), 508–9; *Webster's New Twentieth Century Dictionary*, 2nd ed. (New York: Collins, 1978), 1785.

34. Alain Locke, ed., *The New Negro: An Interpretation* (1925; rpt., Salem, N.H.: Ayer, 1986), 3, 4.

35. *Negro Caravan*, 3. Brown's hand is recognizable in the reiteration of his argument: "Abolitionist authors yielded also to the habit of stereotyping. Besides their idealized victims, they also created the "white slave," the tragic mulatto, who to most abolitionists seemed to be more tragically doomed than darker fellow bondsmen. Later writers have also emphasized, to an even greater degree, the woes of Negroes of mixed blood" (4). A few pages later, William Stanley Braithwaite uses the word "stereotype" in "The Negro in American Literature" in a similar way (29).

36. The same texts may, of course, contain stereotypical and nonstereotypical materials, as well as racialist and unbiased sequences. The recurrence of descriptive details alone cannot be seen as constitutive of the Tragic Mulatto complex. Jacquelyn McLendon has pointed out that Alice Walker uses numerous physical descriptions that resemble those of the Tragic Mulatto tradition. For example, in the short story "The Child Who Favored Daughter," she writes about Daughter's niece: "The long dark hair curls in bits about her ears and runs in corded plainness down her back." And her skin is "full of copper tints and her arms are like long golden fruits that take in and throw back the hues of the sinking sun." McLendon also stresses that Daughter and her niece "meet tragic ends because of their desire for white men." *In Love & Trouble: Stories of Black Women* (New York: Harcourt Brace Jovanovich, 1967), 41. Cited and discussed in Jacquelyn Y. McLendon, "The Myth of the Mulatto Psyche: A Study of the Works of Jessie Fauset and Nella Larsen" (Ph.D. diss., Case Western Reserve, 1986), 182.

37. Kinney, 47.

38. Lydia Maria Child, Letter to Louisa Loring, 15 Jan. 1847 (about a letter from Caroline Gilman, requesting help for the Mulatto grandchild of the Marquis de Lafayette), in *Selected Letters, 1817–1889*, eds. Milton Meltzer and Patricia G. Holland, assoc. ed., Francine Krasno (Amherst: Univ. of Massachusetts Press, 1982).

39. *Negro Caravan*, 6.

40. The excerpts are taken from Harriet Beecher Stowe, *Uncle Tom's Cabin*, 315 (ch. 23, Augustine St. Clare); William Wells Brown, *Clotel*, 211 (narrator); Pauline Hopkins, *Contending Forces*, 87 (narrator).

41. Hoffmann, *Le Nègre*, 231–33.

42. Beane, "The Characterization of Blacks and Mulattoes in Selected Novels from Colombia, Venezuela, Ecuador and Peru" (Ph.D. diss., University of California, Berkeley, 1980), 81–82.

43. J. H. Nelson, *Negro Character*. Zanger, 64–66, also points this out, as does Elfenbein, 5. Nelson was also among the first American literary critics to ascribe the curse of Ham to Jewish origins. Nelson's book is biased but very well researched and includes an informative section on the image of blacks in literary texts from antiquity to modern Europe.

44. J. H. Nelson, 55. He is referring to Barrett Wendell's dismissal of Longfellow's abolitionist poetry in *A Literary History of America* (New York: Scribner's, 1900), 388: "one may fairly doubt whether in all antislavery literature there is a more humorous example of the way in which philanthropic dreamers often constructed negroes by the simple process of daubing their own faces with burnt cork." Wendell made similar comments on *Uncle Tom's Cabin* (355) and on minstrel shows (510).

45. J. H. Nelson, 83–84; see Brown, *Negro in American Fiction*, 45.

46. Wendell and Nelson both clearly supported stable racial boundaries (which the Mulatto character may threaten). Nelson believed that "no nation except our own has made a masterful presentation of the negro in literature" citing "our ablest Southern writers," white, one presumes (14). Brown, in "A Century," 339, criticized Nelson explicitly.

47. Alain Locke, "American Literary Tradition and the Negro," *Modern Quarterly* 3.3 (May–July 1926): 215–22, here 217–18. Surveying the obsession with the "problem of miscegenation" in the Late Reconstruction period, "a time when there was less of it than at any period within a century and a quarter" (220), Locke finds the Mulatto, "the skeleton in the family closet," "trotted out for attention in scrutiny" in works from Howells's *An Imperative Duty* to Stribling's *Birthright*, in which "the typical and dominant figure of literary interest is the mulatto as a symbol of social encroachment, and the fear of some 'atavism of blood' through him working vengeance for slavery" (221). Locke has highest hopes for the literature of the 1920s and its possible realization of the "artistic potentialities of Negro life" in such authors as Waldo Frank, Jean Toomer, Walter White, Rudolph Fisher, and Du Bose Heyward (222).

48. Zanger, 66. Zanger also argued interestingly that the villain of female Tragic Mulatto stories often was a Yankee parvenu who would attempt to take possession of the beautiful Octoroon in order to triumph over her pseudo-aristocratic father.

49. Daphne Patai and Murray Graeme MacNicoll, "Introduction" to Aluísio Azevedo, *Mulatto* (Rutherford: Fairleigh Dickinson Univ. Press, 1990), 21–22.

50. Vauthier, "Textualité et stéréotypes," 88, 89.

51. Arbery, 54, 55.

52. "Introduction" to *Iola Leroy* (1987), xxi–xxii. Carby also questions two underlying premises of the Tragic Mulatto stereotype approach, "first, that the prime motivation for writing was to counter negative images; and second, that social conventions determine the use of literary conventions." See also Houston Baker, *Workings of the Spirit: The Poetics of Afro-American Women's Writing* (Chicago: Univ. of Chicago Press, 1991), 25, and Ann duCille, "'Who Reads Here?' Back Talking with Houston Baker," *Novel* (Fall 1992): 99–100.

53. Stetson, 37–38.

54. See the narrator in Mayne Reid, *The Quadroon* (1856), "why did I not love Eugénie?" (102); and Salem Scudder on Zoe in Dion Boucicault, *The Octoroon* (1859), "When she goes along, she just leaves a streak of love behind her" (5) and "She's won this race agin the white," on Dora Sunnyside, however, "she's a little too thoroughbred—too much of the greyhound" (22).

55. Sánchez-Eppler, 244.

56. Yellin, *Women and Sisters*, 198. It would be interesting to pursue the tradition of Mulatto figures who are attractive to *black* characters.

57. Gerald Early, "'A Servant of Servants Shall He Be,'" 97n8; William L. Andrews, "Introduction," *Three Classic African-American Novels* (New York: Mentor, 1990), 16; Dearborn, 139; Roy, 21.

58. Vauthier, "(Non-)famille romanesque," 174–75.

59. It is not uncommon in the critical literature that authors first suggest the Mulatto as figure of mediation and then proceed to write separate chapters about "black treatments" and "white treatments" of the theme that supposedly makes questionable the either/or approach to race.

60. Roy, 8. Roy illustrates this wide variety throughout her thesis, which is organized so as to follow a historical development from the pre–Civil War period to World War II. She also carefully compares black and white authors for their differences and similarities, and although she describes some divergent strategies in the representation of interracial marriage in 19th-century (though not in 20th-century) literature, and of passing in modern (but not in 19th-century) writing, she ultimately finds "a lack of any clear demarcating-line between the white and the Black authors" (256).

61. *The Negro in American Fiction*, 46 and 8. Brown, Berzon, and Little emphasized Cooper, whereas Mencke and other critics have followed the belief in antislavery origin.

62. Stetson, 199. She adds: "Moreover, the mulatto motif is not and never was created for the sole purpose of adding yet another stereotyped image of blacks to the canon of American literature."

63. From this point of view Zanger's argument about the reversal of fortune theme in the Tragic Octoroon is plausible, though Gerald Early's criticism, in "'A Servant of Servants Shall He Be,'" 97n8, that wasn't the African free in his homeland and suddenly enslaved and forced to labor for someone else the best instance of a reversal of fortune, is also justified. In addition, stories of enslaved Africans, from *Oroonoko* to Prosper Mérimée's *Tamango*, were also very popular in aristocratic countries and among readers who were not used to excessive experience of social mobility.

64. Discussed in Yellin, *Intricate Knot*, 89–90, and mentioned in her *Women and Sisters*, 197n50.

65. Gustave de Beaumont, *Marie*, Eng. trans. Barbara Chapman (Stanford: Stanford Univ. Press, 1958), 66 and 60.

66. *Marie* may have served as a model not only to Séjour and Dumas, but also, since it was translated and serialized in the *National Anti-Slavery Standard* in 1845, for Boucicault's Zoe and Stowe's George; even Robert Penn Warren's Amantha Starr or Langston Hughes's Robert still seem to carry traces of Beaumont's characterization.

67. As Fredrik Barth writes in "Ethnic Groups and Boundaries" (1969), rpt. in *Theories of Ethnicity*, 303: "just as both sexes ridicule the male who is feminine, and all classes punish the proletarian who puts on airs, so also can members of all ethnic groups in a poly-ethnic society act to maintain dichotomies and differences." Thus considered, the Tragic Mulatto is a perfect target for the maintenance of black-white boundaries.

68. 306. Alain Locke, "Wisdom De Profundis," *Phylon* 9.1 (1950): 7, also argued more generally: "Basically these are tragedies only because of the traditional acceptance of false premises. Everything hinges on the impossibility of publicly admitting what every body knows to be true." Cited and discussed in Vauthier, "L'Image du noir," 781. See also Gillman in S. Samuels, 221–43.

69. Robert Bechthold Heilman, "Tragedy and Melodrama: Speculations on Generic Form," in *Tragedy: Vision and Form*, ed. Robert W. Corrigan, 2nd ed. (New York: Harper & Row, 1981), 205–15, here 214. One problem is that when tragedy and melodrama are juxtaposed as mutually exclusive extremes, this seems to be, in itself, a melodramatic antithesis. Some passages from the argument developed here have been taken from "'Never Was Born.' The Mulatto, An American Tragedy?" *Massachusetts Review* 27.2 (Summer 1986): 293–316.

70. Evans Wall, *The No-Nation Girl* (New York: Grosset & Dunlap, 1929),

171. For an even worse passage, see 181. This book may now be best known because it was denounced by Tragic Mulatto specialists.

71. See Hugo Dyserinck's useful distinction in "Zum Problem der 'images' und 'mirages' und ihrer Untersuchung im Rahmen der Vergleichenden Literaturwissenschaft," *Arcadia* 1 (1966): 107–20.

72. A Clytie may be a Clytemnestra, a Cassy a Cassandra in interracial literary naming; Oedipus appears twice in Azevedo's *O Mulato*. Tate, *The Fathers* contains an elaborate Jason and Medea story.

73. See, for example, Charles Chesnutt, "The Sheriff's Children," Langston Hughes, "Mulatto," or Adrienne Kennedy, "The Owl Answers."

74. "Crossing the Color Line," *Outlook and Independent* 158 (26 Aug. 1931): 526–43, here, 526; also cited in Washington, 113.

### Chapter Nine. Passing; or Sacrificing a *Parvenu*

1. (Rpt., New York: Arno Press, 1969), 44.
2. (Rpt., Boston: Beacon Press, 1990), 80.
3. *Independent* 75 (1913): 373.
4. *Saturday Review of Literature* (10 July 1926): 918.
5. The 1982 *Supplement* lists a whole number of examples, including Van Vechten. The original *OED* defines the verb "pass," in the sense II 5, as "to pass for, as." Examples include Shakespeare; Addison's 1711 *Spectator* phrasing, "I sometimes pass for a Jew in the Assembly of Stock-jobbers at Jonathan's" (I, p. 5); Harwill's definition from the 1935 *Dictionary of Modern American Usage*; some South African instances; an article in *Time* (16 Feb. 1948) that was based on *Ebony*; and another Jewish example from Mary McCarthy's novel *The Group* (1954):

> "Freddy's parents were trying to pass," [Norine] went on somberly. "Like so many rich German Jews. They sent him to Choate and Princeton, where he had a searing experience with one of the clubs. When the club found out 'Rogers' was 'Rosenberg,' he was asked to resign."

(Rpt., New York: Signet, 1963), ch. 14, p. 352.

6. Stonequist, *Marginal Man*, 198–99. "Passing as Englishmen may occur for those light enough in colour, but this 'is bitterly resented by those left behind. It leaves Anglo-Indians a rabble without leaders,'" Stonequist, 15, citing *New York Times* (10 Sept. 1932). See also the Kipling story "Kidnapped," discussed in Chapter Five on "Fingernails," and the Jewish passer's life story cited in Stonequist (195–98). For American Jewish tales of passing, see Jaky Solomon who turns into Jacques Hollins in Anzia Yezierska's *Salome of the Tenements* (1923) or Harry Gallen who becomes Henry Gallant in Samuel Ornitz's *Bride of the Sabbath* (1951). Sui Sin Far, in her "Leaves From the Mental Portfolio of an Eurasian," *Independent* 66, no. 3138 (21 January 1909): 131, mentions her sister Winnifred Eaton's attempt to "pass as Japanese." Hisaye Yamamoto, in the story "Wilshire Bus" (1950), in *Seventeen Syllables and Other Stories* (Latham, N.Y.: Kitchen Table Women of Color Press, 1988), 36, mentions "I AM CHINESE" buttons worn by Japanese Americans during World War II.

7. On white-to-black passing, see Nathan Irvin Huggins, *Harlem Renaissance* (New York: Oxford Univ. Press, 1971), 92–93; Huggins also discusses passing in a number of literary texts of the 1920s. There may be no absolute symmetry in

black-white and white-black passing. As Eric Lott has also observed in the case of John Howard Griffin's *Black Like Me* (1961), the purpose of the white-black pass-er may not be the adoption of black culture in order to get accepted as black by blacks, but rather the gathering of information in order to address whites. This may be true for Waldo Frank's trip South with Jean Toomer for the writing of *Holiday* (1923); but it definitely applies to Grace Halsell, *Soul Sister* (1969), and its derivation *Superman's Girl Friend Lois Lane*, issue #106 (Nov. 1970): "I Am Curi-ous (Black)." White passing for black has generated its own parodistic counter-genre such as Eddie Murphy's marvelous *Saturday Night Live* skit "White Like Me," and the Dorothea character in Armistead Maupin's *Tales of the City*. See also Zora Neale Hurston's sarcastic comment, reprinted from an unpublished chap-ter in the Univ. of Illinois Press edition of *Dust Tracks on a Road*, that James Wel-don Johnson was "a man white enough to suit Hitler" who has been "passing for colored for years" "but he just hasn't made it." "Watch him! Does he parade when he walks? No, he smiles. He couldn't give a grin if he tried. He can't even Uncle Tom."

For cases of musicians, see Burton Peretti's discussion of Johnny Otis (also mentioned in Chapter Five); Mezz Mezzrow and Bernard Wolfe, *Really the Blues* (1946); or Jelly Roll Morton.

E. Franklin Frazier, *The Negro Family in the United States* (Chicago: Univ. of Chicago Press, 1939), 254–55, notes the case of two white girls who, in order not to be separated from their colored half-sisters, "identified themselves with the colored race." A white illegitimate son of one of these daughters by a white planter also "was identified with the colored group and . . . married into the mulatto community." R. Roberts, "Negro-White Intermarriage: A Study in Social Control" (M.A. thesis, University of Chicago, 1940), found several cases of white partners in mixed marriages who attempted to conceal their white birth and claimed membership in the Negro community. Myrdal, 138n26, writes, cit-ing Wirth and Goldhamer:

> The only white passers the author has personally observed were two cases of white women married to Negro men, who found it convenient to call themselves Negroes. Donald Young informs us: ". . . occasionally persons of unmixed white ancestry have deliberately passed themselves off as Negroes, presumably in the main because of a preference for Negro asso-ciations and for employment opportunities, as in a colored orchestra." (Research Memorandum on Minority Peoples in the Depression, p. 28.) Sometimes white orphans have been brought up in Negro households and voluntarily retain the caste status of their foster parents.

Wirth and Goldhamer, 305, write: "Day reports that of the 35 persons who passed from the 346 families she studied the majority were married to white per-sons." The most widely disseminated literary scene of a person passing for black in order not to violate miscegenation statutes may be the moment in Edna Fer-ber's novel *Show Boat* (1926)—a moment included in Jerome Kern and Oscar Hammerstein's musical *Show Boat* (1927) and in the Hollywood film version—at which Steve Baker claims to have black blood in him when the Mississippi sheriff investigates him and his wife Julie. (Steve is telling the truth, though not in the sense the sheriff believes.)

For an imaginary affirmative action case with a protagonist who pretends to be black in order to get a fellowship at the Harvard Law School, see the unconvincing film *Soul Man* (1985).

8. Carl Van Vechten, *Nigger Heaven* (1926; 14th printing New York: Knopf, 1928), 286. Reuter, *Race Mixture*, 55, writes: "A larger or smaller number of mixed-blood individuals escape the classification by passing as white persons." In Baker's book of 1908 he specifically contemplates the terminology when he writes that he once asked a very light mulatto why he did not "cross the line," as they call it (or "go over to white") and quit his people (161). And although he quotes a Negro saying about a light-complexioned man, "Thank God, he is passing now for white" (158), Baker puts only the phrase "crossing the line" into the index of his book. George Schuyler's novel *Black No More* (1931) uses the word in quotation marks, as does Caroline Bond Day's *A Study of Some Negro-White Families in the United States* (1932). Thus Schuyler's narrator, who also articulates the ironies in the term, describes two men

> who eyed the beautiful little octoroon appreciatively as they bowed, thinking how easily she could "pass for white," which would have been something akin to a piece of anthracite coal passing for black. (56)

And Bond Day states:

> Dominant mulattoes and 5/8 individuals are frequently mistaken for foreigners of various nationalities, or for white Americans, and, as has been said, I know of no case of a quadroon who could not easily "pass for white." (10; also cited in Williamson, *New People*, 126)

The alternative expression "crossing over" is also used, as it was in Elmer A. Carter, "Crossing Over," *Opportunity* (Dec. 1926): 376–78, and, again, in Schuyler's *Black No More*.

9. Wirth and Goldhamer, 301.

10. Roy, 15.

11. *New People*, 100.

12. Wirth and Goldhamer, 307: "the major objective condition necessary for passing is anonymity. This condition is fully provided in the modern world by the presence of numerous urban centers and by the spatial mobility of the individual." Cf.: "Either for victim or criminal there is no place of concealment so safe as the crowded haunts of the populous city; and in New Orleans—half of which consists of a 'floating' population—incognito is especially easily to be preserved." Mayne Reid, *The Quadroon* (1856; rpt., with subtitle *or, Adventures in the Far West*, London: Routledge, n.d.), 379–80. The narrator says this when he thinks of escaping to New Orleans with his racially mixed beloved Aurore.

13. Fannie Barrier Williams, "Perils of the White Negro," *Colored American Magazine* 13 (Dec. 1907): 421, writes: "Comeliness, culture, genius, wealth, conquering forces when otherwise applied, count for nothing as against the merest, and often unsupported hint of the presence of Negro blood in an individual."

14. Stonequist, *Marginal Man*, 194, 198. See Carla K. Bradshaw in Shirlee Taylor Haizlip, "Passing," here 48. See also Barth, in *Theories of Ethnicity*, 316.

15. "The Mulatto Motif in Black Fiction" (Ph.D. diss., SUNY Buffalo, 1976), 156. See also "God made him, and therefore let him pass for a man" from Shakespeare's *Merchant of Venice* I.ii.61, cited, for example, in Magnus Hirschfeld, *Racism* (London: Gollancz, 1938), 103.

16. Mary C. Waters, *Ethnic Options: Choosing Identities in America* (Berkeley: Univ. of California Press, 1990), 18–19. Molefi Kete Asante recently took a situation similar to the one Mary Waters analyzed in order to argue against the self-definition of racially mixed Americans: to claim, for example, a partly German heritage for black Americans may be "a correct statement of biological history but is of no practical value in the American political and social context. There is neither a political nor a social definition within the American society for such a masquerade." "Racism, Consciousness, and Afrocentricity," in Early, *Lure and Loathing*, 142.

When he commented upon the intermarriage case of William E. Jackson and Helen Burns in 1925, in the course of which Jackson was determined to be "colored" (see below), W. E. B. Du Bois, cited in "Wedding of Wm. E. Jackson and White New Jersey Girl Probably Deferred," New York *Amsterdam News* (11 Nov. 1925), used this occasion to stress the difference between "Jewish" and "black" racial definition in the United States: "I see the whole question of Jackson's color as the stupid prejudice of people who should know better. If I were one-eighth Jew nobody would insist that I declare myself a Jew. The Semitic people, however, are almost as distinct from the Aryan race as the Negro."

17. Anna Dickinson, *What Answer?* (1868; rpt., Boston: Fields, Osgood, 1869), 196–97. See also Mark Twain's description of Roxy, cited in Chapter Four, "The Calculus of Color," which continues, "She was a slave, and salable as such."

18. W. J. Nelson, "Racial Definition." In Captain Frederick Marryat's vignette of slavery in *A Diary in America, With Remarks on Its Institutions* (1838; rpt., New York: Colyer, 1839), 192, the children of a slaveholder find out that "having been born of a slave, and not manumitted, they were *in reality* slaves themselves" (my emphasis). Under slavery, however, matrilineage complicated hypodescent rule. As we shall see, it is probable that the term "passing" comes from slavery times. In Jessie Fauset's *Plum Bun* (1929), 137, the connections between passing and slavery are explicitly established, as Angela Murray reaps the benefits of whiteness: "In a country where colour or the lack of it meant the difference between freedom and fetters how lucky she was!" Nelson's concept of the "hypodescent" society deserves to be compared with George Devereux's notion of a "hypercathected identity" in his "Ethnic Identity: Its Logical Foundation and Its Dysfunctions" (1975), reprinted in *Theories of Ethnicity: A Classical Reader*, ed. Werner Sollors (Basingstoke: Macmillan, 1996), 385–414.

19. Zack, 146.

20. See Frances E. W. Harper, *Iola Leroy: or, Shadows Uplifted* (1893; rpt., Boston: Beacon Press, 1987), 203; Oscar Micheaux, *The Masquerade* (1947); Lydia Maria Child, *A Romance of the Republic* (1867), 277; Albion Tourgée, *A Royal Gentleman* (1881), 369; Azevedo, *O Mulato* (1881), 227; Williams, 423; Pauli Murray, "Mulatto's Dilemma," *Opportunity* 16 (June 1938): 180; Zack, 146; Asante in Early, *Lure and Loathing*, 142; Funderburg, 16; Rhinelander trial transcript, 1352, cited in Wacks, 29–35.

21. Chesnutt's story "The Wife of His Youth" may be seen as making a powerful case for Ryder acknowledging 'Liza Jane, precisely because that endangers his social standing. See also Naomi Zack's comment on the "morally good" and "admirable" acceptance of monoracial categories, cited in the Introduction.

22. Hence one alternative to "passing" is leaving the social system in which these rules apply.

23. Only the assumption of such stability makes some racial jokes work, for example, the Jim Crow era story of the black passenger in the white railroad car who explains, "I done quit the race" (considered an impossibility). Such a presumption of stability—which makes "passing" so different a social phenomenon from the process of ennoblement by which the aristocracy was constantly enlarged—may be all the more desirable as other certainties have been waning under modernity; thus Charles Johnson has argued that art produced on the grounds of presumed racial certainty may be "a retreat from ambiguity, the complexity of Being occasioned by the conflict of interpretations, and a flight by the black artist from the agony of facing a universe silent as to its sense, where even black history (or all history) must be seen as an ensemble of experiences and documents difficult to read, indeed, as an experience capable of inexhaustible readings." This short-circuiting to certainty provided by "race" is more likely to generate kitsch than art. *Being & Race: Black Writing Since 1970* (Bloomington and Indianapolis: Indiana Univ. Press, 1988), 20.

24. Stonequist, *Marginal Man*, 194.

25. Wirth and Goldhamer, 303.

26. The most famous example is Walter White, who in "The Negro and the American Tradition," in *The New Negro*, ed. Alain Locke (1925; rpt., Salem, N.H.: Ayer, 1986), 365, writes about his experience "of investigating some thirty-seven lynchings and eight race riots by the simple method of *not* telling those whom I was investigating of the Negro blood in my veins." White also makes the distinction there between permanent and occasional passing. See also White's "I Investigate Lynchings" in *The Negro Caravan*, eds. Sterling Brown, Arthur P. Davis, and Ulysses Lee (1941; rpt., New York: Arno Press, 1970), 1005–17.

27. Wirth and Goldhamer, 301; Williamson, *New People*, 101 (about Charles Chesnutt); "Life Story" from *Independent* in Wirth and Goldhamer. Spickard, 334, speaks of "unintentional" passing.

28. Wirth and Goldhamer, 301. The involuntary form of passing is often a borderline case.

29. It may be planned, for example, by the father and uncovered by the stepmother as in Spencer's "Tristan," or brought about by a Roxy or an Aunt Katy (in Pickens: the grandmother) as a switch of look-alike boys. And though his story remains marginal in Walter White's novel *Flight* (1926), 182, Petit Jean is raised without knowledge of his racial antecedents according to the decision of his mother Mimi Daquin.

30. Williamson, *New People*, 101. Wirth and Goldhamer, 302–3, "permanent," but "only for special segments of . . . life activities."

31. Reuter, *Race Mixture*, 56. The more openly passing is undertaken, the more it becomes another borderline case as this increasingly implies a socially condoned activity.

32. Roy, 169.

33. Frazier notes that, on the one hand, among Negroes who pass "those who feel an inner conflict despite their physical and cultural identification with whites remain as unassimilated as the dark Negroes. On the other hand, there are mixed bloods who have identified themselves inwardly with whites and have become

assimilated in the white race. The children of such people have no history or memories to connect them with Negroes." E. Franklin Frazier, *The Negro in the United States* (New York: Macmillan, 1957), 690, cited in McLendon, 34n14.

34. "White, but Black," *Century* 109 (1924–25): 492–99.

35. "The Adventures of a Near-White," *Independent* 75 (1913): 373–76.

36. Wirth and Goldhamer, 310, invoking "The Adventures of a Near-White," and "White, but Black."

37. *Invented Lives: Narratives of Black Women 1860–1960* (New York: Doubleday, 1987), 164. Mary Helen Washington characterizes Nella Larsen's choice of the theme of passing as a reflection of her "failure to deal with the problem of marginality." Washington continues:

> "Passing" is an obscene form of salvation. The woman who passes is required to deny everything about her past: her girlhood, her family, places with memories, folk customs, folk rhymes, her language, the entire long line of people who have gone before her.

38. George De Vos, "Ethnic Pluralism: Conflict and Accommodation," in *Ethnic Identity: Cultural Continuities and Change*, ed. George De Vos and Lola Romanucci-Ross (Stanford: Mayfield, 1975), 28–29.

39. Hopkins, 430–31; Johnson, 210, 211; see Davis, 295.

40. Nathan Irvin Huggins, *Harlem Renaissance* (New York: Oxford Univ. Press, 1971), 159.

41. Davis, Gardner, and Gardner, 42. Washington, *Invented Lives*, 164, also stresses that the word "passing" may "connote death—in the black community dying is often referred to as 'passing.'" In Chesnutt's *House Behind the Cedars* (1900) the word "passing" in Rena's letter to George Tryon, 233, also signals death. Phrasings such as "crossing over" or "going over to the other side" may, of course, also denote dying.

42. For example, Jessie Fauset, *Comedy: American Style* (1933; rpt., College Park, M.D.: McGrath Publishing, 1969), 224–25.

43. Williams, 422, wrote this before the cresting of fictions on the subject. See Ottie B. Graham, "Holiday" (1923); or Hamilton Basso, *The View From Pompey's Head* (1954), 386, 392.

44. "Passing," in *The Ways of White Folks* (1934; rpt., New York: Vintage Books, 1962), 50.

45. Henry F. Downing, *The American Cavalryman: A Liberian Romance* (New York: Neale, 1917), 15; see the discussions in Bruce Payton Adams, 103.

46. John A. Williams, *Captain Blackman* (1972), 329, cited in Adams, 150: "In America, today, right now, there are at least thirty million Trojan Horses...."

47. In Funderburg, *Black, White, Other*, 79.

48. Adrian Piper, "Passing for White, Passing for Black," *Transition* 58 (1992): 14.

49. William S. Henry, *Out of Wedlock* (Boston: Richard G. Badger, 1931), 86.

50. Elmer A. Carter, "Crossing Over," *Opportunity* (Dec. 1926): 376–78.

51. *A Man Called White: The Autobiography of Walter White* (New York: Viking Press, 1948), 59; Schuyler's *Black No More* directly parodies the debates surrounding racial integrity acts.

52. According to Wirth and Goldhamer, 302, 303, such cases "presumably constitute only a small percentage of those who pass" and are "often accompa-

nied by marriage to a white spouse." And: "Although no reliable quantitative material is available, it appears that a considerable amount of passing is primarily motivated by a desire to secure better vocational opportunities."

53. I have not found a systematic historical account of the phenomenon of passing or its treatment in literature. The studies by Nathan I. Huggins and Joel Williamson remain pioneering, and the unpublished dissertations, most importantly, the one by Ratna Roy, as well as those by Bruce Payton Adams, John Francis Bayliss, Gayle Wald, and Kathleen Pfeiffer, are of value. Briefer discussions can be found in the books by Berzon, Kinney, and Mencke. It now seems customary to credit Frank Webb with the invention of the theme.

54. See *Maryland Journal and Baltimore Advertiser* (13 July 1787), in *Runaway Slave Advertisements: A Documentary History from the 1730s to 1790*, ed. Lathan A. Windley, vol. 2: *Maryland* (Westport, Conn., and London: Greenwood Press, 1983), 366; see also 422.

55. *The White Slave; or, Memoirs of a Fugitive* (Boston: Tappan and Whittemore, 1852), ch. ix, pp. 54–55. The 1836 edition (rpt., Upper Saddle River, N.J.: Gregg Press, 1968), 71–72, is nearly identical for this episode, though the phrasing in 1836 was that they will "attempt to pass off for white people." Hildreth probably had read real examples of advertisements such as this.

56. Capt. Marryat, C.B., *A Diary in America, With Remarks on Its Institutions* (1838; New York: Colyer, 1839), 191. The passage is followed by a discussion of Jefferson and other white fathers of slave children.

57. *Three Novels*, 129 (ch. 11).

58. See, for example, Charles Eliot, *Sinfulness of Slavery in the United States* (Cincinnati, 1857), II: 65, cited in Johnston, *Race Relations*, 192: "light sandy hair, blue eyes, ruddy complexion; he is so white as to easily pass for a white man," and compare Child, *Romance of the Republic* (1867), 322, and *Letters of Lydia Maria Child*, intro. John G. Whittier (Boston: Houghton, Mifflin, 1883), 126.

59. Since "passing" suggests a person who is both one thing and another, it is logical that the motif sometimes occurs in conjunction with that of the double. For example, an informant in Baker, *Following the Color Line*, 160, explained his double life in an explicit allusion to Robert Louis Stevenson's most famous tale of a double: "When I go back to Atlanta after an absence of two years, I can, if I wish, go back in a Pullman, go out of the main entrance of the station, get my dinner at the Piedmont Hotel, and when I am tired of being Mr. Hyde, I can stroll down Auburn Avenue with my friends in the full glory of Dr. Jekyll." The literature of passing includes stories in which two persons change places, encounter each other as mirror images of themselves, or recognize their interior doubleness. Black-white doubling was articulated in similar terms by Pauline Hopkins in *Contending Forces* (1900), 272, where Will Smith, the character modeled on W. E. B. Du Bois, speaks in "Defense of His Race": "Human nature is the same in everything. The characteristic traits of the master will be found in his dog. Black, devilish, brutal as they may picture the Negro to be, he but reflects the nature of his environments. *He is the Hyde who torments the Dr. Jekyll of the white man's refined civilization!*" (272). Hopkins thus casts the white as Hyde and the black as Jekyll.

60. See Berzon, 53; Kinney, 37; and Little, "Definition," 21–36. Among the many examples for Roy's "Heartbroken Mother Left Behind" are Lyle Saxon, *Children of Strangers* (1937) and John Bennett, *Madame Margot* (1921).

61. (New York: Popular Library, n.d.), 286–87, ch. 28. As we have already

seen, Child, *Romance*, uses the word "counterfeit" in connection with passing. The Cooper scene has aspects of what was to become minstrelsy, and in the U.S. the specific story of "passing for white" may have been preceded by minstrelsy— at the core of which was the acting out of a desire by white "delineators" (as they were called) to be taken for blacks; see Huggins, *Harlem Renaissance*, for a perceptive, pioneering discussion of minstrelsy; see also Eric Lott, *Love and Theft: Black-face Minstrelsy and the American Working Class* (New York and Oxford: Oxford Univ. Press). The crossover effect may have been enhanced in the cases in which white male minstrel artists played not only black men, but also black women. See Marjorie Garber, *Vested Interests: Cross-Dressing & Cultural Anxiety* (New York and London: Routledge, 1992), 275–81. It is noteworthy that even in this early instance there is no symmetry in passing from white to black: there is no need to win acceptance as black in the *black* world.

Another startling white-black transformation appears in Robert Montgomery Bird's novel *Sheppard Lee*, 2 vols. (New York: Harper and Brothers, 1836), the fantastic tale of the titular hero, a young white gentleman, who through metempsychosis enters various bodies, among them that of the Negro slave Tom (2:171).

62. See, for example, Harun al-Rashid's famous disguises "The Story of the Ensorceled Prince," in which this motif includes the variant of a white man's pretending to be a black man in a violent interracial adultery plot. Such disguises are also common in Renaissance novellas. At least one modern passing story, Caroline Bond Day's comic tale "The Pink Hat" (1926), directly incorporates the *Thousand and One Nights* tradition, as the narrator is taken for white due to the magic effect of a new hat that is likened to Aladdin's lamp and an enchanted cloak. See *Blacks at Harvard*, 177–80, esp. 179. And James Weldon Johnson develops the theme in his autobiography, *Along This Way* (New York: Viking, 1933). Granting that "all of us have at some time toyed with the Arabian Nights-like thought of the magical change of race," he still states that he does not wish to be anyone but himself, adding, however, that if a jinnee compelled him to change, he would probably answer, "Make me a Jew" (136).

63. 21; ch. 5. It may only be the nature of this investigation that makes the reader take special notice of Hugo's use of pass (*passez*), but the Hughes text also opens with the son "passing" the mother. In fact, many texts about racial passing seem to make a point of using the word "pass" in other senses as well.

64. "New Orleans," "Creole," and "orphan" are three categories that invite thinking of the discovery of blackness in interracial literature.

65. Translated for the *National Anti-Slavery Standard* (25 Sept. 1845): 68. See also the more recent English translation by Barbara Chapman, *Marie; or, Slavery in the United States* (Stanford, Calif.: Stanford Univ. Press, 1958). See also Yellin, *Intricate Knot*, 89–90. For the original text, see *Marie; ou, L'Esclavage aux états-unis* (Paris: Charles Gosselin, 1840), 91–92.

66. In the essay "Art and Fortune" (1948), in *The Liberal Imagination: Essays on Literature and Society* (Garden City, N.Y.: Doubleday Anchor Books, 1953), 253, Lionel Trilling included a longer footnote in which he wondered but ultimately doubted whether ethnicity provided an American substitute, or equivalent, for the function of class in the European novel of manners. Briefly mentioning the case of American attitudes toward minorities such as blacks or Jews, Trilling answered his question in the negative: "It involves no real cultural strug-

gle, no significant conflict of ideals, for the excluded group has the same notion of life and the same aspirations as the excluding group, although the novelist who attempts the subject naturally uses the tactic of showing that the excluded group has a different and better ethos; and it is impossible to suppose that the novelist who chooses this particular subject will be able to muster the satirical ambivalence toward both groups which marks the good novel even when it has a social *parti pris*." However, at least for the cultural analogies between passer and *parvenu*, this is plausible—though the theme of racial passing seems to come from French texts that American writers only continued and though comparisons between novels of passing and of upward mobility could be fruitful.

67. James, *The Portrait of a Lady*, ed. Robert D. Bamberg (New York: Norton, 1975), 525 and 197 (I: ch. 22). James replaced this reference when he revised the novel for the New York edition by the following phrase: "but he suggested, fine gold coin as he was, no stamp or emblem of the common mintage that provides for general circulation; he was the elegant complicated medal struck off for a special occasion." Perhaps James felt that the allusion to racial passing might have directed the reader too strongly into that direction. James had previously reviewed Rebecca Harding Davis's novel *Waiting for the Verdict* and commented on Anna E. Dickinson's *What Answer?*. See his *Essays on Literature: American Writers, English Writers* (New York: Library of America, 1984), 218–29.

Some novels from *Marie* to *Plum Bun* have thematically intertwined or contrasted stories of *parvenus* with those of characters who cross the racial divide. See especially the Jewish parallels in texts about black-white racial passing. And in Willa Cather's novel *A Lost Lady* (1923; rpt., New York: Vintage, 1972), 92, Judge Pommeroy states: "In my day the difference between a business man and a scoundrel was bigger than the difference between a white man and a nigger." See Williamson, *Crucible of Race*, 665, and Kathleen Pfeiffer, "All the Difference: Race Passing and American Individualism" (Ph.D. diss., Brandeis University, 1994), 13.

68. *The House Behind the Cedars* (1900; rpt., Athens and London: Univ. of Georgia Press, 1988), 66.

69. *Folkways* (Boston: Ginn, 1906), section 112, "Antagonism between an individual and the mores," 107–8; partly cited in Stonequist, *Marginal Man*, 5.

Characters who are not racial "passers" but who do conceal their origins and live with a secret have continued to populate literature in the era of "passing." George Eliot's *Daniel Deronda* (1876; rpt., Oxford and New York: Oxford Univ. Press, 1986) could, in fact, be discussed as a novel of Jewish-Gentile passing—in which black-white interracial relations and half-bloods are also thematized in a conversation (279, ch. 29). One could also think of Thomas Hardy's *The Hand of Ethelberta* (1876). In F. Scott Fitzgerald's *The Great Gatsby* (1925), the transformation of Gatts to Gatsby and Tom Buchanan's racist diatribe against interracial marriage invite comparisons.

70. Stonequist, 6.

71. The character who crosses a racial boundary may elicit either more sympathy or a different kind of censure. Telling for this problem is the way in which Sinclair Lewis feels that he has to shift gears as he transforms Neil from a target of social criticism in *Kingsblood Royal* into a much more positively drawn character once he discovers his mixed race status (while his hypocritical wife remains white and targetable). In the 1924/25 Rhinelander case the lawyer developed a line of

argument against Alice Jones that implied that while "class deception was acceptable, race deception was reprehensible." See Jamie L. Wacks, "Reading Race," 1995, 29–34.

72. See Glenn Cannon Arbery, "Victims of Likeness: Quadroons and Octoroons in Southern Fiction," *Southern Review* 25.1 (Winter 1989): 52–71.

73. Beaumont, ch. 9, *National Anti-Slavery Standard* (25 Sept. 1845): 68.

74. Beaumont, ch. 8, *National Anti-Slavery Standard* (11 Sept. 1845): 60, and *National Anti-Slavery Standard* (18 Sept. 1845): 64. In this aspect, Marie is a precursor of Boucicault's Zoe and Chopin's Désirée.

75. Beaumont, ch. 10, *National Anti-Slavery Standard* (16 Oct. 1845): 80.

76. As Hoffmann pointed out, the play by Paul Foucher and Laurencin [Paul-Aimé Chapelle], *Maria, drame en deux actes, mêlé de chant* (first performed on 3 March 1839 and first published by Marchant at Paris in the same year) presents the title heroine as a runaway slave from Guadeloupe, the daughter of a Mulatto woman from Cayenne and a European father. Maria is light-skinned enough to pass for white; she changes her name to Lucy Dolsey and is about to marry Albert de Prével, one of the most important white men on the island, when Frédéric Bréville recognizes her and wants to take her to Jamaica with him. This prompts Maria to confess to Albert. As in Beaumont, the theme of passing is connected with an interracial romance.

77. The first edition was entitled *The Slave; or, Memoirs of Archy Moore.* "White slave" was to become the subtitle and title of later editions; e.g., the 1852 version *The White Slave; or, Memoirs of a Fugitive.* Kinney (48) credits the second part of Hildreth's novel, first published in 1852, for having introduced the theme of passing; there Archy returns from Europe to Boston and New York with a British passport.

78. 48; ch. ix. This is in connection with the cross-dressing of Cassy as Archy's brother. See also 330, John Colter's account of Cassy.

79. In *Running*, 277, the narrator mentions the "sale of an engraving of my wife in the disguise in which she escaped." William and Ellen Craft, *Running a Thousand Miles for Freedom* (London: William Tweedie, 1860), reprinted in Bontemps, 289, also explains that Ellen's poultice, devised to camouflage the smoothness of her face, "is left off in the engraving, because the likeness could not have been taken well with it on."

80. Garber, *Vested Interests*, 284–85. The use of the masculine pronoun and the term "my master" to refer to Ellen Craft is framed by a narrative explanation: when the disguise is adopted in the public realm of the railroad, the narrator says, "my *master* (as I will now call my wife)" (294); at the end of part one, when the Crafts are in safety, William switches back in writing of Ellen as "my master—or rather my wife, as I may now say" (314). In *Uncle Tom's Cabin* (1852), little Harry is transformed into "Harriet." In William Wells Brown's novel *Clotel; or, The President's Daughter* (1853), the titular heroine becomes "Mr. Johnson" and is also referred to as "he" by the narrator. The black slave, also called William, tells Clotel that she could "easily pass for a free white lady" (167); she accepts the challenge, and cross-dresses in order to pass as a white man with William as her servant (a story line obviously inspired by the escape of the Crafts, though published seven years before the Crafts' narrative). Another famous instance of a cross-dressing on the color line is in *Pudd'nhead Wilson.* It could be interesting to compare racial and sexual crossings; see, for example, Paul Whitaker's statement on passing "as straight and white" in Funderburg, *Black, White, Other*, 218. One cul-

tural boundary often gets crossed in conjunction with another one: this is the case with race and sex as it is with fountain of youth fantasies, which often add class mobility (from rags to riches) to rejuvenation. Generally, characters who are represented as passing may represent a challenge not only to the color line but also to the distinction between men and women. The typically comic treatment of cross-dressing may also turn serious in such contexts.

81. *Liberty Bell* (Boston: National Anti-Slavery Bazaar, 1858), 136, 145, 155, 156.

82. Frank J. Webb. *The Garies and Their Friends* (1857; rpt., New York: Arno Press, 1969), 4. Further references to this edition will be incorporated into the text. Compare this episode to the bragging of Walter White's opposite number in McKay's narration about fingernails.

83. In her dissertation-in-progress, Rosemary Crockett stresses that Mr. Ellis, too, passes temporarily and socially.

84. This point occurs in other instances, e.g., in the passage from *The Autobiography of an Ex-Colored Man*, though he laughs about what Clarence suffers from:

> I frequently smiled inwardly at some remark not altogether complimentary to people of colour; and more than once I felt like declaiming: "I am a coloured man. Do I not disprove the theory that one drop of Negro blood renders a man unfit?" (197; also cited in Wirth and Goldhamer, 306)

Webb's representation of passing in tragic interracial courtship plot may have been the first of many such representations, though the part of Clarence would later often be taken by a mixed race woman.

85. Both George and Clarence are discussed in Roy, 43–44, who focuses on the conflict Clarence experiences between loyalty to the memory of his mother and a love relationship in his new (and racist) world under the formula "Heartbroken Mother Left Behind." See also Richard Yarborough, "Ideology and Black Characterization in the Early Afro-American Novel" (ms., University of California, Los Angeles, 1988).

86. James Weldon Johnson, *The Autobiography of an Ex-Colored Man* (1912; rpt., New York: Hill and Wang, 1960), 3. Further references to this edition will be made parenthetically in the text. I am using the spelling of the title of the first edition, though reprints starting with the 1927 edition have often used the English spelling of "Coloured." The opening of the novel is reminiscent of Edgar Allan Poe's "The Imp of the Perverse," in which an undetected murderer finally cannot resist the impulse to let the "long imprisoned secret burst forth from his soul" (Library of America edition, 831). In choosing anonymous publication Johnson may have been inspired by the first edition of Hildreth's *The Slave* (1836), which did not identify the author and carried the editor's advertisement informing the reader that the ms. had come into his hands "with an injunction to make it public."

87. Perhaps this is what Hazel Carby, "Introduction" to Harper's *Iola Leroy*, xxii, had in mind when she wrote that passing was "not fully explored in fiction" before Johnson.

88. *Along This Way: The Autobiography of James Weldon Johnson* (1933; rpt., New York: Viking, 1968), 238–39.

89. Springfield (Mass.) *Republican* (12 May 1912), JWJ collection.

90. *Nashville Tennessean* (23 June 1912); cited in Eugene Levy, *James Weldon*

*Johnson: Black Leader, Black Voice* (Chicago and London: Univ. of Chicago Press, 1973), 127.

91. *The Crisis* 5 (Nov. 1912): 28; cited in Levy, *James Weldon Johnson*, 127, and Eugenia Collier, "The Endless Journey of an Ex-Coloured Man," *Phylon* 32.4 (Winter, 1971): 365–73, here 363. The *New York Times* review, though subtitled "A Negro Who Passed as a White Tells His Life Story," took the story as an "astute, dispassionate study of the race problem," but mentioned the possibility that the book "may be merely the product of some whimsical imagination." "An Ex-Colored Man," *New York Times* (26 May 1912): 319. See also the review by Johnson's Columbia University teacher Brander Matthews, *Munsey's Magazine* 49 (Aug. 1913): 794–98.

92. The best discussion of ironic and autobiographic elements in the novel remains Joseph T. Skerrett, "Irony and Symbolic Action in James Weldon Johnson's *The Autobiography of an Ex-Coloured Man*," *American Quarterly* 32 (1980): 540–58.

93. Levy, *James Weldon Johnson*, 126–27, citing Johnson's letters to George Towns and Jack Nail.

94. "The Politics of Passing: The Fiction of James Weldon Johnson," *Negro American Literature Forum* 3.1 (Spring 1969): 22. According to Philippe Lejeune's categorical grid, Johnson's novel would pass as autobiography.

95. The tension between wishing to tell and not wishing to tell resembles that experienced by Clarence Garie.

96. See the perceptive discussion by Robert B. Stepto in *From Behind the Veil: A Study of Afro-American Narrative* (Urbana: Univ. of Illinois Press, 1979).

97. This passage was also cited in Wirth and Goldhamer, 306.

98. See Karl Baedeker, *The United States of America*, 4th ed. (Leipzig: Baedeker, 1909), 21, 44.

99. Angelina Dove's mother in Claude McKay's short story "Near-White" (1931) echoes this biblical phrasing from the story of Jacob and Esau (Gen. 25:22–34), 94, when she tells her daughter, "what's the use of selling your birthmark for a mess of pottage that might turn bitter-gall in your mouth afterwards?" On the motif of the "birthright," see Hildreth, 20 and 139; T. S. Stribling's novel *Birthright*; and the discussion of motif by Stetson.

100. Johnson's narrator was hardly exceptional when—despite all his self-styling as man between races—he writes about a white woman and her black companion in a rag-time club: "somehow I never exactly enjoyed the sight" (109).

101. See Barbara Antoniazzi, "Vernon Sullivan: A Modernist Invention" (ms., University of Venice, 1995). Boris Vian, "Préface," *J'irai cracher sur vos tombes* (Paris: La Trompinette, n.d.); and "Postface," *Les Morts ont tous la même peau* (1947; rpt., Paris: 10/18, 1973). My account follows Michel Rybalka, *Boris Vian: Essai d'interprétation et de documentation* (Paris: Lettres Modernes Minard, 1969), 98–113, and Noël Arnaud, *Les Vies parallèles de Boris Vian* (Paris: 10/18, 1970), 137–96. Vian read Herbert Asbury, "Who Is a Negro?," *Collier's* (3 Aug. 1946); and *Newsweek* featured him on 24 Feb. 1947, p. 104. *Romans, Nouvelles, Œuvres diverses*, ed. Gilbert Pestureau (Paris: Livre de Poche—La Pochotèque, 1991), reprints two Sullivan novels, *J'irai cracher sur vos tombes* (1946) and *Et on tuera les affreux* (1948).

102. *The Ways of White Folks* (1934; rpt., New York: Vintage Books, 1971),

49, 53. Other interesting short stories on passing include Caroline Bond Day. "The Pink Hat," *Opportunity* (Dec. 1926): 379–80, and Claude McKay, "Near-White," *Gingertown* (New York: Harper & Brother, 1932), 72–104. Though it would seem to be eminently theatrical, the theme of passing appears to have received weaker treatments in drama from Foucher and Laurencin, *Maria* (1839), to Ottie B. Graham, "Holiday," *Crisis* 26.1 (May 1923): 12–17.

103. Countée Cullen, from *Color* (New York: Harper and Brothers, 1925), reprinted in *My Soul's High Song: The Collected Writings of Countée Cullen*, ed. Gerald Early (New York: Anchor Book, 1991), 88–89.

104. Ernest Gruening, "Going White," *Saturday Review of Literature* (10 July 1926): 918, was struck by the "improbability of a husband—especially of the arch-conventional type—exhibiting no curiosity whatever about his wife's early life and her people."

105. From another point of view, however, it is a surprising move since Mimi spent crucial years in black Atlanta and decided to pass precisely because "the very intolerance of her own people had driven her from them" (212). The use of the phrase "her own people" here as in Mary Helen Washington's excerpt presumes, of course, that mixed-race people are already black, and the use of the word "aping" is unfortunate. Ernest Gruening, "Going White," *Saturday Review of Literature* (10 July 1926): 918, noted that Walter White thrusts "his cultured and intelligent Mimi into a burlesque of Babbittry" and calls it "'white' America." Calling attention to White's representation of black Atlanta as a version of *Main Street*, Gruening wondered whether Mimi's problem and White's theme would disappear if his "heroine had married into the white intelligentsia."

106. The novel contains many other references to Jews (e.g., 158, 289, 290).

107. Jessie Fauset, *Plum Bun* (1929; rpt., Boston: Beacon Press, 1990); references to this edition appear parenthetically in the text. Hugh Gloster, *Negro Voices in American Fiction* (1948; rpt., New York: Russell and Russell, 1965), 134, and Arthur Davis, *From the Dark Tower: Afro-American Writers 1900–1960* (Washington, D.C.: Howard Univ. Press, 1974), 90, have called attention to the theme of passing in *Plum Bun*, although Carolyn Wedin Sylvander, *Jessie Redmon Fauset, Black American Writer* (Troy, New York: Whitston, 1981), 175, criticizes them for overlooking Fauset's formal sophistication in this thematic approach to *Plum Bun* as a novel of passing.

108. It is worth noting that Virginia serves as a double for Angela: whereas Angela quests for exogamy, her sister remains closely connected to her parents and the world of her childhood. Symbolically what may thus also be at work in the differentiation between the sisters is the representation of miscegenation as a way of overcoming incest—even though this course of action may require the betrayal of the sister.

109. This gender division of passing goes back to the lineage from George and Marie in Beaumont and continues with Robert and Sallie/Bertha in Langston Hughes's *Mulatto*—whereas Webb had cast a young man, Clarence, in the part often played by mixed-race women. The theme is always intensified by the possibility of an interracial marriage or the choice between marriage and sexual liaison.

110. What is missing in Fauset's account is any mention of the white lover's response: whereas such novels as *The Garies and Their Friends*, *Caste*, *House Behind the Cedars*, or *Passing* focus in detail on the white lover's or husband's horrified

reaction at finding out the truth about the beloved, Fauset chooses not to represent Roger's story—just as White had not shown such a scene between Mimi and
Jimmie Forester. The first prize for such a melodramatic reaction probably goes
to William Ashby's novel *Redder Blood* (1915), in which Adrian, who has been
passing like his mother, is told by his romance, the white Wanda:

> You leper! You cancer in a man's form, you imp let loose from limbo! You
> deceived me. Acid-like you ate into my pure soul, knowing all the time
> what you were, knowing that you were black as midnight. Let me wipe
> away your kisses, let me tear my flesh from my frame. I was pure; your
> black skin has corrupted me, polluted me. Get out of my sight forever.

(New York: Cosmopolitan Press, 1915), 178; discussed in Mencke, 147–48.

111. The theme of passing is often clustered with that of the "double." See
Spencer's "Tristan" and Don Marquis's "Carter"—as well as Boris Vian's fiction—for obvious examples. The (homo)erotic attraction that Deborah McDowell called attention to may be connected to the rhetoric surrounding the theme of
the double: the woman who passes only sporadically/the woman who passes permanently; Irene's attraction to Clare/Irene's feeling of rivalry for her husband
with Clare—these are all motifs that are related to the doubling strategy. See also
Ann duCille's perceptive comment in *The Coupling Convention*, 103–9, that
homoeroticism is often coded as narcissism in texts.

112. (Rpt., New Brunswick, N.J.: Rutgers Univ. Press, 1986), 157.

113. This was the widely debated New York legal case of 1924 in which a rich
young heir sued for annulment of his marriage on the grounds that his wife had
hidden her racial background from him. Irene wonders: "What if Bellew should
divorce Clare? Could he? There was the Rhinelander case. But in France, in
Paris, such things were easy." See Mark J. Madigan, "Miscegenation and 'The
Dicta of Race and Class': The Rhinelander Case and Nella Larsen's *Passing*,"
*Modern Fiction Studies* 36.4 (Winter 1990): 523–29; and Wacks.

114. Larsen, 216.

115. See Jean Rousset, *Leurs yeux se rencontrèrent: la scène de première vue dans
le roman* (Paris: Corti, 1984), and Deborah McDowell's introduction to the
novel. The passage also gives a genealogy of the eyes in Clare's African ancestry.

116. Matthew Hodgart, *Satire* (London: World University Library, Weidenfeld and Nicolson, 1969), 108.

117. The Reverend Henry Givens seems to stand for William J. Simmons,
the evangelist who resurrected Klan, as well as for the Klan's Imperial Wizard
Hiram Evans, who contributed an essay to the *North American Review*, 223
(1926).

118. See *Literary Digest* (7 March 1925).

119. George B. Schuyler, *Black No More: Being an Account of the Strange and
Wonderful Workings of Science in the Land of the Free, A.D. 1933–1940* (1931; rpt.,
Boston: Northeastern Univ. Press, 1989), 40; see also 63. James Miller's excellent
introduction identifies many of the targets of Schuyler's satire.

120. Many treatments of the theme of passing undermined the apparent certainty of racial boundaries. Hence it could seem inconsistent that the texts also
helped to reestablish this certainty by giving more or less precise genealogical
background information on the characters who were "passing." Some writers
drew consequences from this observation, for example, Langston Hughes,

"Who's Passing for Who?" (1952), or William Faulkner, *Light in August* (1932).

121. This section concerns itself exclusively with the situation in the U.S. George Findlay estimates in *Miscegenation: A Study of the Biological Sources of Inheritance of the South African European Population* (Pretoria: Pretoria News and Printing Works, 1936), 44, that there are at least 733,000 "Europeans" in South Africa with unrecognized coloured ancestry (also cited in Stonequist, *Marginal Man*, 19n14); yet probably the same caution has to be applied to such South African estimates that, as will be suggested, is needed for U.S. figures.

122. James Hugo Johnston, *Race Relations in Virginia & Miscegenation in the South, 1776–1860* (1937; rpt., Amherst: Univ. of Massachusetts Press, 1970), 208–9, citing James D. Davis, *History of the City of Memphis* (Memphis, 1873), 123–24. The episode is also recounted by Caroline Bond Day in "Race Crossings in the United States" (1930), in *Blacks at Harvard*, 186.

123. Ray Stannard Baker, *Following the Color Line*, 160–61. In a footnote Baker spells the name "Manly," which is the version Williamson, *New People*, 100–102, uses.

124. "Negro Blood Divorce Cause," Chicago *Broadax* (28 May 1910): 2, citing as evidence the Cambridge, Mass., *Advocate* (21 May 1910).

125. On 7 November 1925 the *New York Times* reported the news, under the headline "Fiery Cross in Yard Protests Wedding," that a white mob had burned a cross on the front lawn of the Jackson residence at 18 Lexington Avenue, Montclair, N.J., in protest against William Jackson's plans to marry Miss Helen Burns of 16 Walnut Terrace in Bloomfield, N.J. Although Miss Burns had urged him to say that he was white at the License Bureau, he was reported as saying:

> My mother is part negro. Her father was white, but her mother was black. Does that make me a negro? I've always passed as a white man, but I don't know just what to say to this question.

The *Times* continued: "It was ruled that he must describe himself as 'colored.'" This ruling was made by Assistant Corporation Counsel Tarbox. On 8 November, the *Times* reported on its front page, "Mother Says Miss Burns Won't Wed Negro; Contractor and His Fiancee Remain Silent." On 11 November 1925, the New York *Amsterdam News* reported "Wedding of Wm. E. Jackson and White New Jersey Girl Probably Deferred." The article mentions that the Ku Klux Klan had set the fire, that Miss Burns's parents as well as Mr. Jackson's brother, a cafe owner in Harlem, had objected to the match, that Jackson had two children from a previous marriage which ended in divorce, and that James Weldon Johnson and W. E. B. Du Bois publicly questioned "the authority of the Assistant Corporation Counsel to determine the difference between races." Johnson praised Mr. Jackson's honesty as "manly and honorable." He was further quoted as saying:

> I know of no law or even decision in New York State which defines whether a man is colored or white. It seems probable to me that the Corporation Counsel's office exceeded in making a declaration on the race of Mr. Jackson.

See also "Telephone Operator Insists She Will Marry Negro Lover," New York *Age* (14 Nov. 1925), 1.

126. Dan Burly, "The Strange Will of Colonel McKee," *Negro Digest* (Nov.

1951): 17–22. Walter White makes reference to cases in *Flight* that sound as if they are based on true stories.

127. Nancy McLennan, "Near Jury Choice for Sedition Trial," *New York Times* (16 May 1944): 11; "Sedition Defense Attacks Charges," *New York Times* (19 May 1944): 21; and "Two More Fined in Sedition Trial," *New York Times* (23 May 1944): 17; Rogers, *Nature Knows No Color-Line*, 195–96.

128. Spickard, 335.

129. "Five Million White Negroes," *Ebony* (March 1948): 22–28; also cited in Wm. M. Kephart, "The 'Passing' Question," *Phylon* 10 (1948): 336. Ottley's essay includes a graph illustrating the "loss" of more than half a million Mulattoes between 1910 and 1920, apparently derived from Charles S. Johnson and Hornell Hart. *Time* magazine endorsed the figures of "possibly as many as 5,000,000 people with a 'determinable part' of Negro blood" who are "now 'passing' as whites" (16 Feb. 1948): 25; the article is accompanied by four photographs of four women, only one of whom (the darkest one) is "white." The article concludes: "When it comes to deciding which girls are Negro and which white, said *Ebony*, even anthropologists (not to mention Southern legislators) can only guess."

130. Ray S. Baker, *Following the Color Line*, 164.

131. Editorial in *Opportunity* 3.34 (Oct. 1925): 291.

132. Cited in McLendon, 34n14; Washington, 145; Burns Mantle 19 Oct. 1936 review of Samson Raphaelson, *White Man* (play) (New York: S. French, 1935).

133. Kephart, 336.

134. Burton W. Peretti, *The Creation of Jazz: Music, Race, and Culture in Urban America* (Urbana and Chicago: Univ. of Illinois Press, 1992), 31 (thanks to Jim Loeffler); Constance Green, *The Secret City*, (1967), 207–8; cited in Willard B. Gatewood, *Aristocrats of Color: The Black Elite, 1880–1920* (Bloomington and Indianapolis: Indiana Univ. Press, 1990), 337.

135. "Reuter observes that the sex ratio of mulatto men to mulatto women is lower in the North and in the cities, thus suggesting again that it is in the urban areas that passing is most frequent and presumably easiest" (Wirth and Goldhamer, 307).

136. Kephart, 337.

137. Hooton in Wirth and Goldhamer, 311.

138. *Selective Migration as a Factor in Child Welfare in the United States, With Special Reference to Iowa*, University of Iowa Studies in Child Welfare I, first series 192—criticized by Burma, 18–22. See also Wirth and Goldhamer, 312; Myrdal, 1208; and Washington, 125. Reuter, *Race Mixture*, 70–71, writes: "Men are more likely to be doing it than women."

139. Wirth and Goldhamer, 314.

140. Caleb Johnson, "Crossing the Color Line," *Outlook and Independent* (26 Aug. 1931): 526–27. Johnson, 541–52, also gives a glowing account of Davenport's color top researches. Hughes made Caleb Johnson a character in his comic sketch "Who's Passing for Who?" (1952), in which the revelations of the characters' "real" racial identity seesaw so many times that the absurdity of wanting to determine what is "passing" and what is "authentic identity" becomes quite apparent.

141. Washington, 113, also stresses that sensationalist reports inevitably exaggerated numbers

142. Bruce Payton Adams, 133n73, invoking the estimate made by Burma, 20–21, on the basis of Caroline Bond Day's work that probably no more than 10 percent of those who can pass do so.

143. Washington, 106 and 111.

144. Edward Byron Reuter, *Race Mixture*. The high point of fiction of passing was in the years from 1912 to 1931.

145. Nathan Huggins, 1986 seminar presentation entitled "Thoughts on/in Passing," ms. 14pp., here, 8.

146. Spickard, 333.

147. "Testing the Color Line: Dunbar and Chesnutt," in *The Black American Writer*, vol. I: *Fiction*, ed. C. W. E. Bigsby (Baltimore: Penguin, 1969), 121.

148. Wright and Hurston polemicized against Mulatto tradition and did not write passing tales. See V. Lewis, 132–34, for the case of Hurston; and Wright's Mulatto section that he omitted from *Black Boy* as well as his polemics against Mulatto elites.

149. "Passing Is Passé," in Huggins, *Revelations*, 245. In addition to this brief piece from the early 1970s, see also Spickard, 338, who also uses the heading "Passing Is Passé."

150. See for example, John Gregory Brown, *Decorations in a Ruined Cemetery* (Boston: Houghton Mifflin, 1994); Shirlee Taylor Haizlip, "Passing," *American Heritage* 46.1 (February/March 1995): 46–54; or Adrian Piper, "Passing for White, Passing for Black," *Transition* 58 (1992): 4–32.

## Chapter Ten. Incest and Miscegenation

1. *Congressional Globe* (17 Feb. 1864): 710; right after the passing of the Ninth to the Fourteenth Amendments, during the congressional debate on the Freedman's Bureau bill. Thomas Crawford's bronze Statue of Liberty on top of the Washington Capitol was described in the *Miscegenation* pamphlet of 1863 "as a symbol of the future American of this continent," "not white, symbolizing but one race, nor black typifying another, but a statue representing the composite race, whose sway will extend from the Atlantic to the Pacific ocean, from the Equator to the North Pole—the Miscegens of the Future" (63, 64).

2. Albert E. Jenks, "The Legal Status of Negro-White Amalgamation in the United States," *American Journal of Sociology* 21 (March 1916): 666–78, here 676.

3. (Boston: Beacon Press, 1969), 10.

4. (Rpt., New York: Vintage Books, 1987), 445. The typescript, ed. Noel Polk, 437, indicates that Faulkner originally wrote "face" before substituting "bear."

5. Sundquist, *Faulkner*, 122; Ho, 202 and 246–47. Ho writes:

the white supremacist strongly opposes miscegenation between black men and white women because of his overriding concern for "racial purity." Concomitantly, such a taboo perpetuates the myth of the pure white woman. Further, such an attitude of exclusiveness points toward the attitude of incestuous desire as prevalent among whites in Faulkner's fiction. (246–47)

In Faulkner's short story "Evangeline," the narrator and Don have the place that Shreve and Quentin occupy in *Absalom, Absalom!*, and the shared central concern is Sutpen. There are many similar phrasings—see, for example, the word "ghosts" (583), the comment on Judith (584), or the description of the fire as a "holocaust" (607)—and there are some parallel contradictions on small factual details in the story. For example, as in the novel, the picture that Charles has on him when he dies may be the picture of Judith (598) or the picture of Bon's other wife (608). Yet there are obvious differences, too: the narrator, who has Shreve's structural position, is a journalist and an outsider; many facts *do* come out; and the narration is not refracted in so many ways. Most important, as Ho has stressed, incest was not yet present. "Evangeline" is, as Noel Polk writes, one of a "Don and I" series, and it was written two years after Faulkner's first treatment of the Sutpen material in "The Big Shot" (1929).

6. In *To Wake the Nations*, 395–96, discussing Charles Chesnutt's story "The Dumb Witness," Sundquist writes:

> Such melodramatic elements as [395–96] ancestral sins, lost inheritances, and revelations of blood mixture, far from typing Chesnutt's fiction as derivative, gave him the means of exposing cultural segregation at work. "The Dumb Witness" is concerned with the denial of voice and subsequent revenge; but as the story makes clear, Viney's revenge is against Murchison not only as a lover but also as a master—and not just a master but one to whom she is related by blood, in what precise degree we are not told. Yet as African American slave narrators had announced some time in advance of Faulkner, miscegenation was also frequently enough literal incest of just the sort described in Chesnutt's tale, where the . . . quadroon slave mistress and her lover are both descended from the same patriarchal, ancestral tree.

7. Léon-François Hoffmann, an excellent reader, found no instance of a father's incest with his own slave daughter (*Le Nègre*, 233). In nonfrancophone literature, however, representations of attempted and, as we shall see, even of consummated interracial father-daughter incest can be found.

8. *Miscegenation* (New York: 1864). The best accounts of this anonymously published pamphlet and its historical contexts and literary consequences are Kaplan, "Miscegenation Issue"; J. M. Bloch, *Miscegenation, Melaleukation, and Mr. Lincoln's Dog* (New York: Schaum, 1958); and Aaron, "Inky Curse."

9. *Adventures of Jonathan Corncob, Loyal American Refugee. Written by Himself* (1787; rpt., Boston: David Godine, 1976), 72–73. This section invites comparison with Gayl Jones's novel *Corregidora* (1975).

10. Tilden Edelstein, "*Othello* in America: The Drama of Racial Intermarriage," in *Region, Race, and Reconstruction: Essays in Honor of C. Vann Woodward* (New York and Oxford: Oxford Univ. Press, 1982), 182, calls attention to Abigail Adams's reaction to an *Othello* production in 1786 in which Sarah Siddon, who was pregnant, played Desdemona, and her brother John Phillip Kemble starred as Othello "so that both her husband and the virtuous part of the audience can see them in the tenderest scenes without once fearing for their reputation." Edelstein adds dryly: "Obviously, racial intermarriage, *not* any thoughts of incest, caused Mrs. Adams's repugnance for Othello."

11. Ed. with intro. by Mrs. Inchbald (London: Longman, n.d.), 21 (II:i).

12. This is structurally similar to Victor Séjour, "Le Mulâtre" (1837), in which the white father Alfred tries to rape Zélie, the wife of his unrecognized son Georges. See pp. 164–67 above and Hoffmann, *Le Nègre*, 234. The definition of

"incest" to include what we would call in-laws may have been derived from such sanctions in Deuteronomy as those invoked in exegeses of the Curse of Ham.

13. With a new intro. (New York and Auburn: Miller, Orton & Mulligan, 1856). See Kinney, 48.

14. See Karcher, 333. Some of the reviews Hildreth cited at the beginning of the 1856 edition make reference to Archy Moore's "questionable" conduct (xix), to "disgusting instances of isolated ferocity" (xviii), or to the book's details that are "of a character too revolting to be made public" (x).

15. Marc Shell, "The Want of Incest in the Human Family; or, Kin and Kind in Christian Thought," *Journal of the Academy of Religion* 62.3 (1995): 625–50, here, 626.

16. Early, "A Servant," 108.

17. Hildreth previously gave the following explanation of the term "cracker" (now generally "white man"): "it is said from the long whips they employ" (vii).

18. Early, "A Servant," 110–11. Early also stressed that Moore's reaction might have been similar if Archy were not his son, as he is reacting most strongly against the fact that Cassy is no longer a virgin. "But Hildreth has effectively turned the tables on the master by having him usurped sexually by his own son. The irony of the scene hinges on the conflation of the two, actual chastisements which are taking place: Colonel Moore is publicly punishing his runaway, disobedient slaves and, in the same instance, privately, he is punishing his disobedient, incestuous children" (111).

19. Ibid., 115.

20. Published in *Liberty Bell*, 1858, the play was obviously based on the Crafts' escape—Child's main characters have no surname but are called Ellen and William—though this instance of attempted incest does not seem to appear in the Crafts' own narrative.

21. Ironically, this liberal sentiment corresponds, however, to racial notions that racially different "relatives" may not be recognized since "race" has the power to overrule "kinship."

22. *National Era* (8 April 1858). In my comments on *Old Hepsy* I am closely following Simone Vauthier's lead.

23. Nina Baym focused on the specific theme of the erotic attraction of white women for their male slaves and on the incest/miscegenation story. "The attraction of white women for black men is repeated in the Kenneths' legitimate daughter, who falls in love with a slave by whom, in a kind of Romeo-and-Juliet scene, she is poisoned. At the end the Sodom and Gomorrah of the Kenneth household has been reduced to ashes, but Lucina escapes to the North with her father, where they work for abolition and civil rights" (Baym, 271). And Vauthier undertook a most careful close reading of the novel in which the open eroticism and the conflation of incest and miscegenation are clearly delineated. Madeleine B. Stern writes in her entry on Mary Ann Andrews Denison (1826?–1911), in *Notable American Women 1607–1950: A Biographical Dictionary*, eds. Edward T. James, Janet Wilson James and Paul S. Boyer (Cambridge, Mass., and London: Harvard Univ. Press, 1971), 462–63: "Unread and forgotten today, her voluminous writings retain documentary interest. She was a hack to her age, spinning stories that still reflect the fictional heaven to which that age escaped."

24. When young Amy complains somewhat hypocritically about "these white slaves," Mag disagrees: "I'm mighty proud of ours, especially when they travel

with us. It gives us more consequence to carry around an elegant-looking slave, with perfumed locks, gold chain, and kids. And when there are no beaus, it's somewhat amusing to pretend to show them a little extra notice, too. I think it's prime fun, because they do often actually *like* one; and then they are *slaves*, indeed. My! we have one at home who will fly, if I lift my finger, quicker than any gallant I've got!" (88–89).

See also the argument by Edward Le Rux in Harriet Hamline Bigelow, *The Curse Entailed* (Wentworth, 1857), 308–9, that southern plantation daughters and wives "have the same example, the same temptation, as the sons and fathers. They also have the same training. And, although it is wrong, yet the odium which is attached to the female, more than to the male, who commits the same sin, forces them to hide their guilt. . . . But the mother and daughter cannot, so easily as the husband and son, conceal their guilt."

25. Insane mothers of mixed-race protagonists also appear in Azevedo's *O Mulato* and Villaverde's *Cecilia Valdés*.

26. Vauthier, "Textuality," 84–92. Vauthier also sees Lucina, "the fruit of an incestuous interracial relation," as emblematic of America, whose dream of a legitimate white ancestry forms a contrast to Freud's notion of the "family romance," according to which children like to imagine that they are illegitimate. This reading of Lucina invites a comparison with Clara Hohlfelder in Charles Chesnutt's story "Her Virginia Mammy."

27. (1860; rpt., Freeport, N.Y.: Books for Libraries, 1972), 45.

28. See Zanger, 67.

29. *Negro in American Fiction*, 42. See also Kinney, 78.

30. Kinney, 78.

31. "Treatise on Sociology," reprinted in *Faust*, 259–60. Ever since Hughes was cited by Eugene Genovese in the interesting section "Miscegenation," in *Roll Jordan Roll: The World the Slaves Made* (1974; rpt., New York: Vintage Books, 1976), 418, this has become a frequently quoted snippet. See, for example, Mary Dearborn, Richard King, and Eric Sundquist. Eva Saks comments: "The taboo of too different (amalgamation/miscegenation) is interchangeable with the taboo of too similar (incest), since both crimes rely on a pair of bodies which are mutu-ally constitutive of each other's deviance, a pair of bodies in which each body is the signifier of the deviance of the other. Neither body can represent the norm, because each is figured as deviance from an other" (Saks, 53–54).

32. David Lawrence Rodgers, "The Irony of Idealism: William Faulkner and the South's Construction of the Mulatto," in *The Discourse of Slavery: Aphra Behn to Toni Morrison*, eds. Carl Plasa and Betty J. Ring (London and New York: Rout-ledge, 1994), 166–90; here 166, 167.

33. Kaplan, "Miscegenation," 309.

34. "What Is a White Man?," *Independent* (30 May 1889): 6.

35. It was not just expanded but rewritten from an earlier short story and a novel, both published in 1839 under the same title. William Luis, "*Cecilia Valdés*: The Emergence of an Antislavery Novel," *Afro-Hispanic Review* 3.2 (May 1984): 15–19, has carefully compared the three versions of the text and noted that the second and third chapters of the 1882 novel coincide with the short story and the first two chapters of the 1839 novel. Luis suggests that Villaverde may have made use of the short story but not of the 1839 novel in writing the 1882 novel. Luis

also stresses that Villaverde changed the time frame of the novel, which now goes back to 1812—the year of birth of Cecilia Valdés and that of her author and the year of the Aponte conspiracy that aimed to liberate Cuban slaves. On Villaverde, see also the introduction by Raimundo Lazo to *Cecilia Valdés* (Mexico: Porrúa, 1986), xi–xii, the edition against which I have compared the excerpts cited from the (abridged) English translation *The Quadroon; or, Cecilia Valdes: A Romance of Old Havana*, trans. Mariano J. Lorente (Boston: St. Botolph Society, 1935).

36. See Reynaldo González, "Para una lectura historicista de *Cecilia Valdés*," *Casa de las américas* 22. 129 (Nov.–Dec. 1981): 84–92, here 85n.

37. The original, part 2, ch. 4, p. 90, is even more emphatic here.

38. In the original, 62. The phrasing is evocative of the *limpieza de sangre* statutes.

39. Luis, 18, has pointed out that in *Cecilia Valdés* the historical exploitation of black and Mulatto women by white men "began with Magdalena Morales, Cecilia's grandmother," that both 1839 versions predicted that it would "end in the fifth generation," with Cecilia's daughter, but that this reference was omitted in the 1882 edition since Villaverde's hopes for radical changes in mid-19th century had not been fulfilled.

Cecilia's own admission—"I would feel ashamed of myself if I got married and had a child darker than myself" (221; the Spanish text, 162, uses the Calculus term *saltoatrás* in order to render Cecilia's fear of *Natus Æthiopus*)—expresses not only her identification with her father and rejection of her mother, as Williams, 133, argues, but also the widespread rule of the land that encourages mixed-race women to "whiten" their children (see Kaye, 81).

40. Luis, 17

41. Aluísio Azevedo, *O Mulato* (S. Paulo: Série Bom Livro, 1991), ch. xii, pp. 128–31. Eng. trans. Murray Graeme MacNicoll, *Mulatto* (Rutherford: Fairleigh Dickinson Univ. Press, 1990), 201–6.

42. Page numbers refer to the first edition serialized in the *Colored American Magazine*. In the reprint of Hopkins's *Magazine Novels*, ed. Hazel Carby (New York: Oxford Univ. Press, 1988), the decisive passages appear on pp. 593, 607, and 616. Hasty readings of the novel for a racial opposition are in danger of missing this important aspect; thus Elizabeth Ammons, "Gender and Fiction," in *The Columbia History of the American Novel*, ed. Emory Elliott (New York: Columbia Univ. Press, 1991), 275, has viewed the novel as the story of the woman artist who is "doubly vulnerable by race and gender" and offered the surprising plot summary that "the soprano Dianthe Lusk is deceived, sexually violated, silenced, and finally murdered by the book's principal white male character."

43. *The Sins of the Father: A Romance of the South* (New York: D. Appleton, 1912), 335. For comments on the future of the races in America, see 399–413.

44. Kinney, 179; Thomas Dixon, Jr.; "Booker T. Washington and the Negro," *Saturday Evening Post* (19 Aug. 1905): 1–3; see also Mencke, 212–14, and Sharfstein, 33–40. Dixon thus echoed the abolitionist tenet that miscegenation may lead to incest.

45. Michael Rogin, "'The Sword Became a Flashing Vision': D. W. Griffith's *The Birth of a Nation*," in Philip Fisher, ed., *New American Studies* (Berkeley: Univ. of California Press, 1991), 346–91, here 363.

46. Hans Grimm, *Südafrikanische Novellen* (1913; rpt., Lippoldsberg: Kloster-

haus, 1975), 79–134. I am indebted to Joachim Warmbold, "If Only She Didn't Have Negro Blood in Her Veins: The Concept of Metissage in German Colonial Literature," *Journal of Black Studies* 23.2 (Dec. 1992): 200–210.

47. Paul Green, *Five Plays of the South* (New York: Hill and Wang, 1963), 307.

48. Charles Waddell Chesnutt Collection, Western Reserve Historical Society, Microfilm ed., roll #1, frame 809; thanks to David Barron.

49. Wilhelm Reich, *The Mass Psychology of Fascism*, trans. Vincent R. Carfagno (New York: Farrar, Straus & Giroux, 1970), 78–79, 87, 92–93.

50. Freyre, *The Mansions and the Shanties*, ch. 4. Cited from *Herrenhaus und Sklavenhütte: Ein Bild der brasilianischen Gesellschaft* (München: dtv/Klett-Cotta, 1990), 321.

51. *Invisible Man* (1952; rpt., New York: Vintage Books, 1972), 57–58. Here Ellison may be alluding to the scene between Mary and Bigger, and to Bigger's dream, in Wright's *Native Son*.

52. "The Meaning of Narration in *Invisible Man*," in *New Essays on Invisible Man*, ed. Robert O' Mealley (New York: Cambridge Univ. Press, 1988), 46.

53. Smith, 49.

54. Ann duCille, "'Who Reads Here?' Back Talking with Houston Baker," *Novel* (Fall 1992): 104–5. DuCille is reacting against Houston Baker, *Blues, Ideology, and Afro-American Literature: A Vernacular Theory* (Chicago and London: Univ. of Chicago Press, 1984), 183, who sees in Trueblood's act a "type of royal paternity, an aristocratic procreativity turned inward to insure the royalty . . . of an enduring black line of descent." DuCille replies that to "describe a father's sexual violation and impregnation of his daughter as 'an aristocratic procreativity turned inward' is to reduce not *race* to a trope, as Baker has elsewhere been accused of doing, but *rape*."

55. Arens, 148. Arens's witty and highly informative study summarizes research findings which make highly questionable the assumption that royal incest, as in Egypt, was the kind of marriage that led to sex or procreation (102–22) and stresses that since sex is "often used as a means of establishing dominance," the sexual act "becomes doubly significant . . . if it is also antisocial and forbidden" (147).

56. See also Edward La Rux about Judy in Harriet Hamline Bigelow, *The Curse Entailed* (1857), 316: "Nowhere did I meet her equal in worth; all suffered by comparison. Her many virtues stood out in bold relief before me. 'Do I love her only as a sister?' thought I." The tamer Mayne Reid only lets his narrator emphasize that Aurore "had been tenderly reared alongside her young mistress, had received almost as good an education, and, in fact, was treated rather as a *sister* than a *slave*" (138). In Margaret Deland's short story "A Black Drop" (1908), the protagonist Lily is propositioned by—as it turns out—her white half-brother, and with the sentence: "A man feels pretty lonely without any—sisters, don't you know," the phrase which the illustrator selected from this story (244).

57. Arens, 34, mentions that the terms endogamy and exogamy were introduced by John Ferguson McLennan's *Primitive Marriage* (1865); this was at about the same time that Croly and Wakeman coined the term "miscegenation" and that Agassiz pondered the "sterility hypothesis." McLennan, *Studies in Ancient History* (New York: Macmillan, 1886), 80–82, sketched a hypothetical historical development in which shifts from constructing kinship through

females only to a system which acknowledged kinship through males also are central for the development of exogamy and endogamy.

58. Richard H. King, *A Southern Renaissance: The Cultural Awakening of the American South, 1930–1945* (New York and Oxford: Oxford Univ. Press, 1980), 126–27.

59. Citing Charles S. Johnson's *Patterns of Negro Segregation* (1943), Claude Lévi-Strauss argued in *The Elementary Structures of Kinship* (Boston: Beacon Press, 1969), 46, that "endogamy and exogamy are not here complementary institutions and they could appear symmetrical only from a formal point of view." Other observations offered by Lévi-Strauss, whose approach comes out of Marcel Mauss:

> The woman whom one does not take, and whom one may not take, is, for that very reason offered up . . . as soon as I am forbidden a woman, she thereby becomes available to another man, and somewhere else a man renounces a woman who thereby becomes available to me. The content of the prohibition is not exhausted by the fact of the prohibition: the latter is instituted only in order to guarantee and establish, directly or indirectly, immediately or mediately, an exchange. (51)

60. Merton, 362n4.

61. Art. 14, sec. 263, cited in Reuter, *Race Mixture*, 90.

62. Reuter, *Race Mixture*, 84.

63. Saks, 53.

64. Leo Spitz, *Dissent* 6.1 (Winter 1959): 57.

65. Margaret Mead, "Incest," *International Encyclopedia of the Social Sciences*, ed. David L. Sills (New York: Macmillan, 1968), 7:115–22, here 116, writes: "The various laws against interracial marriage in the southeastern United States, the apartheid laws in South Africa, the decrees forbidding the marriage of Jews and gentiles instituted by the Nazi regime in Germany, and the special form of morganatic marriage between royalty and commoner in Europe (a rare occurrence today) exemplify politically enforced endogamy." Emile Durkheim, *Incest: The Nature and Origin of the Taboo* (1898; trans. Edward Sagarin, New York: Lyle Stuart, 1963), 81–96, proceeds from taboos about menstrual blood and views "all kinds of blood" as the "object of analogous sentiments."

66. She has influenced such other readers as Mary Dearborn, Susan Fraiman, Anita Goldman, and Heather Hathaway.

67. Baym, 271.

68. *Foundational Fictions*, 129.

69. Lorna V. Williams, "From Dusky Venus to Mater Dolorosa: The Female Protagonist in the Cuban Antislavery Novel," in *Woman as Myth and Metaphor in Latin American Literature*, eds. Carmelo Virgillo and Naomi Lindstrom (Columbia: Univ. of Missouri Press, 1985), 131 and 133–34. Williams draws on Lévi-Strauss in her reading of Villaverde. Describing Cecilia Valdés, Suárez y Romero's Dorotea, and Zambrana's Camila as Mulattoes "situated between contrary terms," Williams, 124, also writes: "Their beauty, the very quality that renders them irresistible to both black and white men, becomes, in the course of the narrative, their tragic flaw. In all three instances, the women's interaction with black men is seen as socially regressive in that it leads the men to commit some form of murder. On the other hand, the women's relations with white men are

regarded as unnatural because, in each case, that relation results in a form of incest."

70. González, 87, argues, however, that it is the rigid social structure which the love story between the Mulatto woman and the son of a slave trader traverses that leads to the final tragedy and not the incest theme, which he views as a "melodramatic recurrence and a concession to the popular taste of the period."

71. See González for an analysis of *Cecilia Valdés* against the background of Fernando Ortiz, *El Engaño de las razas* (1946); see also Kaye.

72. *Caste and Class in a Southern Town* (1937; 3rd ed. rpt., Garden City: Doubleday, 1957), 153–54. For literary examples, see Reid's *Quadroon* and Boucicault's *Octoroon*, cited in Chapter Eight.

73. *Children*, 276n15.

74. Merton, 368.

75. Ibid., 370.

76. Alain Locke, "American Literary Tradition and the Negro," *Modern Quarterly* 3.3 (May–July 1926): 217–18, fully cited in Chapter Eight.

77. Arthur W. Calhoun, "Miscegenation," *A Social History of the American Family From the Colonial Times to the Present*, vol. III (Cleveland: Arthur H. Clark, 1919), 27–38, here 37.

78. Hans Grimm, *Afrikafahrt West* (1913), 175, cited by Warmbold, who also notes the later deletion of this passage.

79. *Wirtschaft und Gesellschaft*, Eng. *Economy and Society* (Univ. of California Press, 1978), 386, in *Theories of Ethnicity*, 53.

80. Melville J. Herskovits, "Race Mixture," *Encyclopedia of the Social Sciences* 13, 41, writes: "With the possible exception of a few highly inbred groups of an originally homogeneous stock whose members, because of geographical isolation, have had no contact with outsiders, there are no human beings whose genetic composition is such as to fulfill the requirements of the biological concept of the pure strain."

81. Aaron, 184; also in Eric Foner, *Free Soil, Free Labor, Free Men: The Ideology of the Republican Party before the Civil War* (New York: Oxford Univ. Press, 1970), 263, who cites J. A. Lemcke, *Reminiscences of an Indianan* (Indianapolis, 1905), 196. A weaker version from the Buckeye State is cited in Kaplan, "Miscegenation," 312: "Fathers, Save Us from Negro Equality!" from Wood Gray, *The Hidden Civil War: The Story of the Copperheads* (New York, 1942), 150.

82. The question "Would you like your sister (or daughter) to marry one?" constitutes a recurrence that would merit a full discussion with examples ranging from Lincoln to Lois Lane. The racist dimensions of the infamous question are mercilessly explored by Thomas Dixon, who lets George Harris (the Harvard-trained son of Eliza Harris from *Uncle Tom's Cabin*) ask the stunned Boston liberal Everett Lowell for his daughter's hand in the chapter "Equality with a Reservation" of the novel *The Leopard's Spots: A Romance of the White Man's Burden—1865–1900* (New York: Doubleday, Page, 1902), 391–94. The implications of the question are sounded in the outstanding essay by Milton Mayer, "The Issue Is Miscegenation," in *White Racism: Its History, Pathology, and Practice*, eds. Barry Schwartz and Robert Disch (New York: Dell, 1970), 207–17; and taken as the center of a little-known, excellent short story by Delmore Schwartz, "A Bitter Farce," *Kenyon Review* 8.2 (Spring 1946): 245–61.

83. Lévi-Strauss, 481.

84. Among the many critics who, in addition to Sundquist and Ho, have

taken on this issue, John T. Irwin's remarkable attempt, in *Doubling and Incest/Repetition and Revenge: A Speculative Reading of Faulkner* (1975; Baltimore and London: Johns Hopkins Univ. Press, 1980), to read Faulkner inspired by Guy Rosolato's *Essais sur le symbolique* stands out.

85. J. Hillis Miller, "The Two Relativisms: Point of View and Indeterminacy in the Novel *Absalom, Absalom!*," in Betty Jean Craige, ed., *Relativism in the Arts* (Athens: Univ. of Georgia Press, 1983), 148–70, here 160–61.

86. See Elisabeth Muhlenfeld, *William Faulkner's* Absalom, Absalom!: *A Critical Casebook* (New York & London: Garland, 1984), to whose own contribution, "'We have waited long enough': Judith Sutpen and Charles Bon," 173–88, and to Floyd Watkins's "What Happens in *Absalom, Absalom!?*," 55–64, my following discussion is as indebted as it is to Noel Polk's edition of and introduction to the manuscript of *Absalom, Absalom!*. All references to the text, *Absalom, Absalom! The Corrected Text* (New York: Vintage Books, 1987), will be given parenthetically.

87. The question of whose photograph it was that was found on Bon—Judith's or the other woman's, or the Octoroon mistress and the child's—is, of course, one of the unresolvable issues of the novel.

88. Calling attention to the letter that Bon sends to Judith (160–63), Muhlenfeld, *William Faulkner's* Absalom, 182, convincingly writes that she can see "no hint" in it "of any knowledge that he is about to commit incest or miscegenation." That incest and miscegenation are in the air, however, becomes obvious in the momentary belief Mr. Compson ascribes later to Quentin's grandfather that Bon's son Charles Etienne de Saint Valery Bon "might be Clytie's, got by its father on the body of his own daughter—a boy seen always near the house with Clytie always nearby" (252). This brief misunderstanding still suggests a connection with the motif of interracial father-daughter incest.

89. Polk, ed. and intro., *Absalom*, viii.

90. Suzanne W. Jones, "*Absalom, Absalom!* and the Custom of Storytelling: A Reflection of Southern Social and Literary History," *Southern Studies* 24.1 (1985): 82–112, here 106.

91. Irwin, 77–78, discusses the homoerotic theme, connecting it with *The Sound and the Fury* in which Harvard classmates refer to Shreve as Quentin's "husband" and viewing its presence in the story of Bon and Henry as possibly "a projection of Quentin's own state made in the act of narration." See Michaels, 49.

92. For example, the historical setting is precise for the main action in the Civil War period (when the term miscegenation was also created) and the interpretation in 1910 (when the fear of it was at a high peak, and such novelists as Dixon and Durham were popular). The Spanish origin of Sutpen's first wife evokes the history of African slavery and *limpieza de sangre*. Her name Eulalia (that appears only in the genealogy) may go back not only to Longfellow, but also to Child's *Romance of the Republic* (1867) or the "Eulelia" in Henry's *Out of Wedlock* (1931). The scene of the Haitian revolution (314–15) is reminiscent of the tradition of Victor Hugo's *Bug-Jargal*. Henry's difficulties in accepting incest are seen stemming from his Methodist background (424–25)—as did Cassy's in *The Slave* (39). The never-was-born motif appears (256). As in *Old Hepsy*, the house burns down, and the only surviving descendants of the bigoted founding patriarch are of mixed blood.

93. Frederick R. Karl, "Race, History, and Technique in *Absalom, Abalom!*,"

in *Faulkner and Race: Faulkner and Yoknapatawpha, 1986*, eds. Doreen Fowler and Ann J. Abadie (Jackson and London: Univ. of Mississippi Press, 1987), 209–21, here 218–19.

94. Thadious M. Davis, *Faulkner's "Negro": Art and the Southern Context* (Baton Rouge and London: Louisiana State Univ. Press, 1983), 197.

95. For the use of biblical stories, see John V. Hagopian, "The Biblical Background of *Abalom, Absalom!*," in Muhlenfeld, *William Faulkner's* Absalom, 131–34; for the tragic elements, see Ilse Dusoir Lind, "The Design and Meaning of *Absalom, Absalom!*," in *William Faulkner: Three Decades of Criticism*, eds. Frederick Hoffman and Olga Vickery (East Lansing, 1960), and Cleanth Brooks, "Faulkner and the Sense of the Tragic: *Absalom, Absalom!*," in *Faulkner: A Collection of Critical Essays*, ed. Robert Penn Warren (Englewood Cliffs: Prentice-Hall, 1966).

## Endings

1. Alain Locke, ed., *The New Negro* (1925; rpt., New York: Atheneum, 1968), 367.

2. In *Accent on Youth and White Man* (New York: Samuel French, 1935), 196.

3. As cited as an epigraph in Anna Dickinson, *What Answer?* (1868; rpt., Fields, Osgood, 1869), 242.

4. "Narrative Versions, Narrative Theories," *Critical Inquiry* 7.1 (Autumn 1980): 219.

5. See William Wells Brown, *Three Years in Europe; or, Places I Have Seen and People I Have Met* (London: C. Gilpin, 1853), 288 and 292; cited and discussed in Christopher Mulvey, "The Fugitive Self and the New World of The North: William Wells Brown's Discovery of America," in *The Black Columbiad: Defining Moments in African-American Literature and Culture* (Cambridge: Harvard Univ. Press, 1994), 109–11.

6. Sidney A. Story, Jr. [Mary Pike], *Caste: A Story of Republican Equality* (Boston: Phillips, Sampson, 1856), 535, 536.

7. (New York: Harpers and Brothers, [1891]), 149–50.

8. 196. See epigraph to the present chapter.

9. Stonequist, 187.

10. See Antonio Marin Ocete, *Antigüedad y excelencias de Granada* (Madrid: Luis Sánchez); Lope de Vega, *La Dama Boba* (1613), II:21; Don Diego Ximénez de Enciso, *Comedia famosa de Juan Latino* (1652; ed. Eduardo Juliá Martínez, Madrid: Aldus, 1951).

11. For a recent example, Spike Lee's film *Jungle Fever* (1991) was a conservative clustering of interracial sex as adultery. Against this background the significance of Cinthio's novella and of Shakespeare's *Othello* stand out as they imagined the interracial couple as the legitimate one. The theme of jealousy, however, may link *Othello* with interracial adultery tales that the Yiddish version mentioned earlier reintroduced to the play.

12. "Boitelle," in *Complete Short Stories*, vol. 3 (London: Cassell, 1970), 513.

13. The name may indirectly echo "Yarico." Hoffmann, *Le Nègre*, 132n, suggests that "Ourika" comes from Mme. de Staël's "Mirza ou lettre d'un voyageur" (1795), a novella in which Ourika is the cousin betrothed to the prince Ximéo, who is saved from being sold into slavery by the titular heroine Mirza.

14. Hoffmann, *Le Nègre*, 225–27; *Wiener Theaterzeitung* (1824), 427.

15. Mme. [Claire de Kersaint] la duchesse de [Durfort-] Duras, *Ourika*, Eng. trans. [George Wallis Haven] (Boston: Carter and Hendee, 1829), 61.

16. Paul Heyse (1830–1914) wrote a striking poetic version of *Ourika*—he calls her "Urica" (1851), in *Gesammelte Werke*, vol. 2 (Berlin: Hertz, 1872), 1–29, which develops this motif against the intensified background of the revolution. The aristocrat Etienne cannot reciprocate Urica's love because of her skin color, but when he is endangered he tries to kiss the revolutionary Urica in the spirit of *fraternité* in order to save himself. Urica is stunned and accuses him: "Has the fear of death cured you of the repulsion from the Negro woman, that I am good enough to be kissed when you are afraid of the kiss of death?" The Jacobins catch and guillotine Etienne, and in the last part of the poem Urica is a mad beggar woman on the boulevards of Restoration Paris who says only two words, "Egalité! Egalité!" and "Lie! Lie!"

17. "Nègres et blancs, qu'importe l'origine, /Tous les cœurs purs sont égaux devant lui" (27). Franville's comment, 13.

18. *Wiener Zeitschrift für Kunst, Literatur, Theater und Mode* 108 (7 Sept. 1824): 939. Castelli, "Urika, die Negerinn: Drama in einem Akt," *Dramatisches Sträußchen* 11 (1826): 133–78; it was actually adapted from Mélesville and Carmouche, *Ourika; ou, La Petite Negresse* (Paris: Quoy, 1824), so that the Parisian audience had seen an ending in March that was very similar to the one Castelli presented at Vienna in August of 1824.

19. "The Story of *Inkle* and *Yarico*. From the 11th *Spectator*," *London Magazine; or, Gentleman's Monthly Intelligencer* III (1734): 257–58. See also L. M. Price, 9–11.

20. (London, 1787), 45pp, quoted from L. M. Price, here 46.

21. It is conveniently reproduced in Horace Howard Furness's 1886 Variorum Edition of *Othello*, 448.

22. Jan Kott, "The Two Paradoxes of Othello," *Evergreen Review* 10.40 (April 1966): 16.

23. Heinrich von Kleist, *Erzählungen*, ed. Siegfried Streller (Frankfurt: Insel, 1986), 657–58, citing Grimm from *Zeitung für die elegante Welt* (10 Oct. 1811) and Heyse, preface to *Deutscher Novellenschatz* (1871).

24. The text of the Berliner Ausgabe II/4, eds. Roland Reuß and Peter Staengle (Frankfurt: Stroemfeld/Roter Stern, 1988), 76, 83, and 84, renders the often "corrected" text in the manner of all printings in Kleist's lifetime. Reuß in "'Die Verlobung in St. Domingo'—eine Einführung in Kleists Erzählen," *Berliner Kleist-Blätter* 1 (1988—appended to the Berliner Ausgabe): 30–45, here 40, calls attention to Kleist's game with "Nicolo/Colino" in "The Foundling," and argues for a reading of "Gustavgust" (both were considered variants of the same name in Kleist's time). "The 'stranger' is called *by the text* 'August' from the moment at which he, tied in the house to the bed, has lost all faith in Toni. . . . The moment, however, at which he is later on first called 'Gustav' again is— remarkably enough—when Herr Strömli's sons after 'August's' killing of Toni attempt to call the 'stranger' back to consciousness of his self and his deed." The annotation to Helmut Sembdner's edition of Kleist, *Sämtliche Erzählungen und Anekdoten* (München: Deutscher Taschenbuch Verlag, 1978), 301, explains the variant as an error, an oversight.

25. Streller, citing Heyse, preface to *Deutscher Novellenschatz* (1871).

26. Hermann J. Weigand, "Das Vertrauen in Kleists Erzählungen," *Fährten und Funde: Aufsätze zur deutschen Literatur* (Bern and Munich, 1967), 101; cited and discussed in the context of the many incongruities in the novella by Roland Reuß, 5n9.

27. "Toni: Ein Drama in drei Aufzügen," *Theodor Körner's sämmtliche Werke* (Leipzig: Philipp Reclam jun., n.d.), 227–54, here 247.

28. The issue is pursued more fully in Theodor Storm's "Von jenseit des Meeres," in which Toni becomes a stranger in her mother's house and is at home only in the world of her German father and her German beloved. Kleist also provoked two explicit modern retellings: Anna Seghers, "Die Hochzeit von Haiti" (1964), reprinted in *Die Hochzeit von Haiti: Karibische Geschichten* (Neuwied: Luchterhand, 1976), and Hans Christoph Buch, *Die Hochzeit von Port-au-Prince* (Frankfurt: Suhrkamp, 1984).

29. "Heinrich von Kleist und seine Erzählungen" (1954), in Heinrich von Kleist, *The Marquise of O—— and Other Stories*, trans. Martin Greenberg (1954; rpt., New York: Criterion Books, 1960), 21–22. The German text is cited in Heinrich von Kleist, *Erzählungen*, ed. Siegfried Streller (Frankfurt: Insel, 1986), 658–59, Goethe's comment ibid., 657.

30. Lukács, "Die Tragödie Heinrichs von Kleists" ("The Tragedy of Heinrich von Kleist," 1936); cited in Streller, *Erzählungen*, 659.

31. *Theodor Storm—Theodor Fontane: Briefwechsel,* hg. Jacob Steiner (Berlin: Erich Schmidt Verlag, 1981), 124. See Franz Stuckert, *Theodor Storm: Sein Leben und Werk* (Bremen: Carl Schünemann, 1955), 290.

32. Karl Ernst Laage, *Theodor Storm: Studien zu seinem Leben und Werk mit einem Handschriftenkatalog* (Berlin: Erich Schmidt Verlag, 1985), 91. The cover is that of the first edition (Schleswig: Heiberg, 1867). Laage, 196n17, mentions that Storm wrote a similar letter to Pietsch, 10 Dec. 1866, also concerning the tragic ending.

33. Cited in Theodor Storm, *Gedichte Novellen 1848–1867*, ed. Dieter Lohmeier (Frankfurt: Deutscher Klassiker Verlag, 1987), 1195.

34. Lohmeier, 1196–97, points out that Storm did change the ending somewhat by adding Jenni's letter, which partly substitutes for Alfred's (1202–04); but stresses that a fully tragic ending would have been very difficult without major rewriting because of the frame narration; see also Stuckert, 290.

35. *Essays on Literature: American Writers, English Writers* (New York: Library of America, 1984), 218–29.

36. *On Blackness Without Blacks: Essays on the Image of the Black in Germany* (Boston: G. K. Hall, 1982), 47. Christopher Miller, *Blank Darkness: Africanist Discourse in French* (Chicago and London: Univ. of Chicago Press, 1985), 61, uses lines from Radet/Barré in an epigraph.

37. An interracial courtship plot can be rejected as ideological no matter how it is resolved. For Sterling Brown, "the unfailingly tragic outcomes" of interracial unions "supported the belief that mixture of the races was a curse." Sander Gilman similarly assumed that an audience's readiness to accept an interracial match is a progressive sign. For Jonathan Little or for Mary Louise Pratt, however, the interracial marriage at the end of a work may be an "award" for the acceptance of assimilationist goals.

38. Robert Hogan, *Dion Boucicault* (New York: Twayne, 1969), 74–75. See also Lee A. Jacobus, *Longman Anthology*, 102.

39. Kaplan, "*The Octoroon*," 556.

40. Degen, 175. In response to a diatribe from the New York *Herald*, Bouci-cault justified his method by invoking the Greeks and Molière as his models: "I believe the drama to be a proper and very effective instrument to use in the dis-section of all social matters. The Greeks thought so, who founded it; Molière thought so when he wrote the *Tartuffe*; and a very humble follower of theirs thinks so too." Cited in Kaplan, "*Octoroon*," 549.

41. Kaplan, "*Octoroon*," 551.

42. *Times* (12 Dec. 1861); cited in Degen, 175.

43. Degen, 170–78. Nils Erik Enkvist, "*The Octoroon* and English Opinions of Slavery," *American Quarterly* 8 (1956): 166–70, portrayed the change in British public opinion between the productions of *Uncle Tom's Cabin* and of *The Octoroon*.

44. Cited in Degen, 172. For a similar point made in America, see the New York *Herald* of 7 Dec. 1859.

45. London *Times* (20 Nov. 1861), 5:3. Both Degen, 172, and Gary A. Richardson, "Boucicault's *The Octoroon* and American Law," *Theatre Journal* (May 1982): 155–64, here 158, quote parts of this letter.

46. Degen, 176.

47. "Saving the Octoroon," *Punch* (21 Dec. 1861): 253; also cited in Degen, 177.

48. "Our Dramatic Correspondent," *Punch* (4 Jan. 1862): 3.

# Selected Bibliography

Aaron, Daniel. "The 'Inky Curse': Miscegenation in the White Literary Imagination." *Social Science Information* 22.1 (1983): 169–90.

Abbott, Nabia. "A Ninth-Century Fragment of the 'Thousand Nights.' New Light on the Early History of the *Arabian Nights*." *Journal of Near Eastern Studies* 8. 3 (July 1949): 129–64.

Aberigh-Mackay, George. *Twenty-One Days in India: Being the Tour of Sir Ali Baba, K. C. B.* 1881. 6th ed. London and Calcutta: Thacker, 1898.

Adams, Bruce Payton. "The White Negro: The Image of the Passable Mulatto Character in Black Novels, 1853–1954." Ph.D. diss., University of Kansas, 1975.

Adams, Henry. *Mont-Saint-Michel and Chartres.* 1904. Reprint. Boston and New York: Houghton Mifflin, 1913.

Adolf, Helen. "New Light on Oriental Sources for Wolfram's *Parzival* and Other Grail Romances." *Publications of the Modern Language Association* 62 (1947): 306–24.

*Adventures of Jonathan Corncob, Loyal American Refugee. Written by Himself.* 1787. Reprint. Boston: David Godine, 1976.

Allain, Mathé. *"Not Worth a Straw": French Colonial Policy and the Early Years of Louisiana.* Lafayette: Center for Louisiana Studies, 1988.

Allen, Don Cameron. *The Legend of Noah: Renaissance Rationalism in Arts, Science, and Letters.* Urbana: Univ. of Illinois Press, 1963.

Allier, Raoul. *Une enigme troublante: la race Nègre et la malediction du Cham.* Paris: Société des Missions Évangéliques = Les Cahiers Missionaires 26, 1930.

Alvar, Manuel. *Léxico del Mestizaje en Hispanoamérica.* Madrid: Ediciones Cultura Hispánica, Instituto de Cooperación Iberoamericana, 1987.

Amacher, Anne Ward. "The Genteel Primitivist and the Semi-Tragic Octoroon." *New England Quarterly* 29.2 (June 1956): 216–27.

Ammons, Elizabeth. "Gender and Fiction." In *The Columbia History of the American Novel.* Ed. Emory Elliott. New York: Columbia Univ. Press, 1991.

*A Narrative of the Case of Salomé Müller, a German Girl Who Was Reduced to Slavery in Louisiana* [New Orleans, ca. 1845].

Andersen, H. C. *Gesammelte Werke.* Leipzig: Carl B. Lorck, 1847.

———. *Kjendte og glemte Digte, 1823–1867.* København: C. A. Reitzel, 1867.

————. *Mulatten. Originalt romantisk Drama i fem Akter*. 2nd ed. Kjøbenhavn: C.A. Reitzel, 1840.

————. *Skyggen, Fairy Tales*, 1847. Trans. Reginald Spink. London: Everyman's, 1992.

Andrews, William L. "Introduction" to *Three Classic African-American Novels*. New York: Mentor, 1990.

————. "Miscegenation in the Late Nineteenth-Century American Novel." *Southern Humanities Review* 13.1 (Winter 1979): 13–24.

Antier, Benjamin, and Alexis Decomberousse. *Le Marché de Saint-Pierre*. Paris: Marchant, 1839.

Antoine, Régis. *Les Écrivains français et les antilles des premiers Pères Blancs aux Sur-réalistes Noirs*. Maisonneuve et Larose, 1978.

Antoniazzi, Barbara. "Vernon Sullivan: A Modernist Invention." Manuscript, University of Venice, 1995.

Applebaum, Harvey M. "Miscegenation Statutes: A Constitutional and Social Problem." *Georgetown Law Journal* 53 (1964): 49–91.

Arbery, Glenn Cannon. "Victims of Likeness: Quadroons and Octoroons in Southern Fiction." *Southern Review* 25.1 (Winter 1989): 52–71.

Arendt, Hannah. "Race Thinking Before Racism." *Review of Politics* 6 (Jan. 1944): 36–73.

————. "Reflections on Little Rock." *Dissent* 6.1 (Winter 1959): 45–56.

Arens, W. *The Original Sin: Incest and Its Meaning*. New York and Oxford: Oxford Univ. Press, 1986.

Arner, Robert D. "Pride and Prejudice: Kate Chopin's "Désirée's Baby."" *Mississippi Quarterly* 25 (1972).

Arrom, José Juan. "Criollo: Definicion y matices de un concepto." In *Certidumbre de America* (Madrid: Gredos, 1971), 11–26.

Ashby, William. *Redder Blood*. New York: Cosmopolitan Press, 1915.

Atherton, Gertrude. *Senator North*. New York and London: John Lane, 1900.

Avins, Alfred. "Anti-Miscegenation Laws and the Fourteenth Amendment: The Original Intent." *Virginia Law Review* 52 (1966): 1224–55.

Azevedo, Aluísio. *O Mulato*. S. Paulo: Série Bom Livro, 1991. *Mulatto*. Eng. trans. Murray Graeme MacNicoll. Rutherford: Fairleigh Dickinson Univ. Press, 1990.

Azurara, Gomes Eanes de. *The Chronicle of the Discovery and Conquest of Guinea*. Trans. Charles Raymond Beazley and Edgar Prestage. London, 1896. Reprint. New York: Burt Franklin, n.d.

Baedeker, Karl. *The United States of America*. 4th ed. Leipzig: Baedeker, 1909.

Baker, Houston. *Blues, Ideology, and Afro-American Literature: A Vernacular Theory*. Chicago and London: Univ. of Chicago Press, 1984.

————. *Workings of the Spirit: The Poetics of Afro-American Women's Writing*. Chicago: Univ. of Chicago Press, 1991.

Baker, Ray Stannard. *Following the Color Line: American Negro Citizenship in the Progressive Era*. 1908. Reprint. New York: Harper Torchbooks, 1964.

————. "The Tragedy of the Mulatto." *American Magazine* 65 (1907/8): 582–98.

Baldwin, James. *Go Tell It on the Mountain*. 1953. Reprint. New York: Dell-Laurel, 1985.

Ballhatchet, Kenneth. *Race, Sex, and Class Under the Raj: Imperial Attitudes and Policies and Their Critics, 1793–1905*. New York: St. Martin's Press, 1980.

Barker, Anthony J. *The African Link: British Attitudes to the Negro in the Era of the Atlantic Slave Trade, 1550–1817.* London: Frank Cass, 1978.

Barringer, Felicity. "Soviet Vigils Held Widely for Pushkin." *New York Times*, 15 Feb. 1987.

Barron, Milton L. *The Blending American: Patterns of Intermarriag*e. Chicago: Quadrangle Books, 1972.

Barth, Fredrik. *Ethnic Groups and Boundaries.* Boston: Little Brown, 1969.

Barthes, Roland. *Le Plaisir du texte.* Paris: Editions du Seuil, 1973. *The Pleasure of the Text.* Trans. Richard Miller. New York: Hill and Wang, 1975.

Basso, Hamilton. *The View from Pompey's Head.* Garden City, N.Y.: Doubleday, 1954.

Bastide, Roger. *Le Prochain et le lontain.* Paris, 1970.

Battaglia, Salvatore. "Razza." *Grande dizionario della lingua italiana.* Vol. 15. Torino: Unione Tipografico-Editrice Torninese, 1990.

Baudet, Henri. *Paradise on Earth. Some Thoughts on European Images of Non-European Man.* Trans. from Dutch. New Haven & London: Yale Univ. Press, 1965.

Bayliss, John Francis. "Novels of Black Americans Passing as Whites." Ph. Diss., Indiana University, 1976.

Baym, Nina. *Women's Fiction: A Guide to Novels by and About Women in America, 1820–1870.* Ithaca and London: Cornell Univ. Press, 1979.

Beane, Carol Anne. "The Characterization of Blacks and Mulattoes in Selected Novels From Colombia, Venezuela, Ecuador, and Peru." Ph.D. diss, University of California, Berkeley, 1980.

Beaumont, Gustave de. *Marie; ou, L'Esclavage aux états-unis.* 1835. *Marie.* Eng. trans. Barbara Chapman. Stanford: Stanford Univ. Press, 1958.

Bell, Bernard W. *The Afro-American Novel and Its Tradition.* Amherst: Univ. of Massachusetts Press, 1987.

Bell, Derrick A., Jr. "Interracial Sex and Marriage." In *Race, Racism and American Law*, 53–81. 2nd ed. Boston and Toronto: Little, Brown, 1980.

Beltran, G. Aguirre. "Races in 17th Century Mexico." *Phylon* 6 (1945): 211–18 (with chart of terms).

Bentley, Nancy. "White Slaves: The Mulatto Hero in Antebellum Fiction." *American Literature* 65.3 (Sept. 1993): 501–22.

Berlant, Lauren. "National Brands/National Body: *Imitation of Life*." In Hortense Spillers, ed., *Comparative American Identities.* New York and London: Routledge, 1991.

Bernstein, Richard. "Apartheid Laws on Mixed-Race Sex to be Abolished." *New York Times*, 16 April 1985, pp. A1, A12.

Berry, Brewton. *Almost White.* New York: Macmillan, 1963.

Berzon, Judith R. *Neither White Nor Black: The Mulatto Character in American Fiction.* New York: New York Univ. Press, 1978.

Best, George. "A true discourse of the three Voyages of discovery, for the finding of a passage to Cathaya . . ." 1578. In Richard Hakluyt, *Voyages*, vol. 5. London and New York: Dent and Dutton, 1927.

Bezomes, Roger. *L'Exotisme dans l'art et la pensée.* Paris, New York: Elsevier, 1953.

Bigelow, Harriet Hamline. *The Curse Entailed.* Wentworth, 1857.

Bigsby, C.W.E., ed. *The Black American Writer*, vol. 1: *Fiction*. Baltimore: Penguin, 1969.

Birchfield, James D., Albert Boime, and William J. Hennessey. *Thomas Satter-white Noble 1835–1907.* Lexington: Univ. of Kentucky Art Museum, 1988.

Bird, Robert Montgomery. *Sheppard Lee.* 2 vols. New York: Harper and Brothers, 1836.

Bitterli, Urs. *Die Entdeckung des schwarzen Afrikaners. Versuch einer Geistes-geschichte der europäische-überseeischen Begegnungen.* Zürich: Atlantis, 1970.

———. *Die "Wilden" und die "Zivilisierten": Grundzüge einer Geistes- und Kul-turgeschichte der europäisch-überseeischen Begegnung.* München: Beck, 1976.

———, ed. *Die Entdeckung und Eroberung der Welt: Dokumente und Berichte.* Vol. 1: *Amerika, Afrika.* München: Beck, 1980.

Blakely, Allison. *Russia and the Negro: Blacks in Russian History and Thought.* Washington, D.C.: Howard University Press, 1986.

Bloch, Ernst. "Philosophische Ansicht des Detektivromans." *Verfremdungen* I, pp. 37–63. Frankfurt: Suhrkamp, 1962.

Bloch, J. M. *Miscegenation, Melaleukation, and Mr. Lincoln's Dog.* New York: Schaum, c. 1958.

Block, Eugene. *Fingerprinting: Magic Weapon Against Crime.* New York: David McKay, 1969.

Bloomfield, Maxwell. "Dixon's *The Leopard's Spots*: A Study in Popular Racism." *American Quarterly* 16.3 (Fall 1964): 387–401.

Blumenbach, Johann Friedrich. *The Anthropological Treatises.* Trans. Thomas Bendyshe. London: Longman, 1865.

Bochart, Samuel. *Phaleg, Canaan, et Hierozoicon.* 3rd ed. Lugduni Batavorum: Apud Cornelium Boutesteyn, & Jordanum Luchtmans; Trajecti ad Rhenum: Apud Guilielmum vande Water, 1692.

Boddy, Rev. James M. "The Ethnic Unity of the Negro and the Anglo-Saxon Race." *Colored American Magazine* (March 1905): 124–28.

Boelhower, William. *Through a Glass Darkly: Ethnic Semiosis in American Litera-ture.* New York and Oxford: Oxford Univ. Press, 1987.

Bogle, Donald. *Toms, Coons, Mulattoes, Mammies, and Bucks: An Interpretive Histo-ry of Blacks in American Films.* New York: Bantam, 1974.

Bone, Robert A. *Down Home: A History of Afro-American Short Fiction From Its Beginnings to the End of the Harlem Renaissance.* New York: Putnam, 1975.

———. *The Negro Novel in America.* 1958. Rev. ed. New Haven and London: Yale Univ. Press, 1973.

Bontemps, Arna, ed., *Great Slave Narratives.* Boston: Beacon Press, 1969.

Bontemps, Arna, and Jack Conroy. *Anyplace But Here.* 1945, orig. *They Seek a City.* Reprint. New York: Hill and Wang, 1966.

Boucicault, Dion. *The Octoroon.* 1859. Reprint. Upper Saddle River, N.J.: Litera-ture House, 1970.

Bourget, P. *Cosmopolis.* New York: Amblard & Meyer Frères, 1895.

Boxer, C. R. *Race Relations in the Portuguese Colonial Empire, 1415–1825.* Oxford: Clarendon Press, 1963.

Brackenridge, Hugh Henry. *Modern Chivalry, Containing the Adventures of Cap-tain John Farrago and Teague O'Regan, His Servant.* New Haven: College & University Press, 1965.

Braddon, Miss M. E. *The Octoroon*. New York: Optimus Printing. Golden Gem Library, n.d.

Brawley, Benjamin. "The Negro in American Fiction." *The Dial* 40.718 (11 May 1916): 445–532.

———. *The Negro Genius: A New Appraisal of the Achievement of the American Negro in Literature and the Arts*. 1937. Reprint. New York: Dodd, Mead, [1966].

Bredsdorff, Elias. *Bibliography of Danish Literature in English Translation*. Copenhagen: Munksgaard, 1950.

Brewer, David L. "Black-White Marriage: A Norm Conflict Theory." Manuscript, 1977 (quoted by Heer).

Brooks, Peter. *Body Work: Objects of Desire in Modern Narrative*. Cambridge and London: Harvard Univ. Press, 1993.

Brown, Cecil. *The Life and Love of Mr. Jiveass Nigger*. 1969. Reprint. Greenwich, Conn.: Fawcett Crest, 1971.

Brown, Sterling A. "A Century of Negro Portraiture." In *Black and White in American Culture*, eds. Jules Chametzky and Sidney Kaplan. Amherst: Univ. of Massachusetts Press, 1969.

———. "Negro Character as Seen by White Authors." *Journal of Negro Education* 2 (1933): 179–203. Reprinted in James A. Emanuel and Theodore L. Gross, eds., *Dark Symphony: Negro Literature in America*, 139–71. New York: Free Press, 1968.

———. *Negro Poetry and Drama* and *The Negro in American Fiction*. 1937. Reprint. New York: Atheneum, 1969.

Brown, Sterling A., Arthur P. Davis, and Ulysses Lee, eds. *The Negro Caravan: Writings by American Negroes*. 1941. Reprint. New York: Arno Press, 1970.

Brown, William Hill. *The Power of Sympathy*, 1789. Reprint. William S. Osborne, ed. New Haven, Conn.: College & University Press, 1970.

Brown, William Wells. *My Southern Home; or, The South and Its People*. 1880. Reprint. New York: Negro Universities Press, 1969.

Browne, Thomas. "Of the Blackness of Negroes." *Pseudodoxia* (1646), in *The Works of Sir Thomas Browne*, 2: 368–85. Ed. Charles Sayle. London: Grant Richards, 1904.

Brownfeld, Allen C. "Intermarriage and the Court." *Commonweal* 81 (5 Feb. 1965).

Browning, Elizabeth Barrett. *The Poetical Works of Elizabeth Barrett Browning*. Cambridge, ed. Intro. Ruth M. Adams. Boston: Houghton Mifflin, 1974.

Buch, Hans Christoph. *Die Hochzeit von Port-au-Prince*. Frankfurt: Suhrkamp, 1984.

Budde, L. "Die rettende Arche Noah." *Pantheon* 18 (1960).

Bugner, Ladislas, ed. *The Image of the Black in Western Art*. Vol. 2.1. Menil Foundation; distr. Harvard Univ. Press, 1979.

Bullock, Penelope. "The Mulatto in American Fiction." *Phylon* 6 (1945): 78–82.

Bumke, Joachim. *Die Wolfram von Eschenbach Forschung seit 1945: Bericht und Bibliographie*. München: Fink, 1970.

Burly, Dan. "The Strange Will of Colonel McKee." *Negro Digest* (Nov. 1951): 17–22.

Burma, John H. "The Measurement of Negro 'Passing.'" *American Journal of Sociology* 52 (July 1946): 18–22.

Busi, Anna. *Otello in Italia (1777–1972)*. Bari: Adriatica Editrice, 1973.

Butcher, Philip. *George W. Cable*. New York: Twayne, c. 1962.

———. "Mark Twain Sells Roxy Down the River." *College Language Association Journal* 8.3 (March 1965): 225–33.

Cable, George Washington. *The Grandissimes*. 1880. Reprint. New York: Hill and Wang, 1957.

———. *The Negro Question*. New York: C. Scribner's Sons, 1890.

———. *Old Creole Days*. New York: Scribners, 1893.

———. *Strange True Stories of Louisiana*. New York: Charles Scribner, 1889.

Calder, Isabel M., ed. *Letters and Papers of Ezra Stiles*. New Haven, 1933.

Calhoun, Arthur W. *A Social History of the American Family From Colonial Times to the Present*. Vol. III: *Since the Civil War*. "Miscegenation," 27–38; "Race Sterility and Race Suicide," 225–54. Cleveland: Arthur H. Clark, 1919.

Canfield, Dorothy. *The Bent Twig*. New York: Henry Holt, 1915.

Carby, Hazel V. *Reconstructing Womanhood: The Emergence of the Afro-American Woman Novelist*. New York: Oxford Univ. Press, 1987.

Carlut, Charles, Pierre H. Dubé, and J. Raymond Dugan. *A Concordance to Flaubert's Madame Bovary*. New York and London: Garland, 1978.

Carroll, Charles. *"The Negro a Beast," or, "In the Image of God."* St. Louis: American Book and Bible House, 1900.

Carter, Elmer A. "Crossing Over." *Opportunity* (Dec. 1926): 376–78.

Carton, Evan. "*Pudd'nhead Wilson* and the Fiction of Law and Custom." In *American Realism: New Essays*, ed. Eric J. Sundquist, 82–94. Baltimore and London: Johns Hopkins Univ. Press, 1982.

Casper, Leonard. "Miscegenation as Symbol: *Band of Angels*." In *Robert Penn Warren: A Collection of Critical Essays*, ed. John Lewis Longley, Jr., 140–48. New York: New York Univ. Press, 1965.

Castelli, Ignaz Franz. "Urika, die Negerinn: Drama in einem Akt." *Dramatisches Sträußchen* 11 (1826): 133–78.

———. "Die Verlassenschaft des Pflanzers." In *Erzählungen* vol. 4, *Sämmtliche Werke*, vol. 8, pp. 85–110. Wien: Mayer & Compagnie, 1848.

Cather, Willa. *A Lost Lady*. 1923. Reprint. New York: Vintage, 1972.

Catterall, Helen Tunicliff, ed. *Judicial Cases Concerning American Slavery and the Negro*. 1926. Reprint. New York, 1968.

Cavalcanti, Carlos. *Dicionario brasileiro de artistas plásticos*. Vol. 1. Brasilia: Instituto Nacional do Livro, 1973.

Cazenave, Odile Marie. "White Othello: The White Woman and Interracial Relationships in the West African Novels of French Expression." Ph.D. diss., Pennsylvania State University, 1988.

Chametzky, Jules. *Our Decentralized Literature: Cultural Mediations in Selected Jewish and Southern Writers*. Amherst: Univ. of Massachusetts Press, 1986.

Chametzky, Jules, and Sidney Kaplan, eds. *Black and White in American Culture*. Amherst: Univ. of Massachusetts Press, 1969.

Charlier, Victor, and Eugène Chapus. "L'Épave." In *Titime, histoire de l'autre monde*. Paris: Renduel, 1833.

Chase, Richard. "Cable and His Grandissimes." *Kenyon Review* 18.3 (1956): 373–83.

Chellis, Barbara A. "Those Extraordinary Twins: Negroes and Whites." *American Quarterly* 21.1 (Spring 1969): 100–112.

Chesnut, Mary Boykin. *A Diary from Dixie*. Ed. Ben Ames Williams. Cambridge: Harvard Univ. Press, 1980.

Chesnutt, Charles W. *The House Behind the Cedars*. 1900. Reprint. Athens and London: Univ. of Georgia Press, 1988.

———. "What Is a White Man?" *The Independent* 41. 2113 (30 May 1889): 5–6 (693–94).

Child, Lydia Maria. "Annette Gray." *Anti-Slavery Standard* (22 July 1841).

———. *Anti-Slavery Catechism*. Newburyport: Charles Whipple, 1836.

———. *Fact and Fiction*. New York: C. S. Francis, 1846.

———. "Mary French and Susan Easton." *Juvenile Miscellany*, 3rd series, 6 (May 1834): 186–202.

———. *A Romance of the Republic*. 1867. Reprint. Miami: Mnemosyne, 1969.

———. *Selected Letters, 1817–1889*. Milton Meltzer and Patricia G. Holland, eds. Francine Krasno, assoc. ed. Amherst: Univ. of Massachusetts Press, 1982.

———. "Slavery's Pleasant Homes." *Liberty Bell*. Boston: Anti-Slavery Fair, 1843.

———. "The Stars and Stripes." *Liberty Bell*. Boston: National Anti-Slavery Bazaar, 1858.

———, ed. *The Oasis*. Boston: Benjamin C. Bacon, 1834.

Chinard, Gilbert. *L'Amérique et le rêve exotique*. Paris, 1913.

———. "Eighteenth Century Theories on America as a Human Habitat." *Proceedings of the American Philosophical Society* 91.1 (Feb. 1947).

Chopin, Kate. "Désirée's Baby," orig. "The Father of Désirée's Baby." *Vogue*, 14 Jan. 1893.

Clark, William Bedford. "Cable and the Theme of Miscegenation in *Old Creole Days* and *The Grandissimes*." *Mississippi Quarterly* 30.4 (Fall 1977): 597–609.

———. "The Serpent of Lust in the Southern Garden: The Theme of Miscegenation in Cable, Twain, Faulkner and Warren." Ph.D. diss., Louisiana State University, 1974.

———. "The Serpent of Lust in the Southern Garden." *Southern Review* 10.4 (Oct. 1974): 805–22.

Clifford, Deborah Pickman. *Crusader for Freedom: A Life of Lydia Maria Child*. Boston: Beacon Press, 1992.

Clinton, Catherine. *The Plantation Mistress: Woman's World in the Old South*. New York: Pantheon, 1982.

*Code of Alabama 1975*. Vol. 1. Charlottesville, Va.: Michie, 1977.

*Le Code noir; ou, Recueil des reglements rendus jusqu'à présent*. 1767. Reprint. Basse-Terre and Fort-de-France, 1980.

Cohn, Jan. "The Negro Character in Northern Magazine Fiction of the 1860's." *New England Quarterly* 43.4 (Dec. 1970): 572–92.

Cole, Bob. "The Negro and the Stage." *Colored American Magazine* (March 1902): 301–6.

Coleman, Edward Maceo, ed. *Creole Voices: Poems in French by Free Men of Color First Published in 1845*. Washington, D.C.: Associated Publishers, 1945.

Coleman, Elihu. *A Testimony Against That Anti-Christian Practice of Making Slaves of Men.* 1733. Reprint. New Bedford, 1825.

Collier, Eugenia. "The Endless Journey of an Ex-Coloured Man." *Phylon* 32.4 (Winter, 1971): 365–73.

Collins, Harold Reeves. "His Image on Ebony: The African in British Fiction During the Age of Imperialism." Ph.D.diss., Columbia University, 1951.

*Communications* 47 (1988). Special issue on thematics.

Condé, Mary. "Passing in the Fiction of Jessie Redmon Fauset and Nella Larsen." *Yearbook of English Studies* 24 (1994): "Ethnicity and Representation in American Literature," ed. Andrew Gurr, 94–104.

Cook, Mercer. *Five French Negro Authors.* Washington, D.C.: Associated Publishers, 1943.

Copher, Charles B. "Three Thousand Years of Biblical Interpretaion With Reference to Black Peoples." In *African American Religious Studies: An Interdisciplinary Anthology.* Ed. Gayraud S. Wilmore. Durham and London: Duke Univ. Press, 1989.

Cornillon, Charles de. *Odes, suivies d'une lettre sur l'esclavage des nègres.* Paris: Samson, 1806.

Corrigan, Robert W., ed. *Tragedy: Vision and Form.* 2nd ed. New York: Harper & Row, 1981.

Costa, Miriam de. "Evolution of the *Tema Negro* in the Literature of the Spanish Baroque." *College Language Association Journal* 17 (1974): 417–30.

———, ed. *Blacks in Hispanic Literature: Critical Essays.* Port Washington, N.Y.: Kennikat Press, 1977.

Cronholm, Anna-Christie. "Die nordamerikanische Sklavenfrage im deutschen Schrifttum des 19. Jahrhunderts." Ph.D. diss., Freie Universität Berlin, 1958.

Cullen, Countée. "Two Who Crossed a Line" (1925). In *Color.* New York: Harper and Brothers, 1925. Reprinted in *My Soul's High Song: The Collected Writings of Countée Cullen.* Ed. Gerald Early. New York: Anchor, 1991.

Cunningham, Rodger. *Apples on the Flood: The Southern Mountain Experience.* Knoxville: Univ. of Tennessee Press, 1987.

Curtin, Philip D. *The Image of Africa: British Ideas and Action, 1780–1850.* Madison: Univ. of Wisconsin Press, 1964; London: Macmillan, 1965.

D., P. L. "The Constitutionality of Miscegenation Statutes." *Howard Law Journal* 1 (Jan. 1955): 87–100.

Dabydeen, David. *The Black Presence in English Literature.* Manchester University Press, 1985.

Daemmrich, Horst S., and Ingrid Daemmrich. *Themes and Motifs in Western Literature: A Handbook.* Tübingen: Francke, 1987.

Daget, Serge. "Les Mots esclave, nègre, noir et les jugements de valeur sur la traite négrière dans la littérature abolitionniste française de 1770 à 1845." *Revue française d'histoire d'outre-mer* 60 (1973): 511–48.

Daggett, Harriet Spiller. "The Legal Aspect of Amalgamation in Louisiana." *Texas Law Review* 11 (Feb. 1933): 162–84. Reprinted in *Legal Essays on Family Law,* 9–35. Baton Rouge: Louisiana State Univ. Press, 1935.

da Ponte, Durant. "'The Greatest Play of the South.'" *Tennessee Studies in Literature* 2 (1957): 15–24 (on Thomas Dixon).

Darwin, Charles. *The Descent of Man*. 1871. New ed. New York: Appleton, 1888.

————. *On the Origin of Species*. 1859. Reprint. Cambridge: Harvard Univ. Press, 1964.

Daremberg, Ch., and Edm. Saglio, eds. *Dictionnaire des Antiquités grecques et romaines*. Paris: Hachette, 1895.

Dash, J. Michael. *Haiti and the United States: National Stereotypes and the Literary Imagination*. New York: St. Martin's Press, 1988.

Davenport, Charles B. *Heredity of Skin Color in Negro-White Crosses*. Publication #188. Washington, D.C.: Carnegie Institute, 1913.

Davis, Allison, and John Dollard. *Children of Bondage: The Personality Development of Negro Youth in the Urban South*. 1940. Reprint. New York: Harper Torchbooks, 1964.

Davis, Allison, Burleigh Gardner, and Mary R. Gardner, directed by W. Lloyd Warner. *Deep South: A Social Anthropological Study of Caste and Class*. Chicago: Univ. of Chicago Press, 1941.

Davis, Arthur P. *From the Dark Tower: Afro-American Writers 1900–1960*. Washington, D.C.: Howard Univ. Press, 1974.

————. "The Tragic Mulatto Theme in Six Works of Langston Hughes." *Phylon* 16 (1955): 195–204.

Davis, David Brion. *The Problem of Slavery in Western Culture*. Ithaca: Cornell Univ. Press, 1966.

Davis, F. James. *Who Is Black? One Nation's Definition*. University Park: Pennsylvania State Univ. Press, 1991.

Davis, James D. *History of the City of Memphis*. Memphis, 1873.

Davis, Kingsley. "Intermarriage in Caste Societies." *American Anthropologist* 43 (July–Sept. 1941): 376–95.

Davis, Thadious M. *Faulkner's "Negro:" Art and the Southern Context*. Baton Rouge and London: Louisiana State Univ. Press, 1983.

Day, Caroline Bond. *A Study of Some Negro-White Families in the United States*. Foreword and notes by Ernest A. Hooton. Harvard African Studies no. 10. Cambridge, Mass.: Peabody Museum of Harvard University, 1932.

Dearborn, Mary V. *Pocahontas's Daughters: Gender and Ethnicity in American Culture*. New York: Oxford Univ. Press, 1986.

Debien, Gabriel. "Un roman colonial de Victor Hugo: *Bug-Jargal*." *Revue d'histoire littéraire de la France* 52 (1952): 289–313.

De Forest, John William. "A Gentleman of an Old School." Published anonymously in *Atlantic Monthly* 21 (May 1868): 546–55.

Degen, John A. "How to End *The Octoroon*." *Educational Theatre Journal* 27 (1975): 170–78.

Degler, Carl N. *Neither Black Nor White: Slavery and Race Relations in Brazil and the United States*. New York: Macmillan, 1971.

Delany, Samuel R. *The Motion of Light in Water: Sex and Science Fiction Writing in the East Village, 1957–1965*. New York: Arbor House, 1988.

Delesalle, Simone, and Lucette Valensi. "Le Mot *nègre* dans les dictionnaires français d'Ancien régime." *Langue française* 15 (Sept. 1972): 79–104.

Demus, Otto, et al. *The Mosaics of San Marco in Venice*. Chicago and London: Univ. of Chicago Press, 1984.

Derrida, Jacques. *D'un ton apocalyptique adopté naguère en philosophie*. Paris: Galilée, 1983.

Devereux, George. "Ethnic Identity: Its Logical Foundation and Its Dysfunctions." In *Ethnic Identity: Cultural Continuities and Change*, ed. George DeVos and Lola Romanucci-Ross. Palo Alto: Mayfield, 1975.

Devisse, Jean. *The Image of the Black in Western Art: From the Early Christian Era to the "Age of Discovery."* Series ed. Ladislas Bugner. vol. 2.1. Trans. William Granger Ryan, Menil Foundation; distr. Harvard Univ. Press, 1979.

De Vos, George, and Lola Romanucci-Ross, eds. *Ethnic Identity: Cultural Continuities and Change*. Stanford: Mayfield, 1975.

Dickinson, Anna. *What Answer?*. 1868. Reprint. Fields, Osgood, 1869.

Di Segni, Riccardo. *Le unghie di Adama: Studi di antropologia ebraica*. Napoli: Guida editori, 1981.

Dix, Robin C. "The Harps of Memnon and Aeolus: A Study in the Propagation of an Error." *Modern Philology* 85.3 (Feb. 1988): 288–93.

Dixon, Thomas, Jr. "Booker T. Washington and the Negro." *Saturday Evening Post* (19 Aug. 1905): 1–3.

———. *Clansman*. 1905. Reprint. New York: Triangle Books, 1941.

———. *The Leopard's Spots: A Romance of the White Man's Burden—1865–1900*. New York: Doubleday, Page, 1902.

———. *The Sins of the Father: A Romance of the South*. New York: D. Appleton, 1912.

———. "Why I Wrote 'The Clansman.'" *Theatre* 6 (Jan. 1906): 20–22.

Dollard, John. *Caste and Class in a Southern Town*. 1937; 3rd ed. Garden City, N.Y.: Doubleday Anchor, 1957.

Dominguez, Virginia R. *White by Definition: Social Classification in Creole Louisiana*. New Brunswick, N.J.: Rutgers Univ. Press, 1986.

Douglass, Frederick. *Narrative of the Life of Frederick Douglass, an American Slave: Written by Himself*. 1845. Reprint. New York: Modern Library, 1984.

Downing, Henry F. *The American Cavalryman: A Liberian Romance*. New York: Neale Publishing, 1917.

Drake, B. Frank. "The Negro Before the Supreme Court." *Albany Law Journal* 66 (Aug. 1904): 238–48.

Duberman, Martin, ed. *The Antislavery Vanguard: New Essays on Abolitionists*. Princeton: Princeton Univ. Press, 1965.

Du Bois, W. E. B. "Intermarriage." *The Crisis* (Feb. 1913): 181–2.

Duchet, Michèle. *Anthropologie et histoire au siècle des lumières*. Paris: Maspéro, 1971.

———. "Esclavage et préjuge de couleur," "Le Mouvement anti-esclavagiste: théorie et pratique." In *Racisme et société*, eds. C. Duchet and P. de Cormarmond. Paris: Maspéro, 1969.

———. "Le Primitivisme de Diderot." *Europe* (Jan.–Feb. 1969): 121–32.

duCille, Ann. *The Coupling Convention: Sex, Text, and Tradition in Black Women's Fiction*. New York: Oxford Univ. Press, 1993.

———. "'Who Reads Here?' Back Talking with Houston Baker." *Novel*, Fall 1992.

Dunston, Bishop Alfred G., Jr. *The Black Man in the Old Testament and Its World*. Philadelphia: Dorrance, 1974.

Duras, Mme. [Claire de Kersaint] la duchesse de [Durfort-]. *Ourika*. Eng. trans. by [George Wallis Haven]. Boston: Carter and Hendee, 1829.

Durkheim, Emile. *Incest: The Nature and Origin of the Taboo.* 1898. Trans. Edward Sagarin. New York: Lyle Stuart, 1963.

Dykes, Eva Beatrice. *The Negro in English Romantic Thought.* Washington, D.C.: Associate Publishers, 1942.

Dyserinck, Hugo. *Komparatistik: Eine Einführung.* 2nd ed. Bonn: Bouvier, 1981.

———. "Zum Problem der 'Images' und 'Mirages' und ihrer Untersuchungen im Rahmen der Vergleichenden Literaturwissenschaft." *Arcadia* 1 (1966): 107–20.

Early, Gerald. "'A Servant of Servants Shall He Be . . .': Paternalism and Millenialism in American Slavery Literature, 1850–1859." Ph.D. diss., Cornell University, 1982.

———, ed. *Lure and Loathing: Essays on Race, Identity, and the Ambivalence of Assimilation.* New York: Allen Lane, Penguin Press, 1993.

East, Edward M. *Heredity and Human Affairs.* New York: Scribner's, 1929.

Edelstein, Tilden G. "*Othello* in America: The Drama of Racial Intermarriage." In *Region, Race, and Reconstruction: Essays in Honor of C. Vann Woodward,* 179–97. New York, Oxford: Oxford Univ. Press, 1982.

Ekström, Kjell. *George Washington Cable: A Study of His Early Life and Work.* 1950. Reprint. New York: Haskell House, 1966.

Elfenbein, Anna Shannon. *Women on the Color Line: Evolving Stereotypes and the Writings of George Washington Cable, Grace King, Kate Chopin.* Charlottesville: Univ. of Virginia Press, 1989.

Eliot, Charles. *Sinfulness of Slavery in the United States.* Cincinnati, 1857.

Eliot, George. *Daniel Deronda.* 1876. Reprint. Oxford and New York: Oxford Univ. Press, 1986.

Elisséeff, Nikita. *Thèmes et motifs des* Mille et une nuits: *essai de classification.* Beyrouth: Institut Français de Damas, 1949.

Elizondo, Virgil. *L'Avenir est au métissage.* Preface by Léopold Sédar Senghor. Paris: Mame, 1987.

Elliott, Emory. *Revolutionary Writers: Literature and Authority in the New Republic, 1725–1810.* New York, London: Oxford Univ. Press, 1986.

Ellison, Ralph. *Invisible Man.* 1952. Reprint. New York: Vintage Books, 1972.

———. *Shadow and Act.* 1964. Reprint. New York: Vintage Books, 1972.

Emanuel, James A., and Theodore L. Gross, eds. *Dark Symphony: Negro Literature in America.* New York: Free Press, 1968.

Enkvist, Nils Erik. "*The Octoroon* and English Opinions of Slavery." *American Quarterly* 8 (1956):166–69.

Erdman, David V. *Blake: Prophet Against Empire.* Princeton: Princeton Univ. Press, 1977.

———. "Blake's Vision of Slavery." *Journal of the Warburg and Courtauld Institutes* 15.3–4 (July–Dec. 1952): 242–52.

Erickson, Jon. "Fairytale Features in Kate Chopin's 'Désirée's Baby': A Study in Genre Cross-Reference." In *Modes of Narrative: Approaches to American, Canadian and British Fiction.* Eds. Reingard M. Nischik and Barbara Kort. Würzburg: Könighausen & Neumann, 1990.

Erno, Richard Bruce. "Dominant Images of the Negro in the Antebellum South." Ph.D. diss., University of Minnesota, 1961.

Estabrook, Arthur H., and Ivan E. McDougle. *Mongrel Virginians: The Win Tribe.* Baltimore: Williams and Wilkins, 1926.

Estes, Matthew. *A Defence of Negro Slavery, as It Exists in the United States.* Montgomery: Press of the "Alabama Journal," 1846.

Etiemble, René. *Blason d'un corps: récit.* Paris: Gallimard, 1961.

Étienne, Servais. *Les Sources de* Bug-Jargal. Liège: Impr. Vaillant-Carmann, 1923.

Evans, William McKee. "From the Land of Canaan to the Land of Guinea: The Strange Odyssey of the 'Sons of Ham.'" *American Historical Review* 85. 1 (Feb. 1980): 15–43.

Fabre, Michel. "Bayonne or the Yoknapatawpha of Ernest Gaines." *Callaloo* 1.3 (1978): 110–24.

———. *From Harlem to Paris: Black American Writers in France, 1840–1980.* Urbana and Chicago: Univ. of Illinois Press, 1991.

———. *La Rive noire: de Harlem à la Seine.* Paris: Lieu Commun, 1985.

Fairchild, Hoxie Neale. *The Noble Savage: A Study in Romantic Naturalism.* New York: Columbia Univ. Press, 1928.

Fanoudh-Siefer, Léon. *Le Mythe du Nègre et de l'Afrique Noire dans la littérature française de 1800 à la 2$^e$ guerre mondiale.* 1968. Reprint. Abidjan, Dakar, Lomé: Les Nouvelles Editions Africaines, 1980.

Far, Sui Sin. "Leaves from the Mental Portfolio of an Eurasian." *Independent* 66, no. 3138 (Jan. 21, 1909).

Farrison, William Edward. *William Wells Brown: Author and Reformer.* Chicago and London: Univ. of Chicago Press, 1969.

Faulkner, William. *Absalom, Absalom!* 1936. Repr. New York: Vintage Books, 1987.

———. *Collected Stories.* New York: Random House, n.d.

Fauset, Jessie. *Comedy: American Style.* New York: Frederick A. Stokes, 1933. Reprint. College Park, Md.: McGrath Publishing, 1969.

———. *Plum Bun.* 1928. Reprint. Boston: Beacon Press, 1990.

Faust, Drew Gilpin, ed. *The Ideology of Slavery: Proslavery Thought in the Antebellum South, 1830–1860.* Baton Rouge and London: Louisiana State Univ. Press, 1981.

Fawkes, Richard. *Dion Boucicault: A Biography.* London, Melbourne, New York: Quartet Books, [1979].

Ferguson, Mary Anne. "Identifying the Stereotypes." In *Images of Women in Literature.* Boston: Houghton Mifflin, 1973.

Fernandez de Castro, José-Antonio. *Tema negro en las letras de Cuba 1608–1935.* Havanna: Mirador, 1943.

Feuser, Willfried F. "Das Bild des Afrikaners in der deutschen Literatur." Akten des V. Internationalen Germanisten-Kongresses (1975). *Jahrbuch für Internationale Germanistik* Reihe A, Band 2.4 (1976): 306–15.

———. "The Image of the Black in the Writings of Johann Gottfried Herder." *Journal of European Studies* 8 (1978): 109–28.

———. "Slave to Proletarian: Images of the Black in German Literature." *German Life and Letters* 32 (1979): 122–34.

Fiedler, Leslie. *Love and Death in the American Novel.* 1960. Repr. New York: Stein and Day, 1975.

———. *What Was Literature? Class Culture and Mass Society.* New York: Simon and Schuster, 1982.

Fields, Annie, ed. *The Life and Letters of Harriet Beecher Stowe.* Boston and New York: Houghton Mifflin, 1898.

Fields, Barbara Jeanne. "Slavery, Race, and Ideology in the United States of America." *New Left Review* (May/June 1990): 95–118.

Findlay, George. *Miscegenation: A Study of the Biological Sources of Inheritance of the South African European Population.* Pretoria: Pretoria News and Printing Works, 1936.

Fink, J. "Noah der Gerechte in der frühchristlichen Kunst." *Beihefte zum Archiv für Kunstgeschichte* 4. Köln, 1955.

Fischer, Manfred S. "Komparatistische Imagologie: Für eine interdisziplinäre Erforschung national-imagotypischer Systeme." *Zeitschrift für Sozialpsychologie* 10 (1979): 30–44.

Fishkin, Shelley Fisher. "False Starts, Fragments and Fumbles: Mark Twain's Unpublished Writing on Race." *Essays in Arts and Sciences* 20 (Oct. 1991): 17–31.

———. *Was Huck Black? Mark Twain and African American Voices.* New York and Oxford: Oxford Univ. Press, 1993.

Flaubert, Gustave. *Madame Bovary.* Édition nouvelle établie par la Société des Études littéraires françaises. Paris: Club de l'honnête homme, 1971. Eng. trans. from *Best-Known Works of Gustave Flaubert.* New York: Blue Ribbon Books, 1904.

Fletcher, John. *Essays on Slavery, in Easy Lessons: Compiled into Eight Studies, and Subdivided into Short Lessons for the Convenience of Readers.* Natchez, Miss.: Jackson Warner, 1852.

Flynn, Joyce. "Melting Plots." *American Quarterly* 38.3 (Bibliography Issue 1986): 417–38.

Ford, Thomas W. "Howells and the American Negro." *Texas Studies in Literature and Language* 5.4 (Winter 1964): 530–37.

———. "The [Miscegenation] Theme in *Pudd'nhead Wilson.*" *Mark Twain Journal* 10.1 (Summer 1955): 13–14.

Fowler, David H. "Northern Attitudes Towards Interracial Marriage: A Study of Legislation and Public Opinion in the Middle Atlantic States of the Old Northwest." Ph.D. diss., Yale University, 1963.

Fowler, Doreen, and Ann J. Abadie, eds. *Faulkner and Race.* Jackson and London: Univ. of Mississippi Press, 1987.

Fowler, O. S. *Hereditary Descent: Its Laws and Facts, Illustrated and Applied to the Improvement of Mankind.* New York, 1843.

Fraiman, Susan. "Mother-Daughter Romance in Charles W. Chesnutt's 'Her Virginia Mammy.'" *Studies in Short Fiction* 22.4 (Fall 1985): 443–48.

Frazier, E. Franklin. "Children in Black and Mulatto Families." *American Journal of Sociology* 39 (1933): 12–29.

———. *The Negro Family in the United States.* Chicago: Univ. of Chicago Press, 1939.

———. *The Negro in the United States.* New York: Macmillan, 1957.

Fredrickson, George M. *The Arrogance of Race: Historical Prespectives on Slavery, Racism, and Social Inequality.* Middletown, Conn.: Wesleyan Univ. Press, 1988.

———. *The Black Image in the White Mind: The Debate on Afro-American Charac-*

*ters and Destiny, 1817–1914.* New York: Harper Torchbooks, 1972.

Freimarck, John. "*Pudd'nhead Wilson*: A Tale of Blood and Brotherhood." *University Review* 34 (June 1968): 303–6.

Frenzel, Elisabeth. *Motive der Weltliteratur: ein Lexikon dichtungsgeschichtlicher Längsschnitte.* Stuttgart: Kröner, 1980.

———. *Stoffe der Weltliteratur: ein Lexikon dichtungsgeschichtlicher Längsschnitte.* Stuttgart: Kröner, 1963.

———. *Stoff-, Motiv- und Symbolforschung.* Stuttgart: J. B. Metzlersche Verlagsbuchhandlung, 1978.

Freyre, Gilberto. *Casa Grande e Senzela.* 1933. German trans. Ludwig Graf von Schönfeldt. München: Deutscher Tachenbuch-Verlag, 1990.

———. *The Gilberto Freyre Reader.* Trans. Barbara Shelby. New York: Knopf, 1974.

Friedman, Donald M., ed. *Select Poems: Humane and Divine.* Liverpool: Liverpool Univ. Press, 1966.

Friedman, Lawrence J. *The White Savage: Racial Fantasies and the Postbellum South.* Englewood Cliffs, N.J.: Prentice-Hall, 1970.

Frisby, James R., Jr. "New Orleans Writers and the Negro: George Washington Cable, Grace King, Ruth McEnery Stuart, Kate Chopin, and Lafcadio Hearn." Ph.D. diss., Emory University, 1972.

Funderburg, Lise. *Black, White, Other: Biracial Americans Talk About Race and Identity.* New York: William Morrow, 1994.

Gaines, Francis Pendleton. "The Racial Bar Sinister in American Romance." *South Atlantic Quarterly* 25.4 (Oct. 1926): 396–402.

———. *The Southern Plantation: A Study in the Development and the Accuracy of a Tradition.* New York: Columbia Univ. Press, 1925.

Galassi, Frank S. "Slavery and Melodrama: Boucicault's *The Octoroon*." *Markham Review* 6 (Spring 1977): 77–80.

Galton, Francis. *Finger Prints.* London and New York: Macmillan, 1892.

Garber, Marjorie. *Vested Interests: Cross-Dressing & Cultural Anxiety.* New York and London: Routledge, 1992.

Garton, Christiana. "The Portrayal of Negro Character in the American Drama and Novel." Thesis, University of Colorado, 1942.

Gates, Henry Louis, Jr., and Nellie Y. McKay, eds. *The Norton Anthology of African American Literature.* New York and London: W. W. Norton, 1997.

Gatewood, Willard B. *Aristocrats of Color: The Black Elite, 1880–1920.* Bloomington and Indianapolis: Indiana Univ. Press, 1990.

Genovese, Eugene. "Miscegenation." In *Roll Jordan Roll: The World the Slaves Made.* New York: Vintage Books, 1976.

Getman, Karen A. "Sexual Control in the Slaveholding South." *Harvard Women's Law Journal* 7.1 (Spring 1984): 115–52.

Gillman, Susan. *Dark Twins: Imposture and Identity in Mark Twain's America.* Chicago and London: Univ. of Chicago Press, 1989.

Gillman, Susan, and Forest G. Robinson, eds. *Mark Twain's Pudd'nhead Wilson: Race, Conflict, and Culture.* Durham and London: Duke Univ. Press, 1990.

Gilman, Margaret. *Othello in France.* Paris: Champion, 1925.

Gilman, Sander. *On Blackness Without Blacks: Essays on the Image of the Black in Germany.* Boston: G. K. Hall, 1982.

Girod, François. *La Vie quotidienne de la société créole (Saint-Domingue au 18^e siècle).* Paris: Hachette, 1971.

Glasco, Laurence. "The Mulatto: A Neglected Dimension of Afro-American Social Structure." Paper presented at the meeting of the Organization of American Historians, 17–20 April 1974.

Gloster, Hugh M. *Negro Voices in American Fiction.* 1948. New York: Russell & Russell, 1965.

Goldenberg, David. "The Curse of Ham: A Case of Rabbinic Racism?" In *Struggles in the Promised Land: Towards a History of Black-Jewish Relations in the United States,* eds. Jack Salzman and Cornel West. New York: Oxford University Press, forthcoming.

González, Reynaldo. "Para una lectura historicista de *Cecilia Valdés.*" *Casa de las américas* 22. 129 (Nov.–Dec. 1981): 84–92.

Gordon, Charles W. *Select Sermons.* New York, 1887.

Gould, Stephen Jay. *The Mismeasure of Man.* New York: W. W. Norton, 1981.

Graepel, Peter Hartwig. *Die Gärtner-Gedenkstätte im Museum der Stadt Calw.* Kleine Reihe 3, Museum der Stadt Calw. Calw: 1991.

Graves, Robert, and Raphael Patai. *Hebrew Myths: The Book of Genesis.* Garden City, N.Y.: Doubleday, 1964.

Gray, Wood. *The Hidden Civil War: The Story of the Copperheads.* New York, 1942.

Green, Paul. *Five Plays of the South.* New York: Hill and Wang, 1963.

Greenberg, Jack. *Race Relations and American Law.* New York: Columbia Univ. Press, 1959.

Greenblatt, Stephen. *Marvelous Possessions: The Wonder of the New World.* Chicago: Univ. of Chicago Press, 1991.

Grentrup, Theodor. *Die Rassenmischehen in den deutschen Kolonien.* Paderborn: Ferdinand Schöningh, 1914.

Griaule, Marcel. *Schwarze Genesis—ein afrikanischer Schöpfungsbericht.* Freiburg: Herder, 1970.

Griffin, John Howard. *Black Like Me.* Boston: Houghton Mifflin, 1961.

[Griffiths, Mattie]. *Autobiography of a Female Slave.* 1857. Reprint. Miami: Mnemosyne, 1969.

Grimm, Hans. *Südafrikanische Novellen.* 1913. Reprint. Lippoldsberg: Klosterhaus, 1975.

Grønbech, Bo. "Om 'Mulatten' og dens franske forlæg." *Anderseniana,* ser. 3, vol. 3 (1978–79): 43–60.

Gross, Seymour L., and John Edward Hardy, eds. *Images of the Negro in American Literature.* Chicago and London: Univ. of Chicago Press, 1966.

Gross, Theodore L. *Albion W. Tourgée.* New York: Twayne, 1963.

Gruening, Ernest. "Going White." *Saturday Review of Literature* (10 July 1926): 918.

Grünbaum, Max. *Neue Beiträge zur semitischen Sagenkunde.* Leiden: E. J. Brill, 1893.

Gumilla, Joseph. *Histoire naturelle, civile et géographique de l'Orenoque.* Avignon: Desaint & Saillant, 1758.

————. *El Orinoco ilustrado, y defendido.* . . . Madrid: Manuel Fernandez, 1745.

Guttman, Selmen. *The Foreign Sources of Shakespeare's Works.* 1947. Reprint. 1968.

H., L. P. "Constitutional Law—Domestic Relations—Miscegenation Laws Based Solely Upon Race Are a Denial of the Due Process and Equal Protection Clauses of the 14th Amendment." *New York Law Forum* 13 (1967): 170–78.

Haizlip, Shirlee Taylor. "Passing." *American Heritage* 46.1 (Feb./March 1995): 46–54.

Hakluyt, Richard. *Voyages.* London and New York: Dent and Dutton, 1927.

Halsell, Grace. *Soul Sister.* Greenwich, Conn.: Fawcett Publications, 1969.

Hamalian, Leo, and James V. Hatch, eds. *The Roots of African American Drama: An Anthology of Earlys Plays, 1858–1938.* Detroit: Wayne State Univ. Press, 1991.

Hardaway, Roger D. "Unlawful Love: A History of Arizona's Miscegenation Law." *Journal of Arizona History* 27 (Winter 1986): 377–90.

Harper, Frances Ellen Watkins. *Iola Leroy: or, Shadows Uplifted.* 1893. Reprint. Boston: Beacon Press, 1987.

————. "The Two Offers." *Anglo-African Magazine* I. 9 and 10 (Sept.–Oct., 1859): 288–91.

Harris, Joel Chandler. *Uncle Remus: His Songs and Sayings.* London: Routledge, n.d.

Harris-Schenz, Beverly Ann. "Images of the Black in Eighteenth Century German Literature." Ph.D. diss., Stanford, 1977.

Hatch, James V., and Ted Shine, eds. *Black Theater, U.S.A.: Forty-Five Plays by Black Americans, 1847–1974.* New York: Free Press, 1974.

Hathaway, Heather. "'Maybe Freedom Lies in Hating': Miscegenation and the Oedipal Conflict." In *Refiguring the Father: New Feminist Readings of Patriarchy,* eds. Patricia Yeager and Beth Kowaleski-Wallace. Carbondale: Southern Illinois Univ. Press, 1989, 153–67.

Hausherr, Reiner, ed. *Bible moralisée: Codex Vindobonensis 2554 der Österreichischen Nationalbibliothek.* Reprinted in toto. Trans. (from French) Hans-Walter Stark. Graz: Akademische Druck- und Verlagsanstalt, 1992.

Hedrick, Joan. *Harriet Beecher Stowe: A Life.* New York: Oxford Univ. Press, 1994.

Heer, David M. "Intermarriage." In *Harvard Encyclopedia of American Ethnic Groups,* eds. Oscar Handlin, Ann Orlov, and Stephan Thernstrom, 513–21. Cambridge and London: Harvard Univ. Press, 1980.

————. "The Prevalence of Black-White Marriage in the United States, 1960 and 1970." *Journal of Marriage and the Family* 36 (May 1974): 246–58.

Heiberg, Johan Ludvig. "En sjael efter Døden. En apocalyptisk Comedie," 1840. Reprint. *Udvalgte Digtninger.* Kjøbenhavn og Kristiana: Gyldendalske Boghandel, Nordisk Forlag, 1905.

Heilman, Robert Bechthold. "Tragedy and Melodrama: Speculations on Generic Form." In *Tragedy: Vision and Form.* Ed. Robert W. Corrigan. 2nd ed. New York: Harper & Row, 1981.

Heiney, Donald. *America in Modern Italian Literature.* New Brunswick, N.J.: Rutgers Univ. Press, 1964.

Hemenway, Robert. *Zora Neale Hurston: A Literary Biography.* Urbana: Univ. of Illinois Press, 1977.

Hendricks, Margo, and Patricia Parker, eds. *Women, "Race," and Writing in the Early Modern Period.* London and New York: Routledge, 1994.

Henry, William S. *Out of Wedlock.* Boston: Richard G. Badger, 1931.

Hepokoski, James A. *Giuseppe Verdi, Otello.* Cambridge Opera Handbooks. Cambridge, Eng.: Cambridge Univ. Press, 1987.

Herbert, Thomas. *Some Years Travels into Divers Parts of Africa, and Asia the Great, Describing More Particularly the Empires of Persia and Industan...* 4th ed. London: 1677.

Hernton, Calvin C. *Sex and Racism in America.* New York: Grove Press, 1966.

———. *The Sexual Mountain and Black Women Writers: Adventures in Sex, Literature, and Real Life.* New York: Doubleday, 1990.

Herskovits, Melville J. *Man and His Works: The Science of Cultural Anthropology.* New York: Knopf, 1952.

Herzog, Kristin. *Women, Ethnics, and Exotics: Images of Power in Mid-Nineteenth-Century American Fiction.* Knoxville: Univ. of Tennessee Press, 1983.

Hesse, Hans Rudolf. "Herzeloydes Traum." *Germanisch-Romanische Monatsschrift* 43 (1962): 306–9.

Heyward, Du Bose. *Brass Ankle.* New York: Farrar and Rinehart, 1931.

Higginbotham, A. Leon, Jr., and Barbara Kopytoff, "Racial Purity and Interracial Sex in the Law of Colonial and Antebellum Virginia," *Georgetown Law Journal* 77.6 (Aug. 1989): 1967–2029.

[Hildreth, Richard.] *The Slave; or, Memoirs of Archy Moore.* 2 vols. Boston: John H. Eastburn, printer, 1836.

Hildreth, Richard. *Archy Moore, The White Slave; or, Memoirs of a Fugitive. With a New Introduction.* New York and Auburn, Miller, Orton & Mulligan, 1856.

———. *The White Slave; or, Memoirs of a Fugitive.* Boston: Tappan and Whittemore, 1852 (chapters 37–59 added).

Himes, Chester. *If He Hollers Let Him Go.* 1945. Reprint. New York: New American Library, n.d.

Hirsch, Samson Raphael. *Commentary on the Pentateuch.* Trans. Isaac Levi. London, 1960.

Ho, Wen-Ching. "Miscegenation in William Faulkner: A Synecdoche for Slavery/Caste System." Ph.D. diss., Univ. of Michigan, 1989.

Hobart, Benjamin. *History of the Town of Abington, Plymouth County, Massachusetts.* 256ff. Boston: T. H. Carter, 1866.

Hodgart, Matthew. *Satire.* London: World University Library, Weidenfeld and Nicolson, 1969.

Hoffman, Frederick, and Olga Vickery, eds. *William Faulkner: Three Decades of Criticism.* East Lansing, 1960.

Hoffmann, Léon-François. "Balzac et les noirs." In *Année balzacienne,* 297–308. (Paris: Garnier), 1966.

———. *Essays on Haitian Literature.* Washington, D.C.: 3 Continents, 1984.

———. *Le Nègre romantique: personnage littéraire et obsession collective.* Paris: Payot, 1973.

Hogan, Robert. *Dion Boucicault.* New York: Twayne, 1969.

Hoggan, Frances. "La Securité des femmes blanches et la race africaine." In *Mémoires sur le contact des races,* ed. G. Spiller. London: P.S. King & Son, 1911.

[Holland, Edwin Clifford]. *A Refutation of the Calumnies Circulated Against the Southern and Western States.* Charleston: A. E. Miller, 1822.

Hollinger, David A. *In the American Province: Studies in the History and Historiog-raphy of Ideas*. Indiana Univ. Press, 1985.

Holmes, Thomas Alan. "Race as Metaphor: 'Passing' in Twentieth-Century African-American Fiction." Ph.D. diss., University of Alabama, Tuscaloosa, 1990.

Hooton, Earnest Albert. *Up From the Ape*. New York: Macmillan, 1947.

Hopkins, Pauline E. "A Dash for Liberty." *Colored American Magazine* 3.4 (May 1901): 246.

———. "Of One Blood; Or, The Hidden Self." *Colored American Magazine* (November 1902–November 1903).

———. *A Primer of Facts*. Cambridge: P. E. Hopkins, 1905.

———. "Talma Gordon." *Colored American Magazine* 1.5 (Oct. 1900): 271–90.

Hosmer, Hezekiah Lord. *Adela, the Octoroon*. 1860. Reprint. Freeport, N.Y.: Books for Libraries, 1972.

Howells, William Dean. "The Pilot's Story." *Atlantic Monthly* 6, no. 35 (Sept. 1860): 323–25.

Høybye, P. "H. C. Andersen og Frankrig." *Anderseniana*, ser. 2, vol. 11 (1951–54): 146–47.

Huggins, Nathan Irvin. *Harlem Renaissance*. New York: Oxford Univ. Press, 1971.

———. *Revelations: American History, American Myths*. Ed. Brenda Smith Hug-gins. New York and Oxford: Oxford Univ. Press, 1995.

Hughes, Carl Milton. *The Negro Novelist: A Discussion of the Writings of American Negro Novelists, 1940–1950*. 1953. Reprint. New York: Citadel Press, 1970.

Hughes, Langston. *The Ways of White Folks*. 1934. Reprint. New York: Vintage Books, 1962.

Humboldt, Friedrich Alexander von. *Versuch über den politischen Zustand des Königreichs Neu-Spanien*. Vol. 1. Tübingen: Cotta, 1809.

Hunger, Herbert. *Lexikon der griechischen und römischen Mythologie*. Wien: Brüder Hollinek, 1959.

Hurst, Fannie. *Imitation of Life*. New York and London: Harper, 1933.

Hurston, Zora Neale. *Dust Tracks on a Road*. 1942. Reprint. Urbana and Chicago: Univ. of Illinois Press, 1984.

Hutchinson, George. "Jean Toomer and American Racial Discourse." *Texas Studies in Literature and Language* 35.2 (Summer 1993): 226–50.

Hyder, Clyde K. *Wilkie Collins in America*. Kansas Univ. Press, 1940.

Ide, Arthur Frederick. *Noah and the Ark*. Las Colinas, Texas: Monument Press, 1992.

Imbruglia, Girolamo, ed. *Il Razzismo e le sue storie*. Napoli: Edizioni Scientifiche Italiane, 1992.

Irwin, John T. *Doubling and Incest/Repetition and Revenge: A Speculative Reading of Faulkner*. 1975. Baltimore and London: Johns Hopkins Univ. Press, 1980.

Isaac, Ephraim. "Concept biblique et rabbinique de la malediction de Noe," and "Biblical and Rabbinic Understanding of the Curse of Noah." *SIDIC: Service international de documentation judéo-chretienne* 11.2 (1978): 16–35.

———. "Genesis, Judaism, and the 'Sons of Ham.'" *Slavery and Abolition* 1 (1980): 3–17.

Isaac, Rhys. *The Transformation of Virginia, 1740–1790.* Chapel Hill: Univ. of North Carolina Press, 1982.

Jackson, Blyden. "A Golden Mean for the Negro Novel." *College Language Association Journal* 3.2 (Dec. 1959): 81–87.

Jackson, Richard L. *The Black Image in Latin American Literature.* Albuquerque: Univ. of New Mexico Press, 1976.

———. *Black Writers in Latin America.* Albuquerque: Univ. of New Mexico Press, 1979.

Jakoski, Helen. "Power Unequal to Man." *Southern Folklore Quarterly* 38 (June 1974): 91–108.

James, C. L. R. *The Black Jacobins: Toussaint l'Ouverture and the San Domingo Revolution.* 2nd ed., New York: Vintage Books, 1963.

James, Henry. *Essays on Literature: American Writers, English Writers.* New York: Library of America, 1984.

———. *The Portrait of a Lady.* Ed. Robert D. Bamberg. New York: Norton, 1975.

Jason, Howard M. "The Negro in Spanish Literature to the End of the Siglo de Oro." *College Language Association Journal* 9 (1965): 121–31.

Jefferson, Thomas. *The Papers of Thomas Jefferson*, vol. 2. Ed. Jackson Boyd. Princeton, N.J.: Princeton Univ. Press, 1950.

Jenks, Albert E. "The Legal Status of Negro-White Amalgamation in the United States." *American Journal of Sociology* 21 (March 1916): 666–78.

Jobson, Richard. *The Golden Trade: Or, a Discovery of the River Gambra, and the Golden Trade of the Aethiopians.* 1623. Reprint. Ed. Charles G. Kingsley. Teignmouth, Devonshire, 1904.

Johnson, Caleb. "Crossing the Color Line." *Outlook and Independent* 158 (26 Aug. 1931): 526–43.

[Johnson, Charles S.]. "The Vanishing Mulatto." *Opportunity: Journal of Negro Life* 3, no. 34 (Oct. 1925): 291.

Johnson, Charles S., ed. *Ebony and Topaz.* 1927. Reprint. Freeport, N.Y.: Books for Libraries Press, 1971.

Johnston, James Hugo. "Miscegenation in the Ante-Bellum South." Ph.D. diss., Chicago, 1937. Partly printed Chicago, 1939.

———. *Race Relations in Virginia & Miscegenation in the South, 1776–1860.* 1937. Reprint. Amherst: Univ. of Massachusetts Press, 1970.

Johnson, James Weldon. *The Autobiography of an Ex-Colored Man.* 1912. Reprint. New York: Hill and Wang, 1960.

Jonas, Emil, ed. *H. C. Andersens Briefwechsel mit Sr. Königlichen Hoheit, dem Grossherzog Carl Alexander von Sachsen-Weimar-Eisenach und anderen Zeitgenossen.* Leipzig: Wilhelm Friedrich, n.d.

Jones, Eldred. *The Elizabethan Image of Africa.* Charlottesville: Univ. of Virginia Press, 1971.

———. *Othello's Countrymen: The African in English Renaissance Drama.* Oxford: Oxford Univ. Press, 1965.

Jones, Hugh. *The Present State of Virginia.* 1724. Reprint. New York: Joseph Sabin, 1865.

Jones, Suzanne W. "*Absalom, Absalom!* and the Custom of Storytelling: A Reflection of Southern Social and Literary History." *Southern Studies* 24.1 (1985): 82–112.

Jordan, Winthrop D. *White Over Black: American Attitudes Toward the Negro, 1550–1812*. Baltimore: Penguin Books, 1969.

Jourda, Pierre. *L'Exotisme dans la littérature française depuis Chateaubriand*. Paris: Presses Universitaires de France, 1956.

Julien, Claude. "'Et si l'on restait chacun chez soi' ou les liaisons interraciales dans le roman afro-américain." *Revue française d'études américaines* 29 (May 1986): 327–43.

Kaemmerling, Ekkehard, ed. *Ikonographie und Ikonologie: Theorien, Entwicklung, Probleme*. Köln: DuMont, 1991.

Kant, Immanuel. "Bestimmung des Begriffs einer Menschenrace" (1785). *Gesammelte Schriften*, Akademie-Ausgabe, VIII. Berlin & Leipzig: de Gruyter, 1923, 89–106.

Kaplan, Justin. *Mr. Clemens and Mark Twain*. London: Cape, 1967.

Kaplan, Sidney. *American Studies in Black and White: Selected Essays 1949–1989*, ed. Allan D. Austin. Amherst: Univ. of Massachusetts Press, 1991.

———. "The Miscegenation Issue in the Election of 1864." *Journal of Negro History* 34.3 (July 1949): 274–343.

———. "*The Octoroon*: Early History of the Drama of Miscegenation." *Journal of Negro Education* 20 (1951): 547–57.

Karcher, Carolyn L. *The First Woman in the Republic: A Cultural Biography of Lydia Maria Child*. London and Durham: Duke Univ. Press, 1994.

Kasher, Menahem M. *Encyclopedia of Biblical Interpretation: A Millennial Anthology*. New York: American Biblical Encyclopedia Society, 1955.

Katzew, Ilona, ed. *New World Orders: Casta Painting and Colonial Latin America*. New York: Americas Society Art Gallery, 1996.

Kaye, Jackeline. "La Esclavitud en América: *Cecilia Valdés* y *La Cabaña del tio Tom*." *Casa de las américas* 22. 129 (Nov.–Dec. 1981): 74–83.

Kelley, William Melvin. *A Drop of Patience*. Garden City, N.Y.: Doubleday, 1965.

Kephart, Wm. M. "The 'Passing' Question." *Phylon* 10 (1948).

Keyes, Frances Parkinson. *Crescent Carnival*. New York: Franklin Watts, 1942.

Kilpatrick, Jack Frederick, and Anna Gritts Kilpatrick, eds. *Eastern Cherokee Folktales: Reconstructed From the Field Notes of Frans M. Olbrechts*. Smithsonian Institution, Bureau of American Ethnology Bulletin 196. Washington, D.C.: Government Printing Office, 1966.

King, Bruce, ed. *West Indian Literature*. London and Basingstoke: Macmillan, 1979.

King, Richard H. *A Southern Renaissance: The Cultural Awakening of the American South, 1930–1945*. Oxford and New York: Oxford Univ. Press, 1980.

Kingston, Maxine Hong. *Tripmaster Monkey: His Fake Book*. New York: Knopf, 1989.

Kinney, James. *Amalgamation! Race, Sex, and Rhetoric in the Nineteenth-Century American Novel*. Westport, Conn.: Greenwood Press, 1985.

Klein, Holger, ed. *Literary Themes*. Special issue of *New Comparison* 6 (Autumn 1988).

Klein, Leonard S., ed. *African Literatures in the 20th Century: A Guide*. New York: Ungar, 1987.

Kleist, Heinrich von. *Erzählungen*. Ed. Siegfried Streller. Frankfurt: Insel, 1986.

———. *The Marquise of O——— and Other Stories*. Trans. Martin Greenberg. 1954. Reprint. New York: Criterion Books, 1960.

Klineberg, Otto, ed. *Characteristics of the American Negro*. New York and London: Harper, 1944.

Koebner, Thomas, and Gerhart Pickerodt, eds. *Die andere Welt: Studien zum Exotismus*. Frankfurt: Athenäum, 1987.

Körner, Theodor. "Toni: Ein Drama in drei Aufzügen." In *Theodor Körner's sämmtliche Werke*, 227–54. Leipzig: Philipp Reclam jun., n.d.

Kostelanetz, Richard. "The Politics of Passing: The Fiction of James Weldon Johnson." *Negro American Literature Forum* 3.1 (Spring 1969).

Kott, Jan. "The Two Paradoxes of Othello." *Evergreen Review* 10.40 (April 1966): 16.

Kratter, Franz. *Die Sclavin in Surinam*. Frankfurt: Eßlinger, 1804.

Krieger, Heinrich. *Das Rassenrecht in den Vereinigten Staaten*. Neue Deutsche Forschungen, Abt. Staats-, Verwaltungs-, Kirchen-, Völkerrecht und Staatstheorie, vol. 6. Berlin: Junker und Dünnhaupt Verlag, 1936.

———. *Das Rassenrecht in Südafrika*. Neue Deutsche Forschungen, Abt. Staats-, Verwaltungs-, Kirchen-, Völkerrecht und Staatstheorie, vol. 21. Berlin: Junker und Dünnhaupt Verlag, 1944.

———. *Das Rassenrecht in Südwestafrika*. Neue Deutsche Forschungen, Abt. Staats-, Verwaltungs-, Kirchen-, Völkerrecht und Staatstheorie, vol. 18. Berlin: Junker und Dünnhaupt Verlag, 1940.

Kuoh-Moukoury, Thérèse. *Les Couples dominos*. Paris: Juillard, 1973.

Kutner, Nanette. "Women Who Pass as White." *Liberty* (March 1949): 14–15, 44.

Laage, Karl Ernst. *Theodor Storm: Studien zu seinem Leben und Werk mit einem Handschriftenkatalog*. Berlin: Erich Schmidt Verlag, 1985.

Labat, Jean-Baptiste. *Nouveau voyage aux Isles de l'Amérique*. 1722.

Lacan, Jacques. *Écrits: A Selection*. Trans. Alan Sheridan. New York and London: W. W. Norton, 1977.

Lagarde, [Paul de], ed. *Materialien zur Kritik und Geschichte des Pentateuchs*. Leipzig: Teubner, 1867.

Lamore, Jean. "La Mulata en el discorso literario y médico francés del siglo diecinueve." *La Torre (NE)* 1.2: 297–318.

Lang, Hans-Loachim. "The American Novel and Reconstruction." Typescript, c. 1979.

Larsen, Nella. *Passing*. 1929. Reprint with *Quicksand*. Ed. Deborah E. McDowell. New Brunswick, N.J.: Rutgers Univ. Press, 1986.

Lavater, Johann Caspar. "The Effects of the Imagination on the Human Form." In *Essays on Physiognomy; for the Promotion of the Knowledge and the Love of Mankind*, 2nd ed., vol. 3. London: Whittingham, 1804.

Lawson, Hilda Josephine. *The Negro in American Drama. (Bibliography of Contemporary Negro Drama)*. Urbana, Ill., 1939 (abstract of a University of Illinois diss.).

Lazo, Raimundo. "Introduction." Cirilo Villaverde, to *Cecilia Valdés*. Mexico: Porrúa, 1986.

Leaver, Florence B. "Mark Twain's *Pudd'nhead Wilson*." *Mark Twain Journal* 10.2 (Winter 1956): 14–20.

Le Cat, Claude Nicolas. *Traité de la couleur de la peau humaine en général, de cell des Negres en particulier, et de la métamorphose d'une de ces couleurs en l'autre*. Amsterdam, 1765.

Lemcke, J. A. *Reminiscences of an Indianan.* Indianapolis, 1905.

Lemire, Elise. "Making Miscegenation: Discourses of Interracial Sex and Marriage in the United States, 1790–1865." Ph.D. dissertation, Rutgers University, 1996.

Levine, Lawrence W. "William Shakespeare and the American People: A Study in Cultural Transformation." *American Historical Review* 89.1 (Feb. 1984): 34–66.

Lévi-Strauss, Claude. *The Elementary Structures of Kinship* (1949). Rev. ed. Trans. James Harle Bell, John Richard von Sturmer, and Rodney Needham. Boston: Beacon Press, 1969.

Levy, David W. "Racial Stereotypes in Anti-Slavery Fiction." *Phylon* 31 (1970): 265–79.

Levy, Eugene. *James Weldon Johnson: Black Leader, Black Voice.* Chicago and London: Univ. of Chicago Press, 1973.

Lewis, Bernard. *Race and Slavery in the Middle East: An Historical Enquiry.* New York and Oxford: Oxford Univ. Press, 1990.

Lewis, Julian Herman. *The Biology of the Negro.* Chicago: Univ. of Chicago Press, 1942.

Lewis, Sinclair. *Kingsblood Royal.* New York: Random House, 1947.

Lewis, Vashti. "The Mulatto Woman as Major Female Character in Novels by Black Women, 1892–1937." Ph.D. diss., Univ. of Iowa, 1981.

Little, Jonathan David. "Charles Johnson's Revolutionary 'Oxherding Tale.'" *Studies in American Fiction* 19. 2 (Autumn 1991): 141–51.

———. "Definition Through Difference: The Tradition of Black-White Miscegenation in American Fiction." Ph.D. diss., University of Wisconsin, 1989.

Littré, Alexis. "Diverses observations anatomiques." In *Histoire de l'Académie Royale des Sciences: Année MDCCII,* 24–32. Paris: Charles-Étienne Hochereau, 1720.

Locke, Alain. "American Literary Tradition and the Negro." *Modern Quarterly* 3.3 (May–July 1916): 215–22.

———. "Wisdom De Profundis." *Phylon* 9.1 (1950).

———, ed. *The New Negro: An Interpretation.* 1925. Reprint. New York: Atheneum, 1968.

Lockhart, J. G. *Ancient Spanish Ballads, Historical and Romantic.* London: Blackwell, 1823.

Lockridge, Ross, Jr. *Raintree County.* Boston: Houghton Mifflin, 1948.

Lombardo, Paul A. "Miscegenation, Eugenics, and Racism: Historical Footnotes to *Loving v. Virginia*." *University of California Davis Law Review* 21.2 (Winter 1988): 421–52.

[Long, Edward.] *History of Jamaica.* 3 vols. London: T. Lowndes, 1774.

Longfellow, Henry Wadsworth. *Poets and Poetry of Europe.* Philadelphia: Carey and Hart, 1845.

Loos, Dorothy Scott. *The Naturalistic Novel of Brazil.* New York Hispanic Institute, 1963.

Lord, Nathan. *A Letter of Inquiry to Ministers of the Gospel of All Denominations on Slavery.* Hanover, N.H., 1860.

Lorenzetti, Giulio. *Venice and Its Lagoon: Historical-Artistic Guide.* Reprint. Trans. John Guthrie. Trieste: Edizioni Lint, 1985.

Lott, Eric. *Love and Theft: Blackface Minstrelsy and the American Working Class.* New York and Oxford: Oxford Univ. Press.

*Loving et ux. v. Virginia.* In *United States Reports*, vol. 388. Cases adjudged in the Supreme Court at October term, 1966, 12 June 1967, end of term. Washington: Government Printing Office, 1968.

Luis, William. "*Cecilia Valdés*: The Emergence of an Antislavery Novel." *Afro-Hispanic Review* 3.2 (May 1984): 15–19.

McCarthy, Mary. *The Group.* 1954. Reprint. New York: Signet, 1963.

McCloy, Shelby T. *The Negro in France.* Lexington: Univ. of Kentucky Press, 1961.

———. *The Negro in the French West Indies.* Lexington: Univ. of Kentucky Press, 1966.

———. "Negroes and Mulattoes in Eighteenth-Century France." *Journal of Negro History* (1945): 276–92.

McKay, Claude. *A Long Way From Home.* 1937. Reprint. New York: Harcourt, Brace & World, 1970.

———. "The Mulatto." *Bookman* 72 (Sept. 1925): 67.

———. "Near-White." In *Gingertown*, 72–104. 1932. Rpt. Freeport, N.Y.: Books for Libraries Press, 1972.

McKay, Claudette. "Images of the Black and Mulatto Woman in Spanish Caribbean Poetry: Discourse and Ideology." DAI 1987 48.6: 1465A.

McKnight, Joseph C. "Family Law." In *Encyclopedia of Southern Culture*, eds. Charles Reagan Wilson and William Ferris, 806–9. Chapel Hill and London: Univ. of North Carolina Press, 1989.

*McLaughlin et al v. Florida. United States Reports*, vol. 379. Cases adjudged in the Supreme Court at October term, 1964, 5 Oct. 1964 through 1 Feb. 1965. Washington: Government Printing Office, 1965.

McLendon, Jacquelyn Y. "The Myth of the Mulatto Psyche: A Study of the Works of Jessie Fauset and Nella Larsen." Ph.D. diss., Case Western Reserve University, 1986.

McLennan, John Ferguson. *Studies in Ancient History.* New York: Macmillan, 1886.

McLennan, Nancy. "Near Jury Choice for Sedition Trial." *New York Times* (16 May 1944): 11.

Madigan, Mark J. "Miscegenation and 'The Dicta of Race and Class': The Rhinelander Case and Nella Larsen's *Passing*." *Modern Fiction Studies* 36.4 (Winter 1990): 523–29.

Malpighi, Marcello. "Epistolae Anatomicae." *Opera Omnia.* 1686. Reprint. Hildesheim and New York: Georg Olms, 1975.

Mangum, Charles S., Jr. *The Legal Status of the Negro.* Chapel Hill: Univ. of North Carolina Press, 1940.

Marienstras, Richard. *New Perspectives on the Shakespearean World.* Trans. Janet Lloyd. Cambridge: Cambridge Univ. Press/ Paris: Editions de la Maison des Sciences de l'Homme, 1985.

Marker, Frederick J. *Hans Christian Andersen and the Romantic Theatre: A Study of Stage Practices in the Prenaturalistic Scandinavian Theatre.* Toronto: Univ. of Toronto Press, 1971.

Marotti, Giorgio. *Black Characters in the Brazilian Novel.* Trans. Maria O. Marotti and Harry Lawton. CAAS monograph series, vol. 6. Los Angeles: Center for Afro-American Studies, UCLA, 1987.

Marryat, Captain Frederick. *A Diary in America, With Remarks on Its Institutions.* New York: Colyer, 1839.

Martin, Byron Curtis. "Racism in the United States: A History of Anti-Miscegenation Legislation and Litigation." 3 vols. Ph.D. diss., University of Southern California, 1979.

Martin, Tony. *The Jewish Onslaught: Despatches from the Wellesley Battlefront.* Dover, Mass.: Majority Press, 1993.

Martinus-Zemp, Ada. *Le Blanc et le Noir: essai d'une description de la vision du Noir par le Blanc dans la littérature française de l'entre deux guerres.* Paris: Nizet, 1975.

*Massachusetts, Acts and Resolves, Public and Private, of the Province of the Massachusetts Bay,* vol. 1. Reprint. Boston: Wright & Potter, 1869.

*Massachusetts, Acts and Laws of the Commonwealth of.* Reprint. Boston: Wright and Potter, 1893.

Masse, Fernand. "The Negro Race in French Literature." *Journal of Negro History* (1933): 225–45.

Matthews, Victoria Earle. "The Value of Race Literature: An Address Delivered at the First Congress of Colored Women of the United States, at Boston, Mass., July 30th, 1895." Reprinted in *Massachusetts Review* 27.2 (Summer 1986): 169–85.

Maupertuis, Pierre Louis Moreau de. *La Vénus physique.* Geneva, 1780.

Mayer, Milton. "The Issue Is Miscegenation." In *White Racism: Its History, Pathology, and Practice,* eds. Barry Schwartz and Robert Disch, 207–17. New York: Dell, 1970.

Meese, Elizabeth, and Alice Parker, eds. *The Difference Within.* Amsterdam and Philadelphia: John Benjamins Publishing, 1989.

Mélesville and Carmouche. *Ourika; ou, La Petite negresse.* Paris: Quoy, 1824.

Melville, Herman. *Mardi and a Voyage Thither.* 1849. Reprint. Evanston and Chicago: Northwestern Univ. Press, 1970.

Mencke, John G. *Mulattoes and Race Mixture: American Attitudes and Images.* Studies in American History and Culture no. 4. Ann Arbor: Univ. of Michigan Research Press, 1979.

Mercier, Roger. *L'Afrique noire dans la littérature française. Les Premières images (XVIIe et XVIIIe siècles).* Dakar: Université de Dakar, 1962.

———. "Les Débuts de l'exotisme africain en France." *Revue de littérature comparée* 36.2 (1962): 191–209.

———. "Le Naufrage de la *Méduse.* Réalité et imagination romanesque." *Revue des sciences humaines* (Jan.–March 1967): 53–65.

Merton, Robert K. "Intermarriage and Social Structure: Fact and Theory." *Psychiatry* 4 (August 1941): 361–74.

Meyer, Jean. *Sklavenhandel.* Trans. Bettina Wiengarn. Ravensburg: Otto Maier, 1990.

Meyer, Michael. "Thoreau and Black Emigration." *American Literature* 53.3 (Nov. 1981): 380–96.

Michaels, Walter Benn. *Our America: Nativism, Modernism, and Pluralism.* Durham and London: Duke Univ. Press, 1995.

Miller, Christopher L. *Blank Darkness: Africanist Discourse in French*. Chicago: Univ. of Chicago Press, 1985.

*Mississippi Code 1972. Annotated*. Vol. 1, *Constitutions*. Atlanta: Harrison.

Mitchell, John. "Essay on the Causes of different Colours of People in different Climates." Royal Society, *Philosophical Transactions* 9: 65. 1744. London: C. R. Baldwin, 1809.

Mitchell, P. M. *A History of Danish Literature*. Copenhagen: Gyldendal, 1957.

Monahan, Thomas P. "An Overview of Statistics on Interracial Marriage in the United States, With Data on Its Extent From 1963–1970." *Journal of Marriage and the Family* 38 (May 1976): 223–31.

Monash, Samuel. "Normal Pigmentation in the Nails of the Negro." *Archives of Dermatology and Syphilology* 25 (1932): 876–81.

Monnet, Julien C. "The Latest Phase of Negro Disfranchisement." *Harvard Law Review* 26 (Nov. 1912): 42–63.

Moore, Rayburn S. *Constance Fenimore Woolson*. New York: Twayne, 1963.

Morales-Oliver, Luis. *Africa en la literatura española*. 2 vols. Madrid: Instituto de Estudios Africanos, 1957–58.

Moreau de St. Méry, Médéric-Louis-Élie. *Description topographique, physique, civile, politique et historique de la partie française de l'Isle Saint-Domingue*. 1797. Reprint. Paris: Société Française d'Histoire d'Outre-Mer, 1984.

Mörner, Magnus. *Race Mixture in the History of Latin America*. Boston: Little, Brown, 1967.

Mulvey, Christopher. "The Fugitive Self and the New World of The North: William Wells Brown's Discovery of America." In *The Black Columbiad: Defining Moments in African-American Literature and Culture*. Cambridge: Harvard Univ. Press, 1994.

Murray, Albert. *The Hero and the Blues*. N.p.: Univ. of Missouri Press, 1972.

———. *The Omni-Americans: New Perspectives on Black Experience and American Culture*. New York: Avon, 1971.

Murray, Pauli. "Mulatto's Dilemma." *Opportunity* 16 (June 1938).

———. *States' Laws on Race and Color: And Appendices Containing International Documents, Federal Laws and Regulations, Local Ordinances and Charts*. [Cincinnati, Ohio]: Women's Division of Christian Service, 1951.

Musgrave, Marian E. "Kuermann, His Wives, and 'Helen, die Mulattin' in Max Frisch's *Biographie: Ein Spiel*." *College Language Association Journal* 18 (1975): 341–47.

———. "Triangles in Black and White: Sex and Hostility in Black Literature." *College Language Association Journal* 14.4 (June 1971): 444–51.

Myrdal, Gunnar. *An American Dilemma*. New York: Harper, 1944.

Nabokov, Vladimir. *Eugene Onegin: A Novel in Verse*. Trans. Nabokov. Bollingen Series 72. Pantheon Books, 1964.

Navarro, Isidoro Moreno. *Los Cuadros del Mestizaje Americano: estudio antropológico del Mestizaje*. Madrid: José Porrua Turanzas, 1973.

Nelson, Dana D. *The Word in Black and White: Reading "Race" in American Literature 1638–1867*. New York and Oxford: Oxford Univ. Press, 1992.

Nelson, John Herbert. *The Negro Character in American Literature*. 1926. Reprint. College Park, Md.: McGrath, 1968.

Nelson, William Javier. "Racial Definition: Background for Divergence." *Phylon* 47.4 (1986): 318–26.

Newby, I. A. *Jim Crow's Defense: Anti-Negro Thought in America, 1900–1930.* Baton Rouge: Louisiana State Univ. Press, 1965.

Newton, Thomas. *Dissertations on the Prophecies, Which Have Remarkably Been Fulfilled, and at This Time Are Fulfilling in the World.* Northampton, Mass.: William Butler, 1746.

Nielsen, Birger Frank. *H. C. Andersen Bibliografi: Digterens Danske Værker, 1822–1875.* København: Hagerup, 1942.

Nielsen, Erling. *Hans Christian Andersen.* Trans. Thyra Dohrenburg. Hamburg: Rowohlt, 1958.

Nott, Josiah C. "The Mulatto a Hybrid—probable extermination of the two races if the Whites and Blacks are allowed to intermarry." *American Journal of Medical Sciences* 66 (July 1843).

Nott, Josiah C., and George R. Gliddon. *Types of Mankind: or, Ethnological Researches.* Philadelphia: Lippincott; London: Trübner & Co., 1854.

Nuñez, Benjamin. *Dictionary of Afro-Latin American Civilization.* Westport, Conn.: Greenwood Press, 1980.

O'Daniel, Therman B., ed. *James Baldwin: A Critical Evaluation.* Washington, D.C.: Howard Univ. Press, 1977.

Oguntoye, Katharina, May Opitz, and Dagmar Schultz, eds. *Farbe bekennen: Afro-deutsche Frauen auf den Spuren ihrer Geschichte.* 1986. Frankfurt: Fischer, 1992.

Ohl, Hildegard. "Nationale Vorurteile—eine Auswahlbibliographie." *Zeitschrift für Kulturaustausch* 23 (1973): 82–8.

O'Mealley, Robert, ed. *New Essays on Invisible Man.* New York: Cambridge Univ. Press, 1988.

Ortoz, Fernando, and Rafael Marquina. "The Negro in the Spanish Theater." *Phylon* 4 (1943): 144–52.

Otis, Johnny. *Listen to the Lambs.* New York: Norton, 1968.

Ottley, Roi. "Five Million White Negroes." *Ebony* (March 1948): 22–28.

Pagden, Anthony. *European Encounters With the New World: From Renaissance to Romanticism.* London and New Haven: Yale Univ. Press, 1993.

———. "Razzismo e colonialismo europeo: Una indagine storica." In *Il Razzismo e le sue storie,* ed. Girolamo Imbruglia. Napoli: Edizioni Scientifiche Italiane, 1992.

Pagliaro, Harold E., ed. *Racism in the Eighteenth Century: Studies in Eighteenth-Century Culture* 3. Cleveland: Case Western Reserve University, 1973.

Paine, Thomas. *Common Sense.* 1776. Reprint. Harmondsworth: Penguin, 1983.

Park, Robert Ezra. *Race and Culture: Essays in the Sociology of Contemporary Man.* 1950. Glencoe: Free Press; London: Collier-Macmillan, 1964.

Parsons, Dr. James. "Of the White Negro Shown Before the R[oyal] S[ociety]." *Philosophical Transactions* 12. London: Baldwin, 1809.

Pascoe, Peggy. "Race, Gender, and Intercultural Relations: The Case of Interracial Marriage." *Frontiers* 12.1 (1991): 5–18.

Paulding, James Kirke. *Slavery in the United States.* New York, 1836.

Paulitschke, Philip Viktor. *Die Afrika-Literatur in der Zeit von 1500–1750.* 1882.

Paulson, Ronald. *Representations of Revolution 1789–1820.* New Haven and London: Yale Univ. Press, 1983.

Pauw, Cornelis de. *Recherches philosophiques sur les Américains. . .* I. London, 1770.

Pearson, Karl. "Note on the Skin-Colour of the Crosses Between Negro and White." *Biometrika* 6 (1908–09): 348–53.

Peel, Ellen. "Semiotic Subversion in 'Désirée's Baby.'" *American Literature* 62.2 (June 1990): 223–37.

Pennington, James W. C. *A Text Book of the Origin and History, &c., of the Colored People*. Hartford: L. Skinner, 1841.

Peretti, Burton W. *The Creation of Jazz: Music, Race, and Culture in Urban America*. Urbana and Chicago: Univ. of Illinois Press, 1992.

Peterson, Thomas Virgil. *Ham and Japheth: The Mythic World of Whites in the Antebellum South*. Metuchen, N.J., and London: Scarecrow Press, 1978.

Petry, Alice Hall. "'Dey's Quadroons': Love Versus the Code Noir in *Madame Delphine*." In *A Genius in His Way: The Art of Cable's Old Creole Days*. London and Toronto: Associated Univ. Presses, 1988.

Petry, Ann. *The Narrows*. 1953. Reprint. Boston: Beacon Press, 1988.

Pettit, Arthur G. *Mark Twain and the South*. Lexington: Univ. of Kentucky Press, 1974. Excerpts in *Pudd'nhead Wilson and Those Extraordinary Twins*, ed. Sidney E. Berger. New York, London: Norton, 1980.

Pfeiffer, Kathleen. "All the Difference: Race Passing and American Individualism," Ph.D. diss., Brandeis University, 1994.

Pfläging, Wilhelm. *Zum kolonialrechtlichen Problem der Mischbeziehungen zwischen deutschen Reichsangehörigen und Eingeborenen der deutschen Schutzgebiete, unter besonderer Berücksichtigung des Unterhaltsanspruches der unehelichen Mischlinge*. Berlin: Universitätsdruckerei Schade, 1913.

Piacentini, Edward J. "T. S. Stribling: A Checklist for His Southern Novels." *Mississippi Quarterly* 30.4 (Fall 1977): 639–47.

Pierson, George Wilson. *Tocqueville and Beaumont in America*. New York: Oxford Univ. Press, 1938.

Pietromarchi, Luca, ed. *Storia della regina del mattino e di solimano, principe dei geni*. Venezia: Marsilio, 1992.

Piper, Adrian. "Passing for White, Passing for Black." *Transition* 58 (1992).

Piroué, Georges. "Présentation des deux *Bug-Jargal*." In *Œuvres complètes de Victor Hugo*, vol. 1, pp. i–viii, 350ff. Paris: Club français de livre, 1967.

Pittman, R. Carter. "The Fourteenth Amendment: Its Intended Effect on Anti-Miscegenation Laws." *North Carolina Law Review* 43 (1964).

Plasa, Carl, and Betty J. Ring, eds. *The Discourse of Slavery: Aphra Behn to Toni Morrison*. New York: Routledge, 1994.

Plecker, W. A. "Virginia's Attempt to Adjust the Color Problem." *American Journal of Public Health* 15 (February 1925).

*Poétique* 64 (Nov. 1985). Special issue "Vers une thématique."

Polheim, Karl Konrad, ed. *Theorie und Kritik der deutschen Novelle von Wieland bis Musil*. Tübingen: Max Niemeyer Verlag, 1970.

Poliakov, Léon, ed. *Le Couple interdit: entretiens sur le racisme. La dialectique de la alterité socio-culturelle et la sexualité*. Paris, The Hague, New York: Mouton, 1980.

Pope, Edith. *Colcorton*. New York: Charles Scribner's, 1944.

Potter, Richard A. "Negroes in the Fiction of Kate Chopin." *Louisiana History* 12.1 (1971): 41–58.

Pratt, Mary Louise. "From Narina to Joanna." In *Imperial Eyes: Travel Writing and Transculturation*. London and New York: Routledge, 1993.

Price, Lawrence M. *Inkle and Yariko Album*. Berkeley: Univ. of California Press, 1937.

Price, Richard, and Sally Price, eds. *Narrative of a Five Years Expedition against the*

*Revolted Negroes of Surinam.* Baltimore and London: Johns Hopkins Univ. Press, 1988.

Priest, Josiah. *Slavery, as It Relates to the Negro, or African Race.* . . . Albany, N.Y.: C. Van Benthuysen, 1845.

Puckett, Newbell Niles. *The Magic and Folk Beliefs of the Southern Negro.* 1926. Reprint. New York: Dover Press, 1969.

Rabassa, Gregory. "The Negro in Brazilian Fiction since 1888." Ph.D. diss., Columbia University, 1954.

Ramban (Nachmanides). *Commentary on the Torah: Genesis.* Trans. Charles B. Chavel. New York: Shilo Publishing House, 1971.

Rampersad, Arnold. *The Life of Langston Hughes.* Vol. 1, *1902–1941. I, Too, Sing America.* New York and Oxford: Oxford Univ. Press, 1986.

Ramsey, Priscilla. "A Study of Black Identity in 'Passing' Novels of the Nineteenth and Twentieth Centuries." Ph.D. diss., American University, 1975.

Ray, Jane. *The Story of the Creation: Words from Genesis.* New York: Dutton's Children's Books, 1993.

Réda, Jacques, ed. *Album Maupassant.* Paris: Gallimard, Bibliothèque de la Pléiade, 1987.

Reich, Wilhelm. *The Mass Psychology of Fascism.* Trans. Vincent R. Carfagno. New York: Farrar, Straus & Giroux, 1970.

Reid, Mayne. *The Quadroon.* 1856. Reprinted with subtitle *or, Adventures in the Far West.* London: Routledge, n.d.

Render, Sylvia Lyons, ed. *The Uncollected Short Fiction of Charles W. Chesnutt.* Washington, D.C.: Howard Univ. Press, 1981.

Resh, Richard W. "Alexis de Tocqueville and the Negro." *Journal of Negro History* (1963): 251–59.

Reuter, Edward Byron. *The American Race Problem.* 1927. Rev. ed. Jitsuichi Masuoka. New York: Crowell, 1970.

———. *The Mulatto in the United States: Including a Study of the Rôle of Mixed-Blood Races Throughout the World.* 1918. Reprint. New York: Negro Universities Press, 1969.

———. *Race Mixture: Studies in Intermarriage and Miscegenation.* 1931. Reprint. New York: Negro Universities Press, 1969.

Reybaud, Mme. Charles. *Valdepeiras.* Paris: Hachette, 1864.

Richardson, Gary A. "Boucicault's *The Octoroon* and American Law." *Theatre Journal* (May 1982): 155–64.

Richardson, Samuel. *Clarissa; or, The History of a Young Lady.* 1747–48. Reprint. London: Penguin, 1985.

Ricks, Sybil Ray. "A Textual Comparison of Langston Hughes' *Mulatto*, 'Father and Son,' and 'The Barrier.'" *Black American Literature Forum* 15.3 (Fall 1981): 101–3.

Riddell, William R. "Le Code Noir." *Journal of Negro History* (1925): 321–29.

Riepe, Regina und Gerd Riepe. *Du schwarz ich weiß: Bilder und Texte zum alltäglichen Rassismus.* Wuppertal: Peter Hammer Verlag, 1992.

Ringe, Donald A. "The 'Double Center': Character and Meaning in Cable's Early Novels." *Studies in the Novel* 5.1 (Spring 1973): 52–62.

Robbins, Bruce. *The Servant's Hand: English Fiction from Below.* New York: Columbia Univ. Press, 1986.

Roberts, Diane. *The Myth of Aunt Jemima: Representations of Race and Region.* New York: Routledge, 1994.

Roberts, Elizabeth Madox. *My Heart and My Flesh.* New York: Viking, 1927.

Roberts, R. "Negro-White Intermarriage: A Study in Social Control." M.A. thesis, University of Chicago, 1940.

Rodgers, David Lawrence. "The Irony of Idealism: William Faulkner and the South's Construction of the Mulatto." In *The Discourse of Slavery: Aphra Behn to Toni Morrison.* Eds. Carl Plasa and Betty J. Ring, 166–90. London and New York: Routledge, 1994.

Rogers, J. A. *Nature Knows No Color-Line.* 1952. Reprint. St. Petersburg, Fla., 1980.

———. *100 Amazing Facts About the Negro With Complete Proof.* 1957. Reprint. St. Petersburg, Fla., 1970.

———. "Pushkin 'Made' Russian Literature." *Norfolk Journal and Guide.* 25 May 1929.

———. *Sex and Race.* 3 vols. 1944. Reprint. St. Petersburg, Fla., 1984.

———. *From Superman to Man.* Reprint. St. Petersburg Fla.: Helga M. Rogers, 1988.

Rollins, Hyder E. "The Negro in the Southern Short Story." *Sewanee Review* 24 (1916): 42–60.

Romans, Bernard. *A Concise Natural History of East and West Florida.* New York, 1775.

Roscher, W. H., ed. *Ausführliches Lexikon der griechischen und römischen Mythologie.* Leipzig: Teubner, 1884.

Rose, Guy. *My Love, My Love; or, The Peasant Girl.* New York: H. Holt, 1990.

Rosolato, Guy. *Essais sur le symbolique.*1969. Reprint. Paris: Gallimard, 1985.

Rotter, Gernot. *Die Stellung des Negers in der islamisch-arabischen Gesellschaft bis zum XVI. Jahrhundert.* Dissertation. Bonn, 1967.

Rougemont, Denis de. *Love in the Western World.* 1940. Trans. Montgomery Belgion. Princeton: Princeton Univ. Press, 1983.

Rousset, Jean. *Leurs yeux se rencontrèrent: la scène de première vue dans le roman.* Paris: José Corti, 1984.

Rowland, Dunbar, ed. *Jefferson Davis, Constitutionalist: His Letters, Papers and Speeches.* Jackson, Miss., 1923.

Roy, Ratna. "The Marginal Man: A Study of the Mulatto Character in American Fiction." Ph.D. diss., University of Oregon, 1973.

Rubin, Louis D., Jr. "The Division of the Heart: Cable's *The Grandissimes.*" *Southern Literary Journal* 1.2 (Spring 1969): 27–47.

———. *George W. Cable: The Life and Times of a Southern Heretic.* New York: Pegasus, 1969.

———. *Writers of the Modern South: The Faraway Country.* Seattle and London: Univ. of Washington Press, 1966.

Ruchames, Louis, ed. *The Abolitionists: A Collection of Their Writings.* New York: Capricorn Books, 1964.

Rüdiger, Horst. "Nationalliteraturen und europäische Literatur: Methoden und Ziele der vergleichenden Literaturwissenschaft." *Schweizer Monatshefte* 42.2 (May 1962): 195–211.

———, ed. *Komparatistik: Aufgaben und Methoden.* Stuttgart: Kohlhammer, 1973.

S., W. A. "Intermarriage With Negroes—A Survey of State Statutes." *Yale Law Journal* 36 (April 1927): 858–66.

Sachs, Viola, ed. *Le Blanc et le noir chez Melville et Faulkner.* Paris: Mouton, 1974.

Saks, Eva. "Representing Miscegenation Law." *Raritan* 8.2 (Fall 1988): 39–69.

Sampson, Milton J. "The Negro in Anglo-Saxon Literature." *Opportunity* 2 (1924): 168–71.

Samuels, Shirley, ed. *The Culture of Sentiment: Race, Gender, and Sentimentality in 19th Century America.* New York and Oxford: Oxford Univ. Press, 1992.

Sánchez-Eppler, Karen. "Bodily Bonds: The Intersecting Rhetorics of Feminism and Abolition." In *The New American Studies: Essays from Representations,* ed. Philip Fisher. Berkeley: Univ. of California Press, 1991.

Sandiford, Ralph. *Brief Examination of the Practice of the Times.* Reprint. New York: Arno Press, 1969.

Santayana, George. "The Tragic Mask." In *Soliloquies in England and Later Soliloquies.* New York: Scribner's, 1922. Reprinted in *Tragedy: Vision and Form,* ed. Robert W. Corrigan. 2nd ed. New York: Harper & Row, 1981.

Sayers, Raymond S. *The Negro in Brazilian Literature.* New York: Hispanic Institute, 1956.

Sayle, Charles, ed. *The Works of Sir Thomas Browne.* London: Grant Richards, 1904.

Schamschula, Walter. *Der russische historische Roman vom Klassizismus bis zur Romantik.* Meisenheim: Anton Hain, 1961.

Scheick, William J. *The Half-Blood: A Cultural Symbol in 19th-Century American Fiction.* Lexington: Univ. of Kentucky Press, 1979.

Schirò, Giuseppe. *Monreale: City of the Golden Temple.* Palermo: Edizioni Mistretta, 1990.

Schmitt, Franz Anselm. *Stoff- und Motivgeschichte der deutschen Literatur: Eine Bibliographie.* 3rd rev. ed. Berlin & New York, 1976.

Schneider, David M. *American Kinship: A Cultural Account.* 2nd ed. Chicago: Univ. of Chicago Press, 1968.

Schuhmann, George. "Miscegenation: An Example of Judicial Recidivism." *Journal of Family Law* 8 (1968): 69–78.

Schulze, Joachim. "Geschichte oder Systematik? Zu einem Problem der Themen- und Motivgeschichte." *Arcadia* 10.1 (1975): 76–82.

Schuyler, George B. *Black No More: Being an Account of the Strange and Wonderful Workings of Science in the Land of the Free, A.D. 1933–1940.* 1931. Reprint. Boston: Northeastern Univ. Press, 1989.

Schuyler, George S. "Who Is 'Negro'? Who is 'White'?" *Common Ground* 1 (Autumn 1940): 53–56.

Schwarcz, Lilia Moritz. *O Espetáculo das Raças: Cientistas, Instituições a Questão Racial no Brasil, 1870–1930.* São Paulo: Companhia Das Letras, 1993.

Schwartz, Barry, and Robert Disch, eds. *White Racism: Its History, Pathology, and Practice.* New York: Dell, 1970.

Schwartz, Delmore. "A Bitter Farce." *Kenyon Review* 8.2 (Spring 1946): 245–61.

Schwarz-Bart, André. *La Mulâtresse solitude.* Paris: Éditions du Seuil, 1972.

Scribe, Eugène. *Œuvres complètes: opéras comiques.* Paris: E. Dentu, 1879.

Seeber, Edward D. *Anti-Slavery Opinion in France During the Second Half of the Eighteenth Century.* Paris: Les Belles-Lettres, 1937.

Seed, Patricia. *To Love, Honor, and Obey in Colonial Mexico: Conflicts Over Marriage Choice, 1574–1821.* Stanford, Calif.: Stanford Univ. Press, 1988.

Seghers, Anna. "Die Hochzeit von Haiti." 1964. Reprinted in *Die Hochzeit von Haiti: Karibische Geschichten.* Neuwied: Luchterhand, 1976.

Séjour, Victor. "Le Mulâtre." 1837. Reprinted in *Revue de Louisiane* 1.2 (Winter 1972): 60–75.

Sewall, Samuel. *The Selling of Joseph: A Memorial.* 1700. Reprinted with notes by Sidney Kaplan. Amherst: Univ. of Massachusetts Press, 1969.

Shadrach, J. Shirley. "Furnace Blasts. II. Black or White?" *Colored American Magazine* (March 1903): 348–53.

Sharfstein, Daniel Jacob. "In Search of the Color Line: Ferrall v. Ferrall and the Struggle to Define Race in the Turn-of-the-Century American South." Senior thesis, Harvard University, 1994.

Shell, Marc. *Children of the Earth: Literature, Politics, and Nationhood.* New York and Oxford: Oxford Univ. Press, 1993.

———. "The Want of Incest in the Human Family; or, Kin and Kind in Christian Thought." *Journal of the Academy of Religion* 62.3 (1995): 625–50.

Sherman, Joan R. *Invisible Poets: Afro-Americans of the Nineteenth Century.* 2nd ed. Urbana and Chicago: Univ. of Illinois Press, 1989.

Shyllon, F. *Black People in Britain 1555–1833.* Oxford and New York: Oxford Univ. Press, 1977.

Sickles, Robert J. *Race, Marriage, and the Law.* Albuquerque: Univ. of New Mexico Press, 1972.

Skerrett, Joseph T. "Irony and Symbolic Action in James Weldon Johnson's *The Autobiography of an Ex-Coloured Man.*" *American Quarterly* 32 (1980): 540–58.

Small, Stephen Augustus. "Racial Differentiation in the Slave Era: A Comparative Study of People of 'Mixed-Race' in Jamaica and Georgia." Ph.D. diss., University of California, Berkeley, 1989.

Smith, E. Irving. "The Legal Aspect of the Southern Question." *Harvard Law Review* 2 (March 1889): 358–76.

Smith, H. Shelton. *In His Image, But. . . : Racism in Southern Religion, 1780–1910.* Durham, N.C.: Duke Univ. Press, 1972.

Smith, Helena M. "Negro Characterization in the American Novel: A Historical Survey of Work by White Authors." Ph.D. diss., Pennsylvania State University, 1972.

———. "No-Nation Bastards." *Studies in the Humanities* 1.1 (March 1969): 18–28.

Smith, Henry Nash. "Pudd'nhead Wilson and After." *Massachusetts Review* 3.2 (Winter 1962): 233–53.

Smith, J. David. *The Eugenic Assault on America: Scenes in Red, White, and Black.* Fairfax, Va.: George Mason Univ. Press, 1993.

Smith, John David, ed. *Anti-Black Thought, 1863–1925.* Vol. 6, *The Biblical and "Scientific" Defense of Slavery: Religion and "The Negro Problem,"* pt. 2. New York and London: Garland, 1993.

Smith, Lillian. "Three Ghost Stories." *Killers of the Dream.* 1949. Reprint. Garden City, N.Y.: Doubleday Anchor, 1963.

Smith, Milton A. "America's Most Sensational Mixed Marriage." *Tan Confessions* 2.2 (Dec. 1951): 22–78.

Snowden, Frank M. *Before Color Prejudice: The Ancient View of Blacks.* Cambridge, Mass. and London: Harvard Univ. Press, 1983.

————. *Blacks in Antiquity.* Cambridge, Mass.: Belknap Press of Harvard Univ. Press, 1970.

Sollors, Werner. *Theories of Ethnicity: A Classical Reader.* Basingstoke: Macmillan, 1996.

————, ed. *The Return of Thematic Criticism.* Harvard English Studies, 18. Cambridge: Harvard Univ. Press, 1992.

Sollors, Werner, Caldwell Titcomb, and Thomas A. Underwood, eds. *Blacks at Harvard: A Documentary History of African-American Experience at Harvard and Radcliffe.* New York: New York Univ. Press, 1993.

Somerville, Siobhan Bridget. "The Same Difference?: Passing, Race, and Sexuality in American Literature and Film 1890–1930." Ph.D. diss. prospectus, Yale University, 1990.

Sommer, Doris. *Foundational Fictions: The National Romances of Latin America.* Berkeley, Los Angeles, London: Univ. of California Press, 1993.

————. "Sab C'est Moi." *Genders* 2 (Summer 1988): 111–26.

*South Carolina 1976, Code of Laws of, Annotated.* Vol. 21. Rochester, N.Y.: Lawyers Co-operative Publishing.

Southern, Thomas. *Oroonoko; A Tragedy in Five Acts.* 1796. Ed. with introd. by Mrs. Inchbald. London: Longman, n.d.

Spark, Muriel. "The Black Madonna." In *The Go-Away Bird and Other Stories.* Philadelphia and New York: Lippincott, 1958. Reprinted in *Stories in Black and White.* Ed. Eva H. Kissin. Philadelphia and New York: Lippincott, 1970.

Sparks, Alistair. "South Africa to Drop Ban on White-Nonwhite Marriages." *Washington Post* (16 April 1985).

Spickard, Paul R. *Mixed Blood: Intermarriage and Ethnic Identity in Twentieth-Century America.* Madison, Wis.: Univ. of Wisconsin Press, 1989.

Spiller, G. *Comparative American Identities.* New York and London: Routledge, 1991.

————, ed. *Papers on Inter-Racial Problems Communicated to the First Universal Races Congress Held at the University of London, July 26–29, 1911.* London: P. S. King & Son, 1911.

Spillers, Hortense J. "Notes on an Alternative Model—Neither/Nor." In *The Difference Within,* eds. Elizabeth Meese and Alice Parker, 165–87. Amsterdam and Philadelphia: John Benjamins Publishing, 1989.

Stanton, William. *The Leopard's Spots: Scientific Attitudes toward Race in America, 1815–59.* 1960. Reprint. Chicago and London: Univ. of Chicago Press, 1982.

Starke, Catherine Juanita. *Black Portraiture in American Fiction: Stock Characters, Archetypes, and Individuals.* New York: Basic Books, 1972.

Staude, Wilhelm. "Die äthiopische Legende von der Königin von Saba und die Parzival-Erzählung Wolfram von Eschenbachs." *Archiv für Völkerkunde* 12 (1957): 1–53.

Steins, Martin. *Das Bild des Schwarzen in der europäischen Kolonialliteratur 1870–1918. Ein Beitrag zur literarischen Imagologie.* Frankfurt: Thesen-Verlag, 1972.

Stepan, Nancy. "Biology and Degeneration: Races and Proper Places." In *Degeneration: The Dark Side of Progress*, eds. J. Edward Chamberlain and Sander Gilman, 97–120. New York: Columbia Univ. Press, 1985.

Stepto, Robert B. *From Behind the Veil: A Study of Afro-American Narrative.* Urbana: Univ. of Illinois Press, 1979.

Stern, Curt. "The Biology of the Negro." *Scientific American* 191 (1954).

Stetson, Earlene. "The Mulatto Motif in Black Fiction." Ph.D. diss., SUNY Buffalo, 1976.

Stevenson, John Allen. "A Vampire in the Mirror: The Sexuality of Dracula." *PMLA* (ca. 1988): 139–49.

Stolcke, Verena. "Invaded Women: Gender, Race, and Class in the Formation of Colonial Society." In *Women, "Race," and Writing in the Early Modern Period*, eds. Margo Hendricks and Patricia Parker. London and New York: Routledge, 1994, 272–86

Stonequist, Everett V. "Race Mixture and the Mulatto." In *Race Relations and the Race Problem: A Definition and an Analysis*, ed. Edgar T. Thompson. Durham, N.C.: Duke Univ. Press, 1939.

———. *The Marginal Man: A Study in Personality and Culture Conflict.* 1937. Reprint. New York: Russell & Russell, 1961.

Storm, Theodor. *Gedichte Novellen 1848–1867.* Ed. Dieter Lohmeier. Frankfurt: Deutscher Klassiker Verlag, 1987.

———. "Von jenseit des Meeres." 1865. Reprinted in *Gedichte, Novellen, 1848–1867*, ed. Dieter Lohmeier. Frankfurt: Deutscher Klassiker Verlag, 1987.

"The Story of *Inkle* and *Yarico*. From the 11th *Spectator*." *London Magazine: or, Gentleman's Monthly Intelligencer* III (1734): 257–58.

Story, Sidney A., Jr., [Mary Pike]. *Caste: A Story of Republican Equality.* Boston: Phillips, Sampson, 1856.

Stowe, Harriet Beecher. *Uncle Tom's Cabin; or, Life Among the Lowly.* In *Three Novels.* New York: Library of America, 1982.

Striedter, Jurij. *Dichtung und Geschichte bei Puskin.* Konstanz: Universitätsverlag, 1977.

Stuckert, Franz. *Theodor Storm: Sein Leben und Werk.* Bremen: Carl Schünemann, 1955.

*Strumenti critici* 60 (May 1989). Special issue on thematics.

Sue, Eugène. *Les Mystères de Paris.* 1843. Reprint. Paris: Marpon et Flammarion, 1879.

Sullivan, Walter. "*The Fathers* and the Failures of Tradition." *Southern Review* 12.4 (Oct. 1976): 758–66 (on Tate).

Summers, Montague. "Introduction" to *Oroonoko.* In *The Works of Aphra Behn.* Vol. 5: 127–28. London: Heinemann, 1915.

Sumner, William Graham. *Folkways.* Boston: Ginn, 1906.

Sundquist, Eric J. *Faulkner: The House Divided.* Baltimore and London: Johns Hopkins Univ. Press, 1983.

———. *To Wake the Nations: Race in the Making of American Literature.* Cambridge, Mass.: Harvard Univ. Press, 1993.

———, ed. *American Realism: New Essays.* Baltimore and London: Johns Hopkins Univ. Press, 1982.

*Supreme Court Reporter* 87 (June 1967): 1819–24.

Swinburne, Hilda. "Gahmuret and Feirefiz in Wolfram's 'Parzival.'" *Modern Language Review* 51 (1956): 195–202.

Swindler, William F., ed. *Sources and Documents of United States Constitutions.* Vols. 2 and 7. Dobbs Ferry, N.Y.: Oceana Publications, 1973, 1978.

Sylvander, Carolyn Wedin. *Jessie Redmon Fauset, Black American Writer.* Troy, N.Y.: Whitston Publishing, 1981.

Sypher, Wylie. *Guinea's Captive Kings: British Anti-Slavery Literature of the Eighteenth Century.* Chapel Hill: Univ. of North Carolina Press, 1942.

Tate, Allen. *The Fathers.* New York: Putnam's, 1938.

Taylor, Tom. "Saving the Octoroon." *Punch* (21 Dec. 1861): 253.

Taylor, William E. *Cavalier and Yankee: The Old South and American National Character.* 1961. Cambridge, Mass.: Harvard Univ. Press, 1979.

*Tennessee Code. Annotated.* Vol. 1, *1980 Replacement.* Charlottesville, Va.: Michie, 1980.

Tenzer, Lawrence E. *A Completely New Look at Interracial Sexuality: Public Opinion and Select Commentaries.* Manahawkin, N.J.: Scholars' Publishing House, 1990.

Thompson, Lloyd A. *Romans and Blacks.* Norman and London: Univ. of Oklahoma Press, 1989.

Tinker, Edward Larocque. *Les Ecrits de langue française en Louisiana au XIXe siècle.* Paris: Libraririe Ancienne Honoré, 1932.

Tischler, Nancy M. *Black Masks: Negro Characters in Modern Southern Fiction.* University Park and London: Pennsylvania State Univ. Press, 1969.

Tocqueville, Alexis de. *Democracy in America.* 1835. Trans. Henry Reeve, ed. Phillips Bradley. New York: Knopf, 1951.

Todorov, Tzvetan. *On Human Diversity: Nationalism, Racism, and Exoticism in French Thought.* Trans. Catharine Porter. Cambridge, Mass., and London: Harvard Univ. Press, 1993.

Tolson, Melvin. *Harlem Gallery.* New York: Twayne, 1965.

Toth, Emily. "Kate Chopin and Literary Convention: 'Désirée's Baby.'" *Southern Studies* 20.3 (Summer 1981).

Toumson, Roger, ed. *Victor Hugo, Bug-Jargal; ou, La Révolution haïtienne.* Fort-de-France: Éditions Désormeaux, 1979.

Tourgée, Albion W. Letter to E. H. Johnson on Thomas Dixon, 15 May 1902. In Gross and Hardy, 81.

Trilling, Lionel. "Art and Fortune." 1948. In *The Liberal Imagination: Essays on Literature and Society.* Garden City, N.Y.: Doubleday Anchor Books, 1953.

Trotter, David. "Introduction." In: Rudyard Kipling, *Plain Tales from the Hills,* ed. H. R. Woudhuysen. Harmondsworth: Penguin Books, 1987.

Twain, Mark. *Pudd'nhead Wilson: A Tale.* 1894. Reprint. *Pudd'nhead Wilson and Those Extraordinary Twins,* ed. Sidney E. Berger. New York, London: Norton, 1980.

Twitchell, James B. *Forbidden Partners: The Incest Taboo in Modern Culture.* New York: Columbia Univ. Press, 1987.

Tyndall, John W. *The Origins of the Black Man.* St. Louis: Metropolitan Correspondence Bible College Department, 1927.

Vail, Stephen M. *The Bible Against Slavery.* New Hampshire: Hadley, 1864.

van den Berghe, Pierre L. "Miscegenation in South Africa." *Cahiers d'Etudes Africaines* 4 (1960): 68–84.

Vanhelleputte, Michel, and Léon Somville, eds. *Motifs in Art and Literature.* Proceedings of a symposium held on the 8th of December 1984 at the Vrije Universiteit Brussel. Leuven: Uitgiverij Peeters, 1987.

Van Lier, R. A. J. *Frontier Society: A Social Analysis of the History of Surinam.* Koninklijk Instituut voor Taal-, Land- en Volkenkunde, Translation Series 14. The Hague: Martinus Nijhoff, 1971.

Van Vechten, Carl. *Nigger Heaven.* New York: Knopf, 1928.

Vauthier, Simone. "Abolitionisme et féminisme dans *Zoe, or the Quadroon's Triumph.*" *RANAM (Recherches anglaises et américaines)* 12 (1979?): 148–70.

———. "L'Image du noir dans la fiction américaine. Lecture des minores 1789–1850." 3 vols. Thèse, Paris III, 1977.

———. "Jeux avec l'interdit: la sexualité interraciale dans le roman de Joseph H. Ingraham, *The Quadroone.*" *RANAM* 11 (1978?): 133–46.

———. "(Non-)famille romanesque, famille socio-historique, famille fantastique: l'exemple d'*Oran, the Outcast*" (1833). *RANAM* 8 (1975): 163–81.

———. "Of Time and the South: The Fiction of William Gilmore Simms." *Southern Literary Journal* 5.1 (Fall 1972): 3–45.

———. "Textualité et stéréotypes: Of African Queens and Afro-American Princes and Princesses: Miscegenation in *Old Hepsy.*" In *Regards sur la littérature noire américaine,* ed. Michel Fabre, 65–107. Paris: Publications du Conseil Scientifique de la Sorbonne Nouvelle—Paris III, 1980.

Verville, François Beroalde de. *Le Moyen de Parvenir.* Paris: Charles Gosselin, 1841.

Vignols, Léon. "Les Sources de *Tamango* de Mérimée et la littérature négrière à l'époque romantique." *Mercure de France* (15 Dec. 1927): 542–57.

Villareal, José Antonio. *Pocho.* Garden City, N.Y.: Doubleday, 1959.

Villaverde, Cirilo. *Cecilia Valdés.* Trans. Mariano J. Lorente. *The Quadroon or Cecilia Valdes: A Romance of Old Havana.* Boston: St. Botolph Society, 1935.

Virgillo, Carmelo, and Naomi Lindstrom, eds. *Woman as Myth and Metaphor in Latin American Literature.* Columbia: Univ. of Missouri Press, 1985.

Wacks, Jamie L. "Reading Race, Rhetoric and the Female Body: The Rhinelander Case and 1920's American Culture." Senior thesis, Harvard University, 1995.

Wadlington, Walter. "The *Loving* Case: Virginia's Anti-Miscegenation Statute in Historical Perspective." *Virginia Law Review* 52 (1966): 1189–223.

Wagenknecht, Edward. *William Dean Howells: The Friendly Eye.* New York: Oxford Univ. Press.

Wagner, Jean. *Black Poets of the United States: From Paul Laurence Dunbar to Langston Hughes.* Trans. Kenneth Douglas. Urbana, Chicago, London: Univ. of Illinois Press, 19.

Wald, Gayle Freda. "Crossing the Line: Racial Passing in Twentieth-Century American Literature and Culture." Ph.D. diss., Princeton University, 1994.

Walker, Alice. "The Child Who Favored Daughter." In *Love & Trouble: Stories of Black Women.* New York: Harcourt Brace Jovanovich, 1967.

Walker, David. *Appeal in Four Articles.* 1829. Reprint. New York: Arno Press, 1969.

Wall, Evans. *The No-Nation Girl.* New York: Grosset & Dunlap, 1929.

Wallace, Robert W. "Afrocentricity, Multiculturalism, and *Black Athena.*" *Caribana* 3 (1992–93): 45–53.

Walther, Wiebke. *Tausend und eine Nacht. Eine Einführung.* Artemis Einführungen, Band 31. München & Zürich: Artemis, 1987.

Warmbold, Joachim. "If Only She Didn't Have Negro Blood in Her Veins: The Concept of Metissage in German Colonial Literature." *Journal of Black Studies* 23.2 (Dec. 1992): 200–210.

Warren, Robert Penn. *Band of Angels.* New York: Random House, 1955.

———, ed. *Faulkner: A Collection of Critical Essays.* Englewood Cliffs: Prentice-Hall, 1966.

Washington, Joseph R., Jr. *Marriage in Black and White.* Boston: Beacon Press, 1970.

Washington, Mary Helen. *Invented Lives: Narratives of Black Women 1860–1960.* New York: Doubleday, 1987.

Waters, Mary C. *Ethnic Options: Choosing Identities in America.* Berkeley: Univ. of California Press, 1990.

Wauthier, Claude. "L'Immoralité en Afrique du Sud." In *Le Couple interdit: entretiens sur le racisme. La dialectique de la alterité socio-culturelle et la sexualité,* ed. Léon Poliakov, 247–52. Paris, The Hague, New York: Mouton, 1980.

———. *The Literature and Thought of Modern Africa.* 1964. 2nd Eng. language ed. London: Heinemann, 1978.

Weatherley, Ulysses G. "Race and Marriage." *American Journal of Sociology* 15.4 (Jan. 1910): 433–53.

Webb, Frank J. *The Garies and Their Friends.* 1857. Reprint. New York: Arno Press, 1969.

Weber, Max. *Wirtschaft und Gesellschaft: Grundriß der verstehenden Soziologie.* Ed. Johannes Winckelmann. Tübingen: J. C. B. Mohr, 1956. Eng. trans. *Economy and Society.* Univ. of California Press, 1978.

*Webster's New Twentieth Century Dictionary.* 2nd ed. New York: Collins, 1978.

Wedberg, Lloyd Warren. *The Theme of Loneliness in Theodor Storm's Novellen.* The Hague, London, Paris: Mouton, 1964.

Weigand, Hermann J. "Das Vertrauen in Kleists Erzählungen." In *Fahrten und Funde: Aufsätze zur deutschen Literatur.* Bern and Munich: Francke, 1967.

Weinberger, Andrew D. "A Reappraisal of the Constitutionality of Miscegenation Statutes." *Cornell Law Quarterly* 42 (1957): 208–22.

Weisschedel, Wilhelm. *Die philosophische Hintertreppe: 34 große Philosophen in Alltag und Denken.* 1966. Reprint. München: Deutscher Taschenbuch Verlag, 1986.

Weisser, Susan Ostrov, and Jennifer Fleischner, eds. *Feminist Nightmares: Women at Odds. Feminism and the Problem of Sisterhood.* New York and London: New York Univ. Press, 1994.

Wellek, René. "The Crisis of Comparative Literature." In *Comparative Literature,* ed. Werner B. Friederich, 149–59. Proceedings of the 2nd Congress of the ICLA at the University of North Carolina, 8–12 Sept.

1958. UNC Studies in Comparative Literature 23. Chapel Hill, N.C.: Univ. of North Carolina Press.

Wendell, Barrett. *A Literary History of America*. New York: Scribner's, 1900.

Wheatley, C. S., Jr. "Who Is a Colored Person?." *Law Notes* 35 (July 1931): 68–70.

Wheatley, Phillis. *The Poems of Phillis Wheatley*. Ed. Julian D. Mason. Chapel Hill and London: Univ. of North Carolina Press, 1989.

Whitaker, William Joseph, ed. *The Mirror of Justices*. London, 1895.

White, Walter. *Flight*. New York: A. A. Knopf, 1926.

———. *A Man Called White: The Autobiography of Walter White*. New York: Viking Press, 1948.

Whitman, Walt. *The Early Poems and the Fiction*, ed. Thomas L. Brasher. New York: New York Univ. Press, 1963.

Wiese, Benno von. *Novelle*. 5th ed. Stuttgart: Metzler, 1971.

Wilkinson, Doris Y. *Black Male/White Female: Perspectives on Interracial Marriage and Courtship*. Cambridge, Mass.: Schenkman, 1975.

Willey, Norman L. "Exotic Elements in Storm and Sealsfield." *Germanic Review* 14 (1939): 28–31.

Williams, Diana Irene. "New Orleans in the Age of Plessy v. Ferguson: Interracial Unions and the Politics of Caste." Senior thesis, Harvard University, 1995.

Williams, Fannie Barrier. "Perils of the White Negro." *Colored American Magazine* 13 (Dec. 1907): 421.

Williams, Garth. *The Rabbits' Wedding*. New York: Harper and Row, 1958.

Williamson, Joel. *The Crucible of Race: Black-White Relations in the American South Since Emancipation*. New York and Oxford: Oxford Univ. Press, 1984.

———. *New People: Miscegenation and Mulattoes in the United States*. New York and London: Free Press/Collier Macmillan, 1980.

Willis, John Ralph, ed. *Slaves and Slavery in Muslim Africa*. London: F. Cass, 1985.

Wilson, Edmund. *Patriotic Gore: Studies in the Literature of the American Civil War*. New York: Oxford Univ. Press, 1962.

Wilson, Judith. "Optical Illusions: Images of Miscegenation in Nineteenth- and Twentieth-Century American Art." *American Art* 5.3 (1991): 89–107.

Windley, Lathan A., ed. *Runaway Slave Advertisements: A Documentary History from the 1730s to 1790*. Westport, Conn., and London: Greenwood Press, 1983.

Wirth, Louis, and Herbert Goldhamer. "The Hybrid and the Problems of Miscegenation" and "Legal Restrictions on Negro-White Intermarriage." In *Characteristics of the American Negro*, ed. Otto Klineberg. New York: Harper and Row, 1944.

Wolff, Cynthia Griffin. "Kate Chopin and the Fiction of Limits: 'Desirée's Baby.'" *Southern Literary Journal* 10.2 (Spring 1978): 123–33.

Wolters, Wolfgang. *La Scultura veneziana gotica*. Venezia: Alfieri, 1976.

Woodbridge, Hensley C. "Glossary of Names Used in Colonial Latin America for Crosses Among Indians, Negroes, and Whites." *Journal of the Washington Academy of Sciences* 38 (1948): 353–62.

Woodson, Carter G. "The Beginnings of Miscegenation of the Whites and Blacks." *Journal of Negro History* 3.4 (Oct. 1918): 335–53.

Woolson, Constance Fenimore. "Jeannette." *Scribner's Monthly* 9 (Dec. 1874): 232–43.

Wormley, Margaret. "The Negro in Southern Fiction." Ph.D. diss., Boston University, 1948.

Wysong, Jack P. "Samuel Clemens' Attitude Toward the Negro as Demonstrated in 'Pudd'nhead Wilson' and 'A Connecticut Yankee at King Arthur's Court.'" *Xavier University Studies* 7.2 (July 1968): 41–57.

Yamamoto, Hisaye. "Wilshire Bus." 1950. In *Seventeen Syllables and Other Stories.* Latham, New York: Kitchen Table Women of Color Press, 1988.

Yarborough, Richard. "The Depiction of Blacks in the Early Afro-American Novel." Ph.D. diss., Stanford University, 1980.

———. "Ideology and Black Characterization in the Early Afro-American Novel." Manuscript, University of California, Los Angeles, 1988.

Yellin, Jean Fagan. *The Intricate Knot: Black Figures in American Literature, 1776–1863.* New York: New York Univ. Press, 1972.

———. *Women and Sisters: The Antislavery Feminists in American Culture.* New Haven and London: Yale Univ. Press, 1989.

Yerby, Frank. *Speak Now.* New York: Dial Press, 1969.

Young, Donald. "Techniques of Race Relations." *Proceedings of the American Philosophical Society* 91.2 (April 1947): 150–61.

Young, Era Brisbane. "An Examination of Selected Dramas From the Theater of Victor Séjour Including Works of Social Protest." Ph.D. diss., New York University, 1979.

Yourcenar, Marguerite. *Fleuve profond, sombre rivière: Les "Negro Spirituals," commentaires et traductions.* Paris: Gallimard, 1964.

Zabel, William D. "Interracial Marriage and the Law." *Atlantic Monthly* (Oct. 1965): 75–79 (reprinted in Wilkinson).

Zack, Naomi. *Race and Mixed Race.* Philadelphia: Temple Univ. Press, 1993.

Zanger, Jules. "The 'Tragic Octoroon' in Pre-Civil War Fiction." *American Quarterly* 18 (1966): 63–70.

Zeisler, Ernest B. *Othello: Time, Enigma and Color Problem.* Chicago: A. J. Isaacs, 1954.

Zuckerman, Michael. "William Byrd's Family." *Perspectives in American History* 12 (1979): 253–311.

# Index

Aaron, Daniel, 510n8
Aberigh-Mackay, George, 150
Abolitionism, 4–5, 36, 46, 96, 106–7,
    109, 113, 131, 134, 167,
    188–97, 201–13, 215–18, 224,
    230, 233, 236–37, 241, 242,
    285, 294–98, 314, 320–21, 328,
    331, 335, 339, 355, 453n96,
    454n107, 464n72, 476n94,
    490n44, 511n23, 513n44
Adams, Abigail, 6
Adams, Bruce Payton, 508n142
Adams, John Quincy, 6
Addison, Joseph, 493n5
Adulteration and adultery, 5, 7, 36,
    41, 47, 48–77, 110, 130, 150,
    182, 232, 237, 344, 435n81,
    437n98, 500n62, 518n11
*Adventures of Jonathan Corncob*, 288
Aeschylus, 41, 43, 242, 244, 332
Aesop, 22
Agassiz, Louis, 131–32, 297–98,
    514n57
al-Suyūtī, Jalálu 'l-Din, 96
al-Ṭabarī, 89, 91
Allen, Don Cameron, 446n49
Allen, Shirley S., 450n76
Allier, Raoul, 93, 446n49
Alte Apotheke, 32
Alvar, Manuel, 116, 123, 421n14,
    462n46
Amalgamation, 5, 31, 73, 101, 102,
    107, 115, 120, 126, 131, 153,
    262–63, 298–99, 311, 320,
    433n69, 450n67, 465n80

Ambrose, 81, 87, 441n16
Andersen, Hans Christian, 30, 162,
    174–87, 287, 355, 477n29
    *The Moorish Maiden*, 175, 182
    *Mulatten*, 174–87, 193, 287
    "Negerkongens Datter," 178
    "The Shadow," 181
    "The Ugly Duckling," 173–74
Andrews, William L., 13, 238,
    415n35
Animal imagery, 17–23, 32, 55,
    60–62, 101–2, 114, 115, 119,
    127, 196, 476n19
Antier, Benjamin, 180
Antin, Mary, 265
*Arabian Nights*. See *Thousand and One
    Nights*
Arbery, Glenn Cannon, 236
Arendt, Hannah, 316, 412n9
Arens, W., 313, 414n26, 514n55
Aristotle, 49, 51, 63–64
Armstrong, Nancy, 419n80
Asante, Molefi Kete, 495n16
Asbury, Herbert, 283, 504n101
Ashby, William, 435n80, 506n110
"As white as anybody," 461n40
Atavism, 49, 51, 52, 64–66, 70
Athanasius, 429n39
Atherton, Gertrude, 144, 146–48,
    151–52, 157–58, 438n103
Auction, 171–72, 174–75, 179–80,
    181, 184, 186, 222. *See also* Sale
    and marriage; Slavery
Augustine, 60, 61, 83, 429n39,
    441n16